Soviet
Union

FODOR'S TRAVEL PUBLICATIONS

are compiled, researched, and edited by an international team of travel writers, field correspondents, and editors. The series, which now almost covers the globe, was founded by Eugene Fodor in 1936.

OFFICES
New York and London

Fodor's Soviet Union

Executive Editor: RICHARD MOORE
Area Editor: HILARY STERNBERG
Editorial Contributors: JOHN FINCHLEY, GEORGE LEWINSON, GEORGE SCHÖPFLIN, MARY SETON-WATSON, RICHARD TAYLOR, GABRIELLE TOWNSEND, GRAHAM WEBB
Drawings and Maps: BRIAN STIMSON, SWANSTON GRAPHICS
Photographs: ELIZABETH LEE, JOHN MASSEY STEWART
Cover Photograph: CARY WOLINSKY/STOCK BOSTON

Cover Design: VIGNELLI ASSOCIATES

SPECIAL SALES

Fodor's Travel Publications are available at special discounts for bulk purchases (100 copies or more) for sales promotions or premiums. Special editions, including personalized covers, excerpts of existing guides, and corporate imprints, can be created in large quantities for special needs. For more information, write to Special Marketing, Fodor's Travel Publications, 201 East 50th Street, New York, NY 10022. Enquiries from the United Kingdom should be sent to Merchandise Division, Random House UK Ltd, 30–32 Bedford Square, London WC1B 3SG.

Fodor's 89

Soviet Union

Fodor's Travel Publications, Inc.
New York & London

ISBN 0-679-01700-3

MANUFACTURED IN THE UNITED STATES OF AMERICA
10 9 8 7 6 5 4 3 2 1

TABLE OF CONTENTS

FOREWORD

Most visitors to the U.S.S.R. anticipate a trip for earnest reasons of political, social and cultural curiosity. Certainly no one goes to the Soviet Union to find the kind of relaxed fun that you would expect from a holiday in the West. Almost everyone is aware that a visit to Russia has little to do with creature comforts—sun, sand and *après ski,* or any of the other frivolous pursuits associated with having a good time. The reason for going is, pure and simple, curiosity—curiosity about a completely different way of life.

For this reason we have adopted a somewhat different format for this book from the others in our series. In order to satisfy the visitor's need for background information, we have given preponderant coverage to the political, social and cultural aspects of the Soviet Union, as well as including many parts of the country a tourist is not likely to see.

The thaw in U.S./U.S.S.R. relations that began with the Geneva "fireside summit" is proceeding steadily. There is every sign that this gradual warming of the international climate will continue to spread to making the lives of visitors to the U.S.S.R. easier, too. Over the past few years—since the 1980 Olympics, when there was a concentrated training program for guides and others who would be dealing with guests—there has been a noticeable improvement both in standards and attitudes. The remarkable friendliness of President Reagan's reception in May 1988, and the breadth of the media coverage that his visit received, marked a new high in relations. Indeed visitors who are returning to the U.S.S.R. after an absence of several years will notice a world of difference in their welcome.

The complex world of the U.S.S.R. is fascinating beyond belief: your encounters with individual Russians, Latvians, Mongolians or Georgians (to name but a few) can be a heartwarming experience; the Soviet social order, so different from ours, will provoke the imagination if you are politically aware; the fine arts, in the form of museums, theater, dance or music, will impress you by the sheer volume of participants. On a more mundane level, you may enjoy the skill of Soviet athletics, which has more than ten million registered active participant enthusiasts, and the excitement of the very best in competition. And, despite the occasional poor service in restaurants, you will probably enjoy the various regional food and drink specialties of the country.

Special advice for a special visit. You will find throughout this book the theme: "Visiting the Soviet Union is like nothing you've ever done before." Because this is so, we'd like to offer some special advice for visiting a very special country, with our apologies if we sound a bit heavy-handed about it. We're not trying to make the ordinary problems of logistics seem worse than they are, but our experience, and that of many other travelers, indicates that the following hints may help to prepare you for your adventure into another way of life:

1—Go to the U.S.S.R. on a group tour if you can possibly do so, especially if it's your first visit, or if you don't speak Russian. Group tourists get priority over individual tourists, even if the latter do pay more than the former.

2—Be careful not to break any laws, and if you're not sure, follow this rule: if you aren't certain something is allowed, it is safer to assume it is definitely forbidden. Sticking to your pre-arranged itinerary, not photographing any rail stations, instalations, buildings, etc. which might be regarded as "sensitive," not selling your blue jeans, or not offering a dollar bill or pound note for a tip, all these are covered by some law or other and, for ignoring things like these, visitors have run into trouble and some have even been expelled from the country.

4—If you are traveling individually and expect to spend more than a day or two in the U.S.S.R., register with your embassy in Moscow, preferably in person, but at least by mail or telephone, giving your full name, passport number, date and place of birth, occupation, hotel and room number, purpose and dates of visit, home address, and (if applicable) names and addresses of any relatives to be visited in the U.S.S.R.

5—Carry your hotel identity card (which you will get when you register, in exchange for your passport) with you at all times. It is officially accepted as proof of your status in foreign currency shops, restaurants, etc., and may be useful also if, for example, you get lost and want to ask someone the way to your hotel or to take a taxi. If you are allowed to keep your passport as well, keep it in a safe place on your person at all times. There is reported to be a black market in U.S. and U.K. passports.

6—Plan well ahead, meaning that *everything* you want to do in the Soviet Union, and especially all the cities you want to visit or special interests you want to pursue, is arranged before you leave your home for the airport.

7—Finally, and a very basic point, remember that you are going to a country with a very different attitude to life from your own. We have had letters over the years from readers who have been disturbed by their trip to the U.S.S.R. If it is at all likely that you will be unable to approach your trip with patience and an open mind we seriously suggest that you think twice about going at all. But if you like adventure—enjoy!

*

We would like to thank our many friends who have helped in the preparation of this edition, including the staff of Intourist in London, who have given us valuable assistance. We would like also to express our gratitude especially to Mary Seton-Watson, George Lewinson and George Schöpflin for putting their expertise at our disposal, and to Hilary Sternberg for her valiant work on this revised edition.

*

While every care has been taken to assure the accuracy of the information in this guide, the passage of time will always bring change, and consequently the publisher cannot accept responsibility for errors that may occur.

All prices and opening times quoted in this guide are based on information available to us at press time. Hours and admission fees may change, however, and the prudent traveler will avoid inconvenience by calling ahead.

Fodor's wants to hear about your travel experiences, both pleasant and unpleasant. When a hotel or restaurant fails to live up to its billing, let us know and we will investigate the complaint and revise our entries where the facts warrant it.

Send your letters to the editors of Fodor's Travel Publications, 201 E. 50th Street, New York, NY 10022. European readers may prefer to write to Fodor's Travel Publications, 30–32 Bedford Square, London WC1B 3SG, England.

Note: It is now over two years since the Chernobyl disaster. Although the full extent of the long-term effects is still not completely known, tourist trips to the Soviet Union are back to normal. The immediate area around Chernobyl was never a tourist destination anyway, and tours to Kiev and the rest of the Ukraine are perfectly safe.

FACTS AT YOUR FINGERTIPS

FACTS AT YOUR FINGERTIPS

Planning Your Trip

PROS AND CONS. If you are thinking of going to the Soviet Union on the spur of the moment, our advice is: don't. Even if you could get a visa quickly, you might find that there is an All-Union Congress of Tractor Engineers in Moscow or a meeting of international agronomists in Leningrad and accommodations are impossible to obtain. Give yourself time for planning, consider your own likes and dislikes, your special hobbies and interests. In this vast country of which you will be able to explore only a small section, there is so much to see it is essential to make a choice and then make plans accordingly.

Are you allergic to cold? Stay out of the areas of frost and snow and go in summer. Does the heat bother you? Avoid July and August, when Moscow can sizzle like New York and be as humid as London. Above all remember that improvisation following a sudden fancy or urge is rarely possible in the U.S.S.R. The individual traveler isn't really welcome, only tolerated, and pays more. Even if you want to travel only with your family or a small group, it is better to pick a tour that suits your purpose best. If you should decide that you would like to extend or vary it after arrival this is possible through Intourist, who will be represented in your hotel.

WHEN TO GO. In a country as vast as the Soviet Union, it is possible to enjoy a holiday at almost any time of the year. Some experts consider August and September the best months. This is the high season, so you must reserve well ahead to avoid disappointment. In the central part of the Soviet Union, June and July are fairly hot and on the Black Sea coast it is even hotter. But on the Black Sea May is a particularly attractive month and you can bathe from the beginning of that month through October. If you choose June or July, pick the Baltic countries and Leningrad, which will be just pleasantly warm. Central Asia is best visited in March–April or September–October as you will find the climate in summer almost tropical yet dry and dusty.

Winter in Moscow can be fierce in January and early February but the rest of the season is tolerable. There is, of course, plenty of snow and in the dry cold the city looks very attractive under its white cover. Some people find the cold most exhilarating, and Russian interiors are always well-heated.

Here are the average temperature ranges of the five main tourist centers (lowest monthly *average* and highest *average*):

Leningrad: 18.5°F. to 63.5°F. (–7.7°C. to 17.5°C.).
Moscow: 12.6°F. to 65.3°F. (–10.8°C to 18.5°C.).
Odessa: 25.7°F. to 71.6°F. (–3.7°C. to 22.1°C.).
Sochi: 60.0°F. to 73.4°F. (16.0°C. to 23.0°C.).
Yalta: 38.3°F. to 75.2°F. (3.7°C. to 24.2°C.).

In the off season, October through April, deluxe tours are 15% less expensive and the first- and tourist-class tours 25% less, outside Moscow and Leningrad. This is the best time to see the country and have the pick of the full theater and concert season. You can enjoy skiing, skating, troika rides and tobogganing in these months. You'll also sample the best cooking: the hearty winter dishes that Russia is famous for are in season then. In summer, light clothing will be sufficient, but you should take at least one warm suit or pullover. A raincoat and rubber overshoes or boots will also be useful. Evening dress or formal clothes are not necessary for the theaters or restaurants. Do not wear shorts or beach wraps in towns—you may not be allowed into museums or cafés. Women in trousers are now accepted.

1

SEASONAL EVENTS. These include the May Day celebrations, the anniversary of V.E. Day (May 9) and the military parades of the Great October Revolution (actually commemorated on November 7 each year). The parades are followed by mass pageants and sports displays in Moscow's Red Square and the centers of other large cities.

The Russian Winter Festival lasts 12 days from December 25 to January 5. Carnivals take place in the immense Luzhniki Stadium in Moscow and elsewhere there are circuses and special theatrical performances. The Russian New Year is usually celebrated in restaurants and cafés. The Festival is also celebrated in Leningrad, Suzdal, Novgorod and Irkutsk where events are laid on for foreign visitors.

There are the Festival of Moscow Stars (May 5–13), the Kiev Spring Festival (May 18–30), the Leningrad White Nights (June 21–29), various art festivals and the Riga Song Festival (August 1–9), all of which offer a rich fare of ballet, opera and drama. The Moscow International Film Festival is held every odd-numbered year in July, with entries from all over the world.

Sporting highlights include national and international ice-hockey and soccer (football) matches, skating and skiing championships, athletic meets, boxing competitions and many other events.

The November 7 celebrations are particularly brilliant in Moscow, with the whole city decked out in bunting, gaily-colored streamers and flags. The Soviet leaders take the salute on top of the Lenin Mausoleum while the long colorful parade rolls past to the strains of a large brass band. (The exact position of the leaders is supposed to be an indication of their actual standing in the hierarchy of the Party.) Then follows a spectacular gymnastic display after which folklore groups from all over the country perform. The march-past of workers, many carrying their children on their shoulders, can last three or four hours. In the evening, the buildings are illuminated, fireworks light up the sky, and there is dancing and entertainment in the central squares and streets (which are closed to traffic). In Leningrad, the Soviet Baltic Fleet sails up the Neva and drops anchor opposite the Winter Palace. Illuminated at night, the warships draw great crowds to the embankments.

In Moscow, Leningrad, Kiev and other towns the theatrical season usually starts in October.

PRICES. We give figures throughout this *Facts At Your Fingertips* for accommodations, travel and so on. The prices we quote are naturally subject to alteration, many of them being based on the 1988 figures projected through a crystal ball. As of spring 1988 the official exchange rate stood at around 58 roubles per $100 and 1 rouble to the pound sterling; and, although a rouble does sell more cheaply in financial markets abroad, the importation of roubles into the U.S.S.R. is strictly forbidden and severely penalized.

INTOURIST. All travel to the Soviet Union is ultimately organized through the State travel agency, Intourist Moscow Limited. They themselves have tours and a certain amount of useful information. The following are the offices of Intourist in the U.S.A., Britain and Canada—

U.S.A.: 630 Fifth Ave., Suite 868, New York, N.Y. 10111.
Britain: 292 Regent St., London W.1; 71 Deansgate, Manchester M3 2BW.
Canada: 1801 McGill College Ave., Montreal, Quebec H3A 2N4.

Intourist in the Soviet Union. The head office of Intourist in Moscow is at Prospekt Marxa. For general enquiries and help in contacting other tourists call 292–2260. The American Department's phone number is 292–8670; the British Department's 292–2697. The Excursion Department (M.E.O.) has offices in the following Moscow Hotels:
Bucharest, 232–5533, ext. 149; *Metropole* (Excursion Hall), 225–6970/1/2; *National,* 229–6224; *Rossiya,* 298–5437; *Ukraine,* 243–2690.

TOURS. These fall into two main categories: individual and group. (For special-interest tours, see p. 5.)

For the individual tours, any Intourist itinerary can be chosen. According to the latest information at press time, the following places are open to tourists and have Intourist hotels and services available:

Abakan	Frunze	Nalchik	Sochi
Alma-Ata	Gori	Novaya Kakhovka	Stavropol
Ashkhabad	Irkutsk	Novgorod	Sukhumi
Baku	Ivanovo	Novosibirsk	Suzdal
Batumi	Kalinin	Odessa	Tallinn
Beltsi	Karaganda	Ordzhonikidze	Tashkent
Bratsk	Kazbegi	Orel	Tbilisi
Brest	Khabarovsk	Pärnu	Telavi
Bukhara	Kharkov	Pasanauri	Ternopol
Chardzhou	Kherson	Petrozavodsk	Tiraspol
Cherkassy	Khmelnitsky	Poltava	Tselinograd
Chernovtsy	Kiev	Prielbrusye	Tskhaltubo
Chimkent	Kishinev	(groups only)	Ulyanovsk
Dagomis	Kislovodsk	Pskov	Urgench
Dombaiskaya			
Polyana	Krasnodar	Pyatigorsk	Uzhgorod
(groups only)	Kursk	Repino	Viliandi
Donetsk	Leningrad	Riga	Vilnius
Druskininkai	Listvyanka	Rostov-on-Don	Vinnitsa
Dushanbe	Lutsk	Rovno	Volograd
Dzhamboul	Lvov	Samarkand	Yalta
Erevan	Minsk	Simferopol	Yaroslavl
Essentuki	Moscow	Sheki	Zaporozhye
Fergana	Murmansk	Smolensk	Zheleznovodsk

In addition, day sightseeings (no overnight stops) are available from:
Abakan to Minusinsk, Shushenskoye;
Baku to Kobystan, Shemakha, Sumgait;
Batumi to Kobuleti, Tsikhisdziri;
Cherkassy to Kamenka, Korsun-Shevchenkovski;
Chimkent to Kentau, Turkestan;
Donetsk to Slavianogorsk;
Dushanbe to Nurek, Kurgan-Tube;
Erevan to Dilizhan, Echmiadzin, Kirovakan, Tsakhkadzor;
Kalinin to Klin;
Karaganda to Shakhtinsk, Temirtau;
Kiev to Kanev;
Kishinev to Bendery;
Kislovodsk to Teberda;
Krasnodar to Novorossiisk;
Kursk to Zheleznogorsk;
Leningrad to Pavlovsk, Petrodvorets, Pushkin;
Moscow to Klin, Pereslavl-Zalesskii, Podolsk, Rostov, Vladimir;
Odessa to Belgorod-Dnestrovski;
Pyatigorsk to Teberda;
Riga to Sigulda, Jurmala;
Rostov-on-Don to Azov, Novocherkassk, Taganrog;
Samarkand to Pendzhikent;
Simferopol to Bakhchisarai;
Sochi to Gagra, Pitsunda;
Sukhumi to Gagra, Novy Afon, Pitsunda;
Suzdal to Bogolyubovo, Kideksha, Vladimir;
Tallinn to Paide, Tartu;
Tashkent to Angren, Chirchik;
Tbilisi to Bakuriani, Borzhomi, Mtskheta;

Tskhaltubo to Kutaisi;
Urgench to Khiva;
Vilnius to Druskininkai, Kaunas, Trakai;
Yalta to Bakhchisarai;
Yaroslavl to Pereslavl-Zalesskii, Rostov.

Note: These lists are constantly being revised. Check with Intourist for any last-minute changes.

Tourist travel is normally limited to standard itineraries. All travel, hotel accommodations, meals, etc., should be arranged and paid for in advance. By working through Intourist or an accredited U.S. or U.K. travel agent, "special interest" tours can often be arranged encompassing visits to areas of professional interest to the traveler and appointments with Soviet specialists in the traveler's field. However, some travelers have in the past expressed dissatisfaction with Intourist arrangements, noting especially the difficulty in obtaining refunds for travel and services which they paid for in advance but never received. There is substantial evidence that Intourist has sometimes offered travel and hotel facilities, particularly in the higher price range, to more travelers than it has the capacity to accommodate. Because arrangements between traveler and Intourist are based on private contract, the traveler who is dissatisfied with services provided or seeks refund for unused travel coupons must make a claim to Intourist or through his travel agent as provided for in the contract. If the claim for refund cannot be resolved directly the traveler may institute legal action in the city or state where the contract was entered into. Intourist regulations permit refunds for full unused days of Intourist services only if the traveler obtains a certificate *(spravka)* from Intourist while in the U.S.S.R. stating that the services were not used. This system appears to work more smoothly now than formerly and dissatisfaction is rarer. See below under Currency Regulations for the use of charge cards.

Group Tours. Though group tours have fixed starting dates, it is possible to join a group upon your arrival in Moscow; Intourist then organizes the groups. Accommodations (see under *Hotels*) are available only in the first-class category; they include hotel room with bath or shower, full board (three meals a day), guided excursions by bus, entrance fees, transfers upon arrival and departure, transportation while within the U.S.S.R. and porterage for two pieces of hand luggage. The cost is dependent upon the itinerary chosen.

Group tours are offered by American and British travel agents by arrangement with Intourist. Some 250 different tours, each with a number of departure dates, are available, and you can combine the U.S.S.R. with other countries if you want to. Cost naturally depends on type of accommodations, length of stay, method of transportation and the itinerary.

The group tours usually comprise 20 to 25 people. Fixed-date tours are offered to tourists who speak English, French or Italian. From October 1 through April 30, package services are available at a 15–25% discount, depending on the class of the service.

For somewhat cheaper group tours for students, see below under *Special Interest Travel.*

À la Carte Tours. Tourists traveling individually may opt for an *à la carte* tour, making a choice of the cities they would like to visit from the list of places where this service is available. The time you stay in each city is up to you, provided the whole tour does not exceed 8 days/7 nights. Cost is 425 roubles May through October, 342 November through April. The tour can be extended at a cost of 61 roubles per day (49 per day November to April), and there is a single room supplement of 10 roubles per day. What you get for your money are First Class hotel accommodations in a twin-bedded room; two meals daily (breakfast plus lunch or dinner—extra meal 5 roubles); internal air transportation between cities on tour; and private car transfers on arrival and departure in each city on itinerary. There's a 50% reduction for children under 12; excursions can be arranged for an extra payment on request.

The following cities currently accept *à la carte* tourists: Alma-Ata, Ashkhabad, Baku, Bratsk, Dushanbe, Erevan, Frunze, Irkutsk, Khabarovsk, Kiev, Kishinev, Leningrad, Minsk, Moscow, Odessa, Riga, Tallinn, Tashkent, and Tbilisi. Certain hotels, only, are used.

SPECIAL-INTEREST TOURS. Intourist and its associates cater for special interest groups and link their tours to the seasonal events. For the *Moscow Stars Theater Festival* (12 days, from about May 4), a tour is arranged which spends the first 7 days in Moscow, then moves to Leningrad for 4 days. There are sightseeing tours with optional excursions and (for extra payment) 6 visits to theaters, including transport. Return to London is on the 12th day.

The *White Nights Festival* (leaving mid-June) also takes in both Moscow and Leningrad. On your outward trip the first stop is Moscow, where you spend 5 nights (with a day's sightseeing and optional theater visits). On the 6th day you fly to Leningrad. The 7th to the 14th days are spent in Leningrad.

The *Song Festival Tour* to Riga usually departs around July 18, in time for the festival, which is held between July 20 and 24.

The *Golden Autumn Festival* is held at Sochi between September 6 and 20 and the *Georgian Arts Festival* at Tbilisi between September 21 and 26. Of course, it is possible to visit both on one trip.

The *Ukrainian Arts Festival* is at Kiev, between October 1 and 10.

The *Russian Winter Festival* in Moscow, Leningrad, Suzdal/Vladimir, Novgorod and Irkutsk, lasts from December 25 to January 5. *(All the above tours leave from Britain.)*

Although most Western travel to the U.S.S.R. is handled by Intourist, youth and student travel is arranged by *Sputnik,* which offers group tours for students through the Scandinavian Student Travel Service. In the U.S., write to the *Council on International Educational Exchange,* 205 E. 42 St., New York, N.Y. 10017; in Canada apply through the *Canadian Federation of Students-Services,* 187 College St., Toronto, Ontario M5T 1P7. Overseas, apply through any of the S.S.T.S. offices. Ask for the booklet entitled, *SSTS Student Tours to the USSR.* Although Sputnik's tours are cheaper, the number of itineraries available is much more limited than those available through Intourist. Sputnik's address is: International Youth Tourist Bureau, Lebiazhy 4, Moscow G 19. Other study programs are available from the *Institute of International Education,* 809 United Nations Plaza, New York, N.Y. 10017. In the U.K., *East Europe Interchange,* 186 Streatham High Rd., London SW16 IBB, operates tours, including one to Siberia, for teachers and youth groups.

Business travel services are available to representatives of industrial and other organizations who need to travel to Soviet cities to negotiate or to participate in trade fairs. In 1986 *Express Boyd* (a London-based agency specializing in business travel) opened a Moscow office under a formal agreement with Intourist.

Ask Intourist for its brochure *Special Interest Tours* which tells how to organize "subject study" tours for groups. Examples of itineraries are given for Art and Architecture, Flowers and Gardens, Art and History of Ancient Russia, Literature, Palaces, Agriculture, Town Planning, Wine. Other subjects Intourist can now cater for include: Circuses, Puppets, Ballet, Music, Filming, Urban Transport and Fur Breeding.

HEALTH RESORTS. It is also possible to visit the Soviet Union for whatever ails you. There are two types of facilities: complete and out-patient. The first is for **resident patients** and is available at the health resorts of Sochi, Tskhaltubo, Kislovodsk, Essentuki, Pyatigorsk and Zheleznovodsk (all in the Caucasus); and Repino (near Leningrad). In these places the off season runs from January 1 through May 31 and October 1 through December 31, the ordinary season from June 1 through September 30. The rates (available from Intourist offices) cover full medical treatment for 24 days in Kislovodsk, Sochi, Essentuki, Pyatigorsk, Repino and Zheleznovodsk and for 20 days in Tskhaltubo. The classes of services range from deluxe to first class and tourist. The cost includes accommodations at a sanatorium for the duration of the treatment, medical treatment under a doctor's care, medical examinations and analyses, X-rays and therapy, transfer for therapy and other treatments, services of an interpreter-guide during examinations and treatments, all meals (as prescribed by the dietician), transfers upon arrival and departure (except in certain cities), and porterage.

Out-patient medical treatment is available in Sochi, where first-class service only is available. The cost is about 16–26 roubles daily in ordinary season, 12–21 off season; the fee covers doctor's care, medical examinations, laboratory analyses, X-rays and therapy, transfers to the medical center and the services of an interpreter during examinations and treatments. This is available during the off season and the ordinary season. The rates also cover hotel accommodations, three meals daily within the first-class price limit, and transportation on arrival and departure.

Tourists coming to the Soviet Union for medical treatment should bring an up-to-date medical history from their physicians. In some cases, these may be obtained after a thorough examination in the Soviet Union at an authorized clinic for an additional fee of 50 roubles per person. Medical treatment is not usually available to children. Unused days of the treatment are not refundable.

TRAVEL AGENTS AND SAMPLE TOURS. A good travel agent can save you time and money through his knowledge of details which you could not be expected to know about. In the all-important phase of planning your trip, even if you wish to travel independently, it is wise to take advantage of the services of these specialists.

As we have indicated, except for Sputnik (the travel bureau which organizes youth travel on an exchange basis) and the trade unions (reciprocal tours for union functionaries only), *Intourist* is the only organization that deals with tourists inside the Soviet Union; and all arrangements made outside the U.S.S.R. must eventually go through Intourist anyway. Since Intourist generally has only one office in each Western country, there are fortunately a number of regular agencies that have experience in dealing with Intourist and advising on travel in the U.S.S.R., and we have listed some of them below.

Whether you select *American Express, Thomas Cook, Maupintour,* or a smaller organization, is a matter of preference. They all have branch offices or correspondents in Moscow. But there are good reasons for engaging a reliable agent.

If you wish him merely to arrange a steamship or airline ticket or to book you on a package tour, his services should cost you nothing. Most carriers and tour operators grant him a fixed commission for saving them the expense of having to open individual offices in every town and city.

If, on the other hand, you wish him to plan for you an individual itinerary and make all arrangements down to hotel reservations and transfers to and from rail and air terminals, you are drawing upon his skill and knowledge of travel as well as asking him to shoulder a great mass of details. His commissions from carriers (8% to 11%) won't come close to covering his expenses. Accordingly he will make a service charge on top of the actual cost of your trip. The amount of this charge varies with the agent, the complexity of your tour, the number of changes you have made in your itinerary, etc.

If you cannot locate a travel agent near your home, write, if in America, to the *American Society of Travel Agents,* Box 23992, Washington, DC 20026. In Britain, to the *Association of British Travel Agents,* 50–57 Newman St., London W1P 4AH. Any agency affiliated with these organizations is almost sure to be thoroughly reliable.

The following are the offices of Intourist in the U.S.A., Britain and Canada:
U.S.A.: 630 Fifth Avenue, Suite 868, New York, N.Y. 10111.
Canada: 1801 McGill College Ave., Montreal, Quebec H3A 2N4.
Britain: 292 Regent Street, London W.1, and 71 Deansgate, Manchester M3 2BW.

Soviet Embassies, consulates and trade delegations will also provide travel information, and are becoming much more helpful than their traditional reputation would suggest.

There are about 50 travel agencies in the United States linked with Intourist, and more than a dozen in Britain.

Some U.S. Agents Promoting Soviet Travel

American Express, 822 Lexington Ave., New York, N.Y. 10021 (and all branches).

American Travel Abroad Inc., 250 West 57th St., New York, N.Y. 10107.

Bennett Tours Inc., 270 Madison Ave., New York, N.Y. 10016.

Extra Value Travel, 683 S. Collier Blvd., Marco Island, FL 33937.

Four Winds Travel, 175 Fifth Ave., New York, N.Y. 10010.

General Tours Inc., 770 Broadway, New York, N.Y. 10003.

Globus-Gateway/Cosmos, 95–25 Queens Blvd., Rego Park, N.Y. 11374.

Gordon Travel Service Inc., Prudential Plaza, 130 East Randolph, Chicago, IL 60601.

Harvard Travel Service Inc., 1356 Massachusetts Ave., Cambridge, MA 02138.

Hemphill Harris Travel Corp., 16000 Ventura Blvd., Suite 200, Encino, CA 91436.

Kobasniuk Travel, 157 2nd Ave., New York, N.Y. 10003.

Lindblad Travel Inc., 1 Sylvan Rd. North, Westport, CT 06880.

Love Holidays, 15315 Magnolia Blvd., Suite 110, Sherman Oaks, CA 91403.

Maupintour Inc., 1515 St. Andrews Dr., Lawrence, KS 66046.

Orbis Polish Travel, 500 Fifth Ave., New York, N.Y. 10110.

Russian Travel Bureau Inc., 245 E. 44th St., New York, N.Y. 10017.

Travcoa Travel Corp., P.O. Box 2630, Newport Beach, CA 92660.

Sample Tours from the U.S. —Itineraries and prices are representative of recent offerings and are likely to change somewhat from year to year. Use those listed for the basis of comparison when choosing your own package.

Russian Travel Bureau offers 8- to 22-day escorted tours designed to accommodate a variety of interests and budgets. An 8-day jaunt divided evenly between Moscow and Leningrad begins at a very reasonable $1,550–$1,700, including airfare, all meals and 1st class lodgings, per person, double occupancy. The deluxe 16-day *Grandeur of Russia* runs $3,046–$3,699. The less ambitious "standard series" 15-day *Grand Cities Adventure* (Leningrad, Kiev, Odessa, Helsinki, Moscow) averages about $2,550. The 22-day *Russia the Great* through Siberia and Oriental Russia, including Tbilisi, Tashkent, Samarkand, Bukhara and Irkutsk as well as Moscow and Leningrad will cost approx. $2,963–$3,363. They also offer a Russia/China combination tour.

Notes: Visas are extra to prices quoted, though the tour operator will handle acquiring them for you, sometimes for a small fee (about $2–2.50). All prices are for fully escorted tours per person, double occupancy.

Some U.K. Tour Operators

American Express Co., Inc., 6 Haymarket, London S.W.1.

Bales Tours Ltd., Bales House, Barrington Road, Dorking, Surrey RH4 3EJ.

Thos. Cook & Son Ltd., 45 Berkeley St., London W.1.

London Walkabout Club, 20–22 Craven Terrace, Lancaster Gate, London W.2, for Trans-Siberian rail trips, London to Yokohama or vice-versa.

P & O Air Holidays, 77 New Oxford St., London W.C.1.

Page & Moy Ltd., 136–140 London Rd., Leicester 2.

Rankin Kuhn & Co. Ltd., 19 Queen Anne St., London W.1.

Serenissima Travel Ltd., 21 Dorset Sq., London N.W.1.

Sovereign Holidays (British Airways), P.O. Box 410, West London Air Terminal, Cromwell Road, London S.W.7.

Swan Hellenic Art Treasure Tours Ltd., 29–55 Middlesex St., London E.C.1.

Thomson Holidays, Greater London House, Hampstead Road, London N.W.1.

Virgin Holidays, Sussex House, High St., Crawley, West Sussex.

Voyages Jules Verne, 10 Glentworth St., London N.W.1.

Sample Tours from the U.K. —*Serenissima Travel Ltd.,* excellent operators of art-oriented tours, guided by expert guest lecturers, have a 16-day trip to Moscow, Georgia, Armenia and Central Asia (including Samarkand, Bukhara, Khiva and Shakhrisabz) for £1,220 per person. Also a 10-day Moscow-Leningrad trip for around £900. A one-week tour, *Palaces and Gardens of St. Petersburg,* is led by Prince George Galitzine and costs £845.

Intourist have a number of tours from Britain to the Soviet Union; in 1988 there were departures from London, Manchester, and Glasgow. Most tours take in the major cities (especially Moscow and Leningrad); they last for two weeks and cost from £426. Newer to the list of tours is a 15-day fly/bus tour in which journeys to and from the Soviet Union are by air, while travel within the country is by bus or train. The *Ancient Russian Cities* tour visits either Leningrad, Kizhi, Moscow, Suzdal, and Vladimir, or Moscow, Vladimir, Suzdal, Novgorod, Pskov, and Leningrad; it costs £566–£592 for two weeks. The *Transcaucasia* tour, at £571–£601, takes you by air to Moscow and onto Baku, then by bus for a tour of the Caucasus, taking in Tbilisi and Erevan. From here you fly to Leningrad and then back to the U.K.

The *Moscow Weekend Break* is run in conjunction with *British Airways.* For £270–£334 you get three nights in a first class Moscow hotel (twin room), all meals, one sightseeing excursion, all transfers, and porterage. A tour including three or six nights on the Trans-Siberian is available at £643–£683; a one-week winter trip to the Arctic (Murmansk, also visiting Moscow and Leningrad) costs about £325.

Other winter specials (all from Intourist) include *Russian Winter Magic,* a week's trip during the Russian Winter Festival (Dec. 25 to Jan. 5) in either Moscow, Vladimir, Suzdal, and Leningrad, or Moscow and Leningrad, or Moscow alone. Prices from London, Manchester, or Glasgow are £305–£380. Cross-country skiers might like the one-week trip to Olgino, near Leningrad, or to Suzdal, near Moscow. It costs about £350, including ski-hire etc.

Thomson Holidays have several trips lasting seven or 14 nights. Special Moscow-and-Leningrad two-center holidays cost £298–£371 for seven days; a Black Sea tour, including seven nights in either Sochi or Yalta, and three nights each in Moscow and Leningrad at beginning and end, is £527–£545. *Foothills of the Himalayas* takes in Samarkand, Bukhara, Tashkent, Alma-Ata, Dushanbe, Moscow, and Leningrad. This is a May–Nov. tour and costs £593–£599 for two weeks.

Thomson's winter tours include a seven-day *Arctic tour* to Moscow, Leningrad, and Murmansk for £266–£336. Tours of the Caucasus are priced up to £565 for a fortnight, while an *Ancient Golden Cities* tour costs £412 for a week. A luxury two-week tour to the Soviet Union and northern India, visiting Moscow, Leningrad, Delhi, Agra, and Srinagar, costs £1,150. Tours to China and Outer Mongolia were available in 1988 at £1,310 and £899. There are many other Thomson tours; they are experts in the field and arrange about 70% of U.K./U.S.S.R. packages, all of them excellent value.

Tours for train buffs are becoming more and more numerous. *Bales Tours* have a 19-day escorted train package from Moscow to Peking, with stopovers in Moscow, Irkutsk, Ulan Bator (Mongolia's capital), and ending with three days' sightseeing in Peking and a flight from there to London. Cost: £1,499–£1,599 according to season.

For the ultimate rail experience, try for a seat on one of the specially chartered trains that run from London's Charing Cross station to Chang 'An (Xian) in China. *Voyages Jules Verne* of London, who spent five years putting the trip together, now run them with *P & O Air Holidays,* through whom you book a place. It takes all of six weeks, following the original route of the Orient Express from Paris to Istanbul, then on across the Anatolian Plateau to Kars/Mount Ararat, along the "Golden Road to Samarkand," over the Tien Shan Mountains into China, and along the fabled Silk Road across the Gobi Desert to Chang 'An, the historic terminus of the Silk Road. From there, it's air to Hong Kong. £4,000 plus, but well worth it. Dates from travel agents. *P & O Air Holidays* run a 24-day rail trip London to Hong Kong via Moscow and Peking. Two nights in Hong Kong (extendable) and round trip flight, for around £1,800. A 40-day version costs £3,000, as does London–Hong Kong via the trans-Siberian route.

A really unusual trip for English speakers is a study tour on the Trans-Siberian. The 15-day trips start and end in West Berlin and in 1988 cost about $1,500 including air fare from East Berlin to the Russian starting point, train fare, meals, hotel rooms, Russian lessons, and return to East Berlin. Different routes may be chosen. Participants take 30 hours of Russian language study, learn to read signs and maps, and hold basic conversations. They also learn something about literature, geography, and history. Information from: Hans Engberding, *Lernidee-Reisen,* Eberstrasse 27, 1000 Berlin 62 (tel. 49–30–7844745).

WHAT TO TAKE. Local shortages are common and certain items may be hard for the passing tourist to find. You might find it useful to stock up with a modest amount of the following: adhesive (Scotch) tape, ballpoint pens and refills, insect repellent, films, spare radio batteries, laxatives, anti-diarrhoea pills (see p. 13), indigestion tablets, travel sickness pills, aspirins, and any medicine you take regularly. Also take a spare pair of glasses or contact lenses, sunglasses, detergent, clothes pegs, toothpaste, soap, cosmetics, shampoos, a sewing kit, safety pins, buttons, chewing gum (a welcome gift), candy (ditto), a jar of instant coffee (expensive and of inferior quality in Russia), coffee creamer, Kleenex, hand-towel, sanitary napkins, lavatory paper, corkscrew/bottle opener, spare baggage tags. A flat, wide suction-type bath plug might also come in very handy in some hotels and a roll of electrical tape for fixing faucets, etc. A pillow-case is useful for long rail trips. Other items that can make welcome gifts in lieu of tipping are: felt pens, cigarettes, pantyhose, cosmetics—especially eye make-up. Guides are officially not allowed to receive tips, but books—British and American classics in paperback—are appreciated.

For most tourist destinations, airline baggage now goes by size rather than weight, and the free baggage allowance is now: First class, 2 pieces up to 62 inches overall measure each piece; Economy class, 2 pieces, neither one over 62 inches, both together no more than 117 inches; carry-on baggage up to 45 inches. If you go to the U.S.S.R. by Pan Am, your baggage will be carried on this basis, with added proviso that no piece weigh over 70 pounds. Aeroflot's regulations are similar, except that the weight limitation is 45 lbs.

Packing. Travel light. This is the advice of most seasoned travelers who have learned not to take along the things that *might* be needed, only those that *will* be.

Even if you are going on a package tour with baggage handling inclusive, you will save time, money and frustration by sticking to what you can carry yourself without strain. For most people this means one suitcase with a total weight of 30 pounds or less, or two weighing 20 pounds apiece or less. A shoulder bag should weigh not more than 10 pounds. Take a light-weight collapsible one for emergencies.

Keep in mind that some package tour operators will only accept conventional hard luggage or framed soft bags. Duffle bags and the like are considered harder to fit on a tour bus.

It's a good idea to keep important papers, a camera, guidebooks, a change of underwear, your passport and shot card, other personal items, and perhaps a folding raincoat and hat in your shoulderbag. Women may wish to keep a small handbag in it as well. Carry the shoulderbag with you at all times.

Remember your luggage may be thoroughly searched at Soviet customs points. It is worth *not* wrapping up items in fancy paper or protective plastic. They are likely to be picked on.

What to wear. Starting from the bottom up, a good pair of shoes with thick soles and firm arch supports is your best protection against traveler's limp. Many sidewalks in Soviet cities are pot-holed and poorly maintained. Make sure the shoes are well broken-in and also well-heeled. You may have trouble getting repairs done on the spot in the U.S.S.R. Clothes should be light in the summer—cotton rather than synthetic; shirts and underwear drip-dry; laundry service is slow and cleaning facilities are limited though most hotels have ironing-rooms. There are virtually no self-service launderettes except in a few new housing-estates, out of the tourist's reach. A raincoat, a cardigan or pullover (even in summer) are musts. In winter you will need a heavy overcoat plus woolen underwear, fur- or fleece-lined boots and gloves. (Fur hats—*shapki*—can be bought in the country but are now fairly expensive.)

Put together your travel wardrobe by selecting one or two basic colors and coordinating other colors with them to get the most mileage out of the least amount of clothes. Trouser suits are generally acceptable for women nowadays. Beware of *over-dressing,* even for the Bolshoi Ballet. Your Intourist hotel is probably the only place where you might prefer to look really sophisticated.

For cooler weather, try the layer system. Instead of dragging along a heavy coat, wear a lighter one with a sweater, insulated underwear, and extra layers of clothing. It is a more flexible system and will keep you warmer. Also, make sure that your coat has a hook on its collar so that attendants in public buildings can hang it in the coat check. In *really* cold weather wear woolen tights, *never nylon*—it can freeze on your knees! Winter boots should be waterproof, rather than fashionable.

Light indoor clothes are a must for winter. Russian central heating is efficient and you will *swelter* at night in anything woolen.

TRAVEL DOCUMENTS. U.S. Citizens: Apply several months in advance of your expected departure date. U.S. residents must apply in person to the U.S. Passport Agency in Boston, Chicago, Honolulu, Houston, Los Angeles, Miami, New Orleans, New York, Philadelphia, San Francisco, Seattle, Stamford (Conn.), or Washington DC, or to their local County Courthouse. In some areas selected post offices are also equipped to handle passport applications. If you still have a previous passport issued within the past 12 years you may use this to apply by mail. Otherwise, take with you: a birth certificate or certified copy thereof or other proof of citizenship; two identical photographs, 2 inches square, full face, black and white or color, on nonglossy paper, and taken within the past six months; $35 (plus a $7 processing fee if you apply by mail) or $20 for those under 18; proof of identity (with a photo and signature) such as a driver's license, previous passport, work or any governmental ID card. (Social Security and credit cards are *not* acceptable.) If you expect to travel extensively, request a 48- or 96-page passport rather than the usual 24-page one. There is no extra charge. U.S. passports are valid for 10 years or 5 years for those under 18. If your passport is lost or stolen, report it at once to the local authorities and apply for a replacement at the nearest U.S. Embassy or consular office, or the Passport Office, Dept. of State, 1425 K St. NW, Washington, DC 20524. Record your passport's number and date and place of issue in a separate, secure place.

If a resident non-citizen, you need a Treasury Sailing Permit, Form 1040C, certifying that Federal taxes have been paid; if a non-resident alien, you must file form 1040NR; apply to your District Director of Internal Revenue for this. You will have to present various documents: blue or green Alien Registration card; passport; travel tickets; most recently filed Form 1040; W-2 forms for the most recent full year; most recent current payroll stubs or letter; you'd be advised to check that this is all that's needed! To return to the United States you need a reentry permit if you intend to remain abroad longer than 1 year. Apply for it in person at least six weeks before departure at the nearest office of the Immigration and Naturalization Service, or by mail to the Immigration and Naturalization Service, Washington, DC.

Permanent Resident Aliens in the U.S. *Requirements for Departure and Reentry.* A permanent resident alien contemplating travel to the Soviet Union, as well as to most Eastern European countries, is required to apply to the Immigration and Naturalization Service for a reentry permit. To be cleared for reentry after travel to the Soviet Union, an Alien Registration Receipt Card (Form I-151) is valid as a reentry document. If you intend to be absent for a full 12 months, you will need also to file Form 1-131 2 or 3 months prior to departure from the U.S.

A permanent resident alien having doubt as to the validity of Form I-151 for reentry because of the contemplated itinerary abroad, should consult with the nearest Immigration and Naturalization Service office prior to commencing travel.

Permanent resident aliens of the United States, including stateless persons, who plan to visit the U.S.S.R., are cautioned that the Soviet Government does not recognize that the U.S. Government may have a valid interest in their welfare while they are in the Soviet Union. Permanent resident aliens planning to visit the U.S.S.R. should therefore bear in mind that the U.S. Government will be unable to assist them if they should be arrested or detained in the U.S.S.R. for acts allegedly committed during their sojourn or while they were residents of the U.S.S.R. in the past. The Soviet Government is most severe in punishing those whom it considers to have committed "war crimes" against the U.S.S.R.

British Subjects must apply for passports on special forms obtainable from the Passport Office or a travel agent. The application should be sent to the Passport Office according to residential area (as indicated on the guidance form). Apply at least 4 weeks before the passport is required. The regional Passport Offices are located in London, Liverpool, Peterborough, Glasgow, and Newport (Mon.). The application must be countersigned by your bank manager or by a solicitor, barrister, doctor, clergyman or justice of the peace who knows you personally. You will need two photos. The fee is £15 for a 30-page passport, £30 for a 94-page one; valid for 10 years.

Visas. To enter the Soviet Union you need a visa. For the tourist, the necessary application form will be supplied by Intourist or your travel agent. Four passport photographs must be enclosed. You also have to provide a complete itinerary, as well as an Intourist confirmation number. You should make your application either directly or through the travel agent not less than six weeks before you wish to enter the U.S.S.R. If you apply yourself, there is a $15 postage and handling fee (the visa itself is free). Travel agents and tour operators sometimes charge a little more.

Should you wish to make your application for a visa in person, you can do so at the Soviet Consulate, 1825 Phelps Place, Washington, DC 20008, or U.S.S.R. Consulate General in London, at the Soviet Consular Department, 5 Kensington Palace Gardens, W.8. You must enclose a letter from a travel agent confirming your hotel reservation, or you won't get a visa at all.

Transit visas are issued to those wishing to travel through the U.S.S.R. on their way to another country. Visitors applying for such a visa should make sure that their passport carries an entry visa (where required) to the next country to be entered from the Soviet Union and that a confirmed ticket for travel through the U.S.S.R. is submitted in addition to three photographs, a completed form and a confirmation of hotel reservation for any stopovers. Visas for business trips are the same as tourist visas.

Visas for private journeys are granted to people who visit relatives and friends in the U.S.S.R. and therefore do not require hotel reservations. Application should be made to the Consular Department in Washington, DC or London in person. (See below, "Visiting Relatives," also.)

No visas are required for passengers changing planes at a Soviet airport in transit to another country, provided they do not leave the airport and hold a valid air ticket to the country of destination with a clearly-stated time of departure not more than 24 hours after their arrival.

Passengers on cruises calling at Soviet ports *do not* require visas for a stay of up to 48 hours at each port, provided that they arrive and leave by the same ship and do not travel to any other city in the U.S.S.R. and that they use the ship as their hotel and purchase Intourist shore services. Round-trip passengers on regular scheduled sailings, however, must obtain visas in the usual way, supported by a letter from an accredited Intourist travel agent or the shipping agency. Groups of school children under 18 years of age, traveling on educational cruise ships, are allowed to enter ports of call and visit cities in the Soviet Union *without visas.* They must carry either passports or identity cards to be presented to the authorities at the ports of call.

Note. You should carry your passport with you at all times. Without it you may have problems getting into your own country's embassy. If you have to give up your passport when checking into an hotel, they will give you a hotel card which will get you into your embassy and which you must show to get back into your own hotel, especially at night. Passports can usually be reclaimed when you pay the bill, which, in any case, tends to be at the beginning of your stay if you are an individual traveler.

SOVIET CITIZENSHIP. Foreign governments cannot determine whether a naturalized American or British citizen or resident alien who was once a resident of Imperial Russia, the Soviet Union, or territory now under Soviet control may be considered by the Soviet Government to be a citizen of the U.S.S.R. The possibility cannot be excluded that such a person may be detained in the Soviet Union on the claim that he is also a Soviet citizen. Naturalized citizens or resident aliens who may be regarded by the Soviet Government as still possessing Soviet citizenship can clarify their status before leaving the U.S. or U.K. by renouncing Soviet citizenship through expatriation application to the U.S.S.R. Embassy in Washington or London.

A decision as to whether a former resident of the U.S.S.R. or territories now under Soviet administration should travel there can only be made by the individual himself in the light of his background and all other pertinent factors. Former Soviet citizens with a record of what Soviet authorities construed as "anti-Soviet activity" on U.S.S.R. territory have on occasion been harassed or expelled, or imprisoned.

Visiting Relatives in the U.S.S.R. Requires a *Visitor's Visa,* which usually takes a month but can take much longer. It costs nothing if you do it yourself. You must also obtain a letter of invitation from your Russian relatives. You may spend as little or as much money as you like; there is no set amount. If the visa is required for an emergency such as the serious illness or death of a relative, it is usually granted within three days.

In order to avoid delay or refusal of a visitor's visa, tourists have sometimes taken an Intourist tour to the U.S.S.R. and arranged on their own to meet relatives at a Soviet city near the place where the relative resides. This has not always worked out, for the Soviet authorities have sometimes prevented the Soviet citizens from traveling to meet their relatives. In such cases Intourist assumes no responsibility for any failure to meet relatives. The traveler hoping to visit relatives should mention them in his visa application.

Normally, if you are visiting a close relative—husband or wife, for instance—the authorities will turn a blind eye if you travel on a package tour but do not stay in your hotel. However, you do so at your own risk.

In the past, some tourists visiting relatives in the U.S.S.R. have been subjected to harassment by local officials or over-zealous Party agitators. This harassment, which at times was directed against the Soviet relatives themselves, has included press articles attacking the visitor. This does not usually happen nowadays.

HEALTH REGULATIONS. Tourists from other countries do not need to present any health certificates and there will be no medical examination. However, Soviet public health officers may ask for additional proof of health from tourists arriving from countries known to have an epidemic at the time of arrival. This may soon extend to an AIDS test for visitors from certain countries, mostly in Africa. The U.S. Public Health Service does not recommend cholera shots, but does urge all travelers to have had a tetanus vaccination within the last ten years. Medical service in the U.S.S.R. is free and available in any city or town. If a tourist is indisposed he is asked immediately to call in a doctor through his interpreter or through the hotel administration. First aid treatment and doctors' visits are gratis. If hospitalization is necessary a charge of 20 roubles daily is levied; this may be waived against unused prepaid travel services.

Your Health. Don't let us scare you by mentioning the word "health." Unless you have a special problem, such as being allergic to caviar, you are just as safe in the U.S.S.R. as you are in the U.S. or Britain. Nor is there any need to panic about nuclear fall-out after the Chernobyl disaster. The Soviet authorities are unlikely to allow any visitors anywhere where there is a risk, however remote, to their health.

Water is usually safe. There is no risk in the major cities, but if you have any doubts you can stick to the ever-present bottled or mineral water or coffee, tea and beer. Leningrad's water supply has had occasional problems (see below), and tourist hotels there will not warn you when their water is affected.

Food is as safe as it looks or as you see it handled. Greasy-spoon restaurants are a hazard anywhere in the world, so be certain that dairy products—including cheese and ice cream—have been carefully processed and handled, that fresh-vegetable salads are clean, and so on. Generally speaking, only independent travelers going off into the remoter, non-European parts of Russia—Central Asia, for instance—need worry about the food, and then only outside hotel restaurants. *You should, however, be warned that some visitors to Russia, especially in past years to Leningrad, have returned home with a specific form of diarrhea called giardiasis, caused by an intestinal parasite. It can be effectively treated, but needs slightly different drugs from the normal ones for diarrhea. If you find yourself suffering from such an illness after you return home, then consult your physician.*

Prescription medicines can be obtained with your home prescription only rarely. If you take a prescription medicine regularly, bring enough to last. If you are travelling in the winter or spring, take cough and cold remedies, especially for the northern U.S.S.R.

If you wear glasses or contact lenses, carry along an extra pair. Also, have your optician fill in the optical prescription on your yellow vaccination card.

Those with diabetes, people who are allergic to penicillin or other common drugs, those with a rare blood type, should wear a tag or bracelet or carry a wallet card indicating this.

INSURANCE. We suggest that you be fully covered with theft, loss, and disability policies prior to your arrival in the U.S.S.R. This does not mean that thefts are more prevalent here than elsewhere but you will be covering a lot of territory and we advise it for precaution's sake.

Generally speaking, you can insure: yourself and your family, your baggage, and your travel expenses. For personal accident insurance, "family" usually means a spouse and dependent children 14–21 years old.

Baggage and personal possessions can be insured against loss or damage. Usually covered are clothing, luggage, jewelry, cameras and sports equipment. Loss due to governmental seizure is *not* covered.

Trip cancelation insurance covers the non-refundable parts of your transportation and hotel expenses that you may lose from having to cancel because of death, illness, injury or pregnancy.

Liability coverage carried by local transportation, including taxis, is either non-existent or so low that you should take out your own coverage at home before leaving. You may be able to obtain insurance for baggage loss, etc. from *Ingosstrakh,* a Soviet firm, at some airports and border crossings.

Getting to the Soviet Union

FROM THE U.S. BY AIR. Only two airlines fly from North America to the Soviet Union: *Pan Am* (Pan Am Bldg., New York, N.Y. 10166; 212–687–2600) and *Aeroflot* (630 Fifth Ave., New York, N.Y. 10111; 212–397–1660), the Soviet National carrier. Aeroflot flies once a week to Moscow from Washington, New York, and Montreal. Pan Am has two flights weekly, all of which leave New York, stop in Frankfurt, and then proceed to Moscow.

Despite the apparent paucity of options, it is still well worth your while to consult a travel agent before booking a flight. She or he may be able to book you a better flight. Many major European carriers fly to the Soviet Union from the continent and Great Britain; see below for more details.

Fares. Again, consult a travel agent; they can best help you pick your way through the thicket of international air fares. In general, however, there are four categories of ticket: First class, Business, Economy, and APEX. The first three are all quite expensive, offering for their excessive cost the liberty of booking, traveling, and canceling when you please. APEX tickets, on the other hand, restrict when you can buy your ticket (purchase usually must be made 21 days in advance), when you can fly, and how long you stay; minimum and maximum stays are regular parts of the package. They are also quite inexpensive compared to other tickets. In early 1988, the roundtrip fares New York–Moscow, were: First class, $4,122; Business $2,536; Economy $2,060; APEX $885–1,035 (depending on when you fly).

FROM THE U.S. BY SEA. A few years ago it was possible to sail to the Soviet Union from the United States aboard freighters. Check to see if a replacement service is in operation, or call Pearl's Freighter Trips, (718) 939–2400.

FROM THE U.K. BY AIR. *British Airways* and *Aeroflot* operate flights virtually every day from London to Moscow all year round, and once a week to Leningrad. *Japan Airlines* (JAL) stop off in Moscow en route to Tokyo from London; but you can only take advantage of these flights if you are flying all the way to Tokyo. A weekly Manchester–Moscow service was due to come into operation in 1988.

In 1988 the British Airways excursion return fare to Moscow was £418: Club Class return was £716. First Class return £928. Excursion round trip to Leningrad £396. Club round trip £632. Check in London for current reduced rate fares.

FROM THE U.K. BY SEA. The summer sailings from Tilbury to Leningrad by Baltic Steamship Line have now ceased, but there is a chance they may resume if a ship becomes available. Contact travel agents or *C.T.C. Lines,* 1 Regent St., London SW1Y 4NN (tel. 01–930 5833). Freighter buffs might take one of the weekly sailings by United Baltic Corp., from Purfleet to Helsinki, and then on by Estonian Shipping Co. ferry to Tallin. U.K. agent for UBC is John Good & Sons, 71 High St, Hull HU1 1QT (tel. 0482–25781).

FROM ELSEWHERE BY SEA. There is an all-year-round car ferry between Stockholm and Leningrad, and a ship connection in summer between Helsinki and Leningrad. From East Asia there is a regular service to Nakhodka from both Hong Kong and Yokohama. All these services are by the latest Soviet ships of the *Estonia* type, carrying 330 passengers. Bookings from Japan can be made through the *Japan-Soviet Tourist Bureau,* 1–12–20 Awaza, Nishi-Ku, Osaka 550. Tel. 06–531–7416.

FROM THE U.K. BY RAIL. Direct services carrying a Soviet sleeper-coach are available throughout the year from London in conjunction with Harwich–Hook of Holland or Dover–Ostend boats. They offer a comfortable two-day journey through Central and Eastern Europe with no need to change compartments or trains. Soviet sleeper-coaches are designed for long-distance travel—as we shall see when discussing travel within the U.S.S.R.—and the compartments normally have one or two berths (first class) and three or four berths (second class). There are washstands in first class compartments. In winter, a minimum inside temperature of 64°F. (18°C.) is maintained. Each coach has its own conductor. On most sections of the route, a restaurant car is attached. Tea, coffee and biscuits are served by the conductor, but many travelers on long hauls buy food in stations. Dining cars belonging to various railway systems are attached to these trains. In Western Europe there is no currency problem but after you cross into East Germany (The German Democratic Republic) payment is usually accepted only in western currency from Western travelers. And the change, if you do not have the right amount, is likely to be in kind, e.g. chocolate or a bottle of beer. In the U.S.S.R. roubles only are accepted in the dining car. Try if possible to change some of your currency at the Brest station (Polish/U.S.S.R. frontier) into roubles to pay for your meals. There is a long wait there anyway.

During the summer, the through train departs daily from London's Liverpool Street Station, at 9 or later according to season, and goes via the Hook of Holland. In winter it runs on Mondays, Wednesdays, Fridays and Sundays. It arrives at the Byelorussky Station in Moscow at 2.40 P.M. two days later. Trains via Ostend (change at Aachen) run from London's Victoria Station, leaving daily all the year round. The schedule includes stops at Berlin and Warsaw. Cost in 1988: £354 single, first class; £176 single, second class, both including sleepers.

Moscow and other Soviet cities have direct rail connections with most major European cities.

From Finland. A pleasant way to visit the U.S.S.R. is to enter from Helsinki by train. There are two trains from Helsinki. One leaves Helsinki just after 1 P.M. and arrives in Leningrad at 8.45 in the evening. The other leaves Helsinki around 5 P.M. and reaches Moscow at 8.55 the next morning.

FROM EUROPE BY CAR. You can enter the U.S.S.R. by car at the following border points: From **Finland:** Torfyanovka and Brusnichnoye. From **Poland:** Brest and Shegini. From **Czechoslovakia and Hungary:** Chop. From **Romania:** Porubnoye and Leusheny. It is obligatory to plan your trip in advance and notify Intourist of your route and then keep to it. It is possible to ship your car to Leningrad or to the Soviet Black Sea ports.

Automobile travel along certain specified routes is presently permitted, with or without Intourist guides. Only mature and experienced drivers should consider unaccompanied motor trips. Driving conditions are far more rugged than in Western Europe; service stations are rare. Soviet driving regulations are complex and very strictly enforced. Foreign drivers who violate them are subject to the full severity of Soviet law (including trial and extended imprisonment).

Automobile travelers should be fully insured under policies valid for the U.S.S.R. Such insurance may be placed with a number of Western firms or with Ingosstrakh, the Soviet organization which insures foreigners. (See "Traveling in the Soviet Union by Car", later in this section).

Upon entering the Soviet Union, all auto tourists are required to sign an obligation guaranteeing the re-export of their automobiles; this guarantee also applies to damaged vehicles. Tourists have been required to pay quite large sums to ship their damaged automobiles out of the Soviet Union to neighboring countries for repair because necessary repairs could not be made in the U.S.S.R.

FROM EUROPE BY BUS. There are currently no through bus services from western Europe to the Soviet Union. But, as usual, this situation is liable to unpredictable change, so check with your travel agent. See Intourist's summer brochure for its *Grand Central Europe* coach tours, taking in Brussels, Heidelberg, Vienna, Budapest, Uzhgorod, Lvov, Kiev, Orel and Moscow, returning to London by air. Its *Cities of Europe* coach tour, via Brussels, Hanover, Berlin, Poznan, Warsaw, Minsk and Smolensk to Moscow, Novgorod and Leningrad, is another interesting summer route. Both take two weeks.

Arriving in the Soviet Union

CUSTOMS. A customs declaration form must be filled out on arrival which should be retained until departure from the country. This allows you to import free of duty and without any special license all articles intended for personal use, clothing—but remove price tags from new garments—food (except fresh vegetables and fruits, which must be presented for examination), tobacco and cigarettes, alcoholic drinks, perfume, sports equipment, camera, cine-camera—all of this in reasonable quantities for personal consumption or use. It is illegal to sell personal possessions in the Soviet Union. It is prohibited to import weapons and ammunition; opium, hashish and pipes for smoking them; pornographic articles and pictures; printed matter, printing blocks, negatives, exposed film, photos, phonograph records, tape recordings, motion picture films, manuscripts, designs and drawings "harmful to the U.S.S.R. politically or economically." This includes religious literature. You are allowed to import *one* Bible, in your native language, for your own use, but you are expected to take it out again with you when you leave.

You can export the following articles bought in the U.S.S.R. for foreign currency exchanged for roubles at the U.S.S.R. Foreign Trade Bank and the U.S.S.R. State Bank: fur coats, muffs, boas, etc. (one each), pocket or wrist-watches (two), dinner-, tea-, or coffee-sets (one of a kind). You can also take out souvenirs, in reasonable amounts. Of items made of precious metals, you may take out one wrist-watch or bracelet or a pocket-watch without a chain, one wedding ring, one ring with precious stones, one gold-framed pair of spectacles, one pair of earrings with precious stones (only women tourists) and articles made of silver not heavier than 400 grams (less than half a pound). There may be limitations to the export of amber, even if purchased in a Beryozka (foreign currency) shop. But check with Intourist. Other goods bought for foreign currency in the specialized Beryozka shops at the airfields, hotels, railway stations and ports (including cameras, phonograph records, handicraft articles, caviar and musical instruments) can also be taken out upon presentation of the appropriate shop receipts. Books published before 1945 technically need an export permit—Intourist will advise you. In 1981 the restriction was extended to books published before 1975 *in any language,* but check with Intourist.

Never try to smuggle out icons (see page 30) or antique items. On entering the Soviet Union, drivers must sign a declaration that they will re-export their car at the end of their tour. No taxes or customs duties are payable for a temporary import.

Note. Customs and passport officials are the first Soviet citizens you will meet. It has to be said that they can make a very unpleasant impression on the first-time visitor. There is no point in being aggressive to them; simply make it clear that you have nothing to hide and allow them to conduct their very time-consuming ritual of checking and *re*-checking the color of your eyes, etc. They are only carrying out orders, often under the gaze of their superiors. Don't let these bureaucrats sour the rest of your trip. Laugh it off—but not to their faces!

CURRENCY REGULATIONS. You must *not* import or export roubles, Soviet State loan bonds or Soviet lottery tickets. All foreign currency in travelers checks and banknotes which tourists bring with them must be declared on the customs form upon entry and the declaration retained and produced whenever you change money. There is no limit as to the amount you can import and, in fact, Russia is one country where it is more useful to have a fair supply of small denomination foreign cash (especially $ and £) handy than travelers checks—especially for use in foreign-currency stores and bars. Roubles cannot be obtained outside the country. Foreign currency can be converted at the exchange office *(bureau de change)* of the Soviet State Bank at all border points, at the official rate of exchange, now about £1 per 1 rouble, $1 per 58 kopeks. These offices can be found in the hotels, at the international air and sea ports of the Soviet Union, but hours of operation are often irregular, so travelers should plan ahead. Each transaction will be recorded on a receipt which you must preserve (it will be stapled to your original customs declaration). On leaving the country—*and not before*—you can change back the remaining roubles into foreign currency at the airport. It is illegal to carry out any transactions in foreign currency except through the U.S.S.R. State Bank or Intourist or other authorized State Organization. You would be well advised not to change too much of your currency at a time, the more so as the re-exchange rate when you leave the country is less than the exchange rate was when you entered it, so you lose some as you convert back. You will not need, by and large, to use a great deal of Russian money, and changing it back when you leave can be tedious. (There is a black market, but unless you are *very* foolhardy, you will not have any dealings with it.)

Credit Cards. At the moment, both *American Express* and *Diners Club* credit cards are accepted in a limited number of Intourist offices, in hotels and elsewhere, in the Soviet Union for additional tours booked on the spot, some restaurant reservations, theater tickets, goods bought in 'Beryozka' shops, etc. You can be sure they will be recognized in Moscow and Leningrad, and Intourist reports that 21 other major destinations now accept them as well. *Bankamericard, MasterCard, Visa,* and *Carte Blanche* are now widely accepted also.

Staying in the Soviet Union

HOTELS AND OTHER ACCOMMODATIONS. Detailed information about hotels, etc., will be found in the chapters dealing with the different cities and regions, later in this book. You can state your preferred hotel from the list supplied by Intourist but you cannot pick one *not* on this list. You will find, more often than not, that you do not get your first choice. Nor can you normally alter your booking once you have made it.

Many of the Intourist hotels are modern and reasonably comfortable, though their ratings differ according to individual experiences. Only the deluxe class can be considered to be near the highest American and British standards and even in these you will find that the elevator, perhaps, cannot be used for going down less than three stories and that you have to hand over your key every time you leave your room to the rather severe lady sitting at the stairhead. Although these ladies were officially "abolished" in 1986 in most hotels and a Western-style system of collecting keys from a reception desk in the front hall was introduced, reports have it that they are still there! Room service is sometimes less than perfect. Beds can be uncomfortable—and *short!* The water supply may be interrupted and you may find that while you can have milk in your coffee in the coffeeshop, you have to drink it black in the restaurant, a hundred yards away. Dining-room service can range from excellent to poor.

For American and most British travelers, Intourist recommends deluxe or first class.

Hotel Rates. There are three classes of tourist accommodations for the individual traveler, although the cheapest is rarely available, especially in Moscow and Leningrad, and elsewhere in high season.

Prices are given in roubles, for which the exchange rate during 1988 was 58 roubles to $100 and 1 rouble to the pound sterling. This rate is fixed by the Soviet government, bears no relation to the value of the rouble in international markets, and is subject to change without notice—so do check for the latest position.

All prices include breakfast and porterage of two pieces of hand luggage in the hotel on arrival and departure. N.B.: Transfers not included.

Rates in **Deluxe Class** are from 110 roubles per room per day in certain Moscow and Leningrad hotels (up to 200 roubles in particular luxury suites in the *Hotel National* in Moscow); accommodations consist of 3–4-room suites with private bath. Deluxe rates elsewhere range from 52–68 roubles, depending on the season. If the 3–4-room suites are unavailable, you may be offered a 1–2-room suite, at 72 roubles in Moscow and Leningrad (120–150 in *Hotel National*), and 37–48 roubles elsewhere—with the exception of the *Hotels Viru* and *Tallinn* in Tallinn, where the rate is 70–80 roubles all year round. Lunch and dinner add about another 6 roubles per person per day.

First Class accommodations are available in most Intourist locations. Rooms have bath or shower, breakfasts are of first-class standard, and lunch and dinner will add around 4 roubles per person per day to the bill. First Class rates, per person, are 50 roubles for a single, 25 roubles for a double in Moscow or Leningrad (more in top hotels); elsewhere, 22–29 roubles for a single, 14–18 for a double, according to the season (in Tallinn, 60 roubles single, 35 double).

Finally, there is **Tourist Class.** This is limited to certain cities and is more likely to be offered to budget travelers such as youth groups—but check its availability for individual tourists with Intourist. Accommodations comprise hotel room with wash basin, and bath or shower available on the same floor. There is a first-class menu for breakfast, while lunch and dinner costs about an extra 4 roubles per person per day. Price, per person, in a shared room, is 15–19 roubles per day, depending on the season.

Note: the *off season* lasts October through March; the *ordinary season* is April through September—save in Moscow and Leningrad, where *high season* special rates apply all year round. *High season* in Caucasus and Black Sea coastal resorts lasts June through September, in mountain resorts June to October 20 and mid-January through March (skiing).

Discounts are available in cities other than Moscow and Leningrad from October 1 through April 30 (with the exception of transport between cities and separate services) and these range upwards from 15% on medical treatment courses and 25% on group tours (except for bus tours which get only 15%). Children under 12 accompanying their parents as individual tourists are given free accommodations and breakfast in hotels and motels, provided they share their parents' room. On *à la carte* tours children have a 50% discount. As some cities will have only modest hotel accommodations, those on deluxe tours get a discount if they have to stay in a lower category room. Tourists arriving for medical treatment are given a 45% discount on the domestic tariffs for travel to and from the place of treatment.

Motels. These consist of Deluxe 1–2-room suites or else First Class accommodations. Prices range from 50 roubles for a Deluxe suite in Moscow, to 45 roubles for the same but in Leningrad, to 30 roubles per person for a First Class single in either city, to 17–22 roubles elsewhere.

ROUGHING IT. There *are* ways to travel cheaply in the Soviet Union, but you are still subject to Intourist arrangements. Hitch-hiking is practically impossible. There are not enough cars on the roads and long-distance trucks are strictly forbidden to pick anybody up. Nor will you find the native motorist inclined to do so (except for unofficial local taxi services).

Camping, however, has a fairly long tradition, and because of the growing interest in it, Intourist has expanded its facilities for foreign campers. But the number of recommended (i.e. authorized) camping sites is still rather limited (19 as of mid-1988) and special arrangements must be made for each group (more difficult for individual campers to do). You have to follow a pre-fixed itinerary, day by day. Intourist will supply latest information on itineraries and campsites.

One British organization which arranges camping tours by minibus is *Jet-Trek*, 25 Battersea Bridge Road, London S.W.11, tel. (01)–223–2244. Another is *Contiki Travel Limited*, 7 Rathbone Place, London W.1, tel. (01)–637–2121, whose tours run from 4 to 11 weeks. *Top Deck*, 64 Kenway Road, London S.W.5, tel. (01) 373–5095/8406, has coach camping tours running from 4 to 6½ weeks, some taking in Scandinavia or Eastern Europe as well as Moscow, Leningrad, Kiev and Odessa.

Tentrek, 152 Maidstone Rd., Ruxley Corner, Sidcup, Kent DA14 5HS, tel. (01)–302–6426/7828, operates a 25-day coach camping tour through Holland, Scandinavia, to Leningrad, Kalinin, Moscow, Smolensk, Minsk and back to London via Warsaw, Berlin and Cologne. £460–480, meals included.

Intourist itself also offers low-cost camping tours for motorists who travel by bus or private car, *on the Intourist motor trip routes*. It is *not* advisable to wander off these routes, which are discussed in the section on travelling by car within the U.S.S.R. Intourist is also now offering Fly-Drive vacations with a choice of 5 pre-booked itineraries using a mix of hotels, motels and campsites. See the summer brochure.

All campsites are pleasantly located in green belt areas near main cities. They open on June 1, except the Butovo (Moscow) site which opens July 1. Most close on October 1, some in mid-September. Butovo closes on September 1.

They offer three kinds of services: (1) a parking site only; (2) a parking site and bed; and (3) a parking site and 2-bed bungalow, costing 3.50, 4.50 and 6.00 roubles per person per day respectively (prices at presstime). (3) only exists at Kiev, Minsk, Moscow and Odessa. These rates include (according to Intourist) the rental of bedding, kitchen utensils, tableware, use of electricity, showers, laundry, cooking facilities, etc., plus one sightseeing tour in each city on the tourist's itinerary, either in the tourist's own car (a guide joins you) or by Intourist bus. But take whatever basics you can with you, just in case.

While there are food shops in or near the camping areas, you are advised to bring as much food as you can carry with you—coffee and packet soups are two items practically unobtainable. Detergents are also useful.

RESTAURANTS. For eating in the Soviet Union you need, above all, patience, especially in hotels. It is quite useless to rebel against the system that can sometimes involve long waits for lunch or dinner, although some hotels offer self-service buffets. On the other hand, when you reserve a table at a restaurant through your Intourist bureau, you go to the head of the line and get priority over Soviet citizens! On often elaborate menus, ignore all the items where no prices are marked, since they are not available anyway. Except for some of the regional restaurants, the food is likely to be hearty and ample rather than *cordon bleu*. Although service can be slow, you can sometimes speed it up somewhat (relatively speaking!) by asking the waitress what she *suggests* and going along with her suggestions. Placing a packet of cigarettes on the table has been known to work—you imply that the waiter/waitress will get it if the service is good. Order a glass of tea to pass the time—it usually comes quickly. You can also, at some establishments, order your starters when you make your table reservation. That way, they are ready and waiting when you arrive.

It is very difficult to get a late meal in the Soviet Union. Cafés usually close at 10 or 11 P.M. and restaurants at 11 or 11.30 P.M. but diners are *not* admitted during the half-hour before closing time. The best restaurants usually accept Intourist meal coupons. The smaller ones have no foreign language menus, but you can always point and hope!

By the standards of most Western capitals, restaurants in the Soviet Union are modestly priced and not gourmet quality, with the exception of a few. Except when otherwise indicated in our listings, the normal dinner for two will cost between 8 and 16 roubles. This usually includes *zakuski* (hors d'oeuvres, often the highlight of the meal as they are in Russian homes), a main meat course, dessert and coffee. The same food at lunch costs a bit less. With Russian vodka and caviar, or Soviet champagne or brandy, the meal prices can mount rapidly.

Overcharging in restaurants is now common. Check that the waiter brings exactly what you ordered and no more, and that the service charge is shown, if included. Carry plenty of small change as waiters often short-change you if handed a large bill.

At least once during your visit try a snack in a good cafe outside your hotel, in one of the open-air cafes in the culture parks that are the pride of every Russian city, in a cafeteria, or in one of the many places specializing in shishkebab, pancakes, doughnuts, or ice cream.

Most Intourist package tours come with meals included. Tourists are issued with coupons: these have a definite value in roubles which varies according to deluxe, first- or tourist-class reservations. The coupons are valid in the restaurants of your own hotel, in those of other Intourist hotels, but not in outside restaurants. Reservations at the latter are a must; do it through your hotel desk, otherwise the doorman may turn you away. Go early. Wave your foreign passport quite shamelessly. Russian dinner hours are earlier than those in Western Europe.

Drinks are ordered by grams (100 or 200) or by the bottle. A normal bottle, priced at *over 12 roubles* in some restaurants, will hold about ¼ of a liter. Soviet regulations forbid the serving of more than 100 gr. of vodka per person per meal and since 1985 it has been illegal to serve it at all before 2 in the afternoon and the drinking age—for Soviet citizens at least—has been raised from 18 to 21. (Reportedly this does not apply to Intourist establishments.) A small relaxation in 1986 enabled wine shops in Moscow to open at 11 A.M. on Saturdays for the sale of wine and champagne, and extended opening hours to 8 P.M. at weekends. Normal closing time is 7 P.M. There are several varieties: *starka* ("old" vodka); *khorilka s pertsem* (Ukrainian, with hot peppers in it); *tminaya* (caraway flavored) or *yubileinaya* (jubilee); *pshenichnaya* (made from wheat) and *krepkaya* (at 110 proof, the strongest!). The Crimean and Caucasian wines are excellent, though some people will find them rather sweet. Good also is Armenian brandy. Azerbaijani is even better, but expensive. Port, madeira and vermouth have their Russian approximations if not equivalents.

NIGHTLIFE. By and large, there is no such thing in the Soviet Union, no nightclubs or bars, though there is often singing and dancing in restaurants and hotels, and a couple of Moscow and Leningrad hotels have late-night bars (open till 2 A.M.). There are *clubs* in great profusion, attached to various organizations and enterprises and also for writers, artists, etc. Some have restaurants which are not open to the public, though you might find a Russian friend who can take you there. But as factory and office work starts early, generally—except in their own homes or the country cottages (the *dachas*) of the privileged—people go to bed well before midnight and restaurants, bars, theatres, clubs and just about everything else closes by 11.30 P.M. In the summer resorts there is some relaxation of the rule, but even there, with many seeking rest or medical treatment, night-birds are not encouraged. But things are slowly improving, especially in Moscow, Leningrad and Tallinn, where there are now bars on the western model. In some places, they even serve western drinks for roubles, but entry charges are expensive. Not worth it unless you are homesick.

CULTURAL ACTIVITIES. You cannot fail to be impressed with the fact that culture is taken very seriously in the Soviet Union, and by all levels of the population, from the sophistication and elegance of the great opera and ballet theaters to the more "popular" but large and well-kept Culture Parks.

The theater, ballet and cinema are very popular and the number of seats available for tourists is limited, though many of the *best* are reserved for them. You should apply to the Service Bureau at your hotel as soon as possible—don't count on getting in at the last moment, though this may be easier in provincial cities, where programmes may be less impressive, though interesting. Most performances start at 6.30 or 7 P.M. and few end later than 11 P.M. On Sundays there are matinees, usually at 11 A.M. Even if you do ask for your tickets well in advance, you will probably find out only on the actual day whether you have got them—so planning your evening entertainment is not always easy. Tickets cost about 2–5 roubles (but can be several times as expensive through Intourist); they can be bought from kiosks inside the Metro stations or in the street.

The ballet seasons in Moscow and Leningrad last until the end of May and start again early in September. But many of the leading artists perform during the long summer recess in other towns, sometimes at open-air shows. Synopses are available in English at the Intourist service offices.

The Moscow Stars and the Leningrad White Nights festivals (the first in May, the second in June) are very popular and reservations in advance are vital.

The Obraztsov Central Puppet Theater in Moscow is a sheer delight; if some of its plays are rather heavily weighted with propaganda, the puppets are magnificent and the wit is sparkling. The Romany Gipsy Theater at 32 Leningradsky Prospekt, Moscow, in the Hotel Sovietskaya, is quite spectacular. At all theaters you must deposit your overcoat in the cloakrooms and you might want to hire a pair of binoculars for about 50 kopeks at the same time. This will enable you to

A view of Moscow's Kremlin, stretched along the Moskva River (top). A crowd in Red Square waiting to visit Lenin's Tomb.

The facade of the Bolshoi Theater — home of Moscow's opera and ballet companies.

get at the head of the long queue after the performance (persons returning binoculars get priority).

Foreign-language films are always dubbed in Russian—no subtitles. Performances are not continuous: your ticket only entitles you to a certain showing.

There are concert halls in all major cities, many of them attached to organizations—such as the House of Trade Unions, the Army, the Art Workers, etc.

Circus performances are given both indoors and (during the summer), outdoors in parks. There are evening shows, with matinees on Sundays and holidays.

If your schedule permits, be sure to spend an afternoon in the nearest Culture Park. These are a combination of public garden, performing arts center and amusement park or fun fair; and they are green, attractive, well kept, and well attended. You can eat, stroll, listen to music, contemplate monumental statuary, or ride the merry-go-round; and the openness and spontaneous enjoyment of the ordinary Soviet people around you is very catching. They are fun in winter, too!

GUIDE SERVICES. Guides and interpreters are provided by Intourist both for regular and special tourists. These, of course, vary in efficiency and intelligence, but all are carefully vetted by their employers. Many of them are students or language teachers earning extra money during their vacations or between jobs. Within certain limits, you will find that they identify themselves with your needs, interests and tastes; do not embarrass them by discussing politics or making unfavorable comparisons between the Soviet Union and your own country or vice versa.

If you require a guide for shopping trips or excursions to the theater outside the regular arrangements of Intourist, you can hire one for 24 roubles for 4 hours (22 roubles for business negotiations); for each extra hour another 3 roubles are payable (4.5 roubles for business). Guides for large groups of tourists cost 1 rouble per person for a period up to 3 hours; thereafter 30 kopeks per person for each extra hour become payable.

TIPPING. Officially, there is no tipping in the Soviet Union except in some hotels in Moscow and other large cities, where a 5–15% service charge may be added to your bill. But no one is insulted by tipping—especially taxi-drivers, barbers, delivery men and shoeshine boys (20 kopeks for all of them). Sometimes a small gift of a stick of fancy chewing gum or a lipstick or cigarettes will be even more welcome. Be careful about giving foreign coins or notes (even as a gift for collectors)—it is technically illegal. Felt pens, cigarettes and books (non-political!) make welcome gifts in lieu of tips. Tipping is, in fact, now an accepted practice and in restaurants, for example, worldwide techniques for ensuring tips are in operation. Go over your check with care! Suggested for waiters: 5 percent, porters about 30 kopeks each bag. In Moscow's *Cosmos Hotel* porterage costs 1 rouble.

SHOPPING. You will probably buy most items in the foreign-currency **Beryozka** shops. Other Russian shops may prove interesting, educational, and cheaper. They are generally crowded, and in most of them you will find that you have to line up three times—first to pick out what you want to buy and collect a ticket, then at the cashier's desk to pay and get the ticket stamped, and finally to collect your purchase. But at least you will be able to look at the people and see them in action—fighting to obtain some goods in short supply or arguing over this or that piece of merchandise.

In Moscow, **G.U.M.,** on Red Square, and **TSUM,** near the Bolshoi Theater, are the largest department stores and very characteristic of Soviet daily life. In other major cities, there is at least one such store. All of these have special souvenir departments. The larger shops have information desks whose staff speak foreign languages.

In the self-service shops, you are expected to give up whatever bag or case you are carrying in exchange for one supplied by the shop and then transfer your purchases after you have paid. In some ordinary shops, you can pay over the counter without having to stand in line again and again. There is no delivery to the hotels (except food from certain shops) nor will any shop mail presents abroad.

Some of the best presents include black caviar (sold in small sealed jars or large tins), Ukrainian hand-embroidered skirts or blouses, phonograph records, books, traditional silver-gilt and enamel ware, and wood, alabaster or pottery articles. The caviar is, in fact, in such short supply that it is likely to be found only in the special foreign-currency food shops in Moscow. Other good buys are balalaikas, guitars, samovars, fur hats, painted and lacquered boxes, the traditional Russian wooden nest of dolls *(matryoshkas),* clay figurines from Kymkovo, brightly painted bone carvings from Northern Russia; semi-precious ornaments from the Urals, and malachite, jasper and amber from the Baltic republics (this may now be on sale in Beriozka shops and exportable—ask Intourist); Daghestan and Turkoman carpets, Vologda handmade lace, cameras, chocolates, gift boxes of wine and vodka. Half liter bottles costing 8 roubles make vodka an expensive souvenir.

You might like to visit one of the big markets, which you should do as early in the day as possible. Usually you will find good-quality fresh fruit, which the hotels rarely serve, but prices are high. Honey, fresh eggs, dairy products and local handiwork are also available. The markets usually close at 5 P.M.

CLOSING TIMES. Banks, state offices and some shops and service establishments are closed on January 1–2, March 8 (International Women's Day), May 1–2 (May Day), May 9 (Victory Day), November 7–8 (Days of the Revolution) and December 5 (Constitution Day).

Banks and government offices are open from 9 or 10 A.M. until 5 or 6 P.M., with an hour's break for lunch. Groceries, bakeries and dairies open from 8 or 9 A.M. till 8 or 11 P.M., with a lunch break from 1 to 2 P.M. Other stores are usually open from 11 A.M. to 7 P.M., with a break from 2 to 3 P.M. Big department stores are open from 9 A.M. without a break. All shops, except a few food stores, now close on Sundays although in Moscow many of the big central stores remain open, and the Beryozka shops are open all day.

Restaurants are usually open from 11 A.M. till 11.30 P.M.,—sometimes with an hour's closure for a "lunch break"!, cafes from 8 A.M. to 8 P.M., though some open and close later. Movie shows start at different times during the day but mostly run from 9 A.M. until 10.45 P.M. A few Intourist hotels have foreign currency bars that stay open until 2 A.M. Museums have varying hours; on the day *before* their closing day, visiting hours sometimes end earlier than usual. Opening times in our Guide mean the time the museum itself is open. Last entry time is in general one hour before closing time, especially at places where there is an entry charge. The subway (Metro) runs from 6 A.M. until 12.30 A.M. except on holidays when it closes later. Public transportation runs from about 5 A.M. until almost 1 A.M. Taxis are available 24 hours a day, but you may have a long wait after 1 A.M.

MAIL. Any mail addressed to Moscow, Leningrad or other major cities can be sent either "Poste Restante" or care of Intourist. The Moscow address is Hotel Intourist, 3–5 Gorky Street, K-600 Moscow, U.S.S.R. (there is a small post office inside where foreigners can pick up their mail). Messages for tourists in other cities should be addressed c/o Intourist, followed by the name of the city. It is advisable, if mail is sent in advance, to give the date of your arrival at your destination. Intourist will keep letters for you to collect. In Leningrad, the Poste Restante is: C-400, Nevsky Prospekt 6, Leningrad.

Mail from European countries takes 3–10 days, from the U.S.A. and Canada a week or more. The address must be legible. The Post Office in Moscow is open daily from 8 A.M. to 10 P.M., at 1 Gorky Street (National Office). Post offices also handle the sales of stamps, registered mail and coupons for long-distance calls. Airmail letters and postcards abroad cost 45 and 35 kopeks respectively up to $\frac{1}{4}$ of an ounce. Telegrams, ordinary rate, cost 30 kopeks per word to Great Britain, 40 kopeks to all cities in the U.S.A. Express telegrams are charged at double the regular rate.

Parcels are not delivered to hotels but the addressee is notified of their arrival and told where to collect them.

To dispatch parcels, you should not pack their contents but rather purchase a standard wooden or cardboard box at the nearest post office. It will be packed for you by post office personnel. The maximum weight, including packing, is 22 lb. or 10 kg.

TELEPHONES. Most Intourist hotels have dial telephones in each room. Usually, you dial "8" before the town number needed, except in Moscow where it should be "2." With non-dialing telephones, ask the operator for *"go-rod"* (outside) and wait for a dialing tone. If you are unable to speak Russian, use English or, for general assistance or in case of emergency, ask the operator for "Service Bureau" or "administrator." In public booths, drop a 2-kopek coin or two 1-kopek coins in the slot, lift the receiver, wait for dialing tone and then dial. There is a limit of 3 minutes if there is a line of people outside but no extra charge for overtime. If the line is busy, hang up and the coin is returned. For service, dial 05, for telegraph and cables 06, for long-distance 07, for information 09.

Long-distance calls (including international) made from the hotel must be booked through the Service Bureau. Otherwise, go to a long-distance telephone office (called *peregovorny punkt*) where you will be asked to pay in advance. Calls cost 3 roubles a minute to Great Britain (minimum 9 roubles); 6 roubles to the United States. Calls during holiday season (e.g. on New Year's Eve) should be booked well ahead. Urgent calls can sometimes be arranged with much less delay at double the normal charge. Bear in mind that the telephone system in the U.S.S.R. is not of the most modern and that backlogs and delays are common.

PHOTOGRAPHY. Bring your own film and have it developed after you return home. Take a supply of hi-speed film (Kodak ASA 1000 color print is recommended) for interiors of churches, where flash may be forbidden (it damages icons, frescoes, etc.), and for those gloomy winter days on end-of-season tours. A wide-angle and/or zoom lens is another must. Take an X-ray-proof film bag for airport security checks; at some smaller places in the U.S.S.R. the equipment used is not of the most modern variety, and repeated passage through it may affect films, although the official in charge may assure you everything will be fine. At some airports they do not allow films to bypass the machine.

You can photograph most things, but use your common sense: don't photograph anything that is clearly a "sensitive" installation—airports, factories, military installations or personnel, prisons, railway junctions or stations, telephone exchanges, etc. If in doubt, ask your guide. Photography is *un*-restricted in most tourist locations, but it is wiser *not* to take pictures from airplanes or trains, etc. If you intend taking close-ups of people, *ask them,* even if only by gestures . . . this isn't security, just politeness.

LAUNDRY AND DRY CLEANING. Available in Intourist hotels, but service is generally slow and not always punctual. Make arrangements with your chambermaid for laundry, as room service is available only in very few hotels. Try the porter for dry cleaning. Most hotels have do-it-yourself ironing rooms. Technically you are not allowed to wash clothes in hotel bedrooms. Launderettes are few and far between in Moscow and Leningrad, virtually non-existent elsewhere, and you have to remove all buttons first.

ELECTRICITY. Sometimes it is 127V, but mostly 220V, and usually it is AC. Better inquire before plugging in anywhere. Sockets require a continental-type plug or adaptor. The use of hairdryers in hotel rooms is banned.

SPORTS. Mountain Climbing and Skiing facilities are available, for groups only in the Elbrus, Dombai and Tsakhkadzor areas of the Caucasus at the Hotel Itkol in Elbrus and Hotel Dombai. (Skiing only at Dombai. Elbrus only offers tourist-class accommodations and Tsakhkadzor can only be visited as a day trip from Yerevan.) The rates are, generally speaking, the same as at the vacation resorts. The **skiing** season is January to March, **climbing,** June to August. The off season is April

1 to May 31 and November 1 to December 31, and the ordinary season is January 1 to March 31 and June 1 to October 31. Intourist now also offers one-week cross-country skiing holidays from London, combining 3 or 4 nights in Moscow and Leningrad and 3 or 4 nights in the ski centers of either Suzdal (near Moscow) or Olgino (near Leningrad). Price around £330. See their Winter brochure. **Skating** for foreign visitors is available from October to May, excluding March, at the Medeo Rink at Alma-Ata. Inclusive tours can be arranged. N.B. Own skates, no hire.

Horse-riding classes are available through Intourist at Pyatigorsk for individuals and groups. Pack your own clothes.

Hunting and fishing vacations are offered in the Northern Caucasus at the Krasny Les and Krasnaya Polyana hunting preserves, which are, respectively, 50 and 70 km. from Krasnodar. You can hunt deer, bear and boar here and also at the North Ossetian hunting preserve in the Caucasus, about 20 to 45 km. from Ordzhonikidze. Here the hunting is for deer, roe-deer, aurochs (ibex), chamois, boar and bear; trout fishing is also available. At the Rostov hunting and fishing preserve, 125 km. from Rostov-on-Don, game bird shooting and freshwater fishing are offered. In Siberia, there is the Baikal hunting preserve, about 150 km. from Irkutsk, where you can hunt for Manchurian deer and bear. Finally, in Azerbaijan, at the Kubinsk hunting preserve (260 km. from Baku), the Caucasian aurochs (ibex) is hunted.

Extra services are provided: transfers by car to and from the hunting areas (the cost depending on the distance); transportation within the preserve either by car or by horse at a daily rate; services of a huntsman or huntsmen, depending on the type of game; rental of a hunting rifle (with units of ten cartridges); accommodations in hunting lodges or tents with full board. Both individuals and groups are accepted.

You can bring your own hunting gun into the Soviet Union, provided that you carry a voucher issued by an Intourist office or an accredited travel agent to the effect that you intend to hunt on Soviet territory. All sporting rifles must be presented for customs inspection and the serial numbers declared in the customs form. They must be taken out when the hunter leaves the country.

Traveling in the Soviet Union

BY AIR. The Soviet Union claims to have the world's biggest total route mileage. The big cities are all linked by air. The main airport of Moscow is Sheremetyevo, with two modern and very well equipped terminals. Domodedovo and Vnukovo are used mostly for domestic flights. Transportation to and from the airports is supplied by Intourist and is likely to be included in the cost of your group booking. Baggage delivery and customs inspection can be very slow at Sheremetyevo. Foreigners are assigned to a special Intourist lounge—make sure your bus or taxi sets you down at the right building for departure. You usually jump the baggage line for boarding.

Three types of planes are used on the Soviet airline *Aeroflot*,—the Ilyushin, the Tupolev and the Antonov, all named after their designers and identified by the first two letters of their names. The airlines have both jets and turbo-prop planes. The IL–86, a wide-bodied, 350-seater jumbo jet, the first Soviet plane equipped to show in-flight films, is now being increasingly used on some internal and international routes.

While their sound-proofing is not always perfect and you might be disturbed by the unfamiliar noise of the air conditioning, the seats are comfortable, meals are satisfactory (although light snacks only are served on flights under four hours long, so try to take your own food on board) and service fair. Most of the tours within the Soviet Union include air travel—either exclusively or in combination with other forms of transportation. Your average luggage allowance is 44 lb. Sometimes they weigh hand-luggage, too. In late autumn and winter, bad weather often causes considerable delays in air travel in the U.S.S.R. Overbooking on domestic flights can also be a problem; double check your booking!

BY TRAIN. The Soviet rail network is the largest and most heavily used in the world, carrying over 11 million passengers daily on about 150,000 kilometers of track, over a third of it electrified.

All Soviet trains start exactly on time (if they are not mysteriously canceled altogether); there is a broadcast warning five minutes before departure but no whistle or "all aboard!" call, so you must be careful not to be left behind. There are four classes, of which the *deluxe* offers soft seats and private washrooms; the other classes have washrooms at the end of the cars. The *first-class* service is called "soft seat", with spring-cushioned berths; there are two or four berths in each compartment. There is no segregation of the sexes and you might find yourself sharing a two-berth compartment with someone of the opposite sex. The *second* or "hard-seat" class has a cushion on wooden berths, available in two-, three- and four-berth compartments. The *third class*—wooden berths without compartments—is used mostly in local service and rarely sold to foreigners. Most compartments have a small table, limited room for baggage (including under the seats) and usually a loudspeaker which can be cut off other than for arrival announcements on the rare occasions when these are made. In soft class there is also a table lamp.

The busiest and most important route is between Moscow and Leningrad. The new fast—up to 125 m.p.h.—ER-200 trains have been operating on the Moscow–Leningrad route, the fastest services completing the 407 miles in just over four hours. The leading overnight train on this route with sleeping cars in both soft and hard cars is the *Red Arrow* which leaves each city at about midnight arriving at 8 A.M. the next day. Hi-speed trains are also being introduced on the Minsk–Riga, Moscow–Kiev and Moscow–Brest routes. Sleepers to the Baltic capitals are also of very high quality. The longest route is that of the Trans-Siberian Railway, with a mystique all of its own. Although the experience is highly recommended, you have to be fairly easy-going and adaptable really to get the most out of it. Such a long journey inevitably involves some discomfort for the elderly. When you travel on the trans-Siberian you'll find yourself in a different world. People wear pyjamas or dressing-gowns, there is much tea-drinking and talk—and you are likely to find someone speaking some Western language with whom to strike up a friendship. The dining cars are well equipped, the meals have generous portions and tea and snacks are available almost constantly. In every car, the conductor keeps a samovar on the go night and day and serves you refreshing hot lemon tea in tall glasses. It is not always easy to get a meal just when you want it on a Russian train. You won't starve but lunch could be at midday one day and three in the afternoon the next. Likewise with dinner. You are always handed an impressive menu—but are more than likely to find that most of the dishes are "off."

Railway tickets are called coupons and are sold in a stapled cover without which they are not valid—so you must make sure that the conductor removes only the appropriate section. The baggage allowance is 77 lb. in the compartment; any excess must be placed in the baggage car. Soviet trains are either electrically or diesel hauled although steam is still used in places for freight haulage. They use broad-gauge tracks and their running is smooth (albeit relatively slow) and there is more space than in the European trains. The passenger trains are divided into three types: fast, express and long-distance trains of sleeping coaches alone. There are local commuter trains into all major cities.

BY CAR. These are the *official rules* for foreign motorists touring the U.S.S.R.:

1–In the streets of towns, populated areas and on highways, traffic keeps to the right.

2–Touring motorists must follow *only* Intourist routes, according to whichever tour they have chosen.

3–Tourists driving in the U.S.S.R. must have the following papers: a passport that has been stamped at the hotel, motel or camping site at the first stop-over point after their entry; an international driver's license or a national license *with an insert in Russian* (available at the first Intourist service bureau en route for 50 kopeks), an international certificate of registration of the motor car in the country of departure; a voucher for Intourist service coupons; a "Motoring Tourist's Memo" indi-

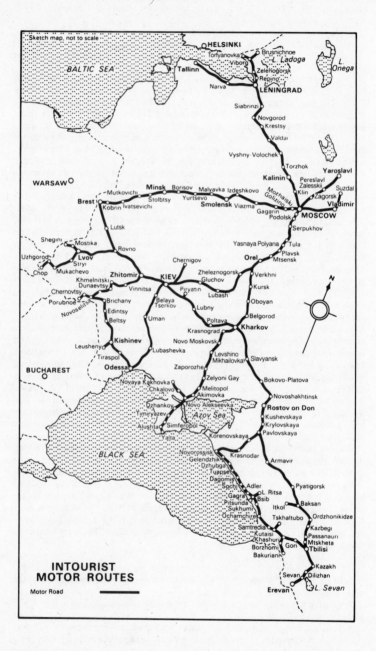

Sketch map, not to scale

BALTIC SEA

HELSINKI
Torfyanovka
Viborg
Brusnichnoe
L. Ladoga
L. Onega

Tallinn
Narva
Repino
Zelenogorsk
LENINGRAD

Siabrinzi

Novgorod
Krestsy
Valdai

Vyshny-Volochek
Torzhok
Yaroslavl

Kalinin
Pereslavl Zalesskii
Klin
Suzdal
Zagorsk
Vladimir

WARSAW

Minsk
Borisov
Malyavka Izdeshkovo
Mozhaisk Golizino

MOSCOW

Mutkovichi
Stolbtsy
Yurtsevo
Smolensk
Viazma

Brest
Kobrin Ivatsevichi
Gagarin
Podolsk

Lutsk
Serpukhov

Shegini
Mostika
Rovno
Yasnaya Polyana
Tula
Plavsk

Uzhgorod
Lvov
Stryi
Orel
Mtsensk

Chop
Mukachevo
Zhitomir
KIEV
Chernigov
Zheleznogorsk
Gluchov
Verkhni

Khmelnitski
Dunaevtsy
Vinnitsa
Piryatin
Kursk

Chernovtsy
Belaya Tserkov
Lubash
Oboyan

Porubnoe
Novoselitsa
Brichany
Edintsy
Lubny
Belgorod

Beltsy
Uman
Poltava

Kishinev
Krasnograd
Kharkov

Leusheny
Lubashevka
Novo Moskovsk

Tiraspol
Levshino Mikhailovka
Slavyansk

Odessa
Zaporozhe

Novaya Kakhovka
Zelyoni Gay
Bokovo-Platova

Chkalovo
Melitopol
Akimovka
Novoshakhtinsk

BUCHAREST

Dzhankoy
Timiryazev
Novo Alekseevka
Rostov on Don
Kushevskaya

Alushta
Simferopol
Azov Sea
Krylovskaya

Yalta
Korenovskaya
Pavlovskaya

BLACK SEA
Novorossisk
Krasnodar

Gelendzhik
Dzhubga
Armavir

Tuapse
Dagomis
Sochi
Adler
L. Ritsa
Pyatigorsk

Gagra
Bsib
Itkol
Baksan

Pitsunda
Sukhumi
Ochamchire
Tskhaltubo
Ordzhonikidze

Samtredia
Kazbegi

Kutaisi
Khashuri
Passanauri

Borzhomi
Gori
Mtskheta
Tbilisi

Bakuriani
Kazakh

Sevan
Dilizhan

Erevan
L. Sevan

**INTOURIST
MOTOR ROUTES**

Motor Road

cating the tourist's name, citizenship, car license number, itinerary, dates and stop-over points. This is presented to you on arrival in the country. You also need a certificate of obligation promising to take the car out of the U.S.S.R., to be registered with the customs at the point of entry. On arrival in the U.S.S.R. you also have to pay a 10 rouble road tax plus 5 roubles for a trailer.

4—Such a "Memo" is not issued to groups traveling in a bus. Such groups must be accompanied by an interpreter-guide and must have a program of visits to towns on the itinerary with indication of their arrival and departure dates from each town, camping site or motel. A coach up to 40 seats is liable to pay a 40-rouble road tax on entry into the U.S.S.R. Over 40 seats and you pay 50 roubles. The fee may be included in group arrangements.

5—The car must have a national license plate as well as an international sign indicating its country of origin, conforming to the rules established by international convention.

6—Motoring tourists must observe the traffic regulations in force in the U.S.S.R. "as well as the rules regulating public order". Any change in their chosen itinerary must be authorized by a written permit registered at the nearest Intourist branch office on the highway.

7—For any breach of law and order, traffic regulations and rules of travel through Soviet territory, tourists are answerable under Soviet law.

8—Motoring tourists must keep their cars in good technical condition and abstain from driving if their cars endanger traffic safety.

9—In all cases, motorists must be observant of traffic safety. They should *avoid night driving,* drive at a safe speed (particularly after rain, in fog and in poor visibility): in towns and populated areas they should not exceed the speed limit of 60 k.p.h. (37 m.p.h.), though it might be pointed out here that on the wide streets of Moscow few people observe this rule. The speed limit on highways is 90 k.p.h. (56 m.p.h.). The official regulations warn you to be careful when passing other vehicles in motion; to dip your headlights at night at least 150 yards from the oncoming traffic; to switch on parking lights in the evening and night when in towns; refrain from halting in forbidden areas or where only transit passage is permitted. Wearing front seat belts is *compulsory.* Speeding or dangerous driving carries a fine of up to 50 roubles.

10—The use of the horn is permitted only on highways outside towns, in thick fog, or when an accident or collision can be prevented only by sounding it.

11—Tourists must give right of way to special-purpose vehicles—such as fire-engines and ambulances—on hearing their sirens. In some big cities a special lane is reserved for "official" cars which speed along apparently in defiance of the 60 k.p.h. limit. They are usually local Party dignitaries, etc. Be prepared.

12—At traffic lights you can only proceed when the light is green—and this includes left and right turns. You must wait for a signal—an arrow—permitting the turn, and give way to pedestrians still crossing.

13—Drunken driving carries *very heavy penalties.*

14—Foreign tourists may travel on Intourist itineraries in their own cars or in cars hired from Intourist, which can be hired with or without drivers. Buses are not rented without drivers.

15—As many foreign insurance companies are unwilling to insure cars touring in the Soviet Union or will charge very high premiums, you may wish to insure with *Ingosstrakh,* 12 Pyatnitskaya Street, Moscow (tel: 231–1658, telex 7144, cables: Moscow, Ingosstrakh). Full insurance cover, including third party liability, may be arranged either in advance, at the point of entry into the U.S.S.R., or in Moscow. Insurance may be arranged in any currency; the premium is paid in the appropriate one and claims will be settled accordingly.

Cars hired in the Soviet Union carry accident insurance and tourist drivers are covered against civil liability arising from the use of the car; the premiums are included in the rental.

Note: In many cases, Ingosstrakh insists on its coverage, even if this duplicates foreign insurance.

Police. Traffic control on Soviet highways is exercised by traffic inspectors who are stationed at permanent posts, patrol in cars and on motorcycles. Information can be obtained from them on rules and specific conditions of travel by car on their itinerary; they will supply directions to hotels, motels, camping sites, restaurants, cafés, telephones, first-aid stations, filling and service stations. In case of any damage to the car, they will help in towing the damaged car to a service station. A tourist involved in a traffic accident must immediately report it to an inspector.

Filling Up. Be sure to refill your tank whenever possible, as service stations are few and far between. They are all listed in the book by Leonid Zadvorny (see below). Gas cost about 4 roubles per 10 liters in early 1988.

When starting, it is much better to leave large towns early in the morning to avoid traffic jams. Use your horn very sparingly.

In some narrow Moscow and Leningrad streets it is forbidden to park or overtake but in general you can park anywhere without looking a parking sign (though you must not park facing oncoming traffic). Night driving is discouraged and, in any case, not pleasant; few cars are equipped with dipping headlights and trucks are often parked along the road without parking lights. Russian pedestrians are not a very disciplined lot—they are likely to cross any time, even with the lights against them, so watch out. Hitch-hiking is discouraged. Keep your car clean—we have heard of people being fined for having a dirty car.

Driving might be a very enjoyable and instructive way of seeing the U.S.S.R. but it is also apt to produce adventures and frustrations. One reason why you must keep to the Intourist-chosen roads is the poor quality of the lesser roads.

Some Other Useful Points. According to the latest information (subject to change), Intourist offers itineraries to motorists (with certain stopovers and local excursions); these are covered by the routes shown on the map on page 29. Contact Intourist for the latest details; ask for their brochure *Motor Tours of the Soviet Union* and their *Motoring Map* leaflet which contains details of the highway code. It is possible to camp in the Soviet Union along the Intourist approved routes. See *Roughing It* earlier.

The British A.A. has issued a route map and guide for motorists traveling to Moscow from the West.

Progress Publishers (Moscow) has brought out a useful, 400-page hardcover book: *Motorist's Guide to the Soviet Union* by Leonid Zadvorny in English translation (2 roubles 80 kopeks if you buy it in the U.S.S.R.; also obtainable in Western bookstores stocking Soviet publications). It contains detailed route maps and descriptions of each available itinerary, city maps and a large fold-out map of Moscow, plus advice and information on everything from hotels and campsites to insurance, gasoline and servicing facilities. Recommended.

Gasoline coupons should be bought in advance; if you stay for a certain length of time you are entitled to a free voucher for 100 liters. The rental arrangements are of three kinds: self-drive cars for a definite rental period; self-drive cars with unlimited mileage; and chauffeur-driven cars. Details from Intourist or allied travel agent offices.

Rental cars without drivers are hard to find. Intourist generally insists you take a driver with the car, especially for out-of-town trips.

Finally, motorists are advised to bring a complete set of tools, a towing cable, a pressure gauge, a pump, a spare wheel, a repair outfit for tubeless tires, a good jack and one or two tire-levers, gasoline (petrol) can, a spare fan-belt, spare windscreen wiper blades and spark plugs. Have also a set of lamp bulbs and fuses, a set of contact-breaker points for the ignition distributor, a spare condenser, a box of tire valve interiors and a roll of insulating tape.

A first aid box, fire extinguisher and an accident warning triangle (or red warning light) are now *compulsory*.

Deviation from Approved Itinerary. Most of the Soviet Union is off limits to foreigners. About one quarter of the U.S.S.R. is officially closed to foreigners and a greater area is in effect barred because Intourist declines to arrange travel there.

Any deviation from a scheduled itinerary will draw immediate and strong reaction from Soviet authorities.

CRUISES on the Black Sea and the Baltic are available in Soviet and foreign ships, calling at Batumi, Odessa, Leningrad, Sochi, Sukhumi, Yalta, Riga, Tallinn and other ports. A 15-day Black Sea cruise has stops of one to two days at the major ports. The cost depends on the class of travel; there are single and double cabins with or without private showers and cabins for four to six passengers. You may not be allowed ashore at Soviet ports unless you have purchased a group excursion in advance or you already have a Soviet tourist visa.

River trips in Soviet ships down the Danube start in May and end in October. Sailings are from Vienna, stopping at Bratislava, Budapest, Belgrade, Turnu-Severin, Lom-Ruse-Djurdjñ, Galaz and Ismail. At the last port, tourists change to a sea-going motorship for Yalta, where a day is spent sightseeing and bathing. You can return by the same route or by air via Kiev and Moscow. In addition, 11-day cruises on the Volga (Kazan to Rostov) and 10-day cruises on the Dnieper river (Kiev to Odessa) are available in both directions from early summer to early fall. In 1988 Intourist began to offer 10-day cruises on the River Lena in Eastern Siberia. Seven-day sailing trips are also available on the rivers, canals, and lakes in the Leningrad area.

Leaving the Soviet Union

CUSTOMS ON RETURNING HOME. If you propose to take on your holiday any *foreign-made* articles, such as cameras, binoculars, expensive time-pieces and the like, it is wise to put with your travel documents the receipt from the retailer or some other evidence that the item was bought in your home country. If you bought the article on a previous holiday abroad and have already paid duty on it, carry with you the receipt for this. Otherwise, on returning home, you may be charged duty again (for British residents, V.A.T. as well). In other words, unless you can prove prior possession, foreign-made articles are dutiable *every time* they enter your own country.

Soviet Regulations. You cannot take out of the Soviet Union works of art such as paintings, sculptures or carpets. Antiques (including icons, old coins, books published before 1975 *in any language,* furniture, or musical instruments) may only be taken with a permit from the Ministry of Culture and after paying 100% *duty* on the item.

U.S. Customs. At this writing, Americans who are out of the United States at least 48 hours and have claimed no exemption during the previous 30 days are entitled to bring in duty-free up to $400 worth of bona fide gifts or items for their personal use. The value of each item is determined by the price actually paid (so have your receipts). Every member of a family is entitled to this same exemption, regardless of age, and the family allowance can be pooled. Infants and children do not get the exemption on alcohol and tobacco. Purchases intended for your duty-free quota can no longer be sent home separately—they must accompany your personal baggage. Do not think that *already used* will exempt an item. If, for example, you buy clothing abroad and wear it during your travels it will nonetheless be dutiable when you reenter the U.S. A flat assessment of 10% is charged on the first $1,000 in excess of the initial $400. Duty after that is based on the type of merchandise purchased.

Not more than 100 cigars and 200 cigarettes may be imported duty-free per person, nor more than a quart of wine or liquor (none at all if your passport indicates you are from a "dry" state, or if you are under 21 years of age). Only one bottle of perfume that is trademarked in the United States may be brought in, plus a reasonable quantity of other brands.

Small gifts may be mailed to friends, but not more than one package to one address and none to your own home. Notation on the package should be "Gift, value less than \$40." Tobacco, liquor and perfume are not permitted.

Do not bring home foreign meats, fruits, plants, soil, or other agricultural items when you return to the United States. To do so will delay you at the port of entry. It is illegal to bring in foreign agricultural items without permission, because they can spread destructive plant or animal pests and diseases. For more information, read the pamphlet "Customs Hints," or write to: Animal and Plant Health Inspection Service, U.S. Department of Agriculture, Washington D.C. 20250.

Canadian Customs. In addition to personal effects, the following articles may be brought into Canada duty-free: a maximum of 50 cigars, 200 cigarettes, or two pounds of tobacco and 40 ounces of liquor, provided these are declared to customs on arrival. The exemption is \$300, and gifts mailed to friends should be marked "Unsolicited Gift—value under \$40."

U.K. Customs. There are two levels of duty free allowance for people entering the U.K.: one, for goods bought outside the EEC or for goods bought in a duty free shop within the EEC; two, for goods bought in an EEC country but not in a duty free shop.

In the first category you may import duty free: 200 cigarettes or 100 cigarillos or 50 cigars or 250 grams of tobacco (*Note* if you live outside Europe, these allowances are doubled); plus one liter of alcoholic drinks over 22% by volume (38.8° proof) or two liters of alcoholic drinks not over 22% by volume or fortified or sparkling wine; plus two liters of table wine; plus 50 grams of perfume; plus ¼ liter of toilet water; plus other goods to the value of £28.

In the second category you may import duty free: 300 cigarettes or 150 cigarillos or 75 cigars or 400 grammes of tobacco; plus 1½ liters of alcoholic drinks over 22% by volume (38.8° proof) or three liters of alcoholic drinks not over 22% by volume or fortified or sparkling wine; plus five liters of table wine; plus 75 grams of perfume, plus ⅜ liter of toilet water; plus other goods to the value of £250 (*Note* though it is not classified as an alcoholic drink by EEC countries for Customs' purposes and is thus considered part of the "other goods" allowance, you may not import more than 50 liters of beer).

In addition, no animals or pets of any kind may be brought into the U.K. The penalties for doing so are severe and are strictly enforced; there are *no* exceptions. Similarly, fresh meats, plants and vegetables, controlled drugs and firearms and ammunition may not be brought into the U.K. There are no restrictions on the import or export of British and foreign currencies.

Anyone planning to stay in the U.K. for more than six months should contact H.M. Customs and Excise, Kent House, Upper Ground, London S.E.1 (tel. 01–928 0533) for further information.

BY WAY OF BACKGROUND

Some Facts and Figures

Geography

The Union of Soviet Socialist Republics—or, to give the Russian appellation, the *Soyuz Sovietskikh Sotsialisticheskikh Respublik,* abbreviated *CCCP* in Cyrillic characters—is the largest country in the world. Sprawling over the continents of Europe and Asia, spreading from the Baltic to the Black Sea, from the Carpathians to the Pacific, from the Arctic to Southwestern Asia, it is almost 7,000 miles from west to east and 2,500 miles from north to south. Of its vast territory 2,110,000 square miles are in Europe and 6,537,172 square miles in Asia. Its total surface is larger than the face of the moon we see from the earth. An express train needs a week to cover the distance from Moscow to Vladivostok. There are 11 time zones in the union; people on the Pacific coast are eating their suppers when the citizens of Moscow are having lunch. It is the only major power in the world that has kept its territory substantially intact for centuries and in fact, in the last forty-odd years, made substantial additions to it.

Its boundaries are over 40,000 miles long. The northernmost point of the continental Soviet Union is Cape Chelyuskin, at 77° 44′ N latitude; its southernmost lies in the city of Kushka, 35° 18′ N latitude, on the frontier of Afghanistan. The western tip of the U.S.S.R. is Mamonovo, on the Baltic, 19° 59′ E longitude. The most easterly point is Cape Dezhnev on the Bering Strait, 169° 40′ E of Greenwich. The Union is bordered by Norway, Finland, the Baltic Sea, Poland, Czechoslovakia, Hungary and Romania on the west; the Black Sea, Turkey, Iran, the Caspian Sea, Afghanistan, China (Sinkiang and Manchuria), Mongolia, the Amur and Ussuri rivers, and Korea on the south; the Arctic Ocean on the north; the Bering Strait, the Bering Sea, the Sea of Okhotsk and the Sea of Japan on the east. Off the northern coast there are four island groups: Novaya Zemlya (New Land), Franz Josef Land, Severnaya Zemlya (North Land) and the Novosibirskiye (New Siberian) Islands. Off the eastern coast lie the islands of Sakhalin and the Kuriles.

The basic outline of the U.S.S.R. is very simple: it is an immense plain framed by mountains. In some places there are impressive plateaus. The complex of mountain chains which form the two great mountain ranges (called knots) of the Pamir and of Armenia are extended and arranged in great arcs, concentric with the so-called Siberian shield. The Siberian mountains, sometimes covered by glaciers, include the Kamchatka, Anadyr, Kolyma, Sayan, Stanovoy, Verkhoyansk and Yablonovy mountains. Some are quite ancient while others are newer with rugged outlines, and there are several active volcanoes, especially in the Kamchatka Peninsula. The peaks of the Altai Mountains rise to 4,620 meters (15,157 feet) on Mount Belukha. Southwest of these, the colossal Tien-Shan (Pobeda Peak, 7,439 m., 24,406 feet) and the Hindu Kush have huge glaciers feeding the rivers of the Turan Lowlands in Soviet Central Asia. West of the Pamir knot, though a considerable distance away, is the barrier range of the Elburz Mountains, forming the southern end of the Caspian basin and the northern frontier of Iran. These extend to the Armenian knot. The lofty massifs are south of the Transcaucasian valley, flanked in the north by the great bastion of the Greater Caucasus Mountains, with few passes. 15 of the peaks are higher than Mont Blanc.

The Ural Mountains are generally considered to be the boundary between Europe and Asia. They are a low range, little above 1,830 meters (6,000 feet), with a general elevation of about 610 meters (2,000 feet). In the center section, the range is divided into individual ranges.

The great rivers of the U.S.S.R., among the largest in the world, are of vital importance as transportation arteries, though both in European Russia and Siberia they are frozen during the winter. In European Russia, the most important rivers rise in the Valday Uplands and the Smolensk-Moscow Hills, flowing outward to the surrounding seas; the Dnieper and Don to the Black Sea, the Western Dvina to the Baltic, and the Volga to the Caspian. The chief rivers of Central Asia, the Amu Darya and Syr Darya, water the alluvial oases of the foothills and the extensively irrigated deserts of Central Asia. The largest rivers east of the Urals, the Ob, the Yenisei and the Lena, follow the dip of the land north to the Arctic. Their lower reaches remain frozen after their upper lengths have thawed and, as a result, vast areas are flooded every spring (especially in the case of the Ob), creating immense areas of permanent and impassable marshes. In the far east, the only important river is the Amur, which flows into the Pacific. Of the great lakes, the Aral Sea and Lake Baikal are the most important; Lake Ladoga and Lake Onega in the northwest are the two largest in Europe.

Climate

The climate of the Soviet Union is largely determined by its geographical situation. It is open to the north, while to the south there is a barrier of high mountain ranges. The cold arctic masses of air sweep across from the Arctic Sea, while the tall southern ranges prevent the warmer currents of air from prevailing.

Over the greater part of the U.S.S.R.'s territory, the western winds from the Atlantic predominate. These cause a good deal of precipitation and, as they move eastward, though their effect gradually decreases, they still have a considerable influence on the climate as far as the Central Siberian uplands. The currents of the Pacific are stopped by the coastal mountain ranges and it is only along a narrow coastal strip, and in the valley of the Amur, that a weakened effect of the monsoon becomes noticeable. The regions far from the oceans have a continental climate, with great differences in temperature between summer and winter. Above Asia, during the winter, the air cools off considerably in the uplands and long periods of high pressure develop, which means that under the cloudless, clear skies, the cold is intense for months on end. From this central area masses of cold air spread out in every direction. During the summer, high barometric pressures disappear in this region. The southern parts of Asia become warmer and a low-pressure area develops over Iran and northwest India. Currents start from the west and northwest and these bring the most rain to the Soviet Union.

Naturally, the higher elevations also play their part in shaping the climate by influencing the movement of air masses. The Caucasus and the Crimean mountains protect the sea coast from the intrusion of northern cold currents. In the Soviet Far East, the mountains also impede the monsoon. The descending currents at the foot of the Central Asian mountains, which are dry and hot, have had an important role in the evolution of the desert regions.

By and large, the climate of the Soviet Union is extremely severe and its effect on agriculture and transportation is fundamental. In January, almost the whole of the country has a mean monthly temperature below 32°F; only the southern Crimea, the lowlands of the Transcaucasus and the southern parts of the Turan Lowlands are above freezing point. All the areas to the north and east are covered by snow for at least some weeks each winter. Of course, this also has some advantages—crops are protected and later, with the spring thaw, watered. The Russians have developed great skill in keeping transport moving over snow and on the frozen lakes and rivers. The Russian winter becomes more intense from south to north and west to east in proportion to the distance from the milder influences of the Baltic, the Black and the Caspian seas. At Batumi, on the Black Sea coast, the mean winter temperature is 43° F; in the same latitude, Tashkent is only 31° F; Leningrad, on the Baltic, with a January mean temperature of 15° F, is three degrees warmer than Moscow, further south. The Leningrad winter, however, begins earlier and lasts longer than Moscow's.

In summer, temperatures are much more even than in winter. The highest occur in some parts of the Turan Lowlands, far from the oceans' cooling effect. July mean temperatures reach 86° F. The lowest temperatures are along the Arctic Ocean, but even here, long hours of sunshine raise the temperature to 45–50° F.

Spring and fall are short. During the spring *rasputitsa* (thaw season), rivers and roads are often impassable; the annual floods are often disastrous, especially on the north-flowing rivers. The end of the fall is a period of alternating frost and thaw, which again makes travel difficult.

The most abundant rainfall is on the Black Sea coast of Transcaucasia, with Batumi recording nearly 100 inches. From the Baltic Coast to Mos-

cow there is a zone that gets more than 24 inches, but as you move east
and beyond the Urals, the rainfall lessens. Most of the rain falls in spring
and summer. In winter there are heavy falls in many parts of European
Russia brought by moist westerly air streams.

The climate of Asiatic Soviet Russia is also severe. In January, the coldest month, most places register mean temperatures below freezing. The
coldest area is northeast Siberia, where Verkhoyansk has a mean January
temperature of –59° F, and –94.4°F has been recorded here and at Oi-
myakon, the lowest temperatures ever found outside Antarctica.

But the Siberian winter is tempered by the dryness of the air and the
comparative lightness of winds. Areas to the south and east often have
much worse weather conditions with cold, piercing winds from the interi-
or. Parts of the Pacific coast are cold for their latitude. The growing season
ranges from 200 days in southern Turkmenistan (Central Asia) to only
80 days in the Siberian Arctic. Rainfall and snowfall are both fairly low;
only a narrow central belt between the Urals and the Tien-Shan gets more
than eight inches. Along the Pacific coast, this increases southwards;
southern Kamchatka and the area southeast of the Amur receive more
than 24 inches. Most of the rain falls in late spring and summer. In Siberia,
there is a permanently frozen subsoil everywhere, except along the coast,
southeast of the Amur, in Kamchatka and in the Kuriles.

Population

The most recent estimate of the Soviet Union's population was 281 million in 1988. The growth is uninterrupted, although the birth-rate overall
is now falling—from 2.5 per cent in the 1960s to 1.85 per cent in 1982,
and life expectancy for men is down from 66 in the 1960s to 62 in 1982
(which some attribute to the nationwide problem of alcoholism). The next
census, in 1989, will show whether these trends are continuing.

We cover the great diversity of peoples in the Soviet Union in a later
chapter, from the East Slavs, representing more than three-quarters of the
total population, through those of Turkic origin living mainly in Central
Asia, those of Finno-Ugrian descent in the north and north-west, right
the way to the east, where there are still several aboriginal communities,
including the Ainus of Sakhalin.

Cities and Villages

As in practically all countries, there is a general movement from the
countryside into the cities. This flow is being balanced in the Soviet Union
by government action, and permits are needed for a change of domicile
or even for travel within the country. The housing shortage, which despite
constant efforts still continues, is another deterrent. In spite of this, the
cities are growing. Moscow is the fifth largest city in the world, with over
eight million people living in the metropolitan area, an increase of over
25% in the last 30 years. Leningrad follows with almost five million. The
other great cities (23 with populations over one million) include Kiev,
Tashkent, Baku, Kharkov, Gorky, Novosibirsk, Omsk, Kuibyshev, Sverdlovsk, Minsk, Odessa, Alma-Ata and Tbilisi. Other cities which are pushing the one million mark are Donetsk (the former Stalino), Chelyabinsk,
Kazan, Dnepropetrovsk, Perm, Volgograd (previously Stalingrad), Rostov-on-Don, Ufa, Yerevan, Saratov, Riga, Voronezh, Zaporozhye, Krasnoyarsk, Krivoi Rog, Lvov, Karaganda, Yaroslavl, Novokuznetsk, Kras-

nodar and Tula. The Soviet policy of settling certain regions either by
compulsory transfer or by holding out particular incentives is shown in
the spectacular population increases of such places as Togliatti (Stavropol)
with 247%, Petropavlovsk-Kamchatsky (259%) or Balakovo (181%).
There are over 60 cities with more than 200,000 inhabitants, and over 270
with more than 100,000. Some 20 new towns spring up every year. Around
20 new towns appear, on average, every year, while—over the last few
years—dozens of new settlements have appeared along the new Baikal–Amur rail link in Siberia.

The main ports of the Soviet Union are divided between the most important stretches of coast line. On the Black Sea, Batumi and Odessa are the
principal ones, followed by Nikolayev, Novorossisk, Rostov-on-Don and
Zhdanov (formerly Maryupol). On the Caspian, Astrakhan and Baku are
the most significant ports; on the Baltic, Leningrad and Riga rate tops with
Kaliningrad, Liepaya, Tallinn and Ventspils following. On the Arctic Sea,
the most important are Archangel and Murmansk, and on the Pacific,
Vladivostok.

How irresistible the lure of the city has been is shown by the simple
statistic that out of the 281 million people of the Soviet Union, over two-
thirds, despite the vital claims of agriculture, now live in urban areas.

It is now over 50 years since the collectivization of agricultural land
in Russia (by 1936 more than 90% of peasant households and almost all
of the country's arable land had been organized into collectives). This, of
course, completely changed the typical Russian village. Living conditions,
still primitive in certain respects, have been greatly improved; electricity
has now reached all but the most remote areas.

The villages are now either in the center or on the borders of collective
farms, of which there are two main types, the *kolkhozes* and the *sovkhozes*.
The former are cooperatives in which the peasant's land, machinery and
most of his animals are the collective property of the farm's members. The
sovkhozes or state farms, much larger than kolkhozes, are financed by the
State and their workers are state employees with fixed wages. There have
been many policy changes and much reorganization in the last 40 years.
The number of kolkhozes dropped from 252,000 in 1950 to only 27,000
in 1979, with an average area of 6,600 hectares (about 16,500 acres) of
land, whereas the number of state farms rose to more than double, and
their average arable area was more than twice as large. In 1967 an experiment was started to end state subsidies to sovkhozes by making more of
them fully responsible for their own profits and losses. The emphasis under
Party leader Gorbachev is on increased personal responsibility, and managers—in agriculture as in industry—are able to offer incentives to increase production.

The many thousands of villages are mostly tied to agricultural production, though some might shelter hunters or fishermen, especially in the
Soviet Far East. Much folk art and folklore has survived here. But the
tourist is not likely to see much of them, except on the main tourist routes.
With a few modern improvements, the Russian villager follows the same
way of life, has the same joys and sorrows as his forefathers, and if he
is young, he is likely to strive hard to escape to the city.

The State

At present, the U.S.S.R. is divided into 15 Soviet Socialist Republics,
sometimes called Union Republics, on the basis of nationalities. They rep-

resent the most populous and culturally most advanced groups of peoples. In administrative respects, they show certain parallels with the 50 states of the U.S.A. The population figures are based on those of the last census, in 1982.

The 15 republics are:

The **Armenian Republic,** population 3,167,000; capital: Yerevan. Area: 11,502 square miles.

The **Azerbaijan Republic,** population 6,297,000; capital: Baku. Area: 33,436 square miles.

The **Byelorussian Republic,** population 9,744,000; capital: Minsk. Area: 80,154 square miles.

The **Estonian Republic,** population 1,496,000; capital: Tallinn. Area: 17,413 square miles.

The **Georgian Republic,** population 5,105,000; capital: Tbilisi. Area: 26,911 square miles.

The **Kazakh Republic,** population 16,000,000; capital: Alma-Ata. Area: 1,064,092 square miles.

The **Kirghiz Republic,** population 4,000,000; capital: Frunze. Area: 76,642 square miles.

The **Latvian Republic,** population 2,551,000; capital: Riga. Area: 24,695 square miles.

The **Lithuanian Republic,** population 3,474,000; capital: Vilnius. Area: 25,173 square miles.

The **Moldavian Republic,** population 4,024,000; capital: Kishinev. Area: 13,012 square miles.

The **Russian Republic,** population 140,000,000; capital: Moscow. Area: 6,593,391 square miles.

The **Tadzhik Republic,** population 4,500,000; capital: Dushanbe. Area: 55,019 square miles.

The **Turkmen Republic,** population 3,000,000; capital: Ashkhabad. Area: 188,417 square miles.

The **Ukrainian Republic,** population 50,310,000; capital: Kiev. Area: 232,046 square miles.

The **Uzbek Republic,** population 18,000,000; capital: Tashkent. Area: 158,069 square miles.

These figures show that the Russian Soviet Federated Socialist Republic is by far the largest in both area and population, representing more than half of the total. Within the Russian Federation, the major nationalities (other than Russian), are subdivided into 16 Autonomous Soviet Socialist Republics. These include the Yakut, Bashkir, Buryat, Dagestan, Kabardino-Balkar, Kalmyk, Karelian, Komi, Mari, Mordovian, North-Ossetian, Tatar, Tuvinian, Udmurt, Chechen-Ingush and Chuvash Autonomous Republics. The Union Republics, except some smaller ones, are divided into *oblasts, krays* and Autonomous Republics. All these are on an appropriate level of jurisdiction and are directly responsible to their respective Union Republics. The oblast is a purely administrative subdivision without any important nationality group other than the one after which the Union Republic is named and of which it is a part. The Autonomous Republics administratively have the same function as the oblasts, but their boundaries serve to give political recognition to some important minority nationality group. The kray is like a combination of the first two. Its lesser policies are based on nationality groups, autonomous oblasts or national *okrugs.* Oblasts are regions and krays are territories, and these are further divided into districts *(rayons),* cities and rural communities.

How does this rather complex system work? At the very top of the state stands the Supreme Soviet of the U.S.S.R., roughly equivalent to a parliament. This is divided into two "houses," the Soviet of the Union and the Soviet of the Nationalities. Both have their standing committees. The Soviet of the Union has a Credentials Committee, a Legislative Proposals Committee, a Budget Committee and a Foreign Affairs Committee. In the House of the Union, one representative is chosen for every 300,000 people; it corresponds roughly to the House of Representatives in the United States or the House of Commons in Britain. In the House of Nationalities (resembling the U.S. Senate), each Soviet Socialist Republic has 32 representatives, each Autonomous Republic 11, each autonomous oblast five and each national okrug one. The House of Nationalities has the same committees as the House of the Union, with the addition of an economic committee.

The next authority, at least in theory, is the Presidium of the Supreme Soviet, with the Supreme Court and the Procurator General of the Soviet Union almost its equal, all three being under the two legislative chambers. The Council of Ministers of the U.S.S.R. supervises the committees and agencies which are above the All-Union Ministries and the Union Republican Ministries. The number and names of these committees and agencies are subject to change at irregular intervals, but there is a board of some kind to regulate almost every facet of life from labor and wages, through television and aviation to foreign economic relations and mineral fertilizers. Under these agencies and committees we find the All-Union Ministries, those of Foreign Trade, the Merchant Marine, Railroads, the Medium Machine Building Industry, Power Station Construction and Transport Construction. The Republican Ministries are those of Higher and Secondary Specialized Education, Geological Surveys, Public Health, Foreign Affairs, Culture, Defense, Communications, Architecture and Finance.

The Party

It is a unique feature of the Soviet Union and one which has been copied by all Communist countries in Europe that the state is controlled by one political party, the Communist Party of the Soviet Union. Through it, the dictatorship of the proletariat is exercised. Its guiding principle is Marxism-Leninism. All the high officials of the state are recruited from the top ranks of the party. Party membership is theoretically open to any working person "if he does not exploit the labor of others, if he accepts the party program and rules, if he actively takes part in the execution of the Party program and if he works in a Party organization and carries out all party decisions." In 1986, over 19 million, about 6% of the population, were members, 30% of them women. The Party has about 200,000 full-time paid officials, the *apparatchiks.*

The Party hierarchy is a complex one. It is headed by the General Secretary who, while the title of his office might be a modest one, is far more important than the All-Union President, usually a figurehead (though the former Party Secretary, Leonid Brezhnev, invested himself with the title of President as well, as did his successors, Yury Andropov and Konstantin Chernenko), or the prime minister of even the largest Republic. Below him is the Politburo and the Secretariat (on a somewhat lower level), and *below* those, the Central Committee. Then follows the All-Union Party Congress, and on the next level, the Congresses of the 14 Republics, the Republic Central Committees and the Secretariats. The next echelon is represented by the Provincial Conferences and the Provincial Committees and Secretariats. One rung lower are the District Conferences, Committees and Secretariats. And at the bottom of the ladder we find the cells, bureaus and local secretariats.

At almost every level, the official state organization is paralleled by a Party organization; it is only at the top that the state and Party pyramids merge. The cells are usually established in factories, farms, villages, army and navy units, educational centers and similar places. The smallest cell or primary unit must have at least three members, but there can be several thousand, as in a large factory or a ministry. Above the primary level, the party units run more or less parallel with the administrative subdivisions of the state. Each city, district, region, territory and Union Republic has a separate Party organization—except the Russian Soviet Federated Socialist Republic, which is run by the central Party organs.

The basic principle, as proclaimed by Lenin, is "democratic centralism," which, in effect, means that the proletariat cannot determine policy but has to be led. This leadership is effectively provided by the Politburo, a select group whose size has varied throughout the years. The Party Congress meets at least once every four years, though it has frequently convened more often. It is supposed to "determine the tactical line of the Party on major questions of current policy," something which it does very rarely. The Central Committee, which carries on in the intervals, is elected by the Congresses. The Central Committee is supposed to meet at least once every six months. It supervises every sphere of the nation's life, and maintains controlling departments for the army, for heavy and light industry, for foreign policy, the arts, propaganda, finances, youth, and, most importantly, for personnel. The last department handles the promotion, demotion or transfer of all top Party officials. The various sections are directed by members of the Central Secretariat of the Party, which meets daily to deal with current political and administrative problems and reports directly to the Party leadership.

How do the State and Party relate? Quite simply: the Party determines policy; the State administers it. The task of government officials is to put into effect the policies originated by the Party, that is by the Politburo and the Central Committee. This has certain advantages: the policy-makers, unlike those in Western democracies, are relieved of routine tasks. The executive of the State is the Council of Ministers and its chairman is the Premier, the formal head of the Soviet national government. While the late Nikita Khrushchev combined the roles of General (or First) Party Secretary and Premier, this was an exceptional situation; Brezhnev, Andropov and Chernenko all held the Supreme Party role, with Nikolai Tikhonov as Premier. Tikhonov was re-appointed Premier at the age of 80 by Party Secretary Gorbachev, but resigned in September 1985, to be replaced by Nikolai Ryzhkov (age 55), a relative newcomer only promoted to the Politburo months earlier.

The Economy

The Soviet Union is the world's leading producer of, among many things, wheat, butter, iron ore, steel, manganese, books, and cigars.

But the figures and "visible" facts, the statistics and the five-year plans tell only part of the story, if they tell it at all. Genuine economic reform has been sometimes blocked by the Party because it would have given too much power to industrial managers, experts, trading concerns and local authorities. It could be argued that the Party's very existence depends to a great extent on the comparative inefficiency of the economy; its main task is to exhort, flatter, and shame people into working harder. As analysts have pointed out, there are really *two* economies in the Soviet Union. Of these, the inefficient one is the visible one. The West knows a good deal about this economy as its faults and irrationalities are quite freely discussed in the press. The main difficulty is the lack of incentives. It is, obviously, difficult to feed people for long with mere promises of a better life. The Soviet leadership under Gorbachev has acknowledged this and is taking vigorous measures to improve economic efficiency, consumer choice, and quality. Limited private enterprise was officially permitted from May 1987.

But there is another aspect of the economy, well-hidden from prying eyes. This is the sector which manufactures arms and spacecraft, handles the U.S.S.R.'s international finances, provides the material base for the police and intelligence services and creates the funds for political action outside the country. No statistics are available about it; in the budget it appears under general and very broad terms. It recruits the most brilliant people and often gives them material rewards which the average Soviet citizen does not even dream about. By all indications, this part of the economy functions more efficiently, perhaps, than the equivalent sectors in any Western country.

Certainly, during the years of Soviet rule immense progress has been made. Czarist Russia was a predominantly agricultural land with few and feeble industries. The First World War and the subsequent civil war disrupted and destroyed the nation's economic life; the difficulties were almost insurmountable. After the period of NEP (a mixed, partly private enterprise economy), it took the U.S.S.R. until 1927 to regain its pre-1914 level of production. The first *pyatiletka* (five-year plan) began on October 1, 1928. The Second World War prevented the completion of the third five-year plan since industry had to switch to armaments. During the war, hundreds of industrial plants were transferred beyond the Urals and these remained in their new locations. The long conflict caused damage and loss costing more than 700 billion roubles. Much of the rebuilding was done within three years after the end of the war.

The following five-year plans demanded tremendous efforts. Industrial production, mostly in capital goods, was multiplied. Until fairly recently, the concentration on heavy industry was aimed to support the country's large military program and to establish a firm base for further economic growth. Today the emphasis has shifted somewhat in the direction of consumer production. The standard of living has risen, though perhaps less quickly than expected; science and technology have accelerated their expansion and Soviet military power has, in many respects, overtaken the West. Apart from the products we have mentioned, new industries are being developed in plastics and pharmaceutical products and computers. Much emphasis has been placed on building up the industries in the eastern and far-eastern territories, which are rich in natural resources—oil, gas, coal and iron ore.

Since the death of Brezhnev his successors have attempted limited economic reforms and the momentum of these appears to be increasing under the present Party Secretary Mikhail Gorbachev.

Energy Production

The Soviet Union is still more than self-sufficient in energy (and in most non-fuel minerals), but readily accessible reserves in the west of the country are becoming depleted and the focus has shifted to Siberia where extraction and transportation costs are much higher.

Coal is still the most important source; according to recent estimates, the Soviet Union has more than 4.86 trillion in reserves. Their value is increased by the fact that the mines produce a good deal of hard coal with a high calorie content. The 1984 production figure was 713 million tons. Of this, over a quarter is used for coke-production in which the Soviet Union leads the world.

The most important mining districts are in the Donets Basin, the Kuznetsk Basin in Western Siberia, the Karaganda Coal Basin (which is semi-desert) and the Pechora Coal Basin, where intensive exploitation began during the Second World War. There is brown coal in the Moscow district and the Urals yield raw materials for the chemical industry from the Kizel and Chelyabinsk mines. In Eastern Siberia, the Irkutsk Coal Basin, centered around Cheremkhovo, is one of the most important. Coal mining in the Soviet Far East is also developing quickly; although investment in these remote areas is costly, they are seen as the main base for the coal industry's future as the more accessible deposits in the older coal basins of European Russia become depleted.

The Soviet Union is also one of the leading oil-producing countries of the world. New areas are continually being surveyed and developed—most recently in the Barents Sea and off the coast of Sakhalin Island—and production in 1984 topped 613 million tons. In former times it was Baku that provided the major portion of oil; today, a substantial though declining percentage also comes from the "second Baku," between the Volga and the Urals with deposits around Kuibyshev, Saratov and Volgograd, from where long distance pipelines deliver the oil to Eastern Europe. The oil fields of Baku have been known for centuries. Hundreds of wells have tapped deposits lying under the Caspian Sea. A pipeline connects Baku with Batumi, the Black Sea port. At the northern foot of the Caucasus, Grozny, Maykop and Neftegorsk are the main centers. The fields along the eastern and northern shore of the Caspian, those in the Nebit-Dag area of the Turkmen Republic, and the Emba fields in the North Caspian Lowland remain important; their reserves are comparable to those of Bashkiria. Local needs are filled by the wells of the Fergana Valley and of the Ukraine and Central Asia. Crude oil is refined partly locally and partly at the terminal points of the pipelines. The Volga is an important oil transportation route and every major Volga port has large oil refineries.

Another and newer pipeline brings oil from the impressive Samotlor field in Western Siberia. Discovered only in 1968 during exploration of the Tyumen oil and gas field just east of the Urals, Samotlor is believed to have recoverable reserves of 3.5 billion tons. However, a variety of problems have meant that promised yields have not been maintained, and since Mr Gorbachev became Soviet leader heads have rolled in the Tyumen region; the Soviet oil minister himself was sacked early in 1985. Despite these troubles, the Western Siberian oilfields currently account for 60% of total Soviet oil production.

Natural gas is found partly in the oil-bearing areas, though in many places it is exploited independently. In 1984 the total production was some 590 billion cubic meters. It is used partly as a source of energy and partly as raw material for the chemical industry. Once again, Western Siberia is the principal producing area, accounting for 40 to 50% of the total. The source of the Siberian gas pipeline to Western Europe, Urengoy—the world's biggest gas field with reserves believed to exceed 10 trillion cubic meters—was discovered in the mid-1970s, along with another giant deposit at Medvezhe. The whole Tyumen region is thought to have reserves of 30 trillion cubic meters. Deposits are next to be developed at Yamburg, 160 miles north of Urengoy in the permafrost (a rail link is under construction) and in the 1990s in the Yamal Peninsula, several hundred miles further up into the Arctic Circle. Other, older gas fields include those at Saratov (the Volga district), in Central Asia (Gazli, Fergana and the new Sovietabad field), in the Northern Caucasus (Stavropol), on the northern slopes of the Carpathians (Dashava), in Transcaucasia and many other places. Oil shale continues to be mined but energy conservation and conversion from oil to gas are priorities.

The Soviet Union, with several of the world's greatest rivers and high mountain regions, has resources of hydroelectricity which have been calculated at 420 million kilowatts, or 11% of the total world potential. More than four-fifths of this is provided by the great rivers of Asian Russia, though the potentials of the Amur and Lena are not yet fully utilized. The principal hydroelectric stations in Siberia are on the Angara, an outlet of Lake Baikal, at Bratsk and Irkutsk. Other large stations are at Krasnoyarsk, on the River Yenisei, at Novosibirsk on the River Ob and at Kamensk, near the mouth of the same river. In the republics of Central Asia, the many rapid mountain rivers have huge potentialities though the power stations so far built are small. The main plants are on the Chirchik near Tashkent, the Farkhadskaya River, the Kayrak-Kumskaya station in the Fergana Valley, the Alma-Ata station on a tributary of the River Ili, the Narin River in Kirghizia, and the Nurek station on the River Vakhsh near Dushanbe. There is a "cascade" of seven stations on the Volga, with others under construction. About 25 stations have been built on rivers flowing from the Greater and Lesser Caucasus, of which the largest is at Mingechaur in Azerbaijan. There are other groups in Armenia, in the Karelian Republic and on the Kola Peninsula.

Nuclear power plants, mainly sited in the Soviet Union's western industrial areas, are considered particularly important because of the great distances between the country's main centers of fossil fuel production and of electricity production. The Russians were the first in the world to complete an experimental nuclear power station for civil use; it opened in 1954 at Obninsk, southwest of Moscow. In 1986 there were 18 reactors operating in 5 plants in European Russia, and the plan is for generating capacity to grow to over 110,000 megawatts in 1990—although the experts' view is that 50,000 megawatts is now a more likely achievement over the period. There are two types of reactor; a controversial graphite-moderated pressure-tube system (PTR) unique to the U.S.S.R., and a pressurized water reactor (PWR) similar to Western plants. The vast nuclear power engineering complex "Atommash" near Volgadonsk in the Ukraine, completed in 1984, is intended to produce equipment for six nuclear power stations a year (some see this as an over-optimistic target). Although there is no official anti-nuclear power lobby in the U.S.S.R., high-level disquiet is growing over the safety risks and environmental consequences of the rapid expansion of nuclear power. Soviet scientists have recently confirmed rumors of a nuclear accident in the Urals in 1958. In April 1986 it was officially admitted that a major disaster had taken place in the Ukraine when a PTR reactor exploded, caught fire and caused many deaths, posing a health risk from radioactivity to neighboring European countries. Since then, modifications have been introduced into all PTR reactors in the Soviet Union, and Chernobyl itself has been inspected by international experts.

Heavy Industry and Its Raw Materials

The iron ore resources of the Soviet Union are the largest in the world. The more important mining centers are at Krivoi Rog (where the proximity of the Donets Basin makes quick smelting possible), on the Kerch Peninsula, in the Urals (Magnitogorsk, Chelyabinsk, Zlatoust, Nizhny-Tagul, the Kuznetsk Basin and Karaganda), in the Central Black Earth Region (Tula and other places), in Siberia (adjacent to the Kuznetsk Basin in the Soria Mountains, in the Angara district and the valley of the Amur). After the Second World War, valuable iron ore deposits were opened up in Kazakhstan, in the Kustanai Oblast.

The development and raw material supply of the iron and steel industries have been assured by the amplitude of different metals needed in refining. The Soviet Union produces 40% of the world's manganese (at Chiatura in the Colchis Lowland of Georgia, the Nikopol Basin, the Urals, Kazakhstan and Western Siberia). Chromium is found in the Urals, Kazakhstan and Eastern Siberia. The deposits of nickel, wolfram, molybdenum, vanadium and titanium are also significant.

In 1984 the U.S.S.R. produced 153 million tons of steel, the largest output in the world. In the Ukraine, this production is based on the coal of the Donets Basin, on hydroelectricity, the oil of the Caucasus, the iron ore of Krivoi Rog and Kerch, and the manganese of Nikopol. The foundries have been built partly in the vicinity of the coal mines and partly close to the iron ore deposits, and a "shuttle system" has been developed between the deposits and the sources of energy. The important cities of heavy industry are Donetsk, Makeyevka, Dnepropetrovsk, Zaporozhye, and Kramatorsk. The Ural's center is the Ural-Kuznetsk *kombinat* (iron and coal cooperative); it was developed mainly during the last war. The centers of iron and steel production coincide with those of iron ore mining. The Central Industrial District (Moscow, Lipetsk and Tula) exploits partly the local iron ore and partly scrap-iron. It plays an important part in the production of refined steel for the machine industry. Some new centers have developed recently: the Cherepovets Combine refines the iron ore of the Kola Peninsula, using the coal of Vorkuta. A similar more recent center is that of Karaganda, using the iron ore of Kustanai. In Transcaucasia, Eastern Siberia and the Soviet Far East, the iron and steel industry is also making considerable strides.

Nonferrous metallurgy is also highly developed. There are deposits in Kazakhstan (Kounradsky, Dzhezkazgan), in Armenia and the Urals. Considerable quantities of copper are exported. Lead and zinc are found primarily in the Altai Region, in Kazakhstan, the Caucasus, Siberia and the Far East. The centers of mercury smelting are Chelyabinsk in the

Urals, Ust-Kamenogorsk in Kazakhstan, Ordzhonikidze in the Caucasus, and some of the cities of the Donets and Kuznetsk basins. Lead is processed mainly at Leninogorsk and Chimkent in Kazakhstan and Ordzhonikidze in the Caucasus.

Aluminum production is based on several ores; the production, being a two-stage process, requires large amounts of electricity and is done mostly near large and cheap sources of current. The bauxite of Tikhvin is processed around Volkhov. The raw material of the important bauxite deposits of the Urals is smelted partly at Zaporozhye, partly locally. The nephelite of the Kola Peninsula also serves to supply Zaporozhye, though the Kandalaksha and Nadvoitsy plants also use it. Recently alumite deposits have been opened up at Zaglik, south of Kirovabad in the Kura River Valley of Transcaucasia. The raw materials are transformed into aluminum at Yerevan and Sumgait. The increase in the capacity to provide energy in the Eastern territories has intensified the development of Siberian aluminum smelting; the most important units are at Novokuznetsk, Krasnoyarsk and Bratsk.

After South Africa, the Soviet Union is probably the world's largest producer of gold, 346 tonnes of which were extracted in 1981. Main production is in Eastern Siberia and the Far East, but older mines still function in the Urals and other mountain areas. Newly discovered lodes have become important in Kazakhstan. Platinum is plentiful in the Urals and the diamond mines of Yakutia are very rich.

The machine industry has been given priority in the Soviet economy. In 50 years, its capacity has been increased by 500% and it is now the second largest in the world. Huge and specialized centers have been developed; the largest are near Moscow and Leningrad, followed by the Urals, the Ukraine and the Volga district. But much progress has been made in the Caucasus and in Western and Eastern Siberia as well.

In the power industry, Moscow, Leningrad, Kharkov, Kiev, Riga, Sverdlovsk and Kuibyshev represent the most important centers providing the equipment for power stations, transportation, etc. The large-scale projects of electrification and the introduction of diesel engines have brought considerable change in transportation. Since 1956, no steam locomotives have been manufactured, and the old ones have been gradually replaced. The Soviet Union is a leading manufacturer of tractors and trucks. While the manufacture of automobiles has lagged behind, Russia has built up a considerable industry, partly with the help of Fiat of Italy, who have built a plant in the U.S.S.R. Production quadrupled between 1975 and 1980, and in 1985 there were said to be 12 million private cars on the road. Agricultural machinery is being manufactured throughout the Union, frequently in specialized form according to local needs. Thus grain-harvesters are made in Rostov, Taganrog and Saratov, in the Black Earth belt; Tashkent produces cotton pickers and, in Zaporozhye, corn pickers are manufactured.

Complex precision instruments and machinery are concentrated most in the plants of Leningrad, Moscow and the Baltic Republics.

Since the end of the war, household equipment—refrigerators, vacuum cleaners, television sets, washing machines—have also found place in the manufacturing program. The home electronics market scarcely exists as we know it but calculators, cassette players, videos and even personal computers are becoming available—sometimes as a result of deals struck with Western suppliers.

The chemical industry had to be created afresh and during the last decade or so, the greatest increase in capital investment was in this field. No detailed statistics are available, but the major categories of finished products are mineral fertilizers, synthetic rubber, artificial and synthetic fibers, plastics, paints and dyes, soaps and detergents, insecticides and weed killers, pharmaceuticals and various products for use in industry, such as chemicals required in oil refining and metallurgy. Superphosphates are manufactured in the Ukraine, the Carpathians, the Baltic Republics, the Urals, Kazakhstan, the Kola Peninsula and elsewhere. The production of sulphuric acid, hydrochloric acid, ammonia and caustic soda has increased over fourfold since 1950.

Like most large industrial countries, the Soviet Union is still struggling with the housing shortage caused by the war and by the planning priorities that gave comparatively little attention to "living space". Though the manufacture of concrete, fireproof bricks, glass and pre-fabricated units has substantially increased, space is still severely rationed and (especially for young couples) an independent, self-contained home often remains a dream. There is ample material for industrial and public building, including granite, basalt, volcanic tufa and other substances and it is claimed that 10 million citizens move into new apartments annually.

Timber, Paper and Light Industries

Though the timber reserves are largely in Siberia, lumbering, woodworking and paper-milling remained until recently more highly developed in European Russia. Intensive development has now raised the participation of the Eastern territories to about 80% and this is still increasing. The majority of the forests consist of pine. The timber is mostly processed locally, much of it having been transported by rafts to the factories. Four million tons of paper are produced yearly, which seems to cover basic needs. Considerable quantities are recycled. However, books, until recently very inexpensive, are becoming less so as paper costs rise.

The most important light industry is textiles, and within it the cotton mills, using almost entirely local raw material. Fine wool fabrics are produced mainly in Moscow, Ivanovo and Yaroslavl. Cotton is grown in Central Asia and Transcaucasia. Hemp is an old crop in Russia, while jute is a newcomer. The largest hemp/jute industry used to be concentrated in ports, but smaller mills have now been built in many localities. The traditional centers of the silk industry are in Central Asia and Transcaucasia, where silk worms are grown, feeding on the mulberry trees planted along irrigation canals. Linen is produced primarily in the Central Industrial Region and the northwest, where the flax is grown.

The shoe industry is being developed rapidly. The latest Five-Year Plan, to 1990, aims to double production of clothing and footwear, along with that of household appliances, televisions and electronic goods, and spare parts for cars—all part of the intensified emphasis on pleasing Soviet consumers. In mid-1985 the Minister for Light Industry was sacked—a victim of the Gorbachev "purge" of incompetent officials!

Food Industries

These are mainly concentrated in the farm districts. Sugar is one of the most important branches and about 10 million tons are produced annually. The flour-milling industry is centered in the big grain-growing areas, the meat-packing industry in the cattle-raising territories and also in the consumer centers. The dairy industry is most highly developed in the Baltic Republics, in the southern zone of the West Siberian Lowlands and around the big cities. The Soviet Union is the biggest producer of butter; even so, she has been happy to buy on occasion a large quantity of cheap European Community surplus. The canning industry has a very important part in supplying the northern industrial districts which are underdeveloped agriculturally. Fish plays a substantial part in feeding the population. Almost seven million tons of seafood, fresh and processed, annually serve this purpose. Vegetable oils are also essential and several million tons are produced each year. Sunflower oil is the leading product, but in Tashkent, vegetable oil production has established a large industry linked to cotton milling. Breweries and tobacco factories have also been developed considerably in recent years.

Agriculture

Although agriculture's share of total investment has risen considerably in recent years, yields have not so far increased as hoped, and it remains the Achilles' heel of the Soviet economy. The charlatanism of Lysenko, a geneticist whose theories flew in the face of common sense but were enthusiastically endorsed by Stalin, caused setbacks that hindered sensible and rational development for years. Nor did Khrushchev's pet scheme for the Virgin Lands fulfill expectations. In recent years the U.S.S.R. has had to import grain almost every year, and much of its gold reserves and exports have gone to pay for this. While collective farms each have about 10,000 acres to cultivate, individual farmers are allowed to have "private plots," varying in size from half an acre to two-and-a-half acres (depending on the fertility of the plot) where they grow vegetables for their families, fodder for their strictly limited livestock and some produce to sell at the nearest town market. Human nature has been changed little, even by the Soviet system, and peasants give priority to their own plots over the collective tasks; nor is it possible to enforce the kind of discipline which prevails in factories and offices. The Soviet Union, in addition, is poorly provided with good soil; even where it is excellent, as in the famous Black Earth areas in the Ukraine and parts of Siberia, the rainfall is often uncertain. Recurrent shortages, bad harvests and inefficient working methods all contribute to the difficulties. Khrushchev's largely irrational schemes failed and his successors are still struggling with the same problems that have bedeviled Russia's leaders for nearly 70 years. The 1970s and early 1980s saw a series of disastrously poor harvests—a situation made even more desperate by the embargos upon exports to the U.S.S.R. imposed by some Western nations. Over the last decade there has been a tenfold increase in food imports by the U.S.S.R., mainly of grain, meat and sugar.

One of the reasons for poor grain harvests is that infrastructure in the countryside is still comparatively primitive. Roads are bad; in winter, access to villages and farms is difficult and it is none too good even in summer. In addition, poor management, inadequate incentives, problems with fertiliser and pesticide applications, and insufficient irrigation all contribute to the country's continuing failure to fulfill its potential. Lack of facilities also makes it hard to keep workers on the land, especially the skilled personnel needed to use and maintain new machinery. In October 1984 the late President Chernenko blamed the weather and put forward a new

Land Improvement Program, due for completion by the year 2000, which would increase the amount of newly drained and irrigated land from the present 33 million to 49–53 million hectares. This would mean that half the country's crops would be produced in conditions which were not subject to drought.

In 1986 a 10-billion rouble river diversion plan under discussion for many years was finally shelved. It would have involved constructing a 2,500-kilometer canal, taking water from the north-flowing rivers Ob and Irtysh, in western Siberia, southwards to the plains of Kazakhstan, and diverting water from the Onega and Dvina rivers (in the Arctic north) into the Volga and thence into the Caspian sea. Senior officials and academics had attacked the project and claimed that the money would be much better spent on soil improvement schemes in traditional farming areas. Party Secretary Gorbachev, who places the emphasis on investment and on raising the quality of exisiting agricultural production, agreed.

According to the official statistics, only 23.6% of the Soviet Union's territory is arable land.Wheat is the main grain product—the U.S.S.R. claims 30% of the world's total production. Earlier it was the Ukraine, Moldavia, the Northern Caucasus and the Volga district that supplied most of it; now Kazakhstan and Western Siberia contribute about 40%. Official Soviet statistics also claim that the U.S.S.R. leads in growing rye, barley and oats. Rice is grown in the Southern Ukraine, in the Northern Caucasus, in Kazakhstan, some irrigated parts of Central Asia and in the Soviet Far East. Sugar beet, cotton and sunflower seeds are other important agricultural products; so is flax (in the Baltic Republics, the Moscow Basin and Byelorussia); jute is grown mainly in the Northern Ukraine and the Volga district's rainier parts. More than 75% of the world's production of sunflower seeds is provided by the Soviet Union. Potatoes, perhaps the most important part of the Soviet diet, are grown throughout the country, but mainly in the northern zone of the steppes. Vegetables are concentrated in the supply districts of the industrial center.The sub-tropical tea plantations and tropical fruit orchards are long-established. Grapes are grown in Moldavia, the Crimea and the Southern Ukraine and the best wine is that of the Caucasus. In 1985 the Soviet Union was the world's third biggest wine producer (topped only by France and Italy).

Cattle breeding still lags behind, and although it has recently been encouraged by increased investment for animal husbandry, there has been recurrent meat rationing in recent years. However, production of meat, mainly beef and pork, rose to 16.7 million tons in 1984 from an average of 14.8 million tons in 1976–80. Output of milk and eggs also rose, perhaps as a result of the Food Program introduced by ex-President Brezhnev in 1982. The Ukraine and the Baltic Republics lead in dairy products. The Ukraine, too, is the center of pig-breeding but this is also concentrated in the areas growing corn, potatoes and sugar beet. Sheep are bred both for their wool and their meat; the centers are in the Ukraine, the Caucasus, the republics of Central Asia and Kazakhstan. The famous karakul sheep provide astrakhan fur. Reindeer, camels and horses are all bred in various areas.

Social Services

About as many doctors graduate annually in the Soviet Union as there were at any one time in the whole of the Czarist empire. Three out of every four Soviet doctors are women. In 1982 there were over 1 million physicians, one to every 270 people. However, the ratio of doctors to inhabitants in rural areas is only one-third that of the urban average.

All medical care is free of charge, except for the purchase of medicines. The Soviet press frequently reports about shortages, especially in the provinces. Doctors can carry on a private practice after their hours at the hospitals and clinics and their charges can be quite high. There are also several private cooperative clinics with some 48 hospitals where patients have to pay—and get much better service. The level of dentistry in the U.S.S.R. seems to be lower than in the West.

Old-age pensions were not introduced until 1956, though previously a very low pension was paid to invalids and the disabled, or granted for special merit. A 1926 law states clearly that children must provide for the needs of their disabled parents. The pensionable age is 60 for working men and 55 for women. The age is 50 for women with 5 or more children. The size of the pension is related to the last basic salary earned before retirement. "Personal pensions" are granted for "heroes of labor," "people's artists," Party and state officials and important scholars. These have no upper limit. State pensions for collective farmers were not introduced until 1965; the pensionable age for farming men is now 65, for women 60. In 1968 the minimum annual holiday was extended to 15 working days; income tax was reduced and the temporarily disabled, if they had worked for eight or more years, now receive 100% of their pay. However, non-union members get only 50% of the regular sickness benefits.

There have been no unemployment figures published in the Soviet Union since 1930. Unemployment benefits were abolished at the same time. In 1960, 78% of able-bodied citizens of working age were employed; in 1965 this rose to 87%, but these figures do not take into account seasonal unemployment and the fact that in 1967 State Committees on the Use of Labor Resources were established with the same functions as Western employment offices (labor exchanges). The essential difference is that they do not pay any benefits but merely help the unemployed to find work. In 1970, there were 1,170.7 females to every 1,000 males in the Soviet Union (the highest recorded imbalance in the world), and 57 million women work outside their homes. Despite claims that there is a labor shortage in the U.S.S.R., technological unemployment is believed to be considerable; even for the trained industrial worker, it takes 20 to 30 days to find employment, yet he is given only two weeks' pay when released from his previous job. In recent months the official press has begun discussing the problem of unemployment—a topic that has surfaced, along with other social problems such as drugs and juvenile crime, in the new "glasnost."

Religion

Before the 1917 Revolution, the Russian Orthodox Church was the established church of the Russian Empire, and most of the Great Russian, Ukrainian, Byelorussian and Georgian people belonged to it. The Czar was also head of the church. The Soviet Government disestablished the Church, confiscated its property and launched a large-scale anti-religious campaign.

Article 124 of the Constitution states that "the church in the U.S.S.R. is separate from the State," and that "freedom of worship is recognized for all citizens." However, the same article also guarantees "freedom of anti-religious propaganda," and this is what appears to prevail in practice. After the Revolution all churches were closed and all religions were persecuted, but during World War II, Stalin, hoping to stimulate nationalism, relaxed these policies and this tolerance has been continued by his successors. All citizens can engage in worship (though it probably does their careers little good), and some new churches have been built since the war. But there are severe restrictions on evangelical activities, and the religious instruction of children is illegal. Few editions of the Bible have been published, and those in limited numbers; the most recent, the fifth since the war, appeared in 1983. The nine main branches of Christianity are represented, as well as Islam, Judaism, Buddhism and smaller communities.

The Russian Orthodox Church, headed by the Patriarch of Moscow and All Russia (assisted by the Holy Synod), is still the largest. Before the revolution it had over 77,000 churches. Until 1959 it had 20,000. Now, only about 6,500 function, though there are still millions of adherents.

The Armenian Apostolic (or Gregorian) Church has more than a million adherents in the Armenian Soviet Socialist Republic. About 40 million Moslems live in Central Asia, European Russia and Siberia, Ciscaucasia and Transcaucasia. Protestantism is represented mainly by Lutherans (in Estonia and Latvia) and the Union of Evangelical Baptists, both with well over a million members.

Roman Catholics are most numerous in Lithuania and the Western Ukraine. Their highest ranking prelates are four bishops. The Buddhists live in the autonomous republic of the Buryat-Mongols, in the Kalmyk and Tuva autonomous regions and around Chita and Irkutsk. They are organized under a Lama.

In spite of the Nazi extermination camps and recent emigration (although this has been hindered since 1980), there are still almost two million Jews in the Soviet Union. Though Jews have occasionally held high Party and state posts, they have always been insecure. There are only a dozen rabbis in the whole country.

There are two main atheist organizations in the U.S.S.R., the Society of the Militant Godless and the All-Union Society for the Dissemination of Political and Scientific knowledge.

In 1988 the millennium of Kievan Christianity was officially celebrated in the Soviet Union. A new legal decree has been issued which redefines the Orthodox Church's legal status and gives it greater rights to hold property, to build new churches on State land, and to establish legal title over regalia, artistic treasures and documents.

Languages

The dominant language of the Soviet Union is Russian, which is officially promoted as a "second native tongue" and, since 1938, has been a compulsory subject in all non-Russian-speaking general and secondary schools. The Indo-European languages are by far the most important; apart from the Slavonic and Baltic tongues, these include the Indo-Iranian tongues. Russian, Ukrainian and Byelorussian all belong to the eastern sub-group of the Slavonic branch of the Balto-Slavic tongues. The Cyrillic alphabet (named for St. Cyril, the apostle of the Slavs who devised it for the translation of the Bible and the liturgy in the ninth century) is in use throughout the Union with the exception of Armenia, Georgia and the Baltic Republics, where it co-exists for official purposes with the Latin or native alphabets. Encouragement has helped the development of national cultures, such as those of the Turkic peoples and Old Asiatics who, in Czarist times, had no written languages, but were given these under the Communist regime, based on the Latin alphabet. The Georgians and Armenians have kept their old Japhetic alphabets (derived from Aramaic and Greek script), while the Latvians, Lithuanians, Estonians and Karelians have retained Latin script. The Mari and the Yakut have established national literatures; the Kazakhs and the Kirghiz have crystallized local cultures which previously were fragmented. Russian, however, serves as a *lingua franca* among the 70-odd languages of the Union. The younger generation of non-Russian nationalities is accepting that bilingualism is a necessity for personal advancement even though the national languages survive.

Many Russians study Western languages. After many years of neglect, English appears to be the favorite. Because of the still prevalent isolation of the country, the results appear to be somewhat uneven; but the English language instruction in secondary schools is excellent in main cities, and, in addition, large numbers of people regularly listen to the B.B.C. and Voice of America. This has not always been easy, especially in large cities where jamming has hindered reception from time to time (although most good shortwave radios can receive unjammed frequencies). However, jamming of the B.B.C. tailed off in recent years and in 1987 ceased altogether.

Education

Before 1917, almost three-fourths of the population were illiterate; by 1950, illiteracy had been almost eliminated. Schooling is universal, compulsory and free from the ages of 6 to 16 (in some cases to 17). There are ample facilities for the care and education of pre-school infants. According to a recent estimate, nearly a third of the entire population is engaged in full or part-time training.

In nursery school, parents must pay one-fifth of the cost. Primary and secondary grades are usually taught in the same school. Until the early 1960s, students attended either four-, seven-, or ten-year schools. The first of these were common mainly in rural areas. The majority of children attended either a seven-year (incomplete secondary) or a ten-year (complete secondary) school. Only a small group of the former went on to higher education. Students in both categories could, however, enter or transfer to a *technikum* (ages 15–19), where various vocational skills were taught. A new system introduced in 1984 calls for students to attend a ten-year school (ages 6–16) and massive structural reform is still in progress, which will eventually re-organize the existing three types of schools. These are: first, a general labor polytechnical school consisting basically of ten classes, though in non-Russian areas (where Russian is taught as a foreign language), an eleventh is added. Graduates receive a school-leaving certificate, needed to pursue higher education. There are four sub-types of part-time general schools: the schools of Working or Rural Youth, Schools for Adults and Correspondence Schools.

Secondly and thirdly are the vocational and the middle-grade specialist schools, of which there are almost 5,000. The vocational schools provide an element of training and workplace experience. In the 3,800 middle-grade special educational institutions, a two- to four-year course is offered for middle-grade specialists. Finally there are the universities and institutes. The universities (of which there are 65), offer training in a wide variety of specialties. The institutes, usually much smaller establishments, are limited to a few closely allied faculties. At present, about one in every five or six of tenth-year school leavers can expect to get a place in a full time institution. Most institutions offer four- to six-year courses in about 350 officially approved specialties; art subjects take about four years, engineering and science five, medicine six. Higher education is free, and some 70% of the full-time students receive modest maintenance grants, depending on their family circumstances, and in some instances, on their grades.

The Press

Like all the other means of communication, newspapers, magazines and all periodicals are state-owned. 8,000 newspapers are published in 58 languages. *Pravda* (Truth) is published every day in 23 cities; *Izvestia* (News) is the next largest daily. All political publications are controlled directly by the government; but censorship is usually exercised by the editors, who are chosen carefully and can be removed at the slightest deviation from the party line. There are signs that this hitherto absolute adherence to the party line is being decisively relaxed. This is one of the most significant and welcome results of Gorbachev's policy of *glasnost,* or openness. Whether there is substance behind the attractive facade remains to be seen, however. Nonetheless, the quite hard hitting criticisms of the system—rather than just individuals—carried in *Pravda* and many other periodicals, now contrast with the stodgy inflexibility of recent years. The Soviet Union set the trend in the Communist world for the so-called "fat" magazines, monthly or quarterly journals either literary, critical or scientific, in whose pages many important ideological battles are carried on. *Novy Mir,* the most liberal of these, had its ups and downs, but is at the moment riding high on a wave of adventurous liberalism and in 1988 is due to publish its long-promised serialization of *Dr Zhivago.* The Soviet Movie Workers' Association has a monopoly of fan magazines and movie stills and does very well out of it. There are, of course, thousands of specialized magazines.

Foreign newspapers are very hard to obtain in the U.S.S.R.—even the New York *Daily World,* the London *Morning Star,* the Paris *Humanité* or the Italian *Unità* can be found only in the big hotels. East European papers are, however, available at street stalls, though by no means always. A select number of Intourist hotels sell limited copies of *The Times,* again, irregularly, depending on the political sensitivity of the contents. They are normally available only to Western tourists. There is *Moscow News,* a Soviet English-language weekly which publishes a small amount of carefully-chosen news and a large number of officially-approved photographs about Soviet achievements. You must be prepared, therefore, while in the Soviet Union, to be cut off almost completely from the world press; nor will radio or television help you in this respect, unless you speak Russian—in which case *do* tune in to the new-style news and political discussion programs, which are a vast improvement on their predecessors of a few years ago. And it is not likely that you will be within reach of the products of *samizdat,* the underground network of typed or mimeographed publications; in any case these deal mainly with unofficial news of domestic interest which would mean very little to the non-specialist visitor from abroad.

THE SOVIET WAY OF LIFE

by
MARY SETON-WATSON

In most countries, tourists notice a discrepancy between the inhabitants' view of themselves and the outsider's view. In the Soviet Union this discrepancy strikes one with particular force. It starts with the tourist's first sight of Soviet streets, usually from an Intourist bus. World peace is in the air: slogans on public buildings call for it, guides provide statistics on peace congresses, and at any official meeting, peace is the first toast. Yet military uniforms are everywhere: not just frontier police, security troops and traffic policemen, but dozens of soldiers and officers in uniform among the crowds on the streets, plus frequent lorry-loads of young conscripts. Town war memorials, always shown to tourists with pride, have an eternal flame guarded by young Pioneers and Komsomols carrying real rifles. It is the first example visitors are likely to encounter of the contrast between the insiders' and the outsiders' viewpoints.

To Russians, it is natural and praiseworthy that children should be taught their patriotic duty to defend their country: to Western tourists, Soviet children carrying guns represent only the militarization of the educational system. But no visitor can fail to appreciate the genuine love of their country which is not just taught to children, but felt by Russians in all walks of life—even if we cannot agree with Soviet educators, for whom a pacifist is automatically a traitor.

Despite the high incidence of uniforms, the Soviet street scene is varied and colorful. Outward appearances have changed enormously in the last

20 years: the red-lettered propaganda slogans adorning public buildings have now been joined by Western-type posters advertising State insurance or Aeroflot, tall apartment blocks ring all the main cities in place of the old one-story wooden houses, private cars are increasing in number every year, and no longer can one always tell the foreigners from the natives in the crowds by their dress.

Groups of schoolchildren or young adults constitute a large element in the throngs on the streets—and here what strikes a Western observer is how quiet and well-behaved the teenagers are. Schoolgirls, for instance, in their black overalls with frilly white pinafores for special occasions, look like parlor-maids from the *Upstairs, Downstairs* television series rather than products of a Socialist educational system. Their behavior suits their clothes: giggling and chattering, certainly, but anti-social behavior— practically never. They seem to have a strong corporate sense, the elder children taking responsibility for the public behavior of the younger ones, an attitude their teachers are very anxious to implant in them from their first day at school.

Yet you may also see gangs of adolescent boys loitering in the streets or parks at night, and you will certainly notice suspicious characters, mostly young, hanging round the entrances of Intourist hotels hoping to buy jeans or currency from foreign visitors. The Soviet Union, like any other country, is worried about its juvenile crime rate, and it has its share of muggers, burglars and car-stealers, very many of whom are still at school. Every week you can read accounts in the press of such crimes, for which the penalty is usually a stiff prison or reformatory sentence. In 1986 there were 46,000 registered drug addicts.

Just like sociologists in the West, Soviet sociologists' favorite explanation for the activities of these young people is that they often come from broken homes, or have alcoholic parents. A deeper reason may be the sharp change in the attitude towards adolescents by adults, once they have reached the end of childhood.

Children are the privileged class in Soviet society, continually told that the future is theirs, and no effort is spared in fitting them for it. Both in pre-school crêches and in regular school, they are surrounded with loving care from parents and teachers, while the State provides nourishing school meals, clothes which are much cheaper than the adult equivalents, summer camps, theater excursions and so on. School lasts for 11 years from the age of six. But at 16, adulthood arrives with a bang: the young person receives his internal passport and, when he or she leaves school, is expected either to compete for a place in a higher educational institution, or to start work and begin repaying the State for its care. Moreover, at the age of 18 young men are called up for two to three years' military service, unless they can obtain exemption on health or family grounds, or postponement if they are continuing their education. Suddenly the pampered child finds himself without his privileges, treated the same as any other adult citizen and subject to all the stresses and difficulties of everyday life, a transition many young people find hard to accept.

But these problems afflict only a small minority: most Westerners who have talked with Soviet schoolchildren are deeply impressed by the sense of security which their privileged childhood has given them. They leave school with a well-founded confidence in their own future: the State is not just bound by law to provide them with jobs, but will in fact certainly do so—even if the work they get is not always what they hoped for. The media are greatly concerned to stress the fulfilling nature, as well as the importance to the country, of manual work and the public services; this is because, like all countries where living standards have risen sharply in recent years, young people in the Soviet Union aspire to better themselves—which usually means that they want white-collar work. There are far too many would-be scientists, artists, actors, and not nearly enough school-leavers going into the factories or the retail trade.

The new school program lays great stress on familiarizing children with various practical trades, in the hope that the girls will discover that commercial cooking or laundry work can be fun, while the boys may find that new skills such as using power-tools will help them mend their motor-bikes. Despite all the efforts of school careers teachers, however, the shortage of people willing to do manual work in central and western Russia remains one of the new Soviet leadership's greatest problems. In the Central Asian provinces of the U.S.S.R., on the other hand, there are far too many manual laborers. But they show no desire to leave their sun-baked villages—and gone are the Stalinist days, when thousands of citizens could be shifted from one side of the country to another at the stroke of a pen. Nowadays Uzbek building workers have to be inveigled into moving to Minsk with the offer of extra wages—which plays havoc with the construction trusts' planned estimates.

Family Life and the Fascination of Food

The long-term solution to labor shortages would be a rise in the west Russian population. But here the planners encounter a formidable obstacle: the unwillingness of modern Russian mothers to have more than one child. Couples with no children have to pay six percent of their earnings in the so-called "childless" tax, and couples with one child are subject to a good deal of social pressure in the form of lectures about their patriotic duty to provide more future Soviet citizens. But although maternity leave is generous and crêches numerous, most women are still reluctant to embark on a large family, much as Russians love children. Indeed, it has been estimated that in central and western Russia, young women are averaging six or seven abortions each (easily arranged, in a State hospital). The chief reason is lack of good living accommodations. Apartments are very cheap to rent, but small and hard to find. Each adult is entitled to 12 square meters of living space, and in theory each child entitles a family to another room; but in practice there is a long waiting-list, or the money must be found to pay for a private exchange. For those with the means, there is the possibility of buying a flat through a cooperative. But the new blocks of flats are located on the outskirts of town, which in Moscow or Leningrad may mean a two-hour journey to work daily.

There is also the problem of shopping, which weighs very heavily on the working mother, often consuming all her lunch-hour and delaying her return home at night. Shopping in Russia used to be dominated by the three-line system: a line to order the goods, another line to pay, and a third line to collect. This system still operates in bookshops, toyshops and the like, so that one wonders how anyone except a tourist ever has time to buy anything. Fortunately, in the big cities food supermarkets are now appearing, and here things have been speeded up in the Western style. The problem then is, to find a shop where supplies of meat or milk have not run out. Most families resort once a week to the collective farmers' open markets, where fresh produce in a greater variety than the shops provide can be had, though at much higher prices. Non-working grandmothers are expected always to carry string bags, and always to join the lines that form at street-corner kiosks with lightning speed: only after a considerable wait may the line discover that it's not oranges today, only cabbage. Apart from meat, the supply of most foodstuffs in the cities has slowly improved in recent years. But the reactions of one Soviet tourist who visited London in the 1970s are still typical: he came home convinced that what he had been told about the situation of the poor in the capitalist west was quite true. "In London," he told his friends, "there are hundreds of shops full of fruit and vegetables—and no lines. That proves that the prices must be too high for ordinary people to buy anything."

Despite the shortages however, food is still a great source of enjoyment to modern Russians, and tourists who get invited into any Soviet home will find a variety of dishes on the table: solid vegetable soup (*shchi*), savoury pasties (*pirozhki*), buckwheat porridge (*kasha*), hors d'oeuvres (*zakuski*) and salads with smoked fish of various kinds, marinated mushrooms, pickled cucumbers, jams—and mounds of both black and white bread. All this should traditionally be washed down with vodka when guests are present; but if Party Secretary Gorbachev's anti-alcoholism campaign has the intended effect, you are more likely to be offered wine or beer, to be followed by many glassfuls of tea, probably accompanied by a sweet cream-filled cake (*pirog*). Perhaps because the ingredients for many dishes are hard to come by, people tend to serve them lavishly when they can and guests are expected to eat every last crumb or risk offending their hosts. Many toasts will be drunk at such a gathering, many questions asked—Russians are insatiably curious about foreign customs and opinions—and warm friendships established, for the Russians are still some of the most hospitable and outgoing people in the world.

After such an occasion, the foreign guest may hope to maintain contact with his new friends after he returns home. Do not be too downcast if this proves impossible. Your letters, if they reach their destination, will probably not receive a reply, and you will find it very difficult to telephone a Soviet home from abroad. Partly this is the result of postal censorship, partly the trouble is old habits of caution which die hard, even though ordinary Soviet citizens no longer need fear the knock on the door at night just because a letter has arrived with a Western stamp on it.

Health for All

Among the more cheerful aspects of Soviet life is the public health service. Medical care is free, for tourists as well as natives, and includes visits to the home by doctors and treatment in hospital: medicines, however, have to be paid for by the patient and many of them are in short supply. Much attention is paid to preventive medicine: whether sick or healthy, most workers have the opportunity to get free or inexpensive holidays in rest homes run by the trade unions in the southern mountains or on the sea coasts. But human nature being what it is, Russians tend to regard paid-for treatment as better than the free kind. Just as Soviet teenagers spurn perfectly good jeans of Russian manufacture, preferring those with a Levi or other foreign label which have scarcity value, so their parents will spend money on private dental care, or if a relative is having an operation in a State hospital, will give expensive presents to the surgeon.

Many people have so little faith in the State health service that they prefer to go privately to homeopaths or faith healers: the most famous of these, a woman from Georgia, is said to include many Ministers among her clients. From time to time quacks offering miracle cures appear, enjoy huge popularity for a time, and then either vanish or are prosecuted by the courts. A few of the old "wise women" (*znakharki*), who appear so often in folk tales, are still alive in remote villages, and their services are still sometimes called on, to read a spell over a sick child or to mix a love potion. The Scientific-Technical Revolution of which Soviet newspapers write with much pride has not yet spread to all corners of this huge country.

Broadening the Mind

Within the Soviet frontiers, traveling for pleasure is expanding every year, both for organized groups and for individuals. At all the main tourist centers, you can find nearly as many Soviet tourists as foreigners, often people from distant Siberia or the Soviet Far East, who spend their summer vacations "doing the sights" of European Russia. Some come in busloads, some on foot with back-packs, some in their own cars.

There has been a great revival of interest in Russia's old church and monastery buildings: the Society for the Preservation of Cultural Monuments campaigns for more State allocations for restoration work, and members of the Society take summer jobs as guides and encourage their friends to travel the northern forest area, studying the carvings on wooden peasant huts and the architectural styles of churches with "tent" or "onion" roofs. The newly restored Tsarist summer palaces along the Gulf of Finland (outside Leningrad) and the old noblemen's estates and mansions on the outskirts of Moscow (Ostankino, Abramtsevo, Kuskovo), have been lovingly restored in all their details—not just as foreign tourist attractions, but as a part of the national heritage which ordinary Russians are now learning to appreciate.

Foreign travel, too, is increasingly becoming part of ordinary people's lives. Intourist guides will tell visitors with pride that the number of Soviet citizens going abroad is nearly as great as that of foreigners coming to the U.S.S.R. Their figures of course include official visitors and businessmen as well as tourists, and there is no attempt to disguise the fact that Soviet tourists going to the West must travel in organized groups, must wait a long time for their turn to come, and finally have to pass a strict security check. But even with these provisos, there certainly are more groups going West every year. The more easily-obtained trips to Bulgaria, Hungary or Czechoslovakia, which offer the possibility of buying a better range of consumer goods than is available at home, are also very popular.

But for most people, the ideal summer vacation is several weeks on the sunny shores of the Black Sea. Those who fail to get a place in a State-subsidized rest home simply take the train to Sochi and then rent a room from one of the private landladies who are usually to be found near the main railway station. This practice has now been semi-legalised by the local authorities, who have lists of rooms which may be rented at officially-fixed prices (not, however, by foreign tourists, who are accommodated in hotels).

Many Russians resent any form of regimentation on vacation: they fill rucksacks, or pile into a friend's jalopy, and set off for a free-and-easy vacation in a tent or in the open air. "We are the 'wild' campers" (*dikari*), they will tell you proudly; and as long as they avoid the restricted areas around the Government officials' Black Sea villas, officialdom leaves them alone. For 11 months of the year they fulfil their norms, attend Party meetings, do what the foreman tells them: for the 12th month, they please themselves. Such people are the exceptions in Soviet life, but they seem to be on the increase. Plenty of them can be found in the official camp sites in the south, to which both foreigners and Russians are admitted.

Rugged Individualism

It may come as a surprise to foreign visitors to discover that among the Soviet people, whom we may think of as willing or unwilling conformists, there are plenty of individualists, even eccentrics. Most people work hard, live in comparatively cramped conditions, and spend their leisure collectively, whether at soccer matches or the theater. But there are also the hobby enthusiasts, who make models of old sailing ships, or go in for yoga, or build their own hang-gliders, or keep pets. For some years now, the really "in" hobby among the young professional Moscow élite has been to keep a pedigree dog, preferably one of the larger breeds—a setter, a boxer or a huge black Newfoundland. It's a form of snobbery: in pre-revolutionary noblemen's households, there were always several big dogs, looked after by the servants and used both for hunting and as a status symbol. So nowadays, "a Muscovite taking a well-groomed setter out for a walk on the lead can feel like a nobleman (*barin*) for a few minutes every day." This, at least, was the explanation offered recently in a novel by Anatoli Ananiev.

There are many other examples of snobbery in modern Soviet life: people who collect antique furniture hoping visitors will think it inherited family property, or who buy up old cupboards and use the doors to wood-panel a room as a study. Anyone who wishes to observe these harmless snobs in action has only to visit any of the Moscow "commission shops" which deal in second-hand goods. As for the pet dogs, cage-birds or gold-fish—they are for sale every Sunday morning at the Moscow "bird market."

We think of Soviet society as regimented: but there are many cases of individuals who refuse to conform—and who apparently get away with it. One hears occasionally of religious drop-outs, young people who refuse to work, but go round preaching universal love and brotherhood, living on their followers' charity until the powers-that-be catch up with them. Then there are the poets and painters who take poorly-paid posts as night watchmen or train attendants, in order to have time to write or paint. There have even been cases of respectable factory managers who suddenly can bear their lives no longer, resign their posts and go off to hunt bears in the Siberian forest or to catch fish on Lake Baikal.

Commoner than all these are the town-dwellers who hold down ordinary jobs but in their spare time build themselves a house in some remote village, where they can spend their vacations growing vegetables and picking wild berries. The "Back to Nature" cult has many followers in modern Russia: people trying to escape from the unhealthy atmosphere of many large industrial towns, and families willing to spend their weekends digging to ensure for themselves a regular supply of fresh fruit and vegetables.

Until recently, such devotees of the "good life" used to encounter a lot of opposition from the local authorities, who were unwilling to provide individuals with the building materials, manure or seeds which they needed. There is no security of tenure for individual weekenders, who are allowed to own their houses but not the land around them. Productivity from private plots, however, is so far above that of the collective (*kolkhozy*) or state (*sovkhozy*) farms, that the Government recently decided to make use of these amateur gardeners and livestock raisers to solve the country's food problems. People are now being encouraged to apply through their place of work for a plot of land outside town, and the State sees to it that any surplus produce is delivered to official collection points and not sold in the open markets. Outside all the main towns, you will see rows of wooden shacks (*dachas*) with their own gardens, where town workers spend their weekends.

Life in the Countryside

Attitudes towards life in the Soviet countryside have changed radically since World War II. Before the war, it was the aim of every rural dweller to escape to the nearest big city: few villages had electricity or running water or proper schools, and collective farm-workers were at the bottom of the social scale, tied to the land where they were born and unable to move. Things have improved greatly in recent years, although many village houses are still without mains water (women carrying buckets with a yoke are still a commonplace sight). Electricity is now almost universal; and since 1974, farm workers have been issued with internal passports at the age of 16 just like all other Soviet citizens—which means they have the legal right to leave and seek their fortunes elsewhere in the Soviet Union. To keep their workers on the land, *kolkhoz* chairmen now have to offer inducements in the form of better wages and living accommodations.

In the 1960s under Khrushchev, an unsuccessful attempt was made at consolidation of villages in western Russia. Outlying hamlets were closed down and their inhabitants moved to bigger centralized settlements (agro-towns), where tall apartment blocks were built to house them with all urban comforts. This policy was never officially withdrawn, but its implementation has been in abeyance for some years. Nowadays the farm workers are demanding individual two-storeyed cottages, one for each family, each with its garden where sheds can be put up to house privately-owned livestock. In some places attempts have been made to retain the collective principle, by building stock-yards at the end of each street of cottages; but these have not caught on, since housewives have clearly indicated that they want the family cow and chickens close at hand. Local authorities now want to encourage private livestock, and their latest problem is that many of today's young wives of farm-hands, who are often girls brought up in the city, are not prepared to keep a cow unless the local *kolkhoz* helps them with fodder, nor will they grow vegetables unless they get the loan of a tractor (plus driver) to plough their allotment. In the past the ploughing would be done by a man on his day off, in exchange for a bottle or two of vodka; now families expect it as a right. Arguments over these matters are going on in thousands of Russian villages: in some places the wives are winning, in others the local bureaucrats.

The worst problem in the Russian countryside, and one which tourists will readily see for themselves if their visit takes place in spring or fall, is the lack of good roads. For about seven months of the year—while the snow is falling or melting, and during midsummer thunderstorms—the village streets are a sea of mud, which only a tractor can get through. What this means in practice has been vividly described by the writer Yuri Nagibin. The hero of his short story, *In the Rain,* an agricultural engineer living in a remote village, has a daily problem in getting from the house where he lives to the truck which is his transport to work at the *kolkhoz,* and which is parked on hard ground at the opposite end of the village. To reach it, he has to circumnavigate the village square, wearing fishermen's thighboots and clinging to the fence, where the ground is firmer. As he struggles through the mire, he notices the village clubhouse, with its posters advertising a filmshow and dance, and comments wryly to himself that to get to that evening at the movies, you would need to wear stilts. No wonder that many of the eight million Russian families who own a house in the country spend only the four summer months (May–August) in their second residences.

Strangely, however, the very backwardness of the rural transport system is an added attraction for many Russians, who would like to escape from the stresses of urban civilisation and return to a simpler way of life. A great wave of nostalgia for the early 1900s is sweeping through intellectual circles in Moscow and Leningrad. People are forming local history associations, looking up their ancestors in the public records, studying old family photographs, reading books of memoirs. After more than 70 years of turbulent history—including two world wars, revolution, civil war, collectivization, industrialization—many Soviet citizens are fascinated by the calmer tempo of life and the greater moral certainties of their grandparents' days. So they search avidly for details to round out the accounts in official history books, finding them in historical novels and in old men's reminiscences.

"The Opium of the People"

Sometimes this fascination with the past can lead to an interest in the Russian Orthodox Church, whose rituals have remained unchanged for centuries, and whose beautiful liturgical music can be heard nowadays at public concerts, as well as in the "working" churches. For some people, this interest leads in turn to religious conversion: believers claim that there has lately been a real upsurge of religion, and that there are as many as 40 million practising Christians in the U.S.S.R. today. In the absence of any reliable statistics, it is impossible to verify this: but the official Party newspaper, *Pravda,* has admitted that eight to ten percent of the Soviet population are believers—in other words, 25 million people. Tourists who visit any Orthodox church or Baptist chapel service cannot but be impressed by the size of the congregation. Elderly women predominate, as official Soviet guides will not fail to point out: but there are also an increasing number of young men and women churchgoers. Most of the congregation seem to be regular attenders, for although there are very few prayerbooks or hymn-sheets in evidence, they obviously know the service by heart. The fervency of their prayers and the intensity of their faith, once witnessed at such a service, can never be forgotten.

The history of the Russian Orthodox Church since the Revolution has been a chequered one: persecuted in the 1920s and 1930s, restored to respectability by Stalin's recognition during the war years, but persecuted again under Khrushchev in the early 1960s, when hundreds of churches were closed. Today's official policy towards the Church is one of limited toleration. Any Intourist office will now provide information on the location of "working" churches, and guides were specially trained to cope with the flood of foreign believers who were expected to visit Moscow in 1988, when the 1,000th anniversary of the conversion of Kievan Russia to Christianity was celebrated. No more churches are being closed; but very few have been re-opened, and any priests or believers who equate Christian teachings with the human rights movement are dealt with severely. To be a professing Christian does a career no good: yet there are Party members who have their children christened secretly, and priests say that these children, after years of making their way in the world as good Communists, often return to the Church in middle age.

Belief in the supernatural is constantly ridiculed in the press; yet people love to tell stories such as that of the Cathedral of Christ the Saviour, which used to stand on the banks of the Moskva river in the center of Moscow. It was dynamited in the 1930s on Stalin's orders; but when construction on its site of a huge Palace of Congresses had to be abandoned because the new building kept sinking into the mud, some saw this as a manifestation of divine vengeance. After the war the authorities very sensibly turned the site into an outdoor swimming pool; and the sequel to the story is that this pool, which is heated in winter and thus covered in clouds of steam, is sometimes the scene of unofficial baptisms.

Russia is full of such real-life stories with unexpected twists, and even on a short visit, the tourist will hear plenty of them. You will also probably meet discontented Russians who hanker after the life abroad they have heard so much about. Never make the mistake of thinking that such people are more than a tiny minority. Most Soviet citizens' grumbles against the powers-that-be are steadily lessening. They regard the constant stream of propaganda under which they live with healthy scepticism: but their patriotism and pride in their country's achievements remain unshaken. For despite shortages and difficulties, they know that things are getting slowly better every year. And now, under Gorbachov, they are more hopeful than ever before.

Russians look back to the war years with horror, and the nightmare which constantly haunts them all is that anything of the sort might ever happen again. Unfortunately, most of them accept what they are told about the outside world's intentions towards the Soviet Union, and their fears echo those of many people in the West, only in reverse. When the Soviet writer Mikhail Roshchin recently asked his 12-year-old son what his friends at school thought about America, the boy replied: "Americans are fine, but why do they want to drop a bomb on us?" And Roshchin remembered that he once asked an American schoolgirl a similar question about the Russians, and got a similar answer. An increase in tourism in both directions may be the best way to remove such dangerous illusions from both children's and adults' minds.

THE PEOPLES OF
THE SOVIET UNION

by
GEORGE SCHÖPFLIN

When is a Russian not a Russian? The answer to this improvised conundrum has in it the essence of the variety of nations that make up the Soviet Union. It might go something like this: a Russian isn't a Russian when he is a Ukrainian or a Georgian or a Central Asian Moslem or a member of any of the hundred or so nationalities that make up nearly half the population of the country. Non-Russians are very insistent on their separate identity.

For most foreigners, ignorant or otherwise, Russia is the same as the Soviet Union. Yet the 1981 population figures give the Russians only a bare majority of the then 265 million population—about 52 percent. Demographers are predicting that the margin will be even closer when the results of the next census are published later in the 1990s—indeed, the non-Russians may even have moved into the majority because of their higher birthrate. By the year 2000 they are expected to have dropped to 44 percent of the population. But even then the Russians will be far and away the largest single national group. In 1981, there were 137 million Russians to 48 million Ukrainians, the next largest national group, and the third largest, the Central Asian Uzbeks, were 13 million and growing. At the opposite end of the spectrum, Soviet enumerators take account of some very small national groups indeed—the 600 Yukagir, for instance, a Siberian group far removed from the 20th century.

Official government policy fully reckons with this ethnic diversity in the Soviet Union. A glance at publications like *Soviet Weekly,* a paper intended for readers in the English-speaking world, will show that Soviet officialdom takes great pride in the continued existence of small, picturesque ethnic groups and insists that this is what Soviet policy is all about, to provide conditions in which their traditions can be maintained. This will probably come as a surprise to many readers, but, in fact, Soviet policy on nationalities goes back to Lenin (but then, *every* Soviet policy goes back to Lenin), who asserted that in the Soviet Union policy towards individual national groups was "national in form and socialist in content." What this was supposed to mean was that Lenin had nothing against the preservation of national languages and national cultures, provided that these were socialist, that they accepted and perpetuated his Communist vision of the world.

Lenin and After

Furthermore, at the time of the Russian Revolution in 1917 and after, Lenin saw the political value of promising full national devolution to the non-Russians, who even then formed a very high proportion of the population. The anti-Bolshevik Whites who opposed him were reluctant to consider autonomy for the non-Russians, so that Lenin's promise of national freedom ensured the Communists the support of many non-Russians, who did, indeed, fight for the Revolution (though, as may be guessed, not necessarily from revolutionary convictions).

In the early years after the Revolution, policy towards the non-Russians followed Lenin's precepts closely. The Soviet Union was established as a federation in 1922, with a complex hierarchical system of union republics, autonomous republics, autonomous *oblasts* or provinces and national *okrugs* or areas. All these administrative subdivisions enjoy different kinds of legal rights and, according to the Constitution, union republics are in theory entitled to leave the Soviet Union and set up on their own. What guarantees the cohesiveness of this apparently loose structure is the disciplined rule of the Communist Party.

In addition, over the years a variety of practices have sprung up which help to keep the country together and prevent fragmentation. So, while in all the non-Russian republics, the head (or First Secretary) of the local party will be a native of that republic, his deputy will be a Russian with close links to Moscow. Control of security, too, tends to be in Russian hands. The Soviet system does give some economic benefits to the non-Russian republics, often in the form of higher investment funds. But in addition to all these, the sheer habit of living in one state, the persistence of the system as the normal order of things has gone some way towards creating a Soviet identity. This does not mean that non-Russians have necessarily given up their Uzbek or Estonian or Georgian national traditions, but many of them accept that they live in the Soviet Union and are to that extent Soviet. The authorities do what they can to encourage this, of course.

At first, in the 1920s, Soviet policy-makers were genuinely concerned to make up for decades of neglect, oppression and Russification under the Czars. The emphasis, in the first place, was to create the bases for national cultures. Languages which had had no literatures (or, in many cases, were not written at all) were encouraged to grow, and institutions were set up to foster national traditions among the non-Russians. The Moslems, who had come under Russian rule through centuries of conquest, were supported in their attempts to give up the Arabic alphabet, which is extremely unsuitable for the Turkic languages that most of them spoke. They chose to write their languages in a Latin alphabet.

Gradually, however, as Stalin consolidated his power, he began to abandon the policy of toleration towards national diversity and pursued an ever more rigid centralization in which there was no room for any divergence from the norm on the part of non-Russians. Many talented non-Russian cultural personalities lost their lives in the purges of the 1930s and, a highly symbolic step, at the end of that decade, the various Latin alphabets introduced earlier were scrapped and replaced with Cyrillic, the alphabet used by the Russians. What this meant in practice was that an educated Moslem, say, born in 1900, would have written his mother tongue in three alphabets by the time he was 40—in the Arabic script, then in the Latin alphabet and finally in Cyrillic characters.

Building the "Soviet Man"

The principal theoretical aim of nationalities policy today is that the peoples of the Soviet Union are entering upon a process of "drawing together," which will lead ultimately to their "merger" into the "Soviet man." The stress is on ultimately. No time limit has been set for this and, indeed, under Brezhnev the "merger" was put off to the remote future. This is seen to be a gradual process, and it is emphasized that the basis on which the "Soviet man" will order his life will be socialism. However, some non-Russians are quick to point out that it looks rather as if this "Soviet man" will be Russian-speaking, and they ask what will happen in the process to their own languages and cultures.

Certainly, enormous emphasis is placed by the Soviet educational system on the learning of Russian. Throughout the Soviet Union, Russian is a compulsory language even for schools in which the language of instruction is *not* Russian, and there is a widespread network of schools, including many in non-Russian areas, where the schooling *is* in Russian. The authorities argue that Russian serves as the means of communication among non-Russians, that it is a window on the wider world, and that advancement can come only on the basis of a sound knowledge of Russian, which is "not just a world language, but even a language of outer space." The non-Russians would like to be able to live a national life with their own national languages and cultures, without having Russian forced down their throats at every turn.

In a word, many non-Russians have the impression that official Soviet policy, Lenin's principles and all, is at times not much more than a gloss on traditional Russian attitudes of regarding the non-Russians within the country as "younger brothers" who should be grateful for the tutelage of the Russian "elder brother." It is well to remember that not every grumble by a non-Russian is automatically evidence of Russian intolerance, and further, that national friction in the Soviet Union is not necessarily a dispute between Russian and non-Russian. In Transcaucasia, for instance (of which more later), relations between the Moslem Azerbaijanis and Christian Armenians have traditionally been tense, and inter-communal quarrels are not uncommon.

Equally, Soviet policy contributed materially to the strengthening of weak national cultures, by providing written languages and encouraging literatures. On the economic side, too, Soviet investment policy has tended to favor the development of poorer areas inhabited by non-Russians, and the latter have benefited from this. Being part of the Soviet Union is, further, undoubted protection for certain non-Russians against outside powers. The small Moslem nations of Central Asia probably prefer rule from Moscow to Chinese overlordship—though it is hard to be dogmatic about this for lack of evidence. And the Armenians, with their tragic history of massacres at the hands of the Turks, have traditionally looked towards Christian Russia for protection.

This said, non-Russians might argue that while they welcome the benefits of membership of the Soviet Union and are fully committed to Communism, they find it irksome that in practice so much of the Soviet system means having to do things the Russian way. Many of them have venerable cultural traditions of their own and see nothing deplorable in favoring their own national ways, not least in an era when small states in Africa and Asia can claim all the advantages of national independence and sovereignty.

The Pattern of Peoples

The various peoples who live in the Soviet Union may be classified into certain broad categories, by language, by religion or by other distinguishing characteristics. By far the largest category is the Slavs—the Russians, the Ukrainians and the Byelorussians. They are almost all Orthodox Christians—it should be understood that religious adherence is in all cases nominal and does not automatically mean that every member of a national group practices his religion—and they speak closely-related Slavonic languages. These are related in turn to the Slavonic languages of Eastern Europe (Polish, Czech, Serbo-Croat, Bulgarian and others). They write their languages in the Cyrillic alphabet, which is, in fact, well adapted to reproducing certain sounds found in the Slavonic languages. So whereas the Cyrillic script can convey the sound *shch* (as in Khru*shch*ev) with one character, Polish, which uses Latin script, is forced to employ the lengthy cluster of letters *szcz*. The Slavs of the Soviet Union originally inhabited the vast plains north of the Black Sea and west of the Ural mountains. Today, they are found everywhere in the Soviet Union. Indeed, northern Kazakhstan, which was once inhabited by nomadic Kazakh tribesmen only, is now a region of Russian settlement and some Russians claim that it should be transferred to the Russian republic. It is worth noting, too, that outside European Russia and the Ukraine, particularly in Central Asia, the friction that sometimes exists between Russians and Ukrainians disappears in the face of the more alien Central Asians, for whom there is little to distinguish a Russian from a Ukrainian anyway. (This may be seen as a neat example by those who believe in the "common enemy" theory.)

The next largest group is the Moslems, of whom those of Central Asia have already been mentioned. Although they are now almost completely settled, there is still a certain difference in outlook between the former nomads—the Kazakh, the Kirghiz and the Turkmen—and the long-settled Uzbeks and Tadzhiks, with centuries of cultivation behind them. Converted to Islam in the early Middle Ages, the Central Asians look back to the empires of Genghis Khan and Tamerlane, whose tomb is still shown at Samarkand. The Azerbaijanis or Azeris, whose capital is the oil city of Baku on the Caspian Sea, are of the Shiite sect of Islam (as distinct from the great majority of Sunni Moslems), and have looked towards Persia rather than the Arab world and Turkey, despite the fact that the Azeri language is virtually identical with that of Turkey. Further to the north, in the central Volga Valley, the Tatars of Kazan and the Bashkirs have had a far longer association with the Russians, and consequently are more open to European influences. The Tatars have been in the forefront of Islamic modernization and were the principal champions of the reform movement known as *jadidism* at the turn of the century. Other Moslem groups are to be found in the northern Caucasus. The Crimean Tatars, who were deported to Central Asia *en masse* during the war, are still lobbying for permission to return to their ancestral homelands in the Crimean Peninsula.

The great majority of Soviet Moslems speak Turkic languages, and as a general rule they all understand one another without too much difficulty. But not all the Turkic peoples are Moslem (the Chuvash of the Volga are Christian) and not all Moslems speak Turkic languages (the Tadzhiks speak a language which is hardly more than a dialect of Persian, though written in Cyrillic). Equally, in the northern Caucasus, Moslem peoples like the Avars speak what are known as Paleo-Caucasian languages, thought to be among the most fearsomely difficult in the world. Another of them, Kabardinian, has four ways of pronouncing the sound *f*, for example, which must make life difficult for a Kabardinian with a lisp!

If one were to ask a Central Asian what he regarded himself as, and he were to reply openly, he might well say, "I am a Moslem first, an Uzbek (or Kazakh or whatever) second and a Soviet citizen third."

Caucasians, Balts, Finns and Others

The next group, although they are in no way related linguistically or ethnically, is formed by the two great Christian nations of Transcaucasia, the Georgians and the Armenians. They were both absorbed by the Czars into their empire, having sought the protection of the largest Christian power in the region against Oriental encroachments. The Georgians speak a Paleo-Caucasian language, while Armenian is Indo-European—hence distantly related to English (*very* distantly).

The Estonians, Latvians and Lithuanians of the Baltic were part of the Czar's empire until the Revolution, after which they clung on to a precarious independence for two decades, and finally were absorbed into the Soviet Union. The Baltic states were long under German and Scandinavian influence; they are undoubtedly part of the mainstream of the Central European tradition which also includes the Poles, Czechs and Hungarians.

The various Finnic peoples of the Soviet Union are small in number and have long been in contact with the Russians, who have been the main influence on them. They are Orthodox Christians (except the Lutheran Estonians) and accept the Russian way of life in most respects. Their various languages are more or less distantly related to Finnish (and even more distantly to Hungarian), and they are quite unable to understand one another. They tend to work in agriculture and forestry, though since the Revolution, urban settlements have arisen in their homelands, which are in various parts of European Russia. The bulk of the population of these towns, as in so many non-Russian areas, tends to be Russian.

In addition to these general groups, there are other peoples who do not fit readily into any of the above categories. Here one might mention those nationalities which are splinters of groups which have a nation-state of their own outside the Soviet Union. These include the Poles (in the western marches of the Soviet Union), the approximately two million Germans (moved to Central Asia and Siberia during the war, but some tens of thousands of whom have been allowed to emigrate to West Germany), Greeks (remnants of the old Greek colonies on the Black Sea, again removed to Central Asia), Koreans (from the Soviet Far East, but removed to Central Asia), Bulgarians in the Ukraine, Hungarians on the Soviet-Hungarian frontier, Finns (mostly in the Karelian Isthmus ceded by Finland in 1944), and a few Czechs and Slovaks. The Moldavians speak a language that is for all practical purposes the same as Romanian, except that (unlike Romanian) it is written in Cyrillic, and that the authorities go to great lengths in insisting that Moldavian is a quite distinct language. There are also some 175,000 gypsies, mostly in European Russia and the Ukraine. The Kalmyks of the lower Volga, removed during the war but allowed to return later, have the distinction of being the only Buddhist people within geographical Europe.

Finally, there is what is best described as the ethnographic museum—the small groups of peoples of the North, Siberia and the Far East, who are regularly cited by official Soviet sources as examples of the success of Soviet nationalities policy. They range from the Uralic Samoyeds—whose languages are remote cousins of the Finno-Ugrian group—on either side of the Ural mountains along the North Sea, to the Chukchi in the extreme northeast of Siberia, not all that far from Alaska. The 1970 census returned only 151,000 representatives of these small peoples put together. Many of them have barely left the Stone Age and continue their age-old occupations of hunting, trapping and fishing. Those who leave assimilate rapidly.

The Russians

The Russians are sometimes known as the Great Russians. This is not a title of honor, but a means of distinguishing them from the Little Russians (now universally called the Ukrainians). The Russians are without a doubt one of the most talented and intriguing peoples of the world, let alone of the Soviet Union. They have the ability to arouse directly contradictory opinions among those who encounter them. Some people find them open, helpful, hospitable and generous; others find them sullen, suspicious, underhand and servile. The truth, for once, is not somewhere between these two extremes, but rather that they both represent aspects of the Russian stereotype, for both kinds of behavior are met with in different contexts.

It is well to bear in mind that these are just stereotypes and that far from every individual Russian will conform to them. But with this proviso, it is probably fair to say that the official Russian—the customs man, the hotel porter, the state functionary—is more likely to exhibit the second, "unpleasant," face of Russia, while the individual met by chance in the street at a person-to-person level will show the "pleasant" face.

Then again, one must distinguish between the Russian intellectual and the great mass of non-intellectuals, a distinction that is far more relevant in the Russian context than in the West. The intellectual stereotype is likely to be someone deeply, even desperately, concerned about whatever he happens to be concerned about, and profoundly committed to gaining his objective.

The Russian intelligentsia is curiously isolated from the great mass of the people. Yet because Russia is a land of paradoxes, the intellectual is looked up to and poets, say, are revered in a way that is most commonly associated with pop stars in the West. The paradox doesn't stop there. While intellectuals may be admired, they are also regarded with more than a breath of disdain by the man-in-the-street. They are set apart, sometimes even alienated from the people at large. This has arisen partly through tradition, in that the Russian intelligentsia—the very word has come into English from Russian—was always something special, consisting of educated people, with a wider view of the world, in what was an overwhelmingly backward, peasant society. This gave them respect in the eyes of the population, but also made them suspect as the practitioners of "special" knowledge. Equally, the intelligentsia is different because its members will tend to be better off, be doing a specialized job and above all because on both sides of the divide, people will be aware of the difference.

It would be foolish to be dogmatic about this, but it is more than likely that the role of the Russian Orthodox Church and the very deep imprint it has left on Russian society have contributed materially to this state of affairs, as well as to a whole host of other Russian attitudes. Because literacy was traditionally associated with the Church (until the 18th and 19th centuries) and because the Church was looked up to by the great mass of uneducated Russian peasants as the only source of guidance in a wicked world, it is arguable that some of the reverence formerly rendered unto the Church has passed to the intelligentsia.

The Russian attitude of suspicion and contempt, touched with a trace of illicit curiosity, towards everything associated with the outside world— for all practical purposes this meant the West until very recently—can also be traced back to the Church, if only in part. The Orthodox Church regarded itself as the Third Rome, the center of Christianity (after Rome and Byzantium) and as the true and only repository of Christianity, not defiled in some way or another as, in its view, both Roman Catholicism and Protestantism are. This has led to what can only be called a kind of messianism, a belief that the Russians are a chosen people, singled out for a special destiny to bring salvation to an otherwise benighted and sinful world. Translated on to a secular plane, this sense of mission spilled over into much of the 19th-century Russian intelligentsia and ultimately it came to infect the Communists too—although they would deny it very strongly. (To be sure, it is next to impossible to give the scientific proof to suggestions of this kind that would satisfy a professional sceptic).

But if one does accept that the Russian Orthodox Church has played a social role along these lines—and a global view of Russian history points in that direction—then, evidently, its influence can be seen in other areas of life as well. A strong candidate is the almost superstitious awe in which all manifestations of authority are held. The individual Russian (and let it be stressed again that this is a stereotype) is far readier to accept administrative abuse and arrogance than his Western counterpart. It has also been suggested that the readiness to put up with inconvenience, and even suffering, which might almost be called fatalistic, can be traced back to the long period of Tatar conquest and Moslem overlordship of Russia. The duality of Russian culture, looking East as well as West, and especially the love-hate attitude towards both, is an undoubted fact of Russian life.

The Soviet state takes a restrictive view of religion, as might be predicted from its Marxist and atheist origins. Religion is supposed to be a relic of the past, suitable only for the "scrapheap of history." Yet in formal terms, under the Constitution, the individual is supposed to be free to practise religion. In reality, numerous obstacles are placed in the way of believers, especially members of the smaller churches, like the Evangelical Baptists. There is, at the same time, evidence of a growing interest in religion in the Soviet Union, possibly as a reaction to the bleakness of so much of Soviet life.

Yet another factor which has had an unmistakable impact on the Russian way of life (though, as before, it is impossible to assess just how far and in what way) is the climate. It is no secret that Russia suffers terrifyingly cold winters and hot summers. This is certainly true of the areas of European Russia and Siberia which have a predominantly Russian population, even if Central Asia and Transcaucasia enjoy a milder climate. True Russia, then, is the land of Generals January and February, who defeated Napoleon and helped to do likewise to Hitler 130 years later.

At the most superficial level, Russians, together with Scandinavians and other inhabitants of northern latitudes, are heavy spirit drinkers and probably every traveler to Moscow has his story of cheerless drunks staggering around the streets, just as in another northern city—Glasgow. The problems of alcoholism and persistent drunkenness have become serious enough (even affecting male life expectancy statistics and the birthrate) for the authorities to mount huge campaigns against them. One of the first moves by Mikhail Gorbachev as leader on taking office in 1985 was to tighten up on drinking. High alcohol consumption was taking an increasing toll by the 1980s, with some statistics suggesting that deaths from alcohol poisoning were reaching epidemic proportions, far above those in the West.

If it is difficult to sum up the character of an individual in a few, brief paragraphs, how much more daunting to attempt to describe the genius of an entire nation in the same space. The truth is, of course, that any comments, like those above, on the Russians (or any other nation for that matter) can only be a broad canvas, showing a few, blurred outlines. The details must be filled in by the visitor to the Soviet Union, who has the extra challenge of knowing that he can never complete the picture.

The Ukrainians

Much of what has been said about the Russians applies to the Ukrainians, too. There is a great deal in common, at least to the complete stranger, between the two most numerous Slavonic nations, whose similarities seem more important than their differences. Perhaps there is a perceptible difference in that there is a certain quickness among the Ukrainians, a great readiness to consider the outside world. There is a good historical reason for this. The Ukrainian nation has never been anything like as isolated as the Russian, having been under Polish, Ottoman, Tatar and other influences. And Galicia, the so-called Western Ukraine, with its capital at Lvov (L'viv in Ukrainian, Lwów in Polish, Lemberg in German—travelers who know Europe east of the Rhine will be aware that most larger towns are known by different names in different languages) was part of Austria-Hungary until 1918.

It is hard to say just how Ukrainians and Russians differ, but the difference is deeply felt by those Ukrainians who are conscious of themselves as Ukrainian. There are not a few Ukrainians who feel that the difference is no more than a sentimental one, and who are, therefore, ready to accept the Russian language and eventually regard themselves as Russian.

Where a definite difference can be detected between Ukrainians and Russians is that the Ukrainians lack the abounding self-confidence that characterizes the Russian attitude towards the rest of the world. The Russians, when faced with non-Russians, seem to know that they are born to rule; the Ukrainians are much less sure.

It is true that a number of major "Russian" cultural figures have been Ukrainian by birth—the writer Nikolai Gogol is an example. However they have made their names through Russian, and much of the Ukrainian political establishment today is more Russian in culture than Ukrainian. It is easy for a Ukrainian to adopt Russian ways. Not only does the Soviet educational system encourage this, but the environment of many Ukrainian cities tends to be Russian rather than Ukrainian. There is a very substantial Russian minority in the Ukraine, some nine million people, and its two best-known representatives are Nikita Khrushchev and Leonid Brezhnev, the former party leaders. One of the few things that may remain to remind an assimilated Ukrainian of his origins could be the characteristic Ukrainian name endings in -enko or -chuk. In other respects, he will be a good Russian.

The Byelorussians

A lot of the above, about the Ukrainians, applies to the Byelorussians, too, except that in the case of the latter, it is only *more* so! They are closer to the Russians in just about every possible way. The Byelorussians are far fewer in number than the Ukrainians (less than 11 million in 1976); they have failed to develop an intense national identity, they remain mostly on the land and speak their language at home. In public, in the towns at least, they accept Russian. A fair comparison may be made here with German-speaking Switzerland, whose inhabitants speak Swytzerdütsch at home and High German in public.

In general, the modesty of the Byelorussian national effort is summed up by the slogan of the first Byelorussian publishing house, set up in 1906: "In our windows, too, the sun shall shine." Even their name, which means "White Russian," indicates that the Byelorussians are barely more than a branch of the Russians themselves. The Byelorussians appear to have accepted the fact that access to the wider world must be via Russian. The great bulk of education in the republic is carried out in Russian—the two languages are fairly alike—even while the Byelorussian Soviet Socialist Republic enjoys full membership of the United Nations (as does, incidentally, the Ukraine). More is published by the republic's presses in Russian than in Byelorussian. The streets of Minsk, the republican capital, resound to the sounds of Russian rather than Byelorussian, and the Byelorussian Academy of Sciences prefers to issue its scholarly output in Russian.

In many ways, it can be argued that the Byelorussians are the greatest success story of Soviet nationalities policy: the Byelorussian nation exists and it has accepted that its existence is expressed through what is the language of "the Soviet man," Russian.

The Baltic States

It is a very different story, though, among the Estonians, Latvians and Lithuanians. There, national self-assertiveness and attachment to national language remain strong, as does pride in local national traditions and achievements. The Balts will go a long way to stress that they have always belonged to Europe—unlike, they may say, the Russians—and that their contacts with the outside world are direct, especially with the Germans and Swedes who ruled the area over the centuries. For less than a generation, the Baltic states enjoyed a precarious independence. They had been part of the Czar's empire, then proclaimed their independence and ultimately found themselves ruled from Moscow after the carve-up of Eastern Europe between Hitler and Stalin in 1939–40. (The Balts fell to the latter.)

The European influence on which the Balts rely is apparent even to the casual tourist. The architecture of towns like Riga, Tallinn (which originally meant "Danes' Town") and Tartu proves that these settlements have had long contact with cultures well to the west of the Baltic lands. They are readily recognizable as stylistic first cousins of German towns like Lübeck and Swedish towns like Lund or Visby.

This difference between Baltic towns and genuine Russian settlements is understood by Russians, too, many of whom have come to live in what they regard as Europe. So many have come that Riga now has more Russians living in it than Latvians. (How the Latvians feel about this can only be guessed at.) In fact, the pace of Russian immigration into the Baltic states is the fastest into Latvia.

The Estonians and Latvians are readily recognizable as Scandinavians of a kind. They prefer the same sort of light and airy style, the clean-cut lines, the feel for simplicity that are so characteristic of the Finns and Swedes. Like the Scandinavians, the Estonians and a large proportion of the Latvians are Protestant. The Lithuanians, on the other hand, are devoutly Catholic and in 1983 a Lithuanian Archbishop became the first Soviet Cardinal. The Lithuanians differ somewhat from the other two Baltic peoples in another respect as well: they look back on a spectacular historical past in association with Poland, to the Polish-Lithuanian Commonwealth, which lasted until the end of the 18th century, when Poland was partitioned.

Latvian and Lithuanian are the only surviving members of the Baltic group of languages. Both these languages, written in the Latin alphabet, are distantly related to the Slavonic group and thus to Russian. Estonian, by contrast, is a Finno-Ugrian language, close enough to Finnish for Finns and Estonians to be able to understand one another. Indeed, many Finns are now able to take weekend trips to Tallinn, the Estonian capital, so reinforcing old links.

A Westerner's impressions of the Baltic states will certainly be conditioned by where he has just come from. If he goes to Tallinn or Riga directly from the West, it will be obvious to him that he is on the far side of the Iron Curtain, with all that that implies. But if, as is more likely, he goes there after having absorbed the atmosphere of Moscow and Kiev, he will react at the familiarity of what is distinctively European and be aware of the more prosperous lifestyle.

Transcaucasia

If the Baltic states form a kind of transition between Europe and Russia, Transcaucasia is very clearly an intermediary between Europe, the Middle East and Western Asia. The Transcaucasians, the three most numerous peoples of which are the Georgians, the Armenians and the Azerbaijanis or Azeris, see themselves consciously in this role, albeit firmly on the European side of the divide. In this sense, there is good reason for regarding Transcaucasia as the Soviet Middle East, the place where East meets West.

The two Christian peoples of the region, the Armenians and the Georgians, have traditionally looked towards Russia as the source of protection against the Moslems of the south, from whom both have suffered during their long history. The Azeris, on the other hand, have been more influenced by the attitudes of their fellow Shia Moslems in Iran. Indeed, there is still a substantial number of Azeri Turks in northern Iran. Despite the eruption of the Ayatollah Khomeini's Islamic revolution in Iran, there has been no evidence that the Azeri Shiites have been in any way tempted to follow his example.

Because of the long history of friendly contact of the Georgians and Armenians with Russians, these two peoples have a somewhat special position in Soviet politics. The elevation in 1985 of the Georgian party boss, Edvard Shevardnadze, to be Soviet Foreign Minister, is indicative of this. Until the early 1970s, they were allowed very considerable latitude in the running of their own affairs in their own way and it took the eruption of major corruption scandals in the 1970s, first in Georgia, and then in Armenia before tighter control was imposed.

The Azeris have always been subject to closer attention, not only because they are Moslem, but also because of the existence on their territory of the earliest substantial oilfield in the Soviet Union. Moscow has understandably regarded this oil as a vital strategic resource and has ensured that it would not be abused. The city of Baku, the Azeri capital and the Soviet Union's equivalent of Houston, has for a long time housed a very large number of Russians involved in the oil industry. On top of this, there is a sizeable Armenian community there as well.

Possibly because of the presence of Baku as an alien center in their midst, the Azeris have been in the forefront of Soviet Moslems in adopting Western ideas, together with the Volga Tatars. They were the first to give up writing their language in the highly unsuitable Arabic script and to use Latin letters instead. (The Arabic script is unsuited to the writing of Turkic languages because it makes virtually no provision for the expression of vowels, whereas the Turkic languages have a complex and essential vowel system.) In the 19th century many Azeris eagerly adopted Western ways, which they had learned through the medium of Russian. Some rose high in the Czar's service. After the collapse of his empire, the Azeris formed part of the short-lived Transcaucasian Federation, and then enjoyed a very brief period of independence before being absorbed into the Soviet Union.

The Armenians

The Armenians, the second of the three great Transcaucasian peoples, have never had much fondness for the Azeris, understandably, since their entire history has been one of persecution by Moslem Turks. The Armenian massacres of the early years of the century were only the culmination of a very long and tragic process. It is not by chance that an Armenian poet has written that his country's history has been marked by a sorrow that was like a shoreless sea.

This has had a number of important results. Armenians have, as already mentioned, looked towards the Russians for protection, and conversely, they have enjoyed a greater trust in the eyes of the Russians than other non-Russians. Secondly, the scattering of the Armenian population has led to an enormous diaspora that can only be compared with that of the Jews. There are substantial Armenian communities all over the Middle East and in North America. Thirdly, the Soviet authorities have encouraged all Armenians to regard Soviet Armenia as their homeland and the Armenian repatriation law is very similar to the Israeli law of Ingathering. It offers full rights and economic assistance to any Armenian who moves to Soviet Armenia. A fair number of expatriates have taken advantage of this and many have settled down to enjoy the benefits of Soviet rule. A few decided that the move was a mistake and have re-emigrated where they could.

Within the Soviet Union, the Armenians have a reputation of being the fixers, the people who get round the system, who operate around the edges of bureaucratic rigidity. They form an internal diaspora within the country, not least because Soviet Armenia is too small to permit all of them to exploit their undoubted talents and high level of education.

Armenians are famed for their entrepreneurial talents, their liveliness and for producing a brandy that is rivalled in the Soviet Union only by the output of Georgian distilleries. Armenians are easily recognized by the fact that virtually every Armenian name ends in -yan or -ian. Their culture is a very ancient one; their script is far older than Cyrillic and the Armenian Church, a focus of loyalty for every Armenian wherever he may be, is tolerated up to a point. In common with other peoples which have suffered long persecution, the Armenians are extremely conscious of their national identity and most of them accept that for want of anything better, the Soviet framework offers them their best chance of survival.

Georgians

The Georgians, too, have a strong self-awareness. They take great pride in being different from everyone else in the Soviet Union. They are ebullient and are inclined to live life larger than it is. If, for example, Georgia is racked by financial and political scandals—as it was often during the 1970s and early 1980s—then these will be the most spectacular the country has ever seen, even including a local "Godfather" who ran a vast network of illegal factories and dispensed patronage with a free hand. The Georgians also claim to have produced the largest concentration of centenarians in the world. It is certainly not unusual to find people over 120 years of age. They attribute this great age to the clean, healthy mountain air which they breathe, the vast quantities of yoghurt they eat and the beneficial effects of the local brandy (vastly superior to the stuff brewed down the way in Armenia).

The Georgians have also given the world another product who preferred to do things on a spectacular scale—in the person of Joseph Vissarionovich Dzhugashvili, better known as Stalin. Another Georgian, Lavrenty Beria, ran the Soviet secret police until his sudden demise in 1953, a few months after the death of Stalin. Stalin's memory is still honored in Georgia; his birthplace at Gori serves as a shrine.

Again, like the Armenians (for whom there is little love in Georgia), the Georgians are heirs to a very ancient cultural tradition. Georgia is supposedly the place where the Argonauts of Greek mythology sailed to find the Golden Fleece. The curlicued Georgian script is centuries older than Cyrillic and suits their complex language, reputedly impossible for an outsider to master, very well. Georgian names are likewise fairly easy to spot, as most of them end in -vili or -dze.

The capital Tbilisi (Tiflis in the 19th century), which derives its name from the warm, sulphurous springs found there, bears out the Georgian preference for being different. It is a pleasant relaxed town, rather Mediterranean in atmosphere, not least because the Georgians are wine drinkers (as distinct from the Russians, who drink the ubiquitous vodka). It is evident that the Georgians enjoy a level of prosperity above that of most areas of European Russia.

The Central Asians

Traditionally, Central Asia was the area bounded by the Kazakh steppes in the north, the Caspian Sea in the west and the mountains and the Oxus River to the east and south. Today, the expression normally includes Kazakhstan as well. The natives of the region, which used to be known as Turkestan, are undoubtedly marked by a certain cultural unity, in that they are all Moslem, that they mostly speak Turkic languages with a high degree of mutual comprehensibility (many of the Iranian Tadzhiks also understand Uzbek), and that they came under European rule in the 19th century. They are conscious of being the heirs of an ancient and glorious civilization, linked with the names of Genghis Khan and Tamerlane, and of having produced a flowering of Islamic culture in the Middle Ages. This had seriously degenerated by the last century and Russian rule has unquestionably raised their educational, social and medical levels. A European going to Dushanbe or Alma-Ata might find them shabby and somewhat dilapidated; an Asian will see that the people are well-fed and clothed, that there are no beggars, and that even the swarms of flies seem less aggressive than further south.

Today, the population of Central Asia is very mixed. There has been an enormous influx of Europeans—Russians and Ukrainians for the most part—to the extent that of its total population of nearly 45 million, over one quarter are Europeans. From the Soviet point of view, Central Asia is a strategically sensitive area, bordering on two fairly unstable states, Afghanistan and Iran (with India and Pakistan beyond), and on China. The Central Asians themselves are not insensible to the presence of the Chinese across the border in Sinkiang, and they are aware that the Turkic population of Chinese Turkestan is often worse off than they are.

This said, the Central Asians are a good instance of how non-European peoples can adopt European ways and go through the process of modernization in the space of two or three generations. Quite apart from the externals of modernization—houses, roads, schools, hospitals—the local languages and cultures have been provided with all the encouragement needed to sustain vigorous standards. Whereas before the Revolution, illiteracy was virtually universal among Central Asians (in 1920 there were only 25 Turkmen women able to read), today literacy is universal and a substantial proportion of the population has been through higher education as well.

Much of this effort has been successful, and the Central Asian nations have increased in self-confidence. They are fully conscious of their separate Islamic traditions and, it would seem, carefully cultivate these. An Uzbek noted on one occasion, "it cannot be considered normal when an educated Uzbek feels that he does not have to know the Uzbek language well." Educated Central Asians accept the need for learning Russian as their means of communication with the outside world (from which they would otherwise be cut off), but insist increasingly on the value of their own native languages, too. It is certainly instructive that in a recent census nearly all the Central Asians said that their native languages were their mother tongues (and not Russian, as is the case with one or two nationalities), and that only an average of about 20 percent of them admitted to speaking Russian at all. Russian, of course, is taught in the schools, and this knowledge is reinforced during service in the armed forces. But this has not always had the desired effect. There were many official complaints in the 1970s and 1980s that too many non-Russian draftees spoke no Russian at all, that months of military service were spent in making this up and that even after that, Central Asians returned home and forgot much of what they learned. So, once back home in Central Asia, apparently, the Moslems prefer to keep to themselves and to restrict their contacts with European settlers to their place of work or when dealing with officials. In the countryside, it is easier to keep up ancient Moslem customs, but even in towns Central Asians will try to have at least one room in the house furnished in the traditional style. Again, while women are not veiled (as demanded by Islamic law), it is still rare for Central Asian girls to pursue careers.

Central Asian attitudes among women are also suggested by the staggeringly high birthrate among the Moslems. This is partly the direct result of better medical facilities and the consequent decline in infant mortality, together with factors like better nutrition and health care; but it is also attributable to the survival of the tradition of large families. Despite the probability that the high Central Asian birthrate will level off eventually, the substantial growth in their absolute number cannot fail to exert an important influence in the years ahead.

The Central Asians seek to point up their national identities in many ways. Central Asian scholars have done a great deal of work on the history of the area, and much of the great literary output of the medieval period has been reissued. National monuments are now better looked after than used to be the case, though this is partly at least the result of a keener awareness of the tourist trade. Mosques and other shrines, including the tomb of Tamerlane in Samarkand, are now kept in a reasonable state of repair and are shown off with a good deal of pride as being the creations of the Central Asians themselves. Indeed, there is good evidence that many Moslems regard a pilgrimage to one of the local shrines as an acceptable substitute for the holy duty of every good Moslem—a pilgrimage to Mecca at least once in their lifetime. The Soviet authorities are reluctant to allow their Moslems to travel in large numbers to Mecca.

Both nationally and culturally, the Central Asians are something of an enigma. They are Europeanized Asians, having adopted European ways to a far greater degree than any other non-European people except the Japanese. At the same time, while accepting modernization on European terms, the Central Asians today are clearly anxious to preserve as much of their traditional culture as is compatible with Europeanization, and perhaps more. But it is impossible to assess with any pretence at accuracy which element in the mix is the dominant, the European or the Asian.

The Non-Russians of the Volga

The non-Russians of the central Volga Valley are far from being a single cohesive group of nationalities, except in one respect—they have all been in very long contact with the Russians and have adopted many of their ways, while retaining their own individuality to a greater or lesser extent. There are six nationalities involved: the Moslem Tatars and Bashkirs, the Finnic Mari, Mordvins and Udmurts, who are all nominally Christian, and the Turkic Chuvash, who are also Christian. They live in a vast area which stretches almost to the River Don in the west and up to the Urals in the east, thinly scattered and often mixed with Russian settlements. The towns of the area, particularly, tend to be predominantly Russian.

The most remarkable and most distinctive, as well as the most numerous, of these nationalities are the Tatars. The descendants of the Tatar conquerors of Russia in the Middle Ages, they had begun to develop a strong middle class two generations before the 1917 Revolution. This middle class, the pillar of a sense of national identity in any community, was based on the merchants of Kazan and the growing number of educated Tatars in the late 19th century, who for a period made Kazan the third most important center of Islamic thought (after Cairo and Constantinople). Indeed, around the turn of the century, the Tatars were actively engaged in converting neighboring peoples, like the Mari and the Chuvash, to Islam, in direct competition with the Russian Orthodox Church.

After the Revolution, the Kazan Tatars pressed for the creation of a separate Tatar republic, which would possibly have included the Bashkirs as well, but Moscow was not prepared to contemplate this. Instead, a Tatar Autonomous Republic (abbreviated to Tatar A.S.S.R.) was set up, where the Tatars now form just under half the population; in addition, there are substantial numbers of Tatars in Bashkiria and elsewhere in the Soviet Union; indeed, there is hardly a major town in the country without a Tatar community. With this kind of a history, it would be surprising if the Tatars were not strongly conscious of their national traditions and identity.

The Bashkirs, a closely related Turkic nationality (which the Tatars in effect attempted to assimilate), were much less advanced culturally at the time of the Revolution. They were still seminomadic in the early years of this century. Since then, they have been encouraged in their efforts to build up an autonomous cultural tradition of their own. Because the Bashkir people are so widely scattered, they form only about a quarter of the population of the Bashkir A.S.S.R., which also contains large numbers of Russians (and Tatars).

Of the Volga Valley's three Finnic peoples (whose languages, incidentally, are only distantly related to Finnish itself), the most numerous are the Mordvins. Once much feared as cruel and pitiless fighters, the Mordvins are now engaged in more peaceful pursuits. About one-third of them live within the Mordovian A.S.S.R. and the rest are scattered over a wide area. There is considerable evidence that the Mordvins have accepted Russian ways for their future and have done so with equanimity.

The Mari are far fewer in number—600,000 as against the 1.2 million Mordvins—but they are conspicuously more attached to their national traditions. They have had a distinctive history, in that they have been in long and intimate contact with the Tatars and Bashkirs, as well as having an extensive record of peasant uprisings against Russian rule. The conversion of the Mari to Christianity is a relatively recent event—some of them are Moslem—and pagan practices among them certainly survived into this century.

The Udmurts live in a fairly compact area to the north of Kazan, around the River Kama, and make up about half the population of the Udmurt A.S.S.R. The rest are urban Russians and some Tatars. The Udmurts are less advanced culturally than the other Finnic peoples of the Volga and their ancient clan system remained in being up to the present century, as did traces of their pagan forms of worship.

The Chuvash are in an unusual position in that they speak a Turkic language, but one very distant from the speech of all the other Turkic peoples of the Soviet Union. There is no question of a Chuvash being able to understand a Tatar, whereas a Tatar and, say, an Uzbek, can make one another out. Secondly, the Chuvash are Christian, and thus more intimately linked with the Russians than with the Moslems. Thirdly, the Chuvash, who are over a million-and-a-half strong, look back to the Bolghar Empire of the 10th and 11th centuries, which ruled over vast tracts of what is now European Russia.

The Northern Caucasus

If the central Volga Valley has a nationally mixed population, northern Caucasia and Daghestan contain a veritable confusion of peoples—one authority cites 32 different nationalities living in a comparatively restricted area. It is interesting that the Daghestan A.S.S.R. is the only one which takes its name from a region rather than from a people or a nationality. Although the Caucasians and Daghestanis are mostly Moslem, they speak a bewildering number of languages—some are Paleo-Caucasian, some Turkic, some Iranian—and until the Revolution, Turkic and Arabic, the holy language of Islam, served as the means of communication. Since then, these have been largely replaced by Russian. Despite the great linguistic and national diversity, the people of the northern Caucasus did unite in the middle of the last century under their great military leader Shamil against the troops of the Russian Czar. Shamil, who is venerated as a hero, fought off the Russians for 25 years. Nowadays, the northern Caucasians and Daghestanis remain attached to their Islamic ways and to their traditional egalitarianism.

The Jews

Whether or not the Jews are a racial entity is a matter for historians and anthropologists. To the Soviet authorities, Soviet Jews are a separate *nationality* and are counted as such—if they wish to indicate their Jewishness—in the census. Some 1.8 million people gave their nationality as Jewish in the 1979 census (in 1970 the number was 2.1 million) and without a doubt many Soviet Jews regard themselves as culturally different, even when their mother tongue is Russian or Ukrainian. Only 14 percent of the Jews, at latest poll, consider Yiddish their mother tongue. The Soviet authorities established a Jewish autonomous province in Siberia, in Birobidzhan on the River Amur, which was to serve as a center of Soviet Jewish life. Less than 10 percent of its small population is Jewish.

Within the Soviet Union, the Jewish communities fall into separate categories. The overwhelming majority are Ashkenazim, who moved eastwards from Central Europe in the Middle Ages and were constrained to remain in the Pale of Settlement in Western Russia under the Czars. Smaller communities were long established in Georgia, in the Caucasian mountains (where they speak an Iranian dialect) and in Central Asia.

Although many Jews accept that their future lies with the Soviet state, some of them have been anxious to emigrate, especially to Israel, where they feel they will have better opportunities, not least to practice the tenets of Judaism which can be difficult in an officially atheistic country. In the last twenty years the Soviet authorities, while simultaneously campaigning energetically against Zionism, have allowed about 260,000 Jews (out of 648,000 who requested invitations from abroad) to leave, over two-thirds of them to Israel and most of the rest to North America, although this contribution to the spirit of international detente came to an abrupt halt in 1980 and since 1982 only a trickle have been allowed to emigrate. In early 1987 new emigration regulations were introduced under which Jewish people with "immediate family members" abroad (i.e. husband or wife) may apply to leave the Soviet Union. How this apparent relaxation will work in practice remains to be seen. At first sight things look encouraging: in 1987, 8,011 Jews left, more than eight times the 1986 number. They included some well-known "refuseniks."

A MINI-HISTORY TABLE

830	Varangians (Vikings) begin to leave Scandinavia
862–79	Great Novgorod, one of the most important Slav towns, falls to Rurik, Varangian chieftain and he is called on to rule

Kievan Russia

879–912	Oleg; 880 he makes Kiev his capital
912–45	Igor; makes treaty with Constantinople
945–62	Olga, widow of Igor; 957 she is baptized a Christian in Constantinople
962–72	Svyatoslav; 968 defeats the Bulgarians; 972 is murdered
973–8	Yaropolk; betrayed by an advisor and murdered
978–1015	Vladimir; 988 he accepts Byzantine Christianity; 977 Novgorod gains freedom from Kiev
1015–1113	Yaroslav the Wise rules until 1019; 1019–54 12 sons of Vladimir struggle for succession; Kiev becomes first center of Orthodox Church in Russia; church law imported from Constantinople; 1054–1113 sons of Yaroslav and heirs feuding
1113–25	Vladimir Monomakh; brief period of unity
1125–1220	Land again divided and in conflict until Mongol invasion

Mongol Invasions and Rule

1220–42	First Mongol-Tatar attack in Caucasus; 1223 first Mongol invasion, Russians and Polovtsy defeated; 1235–40 conquest of Caucasus by Tatar-Mongols; capture of Kiev; 1240 Alexander Nevsky, Prince of Novgorod, defeats Swedes on Neva; 1242 Nevsky defeats Teutonic Knights on the ice of Lake Peipus; Tatar HQ established on lower Volga. Tatar domination for next 250 years, holding 9 principalities in their power. Between 1261 and 1533, Moscow gradually took control of principalities

The Rise of Moscow

1301–10	First territorial acquisitions of Muscovy; 1310 Moscow becomes the See of the Orthodox Church
1325–40	Ivan I, nicknamed "Kalita" (Moneybags) because of the economic hold of Moscow over the other principalities
1359–89	Dimitriy Donskoy; 1367 Kremlin of Moscow begun; 1378 Moscow defeats the Tatars
1389–1425	Vasiliy I; 1393 Nizhny-Novgorod absorbed by Moscow
1425–62	Vasiliy II; 1439 Council of Florence reunites Eastern and Western Churches; 1448 Church of Moscow independent
1462–1505	Ivan III, the Great; 1463–89 many cities incorporated into Muscovy; 1485–1516 building of new Kremlin; 1496–97 war with Sweden; 1502 destruction of Golden Horde by Crimean Tatars
1505–33	Vasiliy III; 1507 Crimean raids on southeastern Russia
1533–84	Ivan IV, the Terrible, first Russian sovereign to be crowned czar (in 1547 in Uspensky Cathedral in Kremlin); marriage to girl with Romanov connections; 1547 Fire of Moscow; 1555–57 war with Sweden; 1558–83 Livonian War; 1571 Crimean Tatars burn Moscow; 1581 beginning of conquest of Siberia; 1582 truce with Poland; 1583 truce with Sweden
1584–98	Fyodor I; 1587–98 Boris Godunov as Regent; 1590–93 war with Sweden
1598–1605	Boris Godunov elected Czar by the Zemsky Sobor; Time of Troubles; 1604–13 civil wars
1605–10	Fyodor Godunov 1605, Czar for a few weeks before army goes over to Dimitriy; Fyodor murdered by pretender's agents; 1605–6 False Dimitriy I; 1606–10 Vasiliy Shuisky; first peasant war in Russian history; uprising led by Ivan Bolotnikov; 1607–10 False Dimitriy II; Polish invasion; 1610 occupation of Moscow; 1611 Novgorod occupied by the Swedes; 1611–12 national uprising led by Minin and Pozharsky; Poles burn Moscow before retreating

The Romanovs

1613–45	Mikhail elected by the Zemsky Sobor; 1618 peace with Sweden, Moscow loses Baltic outlet; truce with Poland; 1632–34 war with Poland again
1645–76	Aleksey; 1653 last Zemsky Sobor summoned to vote on the incorporation of the Ukraine; 1654 beginning of the Schism—Old Believers; 1654–57 Russo-Polish War; truce of Andrusovo cedes Smolensk, Kiev and Ukraine to Moscow; 1656–58 war with Sweden; 1670–71 Stenka Razin's revolt
1676–82	Fyodor III; 1676–80 war with Turkey and Crimea
1682–1725	Peter the Great; in the first outward-looking reign in Russian history Peter opened a window on Western ideas; techniques flooded into Russia; 1686 "permanent" peace with Poland; reform of the calendar; 1700 beginning of Great Northern War against Sweden; 1701–3 foundation of St. Petersburg (later Petrograd and now Leningrad); 1710 conquest of Livonia, Estonia and Vyborg; war with Turkey; 1711 loss of Azov; 1713–14 conquest of Finland; acquisition of Livonia, Estonia, Ingria and Karelia; 1721 Peter adopts title of Emperor; war with Persia; 1722 acquisition of western and southern shores of Caspian
1725–62	Succession of rulers—Catherine I (1725–27) Peter's widow, utterly incapable; Peter II (1727–30) became Czar at 11, died of smallpox; Anna (1730–40) daughter of Ivan V, niece of Peter the Great; 1735–39 war with Turkey; Ivan VI (1740–41), various contesting regents; war with Sweden; Elizaveta (1741–61), daughter of Peter

the Great and Catherine I; Peter III (1761–62); alliance with Frederick II

1762–96   Catherine II, the Great, wife of Peter III; war with Turkey; 1768–74 gets Black Sea steppes; 1772–73 first partition of Poland; 1773–74 Pugachev's revolt; 1781–86 Ukraine absorbed completely into Russian Empire; annexation of the Crimea; 1783 Sevastopol founded; 1783 Russian protectorship over eastern Georgia; 1784 settlement in Alaska; 1787–91 wars with Turkey and Sweden; second and third partitions of Poland; 1793–95 Koscziuszko's rebellion; war with Persia; 1796 campaigns in Daghestan and Azerbaijan

1796–1801   Paul I; enacted new law on succession based on male primogeniture, which gave Russia a series of five more emperors and freedom from dynastic upheavals that had been a feature of previous centuries. 1799 the Russian-American Company (formed in 1797 as the United American Company); 1799 Suvorov's campaigns in northern Italy and Switzerland; 1800 alliance with Napoleon; 1801 Paul murdered

1801–25   Alexander I; involved in his father's murder, he sought to repair the ill Paul had done. He rehabilitated over 12,000 people who had been banished or dismissed from their posts by his father, abolished Paul's secret police, abolished censorship, lifted the ban on foreign books and travel and seemed at one time to want to free the serfs and relax autocratic rule; 1803–13 diplomatic relations restored with England; peace treaty with France; eastern Georgia annexed; conquest of Transcaucasia begun; war with Persia; Russian sovereignty of Georgia; Russia annexes northern Azerbaijan; 1806–12 war with Turkey, Bessarabia annexed; 1807 Treaty of Tilsit; 1808–9 war with Sweden, annexation of Finland; 1812 Napoleon and Battle of Borodino, burning of Moscow, pursuit of retreating Napoleon into France; 1820–37 Pushkin active; 1825 revolt, sometimes called the first Russian revolution, in December

1825–55   Nicholas I, a reactionary czar; 1826 organization of political police force, war with Persia, annexation of Armenia; 1827 war with Turkey; 1830–31 uprising of Novgorod military colonies; 1831–70 Alexander Herzen active; first Russian railway opened between St. Petersburg and Tsarskoye Selo; 1837 Pushkin dies in a duel; 1841 Lermontov, poet, dies in a duel; 1842 publication of Gogol's *Dead Souls;* 1846–81 Dostoyevsky active; 1847–83 Turgenev active; 1849 Russia intervenes in Hungary; 1852–1910 Tolstoy active; 1835–36 Crimean War

1855–81   Alexander II, "The Czar Liberator," a reforming czar; 1858 annexation of Amur and Maritime Provinces; 1859 complete conquest of Caucasus; 1860–73 expansion of railways; 1861 emancipation of serfs; 1862 Russian-American Company liquidated; 1863 Polish rebellion; 1867 sale of Alaska to the U.S.; first Russian translation of Karl Marx's *Das Kapital;* 1873 agreement with England on partition of Central Asia into spheres of influence; 1876 organization of Land and Freedom Party *(Zemlya i Volya);* 1877–78 war with Turkey; 1879 attempted assassination of Alexander; 1880 attempt to blow up Winter Palace and assassinate Alexander; 1881 Alexander accepts proposal for a committee for reform and is assassinated same day

1881–94   Alexander III, conservative and nationalist like grandfather Nicholas I; 1883 organization of the revolutionary group Emancipation of Labor *(Osovobozhdeniye Truda)* by Russian émigrés in Geneva; 1887 assassination attempt on Alexander by Alexander Ulyanov, Lenin's brother; 1891 Trans-Siberian railway begun

1894–1914   Nicholas II, the last Russian czar; he had a marked dislike of elected
                politicians and intellectuals; married Queen Victoria's grand-
                daughter, Princess Alix of Hessen-Darmstadt; 1896 Chinese-
                Russian defensive alliance against Japan; 1898 founding of Russian
                Social Democratic Labor Party in Minsk, Chinese-Russian treaty
                grants Russia lease of Port Arthur and Liaotung Peninsula; 1900
                Boxer Revolt, Russia occupies Manchuria; 1901 Social Revolu-
                tionary Party formed; 1902 Chinese-Russian agreement on evacua-
                tion of Russian troops from Manchuria; Social Revolutionary
                Party member assassinates Minister of the Interior; 1903 Kishinev
                pogrom; Social Democratic Labor Party splits into two factions—
                Bolsheviks (majoritarians) led by Lenin, and Mensheviks (minori-
                tarians) led by Martov; 1904 Japan attacks Russia at Port Arthur
                without declaring war
                1905 Battle of Tsushima; Treaty of Portsmouth; assassination of new
                Minister of the Interior, Plehve, by another Social Revolutionary
                Party member; General Strike in St. Petersburg; Bloody Sunday;
                assassination of Grand Duke Sergei by Social Revolutionary Party
                member; first Soviet (Council) formed in Ivanovo-Voznesensk;
                General National Strike; Convention of Constitutional Democrat-
                ic Party (Cadets); formation of St. Petersburg Soviet; Nicholas'
                October Manifesto summoning Duma (legislative assembly), ex-
                tending suffrage rights, freedom of speech, press and assembly; for-
                mation of Moscow Soviet; formation of Octobrists and Union of
                the Russian People; arrest of members of St. Petersburg Soviet;
                general strike in Moscow; Moscow uprising (December)
                1906 opening of first Duma or Parliament, containing both Bolshe-
                viks and Mensheviks; 1911 Prime Minister Stolypin murdered

                                    War and Revolution

1914–18   1914 Outbreak of the First World War, which Lenin sees as a chance
                for revolution; 1915 Rasputin in effect ruling Russia; 1916 Raspu-
                tin murdered; 1917 February Revolution; abdication of Czar Nich-
                olas II; formation of Provisional Government; Lenin urges "Frat-
                ernization at the Front," "No support for Provisional
                Government" and "All power to the Soviets;" growth of Bolshevik
                influence in the Soviets and in the countryside; October Revolution
                (Nov. 6–7); Lenin, leading Bolshevik faction, overthrows the Pro-
                visional Government in Petrograd in a bloodless coup; issues de-
                cree nationalizing all private, ecclesiastical and czarist land with-
                out compensation; in elections to the Constituent Assembly the
                Bolsheviks poll only one quarter of the votes while the Socialist
                Revolutionaries take 370 of the 707 seats
1918   Bolsheviks and Left Socialist Revolutionaries withdraw from Con-
                stituent Assembly; Lenin claims elections too soon after the Revo-
                lution to be meaningful; the Gregorian replaces the Julian calendar
                (13 days ahead); Treaty of Brest-Litovsk; the Tsar and his family
                are murdered at Ekaterinburg; end of First World War

                                Civil War and Communism

1918–24   1918–20 Bolsheviks introduce press censorship, nationalize heavy in-
                dustry, outlaw strikes, nationalize banks, build up police force (the
                Cheka) and Red Army, and organize requisition of grain for army
                and for urban population; engage in civil war with White armies
                of the Right; emergency measures known as War Communism in-
                cluding seizure of peasants' produce lead to peasant risings, strikes
                and demonstrations; 1921 Kronstadt rebellion (March); famine;
                10th Party Congress introduces New Economic Policy giving peas-
                ants freedom in cultivating their land and marketing its produce,

while State retains control of industry, foreign trade, banking and transport; Congress also votes to prohibit formation of groups or factions within the Party and to limit criticism; 1922 one-fifth of Party membership purged by this year; Stalin becomes General Secretary; Union of Soviet Socialist Republics (U.S.S.R.) established; 1924 Lenin dies; Petrograd renamed Leningrad in his honor

The Stalin Years

1924–38   Stalin asserts his supremacy over the next few years; 1927 Trotsky, co-founder with Lenin of modern Russia, expelled from the Party; 1928–29 first Five-Year Plan and start of collectivization; suppression of *kulaks* (wealthier peasants); 1929 Trotsky deported; 1930 industrialization takes precedence over collectivization; disorganization of agriculture leads to famine; 1932 Five-Year Plan declared completed, nine months ahead of schedule; 1933 Russia establishes diplomatic relations with the U.S.A.; second Five-Year Plan; 1934 murder of Leningrad Party chief Sergei Kirov marks beginning of the "Great Terror;" 1935–38 years of purges and the Treason Trials; destruction of the Old Bolsheviks and Red Army High Command; 1935 rationing system replaces incentives policy, wages graded according to work done; 1936 New Constitution; 1938 Third Five-Year Plan (delayed by German invasion)

1939–45   Second World War; 1939 Molotov–Ribbentrop non-aggression pact; 1940 Trotsky murdered in Mexico; 1941 Soviet Union enters "Great Patriotic War" when Germany invades; Sept. 1941–Jan. 1944 Siege of Leningrad; Nov. 1942 defence of Stalingrad; 1943 German surrender under Paulus at Stalingrad; Russians capture Kharkov, Rostov and Kiev; Russian advance continues; Roumania, Crimea, Bulgaria; 1945 Russians enter Hungary, Poland and Austria; May 2 capture Berlin

1945–53   Occupation of Eastern Europe enables Communist governments to come to power in Poland, Hungary, Bulgaria, Czechoslovakia and Yugoslavia; 1946 famine in the Ukraine; 1948 creation of Israel exacerbates Stalin's anti-Semitism; 1949 German Democratic Republic set up in Soviet Zone of Germany; 1953 campaign against "rootless cosmopolitans" culminates in "doctors' plot" when a group of Jewish doctors are accused of having killed the Soviet Minister of Culture, Andrei Zhdanov, and of having planned to undermine health of Soviet leaders on behalf of an American-Jewish organization; March, Stalin dies; June, uprising in East Berlin smashed by Soviet tanks

The Khrushchev Years

1953–64   Nikita Khrushchev becomes First Secretary of Soviet Communist Party and dominates collective leadership of the U.S.S.R., first with Malenkov, then with Bulganin; 1956 Feb., 20th Party Congress hears Khrushchev's "secret speech" denouncing Stalin; Nov., Hungarian revolt put down by Soviet tanks and troops after Hungary announces intention to leave Warsaw Pact; 1955–57 Khrushchev smashes "anti-Party group" of politicians who disagree with his policies; 1958 Mar., Khrushchev takes over Premiership from Bulganin; 1960 May, shooting down of U2 airplane; 1961 Khrushchev meets Kennedy; Major Gagarin in first manned space flight; 1962 Cuban missile crisis; 1962–63 rift with China becomes public; 1963 partial Nuclear Test Ban Treaty; 1964 Khrushchev's resignation demanded by his colleagues who accuse him of economic failure, agricultural adventurism, unco-ordinated and inconsistent policies, foreign policy blunders and encouraging personality cult of his own

Brezhnev and After

1964–82   Leonid Brezhnev succeeds Khrushchev as Party Secretary, Alexei
           Kosygin is Premier; 1968 "Prague Spring" in Czechoslovakia sup-
           pressed by Soviet invasion; 1970 Solzhenitsyn awarded Nobel
           Prize for Literature, deported to Switzerland 1974; 1975 Helsinki
           Agreement; 1979 Afghanistan invaded by Soviet Union; 1980
           Moscow Olympic Games; Nikolai Tikhonov replaces Kosygin; rise
           of Solidarity trade union movement in Poland and its suppression
           on Soviet orders; 1982 Oct., Brezhnev dies

1982 to   68-year-old Yury Andropov (former KGB chief) succeeds Brezhnev,
Present   but is plagued by ill health throughout 1983 and dies in Feb. 1984;
           Konstantin Chernenko, a 72-year-old protégé of Brezhnev, be-
           comes Party Secretary amid rumors of power struggles; 1985
           March Chernenko dies; 54-year-old Mikhail Gorbachev is elected
           General Secretary by Central Committee; long-serving Foreign
           Minister Andrei Gromyko is replaced by 57-year-old Edvard She-
           vardnadze; Gorbachev campaigns energetically to move U.S.S.R.
           economy forward and appears to favor new style of leadership
           which includes informal contact with people at home and abroad;
           meets Ronald Reagan at Geneva Summit, November 1985; Ch-
           ernobyl nuclear reactor explodes, April 1986; Gorbachev meets
           Reagan at Reykjavik Summit; Gorbachev proclaims a "new atti-
           tude to human rights" and announces other measures aimed at
           "democratization" of Soviet society, February 1987; INF Treaty
           signed in Washington, December 1987; Soviet withdrawal from
           Afghanistan begins May 1988; Reagan pays reciprocal visit to
           Moscow, May 1988

RUSSIAN ART AND
ARCHITECTURE

by
JOHN FINCHLEY

Russian civilization derives from Byzantium, as that of Western Europe derives from Rome. As the English, the Germans, the Scandinavians and the Magyars have taken their written history to begin from the date of their conversion to Christianity by missionaries owing their allegiance to Rome, so the beginning of Russian history is conveniently dated from the acceptance of Christianity from Constantinople by Vladimir, Grand-prince of Kiev, himself married to the sister of the Byzantine emperor, in 988.

The close links with Byzantium, and the adherence to the Eastern arm of Christendom, thus established, were to endure. Though there were signs during the 12th century that Western might displace Byzantine influence, these links were reinforced during the period of the Mongol invasion and domination, from the mid-13th to the later-15th centuries, when, for the greater part of Russia, contact with the West all but ceased, and Byzantium retained the prestige of the citadel of civilization. The relationship was simply reversed after the fall of Constantinople in 1453, and the re-emergence of a united and independent Russia, based on Moscow, under Ivan III (1462–1505). Ivan III saw the new Muscovy as the heir to Constantinople, as the "Third Rome." Married to the niece of the last Byzan-

83

tine emperor, he took the latter's title of "caesar" (czar). It was not until the reign of Peter the Great (1682–1725) that Western Europe replaced Byzantium, and the traditions of Muscovy itself, as the major source of cultural and spiritual inspiration, and Russia began to consider herself as part of the civilization, and of the international political system, of the West.

This fact was to have momentous consequences: for literature and thought; for religion and the Church; for ideas of government and the concept of kingship. Not least is it evident in the development of art and architecture. The forms of Byzantium—the Roman arch, the cruciform domed church and, in painting, the icon—were to remain dominant in Russia and the Ukraine until the 16th and 17th centuries. The history of Russian and Ukrainian art and architecture over this long period is the history of the evolution of these essentially Byzantine themes.

The Influence of Kiev and Novgorod

The oldest surviving building in the European part of the Soviet Union, which amazingly survived both the sack of Kiev by the Mongols in 1240, and World War II, was the finest of the Kievan period of Russian history. St. Sophia, named after Constantinople's cathedral, was built from 1036 to 1046 by Vladimir's son, Yaroslav the Wise. Its exterior has been disguised by 18th-century additions. But its interior remains substantially unaltered, a magnificent example of the Byzantine style, revealing Kiev as a major center of that cosmopolitan Eastern Mediterranean culture, stretching from European Russia to Venice, which had lasted down the centuries since Justinian built Constantinople's St. Sophia and the churches of Ravenna in the sixth century. Now, in the 11th, it produced Kiev's St. Sophia and St. Mark's in Venice: monuments quite outshining anything which contemporary Western or Northern Europe had to offer. The mosaics and frescos of St. Sophia, purely Byzantine in their two-dimensional serenity, laid the foundation for the Russian school of painting.

As this architectural style penetrated northwards it gathered original and specifically Russian aspects. Yaroslav built a second St. Sophia in another important religious center, Novgorod, in 1045–52. Built on the same cruciform plan as its forerunner in Kiev, it is adapted, with its steeper roofs and narrower windows, to the demands of a harsher climate. Its greater external austerity is matched by a similar restraint within—in particular by an absence of mosaics—and already stands in some contrast to the exuberance of contemporary Byzantium.

These tendencies became even more marked in the Church of St. George at the Yuriev Monastery in Novgorod, built at the beginning of the following century. The latter is the first example of the practice, which was to become distinctive, of dividing the outer faces of the north, south and west walls of churches into three vertical sections by means of raised bands of stone or brickwork, matching the three convex protrusions of the main and two side apses at the east end. These three churches also represent the evolution of the dome from the low, rounded Byzantine cupola of Kiev's St. Sophia to the more pointed dome of Novgorod, set in a steadily lengthening drum. From the latter, which was more suitable for the snowfalls of the north, the onion dome was to evolve.

Vladimir

From the 12th century on, the Crusades and the increasing activity of Italian merchants in the Mediterranean—culminating in the sack of Constantinople by the Venetians in 1204—undermined the commercial importance of Kiev as a route between Western Europe and the Near East. The rulers of Russia began to find it more convenient to make their base in the more central and more easily defensible forest area to the east of modern Moscow. Andrei Bogoliubsky, great-great-grandson of Yaroslav the Wise, having sacked Kiev in the course of a struggle for succession, transferred his capital to Vladimir in 1169. It was here, in the area between the Oka and Volga rivers, that the classic phase in Russian architecture opened.

The essential square, cruciform ground plan of Vladimir's churches, and the engineering of arches and domes, remained Byzantine. By taking these elements and molding them in their own way, the (anonymous) Russian architects of the period produced a series of churches in white stone, of modest size and of subtle but disciplined proportions, which were single works of art in themselves. It was as if the grandeur and vulgarity of Rome had given way to the confident simplicity, good taste and human scale of Greece.

As is to be expected of one of the first examples of a new genre, the Church of the Savior at Pereslavl-Zalessky seems at first sight crude and excessively unpolished. But, on second view, the interrelation of the side and main apses, and the perfect balance between the weight of the dome and the body of the church become evident. Vladimir-Suzdal architecture reached its zenith with the Church of the Intercession of the Virgin at Bogoliubovo (1165) and the Cathedral of St. Dmitri at Vladimir (1197). Both show an austerity and a rigorous harmony of proportion which were not to be recaptured in Russian architecture. Though their evolution from the Russian-Byzantine style is undisguised, both display elements of decoration, especially in their porches, and in the carved relief sculptures on the outer walls, which betray the influence of the Western Romanesque.

Such was the young, vigorous and distinctive civilization that went down before the Mongol invasion in 1240. Only Novgorod resisted occupation, and then only at the price of heavy tribute. Cultural, and even national, continuity survived largely thanks to the continued independence of Novgorod, and to the efforts of the Church, and particularly of the monasteries which sprang up in large numbers, especially in the forest land of the northeast. The great monasteries acted as fortresses against attack, as preservers of the new written language and of icons and manuscripts from the past; and, through exchanges with Constantinople and Mount Athos, as links with the outside world. Virtually the only stone buildings to be erected for over 200 years are in Novgorod (or neighboring Pskov) or in monastic foundations. The rest of the country reverted to building exclusively in wood, though no examples of wooden churches, palaces or other structures from the period survive.

Icons

For this newly introverted, impoverished and deeply religious society, the icon acquired a special importance. Small enough to be preserved from the invader; produced, in its simplest form, in sufficient quantities to become, as it remained down to the 20th century, the possession of each household, the icon became the symbol of the strength, extent and survival of Russian Christianity and Russian culture. The earliest "Russian" icons—including, for example, the majestic *Virgin of Vladimir,* dating from the mid-12th century and now in the Tretyakov Gallery in Moscow—had been commissioned in Byzantium or, somewhat later, from Byzantine masters living in Russia. Only from the 12th century on did icons or wall frescos of real merit appear which had been produced by native Russian artists. In the Kievan period the figures retained the cold and stiff remoteness, and glazed expressions, of Byzantine art. But, as the center of gravity of the new civilization moved to the Vladimir-Suzdal region, a new, more informal, spirit was revealed. This tendency became increasingly marked after the Mongol invasions, which, by limiting her contacts with the outside world, forced Russia to build upon her artistic and spiritual heritage largely on her own. The subjects of icon paintings, the saints, the prophets, the Madonna with Child, and the absence of perspective and movement, remained the same. But a new humanity was evident: colors became warmer, faces more life-like and more expressive of feeling and character. Byzantine classicism had given way to a more popular and more spontaneous inspiration.

The political fragmentation of the country during the Mongol period led to the development of distinct schools of icon painting in each major region of Russia, often most easily to be identified by the predominant colors of their works. Novgorod used a characteristic bright red; Tver a light blue; Pskov a distinctive gold highlighting.

It was in independent Novgorod, the wealthiest city of Russia, that, through the re-establishment of artistic links with Byzantium, icon painting reached a new level of technical and artistic distinction and entered its golden age. Theophanes the Greek, as he has been known ever since, came to Novgorod from Constantinople in about 1370. He brought to the native Russian love of color, and concern with human character and emotion, a new confidence of technique and discipline of form. The re-uniting of the two traditions is very evident in the work of Theophanes's Moscow pupil, Andrei Rublyev (c. 1380–1430), and the latter's life-long collaborator, Daniel Chorny. Rublyev is perhaps the only Russian painter of world stature to emerge until the close of the 19th century.

His work is distinguished by a boldness of stroke and economy of line, and a harmony of shape and color, which set him in a class apart. His figures have all the serenity of the subjects of Byzantine painting, but none of their coldness or stiffness. Indeed, his devout religious faith is very clear in the humane, sympathetic treatment of his subjects. His reputation was enormous, both in his lifetime and beyond. His *Old Testament Trinity* (now in the Tretyakov Gallery), in particular, was to be endlessly copied.

After Rublyev, Russian icon painting lost something of its inspiration. Moscow, increasingly unchallenged as the political capital of the country, remained its artistic center. The well-known painter Dionysius (c. 1450–1505) whose elongated and exaggerated figures and more lavish colors represent something of a descent into monumentalism, had a large and productive workshop. Thereafter, there are no names that are worth recording. Rublyev had taken the Russian tradition to its high point of perfection; there was little more that could be done in that direction. But official church and government policy, re-emphasized by the Council of the Hundred Chapters in 1551 and enforced with particular rigor under the patriarchate of Nikon (1652–67) forbade innovation, or the adoption of Western secularism and realism. The result was sterile, and often naive, imitation of traditional themes and techniques. The originality indispensable to artistic achievement was lost, and the distinction between the work of major artists and folk-art became blurred. The visitor to Russia is easily disoriented by the icons and wall frescos of the 16th and 17th centuries: to Western eyes they frequently appear to date from no later than the 14th century.

The Kremlin Churches

But this period was a most productive one for architecture. Ivan III determined to celebrate his final renunciation of the Mongol overlordship (1480), and his annexation of Novgorod and Tver, by launching a major building program, the greatest fruits of which were the churches of the Moscow Kremlin. The art of construction in stone had so declined during the Mongol centuries that architects suitable to the task had to be imported from Pskov (in the Novgorod region, which had escaped occupation by the Mongols) and from distant Renaissance Italy. But Ivan III determined to build in the style of the period before the Mongol invasions, thus affirming the continuity of his newly united realm with the Russia of the 11th and 12th centuries. While the engineering skills and craftsmanship of the Pskov and of the Italian architects (most notably Marco Ruffo, Pietro Solario and Rodolfo Fioravanti) were indispensable, and though the latter left the imprint of the Italian Renaissance on many decorative motifs and in the style of the windows of the Palace of Facets in the Kremlin, the general design of the Kremlin churches represents a deliberate reassertion of the traditions of the Vladimir-Suzdal period.

This was not because architecture had failed to evolve in Russia during the interval. But, except in Novgorod and in Pskov, building had been confined to wood. As a result, the old themes of arches and domes had been transformed. From being a half sphere, the dome had developed into an almost complete sphere on a thin neck: the onion dome that was to remain characteristic. Three other features distinctive to Russian architecture also emerged, all of them owing their origin, in part at least, to the exigencies of the climate: steeply roofed "tent-shaped" churches; the "trapeza," or gallery with open sides, giving shelter outside the western door of the church; and the "Kokoshnik" gable (so named after the curved and winged headdress worn by peasant women), perfectly adapted to heavy snowfalls. Once the need to perpetuate self-consciously the architectural style of the preconquest era had been fulfilled, it was natural that these forms should begin to be reproduced in stone. The Church of the Ascension at Kolomenskoye near Moscow (1533) was one of the first, and finest, stone churches to be built on the tent-shaped pattern and to incorporate a trapeza.

But the most remarkable construction of all was St. Basil's in Moscow. It was built from 1555–60 at the order of Ivan IV (The Terrible) to celebrate his capture of the Mongol capital of Kazan (1552). Its two architects, Postnik and Barma, are reported to have been blinded by the Czar after its completion "in order that they should never produce anything better." St. Basil's is not easy to appreciate by applying conventional criteria; it is a riot of exuberant color and contrasting patterns. To Western contemporaries it must have seemed exotic, compelling but utterly barbarian. It is the result of the flowering, in a new age of confidence and prosperity, of a style nurtured in isolation from the rest of the world, and of techniques mastered when wood was the only material in which it was feasible—or prudent—to build.

Few churches or other monumental buildings were constructed during the Time of Troubles (consisting of civil war and foreign invasion) which followed the death of Ivan IV. When building was resumed in the mid-17th century it was under the conservative and anti-Western regime which culminated in the patriarchate of Nikon.

The ecclesiastical, and indeed the secular architecture of the time represents a deliberate attempt to produce a purely Russian style synthesizing all the major past tendencies in Russian architecture: the onion dome and the trapeza now serving decorative rather than functional purposes. The revolution in color, translated into the stone architecture during the previous century, retained its force: there was no return to the unbroken wall surfaces of the classical period. On the contrary, polychromy became the rule and exteriors were frequently decorated with glazed tiles, carved stone ornamentation and brick patterns; roofs of churches were often blue and the onion domes above gold. But the elements were interpreted in a surprisingly harmonious way, and the churches built by Nikon in particular are distinguished not only by a greater severity, by an insistence on the use of the arch and the dome and the complete rejection of the tent-shaped method of construction, but by the subtle mutual balance of the proportions of the tower, the domes and the long rectangular body of the church. Good examples of the style can be seen in the Church of the Twelve Apostles in the Moscow Kremlin, in the church of Our Lady of Kazan at Kolomenskoye, in the Refectory at Zagorsk and in several churches in Yaroslavl.

The fall of Nikon in 1667 removed the last major obstacle which stood in the way, after such a long interval, of the return of Western intellectual, esthetic and social influences. The next 40 years were a watershed between two ages: in art and architecture neither a xenophobic adherence to native traditions, nor a ruthless Westernization, was enforced: the two influences were allowed to merge and to fertilize each other, almost spontaneously. The result was an architectural style which combines many of the forms of Russian architecture with the spirit of the European Baroque. Of the examples which survive, the most striking is the Church of the Intercession at Fili (now a suburb of Moscow). It is undoubtedly one of the finest gems of Russian architecture.

Peter's New Priorities

The reign of Peter the Great brought this process to an end. Russian styles in architecture and painting (the latter already, it must be admitted, in a state of sterility) were rejected as symbolic of the backwardness of the country. Western models were insisted upon in their place. A decree of 1710 banned all new building in stone except in the new capital of St. Petersburg, where it was especially easy for the government to ensure that, in all new building, the new canons of taste and style were being followed.

Peter's priorities in his new capital were secular. He built only one church. This and other decrees therefore had the additional consequence of bringing the construction of stone churches in Russia to an almost complete, if temporary, halt. The masterpiece of wooden ecclesiastical architecture, the monastery at Kizhi, dates from this time; it represents the final flowering of a tradition which began during the Mongol period. Nevertheless, from Peter's reign onwards the emphasis in architecture shifts permanently to palaces, public buildings and even private houses. Hitherto such buildings had been strictly utilitarian, though there were rare exceptions (such as the Palace of Facets in the Moscow Kremlin). Both during the 18th century and subsequently, few churches of any architectural note were built, except for the St. Petersburg cathedrals.

The new capital was intended to be a purely Western city. It contained elements of Florence, of Venice, of Versailles (then at its zenith under Louis XIV) and of contemporary Holland. The leading architect Peter employed was an Italian, Domenico Trezzini. Nevertheless, for all Peter's determination to avoid any but authentic Western styles, these varied influences could not be brought together in a new northern environment without taking on a distinctive character of their own. Such was the Russian Rococo style, which reached its climax in mid-century with the construction of the Winter Palace and of the Catherine Palace at Tsarskoye Selo (now Pushkin), both built by Bartolomeo Rastrelli. The two buildings are particularly successful and pleasing in the way in which enormous horizontal expanses of outer wall are broken up by vertical lines and the alternate variation and repetition of lintels, pediments, porches and other decorative elements. Rastrelli's two best-known churches, the Smolny Cathedral in St. Petersburg and St. Andrew's Church in Kiev, incorporate in their fluid Rococo designs the Russian onion dome—the first reappearance of this indigenous motif since the reign of Peter the Great.

Holding to her Westernized course, Russia now followed Western classical. The Grand Palace at Pavlovsk, built by the Scottish architect Charles Cameron between 1782 and 1796, is one of the first examples of the latter style in existence. The St. Petersburg Stock Exchange (1804–10) by Thomas de Thomon and the Cathedral of Our Lady of Kazan (1801–11) by Voronikhin are in the same spirit. As in the West, however, neo-Classicism lost its early gracefulness and Greek sense of proportion and evolved towards the heavier, more monumental, imperial style. This tendency is well illustrated by the work of C. I. Rossi (1775–1849), who built, or re-built, much of central St. Petersburg during the 1830s and 1840s. His buildings include the War Office (opposite the Winter Palace), the Michael Palace (now the Russian Museum) and Theater (now Rossi) Street.

From mid-century on, Russia underwent the same urge to imitate the medieval that afflicted the rest of Europe in the Victorian period. The results can best be seen in the gaudy and tasteless interior of St. Isaac's Cathedral (completed in 1858), in the incongruous St. Savior's Church, also in Leningrad, built between 1883 and 1907 to commemorate the spot on which Czar Alexander II was assassinated in 1881, and, in the Ukraine, in St. Vladimir's Cathedral and the refectory of the Pecherskaya Monastery in Kiev, completed in 1882 and 1900 respectively, both in pseudo-Byzantine style.

Russian Painters

In the reign of Peter the Great, artists began equally abruptly—and perhaps still more slavishly—to imitate Western models. In order to enforce the "right" Western standards, Peter set up a school of drawing in St. Petersburg which was later elevated by Catherine the Great to the Academy of Fine Arts. The success of this Westernizing policy was complete—excessively so. In the late 18th century, Russia did produce a number of talented portraitists in the Gainsborough manner—an example is Dimitri Levitski (1735–1822)—and in the 19th a school of artists in the mould of the French and German Romantics (most notably Karl Bryullov (1799–1852) and Orest Kiprensky (1782–1836). But unlike the architects, Russian artists failed to put their own stamp on the foreign styles they had imported or to make a distinctive contribution to the development of these styles.

In 1863 a number of talented painters broke away from the Academy as a reaction against its deadening influence. Inspired by the idea—fostered chiefly by the critic Chernyshevsky (see the chapter on literature)—that art should serve a social purpose, they determined to represent the life and sufferings of the common people with the utmost realism. They organized a series of traveling exhibitions throughout the country—hence the name they adopted: the Wanderers. As with their Pre-Raphaelite contemporaries in England, their art was literary. It was designed to convey a social message or to inspire moral feelings rather than simply to be enjoyed esthetically. Their favorite subjects, alongside scenes evoking the cruelties and abuses of contemporary life, were drawn from the Russian past. In this way, too, they represented a reaction against the Westernism of the Academy.

The supreme artist among this group was Ilya Repin (1844–1930), whose *The Volga Bargemen* and *They Were Not Expecting Him* have remained to this day perhaps the most widely-loved and reproduced of Russian paintings. Their popularity in the Soviet period has been matched only by the historical canvases of V. Surikov (1848–1916)—in particular *The Boyarinya Morozova*—and V. Vasnetsov (1848–1926).

But the Wanderers had a historical importance beyond the value of their own works. By breaking with the Academy, they re-established an authentic Russian school of art. They reintroduced into painting the sense of color that had distinguished early Russian icons from their Byzantine models. Above all, by taking realism and social content to their logical extremes and thus demonstrating the limitations of both, they cleared the way for the remarkable achievements that were to follow.

In particular, three young artists emerged who, though they owed much in their early training to the Wanderers and to the colony of artists brought together by the wealthy Mamontov family at their estate at Abramtsevo near Moscow, would eclipse all their elders, except possibly Repin himself. These three were Mikhail Vrubel (1856–1910), Isaac Levitan (1860–1900) and Valentin Serov (1865–1911). They all displayed in their paintings a bold brushwork, a flair for essentials and a sense of form that contrasted sharply with the obsession with detail and heavy-handed narrative style of the Wanderers.

Levitan is the greatest of Russian landscape painters. His canvases are evocative and perhaps even nostalgic—no one who knows and loves the endless perspectives, the broad rivers and wide skies of Russia can fail to be moved by them. But his effects were achieved, like Cézanne's, through an analysis of the essential shapes, colors and textures of his landscapes.

Serov adopted a similar approach to portraiture. Few artists have ever brought their subjects to life more effectively. Though his study of Nicholas II will probably remain his most famous work, one of his masterpieces was painted when he was only twenty-two. This was *Girl with Peaches,* a portrait of Vera Savishna Mamontova that still hangs in Abramtsevo.

Vrubel was the most original of the three. The metaphysical side of his work is most evident in his series of illustrations for Lermontov's poem, *The Demon.* But it is also revealed in his tortured, dissecting, many-angled studies of still-life and flowers. Though he lacked the cool intellectualism of the Cubists, he foreshadowed them in his tireless investigation, from every viewpoint, of the visual potentialities of his subjects.

"The World of Art"

These artists of the 1890s, nurtured in the circle of Abramtsevo, would have regarded themselves more as the heirs of the Wanderers than as their over-throwers. The first deliberate and full-blooded reaction against the latter came with the new century. It can be dated from the foundation of the magazine *The World of Art* in 1898, or from the first exhibition organized by the group of the same name in the following year. The aim of this group, of which the leading members were Alexander Benois (1870–1960) and Sergei Diaghilev (see the section on ballet), was to proclaim the doctrine of Art for Art's Sake and to introduce into Russia the works of the French Impressionists and Post-Impressionists, whose works were first shown in the country at successive World of Art exhibitions. They thus intended to displace the influence of the Wanderers, who no doubt appeared insufferably provincial to the international culture of St. Petersburg to which Benois and his circle belonged.

The World of Art group brought together artists and avantgarde poets who were simultaneously introducing into Russia the latest French literary ideas. The two movements were characterized by the term Symbolism. Both disdained banal portrayals of reality and sought to create a higher world of beauty and harmony. The canvases of Victor Borissov-Mussatov (1870–1905) and Pavel Kuznetsov depict human figures and themes drawn from nature, but the colors are ethereal, the vision is distant, dreamlike and pantheistic, revealing a still, silent and timeless world.

While St. Petersburg was dominated by Symbolism, a group of young painters in Moscow, most notable of whom were Mikhail Larionov (1881–1964) and his life-long companion Natalia Goncharova (1881–1962), had begun to rediscover the Russian icon and to paint in a primitivist style inspired by it. It was the confluence of Symbolism, of the primitivist insistence on line and pure form, of the experiments of Vrubel and of the influx of new Western styles (French Fauvism and Cubism and Italian Futurism) that produced, in the second decade of the century, a revolution in art no less momentous in its field than the coincident turmoils in politics and society.

The "Rayonnist" paintings of Larionov and Goncharova (which date from 1911–13) represented the first breakthrough into modernism. The Rayonnists' optical experimentalism was inspired, in part at least, by the Cubism of Picasso and Braque, while the intensity of surface working in their paintings and their dramatic representation of movement paralleled the Futurism of Marinetti, Carrà and Severini. A similar kinetic quality is evident in the "Cubo-Futurist" works (so called after the French and Italian influence apparent in them) of Kasimir Malevich (1878–1935) and his followers of the period: but here the aim was no longer, as in Rayonnism, to examine the effects of the crossing of the reflected rays from objects, but to break down figures and background into elemental blocks of color. The massive and rhythmic use of color in Cubo-Futurist paintings derived directly from Russian primitivism.

Primitivism, Rayonnism and Cubo-Futurism were all authentically Russian movements, though they were but one aspect of the contemporary ferment in the arts throughout the Western world—a world of which, in culture as in economic and political life, Russia had never been so fully a part as in the generation before the October Revolution. But for all the talent, technical innovation and achievement of Russian artists, they had not up to this time given any decisive new impetus to the development of Western art as a whole. In the four vital years 1913–17, all this was to change. From having been the precocious pupil of the West, Russia then, if only briefly, took the lead.

In 1913 Malevich began to devise his system of "Suprematism." His earliest paintings in the new style were single geometric forms (squares, circles, crosses and triangles) on contrasting backgrounds, originally black on white. From there he moved on to assemble, in one composition, various geometric elements seemingly revolving on invisible axes, flawlessly balanced. His last paintings, executed in 1917–18, his famous "White on White" series, represented the ultimate rejection of objects drawn from, or relating to, the human or visible world. Meanwhile, Vassily Kandinsky (1866–1944), who returned from Munich to Russia at the onset of war in 1914, had already begun to paint his "free" improvised compositions, containing no geometric or defined shapes at all but only lines, and areas of contrasting color. If Cubism had still been concerned with the traditional analysis of perceived objects, Malevich and Kandinsky, in their different ways, had launched out on a new course altogether: the creation of pure form without reference to visible things. Together with the Dutchman Mondrian, they stand as the founders of abstract painting.

Two further—and quite diverse—trends were to emerge from this fertile period. Marc Chagall (1889–1985), whose early work is Symbolist, evolved his own, deeply personal style. Though he has the instinctive sense of form of all great painters, his primary concern is psychological, even psychoanalytical: his use of fantasy, unreal colors and dream images inaugurated the Surrealist movement.

The Constructivists and the Revolution

Nor did art fail to suffer the politicization experienced by other aspects of Russian life in the period immediately following the 1917 Revolution. Suprematism, with its dynamic interrelation of abstract geometric forms, gave birth to three-dimensional models and to the design of real machines and useful objects, from workers' outfits to furniture and buildings. The artist had become the artist-engineer. Constructivism was born. A great controversy ensued between those who, like Malevich, continued to insist that art was essentially a spiritual activity to be pursued for its own sake, and the Constructivists, led by Vladimir Tatlin (1885–1953) and by two former Suprematists, Alexander Rodchenko (1891–1956) and El Lissitzky (1890–1941), who insisted that art must serve a useful purpose and remain close to life. It followed that art should not pursue its own course in the creation of the esthetically pleasing, but that it should obey the laws and requirements of the real world. Technique replaced style. Easel painting was all but abandoned, while Constructivist design and architecture became distinguished by an uncompromising functionalism.

It was indeed in architecture that the contrast with the immediately preceding period was most marked and the achievements of Constructivism most notable and lasting. Though in St. Petersburg throughout the Czarist period architecture had continued to imitate the latest Western fashions, the new plutocracy which emerged in Moscow from the 1870s to 1914 (years of great economic advance) increasingly built themselves, in the Art Nouveau style, houses whose asymmetry and fantasy reveal direct affinities with contemporary Symbolist esthetic ideas. Moscow, for example, retains the finest collection of Art Nouveau architecture in Europe. The interested visitor should see the former house of Maxim Gorky on Vorovsky Street; the Ryabushinsky House on Tolstoy Street; the Australian Embassy on Kropotkin Pereulok, the Tretyakov Gallery and the Yaroslavl railway station, all dating from the first decade of the century.

When building resumed after World War I and the Civil War, it was evident that an architectural revolution had taken place. The predominantly Constructivist style, its austerity no doubt reflecting the economic stringency of the times as much as esthetic theory, made no concessions either to the imagination or to conventional ideas of comfort or finish. Stark outlines, unrelieved expanses of wall or window, and harsh angular lines became the rule. Among the best examples of the style—which so impressed contemporary visitors as the reflection of a new, iconoclastic, and compellingly single-minded society—are the Izvestia building, built by G. Barkhin in 1926; the Zuyev Club by Ilya Golosov, which dates from the same year; the Ministry of Agriculture building designed by Aleksei Shchusev and erected from 1928–33; and the Central House of Cinema Actors, built by the brothers Vesnin in 1931–34, all of them in Moscow.

Constructivist painters, too, regarding themselves as the natural exponents and inspirers of the new age, put their talents at the service of the Bolshevik regime. El Lissitzky and Rodchenko both spent much of their time producing political posters, often in the Suprematist style of their early paintings. Tatlin labored long and hard on a futuristic design for a grandiose *Monument to the Third International.* Constructivist artists and typographers co-operated with Futurist and Constructivist poets and writers in founding in 1923 the magazine *LEF,* which was to herald the art of the future (see the chapter on literature). But with the enforcement of the doctrine of "socialist realism" from 1932 onwards, the activities of Constructivist artists and architects came to as abrupt an end as those of their counterparts in literature.

Socialist Realism

In art the period since the 1930s saw an officially-induced return to the programmatic and illustrative painting of the Wanderers, with the difference that the conscious aim was no longer to depict the suffering of humanity, but rather the happiness, confidence and optimism of Soviet society. Such are the works of T. N. Yablonskaya (b. 1917). Many of her best-known canvases of contented workers and overflowing grain harvests were executed at the worst moments of the Purges and material privations of the Stalin period. This is not to say that socialist realism has not, if untypically, produced works of real inspiration. There is no denying, for instance, the enormous, pristine force of the sculptured stainless steel group, *Worker and Collective Farm Woman* (1937), by Vera Mukhina (1889–1954).

In architecture, as in art, "socialist realism" demands in theory that works be both easily comprehensible and inspiring to the masses. In practice they had also to conform to the—instinctively philistine—tastes of the Party. The architecture of the 1935–55 period reflects both these requirements. Symmetry and monumentalism became the order of the day. Though these features are common to almost every construction, the buildings of the time display a curious amalgam of stylistic influences: the 19th-century Petersburg of Rossi with its classical themes and columns; a Florentine style (though without any Renaissance sense of proportion) evident, for example, in Moscow's Gorky Street and Prospekt Mira; and, more especially after World War II, the "modern" style of the 1930s West, with its emphasis on scale, and use of external fluting, massive pediments and lintels and other Egyptian motifs. The Manhattan of the 1930s is particularly recalled by the seven prominent skyscrapers erected in Moscow after World War II, though their crenelated turrets and fussy external decoration are all their own. These enormous constructions, together with the older stations of the Moscow Metro—subterranean temples of marble—remain, as they were intended, permanent and evocative monuments of Stalin's rule.

Since 1955, quantity has replaced quality, solidity or style as the overriding aim. The rectangular, barrack-like apartment blocks in grey or yellow brick of the late 1950s and early 1960s—a feature of every Soviet town— have been succeeded by the more elongated, but no less severely utilitarian, blocks in prefabricated concrete sections which characterize the building program of the last few years. There have been several interesting and imaginative advances in design and in town planning, for example in Moscow's Kalinin Prospekt and the New Arbat district, as well as in some of the capital's newer suburbs, such as the Olympic Village, though the results are too often marred by bad workmanship or the use of inferior materials—not failings of the Stalin years. Few Soviet buildings can stand comparison with the achievements of contemporary architecture in the West. One notable exception is the S.E.V. (Council for Mutual Economic Assistance) headquarters in Moscow, built by S. Egorov and Y. Semyonov in 1967.

In art, the imposition of socialist realism was totally effective, at least until the mid-1950s. The creativeness and experimentalism of the first decades of the century were brought to an abrupt end. Those artists who had been associated with the great age of Russian painting but who did not go abroad (Larionov and Goncharova had left at the time of the Bolshevik Revolution, and Kandinsky and Chagall were to emigrate in the 1920s)— virtually ceased to paint. Even the ardent Communists Tatlin and Rodchenko were forced into an intimidated inactivity, their works denounced as "non-objectivist" and "formalist." The latter's family destroyed a large number of his canvases in panic during the Purges. The Union of Artists, at once mutual benefit society and self-regulating guild, on the whole succeeded in maintaining the required conformism without the need for the spectacular repression of individual dissidents that has marked Party regulation of literature.

In the more relaxed atmosphere that followed the Twentieth Party Congress in 1956, a body of "unofficial" artists (not members of the Union) began cautiously to emerge. Such was the spirit of the times that an exhibition of their work was even held in the Manège Gallery in Moscow. But a savage denunciation by Khrushchev himself made it clear that "formalism" was, after all, not to be tolerated. Moreover, the 40 years of close

Party control and isolation from the artistic life of the rest of the world had done their work.

Beneath the official surface of "socialist realism" there indeed lurk a number of original talents—even some outstanding ones. It is not possible to speak of "movements." The work of unofficial artists in the Soviet Union varies from the tense and tortured drawings and sculptured figures of Ernst Neizvestny (who finally emigrated to Israel in early 1976) to the dark and pessimistic paintings of Oscar Rabin, with their telling use of Russian imagery, to the cool abstraction of the canvases of Lydia Masterkova and her former husband Nemukhin. There has been some recent revival of Western interest in contemporary Russian art, and some unofficial artists' paintings bought by foreigners and brought to the West or brought out by emigrating Russians have been displayed in exhibitions large and small in Europe and the U.S.A.

There are signs that the Soviet government is relaxing its attitude towards some of these unofficial artists. Groups are sometimes allowed to hold exhibitions although in recent years they have occasionally been squashed, literally, with the help of bulldozers and police. In 1986 they were given official facilities for holding open-air markets in a Moscow suburban park where permanent stalls have now been set up. And now, in the present atmosphere of experimentation, all kinds of weird and wonderful art forms are emerging—some less inspired than others—to provide a startling variety that has not been seen in "official" art for decades. But there is still a long road ahead if Russia is to regain the ground she has lost and return to the mainstream of international developments in art. So far, contrary to the expectations of so many artists in 1917, political revolution has proved incompatible with creative revolution.

RUSSIAN AND SOVIET
LITERATURE

Few would deny that the Russians have produced the greatest of European literatures, at least in the fields of poetry and the novel. But this achievement, like so much in their country, has been based on a very late start. As late as the year of Pushkin's birth, 1799, it would have been impossible for contemporaries to have foreseen the creation of a modern national literature in Russia. There had been no serious drama or social comedy; no lyrical poetry to speak of. Russia had remained virtually untouched by the literary achievements of the European Renaissance and its aftermath, and had nothing of her own to set against the works of Petrarch, Ronsard, Shakespeare, Molière, Racine and their successors in the West.

This state of affairs is not hard to explain. From the time of its conversion to Christianity in the tenth century, to the beginning of the Mongol invasions in the 13th, Russia had been a full part of a cosmopolitan Christian civilization, in contact alike with Scandinavia, with Western Europe and with Byzantium. The chronicles which have come down to us from this period, written in the old Church Slavonic, are not unlike their contemporary counterparts in Scandinavia and in England. In the generation before the first Mongol invasions, Kievan Russia produced its greatest literary masterpiece, the epic poem *The Lay of Igor's Campaign.* There followed 250 years of Mongol domination, of intermittent resistance to the invader followed by further repression at his hands, of political fragmentation into small princedoms, of the frequent destruction of cities and the interruption of economic life. Russia was effectively cut off from outside influences and ceased to share in the economic and cultural development of the West. If she survived at all as a cultural and political entity, that was the achievement of the Church and of the monarchy, both, from the 14th century on, based in Moscow. No other institution came through. Together they enjoyed a monopoly of the written word until the late 17th century, 200 years after Russia's release from the Mongol yoke.

Throughout all this period, in sharp contrast to the versatility and innovative brilliance of the contemporary West, Russian literature (still written in Church Slavonic) consists of little more than sermons, lives of saints and similar religious pieces; and ballads and other works glorifying the exploits of kings. As the balance of power in the state shifted from Church to monarchy, so the proportion of total literary output devoted to the latter's cause increased. It is interesting that the first work to break out of this mould, and also the first to be written in modern colloquial Russian (as opposed to Church Slavonic), *The Life of the Archpriest Avvakum* by himself (1672–73), was composed by the leader of the Old Believers movement, which represented the first serious challenge to the authority of the centralized monarchy and of the established Church.

Avvakum devoted his life to opposing the encroachment of Western influences in Church and State. But modern Russian literature traces its beginnings to the success of the trends which Avvakum and the Old Believers had attempted to resist. The westernizing reforms of Peter the Great and the construction of the new capital of St. Petersburg as a window on the West opened a new era. By the reign of Catherine the Great (1762–96)—herself a child of the European Enlightenment and a correspondent of Voltaire, Diderot and other philosophers—the westernization of the Russian upper classes, at least in Petersburg, was complete. The widespread circulation, for the first time in Russia, in the original and in translation, of works of contemporary French, English and German literature was a natural part of this process, as was the emergence of a native literature strongly influenced by them.

Mikhail Lomonosov (1711–65) is often regarded as the father of modern Russian literature. He set out, self-consciously, to establish a language suitable for the imitation of the literary achievements of France and England, distinguishing between the old Church Slavonic for elevated prose, a colloquial Russian to be used for fables and comedy, and an intermediate style for general literary use. Lomonosov also published the first Russian grammar. His own verse, written in a formal and philosophical style, for the most part in rhyming couplets, owes something to the influence of Boileau and of Alexander Pope.

Nikolai Karamzin (1766–1826) wrote the first novel in the Russian language, *Poor Liza,* a sentimental story strongly influenced by Richardson's *Pamela.* In the same year, 1790, appeared two interesting, and ultimately influential, prose works; Karamzin's *Letter of a Russian Traveler* and Alexander Radishchev's *Journey from Petersburg to Moscow.* Both are clearly influenced by Sterne's *Sentimental Journey.* But both employ a literary device, the journey through Russia revealing contrasts of human type and social condition on the way, which was to be used to good effect by future writers. And the Radishchev book, with its subtle criticism of serfdom (which caused Catherine II to exile the author to Siberia) inaugurated the tradition of Russian social satire. One further writer of the period deserves mention. Gavrila Derzhavin (1743–1816) is the most important poet before Pushkin, and the first Russian poet to enjoy a major reputation both in his own country and in the West.

Pushkin and Lermontov

Alexander (1799–1837) occupies in Russian literature the position enjoyed by Shakespeare and Goethe in the Literatures of England and Germany; all his immediate successors, and the greatest writers of the remainder of the 19th century, acknowledged their debt to him, and his reputation remains unchallenged today. His works include lyrical and narrative poems, short stories (including *The Queen of Spades* and *The Captain's Daughter*), the verse play *Boris Godunov* and the verse novel *Eugene Onegin*. The latter, a tale of frustrated romantic love which introduced into Russian literature Onegin, the type of the "superfluous man," has remained his most popular work in Russia. Pushkin's characters are neither villains nor positive heroes; they are depicted as a combination of many qualities, and are seen more as the victims than as the arbiters of their own fates. In this respect, Pushkin broke with the conventions and stereotypes of the past and cleared the way for the achievements of Tolstoy and Chekhov.

This human sympathy in Pushkin is no doubt due to his own lack of pre-conceived ideas or fixed credos, to his openness before the experiences of life combined with disillusionment at its reverses and scepticism as to its overall meaning. His own emotional and sexual life, which he lived to the full in true Byronic fashion, is reflected in some of the finest love lyrics, and erotic poems, which exist in any language; though a sense of despair at the superfluity of existence is all pervasive.

Pushkin inspired a generation of poets, including Yevgeny Baratynsky (1800–44), Fyodor Tyutchev (1803–1873) and Afanasii Fet (1820–92), all of whom wrote intense, lyrical poetry of the highest quality, evoking the emotions of love and the sights and sounds of nature in clear, mellifluous language. But the greatest literary figure after Pushkin is Mikhail Lermontov (1814–41). His flights of imagination and his images are more strikingly unexpected than those of his contemporaries, his language more rhetorical and more effortless. These qualities are well illustrated in his poem, *The Demon,* which was to inspire Vrubel's paintings as well as to influence future poets. Of his prose works, the only one to enjoy lasting attention has been his short novel, *A Hero of Our Time,* a work of remarkable modernity, based as it is on the exploits of an anti-hero, Pechorin, bored with life, unable to respond to human affections, aimless and amoral (alienated as we would now say). He reminds the mid-20th century reader of no one so much as the "hero" of Camus' *The Stranger.* Indeed, precociousness, and precocious disillusion, are the hallmarks of Lermontov's career. At the age of 27 he was killed, like Pushkin, in a senseless duel.

The brilliance of Pushkin, Lermontov and their circle, as a result of which Russia was brought for the first time into the forefront of European literature, had its origin in the impact of the Western Romantic movement on a young, vigorous and aristocratic culture. The Napoleonic wars, which carried Russian troops to Paris and ensured the full integration of the Russian Empire into the European political system, and the liberal policies of Alexander I (1801–25) permitted the intensification of these contacts. Both victory in war and relative liberalism at home inspired a new confidence in the future; an assumption that Russia's destiny lay in imitating the political institutions of the West; and, in literature, the neglect of specifically national subjects in favor of more universal themes and the cultivation of individual sensibility.

Poetry is the typical literary mode of expression of the age. The reign of Nicholas I (1825–55) opened with the Decembrists' Rising, which the young monarch attributed to the disrupting effect of foreign ideas, and to which he reacted with a fierce repression, and with the rejection of Western political, industrial and cultural influences. All contact, even personal travel, was made more difficult (Pushkin was himself refused permission to go abroad); and thinking Russians became increasingly aware of their country's isolation, its political backwardness, and its failure to take part in the unprecedented economic expansion then taking place in Western Europe. The great intellectual debate of the reign was between the "Westerners" and the "Slavophiles," i.e. those who believed that Russia had a distinct Slav historical mission of her own. In literature, this mood produced a new national introversion, and a concern with social themes. Its typical form of expression is the novel.

Gogol and Turgenev

The great age of the Russian novel begins with the publication, in 1842, of *Dead Souls* by Nikolai Gogol (1809–52). The story of Chichikov, an amiable rogue, who hits upon the idea of making a fortune by buying up the title deeds to dead serfs and proceeds to visit a series of provincial landowners, reveals a whole gallery of human types. Gogol is less widely read in the West than Turgenev, Tolstoy and Dostoyevsky, perhaps because his characters are difficult to appreciate fully outside a Russian context. But in his ability to paint living and memorable—if caricatured—social types, he has rightly been compared with Dickens; and in his sharp eye for human weakness, petty vices, and folly, with Molière. His secret is perhaps his talent for combining humor and pathos. He is the first of the great Russian humorists, and in his attacks on officialdom in his play, *The Inspector General,* adopts what is to be one of their favorite butts. But he also shows a darker side, most especially in his stories, *Nevsky Prospekt, Memoirs of a Madman* and *The Overcoat,* an exploration of human despair which foreshadows Dostoyevsky.

The works of Ivan Goncharov (1812–91) and of Ivan Turgenev (1818–83), though their appeal is universal, also illustrate, in their various ways, peculiarly Russian themes. In *Oblomov,* Goncharov created, in the hero of that name, the archetypal "superfluous," Hamlet-like character of Russian literature. A man paralyzed by his own weakness, indecision and inertia, who for long periods cannot even bring himself to get out of bed, Oblomov fails to take advantage of any of the opportunities, personal or romantic, with which life presents him, and dies after an existence which appears to have been without purpose or meaning. He remains, in Russia, one of the best-loved of all literary creations.

In his technique, Turgenev is the most Western of the great Russian novelists; like the leading nineteenth-century realist writers of France and England, he is content to describe his characters, and the physical world around them, from the outside; he lacks the philosophical dimension of Tolstoy, or the psychological penetration of Dostoyevsky. But his subjects are entirely Russian. *Notes of a Hunter* depicts, with great sympathy and affection, the Russian countryside and the Russian peasant; it was considerably influential at the time as an indictment of serfdom. *A Nest of the Gentry,* a moving tale of thwarted romantic love, describes the atmosphere of life among the old provincial gentry, as does his play, *A Month in the Country. Fathers and Sons,* inspired by the contemporary conflict of generations in Russia, is the story of Bazarov, the new type of nihilist who rejects all religious values and Russian traditions, in the name of a ruthless materialism.

Tolstoy and Dostoyevsky

There is no need to make out a case for the greatness of Count Lev Nikolayevich Tolstoy (1828–1910). *War and Peace* (1865–69) is perhaps the most ambitious novel ever undertaken anywhere: a vast tapestry of Russian life during the period of the Napoleonic Wars, it embraces the whole range of human experience, from love to death in war, and integrates the story of its individual characters with the flow of the impersonal currents of history. In this respect it was to be followed by the great novels of the 20th century, Sholokhov's *And Quiet Flows the Don* and Pasternak's *Dr. Zhivago.* In *Anna Karenina,* the heroine, by following the impulses of her own heart, transgresses the conventions of society, and is inevitably destroyed. The novel is at once high tragedy in the Greek sense, a horrendous indictment of contemporary social hypocrisy and the double standard applied to men and women, and, above all, one of the finest examples of that sympathetic treatment of human suffering which is so characteristic of Russian literature. *The Death of Ivan Ilyich* and *Resurrection* (1886 and 1899, respectively) were written after Tolstoy's conversion to his own brand of Christianity, and strongly reflect his new religious perception of life; the first is a study in depth of death, the second of the redeeming power of love. Tolstoy also composed in these years his *Confession,* a number of religious and political works, and a series of childlike allegorical stories intended to illustrate his religious and moral convictions. Some have seen in these stories the simplicity of genius; others a regrettable, if deliberate, descent into naïveté.

Fyodor Mikhailovich Dostoyevsky (1821–81) is the originator, and the master, of the psychological novel. His works, of which *Crime and Punishment, The Idiot, The Possessed* and *The Brothers Karamazov* are justly the most famous, exercised a considerable influence on Freud, and on other psychologists and writers of the 20th century. Arrested as a young man on political charges, Dostoyevsky was condemned to death and suffered a mock execution before being exiled to Siberia. Like Solzhenitsyn, therefore, he had himself experienced the moral dilemmas and sufferings of which he writes. Dostoyevsky belongs to the tradition of Russian realism; but it is a realism that is directed, above all, to describing the internal dramas of the soul.

Russian prose in the period between the death of Dostoyevsky (in 1881) and 1917 is dominated, apart from the aged Tolstoy, who continued to write until his death in 1910, by three figures: Anton Chekhov (1860–1904), Maxim Gorky (pen-name of Alexei Peshkov, 1868–1936) and Ivan Bunin (1870–1953).

Though all can loosely be called realists, Chekhov is quite distinct. His medium is the play and short story rather than the novel; his style impressionistic rather than exhaustively descriptive: indeed, no writer has been better able, with a few brief strokes, to conjure up a complete character or convey a situation or a mood. Chekhov's most evident qualities are his acute powers of observation of people, and his great sympathy for them: perhaps both characteristics derive from his early training and experience as a doctor. Chekhov's view of life is stoically pessimistic: he is always conscious of the gulf between ideals and personal aspirations, and reality. Many of the characters of his best short stories (*The Kiss, Lady with the Lap Dog*) and his plays (*The Seagull, The Three Sisters, Uncle Vanya, The Cherry Orchard*) are suddenly made aware of the futility of their current existence but have ultimately to resign themselves to the abandonment of their romantic illusions and to a banal and mindless future.

Gorky and Bunin are firmly in the realist tradition. Gorky's *Former People* and *Mother,* his autobiographical *Childhood,* and Bunin's *The Village* paint unforgettable pictures of the misery, squalor, drunkenness and violence of life among the poor at the turn of the century. Bunin's later writing (*The Gentlemen from San Francisco*) is more metaphysical. A poet as well as a writer of prose, Bunin left Russia after the Revolution and lived the rest of his life in France. He was awarded the Nobel Prize in 1933. Gorky also left Russia after 1917, but subsequently returned. He was retrospectively acclaimed as the founder of "socialist" realism in literature, and in 1934 made Chairman of the new Union of Soviet Writers. He died in mysterious circumstances in 1936, during the Purges.

Poetry after Lermontov

Poetry during the half century from the death of Lermontov to the 1890s was largely eclipsed by the novel. Three names alone stand out, none of them to be compared with their forerunners or successors: Tyutchev, Fet and Nikolai Nekrasov (1821–77). The latter, with his narrative style and his concern with the themes of the Russian countryside and the Russian peasant, is in some ways the equivalent of Turgenev in prose: in the Soviet Union, he is accorded a higher stature than any 19th century poet after Pushkin. But realism and social content—which had reached a high point during the 1850s and '60s, when some critics and writers had argued that literature should serve a strictly utilitarian social purpose—provoked a reaction similar to that which set in against the "Wanderers" in art. Moreover, the headlong course of industrialization and Westernization on which the Russian Empire was embarked, with increasing momentum, from the 1860s until the Bolshevik Revolution, had its impact on literature as on painting: the rich seeds of Western, and especially French, modernism were implanted in the fertile but relatively unsown soil of Russia.

In literature, these two trends combined to produce the Russian Symbolist movement—memorable for its achievements in poetry rather than in prose. The movement begins in the early 1890s with the first works of Konstantin Balmont (1867–1943) and Valery Bryusov (1873–1924) whose poetry is nearest to French symbolism. It reaches its climax in the period 1900–17 with the work of Andrei Bely (pen-name of Boris Bugaev, 1880–1934) and of Alexander Blok (1880–1921). Like their French counterparts, the Russian symbolists were uniquely concerned with the personal vision of the poet, breaking with the Romantics in insisting that this vision could not be adequately conveyed by literal description, by the choice of the "right" word, but only by the use of symbols.

Symbolism gave way to two movements, both of them entirely Russian in origin, which together were to dominate the poetic scene until the 1950s.

Acmeism was an artistic reaction against Symbolism and in favor of a restoration of clear images and precision in the use of language. It produced three great poets: Nikolai Gumilyov (1886–1921), Osip Mandelstam (1892–1940?) and Anna Akhmatova (pen-name of Anna Gorenko, 1888–1966), whose first husband was Gumilyov. Their fates provide good illustrations of the period through which they lived: Gumilyov was shot by the Bolsheviks in 1921; Mandelstam, arrested in 1938, died in a camp perhaps in 1940; Akhmatova, though she lost both her second husband and her son by Gumilyov in the 1936 purges and was herself savagely denounced in the 1940s, survived to be generally recognized by many Russians, by her death in 1966, as their greatest living poet. All three have been officially "rehabilitated" under Gorbachev.

Of the three, Mandelstam's poems are the most classical and polished; their serenity and perfection are in sharp contrast to the turmoil and suffering in which the poet was to end his life. Akhmatova's poetry is more direct and personal; much of it deals with love both in its romantic and its sensual aspects. But the ordeals of her tragic life come through in a series of poems and in 1987 in the Soviet Union, at last, published in the West under the title *Requiem*. They are the most moving poetic document of the Purges.

Futurism

Futurism was another reaction against Symbolism, both technical and philosophical. In place of the mysticism of the Symbolists, their concern with the other world of beauty and art, the Futurists reasserted the material world and delighted in its technology and its politics. Not for nothing was the manifesto of the movement, issued in 1912—over the signatures, among others, of the two major Futurist poets, Viktor Khlebnikov (1885–1922) and Vladimir Mayakovsky (1893–1930)—called *A Slap in the Face of Public Taste*. Their defiance of the rules of grammar and syntax, their stunningly unexpected metaphors and imagery, their exhibitionist behavior and outlandish clothes were all deliberately designed to shock.

Behind the histrionics and the self-advertisement was a serious purpose: to solve the perennial problem of poetry that a feeling once expressed is distorted by the limitations and extraneous associations of the words used. The sound of a word, and its appearance on the printed page, thus acquire a new importance of their own, and the Futurists set great store by their public declamations of their poems, and by their typographical experiments, both of which contributed to their remarkable notoriety in Russia on the eve of the Great War.

The Futurists were intimately linked with the *avant garde* movements in art in their day (Mayakovsky and Kruchonykh were both professional artists; Burlyuk (1882–1967) was even better known as a painter than as a Futurist poet) and their poetry can often be best read as an attempt to use language to build up contrasts and patterns in new and suggestive ways, rather than to convey a literal message, in the manner of contemporary Cubist and Rayonnist paintings.

No country in Europe, in the years before 1914, displayed greater vitality and variety in the arts, greater or more fruitful interaction between them, or greater passion in the controversies between the various movements and cliques within them. It is wrong to see this process as having come to an end with the Revolutions of 1917. Many writers—perhaps initially the majority—welcomed the new order. The Futurists instinctively identified themselves with it and Mayakovsky and others founded in 1923 a new journal, *LEF* ("Left Front"), with the aim of proclaiming the art of the future.

But Futurism, like all experimentalism in the arts, fell into increasing official disfavor, as being both insufficiently susceptible to Party control, and too highbrow to serve the Party's needs (Lenin, whose tastes were nothing if not bourgeois, had already denounced Futurism as "literary hooliganism"). But official censorship and control were at first exercised with a light hand, and the decade saw a lively controversy between, on the one hand, Futurism, and its successor movement, Constructivism (which emphasized the tendency in Futurism towards the creation of a close-to-life, technological literature), and, on the other, the Association of Proletarian Writers, whose attempts to create a popular, realistic and immediately comprehensible literature produced little worthwhile poetry, though a number of important works in prose. Both movements believed with equal passion that they represented the wave of the future. But it was the latter that finally triumphed. Mayakovsky, shortly before his suicide in 1930, was himself forced to join the Proletarians. In 1934, all remnants of heterodoxy were abolished when all literary groups were compulsorily merged in the new Union of Soviet Writers.

The great events in poetry in the 1920s were publication of the first major collections of poems of Boris Pasternak (1890–1960), and of the works of Sergei Esenin (1895–1925). The latter described himself as "the last poet of wooden Russia." The description is apt: his personalized, homely and always melodious lyrics, sometimes on political and patriotic themes, but more often recalling the seasons of love, bear little relation to the work of the myriad movements of the time (though those who insist on labels refer to him as an Imagist). Born of peasant stock, Esenin welcomed the October Revolution; though his suicide, like that of Mayakovsky five years later, has sometimes been attributed, at least partially, to political frustration and disillusionment. He has remained perhaps the most popular of 20th-century poets.

Pasternak, on the other hand, together with Blok and Akhmatova, with whom he shares a world stature, has always been the favourite of Russian intellectuals. His poems published in the '20s show the influence of the Futurists, a movement with which he is often identified and with which he undoubtedly had close personal contacts. But his poetry displays a musical quality, a rhythmical regularity, concision and discipline of form, and above all, a hint of the metaphysical. His poems written after World War II—and particularly the *Zhivago* poems—with their greater simplicity of language and their religious themes, have become well known in the West. Only incomplete editions of Pasternak's works, in very limited numbers, have been published in the Soviet Union. In 1988, *Dr. Zhivago* is due to appear in print.

The Soviet Novel

But, as in other periods in Russian history when political and social themes have come to the fore, the most notable literary achievements of the Soviet period have been in the field of the novel. As in poetry, the 1920s were a period of enormous range and variety. Isaak Babel (1894–1941?) brought realistic description to a new point in his *Red Cavalry* (1926), with its vivid and horrifying verbal pictures of the violence and brutality of the Civil War. *Cities and Years* by Konstantin Fedin (b. 1892) is a thoughtful account of a Russian intellectual, brought up in the humanistic values of the old order, who returns to Russia after a long absence and attempts to come to terms with the new situation.

Both these themes are among those reflected in the greatest Russian novel of the first half of the century, *And Quiet Flows the Don,* by Mikhail Sholokhov (1905–84), a panorama of the lives of the inhabitants of a Cossack village from the pre-1914 period through the vast upheavals of the First World War and Civil War. Though the novel has always been accorded high official acclaim in the Soviet Union, its power and originality, its magnanimous sense of the complexities, contradictions and poignancies of life, owe nothing to dogma. Its sympathetically depicted hero fights for the Whites, while there can be few more unpleasant characters anywhere in literature than the Red, Misha Koshevoi.

But classical realism by no means held the field in the post-revolutionary period. There was also a revival of the tradition of humor and social satire which had lain almost dormant since Gogol. The satirical, and often brilliantly funny, works of Mikhail Zoshchenko (1895–1958) and of Il'f and Petrov (pen names of Ilya Fainzilberg, 1897–1937, and Yevgeni Kataev, 1903–42) won great popularity in the 1920s and have enjoyed a mild revival. Though they do not ridicule the Soviet system as such, their most frequent targets are the absurdities of officialdom.

The surrealistic works of Yevgeni Zamyatin (1884–1937) and of Mikhail Bulgakov (1891–1940) represent, in their different ways, a more profound reaction to the events of the time, and in particular to the growing suppression of dissent and individual freedom and to official insistence on the emergence of a New Communist Man with new standards of morality of his own. Zamyatin's *We* (1924), which has just been published in the Soviet Union, anticipates Huxley's *Brave New World* and Orwell's *1984* in its nightmarish description of the totalitarian state of the future. Still largely known in the Soviet Union as a writer of orthodox plays (and one not quite so orthodox, *The Days of the Turbins,* in which the heroes are White officers), Bulgakov's chief claim to fame lies in his novels *The Heart of a Dog* (written in 1925) and *The Master and Margarita* (written some ten years later, but only discovered in 1967, when it was published in the West, and, in a severely-censored version, in Russia). Mixtures of the fantastic and the allegorical, with frequent satirical allusions to contemporary Soviet themes, both novels can be read as Aesopian attacks on the moral assumptions of the Bolshevik regime.

Threatening ultimately to displace all other trends was the Proletarian movement with its attempts to produce a new Communist literature. *Gorky's Mother* (1907) was subsequently claimed as marking the beginning of the new era in literature. But its real pioneers were Fyodor Gladkov (1883–1958) and Alexander Fadeyev (1901–1956). Gladkov's *Cement,* published in 1925, and Fadeyev's *The Rout,* which appeared a year later, introduced the new type of revolutionary hero: the leader of the proletariat, acting "in tune with history," purposeful, resolute, ruthlessly dedicated to the cause of the Party, and utterly contemptuous of "bourgeois" humane values. Though part of the drama of *The Rout* is provided by the hero's momentary loss of resolution, such heroes normally display little internal conflict or even private emotional life; their opponents, counter-revolutionaries or relics of the past order, doomed by history, appear in equally monochrome tones.

Socialist Realism

It was natural that this style should be adopted as the norm as Party control over the arts was extended and intensified during the period of the First Five Year Plan (1928–33). The Party of the Stalin period had little use for fantasy, allegory or satire. Nor was classical realism an approach to be encouraged. Soviet literature should present positive heroes who would serve as models for the reader. It should be inspiring and optimistic. Socialist realism therefore demanded not that life should be depicted as it is (with all its imperfections), but as it should (and ultimately would) be—in short, it is in *no* way to be confused with realism!

Official direction and control of this kind was a new phenomenon in Russia: Czarist censorship, haphazard and rarely onerous, had been purely negative; it had never attempted to enforce particular subjects, aims or styles upon literature or art. The consequence of the enforcement of socialist realism was certainly not any diminution in the number of works produced. On the contrary, vast numbers of novels appeared, all of them characterized by their didactic and moralizing tone, their idealized "positive" heroes and a remarkable similarity of situation and plot.

Among the most famous examples of the genre are Sholokhov's *Virgin Soil Upturned,* a description of the process of collectivization as seen from the official point of view; *Courage* by V. K. Ketlinskaya (b. 1906), which recounts the story of the building of Komsomolsk-on-Amur; *The Second Day* by Ilya Erenburg (1891–1967), which deals with the construction of a Siberian steel plant; and *How the Steel was Tempered* by Nikolai Ostrovski (1904–36), which tells the story of a young Bolshevik from a poor background who joins the revolutionary cause and succeeds, under the new regime, in realizing his ambition to be a writer.

With World War II, the war itself replaced industrialization as the most favored theme in Soviet literature. The subject was only too natural in the aftermath of the war itself. But its political attractiveness, its scope for creating inspiring "positive" heroes, and, especially, for identifying patriotism and the defense of the Russian homeland with the cause of the Party, have ensured that it would remain, into the 1970s, a dominant motif in officially approved and published writing. The most celebrated of the early war novels were Fadeyev's *The Young Guard* and Boris Polevoi's *The Story of a Real Man.* The subject has been the basis of the careers of Konstantin Simonov (b. 1915), Yuri Bondarev (b. 1924) and innumerable others.

The requirement that literature should serve the Party's ends (and should display *partinost,* or party spirit) and the contention that only the style of "socialist realism" can satisfy this requirement have remained, and are likely to continue to remain, with modifications, the foundations of official policy. Only the narrowness with which these principles have been interpreted, and the rigor with which they have been enforced, have varied. Since 1986 there has been a noticeable thaw in official rigidity, which has led to a real relaxation of curbs on what can be published. The death of Stalin in 1953, and the publication the following year of Erenburg's novel *The Thaw* (which actually dares to mention the Purges of the 1930s) appeared to herald a new era of literary freedom; the denunciation of Stalin at the Twentieth Party Congress in 1956 seemed to indicate that there could be no reversion to the tight control of the past. And, indeed, Khrushchev, in his attempts to outmaneuver and discredit his Praesidium rivals, Malenkov, Molotov and Kaganovich, who had been much more implicated in Stalin's crimes than he, found it very useful to permit the publication of literary works exposing those crimes. By far the most notable of these was *One Day in the Life of Ivan Denisovich,* by Alexander Solzhenitsyn (b. 1918) published in the periodical *Novy Mir* in 1962.

That Party control over literature was not to be relaxed except for particular Party purposes was well demonstrated by the storm of abuse which greeted the award of the Nobel Prize to Pasternak in 1958 for his novel, *Dr. Zhivago,* which had been published in the West. A work entirely in the tradition of *War and Peace* and *And Quiet Flows the Don* in its synthesis of individual with great historical themes, it is nonetheless very much a poet's novel, more remarkable for its insight into the human mind, and its sense of the scale and significance of life, than for the structure of its plot. Its great faults in official eyes have been its refusal to adopt the simple orthodox view of the great events of the Revolutionary period, and the introverted, complex and often ambiguous reaction to them of the hero, Zhivago. This attitude has now softened. A 6-volume edition of Pasternak is reportedly due for publication in 1990.

Victor Nekrasov (1910–87), whose most famous work is *Front Line Stalingrad,* eventually emigrated to France in 1974. Vladimir Maximov, another imaginative writer, followed and is now editor of a literary-political journal, *Kontinent,* published in the West since 1974. Other leading writers who emigrated, voluntarily or involuntarily, in the 1970s and '80s, and who now continue to write in Russian while living in the West include: Georgi Vladimov (author of one of the best Soviet novels about young people, *Three Minutes Silence,* published in Moscow in 1968; Vasili Aksyonov, now in America; the satirist Vladimir Voinovich, whose *Life and Adventures of Private Ivan Chonkin* is available in English translation; and the poet Iosif Brodsky, a pupil of Anna Akhmatova, now writing in both Russian and English in the U.S.A. In 1987 Brodsky was awarded the Nobel Prize for literature.

Khrushchev and After

Notwithstanding the persecution of Pasternak, and of other, lesser, writers and artists, the Khrushchev era, with its illusion of a new literary emancipation, and its relaxation of police controls throughout society, saw a new flowering of literature. The poets Yevgeni Yevtushenko (b. 1933) and Andrei Voznesensky (b. 1934), who have strong affinities with the Futurists, declaimed in public to large audiences. Prose writers, on the whole, were less fortunate: the most original were rarely published. The period saw a remarkable revival of the tradition of satire, coupled often with surrealism, as in the work of Valery Tarsis (1906–83), Andrei Sinyavsky (b. 1925) and Yuli Daniel (b. 1925) (the latter two publishing in the West under the names of Terz and Arzhak). Yet this revival ended badly: Tarsis was confined in a mental hospital and Sinyavsky and Daniel, at a celebrated trial in 1966, were sentenced to long terms in labor camps. (Tarsis and, more recently, Sinyavsky came to settle in the West, while Daniel, after his release, still lives near Moscow.)

But by far the greatest figure has been fully in the tradition of Russian realism. None of Solzhenitsyn's major works, after *One Day . . . ,* has been published in the Soviet Union. *Cancer Ward* and *The First Circle,* like their predecessor, are both set against the background of the 1930s Purges. But they are far more than documents of one of the most extraordinary phases of history. The prisoners in the camp, or the patients in the cancer hospital, form a microcosm of society, with the difference that they are *in extremis:* they daily confront the worst in cynicism, in treachery, in suffering and in death. But, in spite of this, qualities of honor, generosity, self-sacrifice and love survive. Optimism is one of the most notable characteristics of Solzhenitsyn's work: a sense that for all the evil, for all the millions of wasted and broken existences, many tragic examples of which he describes in his massive historical documentary record of the labor camp, *The Gulag Archipelago,* human life is not in vain. Exiled in 1974, Solzhenitsyn has settled in the U.S.A. (Vermont), where he continues to write, and there are signs that his optimism has come to be based on a strong Orthodox religious belief while, politically, he was, until recently, increasingly pessimistic about the prospects for his country.

Comparatively little of the work of authors still living in Russia is published in translation in the West: but it should not be assumed that what they are writing for a Soviet readership is mere propaganda. There are many extremely talented men and women among the "official" Soviet authors. Moreover, despite the system of censorship through which all literary works must pass before publication is authorized, recent "official" fiction has included many scenes of "unofficial" daily life and much criticism of negative aspects of Soviet society. Speculation, bribery, hit-and-run drivers, hooliganism ending in group murder, poaching, cover-up's of all kinds—all these have figured in stories and novels published in the last ten years. The novelist Yuri Trifonov (died 1981) wrote with great insight of the mental stresses affecting intellectuals, particularly their feelings of guilt over the legacy of the Stalinist repressions. Characters in several recent novels have even included religious believers, often portrayed with considerable sympathy.

Some of the best writers are the so-called "country school" (*derevenshchiki*), whose stories are set in the Russian countryside and include much criticism of Soviet agricultural policy over the last forty years. Most of these writers are unknown outside their own country, but two who have been translated are Vasili Shukshin (died 1974) whose short-story heroes (like their author) are peasants who have to make the difficult transition to modern urban living; and Valentin Rasputin, who writes marvellous prose describing nature in his native Siberia, insistently drawing his readers' attention to problems of the environment, pointing out the damage men have been causing to forests and rivers in the cause of industrialisation.

The most widely-read books in the Soviet Union, as in the West, are found in the genres of detective and science fiction. Here the leading authors are two pairs of brothers: in crime fiction, Arkadi and Georgi Vainer; and in science fiction, Arkadi and Boris Strugatsky—the latter couple's books are well known in translation both in the U.S.A. and Germany. Finally, of the few current Soviet authors readily available in the West, perhaps the most interesting is the Kirghiz writer Chingiz Aitmatov. His books combine many strands: he often uses stories from folklore as parables with a contemporary political message, and he expresses not only Soviet but what might be called global patriotism, since he sees Russia's problems as closely linked with the fate of humanity as a whole. In his last book, *The day lasts more than a hundred years* (London 1983), Aitmatov weaves the story of an honest Kazakh working man into the framework of an imaginary Soviet-American joint space exploration—and draws some moral conclusions about the need for international cooperation. This book, with its mixture of folk legend, contemporary life and fantasy, would be an excellent introduction to Soviet literature for any tourist about to visit the U.S.S.R.

THE LIVELY ARTS

by
HILARY STERNBERG, RICHARD TAYLOR
AND JOHN FINCHLEY

The lively arts are easily the most approachable of all Russian creative art forms. This is partly because they are frequently performed in the same programs as "Western" works, making them seem less remote. Music by Tchaikovsky is part of the standard concert repertoire of all Western orchestras; plays by Chekhov and Turgenev appear regularly on most Western stages; the films of Eisenstein are among the greatest classics of all cinematic art; the classic ballets—again to the music of Tchaikovsky—*Swan Lake* and *The Sleeping Beauty* are the cornerstones of nearly every dance company in the West. But these are the mountain peaks of Russian performing art. Below them lie whole vistas of creative countryside, much of it little known outside the borders of the Soviet Union, rarely translated, not often played. These vistas, though, contain much that would open a new understanding of the country's past and its present way of life. All it needs is searching out.

Music

You may be forgiven if the words "Russian music" conjure up a vision of the massed choirs of the Red Army accompanied at breakneck speed by an orchestra of three hundred ebullient balalaikas. They certainly are a part of the picture—but only a part. And you are more likely to see them abroad than in the U.S.S.R., for they are the "image" the Soviet Union likes to export, along with its top ballet companies, conductors, singers and instrumentalists. These people are, however, more than mere musical ambassadors; they have a remarkable popularity and following in their own country, too. The Russians are a music-loving people, and the visitor will be struck at once by the quantity and variety of musical entertainment, the relative cheapness of tickets, and the size and enthusiasm of audiences.

Music in Russia goes back to very ancient origins. In many ways, its development parallels that of Russian literature. Both are facets of a culture that has always been intensely influenced by social and political circumstances. Because of the centuries of geographical and political isolation of the Russian state, punctuated by periods of officially encouraged "Westernization" (under Peter the Great, for example), Russian music has been either entirely reliant upon native folk tradition and Orthodox Church conventions, or suddenly subjected to bouts of imported influence from abroad, whether Italian vocal style or German counterpoint. It was not until the 19th century, at about the same time as the flowering of Russian literature, that a national Russian music came into being.

Slavonic folk music can be traced back long before the birth of Christ. Many of its themes are pagan and relate to old Slav mythology, rituals and ancient festivals. There are wedding songs, funeral songs, and harvest songs. In its purest form, Russian folk music tends to use the natural minor and major modes; present day arrangements have modified and Westernized some harmonies, but the distinctive features of the melodic line remain. When Kievan Russia was converted to Christianity in A.D. 988, Greek and Bulgarian chant was introduced, but later, Russian forms of the Byzantine chant have acquired a Slavonic character and sometimes use Russian modes.

Kievan Russia was closely linked with Byzantium and absorbed much ecclesiastical and secular culture. Music played an important ceremonial and entertaining role in court life. Those were the days of the *skomorokhi,* wandering minstrels and court buffoons, who appear in many Russian operas (Rimsky-Korsakov's *Snow Maiden* is an example). The balalaika, the triangular stringed instrument now so popular, only dates back to the 19th century, while the guitar and accordion used widely today were introduced even later. Early Russian folk music employed a whole range of bowed, plucked and wind instruments; some of them were of oriental provenance, like the 16th-century *domra,* a forerunner of the balalaika, which is still played today in India and elsewhere. A very ancient stringed instrument often mentioned in folk epics and ballads is the *gusli,* which the minstrels used to accompany their songs. Sadko, the 12th-century merchant from Novgorod, celebrated in a medieval ballad (*bylina*), reputedly played his gusli for three days and three nights to placate the Sea King when a storm threatened to wreck his 30 red ships laden with rich wares.

With the growth of the Muscovite state in the period between the 14th and 17th centuries Moscow was hailed as the "Third Rome" and the Church became the dominant influence. In the mid-17th century, the Patriarch of Moscow even ordered the destruction of all folk instruments that could be found in the city. The *skomorokhi,* now regarded as an evil, pagan influence, were forced to flee into the countryside.

Western Influence

By this time a new, urban, Western European culture was developing, and Moscow was acquiring cultural ties as travelers visited Europe and Europeans came to settle in Moscow, foreign musicians among them. In 1586, incidentally, the English Queen Elizabeth I had made a gift of a gilded clavichord to the czar's wife and, according to the description by the English envoy, crowds gathered in their thousands round the palace windows to hear the novel sound. In the mid-17th century, European musical notation was finally adopted—until then a variety of inconsistent and now only partly decipherable systems had been in use in Russia.

In the early 18th century Czar Peter the Great, who professed a great admiration for things European, introduced many Western features into Russia in his determination that his country should not lag behind. German musicians were employed at court and many wealthy nobles followed suit and hired private musicians to play in their homes. By the 1740's, Italian opera was well established in the new capital, St. Petersburg, and there were even resident foreign composers. It was at this time, too, that the first native soloists of repute emerged, and with them, Russian craftsmen—the violins of Ivan Batov (born 1767) were reckoned among the finest in the world.

In the 18th century a large scale revival of interest in folk music (by then contaminated by "urban" harmonies) led to the first methodical compilations of folk song collections. These were to prove very important to the first native composers, who made extensive use of folk material, either by way of direct quotation, or, later, by more subtle composition in the folk idiom. The first Russian operas date from the late 18th century and tend to be, musically, something of a hotchpotch, and dramatically primitive. They did, however, start a fashion for using Russian folklore that was to continue right through the 19th century and produce some of the greatest Russian operatic and orchestral music.

Glinka

It was not until the early 19th century that there came a composer of real stature who was able to transcend the melodramatic and fuse the folk idiom with an accomplished, professional technique and a classical feeling for melodic and harmonic flow, and to create an end product that was not simply a pastiche. He was Mikhail Glinka (1804–57), whose sense of balance and form, general sophistication and indeed innovation have been compared with those of the poet Alexander Pushkin. If the latter formulated the basis of a modern literary language, Glinka did the same for Russian music. Glinka is chiefly remembered for his two operas, based on folklore and historical legend, *Ivan Susanin or A Life for the Czar* (1836) and *Ruslan and Ludmila* (1842), both of which are still performed today. He also wrote many orchestral and chamber works and a large quantity of piano music and songs. The Russian "romance," the lyrical, sentimental or passionate song, also developed with Glinka, and he was one of the first to introduce exotic and oriental material from Turkey, Persia, Arabia and the Caucasus, and to suggest oriental effects by the use of what were then unusual orchestral combinations, including nasal wind instruments (cor anglais and oboe).

A lesser-known, younger, contemporary of Glinka's was Alexander Dargomyzhsky (1813–69). He too composed an opera based on folk legend (*Rusalka,* 1848). Greatly influenced by Glinka, he exercised considerable influence in his turn upon the embryonic Russian "nationalist" school of music. Some of his later music, particularly his opera *The Stone Guest* (1868), a setting of Pushkin's poem, was, by the standards of the day, quite revolutionary, making use of vocal and instrumental motifs that anticipate Wagner, and attempting to reproduce the inflections of human speech. It was completely misunderstood by many critics.

"The Mighty Handful"

The 19th century was one of social, cultural and political ferment, and also of unprecedented fertility in the arts. Naturally, music was somewhat less affected than other cultural fields by philosophical and political argument. Nevertheless, there was a rough division in the musical world between the Westernizing, pro-European Anton Rubinstein, a confirmed supporter of Teutonicism in music; middle-of-the-road Tchaikovsky; and the nationalist, Slavophile, school represented by a group of young composers known collectively as "The Mighty Handful" or "The Five:" Balakirev (1836–1910), Borodin (1833–87), Cui (1833–1918), Mussorgsky (1839–81) and Rimsky-Korsakov (1844–1908). United by their admiration for Glinka and his musical principles, The Five were an extraordinary musical phenomenon—a group of musicians who began largely as amateurs untrained in either instrumental technique or formal musical composition. Under the tutelage of Balakirev, the only one among them to have received some semblance of a professional training (the other four were a chemist, an army engineer, a guards officer and a naval cadet), these men composed some of the finest 19th-century Russian music. Often they composed jointly, suggesting themes and libretti, and criticizing each other's work. Had it not been for the efforts of Rimsky-Korsakov in particular, Mussorgsky's opera *Boris Godunov* and Borodin's *Prince Igor* might never have been completed in the form in which we know them today.

The Five met with a good deal of criticism and direct opposition from the musical establishment of the day, but eventually won recognition. Rimsky-Korsakov went on to become professor at the St. Petersburg Conservatory in 1871 and conductor of the Russian Symphony concerts in 1886–1900. As professor, he taught many young musicians who were later to become the first generation of 20th-century and Soviet composers, including Lyadov, Ippolitov-Ivanov, Grechaninov, Glazunov, Stravinsky and Prokofiev. Balakirev played a leading part in founding the Free School of Music in 1862, an institution which did much to promote the works of The Five and also the music of Berlioz, Schumann and, later, Liszt. A detailed list of the works of The Five is beyond the scope of this chapter. Their main feature, however, is the use of folk motifs from all over Russia and from more exotic lands (for instance, Balakirev's oriental fantasy *Islamey,* Borodin's *In the Steppes of Central Asia,* a musical picture; Rimsky-Korsakov's *Sheherazade;* and perhaps the most well-known piece by Borodin, the *Polovtsian Dances* from *Prince Igor*).

Mussorgsky developed away from the rather romantic orchestrations of his mentor Balakirev and embarked upon a new, realistic style best exemplified in his piano suite *Pictures from an Exhibition* (1874), in which he attempts to depict himself strolling through an exhibition of water colors by his friend Victor Hartmann, whose death the music commemorated. His historical opera *Boris Godunov* (1868–72) was an even further cry from the early days of The Five; its unusual, sometimes stark harmonies, powerful historical atmosphere and massive scale were an entirely new departure in the field. Indeed, much of Mussorgsky's music was more original and ahead of its time than his contemporaries knew. You can see *Boris Godunov* today at the Bolshoi Theater in Moscow; it is one of the most exciting spectacles, both musically and visually, that you are likely to experience during your visit.

Tchaikovsky

Before leaving the 19th century, a word should be said about Tchaikovsky (1840–93), perhaps the best known and most loved Russian composer. You will find his music played all over the Soviet Union today, whether at the Bolshoi or Kirov Ballets or in the countless concert halls. His operas and ballets are lavishly produced and beautifully performed—they are not to be missed! A very personal composer, and a master of brilliant orchestration and rhythm, Tchaikovsky was able to express the whole gamut of emotions from the despair of his *Symphony No. 6 (Pathétique)* to the exuberance of his *1812 Overture* and the passion of the *Romeo and Juliet Fantasy Overture.* His best known opera, *Eugene Onegin,* is a firm favorite in the Bolshoi repertoire, and his great ballets are performed the world over.

A group of composers who form a bridge between the 19th and 20th centuries include Ippolitov-Ivanov (1859–1936), Glière (1875–1956), who was essentially a classical Russian composer although his life spans the first 40 years of Soviet power, and the solitary, mystically-inclined Alexander Scriabin (1872–1915), whose *Poem of Ecstasy* frequently figures in Western concerts. (Scriabin's nephew was also famous, in the political field however—he was Vyacheslav Molotov, Stalin's long-time Foreign Minister.)

The Bolshevik Revolution in 1917 led to a complete break in the continuity of musical development, especially after the first few years of relatively free experimentation. Many composers and musicians, old and young, emigrated. They included Medtner, Grechaninov, Glazunov, Rachmaninov, Cherepnin, Prokofiev and Stravinsky—and the singer Chaliapin. Of these, only Prokofiev returned, in 1936, after a series of visits. Some of these émigré composers were not played or even mentioned for many years in their homeland. Stravinsky in particular was designated the archvillain of them all, and it was not until the relatively liberal 1960s that he returned to the Soviet Union.

Socialist Realism and the Present

By 1932, the new criteria in all the arts, music included, were those of "socialist realism:" patriotism, comprehensibility and accessibility to the masses. This entailed self-imposed isolation from contemporary Western musical experimentation in such fields as dodecaphonic, serial music and musique concrète (in much the same way as abstract art was shunned). Nevertheless, some composers with genuine talent have emerged within these limitations: Nikolai Myaskovsky, for instance, the most prolific Soviet symphonist (he had 27 to his credit when he died in 1950 at the age of 69). Among the few really individual and controversial Soviet composers are Sergei Prokofiev (1891–1953), many of whose works were not played until recently in Russia, and Dmitri Shostakovich (1906–75), who earned a worldwide reputation and now ranks as a great, if uneven, 20th-century symphonic composer. (Shostakovich has the unique distinction of being the only Soviet composer to be awarded an honorary doctorate by Oxford University.) An opera *The Nose,* composed in 1927–28 by the young Shostakovich, was successfully revived in 1979 by London's English National Opera. Based on Gogol's short story, it was first performed in 1930 but was withdrawn after controversial reviews and official disfavour.

There are well over 1500 listed members of the official Union of Composers. Among them, Aram Khachaturian (1903–78) and Dmitri Kabalevsky (1904–87) are known abroad, though their output has been on a lesser, more superficial scale and cannot be compared to the creative individuality of Prokofiev or Shostakovich. Concerts usually include at least one work by a Soviet composer.

Light music and variety concerts are plentiful, and performances by Western pop and rock groups are becoming more frequent. A Moscow sensation in the early 1980s, which later played in Paris and on television in the West, was the U.S.S.R.'s first officially staged rock opera, *Juno and Perchance,* with lyrics by poet Andrei Voznesensky and music, by Alexei Rybnikov, somewhat in the style of *Jesus Christ Superstar*—a blend of hard rock, folk, and Orthodox Church chant.

The visitor who wishes to enjoy the best of Soviet music-making should come for one of the annual music festivals. There is the "Moscow Stars" festival held each May in the capital; the "White Nights," a celebration of the long summer nights in the north (Leningrad, each June); and the "Russian Winter," a New Year festival in Moscow (December 25–January 5). At these festivities you can see and hear the finest folk music and dance ensembles from many of the Soviet republics; the Moscow Chamber Orchestra, the Leningrad Symphony Orchestra, the Kirov Opera and Ballet, the Bolshoi Opera and Ballet, and the finest conductors and soloists. Don't miss the Tchaikovsky Piano Competition in Moscow, at which some of the best young international talent as well as Russia's up-and-coming pianists may be heard.

Tickets for most things can—and preferably *should*—be booked through your hotel or an Intourist bureau.

Soviet records are inexpensive and of increasingly high quality.

Movies

Lenin once observed, "Of all the arts for us the cinema is the most important," and, despite the rapid growth of radio and television as media for communication and entertainment, cinema attendances in the Soviet Union continue to grow: with 572 cinemas per million people, the average Soviet citizen goes to the cinema 23 times a year.

The Russian cinema was in a parlous state when the Bolsheviks seized power in 1917. Before World War I, Russian films had been heavily dependent on foreign capital and raw materials and these supplies had now dried up. During the Civil War that followed the October Revolution, many people active in the cinema fled abroad, taking their much-needed skills, and often even their equipment, with them. In August 1919, the remains of the film industry were nationalized and the world's first state film school was established in Moscow to train new actors and technicians.

The cinema was regarded as a vital weapon in the struggle to unify the country; as the silent film was not hampered by the restrictions of language or the written word, it was ideally suited for the task of propagating Bolshevik ideology to the illiterate and multinational masses. Poets and painters lent their talents; from their midst emerged Eisenstein, formerly a stage designer. His films (*Strike, Battleship Potemkin, October*) characterize the heroic era of the Soviet silent cinema and blazed a trail across the world. He was not, however, alone; equally important, if less well-known, directors from this period include Pudovkin and Dovzhenko, and the documentary film-makers, Vertov and Shub. All their films were strongly visual, full of powerful revolutionary imagery aimed at the masses. But it was not until 1927 that the Soviet Union was able itself to produce the majority of films shown in its cinemas; Mary Pickford and Charlie Chaplin had been the real popular heroes.

With the advent of sound, which reached the U.S.S.R. several years later than the West, the spontaneous exuberance of the '20s gave way to a stale conformism. The dead hand of Stalinism had fallen; the crudest propaganda films date from the Stalin period and include *Peter the First, Lenin in October* and *The Rainbow.* These films are no longer shown; they now seem as dated to a Soviet audience as they would to its Western counterpart. But even at the height of the purges, some films still managed to display a subtle complexity; Eisenstein's two sound masterpieces, *Alexander Nevsky* and *Ivan the Terrible* may be overtly propagandist, but they are at the same time covertly subversive.

In the years since 1956 there has been a general relaxation. The state still controls all branches of the cinema: production, distribution and exhibition. It can thus determine what is produced and what is shown. In addition to an extensive chain of conventional cinemas, the Soviet Union has a larger number of projectors installed in youth clubs, workers' clubs and collective farms, as well as a network of traveling cinemas to serve the remoter areas such as Siberia. All this ensures blanket coverage of the entire country. But what kind of films do they show?

Nowadays the program in a Soviet cinema usually begins with the newsreel *Novosti dnya* (News of the day). Similar in style and structure to a Western newsreel, *Novosti dnya* concentrates on items like party functions, industrial output targets, the progress of the harvest and space or sporting triumphs. Negative news is never reported unless a moral can be drawn. The newsreel is often followed by one or more short films on similar topics, or the preservation of folklore or wild life; the aim is always to uplift the audience, never to depress it. Finally there comes the full-length feature film. The propaganda content in most current Soviet feature films is negligible; if it were otherwise, audiences would not go to see them—they sometimes only barely tolerate the newsreel and the shorts.

Long, but Not Always Boring

The Western viewer, however, should be warned that, in a country where time often seems to be on a different scale, length is no obstacle for the cinema audience. The pace of many Soviet films is therefore very slow by our standards; the classic examples are Sergei Bondarchuk's epic films *War and Peace* and *Waterloo,* with their extensive battle scenes. In its original four-part version, *War and Peace* lasted nearly 12 hours and was shown in sections on consecutive nights. More recently, the U.S.S.R. has produced a similar epic about World War II entitled *Liberation.* Apart from such epics, the Soviet cinema also excels at biographical and historical films and adaptations from literary classics. Amongst more recent films in the first categories, *Tchaikovsky, The Sixth of July, Andrei Rublev* and *Lenin in Poland* should be noted. Many of the adaptations are already known in the West; Kozintsev's film versions of *Hamlet* and *King Lear* have been widely acclaimed, as has Heifits' *The Lady with the Lap Dog,* but *The Seagull, A Nest of the Gentry,* and *The Brothers Karamazov* have also been successfully adapted to the screen. A film version of Goncharov's *Oblomov,* with a virtuoso role for actor Oleg Tabakov, was acclaimed in the West in 1981.

Soviet film-makers have recently begun to explore what are for them new fields: the detective film, the spy film and the science-fiction film. In the latter genre, Andrei Tarkovsky's superb *Solaris* and, recently, *The Stalker* must reign supreme. In 1982 he applied to work in the West, making *Nostalgia* in Italy in 1983. In 1984 he was stripped of his Soviet citizenship. He died, aged 54, in 1986, shortly after the release of his award-winning *The Sacrifice.* In the new, less repressive climate in the Soviet Union, the official press paid tribute.

Colorful folk customs are sometimes used as a basis for films. The Hutsuls, a Slav tribe of great antiquity, were lyrically portrayed by the Armenian director Paradzanov in *Shadows of Our Forgotten Ancestors.* His second major film, *The Color of Pomegranates* (1969), was shown abroad in 1982 to great acclaim. It is a historical work celebrating Georgian and Armenian cultural traditions and filled with religious imagery. One of the Soviet Union's most original film-makers, Paradzanov has served more than one period of imprisonment for his artistic and personal unorthodoxy, most recently in 1982–83 on a charge of homosexuality (still illegal in the U.S.S.R.). In 1985 his newest film *Legend of Suram Fortress,* based on an Armenian folk myth, was shown at the Moscow Film Festival.

Recently, the Soviet cinema has become a little freer in its social criticism. Films such as Vadim Abdrashitov's *A Train Stopped,* Yuli Raizman's *Private Life,* Nikolai Gubenko's *Life, Tears and Love,* and Sergei Mikaelyan's *Love by Request* show a society that is a great deal less perfect, and consequently a lot more human and credible, than the moralistic, utopian visions of not so long ago. Also worth seeing is the lively, witty *Jazzmen,* Shakhnazarov's story of Russia's first jazz band, formed in Odessa in the 1920s. Partly based on the lives of Russian jazz pioneers, it has some wonderful music and evokes a golden age of color and humor. In 1986–87, a remarkable film by Tengiz Abuladze called *Repentance,* released with official approval, dealt frankly with the horrors of life during Stalin's purges. *The Cold Summer of 1953,* released in 1988 to rave press reviews, is reportedly the first film shown in the U.S.S.R. about political prisoners and the victims of the Stalin camps.

There is now a film studio in every one of the 15 union republics, producing films in the local languages and cultural traditions.

The Soviet film industry has been co-producing films with Western countries for over a decade. *Tchaikovsky* resulted from a collaboration with the Americans, *Waterloo* with the Italians, and *The Red Tent,* with Peter Finch, from a similar arrangement with the British. A recent Soviet-Mexican-Italian production is *Red Bells* an "alternative" version of the

John Reed story filmed as *Reds* on this side of the Curtain! The co-production, *The Divine Anna* (1983), a biography of the legendary ballerina Anna Pavlova, a joint Soviet, British and French venture, was shot in six countries using actors from all of them. The British contingent included the unlikely combination of Bruce Forsyth, James Fox and Roy Kinnear! Next in line is a Soviet-French co-production of Victor Hugo's *Notre Dame de Paris*. Nevertheless the U.S.S.R. imports few Western films for general exhibition. Some are films which show Western society in a negative light, such as *If*. Then there are occasional musicals like *West Side Story* or *My Fair Lady*. In tourist centres at the height of the season there is now quite a wide choice of uncontroversial foreign viewing. Many other foreign films are given only a restricted release; on the one hand, Indian flesh-and-blood epics are imported for distribution in Central Asia, on the other, the products of the European avant-garde are shown only to restricted audiences.

Theater

The first recorded theatrical performance in Russia took place in 1662, but it was during the reign of Peter the Great (1682–1725) that the theater, like so many other Western fashions and institutions, first entered Russian life. Though the first theatrical companies in the country were foreign, it was not long before native performers emerged.

So popular, indeed, did the theater become among the upper classes of Russia that, in parallel with the development of distinguished metropolitan theaters in St. Petersburg and Moscow, many landowners began to set up theaters on their own estates, using their serfs as actors. The serf theater, which reached its climax in the first half of the 19th century, became a major feature of Russian provincial life and produced a number of most distinguished actors and actresses who later gained their freedom and became stars of the Petersburg stage.

Until the mid-18th century all the plays produced in Russia were foreign, but the country was not slow to produce its own dramatists. Alexander Sumarokov (1718–77) is generally recognized as the first Russian playwright. Denis Fonvizin (1745–92) was the first native dramatist to move on from mere imitation of foreign models. His satire *The Minor* is still sometimes performed in the Soviet Union. The first Russian play of real literary importance was *Woe from Wit* by Alexander Griboedov (1795–1829). A perceptive satire on the contemporary Russian scene, many of its pithy lines have remained in the language.

The great Russian writers of the Romantic period, Alexander Pushkin and Mikhail Lermontov, both wrote plays. The former's *Boris Godunov* (later set to music as Mussorgsky's opera of the same name), and the latter's *Masquerade* both display the hold exercised by Shakespeare over their authors. But the drama of great conflicts and isolated heroes, so typical of Romanticism, gave way by mid-century to more mundane themes, to the depiction of particularly Russian characters and situations and to the cult of realism which similarly characterized the contemporary novel.

Gogol's plays, of which *The Inspector General* is the best known, with their memorable (if caricatured) characters, their apparent humor and underlying pathos, are of a piece with his novels, as is Turgenev's *A Month in the Country.* The first Russian professional playwright, whose nearly 50 works have remained the backbone of the repertoire of the Russian theater, was Alexander Ostrovsky (1823–86). His work represents the high point of realism on the stage: both characters and dialogue are drawn, unaltered and unembroidered, straight from life. In his earlier works he was content to depict, and to satirize, the contemporary scene, and especially the world of the materialistic Moscow merchant class. But his later plays, *The Ward* and *The Thunderstorm* in particular, were written in a more gloomy and pessimistic vein, and show up the human misery under the surface of respectable society.

Chekhov

Turgenev and Ostrovsky both influenced the greatest of Russian dramatists, Anton Chekhov (1860–1904). His major plays, *Ivanov, The Seagull, Uncle Vanya, The Three Sisters* and *The Cherry Orchard,* have been variously interpreted as tragedy and as comedy, as reflecting a negative, individualistic and essentially despairing view of life, and as looking beyond the apparent frustration of their characters to a more glorious future. In truth, Chekhov's plays seem imbued with a stoical acceptance of the irony of life. His characters are both conscious of the brevity of existence, and bored with it; time is painfully limited and yet hangs heavy on their hands. Only occasionally does this sense of futility appear to be challenged: usually by the incursion of love with its new and sudden, if fleeting, conviction of purpose and hopes; or, as with Colonel Vershinin in *The Three Sisters,* by dreams of a new and better life.

Though all such aspirations seem but pathetic self-delusions, doomed to final frustration, Chekhov is remarkable in that, having analyzed the human condition with such uncompromising directness and honesty, he does not draw his characters with cynicism or contempt, but rather with a warm sympathy that is greater for the excision of the pretensions and illusions with which men generally seek to give significance to their lives.

Chekhov's reputation was made in his own day largely by the performances of his works staged at the newly-founded Moscow Arts Theater by Konstantin Stanislavsky (1863–1938). Stanislavsky, the foremost exponent of realism in the theater, who insisted on strict authenticity of scenery and costume and taught his actors to "live" their parts, has left a permanent mark on the Russian stage and, indeed on the Western theater through the Method School of acting, an offshoot of his theories. Chekhov himself frequently quarreled with his "slice of life" and generally tragic interpretations of his plays, which he considered failed to catch some of their nuances of irony and comedy. Maxim Gorky's *The Lower Depths,* set in a doss house, provided the ideal material for Stanislavsky's technique, and its first production at the Moscow Arts Theater in 1902 was one of the latter's great triumphs.

Stanislavsky's most talented pupil, Vsevolod Meyerhold (1874–1940), took an entirely different direction, turning his back on realism and abolishing the conventional stage set altogether. He became the interpreter of Futurist drama, and his name is as closely linked with the first performances of Mayakovsky's *The Bedbug* and *The Bathhouse* as that of Stanislavsky is linked with Chekhov.

Experimentalism of the type of Meyerhold came to an end with the cult of "Socialist realism" during the 1930s (Meyerhold himself was arrested in 1937 and shot in 1940). The Soviet theater, so alive and influential during the first quarter of the new century, became largely monopolized, so far as new works were concerned, by propagandist works by Nikolai Pogodin (1900–62), Konstantin Simonov (1915–60) and others. Mikhail Bulgakov, whose *The Days of the Turbins* had enjoyed much success in the 1920's, under Stalin wrote plays on the lives of Molière and Pushkin, and dramatized Gogol's *Dead Souls.*

Since the death of Stalin, and more particularly since 1960, the Soviet theater has seen a revival, less in the quality of new plays being staged than in the variety, originality and talent with which classical, contemporary and foreign works are produced. Moscow presents a range of styles of production as wide as New York and wider than London or Paris. In the place of the ephemeral drawing-room comedies or romantic musicals of the West, the Soviet stage displays a high proportion of earnest propagandistic works. But the visitor to Moscow can still see virtuoso acting performances in the Stanislavsky manner in productions of Chekhov at the Moscow Arts Theater, while the modern-dress tradition of Meyerhold lives on in full vigor at the Sovremennik and Taganka theaters, the latter famous for its striking productions of Shakespeare (using the Pasternak translation), of Brecht, and of daring contemporary plays including the unexpectedly popular *Rush Hour.* The Rustaveli Theater, from Tbilisi, the Georgian capital, have also won international acclaim for their boldly experimental productions. In 1986 the Chernobyl nuclear accident was dramatized by Pravda's Science Editor, Vladimir Gubarev. The play makes scathing criticisms of the authorities' handling of the disaster. Soviet theater is entering a new, experimental period, and Moscow theaters are now among the most exciting and creative venues East or West.

Ballet

Ballet in the 20th century has been inextricably linked with Russia, but the art form did not start there. It was introduced from France during the great period of Westernization which began in the last decades of the 17th century and continued throughout the 18th. The first ballet performance in Russia—perhaps it would be more accurate to refer to the first formal dance spectacle—was staged at the Russian court by Czar Alexei in 1672. Empress Anna founded the Imperial School of Ballet in St. Petersburg in 1738.

The ballet during all this period had drawn its inspiration from the West. It first became an innovative force of its own with the arrival in 1801 of Charles Didelot (1769–1837), a refugee from the French Revolution. With an interval during Napoleon's invasion of Russia, Didelot was to remain, and to dominate the ballet in his newly adopted country, for 30 years. He was responsible for three decisive innovations: the use of the *pointes* (the tips of the toes), the development of the *pas de deux* as a "conversation" between two dancers, and the introduction of expressive dancing, inspired by Caucasian and Russian folk dancing, with which he abandoned the courtly and classical dance of the 18th century in favor of a figurative and dramatic style more in tune with the spirit of the contemporary Romantic movement. Under Didelot's pupil, Aram Glouzhkovski, who became its director in 1811, these tendencies were still further developed in Moscow's Bolshoi Ballet (founded in 1776).

The long career of Marius Petipa (1819–1910), who came to Russia as a dancer from his native France in 1847 and who remained as chief choreographer of the Imperial Ballet, spans the Romantic and the modern ages. It was he more than anyone who introduced the great sense of spectacle, and the cult of the virtuoso solo part, that have remained features of the Russian ballet to this day. Together with his deputy Lev Ivanov (1834–1901), he was responsible for the choreography of all the major ballets of Tchaikovsky, still the foundation of the repertoires of all Russian companies—and indeed many Western ones–*Sleeping Beauty* (1890), *The Nutcracker* (1892), and *Swan Lake* (1895). Their choreographies combined a unity of dance and music that marked a return to the precepts of classicism and a lyricism and taste for the spectacular that were the legacy of the Romantic Movement.

While Petipa and Ivanov dominated the St. Petersburg ballet in their day, a rather different direction was taken by Moscow's Bolshoi under the leadership of Alexander Gorsky (1871–1924). Gorsky was the pioneer of realism in the ballet, the counterpart of his contemporary Stanislavsky, whom he much admired, in the theater. His choreography was designed to achieve the dramatization of character and plot; his *corps de ballet* acquired individual dancing roles, so that his crowds appeared as collections of living people. In the 20th century, he abandoned some of his concern with the representation of real life and fell under the influence of Isadora Duncan, with her ideas of free self-expression in dancing, which he did much to popularize in Russia. Gorsky's influence, both on Fokine and the Ballets Russes, and on the "socialist realist" style of the Soviet period, was profound.

Diaghilev

The fantasy and the spectacle of the St. Petersburg tradition, and the dramatic legacy of Moscow, were both evident in the Ballet Russe (founded by Sergei Diaghilev, 1872–1929), which has had a decisive and permanent influence on the development of the art. Determined to evolve a new art form, in which dancing, painting and music would be inseparably combined, Diaghilev brought together a most remarkable group of choreographers, dancers and artists. He employed, in succession, the choreographers Mikhail Fokine (1880–1942), Leonid Massine (1894–1979), Bronislava Nijinskaya (1891–1972) and George Balanchine (1904–83); the dancers Anna Pavlova (1882–1931) and Vatslav Nijinsky (1890–1950)—to name only two immortals—and artists, who were responsible for the sets, of the caliber of Leon Bakst, Alexander Benois, Natalia Goncharova, Derain and Picasso.

Diaghilev's choreographers differed in many ways. But they were alike in their rejection both of the conventions and artificialities of classical ballet and of heavy-handed realism; their assertion of the role of the vigorous male dancer; and their insistence on natural movement. Consistent with his role as a founder member of the "World of Art Society," Diaghilev devoted himself to the creation of his new art for its own sake, permitting no extraneous didactic or literary preoccupations to enter his work. His objective was simply to excite in his audiences a pure—and quite novel—esthetic emotion. For the same reason, he avoided figurative representation in his stage sets, granting full rein to the imaginations of the leading artists he employed, the sensual effects of whose works were to complement those of the dancing and the music.

As for the music, Fokine achieved some notable successes with the work of earlier composers including Tchaikovsky, Chopin (in *Les Sylphides*) and Schumann (in *Carnaval*). But Diaghilev's choreographers were most at home, and his productions most original and striking, when they employed contemporary music. The Ballet Russe made use of many modern composers, including Debussy (*L'Après-Midi d'un Faune*), Ravel (*Daphnis and Chloe*) and, above all, Stravinsky (*Petrushka, The Firebird, The Rite of Spring*). The combination of unfamiliar harmonies and daring rhythm, the exotic and fantastic colors and designs of the scenery, and the uninhibited, sometimes primitive, force of the dancing combined to produce a pantheistic festival of modernism that stunned the Europe of the pre-1914 years. Diaghilev transformed the ballet into a major art form, and brought it a cosmopolitan recognition that it has never lost.

The October Revolution condemned the Diaghilev Ballet to permanent exile, and though some of its greatest successes date from the 1920s, its history no longer belongs to that of the Russian ballet. Diaghilev's two youngest choreographers, Balanchine and Sergei Lifar, have had a dominating influence on the development of ballet in the West during the remainder of the 20th century, Lifar in France (where he died in 1986), and Balanchine in America. The latter, as director of the New York City Ballet until his death in 1983, was the pioneer of the abstract approach to the art which perhaps represents the major contribution to it of the mid-20th century.

Soviet Spectacle

Paradoxically enough the Diaghilev ballet had less influence in Russia itself since 1917 than it had in the West. The 19th-century ballet of Petipa with its emphasis on spectacle, and the ideas of Gorsky, and specially the latter's insistence that his performers should act as well as dance, have been the models chiefly followed. This approach achieved its greatest successes in the 1930s and 1940s, with the works of Leonid Lavrovsky (b. 1905) and in particular with his *Romeo and Juliet* (1940), set to Prokofiev's music and with the great ballerina Galina Ulanova (b. 1910) in the title role. Lavrovsky's production aimed to transmit through the dancing the full dramatic impact of the original play.

As in literature and in art, the 1920s had been a period of experimentation in the Soviet ballet, inspired by the contemporary Futurist and Constructivist movements. Kassian Goleizovsky (b. 1892) had tried to break away entirely from the lyricism and harmony of traditional ballet, as well as from its technical conventions, with his introduction of acrobatic effects. But this interval was not to last. With the 1930s ballet, in common with the other arts, was brought under strict Party surveillance and control. Leading figures whose productions were approved, including Lavrovsky, continued to be allowed relative freedom of expression. But the guidelines for young choreographers and composers were clearly set out: ballet must serve a useful social purpose, its aim should be to tell an uplifting story, to point a moral, above all to adopt a realistic idiom which would be immediately comprehensible to every audience. One of the pioneering works in the style, *Flames of Paris* (1932), on the theme of the

French Revolution, with music by Asafyev and choreography by Vai-nonen, is still one of the stock works of Soviet repertoires.

But it should not be thought that socialist realism has produced only propagandistic and inferior works. Indeed, the style has been the major contribution of the Soviet Union to the development of ballet during recent decades. Among leading examples of the genre are *Spartacus* (1956; music by Khachaturian, original choreography by Jacobson) and *Icarus* (1971).

The Soviet ballet of today shows undiminished vigor. There are 33 companies in 31 cities (Moscow and Leningrad have two companies each, including, respectively, the Bolshoi and the Kirov—among the foremost in the world). But the great tradition of technical mastery, spectacle and lyricism inaugurated by Petipa remains, and nowhere in the world are classical interpretations of the ballets of Tchaikovsky better performed than by the Bolshoi and the Kirov. The Russian ballet also retains its reputation for the power of its virtuoso male dancers, one of the characteristics for which the Diaghilev Ballet Russe was famed: Vasiliev, the male lead at the Bolshoi, Nureyev, his Kirov predecessor, and Baryshnikov, who is currently stunning Western audiences with his vivid portrayals, are all fully in this tradition.

In contemporary choreography, modernism, abstraction and the concept of dance as pure movement continue to be rejected. Instead—and most happily for the variety of ballet, and for the world—the Soviet Union has continued to explore the theatrical possibilities of the medium. The requirement that every production should convey a crude ideological message has been relaxed, but Soviet ballets still tell a story. As a result, Russian performers retain their reputation for combining technical mastery with the power to convey human emotion and character, and a dramatic sense of pathos or excitement. Good examples of this approach have been provided by two of the great successes of the Bolshoi, both written by Rodion Shchedrin for his wife, Maya Plisetskaya; the ballerina-actress *par excellence:* the *Carmen Suite* (first performed 1967) and *Anna Karenina* (first performed 1972).

One of the most striking of recent ballets is *The Golden Age.* Although it has an apparently conservative ideological theme ("communist youth emerges triumphant from a conflict with decadent capitalistic society"), this reworking by the Bolshoi's talented artistic director Yury Grigorovich of the 1930's ballet to Shostakovich's music shows a new daring, including sensuous scenes from the cabaret and nightclub world, with sexy chorus girls and a voluptuous siren danced by Tatiana Golikova. The Bolshoi's recent tours abroad have shown Western audiences a new generation of ballet stars.

FOOD AND DRINK

by
GABRIELLE TOWNSEND

"Russian cooking? Well, there's borshch, and chicken Kiev and . . . beef
Stroganov . . . and . . . " How many people could name more Russian
dishes than that, or even claim to have tasted an authentic version of these?
The cooking of the Soviet Union—the real cooking—is pretty unfamiliar
to us in the West, and those who haven't traveled there or at least sampled
Russian cooking in the home of émigré friends won't have any idea of its
richness and variety. Sadly, we know only the two or three dishes that
have passed into the depersonalized repertory of international restaurant
cuisine and in the process lost all their authentic flavor.

You may doubt that in a monolithic, utilitarian society such as the
U.S.S.R. there can be any time or inclination for such frivolous activities
as creative cookery or gourmet eating. It would be understandable if the
periods of privation and austerity to which the Russians have been subjected at many times in their history had killed their culinary traditions completely. Gratifyingly, as the interested tourist will discover, this isn't true
at all. (After all, music and ballet flourish, and *they're* not utilitarian!) And
the general level of prosperity in the U.S.S.R., despite the occasional shortage of certain commodities, is probably higher now than at any time in
the past.

Having said this, we must admit that it's not always easy to find the
best cooking. The kind of food you'll eat from day to day depends on several factors: the category of accommodations you've reserved, the area of

123

the U.S.S.R. you're staying in, the season, and whether you have Russian friends or acquaintances who will invite you into their homes or show you their favorite restaurants.

Since your hotels and most of your meals are probably prepaid, you may not have a lot of choice; unless you're in the deluxe class (and possibly even then) you may find your daily fare rather monotonous, except in some of the newer hotels which offer Scandinavian-style fare. Hotel meal-times are similar to ours in the West (outside hotels they tend to be more chaotic, random and prolonged). In hotels dinner is usually served from around 7 to 8 or 8.30 and it may be difficult to get a hot meal later in the evening. Breakfast will be tea or coffee with bread, butter and jam or cheese and perhaps cold meat as well; lunch is soup, meat or fish and dessert, and dinner the same. Meat in hotels tends to be served in a thick sauce, garnished with sour cream and dill and accompanied by mashed potatoes or perhaps *kasha,* a kind of buckwheat gruel. What you're most likely to miss, if you're staying in Moscow and the north, is fresh fruit and vegetables. They are often in short supply and pickled vegetables, particularly red cabbage and cucumber, are much used instead. But if you go down to the south, to the Crimea or Georgia, you'll see lush, delicious vegetables and fruits aplenty—huge golden watermelons, green beans, big ripe tomatoes, purple grapes and plums ripening to sweetness in the southern sun.

Regional Specialties

The Soviet Union is, as we have already said, not one country, but a federation of 15 republics, each with its own climate, natural features, language and culture. Though the Moscow administration and centralization have destroyed some of the republics' individuality certain things survive intact; especially language, costume and cooking. Indeed, people seem to cherish them all the more: the regional restaurants in Moscow are immensely popular and very good. (You'll find more about regional food in the chapters dealing with the different areas of the U.S.S.R., but if you don't have time to visit all the places, you can at least get a taste of what they're like from the representative restaurant. It's the best way to vary your meals if you're tired of hotel food.)

You can try chicken *tabaka* in a Georgian restaurant, *shashlik* from the Caucasus, *pilaff* in an Uzbek restaurant, lamb stew with pine kernels in an Armenian one, and honey-cake in a Ukrainian establishment. The problem, though, is not so much what to choose as how to get in. These regional restaurants are popular both with local people who enjoy their novelty and exoticism and with homesick provincials who have been longing for some home cooking. It's very hard to reserve a table, though you can ask your Intourist guide or hotel service desk to try for you. Otherwise you can go along and either join the long line of Russians waiting patiently to get in, or, if you have the nerve, walk right in and hope that someone will give you special treatment as a foreigner. This sounds boorish, but in fact most Russians are so hospitable to tourists and so proud of their country in all its aspects that they prefer to see foreigners take precedence over themselves so that the guests, with less time, shouldn't get a bad impression.

Meals Slow, Meals Fast

Although the Russians made an effort to improve service during the year of the Olympics, with some success, reports you may have heard about slow service in some restaurants are not exaggerated: nowhere does the fatalistic and resigned side of the Russian character reveal itself more than in the way that restaurant patrons uncomplainingly wait to be served. Maybe the restaurants are understaffed or badly managed; more likely it's just because the waiters don't *have* to hurry: people really are *happy* to wait. Probably dining out is such a rare treat for the average citizen that he's determined to make the evening last as long as possible. In the long gaps between courses he's either laughing and drinking with his friends or, in an establishment with music, he and his partner are doing a sedate foxtrot to thirties jazz or, if younger, boogie-ing wildly! "So why don't you do the same?" the waitress will ask if you get impatient. You can always try tipping her in advance (not officially approved of, but sometimes effective). Or you can leave. What doesn't help is to get angry—it'll only spoil your digestion and make the Russians think how rude foreigners are.

If you do want a quick meal, there are plenty of alternatives. You'll find self-service cafes and stand-up snack bars where you can have anything from caviar to a plate of *borshch, pirozhki* (little pastries filled with ground meat or anything else) to a glass of tea. There are also parlors serving ice-cream and sweet champagne which are very popular. Russian ice-cream is excellent and you can also try it at kiosks on the streets and in the parks—the word to say is *morózhenoye.*

Peter Strikes Again

Traditionally, Russian food was always hearty and substantial, with plenty of farinaceous matter to fill the stomachs of the hungry peasants. *Kasha* was the staple and cabbage was the other main element in the diet; in *shchi,* soup containing perhaps only cabbage and potato, enriched with bone stock if you were lucky; also in *golubtsy,* cabbage rolls stuffed with whatever was available. There's a famous Russian saying:

Shchi da kasha
Pishcha nasha

(Cabbage soup and gruel are our food.)

The other basic item was, and is, bread. Most commonly coarse and black, it was, with salt, the symbol of hospitality offered to the guest in even the humblest household. Russians today still take great pride in their bread, and rightly so: they probably have a greater variety than any other nation in the world and its quality is greatly superior to the mass-produced, steam-baked blotting-paper we have grown used to in the West. Fresh meat and fowl were something of a luxury to most people, but fish from Russia's vast lakes and many rivers was more plentiful. Vegetables were salted and pickled and fruit preserved to last through the long winters. Since ingredients were not widely varied, Russian cooks became skilled in the use of herbs and spices to make their dishes more interesting. In the north, onions, parsley and dill are much used, with sour cream as the almost inevitable accompaniment. In the south, particularly in the Caucasus and Georgia, the cooking resembles that of the Middle East, with the use of paprika, cayenne, ginger, sesame seeds, garlic and coriander.

For centuries, the food of the rich differed from the food of the poor more in quantity and variety than in refinement. It was not until the beginning of the 18th century, in the reign of Peter the Great, that the Russian nobles became aware that the preparation and consumption of food could be an enjoyable art, not merely a means of satisfying hunger. Peter, that most Western-looking of rulers, was determined to modernize and civilize his backward and, as he considered, barbaric people. Not only did he build a beautiful city on Western models, employing Italian architects, and summoned to it Western musicians, dancing-masters and teachers to train his courtiers in the manners of polite society, but he also got a French cook who started producing remarkable delicacies such as the Russians had never seen.

His heirs and their courtiers took their lessons to heart. Feasts became more and more elaborate and extravagant. Contemporary accounts tell of the staggering opulence of the table settings—one family had gold plates for a thousand guests—and the expensive and fantastic dishes served. The object was clearly to astound and impress the guests with the host's wealth rather than with his taste. Nevertheless, by the early 19th century every wealthy household had its own chef, and as a result Russian cooking did become more delicate and subtle. But the old customs still prevailed— French cuisine did not disrupt the daily rhythm of life in Russian families. Chekhov's plays show how, even at a later date, the rituals of eating and drinking were the welcome punctuation of the tedium of the long provincial days. The *samovar* was always on the boil, and meal followed meal: breakfast, lunch, dinner (often six courses) preceded by *zakuska* (which will have a few words later) and followed eventually by supper, known as evening tea, which, though simpler, was another meal in its own right.

Home Cooking Today

The food you'll have if you're invited to a Soviet home today is obviously not so extravagant nor so vast in quantity as in rich people's houses in pre-revolutionary days. But Russians still enjoy a feast as much as they ever did and the tradition of hospitality is just as lively.

In the evening, you'll probably be offered *zakuska* before dinner. In the old days this was an elaborately decorated table laid with savory tidbits— different kinds of caviar (the best is black Beluga but there are also red and golden varieties), cold sturgeon in aspic, cheeses, pickles, liver pâté, cold cuts—which guests washed down with a choice of different vodkas. It was enough to constitute an ample meal in itself, though it was only meant to be a light snack for those who got too hungry to wait for the real dinner. Today you'll probably still be offered vodka and perhaps caviar (*ikra* in Russian), though it's scarcer and more expensive than it used to be. It's most likely to be served with *blini,* thin buckwheat pancakes in which the caviar or other filling is rolled and then covered in sour cream. Other likely *zakuski* are *pirozhki,* mentioned above, which might alternatively be served as an accompaniment to soup as the first course of the dinner proper. Or your hostess might have made a *kulebiaka*—a flaky pastry loaf with a savory filling, often salmon. Whatever you're offered, temper your enthusiasm and politeness (you are bound to be pressed to eat more than you can manage) with prudence, in the knowledge that you've still got a long way to go: what follows the *zakuska* may not be a Czarist feast, but it will be fairly substantial and your hostess will be hurt if you can't last the course. Since Russian housewives don't have as many labor-saving devices and convenience foods as we do, an elaborate dinner party is all the more an honor for the guest and a source of pride to the hostess.

The dinner will probably start with soup such as *borshch,* but probably a more interesting and substantial version than any you've tasted before, perhaps with ham and cabbage added to the basic beetroot liquid. Or in summer it might be *akróshka,* a chilled soup of vegetables or meat in *kvas* stock. *Kvas* is that strange beverage that characters in Russian literature are always drinking and which never seems to find an adequate translation; in fact it's a kind of beer most commonly made by adding a yeast mixture to stale black bread and allowing it to ferment.

The main course will be either fish or meat. The fish you are most likely to be served are sturgeon, halibut, or herring, though of course if you are near the sea in one of the Baltic republics or by the Black Sea there will be a wider variety of local fish available. If the main dish is meat, perhaps you'll be lucky enough to have a well-cooked chicken Kiev—at its best a miraculous creation and very tricky to make. When you pierce the lightly-fried chicken breast, a fountain of golden butter shoots forth. Or you might get an authentic beef Stroganov, succulent with little mushrooms and sour cream. Or *pelmeni,* light boiled dumplings filled with meat and again served with sour cream. The possibilities are infinite and depend very much on where the family comes from: as we've said before, people in the Soviet Union are very attached to the cooking of their birthplace and take it with them wherever they move.

For dessert there might be *vareniky,* sweet dumplings filled with fruit, fruit purée, charlotte russe or some of that delicious ice-cream. The meal will probably last a long time, there will be a lot of toasting, and everybody will eat and drink far too much and enjoy themselves thoroughly!

What's On the Menu?

Here are a few names of the more common dishes that you may come across: *borshch*—beet soup; *akróshka*—cold soup with a base of *kvas* (a kind of beer); *beef Stroganov*—beef stewed in sour cream with fried potatoes, not rice; *bliny*—small pancakes, which you then fill with caviar, fish, melted butter or sour cream; *aládyi*—crumpets, with the same filling but also with jam; *ikrá*—black caviar. Ask also for butter (*máslo*) and toast (*tost*); *krásnaya ikrá*—red caviar, excellent with sour cream (*smetána*); *kotlyety po Pozhársky*—chicken cutlets; *kotléta po Kiyevsky*—fried breast of chicken, rich with butter; *pirozhkí*—fried rolls with different fillings, usually meat; *pónchiki*—hot, sugared doughnuts; *prostakvásha*—yogurt; *pelméni*—meat dumplings; *rassólnik*—hot soup, usually made of pickled vegetables; *shchi*—cabbage soup; *morózhenoye*—ice cream.

The Two Essentials—Tea and Vodka

The two most typical drinks you'll be offered in the Soviet Union are tea (*chai*)—usually with a pile of sugar—and vodka.

Russians drink their tea black, often with lemon and with a spoonful of fruit jelly stirred in. It comes in tall glasses with metal holders. The boredom of long train journeys is relieved by frequent refreshment dispensed by the conductor from the steaming samovar kept on the boil night and day in every car. In the Central Asian republics try visiting a local *chaikhana* (tearoom) where you may sit outdoors or indoors and sip *green* tea.

Coffee is generally available with meals and in cafes, though the standard is variable. We recommend taking a jar of instant coffee along (like gold dust in the U.S.S.R.) so that you can ask for hot water in the hotel and make your own. Take your own creamer, too. Soft drinks, fruit juices and mineral waters are obtainable everywhere, though quality varies. If you are pining for a cola, you'll find Pepsi on sale in tourist locations, while many establishments will produce a bottle of "Baikal," not dissimilar to Coke, if you ask.

Vodka is a drink the Russians treat with respect, and so should you. Legends that it never causes a hangover are just that—legends. But that doesn't mean you should sip it slowly and nervously: you should knock it back in one go and then savor the afterglow. With it, you nibble *zakuski*—Russians *never* drink vodka without eating something. Apart from the colorless, almost tasteless drink that we are used to, vodka in the U.S.S.R. is often flavored and colored with herbs and spices for added interest. For instance, there's *zubróvka,* flavored with a particular kind of grass, *ryabínovka,* in which ashberries have been steeped, *stárka,* the dark, smooth old vodka, *pertsóvka,* with hot pepper, or cherry or lemon vodka. You can buy these readymade or take home a bottle of pure vodka and experiment with it yourself.

A note for restaurant-goers: in 1985 a law was passed prohibiting the serving of alcohol before 2 P.M.—part of a series of measures aimed at tackling Russia's eternal problem of over-indulgence. Apparently some establishments catering for foreign tourists have been exempted from this rule.

The Soviet Union also produces its own table wines, which are well worth trying. The best-known wine-producing areas are Georgia and the Crimea, where the grapes ripen through the long hot summers to be made into sweet full wines. You may well find some of them too sweet for your taste, but they go well with desserts. Russian "champagne" (since 1985 officially known simply as "sparkling wine" after the French complained about abuse of the term champagne) is reasonably good, too—an inexpensive luxury here. However, you should make a point of trying the excellent Armenian or Azerbaijani brandies too, even if they are no longer permitted to call themselves "cognac." Beer in the U.S.S.R. compares well with its Western counterpart and, if only from curiosity, you should try *kvas*—it's a refreshing and unusual drink on a hot day.

Finally, you should learn two words of Russian—*na zdoróvie*—which means, literally, "to your health," but is the all-purpose toast. It's a phrase you may be saying and hearing quite a lot.

EXPLORING
THE
SOVIET UNION

MOSCOW

The Seat of Power and Culture

Jerusalem, Mecca, Rome, Moscow—all are places of pilgrimage, whether the faithful come to pray at the Wailing Wall, circle the *kaaba,* be blessed by the Pope or file past Lenin's embalmed body in the great mausoleum on Red Square. Holy Moscow—that was the name for centuries and it has remained the symbolic heart of this vast country. Though Leningrad now bears the name of the founder of the modern state, by the spring of 1918 the Communist regime moved from what was then St. Petersburg to Moscow, which has been the center of government ever since.

Peter the Great, who built his city as a "window onto Europe," had deliberately turned his back on the old traditions; some three centuries later, equally deliberately, the young Soviet Republic transferred itself back to the heartland, for the former capital was too close to the besieged frontiers. And while Napoleon managed to occupy Moscow briefly, for over 170 years since the city has remained inviolate, defying the most violent onslaught, resisting the most determined foe. Moscow is more than a metropolis of over eight million people, one of the world's most populous cities, more than the administrative, legislative, educational and cultural capital of the U.S.S.R.—it is the embodiment of the Russian character and of Russian history.

It is the official capital not only of the Soviet Union, but of the Russian Soviet Federal Socialist Republic, the seat of the Central Committee of the Communist Party, the citadel of Soviet power, of the Supreme Soviet and all other federal government organs and offices.

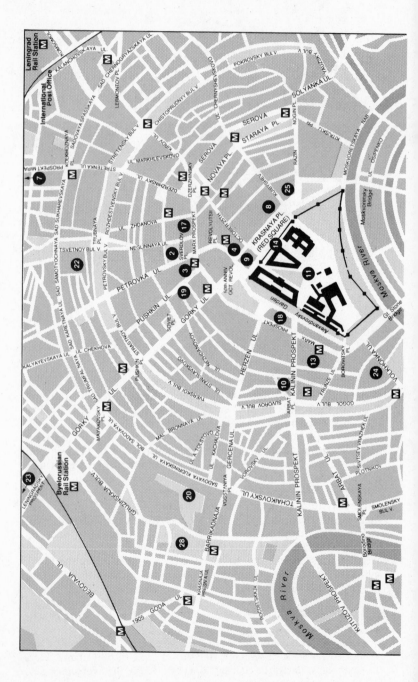

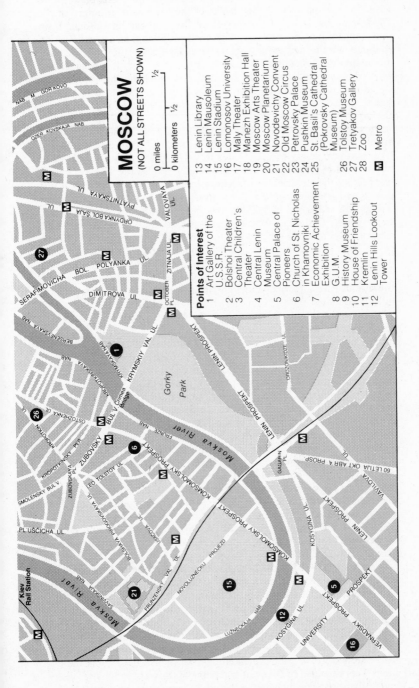

The city lies in the central zone of the great Russian Plain, between the Rivers Volga and Oka, on the banks of the Moskva (a tributary of the Oka), some 360 feet above sea level. All the great rail lines radiate from it; it is the focal point of all air traffic. Centralization is an ancient Russian tradition which has been strengthened under Soviet rule, and whatever autonomy other republics and cities possess, they are all subordinate to Moscow. And while in the old times the oppressed and the dispossessed, sighing for justice, kept on saying, "The Czar, our Father, is far away," today, with modern communications, Moscow keeps the reins tight and the supervision constant.

Moscow's history covers about two thousand years, though the earliest annals set the date as A.D. 1147, which is the official "birthday" of the city (the eighth centenary was celebrated in 1947). The first, wooden Kremlin was erected by Prince Yuri Dolgoruky in 1156. By the 13th century it had become the center of the Moscow principality. Before very long it was destroyed by the Mongolian Tatar invasion, but the rule of Batu Khan did not last very long. In 1326 the foundations of the first stone building, the Uspensky Cathedral, were laid, and in 1380 it was from Moscow that the army of Prince Dimitri set out to defeat the Tatar forces at Kulikovo on the Don. The Kremlin rose to become both the ruling princes' residence and a fortress which withstood Mongolian, Lithuanian and other attacks.

By the 15th century, Moscow had established its paramount rule over the various Russian principalities and its urban area was over three square miles. A hundred years later it had grown into the capital of a strong and prosperous state, one of the largest in the world. A system of concentric fortifications with the Kremlin as its center enclosed Kitai-Gorod and Bely Gorod, new and large sections of the city with two other outer rings; the city had spread to over ten square miles. The Cathedral of the Archangel, St. Basil's Cathedral in the Red Square, the Great Bell Tower in the Kremlin were built and Russia's first printing plant was set up in 1563. And though civil war and Polish invasion ravaged the city in the first two decades of the 17th century, with Peter the Great a new era of stability and development began at the end of the 17th century—even though he favoured his own new capital on the Neva.

Moscow still remained the economic and cultural center of the country. The first university opened in 1775. By the end of the 18th century, the city had a population of 217,000 and a quarter of its buildings were of stone. Then came the Napoleonic invasion in 1812; the French occupation ended with a conflagration in which three out of every four buildings were gutted. But Moscow rose from its ruins; by 1840 it had a population of 350,000 and it was completely rebuilt. A major industrial and cultural center, its limits expanded to the so-called Kamer-Kollezhsky wall, with an area of 50 square miles.

In March 1918, Moscow became the capital of the new Soviet state. There followed years of much suffering and hardship, and the rebuilding and development of the capital were again interrupted by the Nazi invasion. Moscow, in the early stages of the war, was hard pressed; the enemy was stopped during the bitter winter of 1941 almost under the walls of the city and for many months Moscow was repeatedly attacked from the air. The post-war years saw the end of the Stalin era and the realization of the second urban plan, which emphasized housing. In 1960, the city limits were extended to the great outer ring of freeways and many villages and settlements were included in the urban area, while the district known as Yugo-Zapadny Rayon (Southwestern Region) was completed. Since then the city has continued its expansion and many miles of new housing developments have been completed, while parts of central Moscow have been renewed and redesigned. A new development plan catering for the city's expansion up to the year 2010 will take in another 25,000 acres of land, increase the subway (under-ground railway) network to over 300 kilometers and move many industrial enterprises to beyond the city limits.

Exploring Moscow—The Kremlin

The nucleus of Moscow is the Kremlin and its Red Square. This is the oldest, most characteristic part of the Soviet capital, the site of its finest architectural monuments, and symbols of Russian and Soviet power. (Kreml means "citadel.")

We suggest you start your tour at the Metro station on Karl Marx Boulevard (Prospekt Marxa). From the corner of the Hotel Moskva, you'll have a general view of Red Square and two sides of the (roughly) pentagonal Kremlin. The first thing that you see is the red-brick battlemented walls, some 1½ miles in circumference and in some places 65 feet high, 10 to 20 feet thick. The walls are reinforced by 20 towers, five of which are also gates. In their present form they have stood practically unchanged since the end of the 15th century.

Cross under the square named after the 50th anniversary of the October Revolution to the northernmost point of the Kremlin, the so-called Sobakina Tower. More than 180 feet high, this was once an important part of the Kremlin's defenses. Its walls are more than 12 feet thick at the foundations; it was built so solidly because it concealed a secret well (important in time of siege) and also a way out to the Neglinnaya River, which now flows underground. Passing through a huge wrought-iron gate, you enter the Alexandrovsky Garden, which stretches along the northwestern wall. Not far from the entrance there is a grey obelisk, a memorial to the revolutionaries. Close to it stands the grave of the Unknown Soldier, dedicated on May 9, 1967, the 22nd anniversary of the victory over Nazism. The body resting under the red granite slabs is that of an unidentified Soviet soldier, one of those who, in the autumn of 1941, stopped the German attack at the village of Kryukuvo, outside Moscow. To the right of the grave there are six urns holding soil from the six "heroic cities", Odessa, Sevastopol, Volgograd, Kiev, Brest and Leningrad, which so stubbornly resisted the German onslaught.

Looking up from the garden to the Kremlin walls, you can see a large yellow building, the Arsenal. Begun in 1701 by Peter the Great, it was finished only at the end of the 18th century; its present form dates from the early 19th century. The simple, yet impressive, two-floored building was originally intended to be an arsenal and museum; today it houses offices.

Walking along in the garden, you reach a double bastion linked by a stone bridge on nine pillars. The white outer bastion defended the approach to the bridge. The tower is called Kutafya, which in Old Slavonic means "clumsy or confused", and its shape is different from the other towers of the Kremlin. The massive inner tower, the Troitskaya (Trinity) is the tallest in the Kremlin wall, rising 240 feet above the garden. Its deep subterranean chambers were once used as prison cells. Napoleon's army entered the Kremlin in 1812 through this gate.

The Alexander Garden continues beyond the bridge and ends at the western corner of the Kremlin. You'll hear the noise of traffic beyond the iron railing. On the left a sloping path leads from the garden to the Kremlin wall. Here stands the pyramid-shaped Borovitsky Tower, rising to more than 150 feet; at its foot, a gate pierces the thick wall. The slits for the chains of the drawbridge are still visible beside the gate. Vehicular traffic passes through here now, with a separate entrance for pedestrians. This is one of the two pedestrian entrances (the other is through the Sobakina Tower) for touring the Kremlin. Both open at 10 A.M. daily.

The road climbs steeply, as the Kremlin was built on a hill for defense reasons. A few yards away is the entrance of the famous Armory (Oruzheinaya Palata), the oldest museum of the Kremlin and the place where the regalia and ambassadorial gifts were kept. Arms, armor and valuable objects from the country's chief armories and storehouses were gathered here. The present building was erected in 1849–51 to house an expanding collection which had already outgrown three previous sites; some 4,000 exhibits date from the 12th century to 1917 and now include a rare collection of 17th-century silver. Admission is only possible through the Intourist City Tour.

Hall I has a large collection of Russian and foreign arms and armor, with a striking display of helmets (of which the earliest dates from the 13th century and is ascribed to Prince Yaroslav, father of Alexander Nevsky). Here, too, is the helmet of Prince Ivan, son of Ivan the Terrible, whom his father killed in a fit of rage when he was 28. Russian chainmail, battleaxes, maces, arquebuses, German and Dutch muskets, ceremonial armor and Russian and original sabers are also in this hall, together with the large Greek quiver belonging to Czar Alexei, his Oriental saber and a heavy golden mace presented to him by the Persian Shah Abbas. European suits of armor of the 15th-17th centuries, pistols and firearms complete the display. Admission to the Crown Jewel Room ("The Diamond Fund") is by special ticket.

Halls II and III display the work of goldsmiths and silversmiths of the 12th to 19th centuries. In Hall II there is also a collection of Russian and foreign clocks and watches of the 16th to 19th centuries. The gift copper watch in the shape of a book was Ivan the Terrible's and the wooden watch was made by Russian craftsmen in the 19th century. In Hall III there is a collection of 18th- to 20th-century jewelry, including a silver egg on the surface of which a map of the Trans-Siberian railroad is engraved; inside there is a golden clockwork model of a train with a platinum engine, windows of crystal and a headlight made of a tiny ruby.

Hall IV has vestments of priceless silk, velvet and brocade, embroidered with gold, encrusted with jewels and pearls, once worn by Czars, Patriarchs and Metropolitans.

Hall V is filled with foreign gold and silver objects, mostly ambassadorial presents to the Czars.

Hall VI contains the regalia. Here are the thrones; the oldest, veneered with carved ivory, belonged to Ivan the Terrible. The throne of the first years of Peter I's reign, when he shared power with his older brother, Ivan, has two seats in front and one (hidden) in the back, where the Regent, their elder sister Sophia sat, and prompted the young boys to give the right answers to ambassadors' and others' queries. Another throne, covered with thin plates of gold and studded with 2,200 precious stones and pearls, was presented to Czar Boris Godunov by Shah Abbas of Persia; the throne

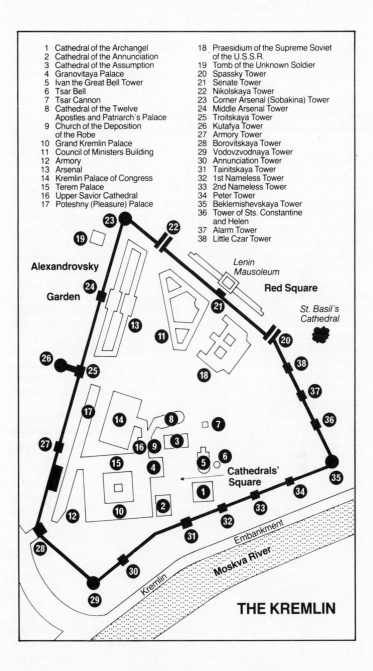

1 Cathedral of the Archangel
2 Cathedral of the Annunciation
3 Cathedral of the Assumption
4 Granovitaya Palace
5 Ivan the Great Bell Tower
6 Tsar Bell
7 Tsar Cannon
8 Cathedral of the Twelve Apostles and Patriarch's Palace
9 Church of the Deposition of the Robe
10 Grand Kremlin Palace
11 Council of Ministers Building
12 Armory
13 Arsenal
14 Kremlin Palace of Congress
15 Terem Palace
16 Upper Savior Cathedral
17 Poteshny (Pleasure) Palace
18 Praesidium of the Supreme Soviet of the U.S.S.R.
19 Tomb of the Unknown Soldier
20 Spassky Tower
21 Senate Tower
22 Nikolskaya Tower
23 Corner Arsenal (Sobakina) Tower
24 Middle Arsenal Tower
25 Troitskaya Tower
26 Kutafya Tower
27 Armory Tower
28 Borovitskaya Tower
29 Vodovzvodnaya Tower
30 Annunciation Tower
31 Tainitskaya Tower
32 1st Nameless Tower
33 2nd Nameless Tower
34 Peter Tower
35 Beklemishevskaya Tower
36 Tower of Sts. Constantine and Helen
37 Alarm Tower
38 Little Czar Tower

Alexandrovsky
Garden

Lenin Mausoleum

Red Square

St. Basil's Cathedral

Cathedrals' Square

Embankment

Kremlin

Moskva River

THE KREMLIN

of Czar Alexei (also of Persian make) is decorated with 876 diamonds and 1223 other stones. Among the crowns, the oldest is the "Cap of Mono-makh," dating from the 13th century, refashioned in the 16th. Russian and foreign orders are also displayed here.

Hall XI holds court carriages, the oldest being an English one, reputed to have been presented by Queen Elizabeth I to Boris Godunov. The most attractive one is a French carriage painted by Boucher.

After visiting the Armory you'll see a courtyard on the left, closed off by a wrought-iron railing. The building on the left, adjoining the Armory, was once the home of the Czars. Today it is used for the visits of foreign heads of state. On the right is the complex of the Grand Kremlin Palace (Bolshoi Kremlyovsky Dvorets) that flanks the road.

Grand Kremlin Palace

This is a group of several buildings. The main section is the newest, built between 1838 and 1849 by the architects Chichagov, Gerasimov, Ton and others. Its 375-foot-long front faces south, overlooking the Moskva River. This was for centuries the site of the palaces of the Grand Dukes and Czars, but the immediate predecessor of the present building, dating from the 18th century, was badly damaged in the 1812 conflagration. This is the seat of the Supreme Soviets of the U.S.S.R. and of the Russian Repub-lic and is only open to visitors on special occasions.

The main entrance leads into a spacious marble hall with several marble chambers on the left. These used to be the imperial reception rooms; today they are used for ceremonial signing sessions.

A sweeping staircase leads to the first floor. Here is the great St. George's Hall, named after the highest military decoration of Czarist Rus-sia, the Order of St. George, whose members are commemorated on mar-ble tablets. They include Suvorov and Kutuzov, two famous generals. Eighteen spiral zinc columns topped by sculpted figures support the roof, the work of Ivan Vitali. Six immense gilt chandeliers and 3,000 lamps pro-vide illumination. The parquet flooring is made up of 20 different kinds of wood. The hall is used for government and diplomatic receptions, youth balls and children's New Year celebrations.

Mirrored doors lead into the octagonal Vladimir Hall, the so-called "sa-cred ante-room." Its foundations were laid in 1487. A beautifully carved, gilt door opens from here into one of the most ancient chambers, the Pal-ace of Facets (Granovitaya Palata), so called because of the shape of the stone facings on the side nearest Cathedral Square. Built in 1473–91 by the Italian architects Marco Ruffo and Pietro Antonio Solario, it is a large low-vaulted chamber, the roof supported in the middle by a rectangular pier. The iron ribs of the vaulting are gilded with inscriptions.

From the Vladimir Hall there is access to the so-called Terem, or Gol-den Czarina Palace, also among the oldest parts of the Kremlin. It was in the gilt rooms of this palace that the Czarina received her official visi-tors. Another passage with wooden stairs and a gilt iron door leads to the Terem Palace, the residence of the early Czars; its furnishings have been preserved in the richly decorated vaulted chambers.

The Supreme Soviet's council chamber is the second largest in the Kremlin, with seating for 3,000. It was created by combining two existing halls. Here the party congresses were held until 1967, when the modern steel-and-glass Palace of Congresses was completed.

Near the council chamber are the former apartments of the imperial family. Their marble walls are covered with silk tapestries. There are statuary and china of great value and substantial inlaid furniture. The walls of the so-called Catherine Chamber are supported by green malachite columns valued at several million gold roubles.

The Square of Cathedrals

After visiting the Grand Kremlin Palace, cross to the other side of the roadway and look down upon the Kremlin Garden, which is in the hollow below. The shady park has huge oaks and fir trees. If you return to the left side of the road, a few steps bring you to the ancient center of the Kremlin, the Square of Cathedrals. The paved square is framed by three large cathedrals in old Russian style, the massive bell tower and the Granovitaya Palace. The side-entrance of the Uspensky (Assumption) Cathedral is opposite. This is one of the oldest edifices of the Kremlin. The present building, which became Russia's principal church, follows the style of the Uspensky Cathedral at Vladimir. It was built in 1475–79 by the Italian architect Aristotle Fiorovanti, who had spent many years in Russia studying traditional architecture. Topped by five gilt domes, it is both austere and solemn, with a spacious interior, illuminated by two rows of narrow windows. It contains rare ancient paintings, including the ikon of the Virgin of Vladimir (the work of an 11th-century Byzantine artist) and the icons of St. George (12th century) and the Trinity (14th century). The carved throne of Ivan the Terrible also stands here. The church is still open for religious services.

The smaller, single-steepled Rispolozheniye (Church of the Deposition of the Robe), built 1484–86 by master masons from Pskov, stands next to the Uspensky Cathedral, on the northwestern corner of the square. This was for a while the personal church of the Patriarchs of Moscow. It was rebuilt several times and restored to its original 15th-century condition by Soviet experts. In 1965 it was re-opened as a museum. The building boasts brilliant frescos dating from the mid-17th century covering all its walls, pillars and vaults. Its most precious treasure is the iconostasis by Nazary Istomin (1627).

The carved stone facade of the Granovitaya Palace stands on the west side, close to the Grand Kremlin Palace with the Blagoveshchensky (Annunciation) Cathedral next to it. This is a remarkable monument of Russian architecture, linking three centuries of art and religion. Its foundations were laid in the 14th century and a triangular brick church erected on them in the early Moscow style in the 15th century. Fire partly destroyed it; during the reign of Ivan the Terrible six new gilded cupolas were added when it was rebuilt. The 16th-century carved stone portals are particularly fine. Inside, look for a beautiful iconostasis and striking frescos, which were recently restored. These were painted in 1508 by the Russian artist Feodosy and his father and brother. The fine icons of the second and third tiers of the iconostasis were painted by Andrei Rublyov, Theophanes the Greek and Prokhor of Gorodets. The floor is covered with polished tiles of agate jasper, given by the Shah of Persia. The cathedral served as the private chapel of the Czars. In the South Gallery, icons and paintings are exhibited.

On its opposite side, the Square of Cathedrals is bordered by the Cathedral of the Archangel. This is a five-domed edifice, built by the Italian architect Aleviso Novi in 1505–9 to replace the original 14th-century church. Its ornate decorations have distinct elements of the Italian Renaissance. Between 1540 and 1700 this was the burial place of the Russian princes and Czars; their likenesses are painted on the walls above each of the 46 tombs, including those of Ivan Kalita (d. 1340) and Ivan the Terrible. The carved wooden iconostasis is 43 feet high. The icon of the Archangel Michael is attributed to Andrei Rublyov. In 1953–55 some outstanding medieval murals, depicting battle scenes, were discovered beneath the layers of centuries. Other murals depict historical, religious and domestic scenes.

The tallest building of the square, and of the Kremlin, is the Ivan the Great Bell-Tower, which forms a splendid ensemble with the adjoining buildings. The octagonal main tower with its 329 steps is 263 feet high—three feet higher than the Hotel Rossia across the Square, in accordance with a tradition that the Tower must be the tallest building in Moscow. The Bell Tower is one of the most unusual structures built in the 16th century. The first tower was erected in 1505–8, the second in 1532–43. The first was rebuilt in 1600, when it was crowned with an onion-shaped dome covered with gilded copper. Originally it served as a watchtower; from it Moscow and its environs could be observed within a radius of 20 miles. The first tower has 21 bells, the largest weighing 64 tons. Both towers together have 52 bells, the largest weighing 70 tons. The Czar Bell, standing on a stone pedestal nearby, is the biggest bell in the world; cast in the Kremlin in 1733–35, it weighs more than 200 tons, is 20 feet high and 22 feet in diameter. The bas-reliefs on the outside show Czar Alexei Mikhailovich and the Czarina Anna Ivanovna. Not far from the Bell is the Czar Cannon, with the largest caliber of any gun in the world, cast in bronze in 1586 by Andrei Chokhov. It weighs 40 tons, its length is 17 ft. 6 in., and its caliber is 35 inches in a barrel six inches thick. It bears the image of Czar Fyodor Ivanovich. Its present carriage was cast in 1835, purely for display purposes.

Leaving the Czar Bell, walk around the large square into which you have emerged. It contains the Church of the Twelve Apostles and the Patriarch's Residence. The Church was built in 1655–56 and served as the Patriarch's private church. The buildings now house (since 1963) the Museum of 17th-Century Applied Art; the exhibits were taken from the surplus of the State Armory Museum and include books, items of tableware, clothing and household linen.

The Seat of Government

Passing the Cathedral of the Twelve Apostles and the former Patriarch's Palace you arrive at the most recent building of the Kremlin, the Palace of Congresses. A glass and aluminum building, it was added to the Kremlin complex in 1961 and completed six years later, much of it underground to avoid clashing with the old Kremlin architecture and ruining the skyline. Its vast stage is fully equipped for opera and ballet, concerts and recitals and wide-screen film projection. Simultaneous translation apparatus is built into the seats. Above the auditorium there is a banqueting hall for 2,500 people. The covered promenade circling this hall provides a splendid view. In addition there are more than 800 different premises—halls and lobbies, conference rooms, accommodations for the diplomatic corps and the press.

Beyond the palace you'll see the façade of the Arsenal, with the French cannon captured in 1812 by Kutuzov's forces.

On the other side of the square stands a two-storied, Classical building with a central dome. This is the Council of Ministers, once the Senate, an 18th-century building by Matvei Kazakov. It was in this building that Lenin lived and worked; his fourth-floor study, with its original furniture and books, is sometimes open to the public. Next to it is the hall where Lenin chaired the meetings of the Council of People's Commissars and other committees. Lenin's apartment can be reached by a corridor from this hall. Four medium-sized and simply-equipped rooms have also been preserved in their original condition.

Next to the Council of Ministers Building is the Kremlin Theater, also in Classical style. Walking past it, we reach the gate of the Spassky Tower, the finest and most ornate of the 20 bastions built to defend the main entrance of the Kremlin. Designed originally in 1491 by the Milanese architect Solario, it was given its present form in the middle of the 17th century. Rising to almost 210 feet, it has an ornamental clock, made in 1851–52, with a carillon marking every quarter hour.

Red Square

Near the Spassky Gate is a pedestrian exit into Red (Krasnaya) Square. Turning right along the descending broad road, stop briefly on the Moskvoretsky Bridge over the Moskva River. The center of the bridge offers an excellent view of the southern part of the Kremlin; the garden behind the tall, crenelated wall with towers and bastions; the facade of the Grand Kremlin Palace, the forest of the gold-and-silver spires of the cathedrals make striking subjects for photographs.

Return now up the slope to Red Square. Its history reaches back to the 15th century when it was known as the *Torg* (Slavonic for "market place"). In the 16th century it became the place for ceremonies. The Lobnoye Mesto (the elevated round platform in front of St. Basil's Cathedral) was built in 1534; from here the imperial *ukases* (decrees) were proclaimed and later it also served as a scaffold. The present-day appellation of the square dates from the 17th century, though in the usage of those days *krasnaya* meant "beautiful" and not "red." For centuries it remained the center of Moscow life, and since the establishment of the Soviet regime it has been the venue of the November 7 and May Day parades.

Apart from the Kremlin, the oldest building in Red Square is the Cathedral of the Intercession (Cathedral of St. Basil the Blessed, or Pokrovsky Cathedral). Built in 1555–60 on the orders of Ivan the Terrible by the Russian architects Barma and Postnik, it is a unique achievement—a combination of nine churches. The central structure is 107 feet high, surrounded by eight tower-like chapels linked by an elevated gallery, and each with a differently patterned exterior. To commemorate the conquest of the Tatar city of Kazan, Czar Ivan dedicated each of the eight subsidiary churches to the saints on whose days he had won battles. Today the Cathedral is a museum. The antechamber provides a history of the building, the story of its construction and specimens of the materials used. In the 16th century, the crypt became the state treasury; in 1595 two nobles decided to rob it, first diverting the city guards by starting fires at different suburban spots. Their plan failed and they were executed. The Cathedral contains the iconostasis of the Trinity Church, the famous *Entry into Jeru-*

salem icon in the church named after it, and some magnificent decorations in the Church of St. Alexander of Svir. In 1588 a church was built close to the cathedral and dedicated to a Muscovite holy man named Basil who had considerable influence over Ivan the Terrible. It was his name that was finally given to the Cathedral complex.

Near the cathedral on the lower corner of Red Square along the Moskva River stands the Rossiya Hotel, a huge block whose central tower houses luxury apartments.

In the small garden outside St. Basil's Cathedral stands the monument to Kuzma Minin, a Nizhni-Novgorod butcher, and Prince Dmitry Pozharsky, who liberated Moscow in October 1612 from Polish-Lithuanian occupation. The work of Ivan Martos, it was erected in 1818, paid for by public subscription.

Red Square is bordered on the east by two look-alike buildings. One is the home of GUM, the state department store, undergoing refurbishment but still open.

At the north end of the Square is the History Museum, built in typical Moscow style in 1874–83. Originally the first building of the Moscow University, the Museum, with 300,000 exhibits, now houses the largest collection of historical material and documents about the origin and history of the peoples of what is now the Soviet Union from their beginnings to the end of the 19th century. It is the oldest museum in Moscow and its unique and fascinating collections include coins and medals, ancient implements, furnishings, manuscripts and early hand-printed books (including 11th-century Greek and 13th-century Byzantine works), Novgorod birch-bark scrolls dating from the 10th century, samples of the arms of Kiev Rus, robes of Ivan the Terrible, the iron cage in which the captured Pugachov, leader of the 1773–75 peasant uprising, was brought to Moscow, and Napoleon's bed which he abandoned when leaving Russia. The museum is engaged in ambitious research work. In 1986 a 3-year renovation program began and many exhibits have been moved to museum annexes. Check with Intourist.

The focus of Red Square is the Lenin Mausoleum, sited beside the Kremlin Wall between the Spassky and Nikolsky Towers, containing his embalmed body. The opening hours are Tuesdays, Wednesdays, Thursdays and Saturdays from 10 to 1 and on Sundays from 10 to 2. There are always long lines, but escorted foreign tourists usually receive precedence or are allowed to join the line during the hour after the mausoleum is closed to Soviet citizens, i.e. from 1–2 PM (2–3 PM Sundays). The place to go is the corner of the red-bricked History Museum on Red Square, opposite the entrance to the Alexandrovsky Garden. From here it takes about half-an-hour in the line. N.B. *Cameras not allowed inside. Take your passport if you go alone.*

Behind the mausoleum is a cemetery with the remains of many leading Soviet politicians, including Stalin, Kosygin, Suslov, Brezhnev and, most recently, Yury Andropov and Konstantin Chernenko. Urns set in the Kremlin wall contain the ashes of Gorky, Ordzhonikidze, Kirov, the astronauts Gagarin and Komarov, and others. From the balcony of the mausoleum Soviet leaders watch the great Moscow parades.

The Heart of Moscow

Start your exploration from the metro station exit at the corner of the Hotel Moskva. The southeastern front of the hotel faces the Ploshchad

Revolyutsii (Revolution Square). Opposite is the approach to Red Square, with the History Museum on the right, and another, similar building on the left. Before the Revolution this was the building of the Moscow Duma (council). In 1936 it became the Central Lenin Museum. Opened in 1936, its 22 halls contain many thousands of exhibits, covering the main periods in the life and work of the founder of the Soviet State. Among the exhibits are Lenin's personal belongings—his desk, with secret drawers, a coat with bullet-holes (after an attempted assassination) and his car. Newsreels of him, from 1917–24, are shown.

The metro station next to the museum is linked by an underground passage with your starting point. Behind it there are some remnants of a red brick wall, similar to that of the Kremlin. This is part of the wall of the so-called Kitai-Gorod, built in the 16th century by the architect Petrok Maly. Kitai-Gorod, adjoining the Kremlin, was one of the oldest quarters of Moscow; from the 14th and 15th century it was a center of commerce and contained many noblemen's mansions.

Climbing the staircase that crosses this wall and through an arcaded house, you reach this former merchants' and artisans' district. Three parallel streets, the October 25th, leading into Red Square, the Kuiby-shev, and Stepan Razin, with numerous cross-streets and lanes, occupy the site. The great merchant houses that developed in the 19th and the early 20th centuries built their headquarters and warehouses here and there are still numerous shops in this quarter. October 25th Street is to be redeveloped as a pedestrian shopping precinct.

One of the few surviving original houses was the home of the first Russian printing works at No. 15 October 25th Street, founded in 1563 by Ivan Fyodorov, at the request of Ivan the Terrible and rebuilt in the 17th century on the site of an earlier wooden building. Its carved stone ornaments and doorway are remarkable. Another surviving monument is the lovely Trinity Church in Nikitniki (1635–53), now a museum with murals by Simon Ushakov (Razin Street, Nikitnikov Pereulok). Most of these buildings now house public offices and institutions but No. 10 Razin Street is a museum—a 17th century "boyar's" house.

If you now go along Vetoshny Street, which runs parallel with Red Square, past the G.U.M. department store, you will reach Kuibyshev Street. Turning left on it, you reach busy Nogin Square. On the right stands the building of the Central Committee of the Communist Party of the Soviet Union. In the park opposite there is an octagonal tower-like monument, commemorating the Russian soldiers who fell in the Battle of Plevna in the Russo-Turkish war (1877). Across the street there is a huge block, housing the Polytechnical Museum devoted to extensive displays of Soviet science and technology.

The Innermost Ring

Moscow's basic plan consists of concentric rings bordered by the main boulevards. The innermost ring is a complex of squares and short thoroughfares which starts on the banks of the Moskva, near Nogin Square, and returns to the river not far from the walls of the Kremlin. Exploring this inner ring, you will next reach Novaya (New) Square. Here stands the Museum of the History and Reconstruction of Moscow. Housed in the former Church of St. John the Baptist, dating from 1825, the museum was founded in 1896 and provides an outline of the history of Moscow's development, showing the city's past and planned future development.

A short distance away is another circular "square" named after Felix Dzerzhinsky, the Soviet revolutionary leader (1877–1926) whose statue stands in its center. From the far side of the square two streets start. On the right, next to the Polytechnical Museum, Kirov Street leads northeast almost to Komsomol Square. On the left, next to a large department store, Dzerzhinsky Street runs up to Prospekt Mira, the Permanent Exhibition of Economic Achievements and the Olympic indoor Stadium and swimming pool. The department store is Detsky Mir (Children's World). It sells everything from baby clothes to camping gear. The large building next door to it with bars on the ground-floor windows is the notorious Lubianka Prison and K.G.B. headquarters.

From the western side of Dzerzhinsky Square the wide Marx Prospekt crosses a number of squares, among them Sverdlov Square and the one named for the 50th Anniversary of the October Revolution. The Hotel Berlin stands on the right-hand side of the avenue; on the left is the statue of the first Russian printer, Ivan Fyodorov. Across the road is the beginning of Neglinnaya Street, with the central building of the State Bank close by.

Marx Prospekt now reaches Sverdlov Square, which is linked to Revolution Square. Karl Marx's statue by Kerbel stands in the center of the square, carved from a 200-ton block of granite on the spot and unveiled in 1964. Opposite stands the Bolshoi (Big) Theater, the oldest in Moscow. Formerly known as the Great Imperial Theater, it was completely rebuilt after a fire in 1854 and now seats 2,155 people. Its ballet company is justly world famous. There are many Russian and foreign works in its opera repertory; its orchestra is also outstanding. The Bolshoi's building is remarkable architecturally, with its monumental colonnade topped by a quadriga of bronze horses, and its crimson-and-gold interior.

To the right is the fine building of the Maly (Small) Theater, with the statue of the satirist Ostrovsky in front of it. The Maly, formerly the Little Imperial Theater, is famous for its staging of Russian classics, especially those of Ostrovsky. Founded over 150 years ago, it was once called by Gorky "the Russian people's university." It seats over 1,000. A more intimate studio theater is in Bolshaya Ordynka Street.

Behind the Maly Theater the art nouveau outline of the G.U.M. Department Store forms an interesting contrast. Between G.U.M. and the Bolshoi, Petrovka Street begins, one of the main shopping streets. It has many specialist shops and a department store. Petrovka Street leads to the Hotel Budapest and its restaurant.

To the left of the Bolshoi Theater in Sverdlov Square is the Central Children's Theater. Pushkin Street starts just behind it, with the Operetta Theater at Number 6, and the Stanislavsky and Nemirovich-Danchenko Musical Theater is further along. This ballet and opera theater shows classical and modern works in both genres, as well as light operettas.

On the corner of Karl Marx Prospekt and Pushkin Street the Dom Soyuzov (House of the Trade Unions), painted green, with a classical facade, is the work of the distinguished architect Kazakov. The Dom Soyuzov was once a club for the nobility. Its famous hall of columns is one of Moscow's most beautiful halls and has seen many historic occasions–Lenin's lying-in-state, for instance. Today festival gatherings and concerts are held here. Next to the House of the Trade Unions is the building of the State Planning Committee, while across Marx Prospekt stands the 14-storied Hotel Moskva.

An underpass leads under Gorky Street, perhaps the best-known Moscow thoroughfare. Here, also, Marx Prospekt again broadens into a square. This is named after the 50th anniversary of the October Revolution. On the corner of Gorky Street and the square stand the twin buildings of the National and Intourist Hotels, the former erected in 1903 and the newer, 21-floor Intourist opened in 1970 with a dozen restaurants, cafés and bars. Continuing past the National's entrance, we reach the old Lomonosov University building (Russia's oldest university), another design by Kazakov, dating from the end of the 18th century. The more recent university complex is on the Lenin Hills.

Passing Herzen Street (with the famous Moscow Conservatory, the Rakhmaninov Concert Hall, the Mayakovsky Theater and the Zoological Museum, with its huge collection of thousands of mammals, birds, amphibians and reptiles, and almost a million insects), you find on your left in the center of the square the former imperial riding school, the Manezh (Manège), since 1957 an exhibition hall. Built in the early 19th century, its huge roof has only the walls, not a single internal column, to support it.

Arriving at the busy corner of Kalinin Prospekt, you have a good view of the central building of the Lenin Library, one of the largest in the world. The most recent part, by Vladimir Shchuko and Vladimir Gelfreikh, was built in 1939–40. Bronze busts of outstanding writers and scientists stand in the niches along the facade. The portico, supported by square black pillars, is approached by a wide ceremonial staircase. Beyond this new building, on a small rise, stands the fine old building of the library, known as Pashkov House, designed by Vasily Bazhenov, one of Russia's greatest architects, and erected in 1784–86. Once the home of a rich family, its graceful, light and harmonious composition makes it one of Moscow's most attractive buildings.

Next is the mouth of Frunze Street, which descends steeply to the Borovitsky Gate of the Kremlin and the Great Stone Bridge of the Moskva River. Continuing straight ahead, however, you reach Volkhonka Street which takes you to the Pushkin Museum, standing in the middle of a small park. Founded by Professor Tsvetayev, the museum was supported originally by private donations. The present building dates from 1895–1912 and was first known as Alexander III's Museum. It is the largest museum in the Soviet Union after the Leningrad Hermitage. There is a fine collection of ancient Egyptian art; Greece and Rome are well represented, though mostly by copies. The art gallery has works by most of Europe's greatest painters—Botticelli, Rembrandt, Rubens, Van Dyck, and Constable among them; a vast selection of French pictures from Poussin and Watteau to Cézanne, Gauguin and Matisse; there are also representative canvases by Picasso. Again, many of these are copies; the museum is used for teaching purposes.

At the end of Volkhonka Street, on the left side, is one of the largest swimming pools in Europe, between the street and the quay of the Moskva River. It is divided into several pools for training, competitions, diving, etc. Its heated pool is open in winter; you reach it from the changing rooms through covered tunnels.

You have now reached the end of the ring of squares and streets enclosing the center of the city. Here, if you are tired, you can board the metro at Kropotkinskaya station. But it is also possible to return along the Moskva River, under the Kremlin walls, to your starting point near Nogin

Square, taking a brief look at the island in the River Moskva. To the right of the Great Stone Bridge, on the island, stand the Estradny (Variety) Theater and the Udarnik cinema. The island is laid out as a park; there are several interesting old houses, former noble mansions, including the British Embassy. At the far end of the island, near the Moskvoretsky Bridge which spans the river from the bottom of Red Square, you will find the Hotel Bucharest. Crossing the bridge, you reach the Zamoskvorechye (Beyond-the-Moskva River) district which was inhabited mainly by merchants before the Revolution. There are few interesting architectural sights here, but not far from the river bank stands the massive Soviet Radio building behind the Novokuznetskaya metro station and the Tretyakov Gallery which now has its own subway station, Tretyakovskaya, with an interchange for Novokuznetskaya station.

This is Moscow's finest art gallery and is devoted to the history of Russian art. The foundations of the collection were laid in 1856 by the brothers Pavel and Sergei Tretyakov, who made a gift of it to the nation in 1892. The exhibits illustrate the whole development of fine arts from unique 11th-century mosaics to the works of contemporary artists: more than 5,000 paintings, 3,000 works of ancient Russian art, about 900 sculptures and 30,000 drawings and engravings. They include the works of Andrei Rublyov, the brilliant 14th-15th-century ikon painter, Alexander Ivanov's *Apparition of Christ,* the canvases of Ilya Repin and Vasily Surikov, the landscapes of Isaac Levitan, Arkhip Kuinji, Alexei Savrasov and Vasily Polenov, the marine painter Ivan Aivazovsky, the portraits of Ivan Kramskoi and characteristic examples of "socialist realism." Examples of the work of the constructivists are, however, conspicuously absent.

Among the sculptures there are a few by Mark Antokolsky, the great 19th-century realist, and works of Sergei Konenkov and Anna Golubkina. The large section devoted to Soviet art features many examples of contemporary painters, sculptors and graphic artists, both traditionalists and, added to the display in more recent years, many examples of the art of the experimentalists.

The Tretyakov had been overcrowded for years and a new Art Gallery of the U.S.S.R. has opened on Krymskaya Embankment, opposite Gorky Park. Its huge, 25,000-square-meter area houses 150 display halls, lecture rooms and workshops.

Down Gorky Street

For your next walk you can start again from the Hotel Moskva, in a more or less northerly direction. Gorky Street was given its present form in the middle thirties, during the first plan of reconstruction, though it has been an important route for centuries—the line of the road that led from the Kremlin to ancient Tver, today's Kalinin. Until the rebuilding, Tverskaya Street was narrow and twisting, lined in places with wooden houses. Today's Gorky Street is a broad, modern boulevard, with considerable traffic and many attractive shops.

Starting on the left-hand side, opposite the building of the Central Planning Committee, you see the tall blocks of the Hotels National and Intourist and the Yermolova Theater (named after a famous actress). At the corner of the first major side street stands the Central Telegraph Office, with a striking semi-circular entrance and a large, illuminated, constantly revolving globe. Glancing right into the side street you will spot a small green building—the Moscow Arts Theater, famous for its productions of the Russian classics, Chekhov in particular, and for versions of major foreign works. Founded in 1898 by the celebrated actor and director Konstantin Stanislavsky (1863–1938) and Nemirovich-Danchenko (1858–1943), here were given the first presentations of Chekhov's and Gorky's plays and here Stanislavsky developed his theories into "the Stanislavsky Method," based on the realistic traditions of the Russian theater. After the production of Chekhov's *The Seagull,* they chose this bird as their emblem. (A new, modern Moscow Art Theater with a seating capacity of 2,000 was opened in 1973 on nearby Tverskoi Boulevard, near Stanislavsky's former home.)

Another short stretch brings you to the small Soviet Square. On the right, at the back of the square, stands the Institute of Marxism-Leninism with Lenin's statue, by S. Merkurov, in front of it; closer to Gorky Street is the monument of Prince Dolgoruky, the founder of Moscow, an equestrian statue, the work of the sculptors Orlov, Antropov and Stamm, erected in 1954 to commemorate the 800th anniversary of the city. Opposite this monument stands the building of the Moscow Town Council (Mossoviet), built at the end of the 18th century by M. F. Kazakov as a governor's palace. It was moved to widen the street. Next to the Town Council is the bookshop Druzhba (Friendship), specializing in foreign, chiefly Eastern European, publications.

Passing the Hotel Central on the right, you reach the beginning of Stanislavsky Street (on the left), which contains the memorial museum of the great Russian stage director. Next comes the so-called Yeliseyevsky Store (officially known as No. 1 Gastronom), which specializes in Russian and foreign food products.

Our next stop is Pushkin Square, where Moscow's first outer ring, the Bulvar (Boulevard), crosses Gorky Street. The boulevard is divided by a wide green strip in the middle. On the right hand, the Bulvar widens into an impressive park. A bronze statue of the great Russian poet after whom the square is named stands at its entrance. It is the work of the sculptor Opekushin, and was erected by public subscription in 1880. Summer or winter, fresh flowers on the pedestal and open-air readings prove that the poet's admirers are still ardent and numerous. There is a fountain behind the monument, illuminated on summer evenings.

On the right, Pushkin Square is bordered by the huge Rossia cinema, opened in 1961 for the Second International Moscow Film Festival.

Pushkin Square is also the home of *Izvestia* (News), an important daily paper (circulation, 8½ million copies). Behind the Rossia cinema are the offices of the Novosti (APN) press agency, and nearby *Trud* (Labor), the newspaper of the trade unions, is edited (19 million copies sold).

Continuing along Gorky Street, we reach the railings of the former English Club, once the social center of Moscow aristocracy. Built by Giliardi in 1787, it now houses the exhibitions of the Central Revolutionary Museum. A little further away is another 18th-century building, the Central Ophthalmic Clinic. It is close to the Hotel Minsk, opened in the middle 1960s.

The grand boulevard of Moscow, the Sadoyava ("Garden") Ring, crosses at Mayakovsky Square. Traffic passes here by a tunnel under Gorky Street and there is an underpass for pedestrians. Mayakovsky's statue by Kibalnikov, erected in 1958, stands in the center of the square.

Mayakovsky Square is one of the centers of Moscow's cultural life. The Tchaikovsky Concert Hall stands on the corner of Gorky Street; seating 1,500, it was opened in 1940. Nearby is the Mossoviet Theater, and on the far side of the square, the Sovremennik (Contemporary) Youth Theater. The tall tower of the Hotel Peking rises off to the left.

Gorky Street ends in the square of the Byelorussian Railway Terminus. Vera Mukhina's Gorky monument stands here. The railway station itself is built in Russian style, with the metro next to it. From here, you can return to the center either by the subway or by a trolley-bus. You can also take a trolley-bus down Leningradsky Prospekt, one of the fast, modern routes of the Soviet capital, divided into six lanes and 118 yards wide.

On the right, the second cross-street is Pravda Street, where you'll see the editorial offices and printing works of *Pravda* (Truth), one of the largest-selling daily papers in the Soviet Union (10 million copies). The next corner is marked by the Hotel Sovietskaya which houses the Romany Theater. Here, too, is one of the most important sports centers of Moscow. On the right are the Dynamo Stadium (60,000 seats) and the covered swimming pool; the wide avenue branching to the left leads to the race course. The Cycling Stadium and the Pioneer Stadium are also in the vicinity.

A few hundred yards more brings you to the striking, crenelated Petrovsky Palace, one of the most characteristic creations of the celebrated Kazakov. Today it houses the Zhukovsky Academy of Aeronautical Engineers, whose students include Soviet cosmonauts. Two monuments outside the academy commemorate Soviet achievements in the conquest of space—one of them, erected in 1962, is the work of G. Postnikov, the other, the statue of Konstantin Tsiolkovsky, "the father of space travel," is by S. Merkurov. Two high-rise buildings mark the other side of the street: one is the Ministry of Civil Aviation (Aeroflot), the other Aeroflot's transit hotel for air passengers.

At the next metro station along Leningradsky Prospekt, you reach the Novopeschannaya district, a housing estate dating from the 1950s.

After the Sokol metro station, Leningradsky Prospekt curves right. The left-hand street leads to Tushino, with its airfield for amateur fliers, and then on to Volokolamsk. Keeping right, still on Leningradsky Prospekt, you can take a trolley-bus to the Khimki Harbor, the starting-point for Volga cruises. The station building is in the shape of the hull of a ship. The modern motorway continues past newer housing developments, crosses the River Moskva and, more than 20 miles from the center, reaches Sheremetyevo, the international airport.

The Kalinin and Kutuzov Prospekts

One of central Moscow's most modern avenues is Kalinin Prospekt, linking the Kremlin through Arbat Square with the western reaches of the Moskva River. The first stretch leads from the Karl Marx Prospekt to Arbat Square. This was formerly known as Novodvizhenskaya Street and has retained some of its pre-revolutionary charm. The second section, built in the 1960s, is a completely new thoroughfare, driven through the former maze of narrow streets and alleys. The pre-revolutionary stretch has been widened and modernized and Kalinin Prospekt is now completed, the showcase of the Soviet capital.

Starting from the Kutafya Tower of the Kremlin (with the Riding School on the right) you cross Karl Marx Prospekt at the Lenin Library.

The first important building, on the left, is the Shchusev Museum of Architecture. The building, by M. F. Kazakov, dates from the 18th century; between 1921 and 1924 it housed the Central Committee of the Communist Party. A little further on, the Central Military Department Store stands on the right. This was established before the First World War; it is open to civilians as well.

The next building of note on the right-hand side is the headquarters of the Association of Soviet Friendship Societies, which also occupies the adjoining house, called the House of Friendship. The latter was once the home of the wealthy industrialist Morozov and was designed by V. A. Marizin at the end of the 19th century. It is almost an anthology of interior decoration styles, ranging from imitation Tudor to Classical Greek and Baroque. This is the regular meeting place of foreign visitors and Soviet artists and writers. Opposite these two buildings, several departments of the Soviet Foreign Ministry occupy a large house in Classical style; here press conferences for foreign correspondents are usually held.

Beyond Arbat Square, nine tall buildings, rising to 23, 24 or 25 stories, mark the start of the second section of Kalinin Prospekt. Before reaching them, however, there are two other interesting landmarks on the corner of Arbat Square. On the left, at the opening to Arbat Street, is the Praga restaurant complex, which contains several excellent restaurants, banqueting and reception rooms. The right-hand corner building is the Dom Svyazi, the House of Communications, containing a very large post office and telephone exchange, together with video-phone studios for transmissions to other Soviet cities. Next to the Post Office building is the small 17th-century church of St. Simon Stylites, with its cluster of domes.

On the right-hand side of Kalinin Prospekt there are five apartment blocks, each of 23 stories and containing 280 units. The ground floor and the first floor of these buildings are occupied by the Malachite Box jewelry shop, the Ivushka Café, a chemist shop, the record shop called Melodiya and the Sireny (Lilac) perfume shop. Here, too, you find in a separate building the Dom Knigi (House of the Book), the largest bookshop in the Soviet Union, with an exhibition room and a department that stocks Penguin books, and the October Cinema together with a large bakery and pastry shop.

On the left-hand side of the Kalinin Prospekt, there are four 25-storied office buildings, accommodating different industrial ministries. A glassed-in elevated gallery links them and contains specialized stores, service enterprises and places of entertainment. They include the Café Valday, the Novo-arbatsky Gastronom (one of the largest, partly self-service food shops in the U.S.S.R.), a shop for philatelists, a large newspaper kiosk, an excellent flower shop, the Transagenstvo travel bureau, the Pechora restaurant and café (mostly frequented by young people), which has a popular jazz ensemble, the Moskvichka dress shop, the Charodeika (Witch), a fashionable hairdresser, and the Institut Krasoti beauty salon. There is also a photographer's studio, the self-service restaurant Angara, the photo and amateur film shop Jupiter, the Sintetika (selling synthetic fabrics and dresses), the Metelitsa pastry shop (with a summer terrace), the Vesna gift shop, a take-away food shop, the Café Biryusa and finally, the Restaurant Arbat, which has a nightly cabaret.

After crossing Tchaikovsky Street, Kalinin Prospekt begins to descend towards the Moskva River. Not far from the river, on the right-hand side, is the new headquarters of the Council of Mutual Economic Assistance, built in the 1960s. It houses the executive committee, secretariat and offices of C.O.M.E.C.O.N., the East European equivalent of the European Community. Adjoining it is the twelve-storied Hotel Mir (Peace), which houses mainly foreign employees and guests of C.O.M.E.C.O.N. Nearby is the palace of the Russian Soviet Federal Republic's Council of Ministers.

Passing across the bridge towards the Hotel Ukraine, you will reach the Kutuzov Prospekt. Some 180 feet wide, it runs west, past new apartment houses and office buildings. At Number 26 a bronze plaque commemorates Leonid Brezhnev, who lived there for 30 years until his death in 1982. Soon you come to the Borodino Panorama, with the triumphal arch commemorating Kutuzov's victory over Napoleon in 1812, and Kutuzov's wooden hut. It was in Kutuzov's hut that the Russian Council of War, headed by Field-Marshal Mikhail Kutuzov, decided that the army would retreat from Moscow. The painting by Kivshenko (1880) shows the Council in session. The Battle Panorama is housed in a cylindrical building, built in 1962 to commemorate the 150th anniversary of the Battle of Borodino. The huge canvases were painted by Roubaud (1856–1912) in Munich. The Panorama stands on a small rise, the Poklon hill, where a memorial complex containing both a Museum of the Great Patriotic War (World War II) and a Victory Monument, is being designed.

The Boulevard and Arbat Square

Your next excursion is to explore the Moscow of the early 19th century. Start from the Kropotinskaya metro station on the bank of the Moskva River, southwest of the Kremlin. From here, the semi-circle of the Soviet capital's lesser ring-road starts off, northwesterly, then curves eastwards and south finally to reach the river bank again after several miles, near the Yauza River's mouth east of the Kremlin.

The Bulvar (Boulevard) was built on the site of the wall enclosing the former White City (Bely Gorod). Running along its center is a broad strip of trees and flowers, playgrounds and benches.

Leaving the metro station, you will see the large open swimming pool to the east. Several roads converge in a little square. Volkhonka Street leads towards the Kremlin; two others start opposite, Ostozhenka (Haystack)—which reverted to this old name in 1978 by public demand, from Metrostroyevskaya—and Kropotkin Street. The former crosses, farther south, Zubovsky Boulevard by a high bridge and runs into the Komsomolsky Prospekt, which, in turn, leads to the Lenin Stadium.

These two streets and the river form the southern end of one of the most interesting quarters of Moscow, stretching roughly to Zubovskaya Square, while on the west it is bordered by the Sadovaya (Boulevard Ring). In the 18th and 19th centuries this was predominantly the quarter of court nobility, where they built their small private mansions, mostly single-storied. Alexander Herzen, the writer and philosopher, compared it with the St-Germain quarter of Paris.

The streets to the left of the Bulvar have many houses marked with plaques showing that eminent writers, artists and thinkers have lived in them. At No. 4 Gagarin Street (near the Kropotkin metro station), was Pushkin's home for a while; the revolutionary poet Ryleev also stayed in the same street. At No. 25 Sivtsev Vrazhek Street, which is the next cross-street of the Bulvar, Herzen had his home; it was here that the Czarist police arrested him. When he returned from his exile, he moved into the neighboring house.

The first section of the Bulvar bears the name of Gogol. A pleasant walk takes you to Arbat Square, the center of the quarter, where the writer's statue stands. The large block of the Ministry of Defense catches the eye. There are two metro stations in the square, with the Khudozhestvenny Cinema beside them. The Kalinin Prospekt crosses Arbat Square, and here Arbat Street, one of the oldest thoroughfares of Moscow, begins. In the 16th century, this was the quarter of court artisans; the street names still recall their names—from Plotnikov (Carpenter) to Serebryany (Silversmith) and Kalachny (Pastrycook). Early in the 19th century it became the district of the aristocracy, while a century later it was a favorite shopping street, a role which has recently been revived. The whole area is now under a preservation order and has become a cobbled pedestrian precinct with gift shops in the restored buildings. There is a museum of the history of the area, a concert hall and two art galleries. The restoration is almost complete and the area has been utterly transformed. At number 26 is the Vakhtangov Theater, named after Stanislavsky's pupil, Evgeny Vakhtangov (1883–1922)—an excellent traditional theater. At number 53, where the poet Pushkin lived, experts have recreated the original layout and interior decoration. Arbat Street continues down to the Boulevard Ring; at the corner is the skyscraper of the Foreign Ministry.

Getting on a trolley-bus on the corner of Arbat and Suvorov Boulevard, go to the next stop, which will be the so-called Nikitskiye Vorota (Gate), where Herzen Street crosses the Bulvar. Setting out to the right, you pass the famous Mayakovsky Theater, and a short walk brings you to the Moscow Conservatory. Alexei Tolstoy Street branches off on the left, with the memorial museum of the writer (nephew of Leo). The small square contains the statue of the botanist Timiryazev (1843–1920).

The next stop north along the Bulvar is opposite the Pushkin Theater, which brings you to Pushkin Square. Take a tram from the far end of the square if you want to explore the Bulvar further. Two stops along is Trubnaya Square. On the left, the Tsvetnoy Boulevard branches off at a right angle. A few yards along stands the Mir Panoramic Cinema's circular building with the home of the Moscow Circus next to it.

The Circus, a very popular form of entertainment with the Russians, is well worth a visit. It has a long, varied and spectacular program which changes every year and often includes an appearance by Popov, the famous clown. The building is so modest in size for a circus that it gives a great sense of immediacy to the performance—there is audience participation in jokes with the clowns. (A large, modern New Circus, at 7 Vernadsky Prospekt, has drawn off many of the top performers, though it lacks the intimacy and folksy feeling of the old circus.)

The Bulvar then crosses several avenues radiating from the center of the city—the Sretenka, famous for its shops, and Kirov Street. The Central Post Office is on the corner of Kirov Street. The next stop is the Chistiye Prudi (Pure Water Reservoir), with a small artificial boating lake.

The semi-circle of the Bulvar reaches the Moskva River again at the mouth of the Yauza. Here, on the Kotyelnicheskaya Quay, is another "Stalin Gothic" skyscraper with a 32-story central tower.

The Two-level Grand Boulevard and Its Avenues

The Grand Boulevard of Moscow, the so-called Sadovaya, was also built on the site of the former city walls. It is more than ten miles long—much too long to explore on foot. But trolley-cars travel its entire length.

Don't start on the Sadovaya itself, but at Komsomol Square, northeast of the Kremlin en route to Sokolniki, a few hundred yards away from the Grand Boulevard. Emerging from the Komsomolskaya metro station, you will find yourself on a vast and busy square. It contains three large railway stations: the Leningrad, the Yaroslavl and the Kazan terminals. The narrow, 26-story tower of the Hotel Leningradskaya rises above the square. Starting from the hotel, pass southwest along busy Kalanchovskaya Street to reach Lermontov Square where it joins the Sadovaya. There is another high rise here: the 24-story headquarters of the Ministry of Railways.

If you board a No. 10 trolley-bus in front of this building, it will take you in a westerly direction along the Sadovaya Boulevard. It passes the Ministry of Agriculture, then stops in front of a palace with a classic central part and a semi-circular wing of columns. Once the home of the Sheremetyev princes, today it is the headquarters of the Moscow ambulance service, housing also an emergency hospital and a medical research institute.

After the Skifovsky Institute (named for a famous surgeon), you will reach the corner of the Prospekt Mira (Peace). This is an important route, running north towards the Riga Railway Station, the Exhibition of Economic Achievements of the U.S.S.R., the Kosmos Hotel and one of the main Olympic stadiums and swimming pool.

The next square, the Kolkhoznaya (kolkhoz means "collective farm"), is spanned by an overpass. On the left, Tsvetnoy Boulevard joins the Sadovaya, which widens here into a square; on the right, another parkway leads out of the city. The pentagonal building of the Soviet Army Theater marks its end. Here, too, is the Central Army House and Memorial Museum. Its large park is the scene of concerts and variety performances in the summer.

The Sadovaya is lined by tall apartment houses; traffic moves on two levels, eliminating crossovers. The trolley-bus emerges on Mayakovsky Square from its tunnel in front of the Hotel Peking, then stops outside the Moscow Planetarium. Here there are illustrated lectures on the structure of the universe, on comets, meteorites, eclipses, the weather and on Soviet space exploration.

Almost exactly opposite there is a narrow, small building—the Chekhov Memorial Museum, once the home of the great playwright. The front door still bears his original physician's brass plate. Heading south now, a tour of the Ploshchad Vosstaniya (Square of the Uprising) brings you to the left-hand side of the Sadovaya (this section is called Tchaikovsky Street), by which point the Moscow "Saint-Germain" district has already begun. The other side is the Krasnaya Presnya, a working-class quarter.

Beside the high-rise building on the Square, a sloping road leads to the main entrance of the Zoo. (Another zoo entrance is on the Sadovaya, next to the Planetarium.)

On the far side of the square, Herzen Street and Vorovsky Street join the Square of the Uprising. Vorovsky Street is one of the main thoroughfares of the diplomatic quarter. There are a good many embassies and legations in the neighboring, quiet streets. Close to the Square of the Uprising, two important buildings face each other: the headquarters of the Soviet Writers' Union and the constructivist-style Dom Kino, the former home of the Association of Cinematic Arts.

Continuing along the Tchaikovsky Street section of the Sadovaya, you will pass the building which now houses the U.S. Embassy. The trolley-bus once again dips underground at the point where Kalinin Prospekt crosses the Grand Boulevard. (Down a gentle slope Kalinin Prospekt continues towards the Moskva River and, crossing the 500-yard long Kalinin Bridge, it reaches the Hotel Ukraine.)

If you pursue your exploration of the Sadovaya, however, you will next pass the 27-story building of the Foreign Ministry and Ministry of Foreign Trade. Opposite, the Hotel Smolenskaya stands on a recently-developed square (Smolenskaya Square). Next to the ministry block, the Sadovaya reaches Arbat Street. On the right there is an attractive view of the River Moskva and the Borodino Bridge, decorated with reliefs commemorating the famous battle. Beyond the river on the right rises the glass-domed building of the Kiev Railway Station.

The next broad avenue, the Bolshaya Pirogovskaya (Great Pirogov) Street, opens from the wide Zubovskaya Square. Named after a celebrated Russian surgeon, Great Pirogov Street contains several hospitals and clinics. Leo Tolstoy Street, running parallel with the Sadovaya, opens from Pirogovskaya Street. The great writer's former home is now the Tolstoy Museum. Sixteen rooms are preserved as they were when Tolstoy and his family lived there from 1872 to 1901. Pirogovskaya Street continues past Novodevichy Convent and cemetery, to the Lenin Stadium.

Beyond the Pirogovskaya the Grand Boulevard reaches the Moskva River, where the Crimea Bridge spans it. Another bridge crosses the Sadovaya itself, carrying rapid transit traffic from the Kremlin, towards Lenin Stadium and the southwestern part of the capital. This route is called the Komsomolsky Prospekt and was opened in 1957. On the right you can enter the Gorky Park station of the metro, beyond which stands one of the finest churches of Moscow with its onion-shaped gilt dome (Church of St. Nicholas in Khamovniki, 1679–82). The Crimea Bridge provides a fine vantage point for the river banks. Along the northwestern side there are tall blocks; this is Frunze Quay, a 1950s housing complex. On the other side, the green expanse of Gorky Park is dominated by two giant Ferris wheels. Gorky Park is the most popular of the city's parks. Stretching along the riverside, its 300 acres include the Neskuchnyi Sad (Happy Garden) and the Zeleny Theatr (Green Theater), which is an open-air one, seating 10,000. The park also has sports grounds, a boating station, cafés, a beer hall and various exhibition halls. Unfortunately, the place is getting a reputation for petty crime.

The trolley-bus stops at the ornamental gate of the park, then continues towards October Square. From this point, the Sadovaya continues to the industrial quarters of Moscow. The largest building on October square is the Hotel Warsaw. An underground line starts here towards New Cheryomushki and Kaluzhskaya Station—parts of the Southwestern District. Nearby, one of the principal thoroughfares of Moscow, Lenin Prospekt, starts. Running parallel with this avenue, the Shabolovka, another wide street, branches off; Moscow Television used to have studios here. Opposite the mouth of Lenin Avenue, Dimitrov Street begins, leading to the center.

The Southwestern District

Board a trolley-bus at October Square if you want to travel along Lenin Prospekt to one of the Soviet capital's model housing developments, the Southwestern District.

The first part of Lenin Prospekt was once called the Kaluga Road. Here the city's first hospitals were built, some distance from the noisy and crowded center. The first of them, on the right-hand side, was designed by Bove, the architect who directed the rebuilding of the capital after the 1812 conflagration; the second, with a colonnade and dome, is even earlier, built at the beginning of the 19th century by M. F. Kazakov.

On the right, in the middle of an ornamental park, there is an old building with a gate decorated with statues. This is the seat of the Soviet Academy of Sciences, the former Neskuchny Castle. Scientists occupy the surrounding apartment houses, while on the left side of the road various research and planning departments of the Academy have been established. Between them, a street leads to Donskaya Square, where the Architectural Museum is housed in a 15th-century monastery.

Lenin Prospekt next crosses the circular Gagarin Square. Two tall ornamental buildings stand on either side. Up to the 1950's this square was at the city limits of Moscow and the buildings, somewhat over-decorated, were intended to greet the arriving tourist. Today they mark the beginning of the Southwestern District, consisting of several large, interconnected housing areas. These include the Lenin Hills and the site of the former village, Cheryomushki. The extensive building program began in 1952 and still continues with mile after mile of ribbon development.

At Gagarin Square the Vorobyovskoye Highway branches off from Lenin Prospekt and runs along the Moskva River on the ridge of the Lenin Hills. To the left Profsoyuznaya (Trade Union) Street leads towards Cheryomushki. On the right the Hotel Sputnik rises. Here too is the headquarters of the Central Council of the Soviet Trade Unions. On the left, several research institutes are housed in a block. Opposite, the Moskva Department Store specializes in men's and women's clothing; it is larger than the G.U.M. store.

The first major crossroads is that of University Prospekt (right), and Cheryomushkinskaya Street. At the next crossing you leave the Lenin Prospekt, which continues for several miles, flanked by tall apartment blocks, passing the student hostels of Lumumba University, and then runs towards Vnukovo airport.

Instead follow the broad Lomonosov Prospekt to the right. This was the site of the first blocks of the Southwestern District and today is one of the busiest traffic arteries in the district. In the distance is the impressive skyline of the Olympic Village, a housing estate for 15,000 Muscovites with a range of shops, entertainment facilities etc.

Turning right from the Lomonosov Prospekt, pass the railings of the Lomonosov University campus. This is the Vernadsky Prospekt where the new building for the humanities faculty of the university has been completed recently, and the new premises of the Moscow Circus opened. Near the Prospekt Vernadskovo metro station is the recent Hotel Druzhba. On the other side, the dome of the Sternberg Observatory can be seen among the trees.

You have now almost come full circle, reaching University Prospekt once again. Turning left, start for the distant, tall building of the Lomonosov University, which can also be reached by metro or one of the numerous buses. Standing on the Lenin Hills, this much-criticized complex was built between 1949 and 1953. Individual visitors need special permits to visit it, but there are regular group tours. From the top of the commanding tower there is a panoramic view of the Soviet capital.

Across the park in front of the university (where, in December 1980, John Lennon's death was commemorated—even in Moscow—with an open-air gathering of students), we find the Lenin Hills Lookout Tower rising above the Moskva River. Offering a panorama of the greater part of Moscow, it has a terrace of red polished granite. From here, you can see the wide loop of the river with the gentle slope of the Lenin Hills continuing on the left. There is a clear view, to the distant left, of the housing estates behind the Mosfilm Studios, the grey block of the Kiev Railway Station and the tower of the Hotel Ukraine on the corner of Kutuzov Prospekt. Nearer, the golden domes of the Novodevichy Convent glitter; directly opposite the lookout tower, at the bottom of the river loop, you will be able to see the stadiums of the Lenin Sports Grounds, at Luzhniki. Far in the background, the golden domes of the Kremlin cathedrals are visible in good weather. On the immediate right, a two-level metro bridge spans the river; its two main spans were manufactured on the spot.

On the lower level of the bridge, the metro runs towards the university; it has a stop on the bridge itself, from which you can reach both the stadium and the Lenin Hills. On the upper level, traffic moves from the Komsomol Prospekt towards one of the main traffic arteries of the Southwestern District, the Vernadsky Prospekt. On the flank of the Lenin Hills (though not visible from this vantage point) spreads the new diplomatic quarter.

To the left of the lookout tower there is a small church. To the right, a shady promenade takes us to the crossing of the Vernadsky Prospekt. Pass the ski jump and arrive at a glassed-in hall, marked by the red *M* of the metro (subway or underground). An escalator takes you down to the station on the bridge. Before descending, look at the complex of the Central Palace of Pioneers, a group of all-glass buildings including a winter garden, a stadium and a domed observatory. The foundations of this young people's center were laid on the 40th anniversary of the founding of the Soviet Youth Organization, the Komsomol, and it was built mostly by young labor.

The Sports City, Novodevichy Convent and Frunze District

This exploration should start at the Lenin Hills metro station on the lower level of the double bridge referred to in the previous section. Leave the station at the stadium exit. Inaugurated in August 1956, the main stadium (site of the 1980 Olympic ceremonies) seats more than 100,000 people; there are more than 140 halls, training courses, stadia, as well as several restaurants and cafes in the large park. The Lenin Stadium complex was converted and enlarged for the Olympics, but even before that it was probably the largest sports centre in the world.

Nearest to the metro station is the open-air swimming pool, which has more than 13,000 places for spectators. There is a separate diving pool. The Great Stadium is reserved for soccer, athletic meets and displays. It is equipped for night matches; the 100,000 spectators are able to leave the place within six minutes through skillfully planned exits. Inside the stadium building there is a covered course for sprinters, training and dressing rooms, a sports hotel, restaurant, cinema, a post office, press rooms for journalists and T.V. and numerous other service installations. The Lesser Stadium is reserved for basketball, volleyball, tennis and boxing matches; in the winter it's used for ice hockey and skating. It seats 16,000. The Sports Palace is one of Europe's largest indoor sport halls, with seats for 17,000 spectators. It can easily be converted into an indoor skating rink or a theater; during the Olympics it was used for gymnastic events.

Leaving the sports center, walking north along the Moskva River, you pass under the railway embankment and come to the Novodevichy Convent and cemetery. Its entrance is on the southern side, in Novodevichy Proyezd, through a small park, from Bolshaya Pirogovskaya Street. One of the finest examples of 16th- and 17th-century architecture, the Convent is enclosed by a crenelated wall with 12 battle towers, and consists of a group of several buildings. It was founded in 1524 by Grand Prince Vasili Iovanovich to commemorate the union of Moscow and Smolensk; it formed a stronghold on the road to Smolensk and Lithuania, besides being a convent for ladies of noble birth. Evdokiya, Peter the Great's first wife, and Princess Sophia, his troublesome sister, both spent part of their lives here and are buried here.

The huge, five-domed Smolensky Cathedral (1525) is dedicated to Our Lady of Smolensk; it was built by Aleviz Fryazin. The iconostasis has 84 wooden columns; the icons of the 16th and 17th centuries were painted by outstanding Moscow masters. Since 1922, the Convent has been part of the Museum of History. It boasts rare and ancient Russian paintings, both ecclesiastical and secular, woodwork and metalwork, fabrics and embroidery of the 16th and 17th centuries. There is also a large collection of 16th- and 17th-century illuminated and illustrated books, decorated with gold, silver and jewels. In the cathedral, Boris Godunov was elected Czar in 1598.

The old cemetery within the convent wall is the burial place of eminent artists, generals, political and public leaders and scientists. Gogol, Chekhov, Mayakovsky, Scriabin (Molotov's uncle), Prokofiev, Stanislavsky, Eisenstein, Khrushchev and Molotov himself rest here among the 270 monuments. In 1984 the remains of Feodor Chaliapin, the famous singer, were transferred here from Paris.

Outside the cemetery you can board a trolley-bus; but you can also walk southeast along the railway embankment, back towards the sports complex. Almost opposite the stadium stands the Hotel Yunost (Youth). Farther away you reach the Sportivnaya metro station, and beyond that, the site of the Moscow Fair. From spring to autumn, many Moscow department stores have their own pavilions here.

Continuing, you will arrive at Komsomol Prospekt, which links the center, by means of a two-level bridge, with the Southwestern District. It is lined by apartment houses.

Northwest of Komsomol Prospekt the modern Frunze District has some Russian Classical buildings near the Sadovaya (Zubovsky Boulevard). These military barracks were built early in the 19th century. The nearby Church of St. Nicholas in Khamovniki dates from the 17th century; it used to be the parish church for the weavers who had settled in considerable numbers in this quarter.

At the end of the Komsomol Prospekt there is an overpass above the Sadovaya. From here you can continue by subway (or underground railway) from the Gorky Park metro station. If you take the trolley-bus back to the center, you will pass the open Moskva swimming pool. The bus continues along Metrostroyevskaya (Street of the Metro Builders) towards the Bulvar—here, too, you can change to the metro at Kropotkinskaya Station—or continue along Volkhonka Street as far as Karl Marx Prospekt and the Kremlin.

Economic Achievement Exhibition and Ostankino Palace

If time permits, a whole day can be devoted to these two; they are best reached by the metro. The station for both is VDNKh, at the northern end of Prospekt Mira, near the Kosmos Hotel.

Occupying 553 acres and including about 80 large pavilions and many smaller structures, the permanent Exhibition of Economic Achievements, renewed annually, has a three-mile circular road served by small buses, open miniature trains, motor-bike taxis, etc. The pavilions (closed between September and end of April) are built in the architectural styles of the different Soviet republics; many large buildings are devoted to different branches of agriculture, industry and science. The exhibition grounds also include a circus, a Cinerama (Circorama) cinema, two theaters, and an open-air theater. There are many restaurants and cafés of which the Golden Ear (Zolotoi Kolos) is the best.

Outside the North Gate is the gigantic steel statue by Vera Mukhina *Worker and Farm-Woman,* designed for the Paris Fair of 1937. Also just outside the Gate is a 295-foot monument to commemorate Soviet space exploration, and nearby is the recent Memorial Museum of Space, where you can see "relics" of the Space Age—satellites, rockets, space-suits, and an audio visual documentary. There is a simulated space trip from the past, through the present and into the future.

Most of the other pavilions are devoted to exhibitions covering almost every facet of national life from atomic energy to art. There are displays of work by contemporary artists and sculptors, graphic artists, stained glass panels by Lithuanian craftsmen and carpets by the famous Turkmen carpet weavers. A cinema shows selected Soviet films. Nearby are several hotels and hostels, some used for youth tourist groups.

A little further on, behind the Exhibition site, is the Ostankino Palace Museum. This timber palace was erected in the 18th century by the serf craftsmen of Count Sheremetyev under the direction of the serf and artist Pavel Argunov. The estate itself was over 2 million acres, with 210,000 serfs and an annual income of $1\frac{1}{2}$ million roubles. The decorations, in excellent taste, include delicate, lace-like gilt carvings on the portals and doors, cornices, columns and walls. All the furniture was also fashioned by the serfs. The floors are masterpieces of parquetry and from the painted ceilings hang ornate crystal chandeliers. Stoves and fireplaces are faced with varnished tiles, marble malachite and bronze. There is a fine collection of 17th- and 18th-century carvings, crystal, porcelain and fans.

The palace theater had its heyday in the 18th century when the company included some 200 actors, singers, dancers and musicians—all of them serfs. One of the stars was Parasha Kovalyova, daughter of a blacksmith, whose talent and beauty captured the heart of Count Sheremetyev; she became his wife and one of the Ostankino streets is named after her. The chairs in the theater were movable so that the auditorium could be transformed into a ballroom within minutes. The devices for scenic, light and sound effects, invented by the serfs, still exist. The large park has many marble sculptures. Trinity Church, just to the left of the main entrance, was built in 1683 by the serf-architect Pavel Potekhin.

Near the Ostankino Palace Museum you will find the new Ostankino Hotel and the headquarters of Soviet Television, with the TV Tower just opposite. This was finished in 1967 and rises to 334 meters. It serves five TV channels and six UHF radio programs. In the middle section of the tower, the Sedmoye Nebo (Seventh Heaven) Restaurant offers a splendid view (on three levels) of the whole Moscow area. It is a revolving restaurant, taking 45 minutes to describe a complete circle. Visits to the TV tower must be reserved well in advance; the tickets are 7 roubles, entitling you to a two hours' tour and a meal at the restaurant.

EXCURSIONS FROM MOSCOW

Within easy reach of the city for half-day excursions are some beautiful old palaces, estates and former noble residences, set in typical countryside. To see them to the best advantage you should try and time your visits to coincide with spring or summer.

Arkhangelskoye Estate Museum

This museum is in the village of Arkhangelskoye, 26 km. (16 miles) from Moscow. Motorists can reach it by leaving Moscow along the Leningradsky Prospekt, then the Volokolamskoye Chaussée, taking the left fork to the Petrovo-Dalniye Chaussée.

The estate, with the former palace of Prince Yusupov, is a striking 18th- and 19th-century group of buildings, whose architecture artfully blends into the landscape. The main complex was built at the end of the 18th century for Prince Golitsyn by the French architect Chevalier de Huerne. Bought in 1810 by the rich landlord Yusupov, a descendant of the Tatar Khans, who at one time was the director of the Imperial Theaters and of the Hermitage Museum, it became the home of his extraordinary art collection.

The classical palace contains paintings by Boucher, Vigée-Lebrun, Hubert Robert, Roslin, Tiepolo, Van Dyck and many others, as well as antique statues, furniture, mirrors, chandeliers, glassware and china. In the study there are portraits of royalty and nobility. Samples of fabrics, china and glassware (all produced on the estate) are also on show.

In the French Park, the avenues are lined with many statues and monuments to commemorate royal visits; there is also a monument to Pushkin, whose favorite retreat was Arkhangelskoye.

In the western part, a small pavilion known as the Temple to the Memory of Catherine the Great depicts the Empress as Themis, goddess of justice. The Estate Theater, on the right side of the main road, was built in 1817 by the serf-architect Ivanov; it seated 400 and was the home of the biggest and best-known company of serf-actors. It now houses a special exhibition. The well-preserved stage decorations are by the Italian artist Gonzaga. Arkhangelskoye is open between 11 and 5, closed Mondays and Tuesdays.

The Kuskovo Palace Museum

The Kuskovo Palace Museum is about 10 km. (6 miles) from Moscow along the Ryazanskoye Chaussée, but can be reached by train from the Kursk Railway Station. It was built in the early 18th century as a summer residence by Prince Pyotr Sheremetyev, who owned more than 150,000 serfs. Designed by Alexei Mironov, another serf-architect, it is a timber structure on a white stone foundation. The palace is the center of the estate, standing on the banks of a lake. It has been a museum since 1918 and its interior decorations, including fine parquet floors and silk wall-coverings, have recently been painstakingly restored.

On display in the inner rooms are paintings by French, Italian and Flemish artists, Chinese porcelain, furniture, ornaments and articles of everyday life from the 18th and 19th centuries. The palace also houses one of the best collections of 18th-century Russian art, with some 200 portraits, and contains a Ceramics Museum with a rich collection of Russian, Soviet and foreign ceramics. The White Hall, the dining room, the nursery, the oak-panelled study, the drawing room and the gallery of tapestries are of special interest. There are several smaller buildings in the French Gardens (including the Hermitage, where dinner tables were raised mechanically from the ground floor to the first-floor dining room), the Dutch House, the Italian House and the Grotto.

Kuskovo is open from 10 to 7, closed on Tuesdays and the last day of each month.

Kolomenskoye Estate

This estate was once the favorite summer residence of the Grand Dukes of Moscow and later of the Czars. It stands on the Kashirskoye Chaussée overlooking the Moskva River.

The most striking part of the large complex is the beautiful Church of the Ascension of Christ (1532), built in the old Russian "tent" style. There is a partly-rebuilt 16th-century iconostasis. The belfry also dates from the beginning of the same century. The 16th-century Dyachkovskaya Church is also very fine. The royal estate was centered around a wooden palace which Catherine the Great had demolished in 1767; only the Main Gate, the Clock Tower and the Water Tower remain, but a full restoration is in progress. The log cabin in which Peter the Great lived in Arkhangelsk has been transferred here. Other examples of Russian wooden architecture are the Prison Tower from Siberia (1631), the Defense Tower from the White Sea (1690) and a 17th-century mead brewery from the village of Preobrazhenskoye. The 17th-century Kazan Church, with five onion-shaped domes, is open for services.

The Museum is housed in the former servants' quarters of the estate. There are displays illustrating the peasant wars of 1606–7, the "Copper Mutiny" of 1662 against the introduction of copper coins in place of silver, exhibitions of Russian woodcarving, metalwork and ceramics. Kolomenskoye is open 10 to 7 daily except Tuesdays.

Istra River Museum of Wooden Architecture

About 48 km. (30 miles) out of Moscow, this new museum of 17th and 18th century village life has been set among coppices on the high banks of the River Istra near the old Novoierusalimsky Monastery. Its churches, peasant cottages, granaries and windmills have been brought from various parts of Russia. Other exhibits are being added all the time.

Pasternak's Grave

Take a local train to Peredelkino, a few stops from Kievsky station in Moscow, to visit the grave of the great Russian writer. (See also page 221.)

PRACTICAL INFORMATION FOR MOSCOW

WHEN TO GO. Moscow's climate is changeable; the winter is cold with plenty of snow; the summers are frequently very dry, though sometimes rainy. Winter, too, is changeable, with low temperatures—though there have been years when they rarely dropped below freezing point. June, July and August are the hottest months, August particularly; cloudbursts and thunderstorms are frequent. The average amount of sunshine is 250 hours in July and 211 in August. Winter often brings long periods of frost; December, January and February, particularly, can be rather grim for stretches of a week or ten days. Spring is late and short, so is fall; snow often arrives early in November. So for tourists, the summer months might be preferable, with May and September the best at either end. The festivals are held in May (5–15, Moscow Stars) and in mid-winter (December 25–January 5, Winter Festival).

GETTING THERE. By air. You can fly to Moscow from practically every capital in Europe and many in Africa, Asia and the Americas. There are many regular flights from Leningrad, from all the Union Republics, the health resorts of the Crimea, the Caucasus, the Ukraine and the Baltic seaboard, from the Far East, Siberia, the Far North.

The City Air Terminal is at 37 Leningradsky Prospekt; the nearest subway stations are *Aeroport* and *Dynamo*. It is open 24 hours a day; after checking in you can go by cab, bus or helicopter to the airports.

Planes of 20 foreign companies land at *Sheremetyevo International Airport,* from which Aeroflot and *major* foreign airlines take off for scores of countries.

Sheremetyevo-Two services passengers on other international airlines.

Domodedovo, the largest airport in the Soviet Union (and one of the largest in the world), is on the Kashira Highway, some 48 km. (30 miles) miles southeast of Moscow. Here the largest and fastest planes land, servicing the bulk of domestic flights.

Vnukovo Airport is on the Kiev Highway, some 29 km. (18 miles) from the center of Moscow.

These last two airports have rail links with the city center: Domodedovo with the Paveletsky station, and Vnukovo with the Kievsky Station.

Air Information. *City Terminal:* 155–5004(5) (Also Aeroflot Service Bureau). And at 7 Dobryninskaya Street: 238–8535.

Sheremetyevo: 158–7926 (Cargo dispatch, *fret*); customs: 158–7996 and 158–7923. Intourist representative: 156–9435 and 158–7912.

Sheremetyevo-Two: 155–5004(05).

Domodedovo: Intourist Representative: 234–0932.

Vnukovo: Intourist Representative: 234–0932.

General enquiries about all airports: 155–5005.

Aeroflot: Reservations: 155–5003; International enquiries: 245–3877 and 238–8535.

Lines are always very busy and you may have to try many times before getting a connection, and often conversations can be interrupted for no apparent reason.

Of course you will not always get an English-speaking representative on the other end of the line. But demand one—it very often works. Patience is the main quality when phoning.

By train. Moscow has nine railway stations, which handle 400 million passengers annually. Railways are electrified. From Moscow to Leningrad, by the comfortable *Red Arrow* night sleeper, traveling time is eight hours.

The Byelorussian Railway Station (Byelorussky Vokzal Square): Trains to and from Berlin, Warsaw, London, Paris, Smolensk, Minsk, Brest and Vilnius.

The Kazan Railway Station (2 Komsomolskaya Square): Trains to and from Rostov-on-Don, Kazan, Volgograd, the Central Asian Republics and Siberia.

The Kiev Railway Station (Kievsky Vokzal Square): Trains to and from Chop, Belgrade, Bucharest, Budapest, Karlovy Vary, Prague, Sofia, Cierna, Jassy, Kiev, Kishinev, Lvov, Odessa, Uzhgorod and Chernovtsy.

The Kursk Railway Station (29 Chkalov Street): Trains to and from the Crimea and the Caucasus, Armenia, Azerbaijan, Georgia, the Mineralniye Vody spas, Kursk, Tula, Orel and Kharkov.

The Leningrad Railway Station (1 Komsomolskaya Square): trains to and from Helsinki, Leningrad, Kalinin, Novgorod, Murmansk, Petrozavodsk, Pskov and Tallinn.

The Paveletsky Railway Station (Leninskaya Square): Trains to and from the Donets Basin and Volgograd.

The Riga Railway Station (Rizhskaya Square): Trains to and from Riga and Baltic health resorts.

The Savelovsky Railway Station (Butyrskaya Zastava Square): Trains to and from Leningrad and Uglich.

The Yaroslavl Railway Station (5 Komsomolskaya Square): Trains to and from Siberia and the Far East, Moscow-Peking Express. The Trans-Siberian departs daily at 2 P.M. Moscow time, an event rail buffs should see.

Rail Information. *The Central Railway Enquiry Office* (tel. 266–9000) will provide information about departures and arrivals. Tel. 221–4513 (the office in the Metropole Hotel) for enquires in English.

By car. It is possible to reach Moscow along the autoroutes which we have described in *Facts at Your Fingertips* (see *Intourist Route Map,* page 26).

By ship. You might be adventurous and try to arrange with Intourist to arrive in Moscow by ship along the Moscow-Volga canal. With a length of some 80 miles, it links the Soviet capital directly with the Caspian, the Baltic, the Black Sea, the White Sea and the Azov Sea. The Moscow-end port for long-distance passengers is the North Port on the Khimki reservoir. This option is not listed among Intourist's current offerings except as a two-way cruise from Moscow and back to Moscow. But you can try asking.

GETTING INTO TOWN. Intourist will provide transportation from the airport either by bus or by taxi; also from railway stations and the landing stage of the Moscow–Volga boats, for those on Intourist package tours.

GETTING AROUND MOSCOW. By metro (subway). There are nine subway (underground) lines with over 200 kilometres of track and 132 stations. The Metro (marked with a large illuminated *M* sign) runs from 6 A.M. to 1 A.M.; on Sundays, half an hour longer. It is the fastest and most convenient mode of transport; during the rush hours, trains leave the stations every 50 seconds. 12 million passengers use it daily and it celebrated its 50th anniversary in 1985.

Pocket maps are available from stations or Intourist offices. Plan your route beforehand and have your destination with you written down *in Russian* to help you spot the station. Each station is announced over the train's public address system as you approach it, and the name of the next one is given before the train moves

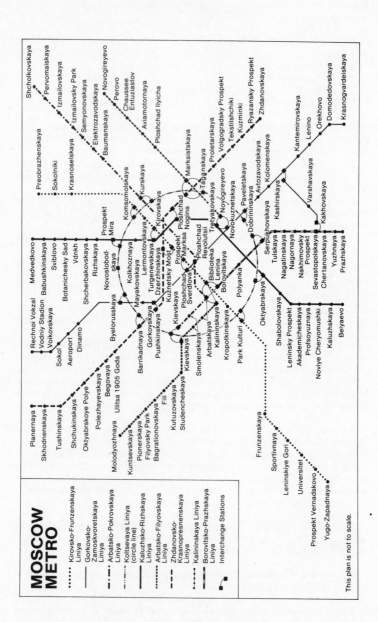

MOSCOW METRO

.... Kirovsko-Frunzenskaya Liniya

───── Gorkovsko-Zamoskvoretskaya Liniya

─ ─ ─ Arbatsko-Pokrovskaya Liniya

·─·─·─ Koltsevaya Liniya (circle line)

═════ Kaluzhsko-Rizhskaya Liniya

─────── Arbatsko-Filyovskaya Liniya

─·─·─· Zhdanovsko-Krasnopresnenskaya Liniya

········ Kalininskaya Liniya

─•─•─ Borovitsko-Prazhskaya Liniya

Interchange Stations

This plan is not to scale.

off. Reminders of interchanges/transfers are also given, so if you understand Russian, keep your ears peeled.

The fare is 5 kopeks regardless of distance; a coin must be inserted into the slot at the turnstile at the entrance to the platforms (as in the New York subway). Another 5 kopeks must be paid for each piece of luggage—whose length must not exceed 3 feet (except skis), and whose width must not exceed one foot or height 16 inches. Most stations now have change machines for 10 or 20 kopek coins. Be prepared for a lot of elbowing and pushing. Escalators run fast—be warned! Every station has a doctor in case of accidents.

Passengers on the Metro rarely speak when traveling and when they do they keep their voices down, foreign visitors can be recognised by their talking. Don't drop any litter on the floor; the Russians are determined to keep the Metro trains and stations clean, an aspect not always characteristic of some other parts of the Soviet Union.

By trolley-bus, bus, tram, and minibus. These carry more than 8 million passengers daily. Most trolley-buses, buses and trams have no conductors; passengers drop the fare into a cash-box and tear off a ticket. All buses etc. are crowded. If you can't reach the cash-box ask someone to pass your money along. The ticket will find its way back to you. This is accepted practice.

The stops are sometimes announced by the driver. The 320 bus and 75 trolley-bus services start at 6 A.M. and the final runs begin at 1 A.M. The trams start at 5.30 A.M. on 52 routes, mostly in the suburbs, finishing at 1.30 A.M. Fares on trolleys, buses and trams were unified at 5 kopeks in 1985. "Microbuses" link points difficult to reach by other means, providing a service on 60 routes every 10 minutes, with intermediate request stops.

River-boats provide a pleasant, if leisurely way of getting about. Small boats ply the Moskva River within city limits, from May-June until September-October, depending on the weather. Two of the 13 routes run through the city center. The first runs from the Kiev Terminal via the Lenin Hills-Gorky Park-Krymsky Bridge-Bolshoi Kamenny Bridge-Bolshoi Ustyinsky Bridge-Krasnokholmsky Bridge-Novospassky Bridge, passing the Novodevichy Convent, the Lenin Stadium, Moscow University, the Moskva swimming pool, the Kremlin and other Moscow landmarks. This cruise takes an hour and 20 minutes and the fare is 20 kopeks. The second route also begins at the Kiev Terminal via the Krasnopresensky Park to Kuntsevo-Krylatskoye. It takes you to the Fili-Kuntsevo Park and the river beach, lasting one hour. The fare is 20 kopeks.

By taxi. There are more than 11,000 **taxis** in Moscow, available at 300 taxi stands marked by a special sign. They can be distinguished by a checkered line on their doors and a green light on the windshield. If this light is on, the taxi is free. You can also hail a taxi in the street by raising your hand. Outside the hotel they have usually been booked by Intourist, so you may have to ask at your hotel desk and pay an extra service charge. The charges are 20 kopeks per kilometer plus a 20 kopek service charge. The waiting charge is one rouble per hour. You pay according to the meter, irrespective of the number of passengers or the amount of luggage. Do not be alarmed if the driver picks up another passenger; if they are going in your direction the fare will be split between you. Russian-speakers may order by telephone. The best numbers are reported to be: 225–0000, 227–0040 or 256–9003 (for freight).

Car rentals. Intourist will provide a private car to tour Moscow with or without driver; either a six-seater Chaika, or four-seater Lada, Zhiguli or Volga. For an excursion outside the city, you can rent a car or bus, with or without a driver. Rentals must be paid in foreign currency and preferably well in advance, at least three weeks if possible. Ask Intourist for latest situation.

On foot. For the pedestrian, the following traffic rules are prescribed:

Traffic moves on the right. Some central streets have one-way traffic. Cross the street only where crossings are indicated by zebra stripes or arrows and at a green light. Use the underpasses where available. If caught in the middle when traffic starts moving, stay put, do not run. Special markings in mid-street indicate where you should stand if caught; traffic will pass *around* the spot, not over you! Cross *behind* parked buses and trolley-buses; only *in front* of stationary trams. As drivers are not allowed to hoot there may be no audible warning.

TOURS. Intourist runs regular city tours, lasting two or three hours, which will be part of your individual or group arrangements, and excursions outside Moscow, ranging from a four-hour trip to Kolomenskoye to a whole day (13 hours) visit to Tolstoy's estate at Yasnaya Polyana. If you have special interests, consult the service bureau at your hotel or your Intourist guide.

HOTELS. Normally, for American, British and most other Western tourists, Intourist uses the top seven hotels—*Rossia, Intourist, Metropole, National, Ukraine* and the new *Belgrade* and *Kosmos.* If these are full, Intourist sometimes directs the overflow to the *Leningradskaya, Ostankino, Berlin* and *Sovietskaya,* or other suitable establishments. Other hotels may be used on special occasions for international meetings and congresses or special cut-rate tour groups. A number of new hotels were completed for the 1980 Olympic Games—the 28-story *Kosmos* is the most luxurious of these.

Aeroflot, 37 Leningradsky Prospekt (tel. 155–5624). This is generally used for transit air passengers and is next to the air terminal.

Altai, 12 Gostinichnaya Street (tel. 482–5879), near the Exhibition of Economic Achievements. Inconvenient location.

Belgrade, 5 Smolenskaya (tel. 248–6692), near the Arbat and Kalinin Prospekt. Nominally Yugoslav, the restaurant serves good Russian food in an imaginative décor. 920 rooms, 20 stories.

Berlin, 3 Zhdanov Street. 83 rooms (tel. 225–6910, 225–6901) rating first-class, atmospheric, with Edwardian elegance. Restaurant quite good. This was formerly known as the Savoy and dates from 1912. Being totally refurbished by Finnair as a Western standard luxury hotel with room-rates in dollars. Unlikely to be open by presstime.

Bucharest, 1 Balchug Street (tel. 283–0029). Restaurant. No private baths. Opposite Kremlin across Moscow River.

Budapest, 2/18 Petrovskiye Linii (tel. 294–8820). Restaurant. Central.

Intourist, 3–5 Gorky Street (tel. 203–4080/0125/4007/0131). Opened in 1970. 458 rooms. Rated by Intourist as first-class superior, but subject of complaints about poor service, plumbing etc. Restaurants, cafés, shops. Finnish furnishings. Intourist Bureau. Basement night bar open till 2 A.M. (foreign currency only). Central location.

Izmailovo, in district of the same name. A luxury skyscraper complex of five 30-story blocks, for 10,000 guests. Concert hall, cinema.

Kosmos, 150 Prospekt Mira (tel. 217–0786), near Economic Achievements Exhibition. New 1980, French-built and equipped, down to the last doorknob. "Four-star prices." 26 stories, 1767 rooms, mostly twin-bedded. Bars, restaurants. Swimming pool, sauna, bowling alley. Good souvenir shop. Far away but close to metro station.

Leningradskaya, 21/40 Kalanchovskaya Street (tel. 225–5300). A 28-floor hotel, near the Leningrad, Yaroslavl and Kazan railway stations. Baroque, medium grade, not particularly convenient location. Less comfortable than it looks.

Metropole, 1 Marx Prospekt (tel. 225–6673, 228–0716). 283 rooms. Rating: Well-located, renovated, first-class. A pre-revolutionary building, it bears three memorial plaques to mark important historical events associated with it. One of them commemorates the battles fought by revolutionary troops in November 1917 to occupy it, another the fact that Lenin spoke frequently in the assembly hall of the building, and the third that Yakov Sverdlov, the first Chairman of the Executive

Committee of the Russian Soviet Federal Republic, had offices here in 1918–19. The hotel was built in 1899–1903 by W. Walcott in the style then fashionable. A historical monument that is also quite a pleasant Intourist hotel. Good restaurant and café. Night bar (foreign currency) open till 2 A.M.

Mezhdunarodnaya ("International"), on Krasnopresnensky Embankment. Built in 1980 as part of the International Trade Center (Sovintsentr). Mainly for businessmen, government delegations and other officials the Russians want to impress. Worth seeing as an eyeopener to how the other half lives! Japenese restaurant, expensive but authentic.

Minsk, 22 Gorky Street (tel. 299–1211). Large, central, often used to house foreign delegations. Restaurant and coffee-shop. Near Mayakovsky Square, theaters and concert halls.

Moskva, 7 Marx Prospekt (tel. 292–1000). Faces the Council of Ministers Building; the two were the first to be built under the reconstruction program launched in 1932. (Not an Intourist Hotel.) Restaurant. Annex next door.

Mozhaiskaya, 165 Mozhaiskoye Highway (tel. 447–3435, 447–3434). First class, 10 story, 153 rooms. The hotel has a campsite and motel with a total capacity of 206 beds.

National, 14/1 Marx Prospekt (tel. 203–6539 and 203–5566). Rating: recently enlarged, traditional leader, handsome, first-class superior. Erected in 1903, but expanded in the 1960's, it has retained some of its original plush atmosphere. The flat roof is designed as an observation platform, from which there is a splendid view of the Kremlin and much of the city center. An Intourist hotel. Good restaurant and foreign currency bar.

Orlyonok, 17 Vorobyovskoye Chaussée on the Lenin Hills (tel. 29–8856). 17 floors, recent. Better-than-average, with friendlier-than-usual service. Food is acceptable. Mostly for foreigners.

Ostankino, near the Kosmos Hotel in the north of the city. No details available at presstime.

Peking, 1/5 Sadovaya Street (tel. 209–2442). Near Mayakovsky Square and the Planetarium. Restaurant.

Rossia (near Red Square) 6, Razin Street (tel. 298–5500). One of the world's largest hotels, with accommodation for 6,000 people. Its rating is first class. Lovely view from 21st-floor restaurant but slow service. It has 3,150 rooms, two cinemas, a concert hall seating 3,000, restaurants, cafés and shops. 5% service charge, and the floor ladies have been known to charge 1 rouble for a cup of tea!

Sevastopol, 1-aya Bolshaya Yushunskaya Street (tel. 119–6450, 318–4963, 119–0567, 318–8370). First class. 4 buildings, 16-story, 1,287 rooms.

Solnechny (tel. 119–7097, 119–8739), just beyond the ring road at 21 Varshavskoye highway, is a 10-story Intourist hotel with 234 rooms, conference hall, shops and bars, plus a campsite and motel with 48 two-room chalets.

Sovietskaya, 32 Leningradsky Prospekt (tel. 250–2342). Near the Dynamo Stadium and the Hippodrome Racecourse.

Soyuz, near Leningradskoye Chaussée, on the banks of the Moscow Canal. Yugoslav-built in 1980, 13 stories.

Tourist, 17/2 Selskokhozyaistvennaya Street (tel. 187–7572). Poor location and appearance. Many student tourist groups end up here. Try not to!

Tsentralnaya, 10 Gorky Street and 2 Stoleshnikov Pereulok (tel. 229–8957). Restaurant.

Ukraine, 2/1 Kutuzovsky Prospekt (tel. 243–3030). Near the Kutuzovskaya Metro Station, close to parks and the Kiev Station. 1,500 rooms, rated as spacious, modern first class. Skyscraper (29 floors) on banks of Moskva River.

Ural, 40 Chernyshevsky Street (tel. 297–4258).

Varshava (Warsaw), 1/2 Oktyabrskaya Square and 1/15 Kotelnicheskaya Naberezhnaya (tel. 233–0032). Fairly recently-built, near the Leninsky Prospekt, the university and three metro stations. Restaurant.

Yunost, 34 Frunzenskaya Val (tel. 242–0353). Operated by the International Youth Tourist Bureau. Pretty spartan.

Yuzhnaya, 87 Leninsky Prospekt (tel. 134–3065).

RESTAURANTS. Russian cuisine (with some regional exceptions) is more nourishing than palate-tickling, but you can eat well in Moscow if you forget any *cordon bleu* pretensions. There are about 7,000 catering establishments, in which two and a half million people eat every day. It is advisable to reserve a table at the more popular restaurants—something which Intourist or your hotel's service bureau will do. As we have said before, reserve ample time for your meal; if you are alone, take a book; if you are in company, practice the art of conversation. Many restaurants have dance orchestras of the Palm Court or Saratoga Springs variety. A few trendy ones have live jazz and even rock.

All the Moscow hotels have their own big restaurants. And there are various establishments for special cuisine. There are also restaurants in all Moscow parks, on the TV tower in Ostankino, at the Exhibition of Economic Achievements, at the Khimki Riverport and the Lenin Stadium in Luzhniki. On a warm day, you might enjoy dinner aboard the floating restaurant near the Krymsky Bridge, the Lastochka or at the Burevestnik in Gorky Park.

Light meals are provided at the cafés. Ice-cream, enormously popular in the Soviet Union, is sold at special ice-cream parlors, open year-round.

Average price in a good restaurant in 1987 was 10–15 roubles per head.

Airline Terminal Restaurant, at the terminal on Leningradsky Prospekt. Modern elegance, fine food.

Aragvi, 6 Gorky Street (tel. 229–3762). Georgian specialties. Has its ups and downs, but can still be very good. Ask for *lobio,* butter beans in a spicy sauce; *kharcho,* a spiced meat soup; *osetrina na vertelye,* sturgeon roasted on a spit; there is also *tsiplyata tabaka,* roast spring chicken, flattened between hot stones. With good wine and vodka a splendid meal can be had for about 12 roubles a head. Reservations essential. Private rooms available at a price. Folk music.

Arbat, 29 Kalinin Prospekt (tel. 291–1403). A modern but uninteresting place. Seats 2,000. Reservations needed; pay 1 rouble to get in. Most expensive restaurant in town. Music, dancing, floorshow. Open till midnight. Typical food. Popular with privileged class.

Baku, 24 Gorky Street (tel. 299–9426). Azerbaijani cuisine, kindred to Turkish. Specialties: *dovta,* a soup made with sour milk and meat; *plov* (pilaff), of which there are well over 20 varieties, all with a rice base. Mediocre food and poor service. Music.

Belgrade, in the new Belgrade Hotel, 5 Smolenskaya Square (tel. 248–6661). Russian and Yugoslav specialties. Good reputation.

Berlin, 3 Zhdanov Street (tel. 223–3581). In the Berlin Hotel. Good, if rather heavy, Russian and German cooking with a dominant Bavarian influence. Old-fashioned atmosphere with fountain, gilt mirrors. Music, dancing. English spoken. Considered by foreign residents one of the best in town. Hotel now closed for refurbishment; restaurant unlikely to be open for '89, but check with Intourist.

Bucharest, 1 Balchug Street (tel. 223–7854). Romanian and Transylvanian cooking. Refurbished with new kitchens, improved dining-room and decor.

Budapest, 2/18 Petrovskiye Linii (tel. 221–4044). Hungarian cooking, with plenty of paprika and sour cream. Good, if not quite up to native standards.

Co-op at 36 Kropotkinskaya Street. An offspring of the 1987 enterprise laws.

Co-op at Tarasovo, about 30 minutes' drive from center up Prospekt Mira. For those with a sense of adventure. Often the venue for wedding or retirement parties. Adequate shashlik, very good hot cheese and hot bread.

Havana, 88 Lenin Prospekt. Fair—but don't expect real Cuban food!

Intourist, 3–5 Gorky Street. In the hotel. Very good food. Sometimes there is a smorgasbord (all you can eat for 4 roubles, not including liquor).

Lastochka, good riverboat restaurant near the Krymsky Bridge on Moskva River. Not expensive.

Lefortovo, Krasnokursantsky Street, suburban. Repellant location near security police interrogation center of same name—if you go by taxi make it clear it's the *restaurant* you want, not the prison. Interesting experience—set lunch costs 1 rouble only. Clientele mostly military and seem to enjoy it.

Metropole, 1 Marx Prospekt. Attached to the hotel. Old-fashioned, but pleasant.

Minsk, 22 Gorky Street. In the hotel. Very good mushroom dishes, soporific orchestra and dancing in the evenings.

Mir, 9 Bolshoi Devyatinsky Per. A hotel restaurant. Average food and services. People living at this hotel get seated and served first. Small dining room.

Moskva, 7 Marx Prospekt (tel. 292–6267). In the hotel. Open-air roof terrace in summer. Large main restaurant on 3rd floor. Music.

National, 1 Gorky Street (tel. 203–5595). In the hotel. There is a third-floor bar in which hard liquor is served for foreign currency, and here you will also find music (an accordion) and *blinis* (pancakes with salmon, caviar and sour cream). Delicious! Restaurant is among the good ones in Moscow, a bit more expensive than average. Dancing. Female balalaika band, folk songs. Good meeting-place on ground floor for morning coffee, cakes etc. Pleasant service.

Praga, 2 Arbat Street (tel. 290–6171). Czech and Russian cuisine. Highly recommended, especially for the Kiev Cutlets and the chocolate cream cake! About 30 roubles for two includes vodka and caviar as well as the aforementioned. Pleasant open-air roof garden. Music and dancing.

Rossia, 6 Razin Street (tel. 298–0552). The hotel has nine restaurants, some of them massive, impersonal, and notable for slow service! One, on the 21st floor, has a lovely view overlooking the Kremlin and St. Basil's, one of the best sights in Moscow. Waiters in this restaurant also speak English. Food is good, and higher-priced than average. The basement restaurant is considered by young foreign residents in Moscow as the best in town for dancing. Good orchestra and music. Floor show.

Russian Country Cabin (Russkaya Izba), a 40-minute drive from Moscow center on the road to Arkhangelskoye (tel. 561–4244). Very pleasant for afternoon drive and meal. Set menu. Excellent *zakuski* (Russian hors d'oeuvres). More expensive than most—about 25 roubles per person. Reservations must be arranged well in advance (two days or so) through Intourist, which will supply car and driver for the trip to restaurant. Taxi fare is about 12 roubles.

Seventh Heaven (Sedmoye Nebo), TV Tower, Ostankino. So-so food, but the view is the main thing.

Slavyansky Bazaar, 13, 25th October Street (tel. 228–4845). Domed market building converted into 19th cent. eating house. Good food and service. Fun, but music can be loud. Excellent private rooms, decorated in traditional styles, for groups only: reserve through your Intourist guide. Intourist can order for you in advance a range of specialties at 20 roubles per person. Or, a four-course meal is about 18 roubles. American Express and other Western cards accepted. English-language menu. Many Russians consider it the best place for Russian food.

Sofia, 32 Gorky Street (tel. 251–4950). Bulgarian and Russian cooking. Food is fair; service, slow. Loud all-girl dance band playing polkas, gypsy music and bouncy 1920's style pop. Moderate prices.

Stolyshniki, in basement of the 1812 cavalry headquarters. It's new; ask Intourist for directions.

Tsentralny, 10 Gorky Street (tel. 229–0241). Attached to the hotel. Traditional Russian dishes of great variety. Music, dancing. Ornate, old-world.

Ukraine, 10 Kutuzovsky Prospekt (tel. 243–3297). In the Ukraine Hotel. Ukrainian cuisine. Try Ukrainian *borshch* (beetroot soup) or *vareniki,* very small dumplings filled with meat, rice vegetables or various fruits. Service and food vary considerably. Russo-Ukrainian music in evenings.

Uzbekistan, 29 Neglinnaya Street (tel. 294–6053). Specialties include: *lagman,* meat and noodle soup; *maniar,* meat and egg soup; *baranina kopecka* (roast mutton ribs); *pilaffs* ("plov") and *Shashliks; tkhum-dulma,* Scotch eggs (breaded boiled eggs, if you can believe it!). Consistently high quality. Service faster than average. Reservations needed after 6 P.M. Colorful.

Varshava, Oktyabrskaya Square 2/1 (tel. 236–8063). In the Varshava (Warsaw) Hotel. Polish dishes. Food fair.

Yakor (Anchor), 49 Gorky Street. Neat little fish restaurant, fast service. Good dishes include King prawns when available and sturgeon Moscow-style with rich cream sauce.

Cafes. Of the many cafes in Moscow, the following deserve listing: **Aelita,** 45 Oruzheiny Pereulok; **Adriatika,** 19/3 Ryleev Street; **Arktika,** 4 Gorky St.; **Arfa,** 9 Stoleshnikov Pereulok; **Artisticheskoye,** 6 Proyezd Khudozhestvennogo Teatra; **Druzhba** (Friendship), Kuznetsky Most; **Krasny Mak,** 20 Stoleshnikov Pereulok; **Ogni Moskvy** (Lights of Moscow), 2 Marx Prospekt, in the Moskva Hotel; **Bar Grill,** at Nikitsky Gates (metro: Puskinskaya); **Georgian Tea Rooms,** 2 Smolensky Boulevard (metro: Park Kultury), for tea and pastries; **Chistiye Prudy,** 8 Christoprudny Boulevard (metro: Kirovskaya), next to skating rink. **Sinyaya Ptitsa** (Blue Bird), Chekhov St, is a jazz club-café favored by Russian and foreign jazz buffs.

OPERA AND BALLET. You can get tickets at the Intourist office beside the Intourist Hotel at the bottom of Gorky Street or at your hotel's service bureau. They will charge you in foreign currency and often at a *very* high price, but it may be your only way of getting in on a popular night. Evening performances 7.30, sometimes earlier, matinees 12 noon, but check.

The **Bolshoi Opera and Ballet Theater,** Sverdlov Square. Tickets from 1 rouble to 5 roubles. Its ballet company is justly world famous; there are many Russian and foreign operas in its repertory, and its orchestra is also outstanding. The Bolshoi also presents regular performances on the stage of the Kremlin Palace of Congresses. (Entrance to this is through the white-washed Kutafia Gate, by the Manège, which leads to the Trinity Gate.) This seats 6,000.

Stanislavsky and Nemirovich-Danchenko Musical Theater, 17 Pushkinskaya Street. For classical and modern operas, ballets and operettas.

The **Operetta,** 6 Pushkinskaya Street. 2,000 seats. Classical and modern works. Obtain tickets for all performances through your hotel service bureau.

Moscow Chamber Opera Theater. Experimental theater; worth a visit.

DRAMA. Even if you do not speak Russian, you might want to explore the dramatic theaters and compare their productions of Shakespeare, Molière, Ibsen, Gogol and Chekhov or of modern playwrights like Arthur Miller or Arnold Wesker with the Western versions. Evenings at 7 P.M.: matinees at 12 noon; puppets at 7.30, but always check ahead. The puppet theater is excellent.

Central Soviet Army Theater, 2 Commune Square, has two auditoria.

Lenin Komsomol Theater, 6 Chekhov Street. The student and youth theater, presenting new plays by young authors.

The **Maly Theater** has *two* houses. The major is at 1/6 Sverdlov Square, its associated studio theater at 60 Bolshaya Ordynka Street.

Mayakovsky Theater, 19 Herzen Street.

Moscow Art Theater (MKhAT), 3 Proyezd Khudozhestvennogo Teatra. An affiliated smaller house, the MKhAT Filial, is at 3 Moskvila Street. New building on Tverskoi Boulevard. The old building was refurbished in 1985.

Moscow Drama Theater, (also known as the Malaya Bronnaya) on Malaya Bronnaya Street.

The **Moscow Music Hall** performs at summer theaters in the parks, in the Variety Theatre, the Exhibition of Economic Achievements, etc.

Moscow Theater of Miniatures, 3 Karetny Ryad, offers popular programs of "witty melodrama, merry tragedy, dramatized songs and dances"; its motto is brevity.

Obraztsov Puppet Theater, 3 Sadovo-Samotechnaya. Puppetry is a particularly popular art form in the U.S.S.R. and this is a world-famous troupe. Though primarily a children's theater it also puts on excellent satirical shows for adults which the visitor can enjoy even without Russian language ability. It also boasts an unusual "puppet cuckoo clock" which, at noon or midnight, is one of Moscow's tourist attractions.

Poezia Hall, 12 Gorky Street. For poetry recitals and experimental drama.

Pushkin Drama Theater, 23 Tverskoi Boulevard.

Romany Theater, 32 Leningradsky Prospekt, in the Hotel Sovetskaya.

Satire Theater, 18 Bolshaya Sadovaya Street, specializes in satirical comedies such as Mayakovsky's *The Bathhouse, The Bedbug* and *Mystery Bouffe.*

Sovremennik Theater, Chistiye Prudy, in its new building. One of the youngest of Moscow's theaters; experimental, with a company of young actors and good designers.

Taganka Drama and Comedy Theater, 75 Chkalov Street. The best known of Moscow's avant-gardist and experimental companies. Almost impossible to get seats for productions like *Master and Margarita,* so popular are they. But keep trying.

Vakhtangov Theater, 26 Arbat.

Variety Theater, 20/2 Bersenevskaya Embankment, also known as the **Estrada,** the center of Moscow's music hall life.

Yermolova Theater, 5 Gorky Street.

Children's Theater. There are four children's theaters in Moscow: **The Central Children's Theater,** 2/7 Sverdlov Square; the **Moscow Children's Theater,** 10 Pereulok Sadovskikh; the **Moscow Puppet Theater,** 26 Spartakovskaya Street; and the **Children's Musical Theater,** now in its beautiful new premises on Vernadsky Prospekt.

There is a **Mime Theater** (Teatr Mimiki i Zhesta) at 41 Izmailovsky Boulevard, which has been praised by no less a master than Marcel Marceau.

CONCERTS. The musical life of Moscow is particularly rich; there are a number of symphony orchestras and song and dance ensembles, and the soloists are often world famous—from Igor Oistrakh to Sviatoslav Richter. The *State Symphony Orchestra* gives a long series of concerts through the season and then tours abroad and within the country. The *Pyatnitsky Choir's* performances of modern and old Russian songs are highly popular. There is Moiseyev's *Folk Dance Ensemble,* well-known in Western Europe and America, while the *Soviet Army Song and Dance Ensemble,* the *Beryozka Dance Ensemble,* the *Beethoven Quartet* and the *Osipov Russian Folk Orchestra* are all equally (and justly) celebrated.

Variety and symphony concerts are given in the **Hall of Columns** (Kolonnyi Zal) of the House of Trade Unions, 1 Pushkinskaya Street. Chamber music is performed in the **October Hall** of the House of Trade Unions, and the **Hall of the Gnesin Music Institute** 30–36 Vorovsky Street, while symphony concerts and solo recitals, oratorios and concert performances of operas are given in the **Grand Hall of the Conservatory,** 13 Herzen Street, the **Rakhmaninov Hall,** also in Herzen Street, and the **Tchaikovsky Concert Hall,** 20 Mayakovsky Square.

Organ recitals are held in the Small Hall of the Conservatory and there are poetry readings in the **Lenin Library Hall,** 5 Kalinin Prospekt, and in the concert hall of the Rossia Hotel. There are scores of excellent halls where concerts are frequently given. A recently opened one is the **Glinka Concert Hall,** in the Glinka Musical Museum at 4 Fadeyev Street. A new **"House of Music"** is to be built with two concert halls, lounges, a library and offices for the Union of Composers, near the new Chaliapin Memorial House.

THE CIRCUS. Often a hit with foreign tourists. The old **Moscow Circus** is at 13 Tsvetnoi Boulevard. **New Circus** at 7 Vernadsky Prospekt. In summer there are tent circuses in the Gorky Park and at the Exhibition of Economic Achievements.

There is a **circus on ice** which claims to rival the great ice shows of the West and has one extraordinary feature, *Bruins Play Hockey,* a troupe of bears playing on skates. The **Moscow Ice Ballet** usually performs in the Palace of Sport of the Lenin Stadium. For times and places of performance check with Intourist.

MUSEUMS. Moscow has about 150 museums and permanent exhibitions. Some of the most important have already been described. Here we list their addresses, as well as some smaller and more specialized museums you may want to visit. Their hours of opening change seasonally, so it is advisable to enquire at the service bureau of your hotel if you are not visiting them in the course of your Intourist group sightseeing. The opening times we give here are according to the latest information but it is still best to check them. *They may close early on days preceding holidays.*

Museums of Soviet Revolutionary History

Central Lenin Museum, 2 Revolution Square, near Red Square. Open Tues. through Thurs. 11–7.30; Fri. through Sun. 10–6.30. Closed Mon. Free. Includes manuscripts by Lenin and his personal belongings.

Karl Marx and Friedrich Engels Museum, 5 Marx-Engels Street. Open 1–7 Monday, Wednesday, Friday; 11 A.M.–5 P.M., Thursday, Saturday, Sunday; closed Tuesday. The exhibits include letters, early editions, documents and photographs of Marx and Engels and their close associates and friends, together with drawings and paintings. Marx's personal belongings, including his armchair and the easy chair in which he died on March 14, 1883, are also on view.

Krasnaya Presnya Museum, 4 Bolshevitskaya Street. A small, one-storied timber house where the Presnya District Revolutionary Committee met in October 1917; one of the headquarters of the armed uprising.

Lenin's House Museum, in Gorki Leninskiye, 85 kilometers (about 50 miles) from Moscow. Open from 11 to 7, closed on Tuesdays. This is where Lenin spent the last years of his life and where he died on January 21, 1924. The furnishings have remained unaltered and documents and manuscripts are on display. Built in 1830, the house stands in a park of 175 acres, with 150-year-old oaks and a number of ponds; it was the home of the Mayor of Moscow before the revolution. Old motor cars stand in the garage, including Lenin's Rolls-Royce, adapted for use in heavy snow. Intourist runs group excursions, 4 hours, 28 roubles.

Mikhail Kalinin Museum, 21 Marx Prospekt, devoted to Kalinin's life and revolutionary activities.

Museum of the Revolution, 21 Gorky Street. Open 10–6, Tues., Sat., Sun.; 12–8 Wed.; 11–7 Fri.; closed Mon., Thurs. Originally built in 1780, rebuilt in classical style after the Moscow Fire of 1812. From 1831 until the 1917 revolution it was "the English Club," for noblemen. The six-inch gun in the yard was used by the revolutionary troops to fire on the Kremlin in October, 1917.

Opened in 1926, the 37-room museum houses relics and mementos of the Revolution, starting with the history of the first worker's organizations in the 19th century. They include the battle-standards of the revolutionary groups, the horse-drawn machine-gun cart of the First Cavalry Army, the texts of the first decrees of the Soviet Government on peace and on land, dioramas and paintings portraying revolutionary battles, and thousands of other relics. Also deals with the 1918–20 Civil War and World War II.

Train of Mourning, at Paveletsky Railway Station, 1 Kozhevnichesky Square. The engine and carriage which brought the coffin with Lenin's body to Moscow.

Underground Press of the C.C., 55 Lesnaya Street. The premises of a revolutionary printing press deep below a house where the newspaper *Rabochii* (Worker) was printed.

Other History Museums

Battle of Borodino (1812) Panorama and Kutuzov's Hut, 38 Kutuzovsky Prospekt. Panorama open 9.30–8; Hut open 10.30–7; both closed Fri.

Museum of the History and Reconstruction of Moscow, 12 Novaya Square. Open 10–6 on Sat., Mon., Thurs.; 2–9 Wed., Fri.; closed Tues. and the last day of each month.

The 16th-17th Century Palace Chambers, 10 Razin Street. A boyar's mansion, furnished as it would have been with all his goods and chattels. Open 10–6; closed Tues. and last Mon. of each month.

Soviet Armed Forces Museum, 2 Soviet Army Street. Open 10–5 Tues., Fri., Sat. and Sun.; 1–8 Wed., Thurs. Closed Mon. and last Tues. of each month.

State History Museum, 1–2 Red Square. Open Mon., Thurs., Sat. and Sun., 10–6; Wed. and Fri. 11–7. Closed Tues., and last Mon. of each month. Russian history to the end of the 19th century. Being refurbished 1986–89; may be partly closed. Check.

Church Museums

(Not used for worship)

Andrei Rublyev Museum, in the Andronikov Monastery, 10 Pryamikov Square. Devoted to one of Russia's greatest icon-painters.

Cathedral of the Intercession Museum, St. Basil's Cathedral, Red Square. Also known as the Pokrovsky Cathedral Museum. Open Wed. through Mon. 9.30–5.30. Closed Tues. Last admission 5 P.M. (See also *Kremlin Museums,* below.)

Kremlin Museums. The churches and cathedrals within the Kremlin have all been converted into museums. Many have recently been specially repainted, restored and cleaned by master craftsmen using traditional methods and materials. They include: **Cathedral of the Archangel; Cathedral of the Annunciation;** the **Cathedral of the Assumption; Ivan the Great Bell Tower.** Detailed descriptions are given in the text of this chapter. Intourist has guided tours round the Grand Kremlin Palace. Expensive but worth it.

Novodevichy Convent, 1 Novodevichy Proyezd, off Bolshaya Pirogovskaya Street (near Sportivnaya Metro Station). Open 10–5.30; from Nov. 1 to April 30, 10–5; closed Tues. and last day of each month.

Art Galleries and Museums

Arkhangelskoye Estate Museum, in Arkhangelskoye village. The **Kuskovo Palace Museum** and the **Kolomenskoye Estate Museum** are described in the section Excursions from Moscow earlier in this chapter.

Art Gallery of the U.S.S.R., Krymskaya Naberezhnaya (Crimean Embankment), opposite Gorky Park. The Tretyakov's extension. Newly opened. Opening hours not available at presstime.

Exhibition Hall of the U.S.S.R. Academy of Arts, 21 Kropotkin Street.

Exhibition Halls of the Union of Soviet Artists, are located at 20 Kuznetsky Most, at 25 Gorky Street, at 5 Chernyakhovsky Street, at 46b Gorky Street, at 7/9 Begovaya Street and 17 Zholtovsky Street. For the various exhibitions and opening times, check with Intourist or the galleries themselves.

Manège Central Exhibition Hall, on Marx Prospekt near the Kremlin. Designed as a riding school, it has Russian and foreign exhibitions of art, textiles, furnishing and glass.

Museum of Horse Breeding. This special curiosity grew out of a collection of paintings belonging to a stud-farm owner who was in charge of Russia's stud farms in the 1920s. All the canvases and sculptures are originals by Russian masters. They depict thorough-breds, Russian trotters and troikas, in decorative and everyday harness—with herds of fine horses galloping across the steppe. The collection also includes drozhki carriages, dress harnesses, various bells and toy horses made of china, clay and glass. Check location and opening details locally with Intourist.

Museum of Russian Folk Art, 7 Stanislavsky Street. Open 12–7 daily; Mondays 12–6. Closed Tuesdays and the last day of the month. Antique and modern pottery, ceramics, glassware, metalware, wood, bone, embroideries, lace and popular prints. In the Naryshkin House (17th century), 22 rooms restored.

Museum of Victor Vasnetsov, 13 Pereulok Vasnetsova. The former home, "a typical Russian fairyland house," of the famous 19th-century Russian artist. Open 10–6; closed Sat. and Sun.

Ostankino Palace (Museum of Serf Art), 5 Pervaya Ostankinskaya Street. Open 11–5 from May to September; 10–4 from October to April. Closed Tues. and Wed., also Sun. at 2, except in summer.

Pushkin Fine Arts Museum, 12 Volkhonka Street. **New Gallery,** 4 Marshal Shaposhnikov Street. Mostly reproductions and copies. Open 10–8; Sun. 10–6. Closed Mon.

Tretyakov Art Gallery, 10 Lavrushinsky Pereulok, near Novokuznetskaya Metro Station. Open 10–8 (but Ticket Office closes at 7), except Mon.

Economic, Scientific and Technical Museums

The Anthropological Museum, 18 Marx Prospekt, has an excellent collection of fossils of primitive man.

The Darwin Museum, 1 Malaya Pirogovskaya Street, is open 10–5, closed on Sat. and Sun. Devoted to life of Charles Darwin.

Exhibition of Economic Achievements of the U.S.S.R., Prospekt Mira, Metro: VDNKh. Open 9.30 A.M. to 10 P.M., Mon. through Fri.; 9.30 A.M. to 11 P.M. Sat. and Sun. From September 1 to May 1, the pavilions closed for refurbishment.

The Frunze Central Museum of Aviation and Cosmonautics, 4 Krasnoarmeiskaya Street. A museum devoted to the history of Russian aviation. Open 10–6; closed Mon.

Memorial Museum of Space, Prospekt Mira (see Exhibition of Economic Achievements). Open 11–7 Wed., Fri., Sat., Sun.; 12–8 Tues., Thurs. Closed Mon.

The Mineralogical Museum, 14–16 Leninsky Prospekt, has a large collection of minerals (including precious stones) of the Soviet Union and other countries.

Museum of Bread, a new museum on the scene. (Details not available at presstime.) You can see and taste replicas of bread as baked in the times of Peter the Great, and the mini-loaves that Soviet cosmonauts take on their space flights. Old recipes and processes have been revived, and bread from different parts of the Soviet Union including the Caucasus and Central Asia is baked in special stoves. One display is devoted to Leningrad "siege bread." Tiny morsels made from flour, wood bark, cottonseed cake and pine needles lie next to wartime ration cards.

The Palaeontological Museum, 16 Bolshaya Kaluzhskaya, one of the oldest in the country, a successor of Peter the Great's *Kunstkamera.*

The Planetarium, 5 Sadovaya-Kudrinskaya Street, is open 12–7 in summer, 1–7 in winter, closed on Tues.

Polytechnical Museum, 3–4 Novaya Square. Open 10–5 Wed., Fri., Sun.; 1–8 Tues., Thurs., Sat.; closed Mon. and the last day of the month.

The Timiryazev Biological Museum, 15 Malaya Gruzinskaya Street, is open daily from 10–6, but from 12–8 on Wed. and Fri.; closed on Mon. Plant and animal life, its origins and development.

U.S.S.R. Merchant Marine Exhibition, 3 Sretenka Street.

The Zhukovsky Memorial Museum, 17 Radio Street. Illustrating the development of Soviet aviation and space exploration.

The Zoological Museum, 6 Herzen Street. Thousands of exhibits of mammals, birds, amphibians, reptiles and almost a million insects. A collection of more than 100,000 butterflies was recently donated by a citizen of Moscow. Open 10–6; Wed. and Fri. 12–8 P.M.; closed Mon.

Literary, Musical and Theatrical Museums

Alexei Bakhrushin Museum, 31/12 Bakhrushin Street. Open Thurs., Sat., Sun., and Mon. 12–7; Wed. and Fri. 2–9; closed on Tues. and first Mon. of each month. It presents the history of Russian drama, opera and ballet theaters from the 18th century to our own time.

Chekhov Museum, 6 Sadovo-Kudrinskaya Street. Open 11–5.30 Tues., Thurs. Sat. and Sun; 2–8.30 Weds. and Fri. Closed Mon.

Dostoyevsky Museum, 2 Dostoyevsky Street, open 11–6 Thurs., Sat., Sun., Mon.; 10–4, Wed. and Fri. 1–9; closed Tues.

Glinka Museum of Musical Culture (and Concert Hall), 4 Fadeyev Street. Open 11–7; 2–10 Mon., Thurs.; closed Tues. and last Fri. of each month.

Gogol Museum, Suvorov Street, in Gogol's former apartment.

Gorky Museum, 25a Vorovsky Street, and the **Gorky Memorial Museum,** 6/2 Kachalov Street. The Memorial Museum, a fine example of Russian art nouveau architecture, is the house where he lived from 1931 to 1936; the Gorky Museum itself is open Tues. and Fri., 1–8; Wed., Thurs., and Sun., 10–5, and on Sat. 10.30–4 (closed Mon.).

The **Leo Tolstoy Museum** and the **Tolstoy Home** are, respectively, at 11 Kropotkinskaya Street and at 21 Lev Tolstoy Street. The Museum is open 11–5 Thurs., Sat., and Sun., 10–3; Mon. 2–8; Wed. and Fri.; and is closed on Tues. The Moscow Tolstoy Home can be visited every day 10–4.30, except Mon.

Lermontov Museum, 2 Malaya Molchanovka Street. Restoration is under way. Guided tours only.

Mayakovsky Library and Museum, 3/6 Proyezd Serova. In the poet's former home. Open 10–6 (12–8 Mon. and Thurs.); closed Wed.

Museum of Literature, 28 Petrovka Street. Open 11–5.30 Tues., Thurs., Sat., and Sun., 2–8 Wed. and Fri. Closed Mon. and last day of the month. A fine collection of material on Russian writers.

Puppet Museum, 3 Sadovaya-Samotechnaya. The Obraztsov Puppet Theater has a collection of old and modern theatrical puppets from over 30 countries.

Pushkin Museum, 12/2 Kropotkinskaya Street. Open on Sat., 1–7.30; Sun., 11–5.30. New branch at *Pushkin's House,* 53 Arbat Street.

Theatrical Museums. There are theatrical museums attached to the **Bolshoi, Maly, Art** and **Vakhtangov** theaters. Others include **Konstantin Stanislavsky's,** 6 Stanislavsky Street; **Vladimir Nemirovich-Danchenko's** at 5/7 Nemirovich-Danchenko Street; **Yevgeny Vakhtangov's** at 12 Vesnin Street; **Boris Shchukin's** at 8a Shchukin Street, and **Alexander Scriabin's** at 11 Vakhtangov Street. This last is primarily concerned with music.

PARKS AND GARDENS. Gorky Park, 9 Krymsky Val. Open 10 A.M.–11 P.M. The most popular in Moscow.

Hermitage Garden, 3 Karetny Ryad. Open May 1 to Sept. 1, 10 A.M.–11 P.M. This is a small park in the center of the city, in which there are concerts and variety and puppet performances in the summer. Several cafes and a restaurant.

Izmailovo Park, 17 Narodny Prospekt. Covering almost 3,000 acres, it includes large stretches of pine forest. Once the manor of the Romanovs, a favorite retreat of the Czars. Amusement park, open air theater and several cafes.

Main Botanic Garden of the U.S.S.R. Academy of Sciences, at Ostankino, (trolley buses 36 or 9 go much nearer than the "Botanicheskaya" metro station) covers an area of some 900 acres and has been planted in and among the original beech-oak-spruce forests of the Moscow area. One large landscape section has nearly 3,000 species of native plants of the U.S.S.R., from the Carpathians to Vladivostok, arranged in naturally landscaped areas; over 1,700 kinds of trees and shrubs are planted in the dendrarium. Another smaller botanical garden, belonging to the University is at 26 Prospekt Mira.

Sokolniki Park, 62 Rusakovskaya Street. Open 10 A.M.–11 P.M. Named after the falconers *(sokolniki)* who used to live here. Open-air theater, an amusement park, a shooting gallery, restaurants and cafes. There are bicycles and horses to hire, which you may need to explore all 1,530 acres of the park, including part of an ancient forest.

The Zoo is at 1 Bolshaya Gruzinskaya Street. Open 10–5.

Bitsa Forest Park, outside the city, features an arts and crafts market. Weekends only.

SHOPPING. Most of the stores in Moscow are open Monday through Saturday 8 A.M. to 8 or 9 P.M., and many are closed Sundays. Foodshops in the city center are increasingly staying open on Sundays, though. There is a one-hour lunch period (which varies) during which shops are closed—except the big department stores GUM and Central.

What to buy and where to buy will depend on your taste, how much you want and how much you can spend. According to most recent information, the best buys seem to be fur hats, blouses and shirts, chess sets, books, records, silver tea-glass holders, lacquered and burnished boxes, ceramics (small vases and cups), balalaikas, pencil boxes, cigarette cases, nests of dolls, pure wool scarves and *babushkas;* also ivory carvings, miniature counting toys and dolls in peasant dresses. Electrical and medical instruments, guitars and educational toys are reasonably priced. Kitchen utensils like cast-iron pots and pans are a bargain.

Though there is a restriction on their export, the famous Russian furs—sable, mink, polar fox, karakul, red, silver and blue fox—are usually available. So is North Russian lace, Lithuanian amber, jewelry, trinkets made of Ural gems, Ukrainian embroidery and inlaid woodwork, Georgian, Ukrainian and Baltic ceramics, Byelorussian linen, etc. Cameras, Armenian brandy, Georgian and Moldavian wine are reasonably priced, though the price of spirits, especially vodka, has virtually doubled in the last two years. Soviet watches, champagne, caviar (now in short supply), Uzbek gowns and gold-embroidered skull caps, Georgian inlaid silver wine horns, accordions and harmonicas might also tempt you. The main shopping streets are Gorky Street, Arbat, Kuznetsky Most, Petrovka, and Stoleshnikov, but there are several other newly established districts. Try the elegant Kalinin Prospekt for records, photographic equipment or gourmet goods.

Beryozka Foreign Currency Shops

It is perfectly possible, and many visitors find it simplest, to do all your shopping in Moscow at the duty-free **Beryozka** ("little birch tree") stores. These tend to be cheaper than the normal Russian shops; they also stock various "luxury" goods unavailable elsewhere. Payment is by cash, travellers' cheque or Bank card. Change, however, will come in whatever combination of western currency the shop has in its till. Come well prepared with an assortment of notes and coins to avoid this.

Beryozka Gift Shops are to be found in all the Intourist hotels, best at the Rossiya and the Ukraine. The Beryozka opposite the Novodevichy Monastery (open Monday-Saturday 9–7) is good for souvenirs, watches, radios and musical instruments. The Beryozka at 9 Kutuzovsky Prospekt (almost opposite the Ukraine Hotel) has a good selection of china, glass, "Palekh boxes," cosmetics and furs. Open Mon. to Sat., 10–2 and 3–7.

Book Shop, 31 Kropotkinskaya Street. The best place to buy Russian classics, also Russian editions of Pasternak, Mandelstam, Bulgakov, Tsvetaeva etc. which can almost never be found anywhere else in Moscow. Also good for art books and records. Open Mon. to Sat., 10–7.

Gastronom, 60 Dorogmilovskaya Street—for food, American cigarettes and drink, caviar, vodka and Russian champagne. Open Mon. to Sat., 9–2 and 3–7.

Jewellery, 32 Gorky Street.

Vneshtorgbank Gold Store, 9 Pushkin Street, for gold, silver and precious stones. Open Mon. to Fri., 10–4 and Sat., 10–2. Expensive, but a bargain if paid for in hard currency.

Shops Accepting Russian Roubles

Although self-service stores are appearing in Moscow, you will still often find that you have to collect a ticket for the goods you want, take it to the cashier to pay, then go back to the first counter to collect everything. In crowded shops this can mean standing in line three times over. The most useful shops are:

Art Galleries—selling works of art (paintings, prints etc.) at 25 and 46b Gorky Street, 24 Kutuzovsky Prospekt, 8/1 25th October Street and 12 Petrovka Street.

Book shops. Dom Knigi ("House of Books"), 26 Kalinin Prospekt. Largest bookshop in Moscow, reasonable selection of English paperbacks. Bookshops at 21 Zubovsky Boulevard and at 8/10 Vesnin Street have a big selection, including some Penguin Books. **Druzhba** ("Friendship"), 15 Gorky Street, for books in languages of the Communist countries, 18 Kuznetsky Most and 17 Zubovsky Boulevard for books in other foreign languages. **Moskva,** 8 Gorky Street for books, stamps and postcards. **Secondhand Bookshop,** 16 Kachalov Street. But please note that you cannot export books published before 1975 without a special permit! Ask Intourist or check with the shop.

Clothing—there are plenty of clothing stores in Moscow. To get an idea of what is on sale try **G.U.M.** or one of the big new shops on Kalinin St.

Commission Shops. Second-hand shops selling goods brought in by private individuals. Can be good for china, samovars, paintings etc., but prices are high and you will probably not be allowed to export anything you buy. The best are at: 56 Dimitrov Street, 46 Gorky Street and 32 Arbat.

Detsky Mir ("Children's World"), 2 Marx Prospekt. Department store with wide range of children's goods, including clothing, toys, nursery furniture etc. Arguably the most crowded shop in Moscow. Open 8 A.M. to 9 P.M.

Dom Igrushki ("House of Toys"), 8 Kutuzovsky Prospekt. 3 separate toyshops in one building, wide selection of toys, models etc. for all ages. Flowers (Tsvety), 1 Sretenka Street, 23 Kalinin Prospekt, 4 Arbat and Nature (Priroda) a garden shop with seeds, fertilizer, etc. at 5/3 Kutuzovsky Prospekt.

Food Markets (Rynoks). For flowers, fruit and vegetables—well worth a visit if you want to see more of Soviet life. Farmers bring in the produce of their private plots, Russian peasants vie with traders from the warmer southern republics of Georgia, Armenia and Central Asia. Huge mounds of berries and salad in summer; steaming vats of pickles in winter; amazing varieties of wild mushrooms in the autumn; cheese, smetana and honey all year round. You can taste before you buy. No bargaining, fancy prices in the winter. Recommended: **Tsentralnyi rynok** (Central Market), 15 Tsvetnoy Blvd. Largest indoor market, next door to Old Circus just off the Sadovoye Ring road. Open 7–6, Mon. to Sat., 7–4 Sun. **Chermyomushkinsky Rynok,** 3 Lomonovsky Prospekt. **Kievsky Rynok,** near Kiev Station and Ukraine Hotel. Poor in winter but good for peasant handiwork. Opens 8–4 every day. **Rizhsky Rynok,** at Rizhskaya Metro Station. **Tishinsky Rynok,** 50 Bolshaya Gruzinskaya Street, for second-hand shops.

Gastronom No. 1, 14 Gorky Street. Food and drink, better than average supplies, pre-revolutionary decor. Open 9–10.

Gifts and Souvenirs. Russkiy Souvenir, 9 Kutuzovsky Prospekt (Open Mon. to Sat., 11–8). *Podarki* (Presents)—4 Gorky Street. *Art and Craft Shop* (Izdelia Khudozhestvennykh Promyslov), 17 Kutuzovsky Prospekt, specializes in mass-produced folk art from all over the Soviet Union, also some paintings and sculptures.

G.U.M. State Universal Department Store, 3 Red Square. A series of small shops and stalls inside a splendid nineteenth century building. Well worth a visit. With perseverance you can find in GUM almost everything that is to be found in any of the Moscow shops. Also food sections, ice-cream and doughnut stalls and cafes. Open Mon. to Fri., 11–9; Sat., 8–9.

Ice-cream Stalls and Bakers' Shops. Universally recommended, always well-stocked with fresh supplies (you poke the bread with special forks to make sure it's fresh!)—much better than cafés for quick snacks.

Khrustal (Cut-glass), 15 Gorky Street. Sells vases, wine glasses, bowls.

Melodiya, Kalinin Street (next door to Dom Knigi)—two floors of records and sheet music. Good value.

Morozko, 3 L. Tolstoy Street and 7a Kedrov Street—for Polish frozen fruit and vegetables.

Pet Market, Sundays, Kalitnikovskaya Street, south-east of Taganka Square. Hard to find but a taxi-driver will know where it is. Birds, dogs, fish—a fascinating glimpse of Russians and their pets. Ask for "Ptichii Rynok."

Posters, at Iskusstvo, 4 Old Arbat Street. Some are very anti-West—fun buys!

Stamp Collectors' Shop, 16 Dzerzhinsky Street.

T.S.U.M. Central Department Store, 2 Petrovka Street. Shopping center of 12 shops. Open Mon. to Fri., 11–9; Sat., 8–9.

Wanda, 30 Polyanka St. Polish gift shop.

MEDICAL SERVICE. Medical service in the Soviet Union is free and available in any city or town. When feeling ill, immediately call a doctor through your interpreter or through the hotel desk. First aid administration and doctors' visits are free, but you will have to pay for medicines, and for hospitalization at 16 roubles a day. Normally this is offset against the value of unused tourist services per day, and the difference is refunded where the unused amount is greater, or paid by the tourist if hospitalization costs exceed hotel or other pre-paid costs.

There is a **special clinic** in Moscow which cares for foreign visitors. Its address is 12 Herzen Street, the telephone numbers 229–7323 and 229–0382. Its staff includes qualified doctors and nurses, and there are X-ray, physiotherapy, dental and other departments. A **Tourists' Polyclinic** also reportedly exists near Belorusskaya Metro (tel. 254–4396), catering for foreign students and employees.

There is a **Diplomatic polyclinic** at 3 Sverchkov Per. (tel. 221–5992 and 221–4911, day and night). It has a **children's section** (228–0725) and the director can be reached at 223–5515. The **Botkin Hospital,** 5, 2nd Botkinsky Proyezd, tel. 255–0015, ext. 268, has a Diplomatic Block (Korpus 5).

First Aid and Ambulance: dial 03; people in hospital, dial 294–3152.

SPORTS. Spectator Sports. Many facilities were re-equipped or extended for the 1980 Olympic Games. The **Lenin Stadium** and the **Palace of Sports,** Luzhniki, provide the largest complex of facilities.

The **Dynamo Stadium,** 36 Leningradsky Prospekt, is the second biggest stadium, accommodating 60,000. It has a large indoor swimming pool. The **Army Palace of Sports** is at 39 Leningradsky Prospekt.

Football matches, track-and-field competitions and mass sports pageants are held in the Lenin and Dynamo Stadiums; hockey games at the Lenin Stadium and in Sokolniki. There is a recent gymnasium in the **Izmailovo Park.**

Swimming. Moskva Open-Air Pool, 37 Kropotkinskaya Embankment is open all year, 7 A.M.–11 P.M. Heated pool. The **Dynamo Bathing Beach** is at Seryebryany Bor. At these places swimming and boating are available. The Rossiya and Kosmos hotels both have heated indoor pools open to non-residents.

Winter sports. For skiing and skating there is ample opportunity in the large parks—especially Gorky Park. Moscow has snow on 164 days a year (on average). Artificial ice-rinks are open throughout the year. There is a ski-jump on the Lenin Hills. Intourist will organize a day's cross-country skiing outside the city, with boots, poles and skis provided.

Horses and Bicycles. The race course (Hippodrome) is at 22 Begovaya Street. Racing begins at 5 on Wed. and Sat.; there is racing also at 1 and 5 on Sun. Tel. 256–1562. An **Equestrian Sports Center** has been laid out at Bitsa Forest Park outside the city (33 Balaklavsky Prospekt: tel. 318–8955) and there is also riding at the **Urozhai Riding Center** in Sokolniki: tel. 286–5922. A new cycle track has been constructed at Krylatskoye to the northwest.

Chess. The **Central Chess Club** is at 14 Gogolevsky Boulevard.

CHURCH SERVICES. Protestant church service and Sunday school is held on alternate Sundays at Spaso House (U.S. Embassy) and the British Embassy, 14 Nab. Morisa Toreza, at 10.30 A.M. The chaplain (according to most recent information) is the Rev. Alphonz Lamprecht (tel. 143–3562, 38 Lomonosovsky Prospekt, Apt. 59–60.). The visiting Anglican chaplain (who normally resides in Helsinki) can be contacted at the British Embassy.

Baptist services are held on Sundays at 10, 2, and 6; and on Thursdays at 6 P.M. at 3 Maly Vuzovsky Per (tel. 297 5167).

Catholic services: St. Louis des Français, 12 Malaya Lubyanka (masses in Latin, sermons in Polish and Russian); Sundays 8.30, 11.30, and 7. Chapel of our Lady of Hope, 7/4 Kutuzovsky Prospekt, Korp. 5, Entr. 3, Fl. 3, Apt. 42. The Chaplain is Father Robert J. Fortin, A.A. (tel. 243–9621). Saturday evening Mass in English and French at 6 P.M. at Our Lady of Hope Chapel. Sunday Masses at the American Embassy Snack Bar, 19/23 Tchaikovsky Street, at 10 A.M. in English and at 12 noon in French. Weekday Masses at Our Lady of Hope Chapel Mon., Tues., Wed. and Fri. at 8.30 A.M., Thurs. at 7 P.M.

Synagogues: 8 Arkhipova Street. Services daily at 10 A.M. and one hour before sundown; also at 8 Bolshoi Spasoglinischchevsky.

Russian Orthodox churches open for worship include: Yelokhovsky Cathedral, 15 Spartakovskaya; Uspensky Church, in the Novodevichy Convent, 2 Bolshaya

Pirogovskaya Street; Ivan Voin Church, 46 Dimitrov Street; Voskresenskaya Church, on the Brusovsky Per.; The Old Believers' Cathedral, 29 Rogozhsky Per.; and the Moscow Patriarchate at Kropotkin Street, 5 Chisty Per. There are 30–40 in Moscow. Most have services at 8 A.M. and 6 P.M. every weekday and at 7 A.M. and 10 A.M. on Sundays and holidays. Women should always wear a head covering when visiting, especially if service is in progress. Men should remove hats. Do not put hands in pockets; it is considered disrespectful.

In the South of Moscow, exact address unavailable, is the Danilovsky Monastery which was restored for the celebrations of 1,000 years of Kievan Russia's Christianity in 1988. One of its churches, the Church of the Intercession, is already used for worship, and two others, the Church of the Resurrection and the Trinity Cathedral, were to be reconsecrated. Eventually the Patriarch, head of the Orthodox Church, will move his seat here from Zagorsk.

Mosque: 7 Vypolzov Per. The *Hamaz* is recited five times daily and on Fridays at 1 P.M.

MAIL, TELEPHONE AND CABLES. For general information, see *Facts at Your Fingertips.* In Moscow: The **International Telephone Call Office** is at 7 Gorky Street, tel. 295–9268 (enquiries). Incoming telegrams can be collected here; tel. 294–4750.

Long distance calls within the U.S.S.R.: (a) the Caucasus, Central Asia, the Far East, Kazakhstan, Siberia, Belgorod, Kherson, Kursk, Odessa, Orel, Tula and Voronezh, dial 08

(b) Crimea, Arkhangelsk, Kaluga, Kazan, Kharkov, Ryazan & Yaroslavl, dial 06

(c) Kalinin, Leningrad, Murmansk, Novgorod, Petrozavodsk and Pskov, dial 225–1003

(d) Kiev, Kharkov and Volgograd, dial 225–1100

(e) The Baltic countries, Byelorussia, Donbas, Moldavia and the Western Ukraine, Chernigov, Poltava, Vinnitsa and Zhitomir, dial 245–0000

(f) Ulyanovsk, Vladimir and Ivanovo, dial 271–90–21

(g) towns in the Moscow area, dial 00

(h) long distance enquiries, dial 07. For dialing codes for most places in the U.S.S.R. dial 09. For enquiries in English, dial 8194.

International Telephone Exchange: 271–9103; 295–1020 (if you have an account); 272–0614 (enquiries); 271–2585 (supervisor).

Cables by phone within the U.S.S.R.: 225–2002.

International Post Office, la Komsomolskaya Square. Tel. 294–7555 (enquiries); enquiries about incoming parcels: 295–4794. *Telex Center:* 229–6306.

READING MATTER. We have mentioned foreign-language bookshops under our shopping information. Foreign (American and British) newspapers are rarely available, though there has been some relaxation in the kiosks of the principal Intourist hotels. Buy foreign (Western) magazines in your hotel for gifts—much appreciated. There is a foreign literature **lending library** at 3/5 Ulyanovskaya Street, which is open 10 A.M.–10 P.M., closed first day of the month; another is located at No. 1 Petrovskiye Linii. **Reading Rooms** are situated at 12 Razin Street.

USEFUL ADDRESSES AND PHONE NUMBERS. Emergency and information numbers in Moscow–Fire (dial) 01; Police 02; Ambulance 03; Enquiries about Moscow phone numbers (if you speak Russian) 09; Speaking clock 100; Lost property, if in metro 220–2085, if in tram or trolleybus 223–0018, extension 139; Lost children, 401–9982; Tracing people in hospital 294–3152.

Embassies. *United States of America:* 19/23 Tchaikovsky Street (tel. 252–2451/59; telex 429). Mon. to Fri., 9–1, 2–6.

United Kingdom: 14 Nab. Morisa Toreza (tel. 231–8511). Office hours Mon. to Fri., 9–12, 2.30–5. Consular section same hours. Commercial and Cultural section (tel. 233–4507). Will move to "another riverside site" in 1990s.

Canada: 23 Starokonyushenny Per. (tel. 241–9034/9155/9698/5070; night 241–9034). Mon. to Fri., 9.30–1, 2–6.

Foreign Airlines and Travel Agencies. *Air Canada:* Hotel Metropole, Room 333 (tel. 225–6926). Open Mon. to Fri., 9.30–6, Sat. 9.30–2.

British Airways: Sovincenter, Room 1905, on Krasnopresenskaya Embankment (tel. 253–2482/84. Telex 413197). New computerized office. Office hours: Mon. to Fri., 9–6. At Sheremetyevo, tel. 158–7965; Mon., Wed., and Fri., 12–6.

PanAm: Hotel Metropole, Room 237 (tel. 223–5183). Open Mon. to Sat., 9–6.

American Express, 21A Sadovo-Kudrinskaya (tel. 254–2111/4495). Mon. to Fri., 9–5.30.

Barry Martin Travel, Room 940, Mezhdunarodnaya Hotel (tel. 253–2940). For business travelers.

LENINGRAD

The Magnificent City

by
GEORGE LEWINSON

Leningrad, once Peter's and now Lenin's, is a revelation. The traveler entering Russia from the West is bound to be struck by its beauty, so European and yet so unlike anything else in Europe. The traveler coming from Moscow is also bound to have a new experience, seeing something quite different from the country's present capital and, for that matter, unlike any other city in the Soviet Union. Yet, Leningrad is both West European *and* Russian. It is unique in being most perfectly planned; its beauty lying in the unsurpassed blend of Russian and West European architecture and art. The builders of the city treated color as an essential part of their scheme, and Leningrad owes much of its special atmosphere to these painted facades that come into their own in the Northern light and especially when seen against the snow; they would look garish and cheap in the bright light of Paris or under the skies of southern Europe.

As European cities go, Leningrad is a young city. It was founded less than 300 years ago in 1703 and for most of its history was known as St. Petersburg. Russianized as Petrograd from 1914 till 1924, it was then renamed Leningrad, and ceased to be the capital.

This glorious maritime city, built on the shores of the Baltic, on the mainland and on the islands, is a supreme monument to its founder Peter the Great, who wrenched Russia from her past and pulled her towards

Europe and the sea. Undaunted by the harsh climate, the marshlands and the distance from the heartland of Russia, using prisoners of war and forced labor, this forward-looking Czar opened "a window on Europe." He laid the foundation of the superb setting in which his successors, especially the women who later ruled Russia—his daughter Elizabeth, and Catherine the Great—aided by their architects and builders, foreign and native, created a fitting capital for the Russian Empire. And St. Petersburg too, stood witness to the struggle against oppression and for justice. Here some of the Czars were assassinated by palace guards or revolutionaries, here the early fires of revolution were kindled, first in 1825 by a small band of starry-eyed aristocratic officers, then by organized workers' movements—the crowds being shot at in the streets of the capital in 1905 on the Czar's orders, then again in 1917 when the Revolution broke out.

Out of the turmoil of war and revolution, Lenin and his associates reaped the harvest of the biggest change in the country's history since the days of Peter, and replaced the Russian Empire with the Union of the Soviet Socialist Republics. But the city's worst ordeal came during World War II when it withstood a three-year siege, between September 1941 and January 1943, nearly 650,000 people died of starvation and more than 17,000 were killed in air raids and by indiscriminate shelling. After the ravages of war, the city restored its buildings and now looks as supreme and beautiful as ever. It has been further enriched by recently developed areas, new housing, office blocks, factories, and parks. Under a 30-year plan, over 200 km. of streets, embankments, and monuments are to be renovated. The city center will become a protected area with growth restricted to outlying districts. Small river bridges are to be strengthened, the waterfront improved, more parkland provided, and a new coastal road built to link with the seaside. Industry is to be dispersed in order to reduce pollution.

Leningrad's strength is that it is not a monument to the past; it is not an ossified repository of past glories, despite its great architectural and art treasures. It is a thriving city, the home of some five million people, proud of living there and who often say that they consider their city superior to other towns—especially to Moscow!

Much of what is known outside the Soviet Union about Russian culture has come from Peter's city. It was the birthplace of Russia's modern literature, the setting for the themes of Pushkin and Gogol, Dostoyevsky and Bely. Tchaikovsky and Rachmaninov not only worked here, but are buried here too. It was from St. Petersburg that Diaghilev and his Russian Ballet swept the West at the start of this century. It was from here that Pavlova, Nijinsky and Ulanova showed the world what ballet was about. It was in St. Petersburg that the Fabergé craftsmen created splendid objects, fit to adorn the collections of royalty and millionaires. To appreciate Leningrad and its spirit one has to look for these links, but there is plenty more to be enjoyed.

White Nights and Ice Floes

Leningrad is one of the world's most northerly cities. It lies on the same latitude as southern points of Alaska and Greenland, and yet its climate—which to a large extent depends on the proximity to the sea and the many waterways that criss-cross the city—is frequently described as fairly mild. Winters are much warmer than Moscow's, and the January average temperature is about −8°C (17°F), with a July average of 18°C (64°F). The annual average is 4°C (39.2°F) but, on the whole, the atmosphere is humid, fogs are frequent, and the rainfall heavy. The weather is very changeable. The White Nights are an unusual phenomenon, lasting from June 11th to July 2nd. During their brief twilights, lasting no more than 30 to 40 minutes, the streets and squares acquire an unusual charm. This was the inspiration for Dostoyevsky's *White Nights,* and they are now the occasion for Leningrad's annual festival of music and the arts.

Water plays an enormous part in the life of the city. Much of Leningrad lies practically at sea level, and hence there is often danger of flooding, at times severe, as in 1824—the subject of Pushkin's poem, *The Bronze Horseman*—in 1924, and again as recently as in 1977 and 1984. The River Neva (a very short one of only 74 km. (45 miles), half of which is within the city's boundary), as it reaches the Gulf of Finland divides into four arms: the Great and Little Neva, and the Great and Little Nevka, which, with numerous affluents, combine to form an intricate delta made up of more than 40 islands. From early November to the beginning of April, the Neva freezes solid enough to bear the weight of pedestrians for most of the time. There are two thaws: the first when the ice in the river melts, usually during April, and the second early in May when the ice floes float down from Lake Ladoga to the sea.

Public transport is good and cheap, but many of the most interesting sites, especially those on the left bank of the Neva, along and around the embankments, are located in a relatively compact area which can be easily explored on foot. There is no better place to get an overall picture than from the viewing gallery of Saint Isaac's Cathedral which is open to tourists (though special permits are required for taking photographs). Another vantage point is the Kirov Bridge which links the left bank with the Vasilevsky Island, from where there is a panoramic view over the Spit of the Island with its fine buildings, of the Peter-and-Paul Fortress and of the palaces lining the Embankment. Conversely, from the Spit there is a superb panorama of the Winter Palace and the left-bank quays.

Palace Square and the Winter Palace

Palace Square (Dvortsovaya Ploshchad) is possibly one of the best starting points for exploring Leningrad. In a way it symbolizes the city's past, the transition years, and the present. Here was not only the center of power in the days of St. Petersburg—the Czar's residence and the great offices of State—but also the splendid repository of art in the Hermitage. In the twilight of the Czar's Empire, it was here that troops were ordered to disperse a workers' demonstration on Bloody Sunday in 1905, and here, too, the fate of the 1917 Revolution was finally sealed when the Provisional Government was ousted from the Winter Palace, and the Bolsheviks took over the capital and the country.

Today the art collections have been expanded to form the richest accumulation of paintings in the world, gloriously housed in one of the world's greatest architectural set pieces—a grouping of buildings and open spaces, making a harmonious whole which the Russians call by the French term *ensemble.* Palace Square is the supreme example of this. Here you can best see the way that St. Petersburg grew out of a total concept and not piecemeal, like most other cities.

The Winter Palace which dominates the Square replaced earlier crowded royal residences and rose in its present form between 1754 and 1762,

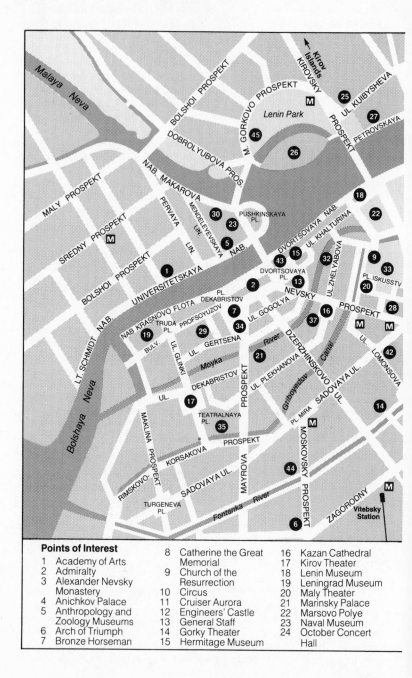

Points of Interest

1	Academy of Arts
2	Admiralty
3	Alexander Nevsky Monastery
4	Anichkov Palace
5	Anthropology and Zoology Museums
6	Arch of Triumph
7	Bronze Horseman
8	Catherine the Great Memorial
9	Church of the Resurrection
10	Circus
11	Cruiser Aurora
12	Engineers' Castle
13	General Staff
14	Gorky Theater
15	Hermitage Museum
16	Kazan Cathedral
17	Kirov Theater
18	Lenin Museum
19	Leningrad Museum
20	Maly Theater
21	Marinsky Palace
22	Marsovo Polye
23	Naval Museum
24	October Concert Hall

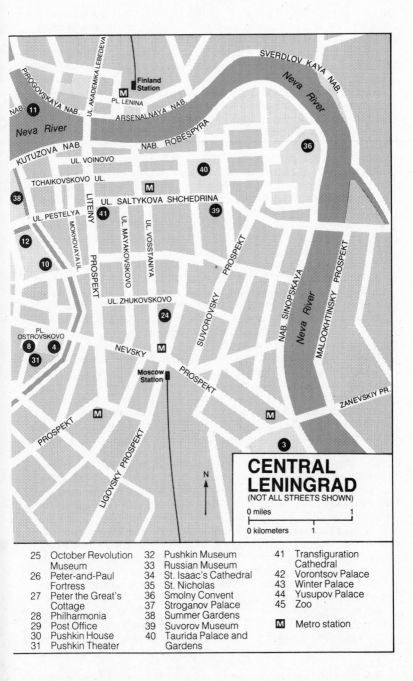

CENTRAL LENINGRAD
(NOT ALL STREETS SHOWN)

0 miles ————————————— 1

0 kilometers ————————————— 1

25	October Revolution Museum	32	Pushkin Museum
26	Peter-and-Paul Fortress	33	Russian Museum
27	Peter the Great's Cottage	34	St. Isaac's Cathedral
28	Philharmonia	35	St. Nicholas
29	Post Office	36	Smolny Convent
30	Pushkin House	37	Stroganov Palace
31	Pushkin Theater	38	Summer Gardens
		39	Suvorov Museum
		40	Taurida Palace and Gardens

41	Transfiguration Cathedral
42	Vorontsov Palace
43	Winter Palace
44	Yusupov Palace
45	Zoo
M	Metro station

in the reign of Empress Elizabeth. Bartolomeo Francesco Rastrelli (later ennobled by his patrons) succeeded in creating an outstanding example of what is known as Russian Baroque. The Palace consists of four large blocks stretching between the Square and the embankment which contain the main State apartments (including the Throne Room, Ceremonial Staircase and Church) and more than a thousand halls and rooms. The blocks are linked by galleries, forming a cross-shaped parade ground in the center. By the time the building was completed Catherine the Great was on the throne and Baroque was out of fashion, Classicism being the vogue. The outside was not tampered with, but the interiors were entrusted to new craftsmen, Yuri Felten, Vallin de la Mothe and Giacomo Quarenghi, who all worked in the latest style. Quarenghi's Throne Room is rich in colored marble and bronze. Later, Carlo Rossi designed a military gallery to commemorate the war against Napoleon, with portraits of the Russian commanders by the English painter George Dawe. In 1837 the Winter Palace was gutted by fire, and all that remained was the walls. But within two decades it was restored, and most of its present interiors date from then. Under the czars it was the main Imperial residence, and was used for ceremonial occasions, grand balls, and receptions.

The complex next to the Winter Palace is the Hermitage. Its building was started by Catherine II who wanted to have a home for the art collection which she was just beginning to acquire abroad, and a retreat (hence the name) connected to her private apartments in the Winter Palace. This is known as the Small Hermitage. It is adjoined by the Large (or Old) Hermitage which was built in stages, and which for a number of years served as a conference chamber for the Czar's ministers. A wing of this building, called the New Hermitage, built by the German Leo von Klenze (the designer of many other European art galleries) is in fact Russia's first purpose-built museum. Of interest also is the Hermitage Theater, created by Quarenghi for Catherine's private theatricals. It is linked with the Large Hermitage by an arch over the Winter Ditch (Zimnyaya Kanavka)—a touch of Venice in this northern city. Another example of Italian influence is the Raphael Gallery, a replica of the Vatican's, with copies of the great painter's works.

The whole museum complex (i.e. the Winter Palace and the various Hermitage buildings) is now known as the "State Hermitage." The setting is magnificent and lavish; malachite, jasper, agate and marble provide a fine backdrop to the treasures. In the 19th century tourists visiting the Winter Palace had to wear court dress or military uniform, but now the treasures of the czars and the hoarded wealth of the nobility and rich merchants has become the property of the State and available to all. In 1987 an 18-year renovation program of the entire complex began. All the rooms will be redesigned, and the organization of tours improved. Several areas of the museum will be closed at any one time (it is a maze at best, and no plans are on sale).

Seeing the Hermitage on your own is recommended; the Intourist tour is very rushed. If you start at around 11:30 A.M., the early crowds will have gone. Try to find a plan if you can—some routes through are blocked by closed rooms, and it is easy to get lost. The collection has seven main sections.

The first section covers Russian history and culture; the second concentrates on prehistoric times showing the discoveries made in the U.S.S.R., including examples of Scythian relics and artefacts; section three is devoted to Central Asia, the Caucasus, and their peoples; section four contains riches from Ancient Egypt, Babylon, Assyria, Byzantium, China and Japan; Greece and Rome are the subjects of section five, where the so-called *Venus of Taurida* (in Room 109) and Greek vases also found on Soviet territory (Room 120) are on display; West European art is covered in six; and the seventh and last section has Russian and foreign medals and decorations.

The sixth section is of particular interest to most art lovers. To mention just a few highlights—there are the two Leonardos, *Madonna with Flowers*—also known as *The Benois Madonna*—and *Madonna Litta* (in Room 214); two Raphaels—*Madonna Connestabile* and his *Holy Family* (in Room 229); and Michelangelo's *Crouching Boy* (in Room 230). Titian has nine fine canvases (in Room 219). The Spanish art collection is second only to the holdings of Madrid's Prado—works by El Greco, Velazquez, Zurbaran and Goya can be seen in Rooms 239 and 240. In Room 245 one can see Flemish art of the 17th century including a splendid *Self-Portrait* by Van Dyck. The Hermitage has more than forty canvases by Peter Paul Rubens and twenty-five Rembrandts, including *Danae* and *The Prodigal Son* (Room 247). French art is very strongly represented—Poussin's *Landscape with Polyphemus,* Watteau's *A Capricious Woman* and Houdin's statue of *Voltaire* (Rooms 272–279). Many works of late-19th–20th-century art, amassed with great foresight by rich Moscow merchants, are now in the Hermitage: Degas and Renoir are in Room 320, Claude Monet and Cézanne (including *The Banks of the Marne*) are in 319 and 318 respectively. Van Gogh is in Room 317. There are 35 paintings by Matisse (Rooms 343–345), including *The Dance.* Picasso—in his various periods, Blue, Pink and Cubist—can be seen in Rooms 346 and 347. British art is well represented by many paintings of Sir Joshua Reynolds, Thomas Gainsborough and also William Morris (Rooms 289–303). Here too is the celebrated *"Frog" dinner service* made by Josiah Wedgwood for Catherine the Great who ordered the 952 pieces decorated with 1,244 views of England. It was intended for use in the Chesma palace which has a green frog in its coat of arms.

Return to the Palace Square and look at some other parts of this splendid complex. Shortly after the Napoleonic wars, the government bought out all the private houses on its south side. Now the General Staff building stands here, the prime example of St Petersburg's Classical style. The enormous three-story semi-circle broken by a large archway, the whole painted yellow and black, was designed by Carlo Giovanni Rossi and built between 1819 and 1829. Rossi, who was half-Italian and half-Russian and worked mainly for Nicholas I, set out to create a complex that would convey both tranquility and movement. The building formerly housed not only the military headquarters but also the Ministries of Foreign Affairs and Finance. The arch is surmounted by a bronze group of a victory chariot (by Demut Malinovsky and Pimenov) commemorating the 1812 war.

In the Square's center stands another memorial to the same victorious campaign and to Napoleon's defeat—the Alexander Column erected by Nicholas I in memory of his brother, after a design by Auguste Richard Montferrand. A huge pillar which is 25 meters (82 feet) high stands on a pedestal hewn out of a single piece of granite. In 1832 it took more than 2,000 soldiers and 400 workmen, using an intricate system of ropes and pulleys, to erect the Column on its high base, where it still stands without any additional support. An angel symbolizing peace in Europe crowns the monument.

On the east side of the square is the building of the former Guards Corps Headquarters built in the 1840s by Alexander Bryullov.

The architectural complex of the Palace Square is completed by the Admiralty. In the early days of St. Petersburg a moated fort containing a well-protected wharf was here. This Admiralty yard, with its stores, workshops and slipways was at first the largest industrial undertaking in the new capital. The present Admiralty, built in 1806–23 after a design by Andrei Zakharov unites two styles—Baroque and Classical. The extensive use of sculpture to adorn the building follows a single theme—the glory of Russia's navy. Neptune handing over his trident to Peter the Great sums it all up. The tapering, gilded spire of the Admiralty is one of Leningrad's landmarks and can be seen from many parts of the city. The weather vane is in the shape of a sailing vessel. Ships continued to be built here up to the 1840s but, in the later part of last century, canals leading into the site were filled in as the embankment was laid leading away from the Winter Palace to what was then Senate Square and is now the Square of the Decembrists.

The Bronze Horseman and the Left Bank

Decembrists' Square (Ploshchad Dekabristov) was the scene of the dramatic attempt by a group of officers to press for reforms in the interregnum after the death of Alexander I. The events of December 14th, 1825, did not bring about a change in Russia, and the ring-leaders were executed or sent to Siberia, but their vainly heroic effort is commemorated today in this square.

Here, too, now stands the monument to the city's founder—the equestrian statue of Peter the Great, known as the *Bronze Horseman.* This brilliant creation by the Frenchman, Etienne-Maurice Falconet, shows Peter on a rearing horse that symbolizes Russia, trampling a serpent that stands for the forces opposed to his reforms. (The serpent, in fact, provides an additional point of support for the horse balanced on its two legs.) The great Czar, to quote Pushkin, "by whose fateful will the city was founded beside the sea, stands here aloft at the very brink of a precipice having reared up Russia with his iron curb." There is stark simplicity in the inscription in Latin and Russian: *To Peter the First from Catherine the Second, 1782.*

In the southern part of the square, stands St. Isaac's Cathedral designed by the same Montferrand who was the designer of the Alexander Column. This, the largest church in the city, took forty years to build. No expense was spared to glorify Peter's patron saint, and some 100 kilos of gold went into gilding the dome. The richly adorned interior, lined with marble, and with malachite and lazurite columns, was intended for up to 13,000 worshippers. It is now a museum. Entrance to the dome balcony is 30 kopeks. No photography is allowed, but it's worth going up for the view.

The Cathedral's main entrance faces Isaac Square (Isaakievskaya Ploshchad), the center-piece of which is the statue of Nicholas I during whose reign the Cathedral was completed in 1858. This square is mainly of the same period, including the Mariinsky Palace built by the Tsar, after a design by Stackenschneider, for his favorite daughter Maria. The Kerensky Provisional Government met here before it was overthrown by Lenin's

Bolsheviks. Today the palace houses the City Soviet, a sort of town hall for Leningrad.

On the eastern and western sides of Isaac Square are some more of the great State buildings, the former Ministries of Agriculture and of State Domains, now used as research institutes. Also in this Square is the Astoria Hotel, dating back to 1912, combining period charm with the functional comforts of a modern establishment. Of the same age is the former German Embassy building (designed by Peter Behrens and Mies van der Rohe) which was sacked at the outbreak of World War I; it now houses Intourist. Another useful place to know about in the area is the General Post Office (Glavny Pochtamt) built as early as 1780.

Returning across the square to the Neva and continuing down the embankment you soon reach Labor Square (Ploshchad Truda). Here is another of the palaces given by Nicholas I to his children, this time to his son Nicholas. Like the Mariinsky Palace, it also was built by Stackenschneider. It is now the home of the Leningrad trades unions. The Naberezhnaya Krasnogo Flota (Red Navy Embankment) was once the center of the English community in the old capital and was then called the English Embankment. One of its outstanding buildings is the former Rumyantsev Palace, originally built for an English merchant and then bought by a scion of the great noble family and used as one of the first private museums in Russia. Its treasures are now elsewhere, and the building is the home of the Museum of the History of Leningrad containing much material about life during the war-time blockade. A modern bridge, named after the leader of the Black Sea sailors' revolt in 1905, Lieutenant Schmidt (Most Leitenanta Shmidta), links the mainland with Vasilevsky Island. On the embankment is a tablet marking the original spot from where the cruiser *Aurora* trained her guns on the Winter Palace in 1917. She is now permanently moored opposite the Hermitage, not far from the Leningrad Hotel (but has been removed to dry-dock for repair and refurbishment, reportedly until 1987).

Vasilevsky Island

Now cross over to Vasilevsky Ostrov, the largest of the islands in the Neva delta. You can use either the Lieutenant Schmidt Bridge or the Dvortsovy (Palace) Bridge. Traveling by subway, get off at Vasileostrovskaya station.

Vasilevsky Island was one of the first areas of the city to be developed. In Peter's grand plan it was to be a kind of Venice, but only a few of the smaller canals were dug (and later filled in when the idea was abandoned). The streets cross the three Great, Middle and Small Avenues (*Prospekts*) which run parallel to the axis of the island, and are called "lines;" instead of names they bear numbers.

The Spit (*Strelka*, in Russian) at the eastern point of the island is one of the best vantage points for a panoramic view of the city. The square on the Strelka (known as Pushkin Square) has two Rostral Columns (Rostralnye Kolonny), another of the city's landmarks. They were erected early in the 19th century to serve as signal towers, for here—for most of the time—was St. Petersburg's commercial harbor. The columns, modeled on similar memorials in ancient Rome, are decorated with ships' prows, with colossal figures symbolizing Russia's rivers—the Volga, Dnieper, Volkhov and Neva—at the base.

The Rostral Columns form part of the magnificent architectural complex of the Spit, the focal point of which is the Stock Exchange (Birzha), erected in 1804–10 and like the Rostral Columns designed by the Swiss architect Thomas de Thomon. It is modeled on the Greek temple at Paestum with Doric columns. The Stock Exchange shared the fate of other institutions of the old regime and was closed down at the time of the 1917 Revolution. The building was then given over to the Central Naval Museum already formed in the days of Peter, who ordered that a model be kept of every ship built in Russia. The Museum's treasury of seafaring memorabilia includes a 3,000-year-old dug-out found on Soviet territory, and also Peter's personal effects, among them the axé with which he built his own *botik* (boat), which is also on show. On display too are models and photographs of modern Soviet warships and submarines.

The *ensemble* of the Spit includes early-19th-century warehouses and the old Customs House, bearing witness to the trading traditions of this part of the city. The latter building, renamed Pushkin House, is the home of the Russian Literature Institute of the Academy of Sciences, a treasure-house of much archival material and of rare editions of printed books. The warehouses, also in the Greek Classical style, are now the Zoological Museum and house nearly 40,000 different species of animals from all over the world. Among the more unusual exhibits is the stuffed mammoth that lived thousands of years ago and was recovered from its permafrost grave in 1901, as well as a mummified baby-mammoth found in 1977.

Continuing along the University Embankment (Universitetskaya Naberezhnaya) you will come to the first Russian natural science museum, the embodiment of another of Peter's ideas, the Kunstkammer. Here is the Czar's own collection of curios, ranging from rare stones to anatomical preparations. The fine Baroque building houses several research institutes.

Next to the Kunstkammer is the building of the main and oldest learned body in the country, the Academy of Sciences. Erected on strictly Classical lines in 1783–89 it is considered to be Quarenghi's grandest design, with an eight-column portico, a pediment and a double staircase. The Academy (founded in 1724 and called "Imperial") had its main administrative offices transferred to Moscow in the 1930s, but some of its branches continue working in Leningrad.

The next group of buildings is that of the Leningrad State University, called after Andrei Zhdanov, the city's party boss in Stalin's time. It is the successor of the University of St. Petersburg founded in 1819. The first and main building is one of the oldest in the city. Designed by Domenico Trezzini in the Baroque style and completed in 1741 it was intended to conform with Peter's idea of siting the center of the city on the Vasilevsky Island. In his days it housed the twelve ministries of state, then called Colleges (*kollegii*), with each department having its own frontage.

The spirit of the 18th century is most evident in the house next to the University buildings, the former palace of Alexander Menshikov, Peter's companion since the days of his youth who rose to become a military commander and statesman. This, the first stone building in St. Petersburg, combines Russian and West European forms of architecture, and provides an insight into how the nobles of the time lived. Giovanni Fontana and Gottfried Schaedel designed the mansion which was built in 1710–16.

Another notable edifice on the University Embankment is the Academy of Arts, designed by Alexander Kokorinov and Vallin de la Mothe and built between 1764 and 1788, a vivid example of early Classicism. The Museum has works by many "academic" painters who worked and taught here, among them Bryullov, Repin and Surikov. The pier in front of the building has two Egyptian Sphinxes of the 15th century B.C. brought to Russia in the last century.

In the Great (Bolshoi) Prospekt stands the huge Kirov Palace of Culture with a 1,300 seat auditorium, an interesting example of Soviet urban architecture of the 1930s. At the end of the avenue is Leningrad's Port and Sea Terminal (Morskoy Vokzal) deep enough to provide a port of call for ocean-going liners.

The Peter-and-Paul Fortress

St. Petersburg was born in the battles of the northern wars, and it was here that it all began when Peter laid the foundation of the first fortress on an islet in 1703 to protect the mainland and to secure Russia's outlet to the sea. This has become the chief monument to the founder's reign. The small hexagonal Hare Island (Zayachi Ostrov) right opposite the mainland and just off what is known as the Petrograd Side of the city, forms—as it were—the hub around which the city revolves. From Vasilevsky Island it is accessible across the Builders' Bridge (Most Stroiteley), and from central Leningrad by the Kirov Bridge from the Palace Embankment. If going by subway, Gorkovskaya station is the closest; from there it is a short walk through Lenin Park and over a footbridge.

The building of the fortress commenced in May 1703 and this date is regarded as the beginning of the city's history. At first only earthworks were raised, and it was not until three years later that the wooden walls began to give way to stone fortifications. The most important architectural feature of the fortress is the St. Peter-and-St. Paul Cathedral started in 1712 and built by Domenico Trezzini, later improved and embellished by Rastrelli. The golden spire—so different from the bulbous domes of Orthodox Churches of pre-Peter days, and almost Protestant in character—rising high above the Neva became the symbol of Russia's outlet to the Baltic Sea. The Cathedral, which is 122 meters (400 feet) high was Leningrad's tallest building until the Television Tower was put up. Peter the Great lies buried inside the Cathedral at a spot he chose himself, and nearly all his successors were buried there too. All, that is, but the last of the Romanovs, Nicholas II, shot dead with his family after the Revolution. He was, of course, denied this honor.

The many interesting structures of the fortress complex include the Neva Gate leading out on to the Commandant's Pier from where a canon is fired every day at midday. Peter's Gate, also built by Trezzini, which looks a bit like a triumphal arch adorned with wooden bas-reliefs, stands almost unchanged since the days when it was erected in 1717–18. The House of Peter the Great (Muzey "Domik Petra Pervogo") stands to the east of the Cathedral. The Czar lived here while supervising the building of his new capital. Its logs were painted to resemble bricks. The cabin has two rooms: a living area and a study, the whole enclosed within a stone structure erected by Catherine II to protect it.

From the early 18th century the Peter-and-Paul Fortress served as a prison, reserved for the most important State prisoners, and rarely holding more than 30 to 40 inmates. One of the first was Czarevich Alexis, Peter's son, who died under torture in its dungeons. The impostor, Princess Tarakanova, whom Catherine had abducted in Italy was also brought here to die. Another of Catherine's foes, the first revolutionary aristocrat in Russia, Alexander Radishchev (author of *A Journey from St Petersburg to Moscow*) was also held here. Later, the cells became overcrowded when the participants in the Decembrist uprising were thrown into prison before being executed or exiled. In time, as opponents of the autocracy became more numerous, a modern prison—the Trubetskoy Bastion—was built in the 1870s to supplement the old dungeons. Among the revolutionaries who were held here were some of the "People's Will" terrorists who assassinated Alexander II, as well as Lenin's elder brother, condemned to death for his part in the attempt on the life of Alexander III. Leon Trotsky and Maxim Gorky were detained in the fortress after the 1905 revolution. The upheavals of 1917 and of the Civil War also yielded prisoners and hostages who were incarcerated or put to death in the Trubetskoy Bastion. The last prisoners were apparently the sailors who mutinied against the Communist regime in Kronstadt in 1921. Since then, the fortress has been turned into a museum and memorial to its former inmates.

The Nevsky Prospekt

Having savored the architectural glories of the complexes on the banks of the Neva, you might like to return to the inner city and to its main thoroughfare, the Nevsky Prospekt. In the early master plan of St. Petersburg this was the "Great Perspective Road" which explains the term *prospekt.* The Nevsky (as the Leningraders call it) runs for about five km. (three miles).

"There is nothing finer than Nevsky Prospekt, not in St. Petersburg at any rate, for in St. Petersburg it is everything ... " wrote the great Russian writer, Nikolai Gogol, some 150 years ago. Today, it is perhaps less resplendent than in the 1830s when fops and their ladies paraded along the fine avenue in horse-driven carriages or strolled in the elegant surroundings. In those days it was a single esplanade, the central artery in a spatial composition intersected by streets and canals, with blocks of mansions punctuated by gaps of varying sizes which allowed adjoining squares to form a part of the architectural whole. The styles along the Nevsky range from 18th-century Baroque to modern versions of urban development; there is a preponderance of fine Classical buildings, but some of the original composition has been spoilt by houses erected early this century.

If you walk from west to east in the direction of the Alexander Nevsky monastery, taking the Gorky Gardens as the starting point, you will soon come to the intersection with Gogol Street (Ulitsa Gogolya), named after the writer who lived for a time at No.17 Nevsky Prospekt where he wrote his play *The Government Inspector* and the beginning of his novel *Dead Souls.* At No.9 the Leningrad Air Terminal and Aeroflot ticket office are located in a former banking house built in the Italian Renaissance style, a mixture of the Doges' Palace in Venice and Florence's Medici Palace. No.10 (across the road) is called *The Queen of Spades* house, this being the home of the old countess on whom Pushkin modeled his masterpiece. The next intersection, Ulitsa Gertsena (Herzen Street) was the street of banks, expensive shops and fashionable eating places before the Revolution. The Imperial Court jewelers Fabergé kept their shop at No. 24 (next to it—No.26—is now a foreign-currency Beryozka shop). The silversmith Ovchinnikov was at No.35.

Cross the River Moyka, where a magnificent building stands, the green-colored former Stroganov Palace, one of the finest of Rastrelli's achievements, completed in 1754. An outstanding example of Russian Baroque, the outside remained intact when the interior was ravaged by fire at the end of the 18th century. While owned by the Stroganovs, the Palace housed one of the great private art collections, now in the Hermitage. On the even-numbered side is an enclave that is a telling reminder of the various religions that co-existed in old St. Petersburg. At No. 20 is the Dutch Church (completed in 1837) and further along, set back from the Nevsky, the Lutheran Church designed by Alexander Bryullov with rounded arches and simple towers that owe much to the Romanesque tradition.

The first major break in the perspective of the Nevsky occurs now as it opens on one of the finest buildings in the city, the Kazan Cathedral. Erected between 1801 and 1811 to a design by Andrei Voronikhin, it is approached by a semi-circular colonnade modeled on St. Peter's in Rome. The huge Cathedral that cost four million roubles to build is surmounted by a high (80 meters, 260 feet) dome set on a drum with 16 pilasters and 16 windows. On the Nevsky side the frontage has niches with colossal statues of St. John the Baptist and of saints prominent in Russian history: Vladimir, Alexander Nevsky and Andrei. The bronze doors are copies of the Baptistry's in Florence and the interior has yet more statues. The Cathedral was completed just before Napoleon's invasion of Russia, and it was here that Field Marshal Kutuzov prayed before taking over command. His statue and that of the other commander in the same war, Barclay de Tolly, stand at the ends of the colonnade. Kutuzov's grave is in the crypt of the northern chapel. Since 1932 the Cathedral—conceived as the Orthodox rival to Rome's St. Peter's—has been the Museum of the History of Religion and Atheism. Its purpose is anti-religious propaganda and it contains much that may seem tasteless and often offensive to visitors from abroad.

Opposite the Cathedral, in what was formerly the offices of the Singer Sewing Machine Company with the distinctive globe trademark on the roof, is Dom Knigi (The House of the Book), Leningrad's main bookshop.

From the Kazan Bridge crossing the Griboyedov Canal (actually a river) you can see a most unusual—for Leningrad—onion-domed church. It is the Church of the Resurrection of Christ (Khram Voskreseniya Khristova), built in the old Russian style of granite, marble and colored bricks to mark the spot where Alexander II was mortally wounded by a terrorist's bomb in 1881. The church has nine domes, the largest decorated with mosaic, the others with enamel.

Further down the Nevsky (on the even-numbered side) is the Philharmonia's Glinka Hall, a center of the city's musical life since the middle of the 19th century. Next door is the theater booking office (*teatralnaya kassa*) where seats can be booked for all major concerts, opera and ballet. Further along at Nos. 32–24 is the Roman Catholic Church of St. Catherine, built between 1762 and 1783 in a mixture of Baroque and Classical styles by Vallin de la Mothe and Rinaldi. The grave of the last king of Poland (and a lover of Catherine II), Stanislaw Poniatowski, is here.

Across the road stands the building of the former city hall or *Duma*, now used as a rail-ticket office. The short Brodsky Street leading off the Nevsky contains a well-known hotel, the Evropeiskaya, formerly called the Hôtel de l'Europe, which was built in the '70s of the last century but given an Art Nouveau look around 1910.

The largest single frontage along the Nevsky is that of the Gostinny Dvor, or Bazar, containing several courtyards. Like many other buildings in the city it was started by Rastrelli in 1757 and then completed by Vallin de la Mothe in 1785 with two tiers of arches. It was completely rebuilt in the last century when it contained some 200 general-purpose shops which were far less elegant than those in other parts of the Nevsky. The bazaar remained the city's main shopping area until recent alterations which turned most of its little boutiques into Leningrad's largest department store.

While still on the same side of the Nevsky, cross Sadovaya (or Garden) Street, at the corner of which is the Saltykov-Shchedrin Library, the largest in the Soviet Union after Moscow's Lenin Library. At the close of the 18th century Yegor Sokolov started work on this first purpose-built library in Russia; it was later extended by Carlo Rossi. The institution opened in 1814 as the Imperial Public Library, and is now said to have some twenty million books. Its holdings in a number of fields, including those of foreign works about Russia, are extensive and often unique. It also boasts of having a copy of all books published since printing was introduced in Russia. The facade is enriched with Ionic columns and statues of Greek philosophers.

The Library is part of Ostrovsky Square (Ploshchad Ostrovskogo), another of Rossi's masterpieces. The square's most important component is the Pushkin Theater, built as the Alexander Theater in Empire style between 1828 and 1832 with six Corinthian columns adorning the frontage facing the Nevsky. Apollo's chariot dominates the building, with statues of the muses Terpsichore and Melpomene to keep him company.

In a small garden in the square stands a monument to Catherine the Great, showing the Empress surrounded by the principal personalities of her reign, and towering above all of them; here you can see Potemkin and Suvorov, Princess Dashkova and the poet Derzhavin, and others who made her age so famous.

Behind the Pushkin Theatre is the Theater Street of the ballerina Karsavina's memoirs. This extraordinary street, now aptly named after its creator, Carlo Rossi (Ulitsa Zodchego Rossi), has two buildings of the same height which are painted yellow with bold white columns. The width of the street (22 meters, 68 feet) equals the height of the buildings, and the street's length is exactly ten times its width. One of the buildings is the Theatrical Museum, the other the Ballet School (founded in 1738) whose pupils included Karsavina as well as Pavlova, Nijinsky and Ulanova.

Return to the Nevsky Prospekt and the corner house that you see facing Ostrovsky Square is what was once St. Petersburg's most luxurious food store, Yeliseyev's, built in the early years of the century. Now it is the city's largest delicatessen. Its elaborate decorations—worthy of Harrods' food hall in London—are well worth seeing.

At No. 60, in the Aurora Cinema building is the Visas and Registration Office. Foreigners not staying in hotels must register here.

Crossing the street once more, you will find yourself in front of the Palace of the Pioneers, formerly the Anichkov Palace built by Empress Elizabeth for her lover Alexei Razumovsky between 1741 and 1750. As if to continue this tradition, Catherine the Great gave it later to *her* favorite, Potemkin. Originally designed by Zemtsov and completed by Rastrelli, the building underwent a number of changes. It once stood in a suburban area, and this explains why its main entrance faces the Fontanka rather than the main street, the Nevsky, where there is only a side entrance. The Palace caters now for all sorts of activities of youth organizations, and has its own planetarium, puppet theater and dance hall. Tourists can only visit it in groups, but usually, after a short wait, enough people gather for a group tour. On the east side of the Palace, the Fontanka is crossed by the Anichkov Bridge—one of the most beautiful in the city—set off by four colossal bronze groups of horse tamers, cast to the design of Peter Klodt.

On the far side of the Fontanka, at No.41 stands the mansion built by Stackenschneider for another nobleman, Prince Beloselsky-Belozersky in the 1840s. Similar in style to the Stroganov Palace at the beginning of the Nevsky, it now houses the local Communist Party headquarters.

The Nevsky leads into Uprising Square (Ploshchad Vosstaniya) which derives its name from the demonstrations and mass meetings held there in 1917. This is a busy spot as it contains a subway (Metro) station and the Moscow Railway Station, serving both long-distance and commuter traffic. There is a hotel in the square, the October (Oktyabrskaya) dating from the 1890s.

Farther along the Nevsky you reach the new Moskva Hotel in Alexander Nevsky Square. Nearby is one of the great monuments of the city, the Alexander Nevsky Monastery (or *Lavra*), one of the four most important monasteries in pre-revolutionary Russia. It was founded by Peter the Great in 1710 on the spot where the Novgorod prince, Alexander Nevsky, is said to have won a great victory over the Swedes and the Teutonic Knights in 1241. The complex includes the Holy Trinity Cathedral (one of the few churches still functioning in the city), a theological seminary, and the Church of the Annunciation. The latter, by Domenico Trezzini (built in 1717–21) is now the Museum of Urban Sculpture. The Cathedral itself, in the Classical style as against the Baroque of the rest of the complex, was designed by Starov and built between 1776 and 1790. The monastery area contains several cemeteries, including the Lazarevsky where a number of St. Petersburg's architects—including Rossi, Voronikhin and Zakharov—are buried, and the Tikhvinsky where there are the graves of many composers—Tchaikovsky, Mussorgsky, Rimsky-Korsakov and Rachmaninov among them. The great soldier, Generalissimo Suvorov is buried under a simple slab in the Church of the Annunciation said to have been designed by himself, which reads simply "Here Lies Suvorov."

The Square of Arts and a Walk Towards the Neva

The next quarter to explore lies north of the Nevsky, roughly enclosed by Sadovaya Street, the Moyka River and the Griboyedov Canal, and has as its central point the Square of Arts—one of Leningrad's largest and finest architectural complexes. Right in the middle stands Rossi's Michael Palace (Mikhailovsky Dvorets) built in 1819–25 in the style of a nobleman's town estate with a principal residence and two service wings. In front of the central portico with its eight Corinthian columns lies a large courtyard with an attractive railing. The original owner of the palace was Grand Duke Michael, the youngest son of Emperor Paul. In 1896 Nicholas II turned it into a museum to commemorate his father, Alexander III; it is now the Museum of Russian Art. A second building, designed by Benois and Ovsyannikov was completed in 1916, and then rebuilt after World War II.

The Museum's holdings of Russian art are next in importance to those of the Tretyakov Gallery in Moscow. Outstanding is its collection of icons (in Rooms 1–4) including the 12th-century *Angel with Golden Hair* and many works by Rublyov and Ushakov. 17th and 18th century Russian paintings are well represented, but most important are those of the 19th century, such as the seascape painter Aivazovsky's *Ninth Wave* (Room 13), and the huge canvases of Ilya Repin including his *Volga Boatmen* (Rooms 47–50). There are many fine portraits by Valentin Serov, amongst them the beautiful *Countess Orlov* (Rooms 76 and 77), and Vrubel's strange *Demons* (Room 78). Painters of the World of Art Movement—Bakst, Benois and Somov—are here too (mainly in Room 80). The Soviet period is chiefly represented by examples of Socialist Realism but there are some Kandinskys and Tatlins (in Room 91) and Altman's striking portrait of the Leningrad poet, *Anna Akhmatova* (in Room 89). The eastern wing of the Michael Palace is the Museum of Ethnography of the Peoples of the U.S.S.R. This contains fascinating collections of applied art.

Carlo Rossi spent some 15 years creating the square and another notable example of his design is the facade of the former Nobles' Club which now houses the Leningrad Philharmonia and is called after Shostakovich. In the main hall of this building, with its marble columns, the composer's *Seventh Symphony* was first performed during the German blockade.

Next to the Philharmonia is the Maly (or Small) Theater, designed by Rossi and Bryullov for the northwest side of the Square in 1831; it was rebuilt by Albert Cavos. This theater known before the Revolution as the French Theater because French companies used to perform here, is now used for opera and ballet performances.

Yet another Rossi building of the 1820s, created for the Golenishchev-Kutuzov family, houses the museum of the painter of revolutionary scenes, Isaak Brodsky, who lived here through the 1920s and '30s. On show are not only works by Brodsky, but also by the main artists from the turn of the century.

In the middle of the square stands a fine statue of Pushkin reading his poetry; sculpted by Mikhail Anikushin, it was put up in 1957.

If you are feeling energetic, you can now continue your tour by leaving the square and walking past the Russian Museum to another palace which is in fact a castle. Here once stood an Imperial summer palace in which the future Emperor Paul was born. The legend has it that when Paul finally succeeded his mother, the Archangel Michael appeared to him in a dream, and told him to build a church on the site of his birthplace. The demented czar proceeded to build not only a shrine but a fortress, surrounded by water on all sides, with secret passages between the ramparts and the moats. St. Michael, however, brought his servant little luck. Paul was strangled by his own courtiers in this same fortress. The palace, which stood empty for a number of years, was later renamed Engineers' Castle (Inzhenerny Zamok) and was used as a place of higher technical education. During Paul's brief occupancy he pursued his favorite pastime on the square to the south—drilling troops. He also had a statue erected here to Peter the Great. Sculpted by Bartolomeo Carlo Rastrelli (the great architect's father), it shows the czar as a Roman Emperor crowned with a laurel wreath. Its formality contrasts with the simplicity of Falconet's Bronze Horseman. Catherine did not like Rastrelli's statue and had it put in store. Paul—always intent on adopting a different line from his mother—had it brought out of storage and re-erected with the inscription *To the Great Grand-father by the Great-grandson,* trying clumsily to paraphrase his mother's tribute to Peter at the foot of the Bronze Horseman.

In the area enclosed by the Fontanka and Lebyazhaya Kanavka, and continuing from the Engineers' Castle in the direction of the Neva, you will come to the Summer Garden, one of the most attractive of Leningrad's parks and widely enjoyed by the people of the city for rest and recreation. The laying out of the Summer Garden began as early as 1704 when it was planned in a regular, geometrical style. There were at the time many fountains fed from the nearby river which was given the name of Fontanka (*fontan* being the Russian word for fountain). These were damaged by floods by the end of the 18th century and never restored. The Garden is decorated with many fine sculptures; one of these, *Peace and Abundance* by Pietro Barrata, dates back to 1722 and allegorically depicts Russia's victory over Sweden. As in many other Leningrad parks, the outdoor sculptures are protected against the severe weather from early fall by wooden covers.

Inside the Summer Garden is a fine example of early 18th-century architecture—Peter's Summer Palace. This two-story stone building, designed by Domenico Trezzini in 1710–14, has survived without major alterations. The walls are of stucco-covered brick and are painted primrose yellow. There are several other attractive buildings in the Garden, including the Coffee House (rebuilt by Rossi in 1826) and the Tea House (by I.L.Charlemagne in 1827). In the park is the monument to Ivan Krylov, the "Russian La Fontaine," by Peter Klodt, 1855. Scenes from his fables appear on the pedestal.

On the Neva embankment side of the Summer Garden is a splendid screen, another of the city's great landmarks. It was made in 1770 after a design by Yuri Felten and P.M. Yegorov. The granite columns are linked by light grillwork which looks as if it were suspended in the air.

Continuing along the river bank you will come next to a monument to the great military commander, Alexander Suvorov (not a portrait likeness but rather the glorification of military valor) and here opens a splendid panorama onto the Field of Mars (Marsovo Poly), the venue of great military parades in the 19th century. It is now a park and in its center an eternal flame burns in the 1919 Memorial to the Victims of the Revolution whose remains were brought here.

The buildings near the Field of Mars were erected at the end of the 18th century, and show the change from Baroque to Classical style. The Marble Palace is a case in point. Designed by Arnoldo Rinaldi it was built between 1768 and 1785 for one of Catherine's foremost favorites, Gregory Orlov, but was in fact completed only after his death. The name of the Palace is derived from the pale-pink marble facings on the walls. The sides are strictly Classical, while the main frontage, which faces inwards to the forecourt with its columns, is vaguely Baroque. The Marble Palace how houses the Leningrad branch of the Central Lenin Museum whose exhibits depict the life and revolutionary activities of the founder of the Soviet state. On show is the Austin armored car from the turret of which Lenin made his first public speech at the Finland Station on his return from exile in April 1917.

Khalturin Street (Ulitsa Khalturina), which runs parallel to the embankment, leads from the Marble Palace to the Winter Palace and Palace Square. It was once the Millionaires' Row of St. Petersburg (it was in fact called Millionnaya). The exclusive English Club was at No. 16. The British Embassy was at No. 4 of the Palace Embankment (Dvortsovaya Naberezhnaya), also in this area, between 1863 and 1918.

The Kirov Theater and Sadovaya Street

This tour will show you some more of the inner city. If you turn south at the Nevsky's intersection with Sadovaya Street you will find yourself in a quarter which was originally one of suburban gardens and estates, but which in the last century acquired the character of an important business and shopping district.

Of note is the Vorontsov Palace (just beyond the Saltykov-Shchedrin Public Library), built by Rastrelli in 1749–57 for the then Vice-Chancellor of the realm, Prince M.I.Vorontsov, and which later became the home of the Corps of Pages (Pazhesky Korpus). Further along Sadovaya Street is the State Bank (Quarenghi's achievement in 1783–90) in the Classical style. You now reach Peace Square (Ploshchad Mira), the former Sennaya Ploshchad (Haymarket), once the chief open market of the capital surrounded by slum dwellings, drinking dens and the like, the real-life setting for Dostoyevsky's *Crime and Punishment*. The writer lived in the area for some time in the 1860s, and the house in which Raskolnikov murdered the moneylender is still shown to tourists—No. 104 Griboyedov Canal Embankment (Naberezhnaya Kanala Griboyedova).

Further along, beyond the Nikolsky markets stands the Cathedral of St. Nicholas built in 1753–62 by Savva Chekavinsky in Russian Baroque style, which looks a bit like some of Rastrelli's creations, especially the Smolny. With its imposing belfry, standing beside the canal and surrounded by green spaces, it is very picturesque and romantic. It is also a working church.

Glinka Street (Ulitsa Glinki) leads into Kirov Square where the Kirov Theater and the Conservatoire stand. This area, around the Kryukov Canal, was for years a place of public entertainment with fair grounds, carrousels, booths, and so on. It was formerly called Karuselnaya Ploshchad. In 1783 the Bolshoi (or Great) Theater was built here, but it was declared unsafe and pulled down some 100 years later, to be replaced by the Conservatoire, which has been the premier place of musical education in Russia ever since Peter Tchaikovsky was among its first graduates.

Until the middle of the last century a theater which was mainly used for circus performances also stood here. It burned down and Albert Cavos built the Mariya (Mariinsky) Theater on the spot. Now called the Kirov Theater it has been the main home of the Russian ballet since the 1880s. The blue-and-gold auditorium is splendidly elegant and the list of artists who have performed there includes all those who made Russian opera and ballet famous throughout the world.

Walking past the Kirov as far as the Moyka River and turning right, you will soon reach the Yusupov Palace which stands beyond the Potseluyev Most (Bridge of Kisses). Built by Vallin de la Mothe in 1760 its claim to fame is as the place where Prince Yusupov murdered Rasputin, the Mad Monk, in 1916. (The Palace is at No.94 Naberezhnaya Reki Moyki). On the same embankment (at No.12) is the Pushkin Memorial Museum, the poet's last home. Here he spent the last night before the fatal duel in 1837, and here he died of his wounds. Also not far from the Kirov, across the Kryukov Canal at 2 Lermontovsky Prospekt, is Leningrad's remaining synagogue.

If you retrace your steps along Sadovaya Street to Peace Square, and turn into Moscow Prospekt, you come to the Moscow Triumphal Arch erected to commemorate victories over the Turks in 1828–29. Not far from it are the Elektrosila electrical engineering works, once the Siemens-Schuckert company plant, and now one of the largest factories of its kind in the Soviet Union. Further along is the Moscow Victory Park started in 1945 with its Lenin Sports and Concert Complex completed in 1980. Past the 10-floor Rossiya Hotel you come to the Chesma Palace and Church built by Yuri Felten for Catherine II as a staging post on her journeys to Tsarskoye Selo (now Pushkin—see page 203). The graceful Chesma Church is one of the rare mock-Gothic churches in Leningrad. Also in this area is the wide Moscow Square with the huge House of Soviets built in the 1930s in the prevailing style of the period. Further along is Victory Square with the Monument to Leningrad's Defenders, unveiled in 1975.

Along the Neva towards the Smolny

Continuing along the Neva embankment (away from the Winter Palace) you can cross the Liteiny (Foundry) Bridge in order to visit the rebuilt Finland Station, and the imposing Lenin Square complete with his statue. At the back of the Pirogov Embankment (Pirogovskaya Naberezhnaya) stands the 17-floor Leningrad Hotel.

If you remain on the left bank of the River, you will soon reach the Taurida Palace, also built at Catherine's command between 1783 and 1789 for her greatest favorite (and lover) Gregory Potemkin who, unlike his predecessor Orlov, lived long enough to enjoy the home his Imperial mistress had built for him. Potemkin's military successes—his conquest of the Crimea (the Tauris of the classical world) brought him the princely title which also gave its name to the Palace. Designed by the greatest Russian architect of the period, Ivan Starov, it shows Classicism at its best, with precisely defined lines, modest decorations, use of ancient architectural motifs and with a pediment above the portico entrance. The interiors are rich and opulent, and it was here, before setting out once again for the south (and this time, for death), that Potemkin gave a farewell ball for his Empress. 3,000 guests were entertained by 300 singers and the whole place was brilliantly lit with 140,000 lamps and 20,000 candles. When the mad Paul succeeded Catherine, he turned this fairy-tale palace into stables to show his hatred for his mother and her lover, but Catherine's grandson, Alexander I, restored it to its former glory. In later years, the *Duma,* the czarist parliament sat in the Palace, and when the first revolution broke out in 1917 it was here that the Petrograd Soviet of Workers' and Soldiers' Deputies held its meetings.

The most important complex in this part of the city is the Smolny group of buildings, reached along the Suvorovsky Prospekt. (By subway to Ploshchad Vosstaniya Metro Station and then by Trolleybus No.5). The Smolny Convent marks Rastrelli's greatest achievement, his success in brilliantly reworking Russian architectural designs from the days before Peter the Great, incorporating them in the Baroque style of the period. The site chosen for the convent had in Peter's day been a tar yard (*smolny dvor,* hence the name). His daughter, the pleasure-loving and yet deeply-religious Empress, commanded the future designer of the Winter Palace to build a nunnery for orphan girls. Rastrelli—who now has a square named after him on the approaches to the complex—started working here in 1748. His strictly regular and symmetrical buildings were to occupy a commanding position over the low-lying banks of the river. His Cathedral, the framework of which was completed in 1764, is in the shape of a cross with adjoining living quarters, forming an open square in the same shape. Small churches stand at the four points of this internal square. In the 1760s an educational institution for the daughters of the gentry was established in the convent's living quarters, but in the early 19th century the girls were moved to a purpose-built edifice, designed by Quarenghi.

The Smolny occupies a significant place in Russia's revolutionary history. In August 1917 the Central Executive Committee of the Petrograd Soviet moved here from the Taurida Palace. Two months later, the revolt against the Provisional Government, masterminded by Trotsky, was directed from the Smolny. Lenin came here in October to take charge of the headquarters of the Bolshevik Party. The Second Congress of the Soviets opened in the ceremonial hall of the Smolny on November 7th 1917, and elected the Council of Commissars with Lenin as its chairman. The Smolny remained the seat of the Soviet Government until it moved to Moscow. It was in the news again in 1934 when the city's party boss, Sergei Kirov was assassinated there, an event which triggered off the trials and purges. The Smolny is now the local Communist Party headquarters for Leningrad; special passes are needed for entry, but there are frequent guided group tours.

The Kirov Prospekt and the Kirov Islands

By crossing the Kirov Bridge from the River's left bank to the Petrograd side and *not* turning at Revolution Square towards the Peter-and-Paul Fortress, you find yourself in the great Lenin Park which was laid out in the middle of the last century, when it was known as the Alexandrine (Aleksandrisky) Park. In addition to theaters, cinemas, a planetarium, and so forth, the park also contains Leningrad's Zoo which was founded at the end of 19th century with Arctic animals—polar bears and seals—as its main attraction; other species to be seen there now include aurochs, black rhinos, and the Tien-shan panther.

The Kirov Prospekt (Kirovsky Prospekt) leads north in a straight line. Built at the turn of the century, it was once a street of luxury apartment blocks. Near Tolstoy Square is the so-called House with Towers, a block of pre-World-War-II apartments built in the style of an English medieval castle.

Off Revolution Square is Kuibyshev Street (Ulitsa Kuibysheva) where the Museum of the October Revolution stands. Its main building was originally the residence of the great ballerina Mathilda Kshessinskaya, once a mistress of Nicholas II. This 1904-built villa is a good example of architecture in the Modern Style. It was seized by the Bolsheviks when the revolution broke out, and it was here that Lenin set up his first office upon returning from exile. Not far away is the Mosque, built in the same period and modeled on one of the great Moslem shrines of Samarkand, the Gur Emir Mosque.

The large film studios of Lenfilm are on the Kirov Prospekt, and nearby stands Leningrad's Television Tower. The Prospekt ends at the Stone Island Bridge (Kamennoostrovsky Most). The Kirov Islands begin here, an archipelago noted for its picturesque landscapes, parks, rest homes, and recreation areas. Workers' Island (Ostrov Trudyashchikhsya), formerly Stone Island (Kamenny Ostrov), was built on even back in the days of

Peter. The palace on the island, dating from the reign of Paul, has survived in its original shape today. There are other stately residences of the nobility as the island was a favorite spot for the rich and the famous to spend their summers away from the capital.

To the northwest lies Yelagin Island (Yelagin Ostrov) named after its aristocratic owner in the late 18th century. By the beginning of the 19th century, the island had become a summer residence for the Imperial family. It was here that Carlo Rossi started his successful career by executing one of his first commissions, a palace for Alexander I in the style of Russian Classicism. This palace, dating from the 1820s, still dominates the island which is now mostly occupied by the Kirov Central Recreation Park with a large open-air theater, exhibition pavilions, a sports centre, boating stations and a beach.

Krestovsky Island, the largest of the group was not well developed in the Czarist days. In 1925 the Dynamo stadium was built here, but the main attraction now is the Primorsky (Seaside) Park of Victory. It has several artificial lakes with swimming pools and boat houses. On the island is the Kirov Stadium which seats 80,000 people—built in the early 1950s, not of stone or reinforced concrete but of earth, and more than a million cubic yards of soil had to be moved for its construction.

The Environs of Leningrad—Petrodvorets

St. Petersburg's isolation was emphasized by its being sited in an inhospitable, thinly-populated wilderness. Peter the Great was the first to realise that he would need not only a new capital and a naval base on the Gulf of Finland, but also a country palace. He commissioned a Versailles by the sea from the French architect, Alexandre Jean-Baptiste Leblond, and like many of the Czar's ideas it was soon translated into reality. Peterhof, now Petrodvorets, came into being. Its palaces, however, owe more to Peter's daughter, Elizabeth, and her architect Rastrelli.

Petrodvorets is some 29 km. (18 miles) from the center of Leningrad and is easily reached by local train from the Baltic Railway Station, by bus from Riding School (Manezh) Square, and—best of all—by hydrofoil from Makarov Quay. The visitor to Petrodvorets and to the other Imperial residences we shall describe will find it difficult to believe that when the Germans were finally driven out of the area towards the end of World War II, everything (or almost everything) was in ruins. Many priceless objects had been removed to safety before the Germans advanced, but a great deal had to be left behind for the invaders to loot and destroy. Now, most of the damage has been made good. Painstaking work, using old plans, photographs and descriptions has made it possible to recreate these palaces and bring them back to their original splendor. Art historians and craftsmen have combined to make the reconstruction a great success.

Petrodvorets is a case in point. To appreciate it best, start at the square where the bus terminus is. On its northern side there is a balustrade, beyond which a green slope descends steeply to a small plain stretching right to the shoreline. This is part of the Lower Park. Having had this first view, now continue walking towards the Great Palace (open 11–8, closed on some Mondays). From here a marble terrace gives you a magnificent view over the Great Cascade, made up of three waterfalls, 64 fountains and 37 statues. The system of waterworks has remained virtually unchanged since 1721. Ducts and pipes which convey the water over a distance of some

20 km. (12 miles) work without pumping stations: the water flows down-hill, while the fountains operate on the principle of communicating vessels. The view from the terrace is breathtaking. The centerpiece of the water-falls is a gilded Samson, tearing apart the jaws of a lion from which a jet of water spurts into the air. The statue represents the Russian victory over the Swedes at Poltava on St Samson's day. The present figure is a meticu-lous replica of the original which was carried away by the Germans. From the foot of the Great Cascade there is a canal leading into the Gulf of Fin-land, flanked by formal gardens in the French style and by many more statues, fountains and cascades.

The Great Palace crowns the hill. The location apart, little remains of Peter's original concept executed by Leblond, Braunstein and Machetti. It was under Elizabeth that Rastrelli accomplished yet another blend of medieval Russian architecture and Baroque. The State apartments are sumptuously appointed, especially the Partridge Drawing Room with bril-liantly restored silk-covered walls adorned with the birds which give the room its name. The White Dining Room in early Classical style with white moldings, and the large Throne Room used in the past for great receptions and official ceremonies, are well worth visiting.

The Upper Park, which you can enter from the Palace, has as its focal point the Neptune fountain originally made in Germany in the 17th centu-ry and then bought by the czars. During the war the three-tiered group of bronze sculptures was carried away by the Germans. It was eventually recovered and re-installed in 1956.

If you return to the foot of the hill by the waterside, you will find your-self in the Lower Park with its very attractive 18th-century buildings. Es-pecially charming is Monplaisir, Peter's favorite palace, built between 1714 and 1723 by the same architects who worked on the Great Palace. This, too, sustained serious wartime damage but was reopened in 1961. One of its most interesting rooms is the Lacquered Study, decorated with replicas of the destroyed Russian panels painted in Chinese style. The Naval Study offers a fine view of the sea. Two more palaces stand in the grounds—the Hermitage Pavilion and the Marly Palace, both dating back to the same period.

Lomonosov

The town of Lomonosov, some ten km. (six miles) west of Petrodvorets and facing the Kronstadt naval base, was founded by Peter's favorite, Al-exander Menshikov, and was first called Oranienbaum. It is also reachable by train from Leningrad's Baltic Station. Menshikov, like Peter, wanted to have a summer residence and between 1710 and 1725 the desolate site was transformed into an elegant nobleman's mansion. Giovanni Fontana and Gottfried Schaedel, who were also building Menshikov's Palace on Vasilevsky Island in the city, created a Great Palace here with its main facade turned towards the sea, and with a formal garden in front of the terraces peopled by sculptures. The Summer Palace of Peter III (Cather-ine's ill-fated consort) is the only relic of fortifications raised in Oranien-baum in the middle of the 18th century. This small stone mansion (built by Arnoldo Rinaldi) now houses an arts and crafts collection. To the southwest is the Chinese Palace (also by Rinaldi) which Catherine used as a summer residence.

Pushkin

Pushkin—formerly Tsarskoye Selo, or the Czar's village—was the home of the Imperial family from the days of Peter the Great right up to the time of the last Czar. Next to the parks and palaces stands the town developed mainly in the 19th century as a summer resort for the aristocracy and well-to-do of St. Petersburg. In 1837 the first railway line in Russia was built here, linking St Petersburg with Tsarskoye Selo. Pushkin is about 25 km. (15 miles) from central Leningrad, this time traveling south. Train service is from the Vitebsk Railway Station (90 kopeks return) or by bus from Riding School (Manezh) Square.

Pushkin is quite different from Petrodvorets and Lomonosov. Here, there are no massed fountains and no vistas over the sea. Here you are very much inland, in beautiful English-style parks, unrestrained by the geometrical formality of the Russian Versailles. The palaces again bear the stamp of the Baroque days of the Empress Elizabeth, the paramount example of which is the Catherine Palace (Yekaterinensky Dvorets) built by the Empress and named after her mother, Catherine I, Peter's second wife. (Open 10–6; closed on Tuesdays and on last Monday of the month.) The palace rose on the site of previous royal residences, and its present form is primarily the work of Bartolomeo Rastrelli who took on the job in 1752 after he had completed the Hermitage pavilion nearby and before turning his attention to the Winter Palace in the city itself. Like Petrodvorets and its residences, the Catherine Palace sustained much damage during the war but today it stands again in all its glory with its 300-meter-long facade, featuring a row of white columns and pilasters with gold Baroque moldings boldly set against a blue background. At the northern end are the golden domes of the Palace Church, and on the courtyard side sparkle the gilded gates designed by Rastrelli himself. Under Catherine the Great the building underwent substantial changes, Rastrelli's interiors being altered to conform with the canons of Classicism. Charles Cameron, the Scottish architect of genius, and the Italian Giacomo Quarenghi were mainly responsible for carrying out the many alterations and additions accomplished at Catherine's command between 1760 and 1790.

Entering the palace by the main staircase you can see several chambers that have not yet been fully restored and contain displays showing the extent of wartime damage and of the restoration work. One of the most handsome rooms in the palace, the Picture Gallery, runs right across the building. Magnificent period pieces are on display in the State Study of Alexander I, with its grand marble fireplace. The Blue Room, restored on the basis of Cameron's original drawings, is very close to its appearance as envisaged by the architect. Restoration work still continues in the Amber Room, whose amber walls vanished during the war. The Cameron Gallery, which adjoins the palace and forms a continuation of its parkside frontage, offers one of the best views of the parks and lakes of Pushkin. There is much to be seen, too, in the Catherine (or Old) Park to the east of the palace, including the Upper and Lower Bath Pavilions, Rastrelli's Hermitage and the Grotto. Next to the Great Pond, an artificial lake, stands the Chesma Column, marking the naval victory in the Aegean in 1770.

Outside the Catherine Park, a visit ought to be paid to the Alexander Palace built by the Empress for her grandson. This yellow-and-white Clas-

sical structure by Quarenghi looks serene and restrained in its own Alexandrine Park. Before leaving Pushkin you should drop by the Lyceum,
a building originally intended for the education of Catherine's grandchil-
dren. It then became a school for sons of the nobility, and Alexander Pushkin, the poet after whom the town is now named, enrolled there in 1811.

Pavlovsk

Pavlovsk is about four km. (two miles) from Pushkin, and it is possible
to combine the visit to the two towns. (Traveling from Leningrad, again
use the Vitebsk Railway Station). Pavlovsk, originally the site of the royal
hunt, was given by Catherine the Great to her son Paul in 1777. Charles
Cameron was commissioned to build the heir-apparent's residence, but
when Paul came to the throne he brought in Vincenzo Brenna who added
some romantic touches to Cameron's Classical design. Brenna built the
stone staircase leading down to the Slavyanka River and landscaped the
romantic Great Circles in the park. But in spite of these and other changes
and additions, Cameron's basic design has survived.

The golden-yellow Great Palace's flat dome is supported by 64 white
columns. (Open 10.30–5.30; closed on Fridays, only the main buildings
are open on Thursdays). It stands on a high bluff overlooking the river
and dominates the surrounding parkland. In front of the palace is a statue
of the snub-nosed Emperor who had his official summer residence here,
while inside there is much of interest—especially the State Apartments
on the first floor. Brenna's Greek Hall, adorned with Corinthian columns
served as a ballroom and, together with the Hall of Knights (created for
Paul as the Grand Master of the Maltese Knights of St John), adds much
to the beauty of the Palace. There is an intriguing contrast between the
Hall of Peace in the Czarina's quarters, which is decorated with such motifs of peace as musical instruments and flowers, and the martial decorations of the Hall of War in her husband's wing.

The Pavlovsk Park—the length of its paths and lanes is said to equal
the distance between Leningrad and Moscow (some 400 miles)—displays
a combination of styles, with areas fashioned in the French, Italian and
English manner, over 1,500 acres of undulating hills and valleys with a
river, ponds, cascades and waterfalls. Just outside the Palace is the Czar's
own Little Garden from the main avenue of which you can see The Three
Graces' Pavilion built by Cameron. Another of Cameron's creations in
the park is the sentimentally named Temple of Friendship, a circular yellow pavilion with a colonnade.

Kizhi and Vyborg

The Island of Kizhi can be visited from Leningrad, a rather lengthy excursion of about 400 km. (250 miles) to the northeast. Kizhi is in the middle of Lake Onega, one of the natural lakes forming part of the White
Sea–Baltic Canal (Belomorkanal) built in the 1930s by convict labour with
terrible loss of life. The nearest town is Petrozavodsk; it has an Intourist
hotel, and is best done as a trip over a weekend. The pleasantest way is
by boat from the Ozernaya River Station, though there is also an Intourist
rail tour.

The Island of Kizhi is one of the most ancient inhabited sites in Russia.
It was an early pagan center and is now an open-air architectural museum
and reserve. Many wooden churches and other shrines were brought here

from other parts of the Russian north. One of the most splendid is the Church of the Transfiguration (1744) with its 22 timbered onion domes. It was restored in 1984–85.

The city of Vyborg, close to the Finnish border, is believed to be open to foreign tourists, in transit, but it still does not appear on official lists—check first.

PRACTICAL INFORMATION FOR LENINGRAD

WHEN TO GO. The people of Leningrad claim that their city is a year-round attraction. In winter you can go skating or ice-fishing, take a ride on a Finnish sled (a chair mounted on long steel runners), and ski (there are two ski-jumps at Kavgolovo, some 32 km. (20 miles) from the center). The end of the winter is marked by special festivities. There is tobogganing, riding in horse-drawn sleds (*troikas*) and snow-ball fights, and the traditional *blini* (pancakes) are served.

The spring draws the first sun-worshippers to the Peter-and-Paul Fortress—though they have to sunbathe well wrapped up and leaning against the warm stone blocks of the fortress. The open-air stadiums start their soccer season. Rowing, yachting and cycling are the favorite spring sports.

In summer the White Nights Music and Arts Festival runs from June 21–29. You can spend a white night on a ship sailing out into the Gulf of Finland. Arts festivals fill the theaters and concert halls. There are fireworks at Petrodvorets, "the town of fountains," some 29 km. (18 miles) from Leningrad.

Autumn brings the 30-kilometer race between the center of the city and the town of Pushkin and the celebration commemorating the October (or, rather, November) Revolution. But the autumn is mostly rainy and cold; if there is a snowfall, it does not last. Life is largely restricted to indoor activities and of course the theaters and concert halls are in full swing.

GETTING THERE. By air. There is a plane from Moscow to Leningrad almost every hour, covering the distance in an hour, for 18 roubles. The fare is less than the first-class sleeper; but as the airports in both cities are some distance from the town center, not much time is saved. At presstime there is a weekly summer service (British Airways) from London Heathrow direct.

By rail. There are 15 express trains linking Leningrad with Moscow each day, of which six are by day (additional services in peak holiday periods), and the fastest now doing 410 miles in just over 4 hours. The *Red Arrow* is the prime overnight express. A daily express to and from Helsinki takes 8 hours. Change your roubles for foreign currency before boarding the train, if leaving the country.

By boat. Cruise ships and ships of the regular Soviet Baltic passenger line and foreign liners call at Leningrad. There is a year-round car ferry from Stockholm.

By car. You can also approach the city by car along the transit highway that runs from Finland, via Vyborg. The road into the city from the north runs along Primorsky Prospekt past the gasoline and service station and over a bridge to Kirovsky Prospekt which leads straight to the Palace Embankment. If you are traveling to Moscow, you follow the main Leningrad-Moscow highway, leaving the city near the Varshavsky (Warsaw) Railroad Station, close to Izmailovsky Cathedral.

GETTING INTO TOWN. Intourist will arrange for you to be met at the docks, the railway stations or the airport. The city air terminal is on Nevsky Prospekt in a remarkable building called Dvorets Dozhei (Palace of Doges), 9 Nevsky Prospekt. Taxis are available at the stations and terminals.

GETTING AROUND THE CITY. By tram and bus. There are 39 streetcar (tram) lines, 17 trolley-bus lines, 68 bus lines and three subway lines. Leningrad's first electric tram, dating from 1907, now runs on a sightseeing route through the city. Tickets are sold on a self-service basis—you put the fare into a collecting box. Standardized fare is 5 kopeks. Books of tickets are available at newspaper kiosks. Further details from your hotel desk.

By boat. Within the city limits water-buses ply on the Neva between the Academy of Arts and the Victory Park and between the Summer Garden and Kirov Stadium. The fare is 10–30 kopeks.

By train. The suburbs and outlying parks are best approached by local trains. There are also buses which mostly start from Riding-School Square (Manezhnaya Ploshchad) which is also the starting point for the airport buses. There are boats from the harbor for Petrodvorets, Zelenogorsk and Lomonosov.

By subway. Of the three subway lines the first, completed in 1955, links all the railroad stations: Moscow, Finland, Vitebsk, Baltic and Warsaw. It is marked red on subway maps. The second (blue) connects the district at the end of the Leningrad–Moscow highway with the Petrograd District. The third (green) runs across town. In December 1978 a new section of the blue line out to the islands was opened, to cater for people in the new residential districts. The overall length of all lines is now 38 miles; a total of 2,730 trains operate daily, carrying several million passengers.

By taxi. Taxis are available at stands and can be ordered by telephone. If you order through your hotel you have to pay an extra 50 kopeks service charge. Many taxi-drivers seem to dislike relatively short distances—under 2½ miles. Some drivers of private cars will offer their services at very reasonable rates.

HOTELS. As in Moscow, Intourist uses only a handful of the better hotels for Western tourists and normally does the assigning of hotel space. The choice hotels are the *Astoria, Evropeiskaya, Moskva, Pribaltiiskaya, Pulkovskaya,* and *Leningrad,* and they are normally used for tour groups. The rates are generally the same as in Moscow for top, deluxe-class hotels. All listed here have restaurant or café attached.

Astoria, 39 Herzen (Gertsena) Street (tel. 219–1100). Leningrad's best all round, ageing but full of atmosphere and certainly the most famous hotel in town. Closed in 1986 for 3-year refurbishment. When finished they say it will be Leningrad's most luxurious hotel.

Evropeiskaya, 1/7 Brodsky Street (tel. 211–9149). Old like the Astoria. Centrally located. 257 rooms, rated first class by us, "deluxe" by Intourist. Self-service lunch is good value. *Vostochnyi Restaurant* quite good.

Gavan, 88 Sredny Prospekt, on Vasilevsky Island. Used often by visiting trade union groups. Reported to have good restaurant with speedy service. Clean, friendly; no Beryozka shop but small bookstall and gift counter.

Leningrad, 5/2 Pirogovskaya Embankment (tel. 242–9123). The place to stay if you want a modern hotel at any price or if you plan a very long stay. This Finnish-decorated hotel is very elegant by Soviet standards. Rated as deluxe. Breakfasts recommended, excellent dining room. Entertainment nightly including variety show, jazz and dancing in restaurant. You are expected to eat a 4-course supper with it. Three late bars; best one on 10th floor has lively balalaika and disco music—foreign currency only, expensive. Other bars are 2 roubles entrance charge. Located across the Neva but only a short ride from the center. 650 well-furnished, smallish rooms all with own bathroom. Ask for waterfront rooms overlooking river. One suite has a sunken bath, Japanese style.

Moskva, 2 Alexander Nevsky Square (tel. 274–2051, 274–9515 or 774–2115). Newish, seven floors, 777 rooms. Dancing nightly. Good breakfast.

Pribaltiskaya, 14 Korablestroitelei (Shipbuilders' Street), tel. 356–4528. On Vasilevsky Island. One of the U.S.S.R.'s largest and pleasantest. 2,400 beds, four restaurants, 7 banquet halls, 6 bars and snackbars seating 3,200 people. Swedish built, with elegant indoor decor. Good souvenir shop. Saunas, small swimming pool (very pricey!), bowling-alley, car park run by computer!

Pulkovskaya, Pl. Pobedy 1 (tel. 264–5111). Big new Finnish-built hotel, voted one of the Soviet Union's best—by Intourist at least. With all the attractiveness of Scandinavian design and a full range of restaurants, saunas, Western currency shops, and other comforts. 540 rooms, each with TV, radio, refrigerator etc. Recent visitors have had no complaints. One late-night restaurant is patronized by the city's gilded youth.

Also-rans. All in the official secondary category, and ranking with us as mixed moderate to rock-bottom, are:

Moskovskaya, 43/45 Ligovsky Prospekt; **Neva,** 17 Tchaikovsky Street; **Leningradskaya,** 10/24 Mayorov Prospekt; **Oktyabrskaya,** 10 Ligovsky Prospekt (opposite Moscow Railway Station); **Rossia,** Chernyshevsky Square, on Moskovsky Prospekt; **Severnaya,** 21 Lenin Prospekt, Petrozavodsk (situated on Lake Onega, some 320 km. (200 miles) out, recommended for visitors to Kizhi); **Baltiskaya,** 57 Nevsky Prospekt (cheap, clean, very central—a bargain for the low-budget traveler); **International Seaman's Club,** 166 Griboyedov Naberezhnaya (not generally used for foreign tourists). All have restaurant or café.

RESTAURANTS. Hotel restaurants open at 8.30 (*Astoria, Leningrad*) or 9 A.M. Hot dishes served until 11.30 P.M. The *Evropeiskaya* and *Leningrad* hotels each have a "Swedish table" where for 4 roubles you can eat all you want. The *Leningrad* is a much better bargain—fantastic selection of soup, fish and salads. The *Evropeiskaya* had run out of most things when your editor stopped in for a *late* lunch; supplies at *Leningrad* seemed endless. Large help-yourself breakfasts for 1 rouble.

Others include: *Neva,* 44–66 Nevsky Prospekt, the largest restaurant in Leningrad, seating more than a thousand. It has the *Sever Café,* a cocktail lounge and banquet hall. The *Sever* is famous for its cakes. The *Neva* prides itself on its *Leningrad* salad, *Neva*-style *shchi* (soup) and fish fillet, its ice-creams and pastries. We have had reports of tourists with young children having trouble getting into some Leningrad eating-places.

Baku, Sadovaya Street between Rakov Street and Nevsky Pr. An Azerbaijani restaurant with spicy Caucasian food and good bread. "Remarkable" is one visitor's description of the *zakuski,* which included smoked sturgeon, herb cheeses, mild pickled peppers, fish in walnut sauce. One of the most popular restaurants in town, with good service. There is a 2-rouble cover charge in the evenings for the upstairs dining room, which offers a quite good dance band. Reservations needed. If you call in during the day to reserve for the evening, you can make an advance order for starters and drinks, which will be ready on your table when you arrive. Saves time and ensures your reservation is taken seriously! 15 to 20 roubles a head including wine and spirits.

Kavkazsky, 25 Nevsky Prospekt. One of the most popular restaurants, specializing in spicy Caucasian dishes. Not as well decorated or expensive as the Baku. Definitely welcomes children.

Metropol, 22 Sadovaya Street. Near Nevsky Prospekt and the Public Library, the oldest restaurant of Leningrad. It's famous for its meat and fish dishes, and for its cakes, pies and tarts. Attached to the restaurant is a shop for take-away food. Indifferent service, but Leningraders claim it has the best Russian food in town. Rarely frequented by tourists, so waiters do not speak English (or any other foreign language).

Moskva, 49 Nevsky Prospekt. Specializes in good Russian cuisine. Service reported "fairly fast," but no English menu.

Okolites, 15 Primorsky Prospekt (en route to Helsinki). A small restaurant with good food and interesting decor. Worth a try for travelers going by car.

Sadko, corner of Nevsky Prospekt and Brodsky Street, practically next door to Evropeiskaya Hotel. Traditional Russian cooking with folk music and occasional, quite lively floor shows. Food has generally good reputation. Hard currency bar in cellar. In summer, it is jammed with tourists, so book reservations well in advance. Few Russians can get in during the tourist season, so you will mingle mostly with foreigners. Good *blini.* Fixed-price dinners.

Volkhov, Liteiny Prospekt, near Chernyshevsky Street. A pleasant-looking, small restaurant which American students have liked.

Other Restaurants. All officially open until midnight, but often turn customers away earlier:

Airport, in Air Terminal, 2nd floor, Manezhnaya Square. Good reputation.

Austeriakh, in the Peter-and-Paul Fortress, has "decent food" with good modern music.

Chaika, 14 Griboyedov Naberezhnaya.

Kronverk, a floating restaurant at 3 Mytninskaya Naberezhnaya, with a pleasant atmosphere.

Primorsky, 32 Bolshoi Prospekt, Petrogradskaya Storona.

Severny, 12 Sadovaya Street.

Universal, 106 Nevsky Prospekt.

CAFES. Aurora, 60 Nevsky Prospekt. Specialists in dairy dishes; also special food, both hot and cold, for people on diets.

Avtomat Cafe (Self-service), 45 Nevsky Prospekt.

Blinnaya, 74 Nevsky Prospekt. A cellar cafe, specialties include pancakes, black and red caviar, salmon, etc.

Children's Cafe, 42 Nevsky Prospekt. Catering particularly for the young, with a staff of experienced dieticians.

Druzhba, 15 Nevsky Prospekt. Open from 8 in the morning, it serves a wide assortment of breakfast, lunch and supper dishes.

Hermitage Museum is reported to have a very good buffet.

Kafe Fregat, Vasilevsky Island, Bolshoi Prospekt 39/4, a cafe near Leningrad University frequented by students; clever decor and good traditional Russian cooking. Inexpensive. No smoking allowed. Champagne and "cocktails" 3–6 roubles; no drinks without food. Quiet by day, livelier in the evenings when there is loud pop music.

Lakomka, 22 Sadovaya Street. Near the Nevsky Prospekt, attached to the Metropol Restaurant. Great variety of pies, cakes and pastries.

Leningrad, 96 Nevsky Prospekt. Sugar-free and other low-calorie diet dishes are the specialties here.

Literary Cafe, on the Nevsky Prospekt at the Neva Embankment. Restored to its 19th-century glory, with old prints and antique-style menu cards. Music and literature recitals.

Minutka, 20 Nevsky Prospekt. Quick-service snacks, coffee, tea, cocoa, clear soup, small pies with a tremendous variety of fillings.

Ogonyok, 24 Nevsky Prospekt. Ice-cream and liquid refreshments—especially popular on hot summer days.

NIGHTLIFE. The situation in Leningrad is the same as in Moscow: desperate. No real nightclubs and fairly early closing times in most cafes, bars and restaurants. Of the latter, **Sadko** has the best music and atmosphere if you don't speak or understand Russian, and its foreign currency bar stays open till 2 A.M. See under hotel listing for details of other bars. Things are improving all the time. A surprisingly good selection of Western pop music is played in the handful of hotel discos. **Baku Restaurant** has good pop group some nights.

OPERA, BALLET AND DRAMA. Academic Maly Theater of Opera and Ballet, 1 Ploshchad Iskusstv (Arts Square).

Comedy Theater, 56 Nevsky Prospekt.

Gorky (Bolshoi) Drama Theater, 65 Fontanka Naberezhnaya. Founded in 1919 by the writer himself.

Great Puppet Theater, 10 Nekrasov Street.

Kirov Academic Opera and Ballet Theater (often known as the Marinsky Theater), 2 Teatralnaya Square.

Komsomol (Youth) Theater, 46 Zagorodny Prospekt.

Musical Comedy Theater, 13 Rakov Street. The only theater that continued to perform throughout the siege of Leningrad. Mainly operettas.

Pushkin Theater, 2 Ostrovsky Square. Classical and modern drama.

Theater of the Music and Drama Institute, 35 Mokhovaya Street, also presents musical productions.

CONCERTS. Leningrad has a very intensive musical life; the concert halls include:

Glinka Kapella (Choral Hall), 20 Moyka Naberezhnaya. Built in 1880 by L.N. Benois; the choir was founded by Peter the Great in 1713. Glinka, Rimsky-Korsakov and many other famous musicians have appeared here.

Leningrad Philharmonia Concert Hall, 2 Brodsky Street. A second, smaller hall of the Leningrad Philharmonia is at 30 Nevsky Prospekt.

October Concert Palace, 6 Ligovsky Prospekt, three minutes from the Ploshchad Vosstaniya Metro station.

CIRCUS. The **Leningrad Circus** is at 3 Fontanka Naberezhnaya. Designed in 1876 it is one of the oldest circuses in the country. Its programs feature many Soviet and foreign artists.

CINEMA. Movie theaters have fixed program times and tickets must be bought for a specific performance. As on public transport, in museums, theaters, etc., smoking is not allowed. Foreign movies are usually dubbed into Russian.

The most important movie-theaters are: **Aurora,** 60 Nevsky Prospekt; **Barrikada,** 15 Nevsky Prospekt; **Gigant,** 44 Kondratyevsky Prospekt; **Khudozhestvenny,** 67 Nevsky Prospekt; **Kolizey,** 100 Nevsky Prospekt; **Molodezhny,** 12 Sadovaya Street; **Neva,** 108 Nevsky Prospekt; **October,** 80 Nevsky Prospekt; **Primorsky,** 42 Kirovsky Prospekt; **Rodina,** 12 Tolmachov Street; **Saturn,** 27 Sadovaya Street; **Smena,** 42 Sadovaya Street; **Stereokino,** 4 Lenin Park (stereophonic films); **Titan,** 47 Nevsky Prospekt; **Velikan,** 4 Lenin Park; **Khronika,** 88 Nevsky Prospekt (newsreel).

MUSEUMS AND GALLERIES. Leningrad, as we have already asserted, has some of the greatest collections in the world—indeed, many people visit the city simply to see the paintings and other treasures in the Hermitage alone. Whatever your historical or artistic interest, it is likely to discover a great deal to feed on in these fascinating galleries.

Museums of Fine Art and Art History

I.I. Brodsky Museum, 3 Ploshchad Iskusstv. Open daily 11–8 except Thurs. A memorial museum to the artist, well-known for his revolutionary scenes, portraits of Lenin, etc. Rather a matter of taste. Closed for restoration at presstime; may open in late 1986.

Hermitage Museum, Winter Palace, 36 Dvortsovaya Naberezhnaya, open 10.30–6; closed Mon. Entrance 1.5 roubles. One of the world's great museums. Intourist charges over 4 roubles for tour—better to go alone at your leisure, preferably several times. Last entry 5. Some parts closed for refurbishment.

Monastery of the Holy Trinity and Alexander Nevsky, 1 Alexander Nevsky Square. Containing the *Museum of Urban Sculpture* and the Lazarevsky and Tikhvinsky cemeteries. Open daily 11–6, except Thurs. Last entry 5.

Permanent Exhibition of Leningrad Artists, 8 Nevsky Prospekt. Open every day 10–9. Various exhibitions of contemporary work.

Peter I's Cottage (Domik Petra), Petrogradskaya Storona, 1 Petrovskaya Naberezhnaya. Open May to November, 12–7, except Tues.

Repin Museum, (Penates), Repino Railroad station, on the Karelian Isthmus, in the resort region of Leningrad. Open from May to September daily, from October to April daily except Tues. This was the estate of the Russian painter Ilya Repin (1844–1930). A characteristic memorial museum, its exhibits span almost a century. Entrance 20 kopeks.

St. Isaac's Cathedral, Isaakyevskaya Square. Open as a museum 11–5. Closed Tues. Entrance to cupola balcony 30 kopeks.

State Museum of Russian Art known as the "Russian Museum," 4/2 Inzhenernaya Street. Open daily 10–6.15 except Tues; Thurs. 10–8.15. Last entry 1 hr. before closing.

The Summer Palace, in the Summer Gardens (see under *Parks and Gardens*). Open May to November, 12–8, closed Tues.

Environs. The palaces and museums in the environs of Leningrad are generally open every day from the end of May until September 15 (depending on the weather) from 11–8. Times vary; check with Intourist.

The museums of Lomonosov are closed on Tues.

Petrodvorets is open 11–8 daily, except some Mons., from 1 January to 25 September. The *Monplaisir Palace* there is open 11–5 except Wed. as is the *Hermitage Pavilion.*

Pavlovsk is closed on Fri., and on Thurs. only the main buildings are open, but check.

The Palaces in Pushkin are open 10–6; closed on Tues. and last Mon. of the month. The *Lyceum* is also closed on Tues.

Historical, Revolutionary and Military Museums

Aurora. After repairs, the Cruiser is back at her mooring on the Neva near Nakhimov Naval College.

Central Naval Museum, Vasilevsky Ostrov, 4 Pushkinskaya Square. Open 10.30–5.45 weekdays, Sun. 11–6, closed Tues. and last Thurs. of each month. Last entry 4.45.

History of Leningrad Museum, 44 Krasnovo Flota Embankment. Open Mon., Thur., Sat. and Sun., 11–6 and Tues. and Fri., 1–9; Closed Wed.

Kirov Museum, 26/28 Kirov Prospekt. Open 11–7 weekdays, Sun. 10–6; closed Sat. Commemorates the Bolshevik politician who was assassinated in Leningrad.

Lenin Museums, 5/1 Khalturin Street. Open 10.30–6.30 weekdays; 11–5 Sun.; closed Wed. Other memorial museums are at Lenin's various homes scattered throughout the city. Among them: 7 Ilyushin Street, Apt. 13; 52 Lenin Street, Apt. 24; 5 Khersonskaya Street, Apt. 9 and the Shalash (Straw Hut) at the Razliv Railroad Station. All these are open every day except Wed.

Museum of the Great October Revolution, 4 Kuibyshev Street. Open Mon. and Fri. 12–8; Tues., Wed., Sat. and Sun. 11–7. Closed Thurs. Housed in the former mansion of Mathilde Kshessinskaya, the famous ballerina and mistress of Czar Nicholas II.

Museum of the History of Religion and Atheism (in the Kazan Cathedral), 2 Kazanskaya Ploshchad. Open 11–6 daily except Wed. Last entry 4.30.

Peter-and-Paul Fortress (Petropavlovskaya Krepost), Revolution Square. Open 11–7, closed Wed. and last Tues. of each month. Last entry 6, Tues. 5. Entrance 30 kopeks. Part of the History of Leningrad Museum.

Smolny (see page 199). Group tours only, individuals need special passes.

Ethnographic, Literary and Theatrical Museums

Anthropological and Ethnographical Museum of the U.S.S.R. Academy of Sciences, 3 Universitetskaya Naberezhnaya. Open daily, except Fri. and Sat., 11–6. Last entry 5.

Circus Art Museum, 3 Fontanka Naberezhnaya. Open daily 12–5, except Sun. A collection illustrating Soviet and world circus history: posters, programmes, photographs, costumes, models, large library, 6,000 postcards.

Museum of the Ethnography of the Peoples of the U.S.S.R., 1/4 Inzhenernaya Street. Open 10–6 daily, except Mon. and last Fri. of each month. Last entry 5.

Pushkinsky Dom (Pushkin House, Literary Museum of the Academy of Scinces), 4 Naberezhnaya Makarova. Open daily 11–5.30; closed Mon. and Tues. Last entry 5. The Pushkinsky Dom is so called because it was founded in 1899, the centenary of Pushkin's birth. It has a vast collection of manuscripts and books illustrating the life and works of Pushkin, Lermontov, Gogol, Turgenev, Dostoevsky, Tolstoy, Gorky, Mayakovsky and other writers. The archives contain over half a million items. There are regular special exhibitions and the institution is a meeting place for Soviet writers and their official foreign guests.

Pushkin Memorial Museum, 12 Moyka. The poet's last residence. English-speaking guide available. Now re-opened after major restoration. You may see this one also called Pushkinsky Dom—but it's not to be confused with the previous entry.

Theater Museum, 6 Ostrovsky Square. Open daily 12–7; closed Tues.

Technical and Scientific Museums

Arctic and Antarctic Museum, 24 Marat Street, open daily 10–6; closed Mon. and Tues. Last entry 5.15.

Komarov Botanical Gardens, 2 Professor Popov Street, is open from May to October daily; the hot-houses are open every day, except Fri., 11–4 in summer and 10.30–3 in winter. Entrance 20 kopeks.

Mikhailovsky Garden, 1 Sadovaya Street, near the Field of Mars; **Garden of Rest,** 39 Nevsky Prospekt.

Popov Communications Museum, 4 Podbelsky Street, near the Central Post Office. Open daily 12–6; Mon. 12–3. Closed Tues.

Railway Museum, 50 Sadovaya Street. Open daily, 12–6; Mon. 12–3. Closed Tues.

The Zoo is at 1 Lenin Park, Petrogradskaya Storona. Open from May to August 10–10, from September to November, 10–6, from December to February, 10–4, in March and April, 10–7.

Zoological Museum, 1 Universitetskaya Embankment. Open daily 11–5, except Mon.; Tues. 11–4.

PARKS AND GARDENS. Botanical Gardens, 2 Professor Popov Street, and the **Zoological Gardens** in Lenin Park have already been mentioned under the *Museums* section.

Kirov Park on Yelagin Ostrov (Island). The park was laid out in 1932; more than 18,000 trees have been planted in recent years. There is a summer theater, seating 1600, a variety theater, movie-theater, exhibition halls, boating facilities and a bathing beach.

Lenin Park, Maxim Gorky Prospekt, a crescent-shaped strip of land on Kronwerk Strait, is not very large but a favorite spot for walkers and lovers.

Park Pobedy (Park of Victory), Moskovsky Prospekt. Leningrad has two victory parks, both established in 1945. The second is the Seaside Victory Park (**Primorsky Park Pobedy**) at 7 Rubin Street on Krestovsky Island.

Piskarevskoye Memorial Cemetery, just outside the city. The graves of well over half-a-million Leningraders who died in the siege. Reported by one visitor as "a must to understanding the basic spirit of Leningrad—our guide was honored that we asked to see it." The three-hour trip costs 22 roubles including Intourist car seating 3 people. It is part of some city tours.

Summer Garden. 2 Pestel Street, founded by Peter the Great.

SHOPPING. Leningrad shopping is much the same as elsewhere in the Soviet Union. **Beryozka** shops provide the simple way of going about it, just as they do elsewhere. The main Beryozka stores are at 26 Herzen (Gertsen) Street, off the Nevsky Prospekt, and at No. 9 Nevsky Prospekt. They can also be found in all the Intourist hotels. Closed 1–2.

The main Leningrad department stores and most of the specialist shops are either on or near the Nevsky Prospekt: **Gostinny Dvor,** 35 Nevsky Prospekt on the corner of Sadovaya and Dumskaya Streets is a large department store; another is **Dom Leningradskoi Torgovli,** 21/23 Zhelyabov Street; **Passage,** 48 Nevsky Prospekt, built in 1848, specializes in women's wear, perfume, household goods; **Apraksin Dvor,** Sadovaya Street (from Lomonosov Street to Apraksin Pereulok).

As we have said, Nevsky Prospekt offers the best array of specialist shops. We give below the house numbers of shops where known, but these are not always displayed. Sometimes a whole block is numbered at each end, e.g. 23–37 Nevsky Prospekt, but no intervening numbers are shown.

No. 55 machine- and hand-made carpets with ethnic designs of the various republics, mainly from Central Asia.

No. 53: cheeses—Altai, Dorogobuzh, Lithuanian, Swiss.

No. 51: national handicrafts, bone and wood carvings, tooled leather, embroidery, ceramics, Palekh caskets, toys.

No. 78: stamps, both foreign and Soviet, match-box labels.

No. 76: Soviet perfumes and cosmetics.

No. 72: prints and engravings, reproductions of works in the museums, postcards and albums. In the same building the Mechta (Dream) shop sells sweets and confectionery (one of the largest selections in the country).

No. 64: machine- and hand-made laces and embroidery. In the same building are tobacco shops selling cigarettes, cigars and the Russian *papirosi* (cigarettes with long cardboard mouthpieces). Still another shop at the same number sells glassware, crystal and china from the Lomonosov Porcelain Factory.

No. 60: for the hunter and fisherman; also other sports goods.

No. 56: is the largest foodstore in the city with meat, fish, dairy produce, cakes, fruit, wine, brandy, vodka. Still called the "Yeliseyev shop" after its pre-revolutionary owner.

No. 54: a gift-shop with a wide assortment of haberdashery, souvenirs, candy.

No. 52: a government-owned "commission store" where antiques, paintings, sculptures, china and bronze are on sale. It also has a recording studio for making your own disc.

No. 50: the largest sheet-music shop in Leningrad.

No. 44: The Sever shop, in the basement, is known for its cakes and tarts. The neighboring shop specializes in sausages.

No. 34: one of the largest record shops.

No. 28: The House of the Book (Dom Knigi). The building also houses several publishers; the shop occupies two floors. Foreign-language publications can also be found here.

No. 26: souvenirs.

No. 18: everything for the artist: brushes, paints. The same building houses a wine and spirits store.

No. 16: Mir (Peace), a bookshop specializing in the arts, and work published in the Socialist countries.

No. 12: a dressmaker—garments in knitted fabrics made to measure.

TOURS are available through the Intourist offices in the city and in hotels, including visits to museums, opera, ballet and theaters. These are either pre-packaged in your trip or can be arranged individually (more difficult) once you have arrived. Be warned that tours arranged via Intourist work out considerably more expensive than doing it yourself. For example, you can get to Pushkin (15 miles outside the city) on your own for about 90 kopeks return. The advertised excursion rate is 4 roubles per person by coach, 30 roubles for a 3-seater car! For longer trips, more distant excursions, e.g. a 10-hour trip to Novgorod, it may be worth paying the advertized rate (94 roubles for a car) for the convenience of door-to-door travel and guide services.

There are also excursions to Petrodvorets (formerly Peterhof), by bus or river-boat (7 or 1.4 roubles return), 29 km (18 miles) from the city on the Gulf of Finland; to Pushkin (formerly Tsarskoye Selo, some 24 km. (15 miles) from Leningrad), to Pavlovsk (17 miles), Lomonosov (formerly Oranienbaum, 40 km., 25 miles), to Gatchina (a former imperial castle and park) and to the Sanatorno-Kurortnaya district, consisting of fifteen spas and resorts along the Gulf of Finland of which Sestroretsk and Zelenogorsk are the best known. We have already mentioned Repino under *Museums*.

The town of Vyborg near the Finnish border can now also be visited in transit. Check this out on the spot. Petrozavodsk (for Kizhi Island) is a lengthy rail trip and can be undertaken individually or in tour groups.

SPORTS. Spectator sports are served by: **Lenin Stadium,** Krestovsky Ostrov, and **Kirov Stadium,** also on Krestovsky Island, the sports center of Leningrad. Seaside Victory (Primorskoi Pobedy) Park was laid out in 1945 and the **Dynamo Stadium** was built in 1925. **Jubilee Sports Palace,** 2 Zhdanovskaya Street; **Winter Stadium,** 6 Manezhnaya Ploshchad.

Swimming. Winter swimming pools are available at: 11 Pravda Street, (only for training); 20 Bolshaya Raznochinnaya Street; Krestovsky Ostrov, 44 Prospekt Dinamo; 38 Dekabristov Street; 5a Novocherkassky Prospekt; 22–25 Nevsky Prospekt; Litovskaya Street (at the corner of Lesnoi Prospekt).

Outdoor swimming pools and aquatic sports centers: 6 Olginskaya Street; 2 Prospekt Dinamo; 2 and 4 Vyazovaya Street; 24 Naberezhnaya Bolshoi Nevi; 11a and 15 Deputatskaya Street.

Beaches, open in summer, are in the Central Recreation Park and the Park Pobedy (Victory Park).

Cycling. Cycling Track: 14 Vyborgskoye Chaussee; Cycling Stadium: 81 Engels Prospekt.

Skating and Skiing. The summer skating rink is at 2,15th Liniya. Open-air skating rink: Central Recreation Park, Tavrichesky Sad (for children).

A ski center within the city limits: Central Recreation Park. Cross-country skiing, at Olgino, on the Gulf of Finland.

CHURCH SERVICES. Orthodox Russian churches open for worship: **Saint Nicholas,** 13 Ploshchad Kommunarov, open daily 8–7. Sun. and holidays, 9, 11.30, and 7. **Trinity Cathedral,** Ploshchad Alexandra Nevskogo, open daily 9–6; Sun. 9–7.

Baptist Church, 29a Bolshaya Ozornaya (in the suburbs), open Tues. and Thurs. at 7 P.M., Sun. 10, 2, and 6; **Roman Catholic Church,** 7 Kovensky Pereulok, open daily at 7, 10 and 6; Sun. at 1, too.

Synagogue, 2 Lermontovsky Prospekt, open daily 10–12, Sat. 10–2.

Mosque, 7 Maxim Gorky Prospekt, open Fri. 1 P.M.

Check times of services at your hotel or at the Intourist office; or, if the information is not forthcoming, visit the church itself.

MAIL, TELEPHONE AND CABLES. The same rules and regulations prevail here as in Moscow (which see). The **Central Post Office** is at 9 Soyuza Svyazi Street, open 9–9, tel. 06; **Central Telegraph Office,** Soyuza Svyazi Street 14, tel. 06 (24-hour service); **Post Office C-400** at 6 Nevsky Prospekt, open 10–8. Handles foreign parcels, telegrams and phone calls. Receives all mail from abroad for foreign tourists in Leningrad when no hotel address is given or when letters are addressed to: Leningrad C–400, Do Vostrebovaniya (Poste Restante).

Post Office at the Oktyabrskaya Hotel is open 9–10 P.M., Sundays 9–4 (Telegrams 9–10 P.M.).

Leningrad-Moscow telephone exchange: tel 10–0020; Telephone exchange: 07; Telegrams on credit: 06 (24-hour service). Enquiries for private telephone numbers: 00; Enquiries for office telephone numbers: 09.

USEFUL ADDRESSES. The following useful telephone numbers and addresses, together with emergency numbers, cover everything you'll need to know in Leningrad: Weather Service: dial 13–6218; time clock: 08 (24 hours).

U.S. Consulate-General, 15 Petr Lavrov Street (tel. 274–8689). Residence of the U.S. Consul-General, 4 Grodnensky Pereulok (tel. 772–8407).

Auto information. Service Station No. 3, 3 Novaya Derevnya, Liniya 5, tel. 33–6930 or 33–8704. (Open 8–11 for overhauls, checking cars; 9–4.30 for repairs. Closed on Sundays.) Filling Station No. 30, at the Service Station; 24-hour service. Filling Station No. 2, 10 Klinicheskaya Street; 24-hour service. Filling Station, No.

3. Moskovsky Prospekt 100; 24-hour service. Filling Station No. 12, 18 Dnepropetrovskaya Street; diesel oil also available.

Recommended parking lots: St. Isaac's Square near Astoria Hotel; Moskovsky Prospekt near Rossia Hotel; 5 Pervaya Staroderevenskaya Street, on the Vyborg side of the city; Torzhkovskaya Street, near Vyborgskaya Hotel, next to Primorskoye Highway; near Olgino Campsite, on Primorskoye Highway. Charges: 30 kopeks per car, per day; 50 kopeks per coach, per day. Parking is allowed anywhere, unless there is a sign to the contrary.

Travel phone numbers. Taxi hire: tel. 10–0022 (24-hour service); arrival and departure of trains: tel. 15–0048 (24 hours); air terminal: tel. 15–0018; Intourist Service, airport: tel. 93–0927; Intourist rail, air and ship tickets: 29 Herzen Street (in the Hotel Astoria) tel. 12–6553; merchant ship harbor: tel. 16–4063; Vasilevsky Island harbor: 17–0320, 17–1038.

International airline offices. *Aeroflot:* 7/9 Nevsky Prospekt (tel. information, 215–0018; tickets, 210–0077). Aeroflot flights to the Baltic and northern U.S.S.R.: 36 Herzen Street.

Finnair: 19 Gogol Street (tel. 12–4228). *Interflug* (G.D.R.): Airport (tel. 13–5566). *SAS:* 19 Gogol Street (tel. 12–0959).

Medical services. These are available on the same basis as in Moscow and other Soviet cities. Emergency ambulance service: dial 03 (24-hour service) but be prepared to wait up to 2 hours. Eye clinic (accidents or other treatment): 38 Mokhovaya Street (tel. 73–1631) 24-hour emergency service. Ear, nose and throat clinic: 9 Bronnitskaya Street (tel. 92–2841) 24-hour service.

The Central Chemist Shop (Pharmacist) is at 63 Nevsky Prospekt (tel. 12–8978). Here, too, there is a round-the-clock service.

Emergencies. Fire alarms, 01; militia (police), 02. Lost property—general, tel. 97–0092; if lost on trolley-buses, 15–1862; in trams, 10–9897. Visa and registration office, 60 Nevsky Prospekt, tel. 11–6749.

EUROPEAN RUSSIA AND
BYELORUSSIA

Ancient Cities and Writers' Homes

We have previously described the Russian Soviet Federal Socialist Republic, the largest republic in the Soviet Union. The Russian S.F.S.R. occupies 6,593,391 square miles in both Europe and Asia, with a population of almost 140 million, made up of more than 40 nationalities.

This huge territory is divided by the Urals into two main areas: European Russia and Siberia. The former occupies the lesser half of the Republic's territory but the majority of its population lives here.

To the east, the European half is bordered by the Ural mountains; to the southwest is the "second Baku," the oil fields between the Volga and the Ural rivers, lying north of the border with Kazakhstan; southwest again are the Caspian plain, the wheat-growing expanse of Krasnodar and Stavropol (the "waving sea of Kuban," as Russian poetry calls it) and the Black Sea Riviera as far as Sochi. To the west it is bordered by the iron ore deposits on the edge of the Ukraine, the district of Kursk, the forests of Bryansk, and further north, by Byelorussia, Latvia, Estonia and the Baltic (in the Gulf of Finland).

The 10,000-square-mile Kaliningrad Territory also belongs to the Russian Federal Republic, though it has no direct territorial link with it: it lies between the Baltic Sea, Lithuania and Poland. This is a district which was added to the Soviet Union by the Potsdam Agreement of 1945, dividing East Prussia; one-third was handed to the Soviet Union, two-thirds to Poland. Thus the former Königsberg and its surrounding area became Kaliningrad and the Territory of Kaliningrad. Here is the westernmost point of the U.S.S.R.

To the northwest, European Russia is bordered by Finland; at the Kola Peninsula the Soviet Union and Norway meet. This is a district rich in nickel, copper and other rare metals. On this peninsula we find the western gateway to the Soviet Union for northern shipping lines: the ice-free harbor of Murmansk. This is the northernmost metropolis in the world and the largest city inside the Arctic Circle, where "night" lasts three weeks in winter and "day" lasts three weeks in summer. The northern limit of European Russia is the North Polar Sea (the Barents Sea and White Sea). Until the foundation of Petersburg, Arkhangelsk was Russia's only sea port. From here the Siberian forests reach almost to Vorkuta, where there is still a vast complex of labor camps.

We will deal with European Russia in various sections, beginning with the territory west of Moscow (from its borders with Byelorussia), moving next northeast of the capital, then northwest and south and, finally, to Byelorussia. The Volga deserves a chapter to itself.

West of Moscow

Smolensk, some 338 km. (210 miles) from Moscow, standing on both banks of the Upper Dnieper, is an important district center. It is also a rail and road junction which, in the former frontier region, was the "Key to Moscow" three times between the 16th and 20th centuries against the Polish and Swedish conquerors, in the Napoleonic invasion, and, finally, during the Nazi assault.

Since 1949 there have been systematic archeological researches in Smolensk and its neighborhood and these have established the presence of Slavs in the sixth century—but human habitations have been traced back to the Later Stone Age. The excavations within the city limits among others on the Sobornaya Gora, Temple Hill—have uncovered the relics of Slav settlements of the sixth to eighth centuries, while about 14 km. (nine miles) west, in Gnyozdovo, there were rich finds at a pagan burial site.

Smolensk was thus one of the oldest Slav settlements; in the ninth century it was already known as a "big" city, compared to Kiev. Russian historical sources mention it as the center of the Krivich tribe in A.D. 865. We know that it was an important industrial and trading town; its name probably derives from the caulking of ships (*smoleniye* —which means tarring). Its prosperity was due to the fact that it lay on the famous waterway linking the Baltic and the Black Sea, of which the Dnieper was an important section. As such, it was mentioned in the famous work of Constantine Porphyrogenitus (A.D. 912–59), *De administrando imperio.*

Excavations at the so-called Dnieper Gate uncovered many layers of wood dating back to the 11th century when the swampy soil of the Dnieper shore was covered with fallen trees. The excavators also found traces of ancient wooden houses, agricultural implements and documents written on birch bark.

In the 12th century Smolensk became the capital of an independent principality. Prince Rostislav enclosed it with walls and battlements. In the 13th century it was annexed by the Lithuanian Grand Duchy. After

110 years of Lithuanian rule, the Russians reconquered it in 1514. In the 16th, 17th and 18th centuries it developed further; its defensive walls date from this period. Early in the 17th century, when Poles and Swedes attacked it together, it was besieged for 20 months and fell only because of its betrayal by three local nobles. Those who did not fall in the battle died under the ruins of the cathedral built by Prince Vladimir Monomakh in 1101, which was blown up at the last moment. One of the ruined bastions of the city walls still bears the name of the Voivode Seyin who commanded the defense. After the fall of Smolensk, the 1618 truce handed it again to Poland. It returned to Russia at the end of the same century and soon became a regional capital. In 1812 it was the scene of a great battle with the French which lasted for two days and ended in a retreat by the Russians after they had set fire to the city and blown up the arsenal.

In the 19th century Smolensk became an important commercial and cultural center. The building of railways, starting in 1856, increased its importance, but its industries mainly developed under the Soviet regime. In the Second World War, the battle of Smolensk lasted from July to September 1941. During the Nazi occupation all but 300 of its dwelling houses were destroyed. It was liberated on September 25, 1943, and since then has built up significant textile, metallurgical and machine-plant industries.

Exploring Smolensk

In the center of the city, next to the Rossiya (Intourist) Hotel in Marx Street if you turn right to Marx Square, you find the House of Soviets (Dom Sovietov) built in the constructivist style of the early thirties. The theater at 4 Marx Street is an eclectic building dating from a little later.

If you take the No. 1 bus traveling north towards Kolkhoznaya Square and get off beyond the Dnieper bridge, at the terminus, you have reached the so-called Gorodnanka District. Here, between Kachin Street, opening from Kolkhoznaya Square, and the railway station, is the oldest architectural monument in Smolensk, the Church of St. Peter and St. Paul (12th century). To the west stands the Episcopal Palace (17th century) and the Church of St. Barbara (Varvarovskaya), also 17th century. The Peter-and-Paul Church was built in 1146, largely in Byzantine style. Its gleaming majolica floor is particularly attractive. In the 17th century it was turned into a Unitarian Church and the Unitarian Episcopal Palace next to it was built in 1632. The Church of St. Barbara is typically Russian Baroque.

The Church of St. John the Divine (Tserkov Ivana Bogoslova) is roughly contemporary with the Peter-and-Paul Church. It was built by Prince Roman Rostislavich in 1173; it stands in Krasnoflotskaya Street, on the left bank of the Dnieper, downstream at the next bridge.

The nearby Svirskaya Church on Malaya Krasnoflotskaya Street, near the Smyadinka river, was erected by Roman's brother, David Rostislavich, in 1191–4. It was intended as a court church and its size and shape symbolize the princely intentions. It is particularly interesting to see how the form of the earlier wooden architecture was imitated in a brick building.

Returning to the Bolshaya Sovietskaya, climb away from the river to Cathedral Hill to find Kutuzov's life-size equestrian statue (erected in 1954, sculpted by Motvilov). On Cathedral Hill the first, wooden, church was erected by Vladimir Monomakh in 1101. This was destroyed five centuries later in the siege of Smolensk; in the 17th century the local people began to build the Cathedral of the Assumption (Uspensky Sobor) on its site on the model of similar Moscow churches. The first architect (in 1677) was the Moscow master Korolkov; his work was continued early in the 18th century by Sedel, and it was according to his designs that the cathedral was finished in 1740. Its bell tower was rebuilt in 1767 in the Petersburg Baroque style; at the same time its stone wall and the triumphal arch of the pedestrian approach road were added. The stairway leading from the Bolshaya Sovietskaya was completed in 1767 by Obukhov with Baroque brick columns and granite steps; but in 1784 it was reshaped by Slepnev with classical elements.

The cathedral is used for services today. It stands 229 feet high and 140 feet wide; the central dome is built of wood and decorated. The iconostasis of gilded limewood is 33 feet high; ten people worked for 12 years to complete it. The principal treasure is a reputedly wonder-working icon of the Virgin, said to have been painted by St. Luke for the ruler of Syria. There are other valuable icons.

Continuing uphill on the Bolshaya Sovietskaya you reach, at Smirnov Square, the city wall, built under the reign of Boris Godunov. The wall continues left to Krasnoznamyonnaya Street and right, crossing the Kutuzov Park, to the City Park. The section between Smirnov Square and Krasnoznamyonnaya Street includes the Seyin Bastion, where the restoration work is most advanced. Built in 1595–1602, the wall, a striking combination of architectural beauty and military utility stretches for four miles. Boris Godunov called it "the pearl of Russia" and it received its first baptism of fire soon after completion, when the Poles besieged Smolensk.

After visiting the wall and the bastions, you can go back down Krasnoznamyonnaya Street, following the lines of the No. 1 tram westwards towards the Hotel Smolensk. This will take us down Glinka Street. The building of Number Three Hospital is the former mansion of the Engelhardt family, built in the 18th century. It was originally Baroque but was later rebuilt in a Constructivist style.

Glinka Street ends at the Town Park of Smolensk, which bears the composer's name. His statue by the sculptor Bok, erected by public subscription, stands near the entrance. The iron railing around it skilfully incorporates several of Glinka's melodies, reproducing the actual musical notes from *Ruslan and Ludmila, A Life for the Czar* and other operas.

Crossing the Glinka Park, (also known as the Blonye, the Flat Meadow), you reach October Revolution Street. Starting uphill, to the left, you find, after the first crossing, Smolensk's other important park, the Kutuzov Garden. Near the city wall (of which a section stands within the park) is the burial place of several illustrious figures in Russian military history, including that of Maria Oktyabrskaya, a Heroine of the Soviet Union who fell in the battles for the liberation of Smolensk in the autumn of 1943.

Kutuzov's bust, by Strakhovskaya, is placed on the central promenade of the Kutuzov Garden. It was unveiled in 1912, the centenary of the Battle of Borodino. The Eagle Monument at the end of the promenade was also erected on the same occasion; a heavily symbolic work by Sukman and Nadolsky, it includes a number of allegorical figures, a stylized bronze map of European Russia and the names of the Russian generals who led the armies against Napoleon. An even more elaborate memorial to the 1812 campaign is at the entrance of the Park Kultury (Cultural Park).

The sights and the history of Smolensk are summed up in the Museum of Natural History on Cathedral Hill. Other museums include the Local History Museum on Lenin Street, which contains exhibits from local archeological excavations, including the Gnyozdovsky tumuli, and some birch-bark writings. Several halls are devoted to the region's past from the 17th century until the Second World War, with the emphasis on revolutionary leaders and activities. A section deals with the first cosmonaut, Yuri Gagarin, including his personal effects and the gifts he received after his first flight in space.

The Art Gallery, 7 Krupskaya Street, contains Russian classical paintings and works by Soviet and foreign artists. The native artists include Ilya Repin and Isaac Levitan; there is also an interesting collection representing the Italian, Dutch, Flemish, Spanish and German schools. Murillo, van Ostade, Claude-Joseph Vernet and Kaulbach are the most important artists represented.

The Smolensk Museum of Local Lore has a branch in the village of Talashkino, 13 km. (eight miles) from Smolensk on the Roslav highway. (Intourist can arrange an excursion.) Here, on the former estate of Princess Maria Tenisheva, stands the Teremok Museum, a wooden chalet built in 1901–3, in Russian "fairy-tale" style, designed by Malyutin. The museum has some 2,000 items of folk art; the woodcarvings are of particular interest. Close by is a small family chapel with a striking mosaic over the entrance. Many prominent Russian artists worked here in the late 19th and early 20th centuries to revive their native folk art.

Gnyozdovo, the site of archeological excavations, is also 13 km. (eight miles) from Smolensk, along the Vitebsk highway. It can be reached easily by the Koltso line on the local train system or by No. 2 bus to the Vtoraya dachnaya, Gluschenki and Belaya Stantsiya stops. Gnyozdovo is a protected area and the taking of any souvenirs—even a stone—is frowned upon. More than 3,000 graves, mostly from pre-Christian times, have been found on the site, which extends over two square kilometers. A number of *kurgans* (burial mounds) date from the tenth century. Many Byzantine and Arab coins, Scandinavian jewelry and Russian tools were found here. The excavations began in 1874 and, with some interruptions, have continued ever since.

The Road to Moscow

Passing Yartsevo, northeast of Smolensk, on the tourist highway to Moscow, you come to another industrial center, Safonovo, the second-largest town of the Smolensk region. The ancient town of Dorogobuzh-on-the-Dnieper and its regional electric power station are close to Safonovo.

Vyazma was first mentioned in an 11th-century manuscript. It stands on the Vyazma River, a tributary of the Dnieper. Until the 18th century it was a place of great military and economic importance and was seized several times by Poles and Lithuanians. During Napoleon's retreat in 1812 it was burnt down. Once among the largest dairy centers of Russia, Vyazma is now a light industrial town. Among its products are jam-filled cookies, famous throughout the Soviet Union, called *vyazemskiye pryaniki.*

Trinity Cathedral, dating from the 17th century, is on Nagornaya Street. It has a copy of a miraculous icon, the Virgin of Iberia, and is open for services. The buildings of the St. John the Baptist (Predtecha) Monastery date roughly from the same time. The Ascension Church (1650) is lavishly decorated with pilasters and small columns, and an arcade extending around practically the whole circumference. The Arkadievskaya Church (1661), with its traditional five cupolas, is also a remarkable monument.

Gagarin (Gzhatsk) stands on the banks of the Bolshaya Gzhat River, which is a tributary of the Vazuza. The river, 97 km. (60 miles) long, used to be an important waterway, and is now used mainly for floating timber. The most interesting monument in Gzhatsk is the Kazanskaya Church (1794), a singular example of Russian Baroque. The town was renamed in honor of Yuri Gagarin, the astronaut, who studied here and who spent his childhood in the nearby village of Klushino.

Mozhaisk, some five km. (3 miles) off the main road, is one of the oldest cities in Russia, first mentioned in a document of 1231. From the 13th century to the 15th century, it was the capital of a princely state. The remains of the Luzhetsky Monastery (16th–17th centuries) and the Cathedral of St. Nicholas (19th century) are both worth visiting. The battle of Borodino took place about 13 km. (eight miles) from Mozhaisk which is a good base for exploring the famous battleground with its various monuments. This can be reached along a side road which branches off from the main Minsk–Moscow road at the 96 or 108 km. stone. Founded in 1903, the museum is now located in a building erected in 1912 to commemorate the centenary of the 15-hour battle between French and Russian armies on August 26, 1812. The collection includes guns, pictures and personal relics. Over 30 other monuments are scattered over Borodino Field, most of them erected in 1912, dedicated to Field Marshal Kutuzov and other generals and to whole regiments. There is also a monument to French soldiers and officers.

There was another battle of Borodino in 1941, and the city was retaken by the Russians in January 1942. A large reservoir, "the Mozhaisk Sea," has been built here and a hydroelectric power station spans the Moskva River.

Zvenigorod, 15 km. (nine miles) off the main road, is an ancient town of the Moscow Region. The earliest recorded references to it date from 1328. For more than 150 years it remained the center of a principality subordinate to Moscow. Situated on the Moskva River on high hills cut by ravines and surrounded by forests, it was an important stronghold protecting Moscow on the west. It lay on the old Smolensk–Moscow road leading from Lithuania and Poland.

The most ancient part of Zvenigorod, Gorodok, is an earth fortification rising 150 feet above the Moscow River. The stone Cathedral of the Assumption, also known as the Sobor na Gorodke, is a striking monument of early Moscow architecture, built in 1400. It has a single dome and is rectangular in shape, similar to the Vladimir Cathedral. The narrow windows show that in wartime it served as a fortress. The decorations are unique, with remnants of ancient frescos.

The Savvino-Storozhevsky Monastery, on Storozha Hill, a mile up the Moskva River, was founded in 1398 under Prince Yuri Zvenigorodsky, whose confessor, Sava, was the first abbot. Ivan the Terrible visited the place frequently; young Peter I, his brother Ivan and his sister Sophia took refuge within its walls in 1682 during the Rebellion of the Streltsy (imperial guard). Today some of the monastery buildings have been turned into a sanatorium and the Zvenigorod Museum of Local Lore. The most ancient and interesting building is the Cathedral of the Nativity of the Virgin, erected in 1404. Though the exterior has changed considerably, the interior walls still have some of their 15th–17th-century frescos. The five-tier iconostasis also dates from the 17th century. The four-story former refectory, built between 1652 and 1654, is also quite distinctive. The Transfiguration Church, built in 1639 by the order of the Princess Sophia, has striking light stucco decorations contrasting with the dark-red walls. Other monastery buildings include the Holy Trinity Church (1652) and the former palace of Czar Alexei Mikhailovich (1652–54), son of the founder of the Romanov dynasty.

The Zvenigorod countryside is very lovely, resembling the foothills of the Alps. Many famous Russian artists spent their summers here. Zvenigorod was also associated with well-known Russian writers and composers, including Herzen, Chekhov (who worked as a doctor at the hospital in Lermontov Street) and Tchaikovsky.

Bakovka and Kuntsevo are the last two towns on the road to Moscow. The former is a popular place for *dachas* (country villas); Boris Pasternak lived in the nearby village of Peredelkino until his death in 1960. His simple grave in the village churchyard may be visited. It is not officially signposted, but if you mention Pasternak's name to any passing local, he will direct you there with great pride. On 30 May, the anniversary of Pasternak's death, his family and admirers gather at the graveside to read his poetry. This is a very special occasion and, while foreign tourists are welcomed, do respect Russian feelings and be discreet if you take photographs.

Bakovka has a motel, a restaurant and a camping site. Kuntsevo is famous for its "Farewell Hill," where Muscovites would say goodbye to relatives and friends going on a long journey. From here, the Kutuzov Prospekt leads straight into the heart of Moscow.

PRACTICAL INFORMATION FOR
WESTERN EUROPEAN RUSSIA

WHEN TO GO. Summer is the best season to visit European Russia, unless you are a winter sports addict. June, July and August are warm and sunny but less humid than in Central Europe. The early autumn is often a true Indian Summer, dry and sunny. October is usually windy and cool; by early November it begins to snow. The winter in the European part of the Russian Federal Republic is cold but seldom wet or windy.

GETTING THERE. By train from Warsaw and other cities west of the Soviet Union; there are good connections from Hungary via Chop. Direct trains both from Moscow and Leningrad. **By car.** The Intourist motor route runs from Minsk to Smolensk and then on to Moscow.

TOURS. Bus or car tours will be arranged by Intourist starting from Moscow or included in your itinerary on the way to Moscow.

Hotels and Restaurants

Gagarin. Has a pleasant restaurant, central, on river bank.

Kuntsevo. Has an adequate restaurant on the Moscow Road.

Smolensk. *Tsentralnaya,* 2/1 Lenin Sq. (3–3604). *Phoenix Motel* (tel. 2–1488), at campsite 1 mile off the Brest–Smolensk road, at 384 km. stone, sited in the woods. Cafe, bathing and shopping facilities, post office, telephone, etc.

Restaurants. In the Rossiya Hotel; the *Dnepr Restaurant* in the Smolensk Hotel. Others: *Sputnik* on Nikolayev Street; *Zarya* on Kommuna Street; *Otdykh* in the Glinka Gardens; *Vityaz,* at crossing of Kutuzov and Frunze Streets.

PLACES OF INTEREST. Smolensk. *Local History Museum,* 9 Lenin Street. The *Local Natural History Museum,* 7 Soborny Dvor, beside Uspensky Cathedral. *The Art Gallery,* 7 Krupskaya Street. *Historical, Architectural and Art Museum,* in the monastery at 7 Mayakovsky Street.

The *Smolensk Museum of Local Lore* in **Talashkino,** 13 km. (8 miles) from Smolensk on the Roslav Highway. Open 10–4, Wed. and Sun.

"Teremok" Museum of Folk Art. 18 km. (11 miles) from Smolensk. Displays of lace, embroidery, carvings, paintings, etc.

Near **Mozhaisk:** *Borodino Museum,* open 10–6.

THEATERS AND CONCERTS. In **Smolensk** there is a *Drama Theater,* 4 Karl Marx Street; a *Puppet Theater,* 1 Sobolev Street, and a *Philharmonic Concert Hall* at the same address.

SHOPPING. Smolensk. The *Smolensk Department Store* is at 1 Gagarin Prospekt; a *Beryozka* souvenir shop is located at 22 Kommunisticheskaya Street; special souvenirs of Smolensk can be found at 11/1 Lenin Street. There is a *Central Bookshop* (18 Bolshaya Sovietskaya Street), a good jeweler's shop (33 Bolshaya Sovietskaya Street) and a well-stocked tobacconist at 10 Lenin Street.

USEFUL ADDRESSES. Smolensk. *Intourist:* 2/1 Marx Street, (tel. 3–3508). *Railway Station:* on the right bank of the Dnieper, at the terminus of No. 1 tram. *General Post Office:* October Revolution Street including International Telephone Office. *Address Bureau:* 12 Dzerzhinsky Street.

Northeast of Moscow

If you set out northeast from the Soviet capital, after passing the first few towns (Pushkin, Abramtsevo and Zagorsk), there are three old Russian cities which have many ancient monuments: Pereslavl-Zalessky, Rostov-Veliky and Yaroslavl. Beyond them lie Vladimir, Suzdal, Ivanovo and Palekh, all of which deserve to be visited.

Zagorsk

Situated 71 km. (44 miles) from Moscow, the town of Zagorsk can be seen from a distance, easily identifiable by the huge fortified monastery of Trinity-St. Sergius, founded in 1340 by Sergius during his evangelizing crusade. It rapidly became the nucleus of Sergievo, (now Zagorsk), and in 1550 the complex of buildings was surrounded by imposing white walls. The Church of the Trinity used to contain famous paintings by Andrei Rublyev, but they have been replaced by copies and the originals taken to the Tretyakov Gallery in Moscow. In 1554 the Cathedral of the Assumption was built, its five enormous bulb-shaped towers, in blue and gold picked out with stars, adding to the already vivid richness of the town's architecture. Near the cathedral is a tiny colorful chapel with a miraculous fountain. Beside the chapel stands the tomb of Boris Godunov and his family. The elegant Baroque belfry in the main square was built in the middle of the 18th century, following the plans of Rastrelli.

For five hundred years this monastery has been one of the most important centers of pilgrimage in Russia. After the Revolution it was converted into a museum, but now almost all the churches are open again for worship. There is even a flourishing theological college. Zagorsk should unquestionably be included in every modern traveler's pilgrimage. The town is, incidentally, often used as a location for costume films.

Pereslavl-Zalessky

Pereslavl-Zalessky, "the city of waters," the birthplace of Peter the Great's fleet, was founded by Yury Dolgoruky in 1152, five years after the foundation of Moscow. It lies on the shore of Lake Pleshcheyevo, framed by numerous tributaries of the Trubezh River—a Russian Venice in miniature.

If you set out from town on the right-hand shore of the lake, you'll have a fine view of Pereslavl and the water from Mount Alexander (Alexandrova Gora), named after Alexander Nevsky who, in the 13th century, was co-ruler of the city. About two miles on the other shore, near Thunder Mountain (Gremyachaya Gora), stands the Nautical Museum housing Peter the Great's ship, *Fortuna*. It was here that the future Czar built a toy fleet in anticipation of the first real one which he launched in the last years of the 17th century.

The heart of the town is Red Square (Krasnaya Ploshchad) with the Cathedral of the Transfiguration of the Savior, erected by Yury Dolgoruky in 1152. The cathedral was linked to the palace of the prince (near the northern city walls) and to the fortifications; it was part of the defenses. Its single dome, apse and the clean lines of its facade make it an impressive and powerful building. The Church of the Metropolitan Peter, on the western side, was built in 1585. It is also known as the Shatrovaya Church. Its cellar, once a treasury, now houses the Alexander Nevsky Museum.

There are large monasteries both north and south of Pereslavl. The northern one is the Nikitsky Monastery, founded in the 12th century, with most of its monuments dating from the 16th. Its compound includes the Cathedral of St. Nicholas and the Church of the Annunciation, joined by the *trapeza,* the rather grim and solemn refectory. The monastery walls are divided by six bastions of different shape.

To the south at the approach to the town stands the Goritsky Monastery with its churches (the Cathedral of the Assumption and the Vsesvyatskaya), and its 17th-century murals. Its chief feature is the richly-carved Holy Gates (17th century). Today it is a museum of local lore, especially rich in icons and wood carvings. There is an art gallery featuring the works of Dmitri Kardovsky (1866–1943), born in this region, and other 19th-century Russian painters. The Czar Gates from the Vedenskaya Church, Peter the Great's live plaster mask (1719), and Falconet's original model for the Bronze Horseman are also here.

Rostov-Veliky

Rostov-Veliky is 64 km. (40 miles) from Pereslavl and about 193 km. (120 miles) from Moscow. Founded in A.D. 862, it was the capital of a principality in the 11th and 12th centuries. Its earliest architecture has been destroyed but in the 17th century the Metropolitan Iona Sisoyevich, a man of both ambition and taste, inspired many outstanding buildings.

Of these, the Metropolitan Palace (actually a fortress) close to Lake Nero, is perhaps the most impressive. Today it houses the local museum, established in 1883 when the kremlin was first restored. The museum has collections of porcelain, icons and woodcarvings of the 16th–20th centuries. There is a small prison cell called the "stone sack." Though it was built in 1670–83 as the Metropolitan's residence, the Palace has something of a medieval castle about it; the high church dignitary wanted it to symbolize the triumph of "the sword of religion" over the "saber of laity." Also known as the White Palace (because of its white-painted walls), it stands in Rostov's Kremlin, close to the town center.

The center of the Kremlin (also known as the Metropolia, as it was fortified only for the purpose of protecting the metropolitan, or archbishop) is a spacious courtyard with a small lake in the middle. This is the actual residence, the so-called Samuilov Corpus, with the remnants of the Krasnaya Palata (Fine Palace) on the right. Beside it stands the five-domed Church of St. John the Divine (Ivan Bogoslov) built in 1683 over one of the gates. Skirting the Metropolitan's Palace you reach the single-domed Church of the Savior (1675), the chapel of the Metropolitan, which had a direct passage linking it to the palace. The murals are truly impressive both in this chapel and in the Church of the Resurrection (1670), built over the other gate.

The Church of the Savior is linked by a gallery to the Belaya Palata (White Palace) and the Otdatochnaya (Ceremonial) Hall. The hall has an area of some 300 square yards, with a huge column in the center and resembles the Granovitaya Palace of the Moscow Kremlin. From the hall you can go on to the castle walls; its open gallery provides access to the whole Metropolitan Courtyard, its bastions and its gate-churches.

The Uspensky Cathedral (built in the 15th century) and the four-domed belfry (1680–2) stand outside the Kremlin. The latter has 13 bells which play four different carillons. On the north the Church of the Resurrection is bordered by the Holy Gates, where the Metropolitan made his ceremonial entry. The best view of all this is from Lake Nero. Take a boat (they can be hired in the lakeside park) and see.

Yaroslavl

Yaroslavl, on the bank of the Volga, is where the highway from Moscow ends. It is not only an important industrial centre but an ancient city, rich in monuments. According to tradition, it was founded by the Kiev Grand Prince Yaroslav the Wise.

Yaroslavl became the regional seat in 1777 when it was rebuilt. The groundplan of the center has remained largely unchanged mostly because this was the residential Inner Town with massive stone houses, and industry therefore could only be established in the outskirts. The center is Sovietskaya (formerly Ilyinskaya) Square, from which the main streets (Sovietskaya, Kirovskaya and Bolshaya Oktyabrskaya) radiate.

The finest feature of Sovietskaya Square is the Church of Elijah the Prophet with its ancient pews, 18th-century iconostasis and 17th-century icons and murals, several of them masterpieces by Yury Nikitin and Sila Savin. Also on the square is an 18th-century classical building, formerly the Governor's Palace, now the seat of the regional government.

A walk from Sovietskaya Square takes you down Narodny Street to the Volga quay, which was built in 1825–35. To the left along the quay, called Volzhskaya by the locals, in the courtyard of No. 2–4, you will find the Nikoly Nadena Church; its murals date from 1640. At No. 5, the Ilinsko-Tikhonovskaya Church, built in 1825–31 and a masterpiece of 19th-century classicism, is now in rather bad repair. Further along, you can turn left into M. Fevralskaya Street (running parallel with Narodny) where No. 1 (on the quay corner) is the Church of the Nativity (1644), which has a mid-17th-century bell tower and a gate-church attached.

Coming from the railway station northward to the main part of the city, you find, at the bridge and Medveditsky Ravine, and the Volga Bastion (1658–68), the area of the former kremlin. From here, going eastwards along the Kotorosl River, you reach the Strelka Point which offers a fine view of the stream's confluence with the Volga. Along the Kotorosl, there is a whole series of monuments: the Nikolai Rublenov Church (1695), once adjoining the wall of the kremlin; the Church of the Redeemer, with its beautiful murals of 1896; and the Church of St. Michael the Archangel, built in 1657–80. Its frescos, painted by local artists, are particularly noteworthy.

The important complex of the Spaso-Preobrazhensky (Transfiguration of Our Savior) Monastery is behind you on the bank of the Kotorosl (at 25 Podbelskov Square). It was there that the only copy of the *Lay of Igor's Campaign* was discovered—and, sadly, lost again when Napoleon invaded Moscow, where it had found its way into the personal library of the nobleman Musin-Pushkin. The opera *Prince Igor* was based on this national epic. The monastery, founded at the end of the 12th century, was converted into a bishop's palace in 1787. The entrance gates date from 1616. The murals inside the archway illustrating St. John's apocalyptic visions were painted in 1664. Within the walls is the Transfiguration Cathedral, built in 1516 but altered several times during the centuries. The frescos were painted in 1563–64 by several local artists; others were added in 1782. Besides the cathedral the monastery also contains a 16th-century refectory, the Church of Yaroslavl Miracle-Workers (1831), now used as a cinema and meeting hall, a 16th-century bell tower (reconstructed) and monks' cells dating from the same period. Parts of the local Art Museum are now housed in the monastery.

South of the monastery is the Kotorosl Bridge. Beyond the river, there are two important architectural monuments. One, to the left, is the Church of St. John Chrysostom, built in 1649–54 in the Korovniki District, with its 17th-century iconostasis and frescos dating from 1732–3; the other, to the right of the bridge, upriver, is the Church of St. John the Baptist (1671–87) with 15 domes, bricks imitating woodcarvings, colored tiles and some outstanding murals. There are an 18th-century bell tower and iconostasis.

Vladimir

Vladimir, founded by Prince Vladimir Monomakh, Grand Prince of Kiev, in 1108, is attractively situated on the River Klyazma, a small tributary of the Volga. Enlarged in the 12th century by Andrei Bogoliubsky, it was destroyed by the Tatars in 1238 and came under the rule of Moscow in the 15th century.

The first striking monument on the way in from Moscow is the Golden Gate, built in 1164. This was not only the ceremonial gate of the city, but one of its important fortifications, rising to two stories and still accessible by a stairway. The actual gates were defended by platforms supported by oak columns.

Behind the Golden Gate, Vladimir rises on a semicircular hill on the riverside. The Cathedral of the Assumption (Uspensky Sobor) stands on the eastern summit. Originally it was built as a single-domed church in 1158–61 but after a fire it was enlarged in 1185–89; it was given another four domes, among other improvements. There is much gilt, fine majolica tiles and some remnants of the old murals. The other frescos (1189) were restored in 1408 by Andrei Rublyev and Daniel Chorny.

It is thought that the palace of Vsevolod III stood close to the cathedral. Its church, the Dimitri Cathedral (1194–97), is the finest in Vladimir, and one of the most outstanding in the whole country. Its high reliefs are quite sensational; carved on the cathedral front, they represent a strange mixture of subjects from the Scriptures and classical history—Alexander the Great and King Solomon, for example, are both represented.

The rest of Vladimir's monuments belong to the 17th–19th centuries; many of these are concentrated in the Street of the Third International, where the Intourist Hotel is located. Here is the Monastery of the Nativity, the Church of the Assumption, the classical Dvoryanskoye Sobranye (Diet of the Nobles) and Torgovy Ryad (Merchant Row).

The Cathedral of the Princess (Knyagini) at the Vorovsky Settlement was built in the 16th century on the site of an earlier church and named after the wife of Vsevolod III. Its 17th-century murals were restored in 1947.

Note: you cannot travel individually to Vladimir unless you are driving, so trips must be arranged from Suzdal or Moscow through Intourist, either in groups or individually, with a guide.

Suzdal

Along the road from Vladimir to Suzdal, the villages evoke ancient times. Batiyevo (from the name of Batu Khan) recalls the Tatar invasion. Pavlovskoye and Borisovskoye, the estates of the medieval Princes of Moscow. Suzdal, a holy city, is in itself an entire museum—its thronging monuments, towers and domes enable the visitor to follow the history of Russian architecture from the 12th to the 19th centuries.

Suzdal's name figures in the annals for the first time in 1024, but excavations have proved that there was already a settlement here in the tenth century, in the bend of the Kamenka (a tributary of the Nerl). The smiths and bricklayers who lived here bartered with the villagers farming the black soil of the district. The coins found in the pagan burial grounds show that traders from distant lands visited Suzdal regularly. At the end of the 11th century, Suzdal came under the rule of the Grand Prince Vladimir Monomakh and under the influence of Kiev architecture. It was in the 12th century that Monomakh built the first stone church. In the same century, Yury Dolgoruky transferred here the capital of the Rostov-Suzdal principality, though his son and heir moved it to Vladimir. Suzdal was almost destroyed by the Tatars; invasions of Poles and Crimean Tatars followed each other; there were fires and plagues—the last one in 1719—but it rose again after each disaster. Today it is more an overgrown medieval village than a town.

The kremlin, perched on the left bank of the Kamenka, represents a strange amalgam of church and lay architecture. It was a princely residence and (in the 16th century) an archiepiscopal seat; but some remnants of Monomakh's church were also uncovered. Within the walls, protected by 15 bastions, the people of Suzdal found temporary safety. Nowadays, the Cathedral of the Nativity of the Mother of God (1222–25) dominates the panorama of the Suzdal kremlin, a monumental building with five domes. It forms a harmonious whole with the belfry (1636) and the snow-white archiepiscopal palace, whose carved window-frames are particularly attractive (16th and 17th centuries).

While in other cities the castle, or kremlin, is usually in the center of the community, here it was built in the southwestern district; the center is occupied by the Torg (Market), the settlement of artisans and traders. In the middle of the Torg, the steeple of the Church of the Resurrection (17th century) rises with exquisite entablatures. The main square is bordered by the Merchants' Row (Torgovy Ryad), with its characteristic double columns. Around the main square are a number of churches, built in the 17th and 18th centuries, simply designed but with elaborate internal decorations: the churches bear names such as Entry into Jerusalem, Nikolskaya, Kare-Konstantinovskaya (the latter has most impressive domes). The Church of Mary Magdalene shares its belfry with the former edifice. The churches stand more or less in pairs, close to each other, with a less-richly decorated building next to a more ambitious one. The richly-decorated ones with several domes were the "summer" churches, opened at Easter, while the "winter" churches, identifiable by their belfries, were for regular services. The domes of the Suzdal churches, generally built on a drum base, have varied forms and decoration. The helmet-shaped belfries are handsome and imaginative.

The Monastery of the Lament of Christ (Spaso-Efimievsky Monastery) has a 180-feet-high belfry. It stands at the northern end of the main street above the bank of the River Kamenka and is in an entirely different style than its neighbors. Its Holy Gate is one of the finest treasures of 17th-century Suzdal architecture. The gate barely rises above the enclosing wall, yet it draws the eye with its asymmetric composition underlined by the symmetrical double "helmet" of the steeple. The yellow-and-green tiles are decorated with botanical motifs; the carvings of the facade and its splendidly human proportions convey an impression of airiness and joy.

The Spaso-Efimievsky Monastery dates from the 16th century. Its walls, over a kilometer long and punctuated by 12 mighty towers, give it the air of a fortress—and indeed for centuries it served as a sort of Russian Bastille, the prison for disgraced courtiers, free-thinkers and political hotheads. Only one tower served as an entrance—and then only once a year, on the day of the Easter Procession. Within the red-and-white walls, the most outstanding building is the Cathedral of Spaso-Preobrazheniye (Transfiguration) with its five domes and fine murals, dating from 1594. Beside it are the Annunciation gate-church (Blagoveshchenskaya, 17th century) and the square belfry (16th century), which are also remarkable buildings.

Walking down along the monastery wall to the river, you see on the opposite, low bank of Kamenka, the Monastery of the Intercession of Mary (Pokrovsky Convent). Founded in 1364, it was built practically as a redoubt of the castle; its walls date from the 17th–18th centuries. It has a three-domed cathedral and two churches: that of the Annunciation (Blagoveshchenskaya) and that of the Immaculate Conception (Zachatievskaya); these are still being restored. Vasily III, the father of Ivan the Terrible, exiled his first wife to Suzdal, having condemned her for barrenness; the churches were built in her time, the 16th century. Ivan the Terrible followed his father's example: his wife was a prisoner here, and so was

the first wife of Peter I. In the crypt of Pokrovsky Cathedral you can still
see the graves of the exiled Czarinas.

Two-and-a-half miles from Suzdal, in the village of Kideksha, you will
find the Church of Boris-and-Gleb (on the banks of the Nerl, near the
mouth of the Kamenka), erected by Prince Yury Dolgoruky in 1152, on
the pattern of churches in Kiev.

Ivanovo and Palekh

On the way to Vladimir, some 97 km. (60 miles) from Moscow, you
pass the textile center of Orekhovo-Zuyevo. A sister city is Ivanovo, beyond Vladimir, some 130 km. (80 miles) by train, on the banks of the Uvod
River. Here, in 1905, the first workers' council *(soviet)* was founded when
80,000 men went on strike. In the 19th century, Ivanovo became known
as the "Russian Manchester." Its museum traces its evolution. It has a
collection of fabrics illustrating the progress of the textile industry, as well
as local folk art, including miniatures of papier-mâché.

The folk artists of the nearby village of Palekh (48 km. (30 miles) away)
are famous for their fairy-tale paintings on the familiar black lacquered
boxes. The murals of the Ivanovo Palace of Pioneers are also their work
and the artists of Palekh were responsible for the restoration of the murals
of the Moscow Kremlin in 1946. In 1935 an art school was opened in the
village to preserve and nurture its traditions. Today 120 local artists work
here, painting lacquer boxes. The museum of Palekh has a large selection
of their work but they are also represented in the Russian Museum in Leningrad and in the Tretyakov Gallery in Moscow.

PRACTICAL INFORMATION FOR

NORTHEASTERN RUSSIA

WHEN TO GO. The climate of this area is similar to that of Moscow and the
territory west of the capital though a little colder in the winter. Summer is the recommended time for a visit unless you are interested in winter sports.

GETTING THERE. Rostov-Veliky and Yaroslavl can be reached from Moscow
by train from the Yaroslavl Railroad Station. Pereslavl-Zalessky is not on the railroad line and it's best to go **by car**—the nearest railroad station is 19 km. (12 miles)
away. All three are on the Moscow-Yaroslavl highway, which passes through Ba-
bushkin, Mytishchi, Pushkino, Novaya Derevnya, Bratovshchina, Rakhmanov, Zagorsk, Novoye-Glebovskoye to Pereslavl and then through Slobodka, Petrovsk,
Rostov-Veliky and Karabykha to Yaroslavl. The total distance to Yaroslavl is 240
km. (150 miles). You can also get there **by boat** down the Volga.

Vladimir can be reached from the Kursk Station in Moscow by taking a train
in the direction of Gorky and Kirov and traveling some 194 km. (120 miles) east.
From Vladimir, Suzdal is only 27 km. (18 miles) by train; the road winds between
hills and through meadows.

Ivanovo is 129 km. (80 miles) from Vladimir; Palekh is a further 48 km. (30
miles) away. Both can be reached by train and road.

It is always advisable and on the whole very much simpler to get train and boat
tickets from Intourist rather than direct from the station or pier. Often at the latter
they are none too keen on selling to tourists.

TOURS. Intourist runs day excursions from Moscow to Zagorsk and also arranges tours by train to Suzdal with a side-trip to nearby Vladimir possible.

Hotels and Restaurants

Suzdal. *Pokrovskaya* (tel. 2–0131). First class, 13 rooms and 32 beds in log cabins; 3.2 km. (2 miles) out. *Intourist,* Lenin Street on the central square, modern, first class. *Suzdal Hotel* and *Motel,* Ivanovskaya Zastava (tel. 2–1137). 3.2 km (2 miles) from town.
Restaurants. Aside from hotels, try *Trapeznaya,* in the kremlin, closed Monday. *Sokol,* on Lenin Street. *Pogrebok,* on Kremlyovskaya Street; open 11–7, closed Monday.

Vladimir. *Vladimir* (Intourist), 74 Third International Street, (tel. 30–42). *Klyazma,* 2 Lenin Street.
Restaurants. In hotel or at *Dieteticheskaya* on Frunze Street.

Yaroslavl. *Volga* (Intourist), Kirov Street. Tsentralnaya, Volkov Square. *Yaroslavl,* 40/2 Ushinsky Street, (tel. 2–1258). 150 rooms, moderate.
Restaurants. In Volga and Yaroslavl hotels or *Moskva,* 1 Komsomolskaya Street; *Konditerskaya* on Volzhskaya Embankment; *Yevropa* on Svoboda Street; *Chaika,* Lenin Street or *Rossiya* on Chkalov Street.

Zagorsk. Proximity to Moscow makes day-trip feasible.

Other **restaurants** include:
In **Pereslavl-Zalessky.** In hotel of same name.
In **Pokrov.** *Druzhba Restaurant.*
In **Rostov-Veliky.** In hotel of same name on Karl Marx Street, or *Beryozka,* a special restaurant for foreign tourists.

PLACES OF INTEREST. Ivanovo. *Museum of Local History,* textile industry, folk art and political.

Palekh. *Museum and Co-operative of Folk Artists.*

Pereslavl-Zalessky. *Alexander Nevsky Museum,* in cellar beneath Church of Metropolitan Peter.
Botik Museum near the village of **Veskovo** 3.2 km. (2 miles) from the town. Open 10–4; closed Tues. Formerly part of the Botik Estate, with a wooden palace, a triumphal arch (1852) and a monument to Peter the Great, designed by Campioni, with some of the great Czar's naval guns and relics of the flotilla.
Museum of History and Fine Arts, housed in the Goritsky Monastery, Kardovsky Street, reached before entering the town on the way from Moscow; follow an arrow pointing left. Open 10–4; closed Tues.

Rostov-Veliky. The *Kremlin* buildings. *Local Museum,* in the Metropolitan's Palace in the kremlin. Open 9–5, closed Wed.

Suzdal. The entire old city is a vast museum. *Local Museum,* in kremlin.
Museum of Wooden Architecture, across river from kremlin. Contains churches, houses, windmills.
In **Kideksha** village 4 km. (2½ miles) away, *Church of Boris and Gleb.*

Vladimir. *Local Museum,* 64 Third International Street.

Yaroslavl. *Local Museum and Art Museum* in the Spaso-Preobrazhensky Monastery, 25 Podbelskov Square.

Museum in the Church of Elijah the Prophet, Sovietskaya Street. If closed, apply to the museum authorities in the Spaso-Preobrazhensky Monastery.

Historical and Local Museum, 19/1 Sovietskaya Square. Open 10–5, closed Sat.
Art Museum, 2 Chelyuskintsev Square. Open 10–5, closed Tues.
Planetarium, 20 Tefolev Street. Open 11–7, closed Tues.
Ferry boat excursion along the Volga, one hour, 20 kopeks.

Zagorsk. The *Trinity-Saint Sergius Monastery* and the *tomb of Boris Godunov.*

THEATERS AND CONCERTS. Ivanovo. Three theaters—dramatic, musical comedy and puppet; *House of Culture.*

Vladimir. *Drama Theater,* 3 Lenin Street.

Yaroslavl. *Volkov Drama Theater,* Volkov Square; *Puppet Theater,* 8 Komitetskaya Street; *Concert Hall,* Komitetskaya Street.

USEFUL ADDRESSES. Yaroslavl. *Intourist:* 40/2 Usinsky Street. *Railroad Station:* Privokzalnaya Square. *Bus terminal:* Moskovskoye Road. *Harbor:* Flotsky Spusk.

Northwest of Moscow

Setting out from Moscow in a northwesterly direction, you have to cover 480 km. (300 miles) to reach Novgorod, one of the most ancient cities of the Soviet Union. It is possible to do the trip in five hours: first to Klin (97 km., 60 miles) where the memorial museum to Tchaikovsky is located; then on to Kalinin (called Tver in pre-revolutionary times), 160 km. (100 miles) away, which is an important stop on the Moscow-Leningrad railroad line. After Kalinin the route leads on through Vyshny-Volochek along the Valday Ridge to your destination.

Starting from Moscow towards Klin, near the settlement of Solnechno-gorsk (Sunny Hills), you will reach the large Lake Senezhskoye, a favorite place for Moscow anglers and hikers. It is a reservoir, originally part of a large-scale canalization scheme which Peter the Great had planned. 16 km. (ten miles) farther on, you reach the village of Frolovskoye, where Tchaikovsky composed his *Fifth Symphony* and finished his opera *The Queen of Spades.* Another few miles and you are in Klin, at the great composer's memorial museum, where on May 7 and November 6 (his birthday and the anniversary of his death), outstanding Soviet pianists give special concerts.

Klin was Tchaikovsky's home in 1892–93, though he had lived in the district from 1885 onwards. Here he composed his *Pathétique Symphony,* his *Third Piano Concerto* and the music for the *Nutcracker* and *Sleeping Beauty* ballets. The two-story building is decorated and furnished as it was in Tchaikovsky's lifetime, and contains his books, paintings, piano and other personal possessions. The Tchaikovsky archives contain 50,000 items and are an important source for researchers.

Beyond Klin, at the 125-kilometer stone, we reach Bezhorodovo, the huge expanse of the "Moscow Sea," a reservoir which was built at the time of the Moscow-Volga canal's construction (1932–37). This section, at the confluence of the Sosa and the Volga, is a favorite excursion spot.

Kalinin

Kalinin is an important regional seat. It lies on the Upper Volga and is also an ancient trading port. Formerly called Tver, it was renamed after Kalinin, the President of the Soviet Union from 1919 to 1946.

The early architectural monuments of Tver-Kalinin were almost all destroyed during the years of feudal strife; the rest were devastated by the great conflagration of 1763. But the White Trinity Church (founded in 1563–64 and built by Tushinsky during the reign of Ivan the Terrible) is still standing. The Transfiguration Cathedral, late-17th century and following the pattern of the Uspensky Cathedral in Moscow, has also survived; the belfry, dating from the middle of the 18th century, recalls that of the Trinity-St. Sergius Monastery at Zagorsk.

Following the great fire of 1763, the Moscow architects Nikitin and Kazakov redesigned the town, and the main lines of their plan can still be followed. The heart of the city was the Moscow–Petersburg highway (today called Sovietskaya Street), from which two avenues fanned out left and right. The Sovietskaya crosses three squares: the Pushkinskaya, the Pochtovaya and Lenin Square. The last is octagonal. Among the town's outstanding architectural features are the Putyevoi Dvorets, the seat of the Municipal Council (built 1770–80), the building of the city Party Committee (formerly the Noblemen's Diet, 1766–70) and the Youth Theater (1786, originally a school).

The Putyevoi Dvorets on Sovietskaya Street, was erected as a palace for Catherine II, so that she could break her journeys between Moscow and St. Petersburg. It was built by Kazakov in 1763–75; Rossi redesigned it in 1809. The Church of the Ascension (1813, designed by Lvov) today houses the local museum.

Ostrovsky, the Russian dramatist, lived here in 1856; in 1859, Dostoyevsky spent a few months at No. 1 Pushkin Street, while Saltykov-Shchedrin worked here as deputy governor of Tver in 1860–62, gathering material for several of his satirical works.

On May 1st Quay (Pervomaiskaya Naberezhnaya) stands the Nikitin Monument, commemorating the Russian merchant and explorer who traveled to India in the mid-15th century and wrote about his trip. It is close to the spot whence, according to tradition, he set sail.

Vyshny-Volochek is an industrial town and the starting point of the canal system of the Upper Volga. It was here that Peter the Great built the first canal in Russia (1703–9). The first barges passed through in 1790, putting an end to the laborious overland transport of goods. Later, this was the place where those exiled to Siberia gathered to start their long journey.

Novgorod

Situated four miles from Lake Ilmen, on both banks of the Volkhov River, this city is a regional center and, with a history of 11 centuries, is perhaps the Russian city richest in art treasures and monuments. Its story, in some ways, has mirrored the history of Russia.

Start your exploration at the castle (kremlin) and then continue along the western or left bank, Sofiskaya Storona (Sophia side), following with the right bank, Torgovaya Storona (Market Side), and ending with the monuments in the environs of Novgorod.

The kremlin is certainly the most striking landmark in Novgorod. Its historic character has been carefully preserved, even though its buildings have been adapted to house the city's most important cultural institutions: the museum, theater, library and lecture hall. There is now even a restaurant in this evocative building.

If you enter the castle's grounds through the entrance on the Volkhov River side, under the 19th-century arcades (formerly the site of the Prechistenskaya Bastion), you will find to the right the most important monument in the city, the Saint Sophia Cathedral, built with six domes by Greek architects between 1045 and 1052. Opposite is the central square of the kremlin with the Millenary Monument, which can serve as a central signpost for your walk. It is shaped like a bell and was erected in 1862 to commemorate 1,000 years of Russian history.

Crossing the square in front of the monument, stand in front of the oldest stone building in Northern Russia, the Cathedral of Saint Sophia. It has three apses—the apse became the most important external feature of all subsequent typical church architecture. The central dome is a huge copy of the helmet of a warrior, capped by a bronze dove and a cross. (Legend says that Novgorod will remain in existence until the dove flies away.) At the west entrance is the Korsun bronze door, supposedly brought from Magdeburg as booty in the 12th century. It depicts scenes from the Old and New Testaments, with Latin and Slavonic inscriptions. The murals are much later, having been painted over earlier ones in the 1830's. The best frescos are in the southern part of the cathedral.

The Vladichny Dvor (Archbishop's Palace, 1436) is northwest from St. Sophia. This was the "fortress within the fortress" of the Archbishop of Novgorod; its entrance was at the passage where today there are some stone cannon balls. But first, adjoining the cathedral, is the 15th century porch where the miraculous icon and the sacrificial bread were kept. Leaving the passage you will find a large, one-storied building, the Nikitny Corpus, today a department of the Museum of History and an art gallery showing 18th to 19th century Russian art.

The Historical Museum has 11th-century mosaics and many other items of interest; over 80,000 exhibits in 35 halls, including letters dating from the 11th to 15th centuries written on birchbark; the Nikitny Corpus dates from the 12th century. Until the middle of the 14th, this was the archiepiscopal residence and was remodeled in the 17th century. In the palace itself is the Granovitaya Palata (Faceted Palace), actually a massive Gothic hall on the second floor. The beautiful interior decoration of the hall is particularly fine. It was in this palace that Ivan the Terrible gave the banquet in 1570 at which the stubborn Novgorod prelates and magnates were killed at the Czar's prearranged signal. Today it houses a collection of icons and other church treasures.

The former apartments of the archbishop now house the Regional Library, with 250,000 volumes: next to it, further west, lies the Sergei Church (1463). Linked to it is the Giant Bell of Yevfimy inspired by the Archbishop Yevfimy, the militant apostle of Novgorod's independence (1443). The 155 ft. high tower was originally a watch-tower.

The next building on the kremlin-wall side is the 17th-century Prikaz (Law Court); between the Prikaz and the section of the castle wall lying to the north was the archiepiscopal farmyard. (Today it houses the local architectural and planning offices.) South of the Prikaz, sharing its entrance, is the Likhudovsky Corpus (a former school-building of the 15th century, rebuilt in the 17th and 18th centuries).

Pass through the archway in front of St. Sophia to the "main street" of the castle (actually a square), where the Millenary Monument stands. On the right is a one-storied building (1670) which served in the 17th–19th centuries as the residence of the Metropolitans. Today it is the administrative headquarters of the Novgorod region. It occupies the site of the Church of St. John Chrysostom, built by Archbishop Yevfimy. Excavations in its courtyard carried out in 1923 uncovered some church plate and vessels buried in the 15th century.

Setting out in the opposite direction from St. Sophia, you will pass the Lecture Hall; opposite, at the castle wall, is the Sofiskaya Zvonnitsa (15th–17th centuries), the belfry of St. Sophia's Cathedral. The additions to the tower (among them the porch) belong to the 17th century. The three bells exhibited outside used to hang in the belfry. (The heaviest weighs 26.5 tons; it was placed in the tower in 1650 but fell and shattered nine years later, after which it was recast.) The bell on the right was the gift of Boris Godunov to the Dukhov Monastery in 1589.

Returning to the block of the Prisutstvennoye Mesto (1783–1822), which stretches the width of the castle and was originally the Treasury, you will find the City Library and the Historical Museum of the Revolution. Turning left here, walk to the Andrei Stratilates Church, where excavations are still in process. It has been established that, from the 15th century, this was the artisan quarter of the castle.

Between the excavations and the Prisutstvennoye Mesto there are three single-storied houses. They were built in 1781, paid for by Catherine II, to house the local clergy. Past them, near the castle-wall is the 14th-century Pokrov (Intercession) Church. It was remodeled in the 17th century. The next tower is named after St. John Chrysostom; nearby the dead of the 1917 Revolution were buried, and in front of the arcade opposite are the graves of the Soviet soldiers who died liberating Novgorod in the last war.

Outside the Kremlin

Passing through the western gate of the kremlin (away from the river) you will enter Victory (Pobeda) Square and the Sofiskaya Storona (Sophia Quarter), the heart of Novgorod. Opposite we see the House of the Soviets, on the right Merkurov's Lenin statue.

Turning left in Pobeda Square, at the meeting of three streets, is a typical monument of 15th-century Novgorod architecture: the Vlasiya (St. Blasius) Church, built in 1407 on the site of a much earlier wooden church and recently restored. Its square groundplan and its single dome are repeated in several other churches. Walking upstream (south) and leaving the kremlin behind, you will reach the Uvereniye Fomi (St. Thomas) Church, built in 1463 on the shore of Lake Myachino. It is a masterly imitation of 12th-century style—so much so that experts until recently believed it to be the 1195 church which once stood on this site. The adjoining Ioanna Milostivogo-Myachinye (St. John) Church has preserved few of its original 15th century features.

West of Lake Myachino, in the middle of the Sinichya Gora cemetery, the Church of Petra-i-Pavla-na-Sinichei-Gorye (Peter-and-Paul on Blue-tit Hill) has remained (with the exception of its flat roof) exactly as the inhabitants of nearby Lukina Street built it in 1185–92. Half a mile away, further west, stands the Blagoveshcheniya-u-Arkazhi (Annunciation) Church. This was built in 1179 and its lower parts are still in the original form while its vaulted roof and dome were rebuilt in the 16th century. Some fragments of murals in the sanctuary are interesting examples of the late 12th-century Novgorod school.

Returning to the city and following the line of the original ramparts (Great Earthwork Fortifications), we find several important monuments. The first, directly west of the kremlin, is the Church of Twelve Apostles, in Leo Tolstoy Street, dating from 1454. The next, the Feodor Stratilates Church on Komsomolskaya Street northeast of the kremlin, belongs to the 13th–17th centuries and has good murals. The Petra-i-Pavla-v-Kozhevnikakh Church in Zverinskaya Street north of the kremlin and nearer the river dates from 1406 and is outside the fortifications; it is one of the most characteristic Novgorod churches of this period. Its fabric is half-brick, half-limestone; the decorations of the front, the vaults, the supporting pillars and the dome itself are all of brick. Continuing north, near the little Gzena River are the three churches of the Zverin Monastery: the Pokrov (Intercession), the Nikolai Byelov (St. Nicholas the White) and the St. Simeon. The latter was built in 1467 and, apart from its disproportionately large dome, invokes the shape of the Twelve Apostles Church. The original murals have been preserved but they have been only partially uncovered.

The Trinity Church in the Dukhov (Holy Spirit) Monastery, built in 1557, is in Molotovskaya Street, along the highway to Leningrad. It reflects the influence of Muscovite architecture.

Across the River

On the right (eastern) bank of the Volkhov, the Torgovaya Storona (Merchant Quarter) with its gridiron streets is a reminder of Catherine the Great's city planning endeavors. The original center of the quarter was the Yaroslav Court, opposite the kremlin on the left bank. It is first described as a "court" in the chronicles of the 13th century and it is known that public meetings were held here. The partly-enclosed complex is dominated by the St. Nicholas Cathedral (Nikolo-Dvorishchensky), built in 1113 in Kiev style, with three naves; under its roof the remnants of the original four domes still exist. The graphic quality of its partially surviving murals is quite remarkable.

South and southwest of St. Nicholas are the churches of Zhen-Mironosits (Myrrh-Bearing Women) and Prokopy, both dating from the 16th century and built entirely of brick, though the roof of the former is wood. Northwest from St. Nicholas Cathedral we see the two-level gatehouse of the Gostiny Dvor (Market Hall), with its double archways; its octagonal helmet-crowned tower dates from the 1690's. One of the other churches of the Torg, the Paraskeva-Pyatnitsa (1207), is one of Novgorod's most original monuments though it was somewhat modified in the 16th century. The other church, the Uspensky (Assumption), has retained only the groundplan of the 12th-century original. North of it in Pervomaiskaya Street the Church of St. George belongs to the 17th century with the exception of its lower walls. West from here the Ioannna-Opokakh (St. John) Church (1127–30) was the headquarters of the Ivanovskoye Sto merchant guild, housing its civil courts, and the depository of the weights-

and-measures officials. The church was demolished in 1453 but its successor was an almost exact imitation of the original.

Southeast from the Yaroslav Court, across the street, a brick passage connects the churches of St. Michael (Mikhail-na-Mikhailovye) and of the Annunciation (Blagoveshchenie). The former was extensively rebuilt in the 19th century; the latter (though built in the 15th century) survives in its rebuilt form dating from the 16th century, when the octagonal belfry was added.

If you walk eastward from the Church of the Annunciation to Ilyinskaya Street, the Filippa (St. Philip) Church is the next point of interest. Built in 1383–4, it was rebuilt in the 16th century but its square groundplan with single apse has been preserved and so has much of its original wall. Interestingly, the upper facade (16th-century) follows a 12th-century style.

North of St. Philip's on Ilyinskaya Street is the Znamensky (Apparition of the Cross) Cathedral (17th century), a classic example of Moscow architecture with its five onion domes, the brick balustrade of the facade and the murals of its tympana.

The Spas-na-Ilyine (Redeemer) Church stands to the north, at the corner of Ilyinskaya and Pervomaiskaya streets. Built in 1378, it is one of the masterpieces of Novgorod architecture; compared to its simple groundplan, its wall-decorations, apse and tympanum appear a little over-rich. But its murals, recently restored, are quite extraordinary. Their creator was the Byzantine master Theophanes (1378). Using only brown, red and white, the artist has worked with superb virtuosity.

The Dmitriya Solunskovo (Dmitri of Salonika) Church (1383) on Moskovskaya Street, the town's main road, has been restored. The nearby Klimenta (St. Clement) Church, though built by a Moscow master in 1386, reflects the local Novgorod style.

Novgorod's second Feodor Stratilates Church stands on Moskovskaya Street, the Moscow-Leningrad highway, on the market side of Feodorovsky Ruchei Street. (The first is on the other side of the river.) Built in 1360–61, it created a new school of Novgorod architecture. Its murals— uncovered in 1910—show considerable Byzantine influence and may also be by Theophanes. On Molotovskaya Street, near Feodorovsky, the Rozhdestva Bogoroditsy (Nativity of the Virgin) Church (1379) has also recently been restored. It is the Feodor Stratilates's contemporary but has a simpler groundplan and is less ornate. However, its murals (some of which date back to 1125) are of great splendor. Some parts of the building date back to the 12th-century Antonius Monastery.

Returning along Krasnaya Street to the city center, turn right into the Moskovskaya, off which to the right is the Nikita Church built in 1557, most probably by Ivan the Terrible. Turning westward on Moskovskaya to the bridge, then turning right, you can walk downstream (north) to the point where the fortifications and the river meet. Here the Borisa-i-Gleba (St. Boris and Gleb) Church is an example of the 16th-century style, based on ancient traditions. Beyond the earth wall the Church of St. John the Divine (Ioanna Bogoslova) is one of the best-preserved examples of 14th-century Novgorod architecture.

Excursions around Novgorod

The important sights of Novgorod's environs are mostly on the Volkhov River and on Lake Ilmen. The best way to approach them is by water.

The first stop, on the right (east) bank of the river, is the village of Gorod-ishche, which may have been Novgorod's ancient Old Town. When the feudal republic was declared in the 12th century, this became the ducal residence; Mstislav, son of Prince Vladimir Monomakh of Kiev, had the Church of the Annunciation built about the same time. It was rebuilt in the 14th century but destroyed in 1941. Opposite, on the left bank, the Yuriev monastery and church of St. George (1119), resembling in its proportions and size the St. Sophia Cathedral. Its murals were largely ruined during the 19th-century restoration, the remainder were salvaged in 1935; the fragments show a Byzantine-Kiev influence.

East of Gorodishche, beyond the small Spasovka River, stands the Church of the Redeemer on Mount Nereditsa, built in 1198 by Prince Yaroslav Vladimirovich and restored after World War II. Though it was a prince's church, it had a single dome and resembled the small churches erected by merchants. The priceless murals were totally destroyed during the war and only remain in reproductions.

The other great architectural monuments, churches and chapels on the right bank of the Volkhov were also heavily damaged but have now been mostly restored.

West of Gorodishche, near the St. George Monastery, postwar excavations on Perun Hill have uncovered the ruins of the temple of the pre-Christian god, Perun. His idol was destroyed with the triumph of Christianity and a monastery was built on the spot—the Our Lady of Perun Monastery, whose 13th century church has been restored. South of here, on the northeastern shore of Lake Ilmen, the Church of St. Nicholas the Miracle-Worker has also been restored in Lipna. North of Novgorod, along the Volkhov you can visit two partly-ruined churches at the Derevy-anitsky Monastery some two-and-a-half miles from the city: the Cathedral of the Resurrection (1700) and the Uspensky (Assumption) Church, dating from 1725.

Pskov

Pskov, another ancient Russian city, lies on the highway between Novgorod and Riga. During the ten centuries of its existence, this regional capital has been the scene of many important historical events. It was at the Pskov railway station that Nicholas II abdicated in March 1917; and in and around the city several decisive battles of the ensuing civil war were fought. Lenin lived here from March to May of 1900, preparing his underground newspaper, *Iskra* (Spark).

But many centuries before these events, Pskov was the advance post of the Eastern Slav drive towards Estonia and Livonia and the base of the Teutonic Knights. It was first mentioned in tenth century chronicles, having been in all probability founded in the reign of Rurik. For many years it was ruled by the Novgorod Republic, but it also intermittently had its own princes. In 1348 an independent republic which survived for a long time was established, though it was constantly at war with the Teutonic Knights and the Grand Prince of Lithuania and withstood no less than 26 sieges. But in the 15th century it yielded to the might of Moscow. Later, Pskov was an important commercial center, still repulsing attacks from Livonia and Sweden. Only at the end of the 18th century, when Byelorussia became a dependency of Russia, did Pskov lose its strategic importance. It was badly damaged during World War II but has been almost completely rebuilt and now has considerable heavy industry as well as traditional plants for processing flax.

Though its urban structure was partly rearranged in the 18th and 19th centuries, Pskov still has many monuments dating from the 12th to 17th centuries: two castles, the remnants of its 14th- and 15th-century Old Town, and the newer quarter developed on the left bank of the Velikaya and the right bank of the Pskov rivers.

The kremlin deserves to be seen first; here, on the romantic limestone cliffs at the confluence of the two rivers, was the cradle of today's city. The kremlin was an important fortress by the 11th century though its stone walls were only raised in the 13th. Its most important monument is the Trinity Cathedral, built in 1699 on the site of the 13th century church. This was the center of the feudal republic of Pskov: the princes set out to do battle from the cathedral; here the treasures were kept, foreign ambassadors received, dignitaries buried. Through the arcade that stretches under the cathedral you can reach the assembly square which extends to the southern castle walls. (Here Alexander Nevsky was acclaimed in 1242.) The restoration work on the bastions and walls has been in progress for some years. The Greblya moat under the castle originally linked the Velikaya and Pskov rivers but has now been filled in.

From the south the Dovmontov Gorod wall, named after Prince Dovmont, was linked to the kremlin in the last third of the 13th century. In the 12th to 14th centuries there were no fewer than 19 churches in this area; the foundations of some of them have been uncovered during recent excavations. Part of the kremlin's southern wall can be seen at the Prikaznaya Palace; this was the administrative center of 17th-century Pskov, an interesting example of civil architecture. The western wall of the Dovmontov Gorod has been restored and a replica of its original Vasilyevskaya Tower erected.

The fortifications of Pskov were built in the 13th and 14th centuries from local limestone and extend about six miles. They defended the two castles and the Central (Sredny) and Suburban (Okolny) quarters, south of the Dovmontov Gorod and the Zapskovye district (the quarter on the right bank of the river) to the north.

From the Dovmontov Gorod there is a fine view of the medieval center of Sredny Gorod, the Torg (Market Place), today called Lenin Square. Setting out along Sovietskaya Street towards October Square, you will see, next to the Central Post Office, the first stone church of Pskov's Old City, the Church of the Archangel Michael, built in 1339 and later remodeled. Its courtyard is bordered by a belfry (17th century) on the street side. Along the Sovietskaya, it is worth climbing the hill to the Vasily-na-Gorke Church (1413), whose tympanum and apse retain their original decorative carvings. Some of the special features of the Pskov architectural school can be seen here: in the tympanum, the belfry above the gate, the loophole-like windows, the inner vaults and the semi-circular arches upon which the roof-structure rests. Across the street the Nikola-na-Usokhe Church (1371) was rebuilt in 1573 and partially restored after the last war. West of it, the ruins of the Odigitria Church (1537–1685) indicate a Moscow influence.

In the Stary Torg (Old Market), the house at 10 Marx Street, with its vaulted ceremonial halls and its attic store-rooms (it had no cellar) recalls the merchant houses of the Baltic (17th century). Also in Marx Street is the Peter-and-Paul Church, built on the site of a 1299 wooden church in the 15th century and rebuilt in 1540. Its restoration in 1962 emphasized its original style.

Walking along the banks of the Pskov in the direction of Krasny Partizan Street, you can drop into No. 6 Yedinstvo Street, the 17th century home of the merchant Yamsky, an interesting survival of the old, picturesque Pskov quarter of Okolny. (In 1710 Peter the Great stayed here.) No. 10 Krasny Partizan Street, the Guryev Mansion, was built somewhat earlier. Continue along Ostrovok Quay to No. 42 Gogolevskaya Street, the so-called Malt House (Solodezhnya). Perhaps this is the most typical of the 17th-century Pskov houses. Its verandah has cross-vaulting, with a rare stone icon-stand and lampholder. It has two large vaulted rooms, a smaller one, an attic and a courtyard. Of the gates, only the iron one is original. Opposite, the Pechenko House (17th century) has been restored. Going southwest towards the Polonishche Quarter, along Mikhailovskaya and Nekrasovskaya streets, you will reach the St. Nicholas (Nikolai-ot-Torga) Church (1676) and the Pokrov-ot-Torga (The Intercession of the Virgin) Church (17th century). The proportions of the Anastasia Church at October Avenue show that in the 16th century it was one of the finest ecclesiastical buildings of Pskov. Farther along Nekrasov Street is the Church of the Ascension (1467), which has been rebuilt several times; only the belfry has preserved its original charm.

Between Nekrasov, Gogol, Museum and Komsomol streets, the 17th-century Pogankin House today contains the historical section of the Art and Historical Museum of Pskov. Pogankin House, consisting of three buildings, was once a fortress. The staircases between the warehouses, the shop and the apartments are lined with six-foot-thick walls; there are double iron gates and the 105 loophole-shaped windows are of the barred-and-shuttered variety. The Menshikov mansion, home of another merchant family (50 Sovietskaya Street), differs somewhat from the traditional 17th-century Pskov style; the barrack-like exterior is relieved by the carved limestone decorations of the windows.

From Sovietskaya Street you can reach the Joachim-and-Anna Church through Sverdlov Street. This has been restored to its original 16th-century condition. On the riverbank, in the 15th-century St. George Church on the corner of Uritsky and Liebknecht streets, only the mosaic decoration of the tympanum under the dome is preserved, though the loophole-windows of the apse also date from that century. Finally, after visiting the 16th-century Double Church of the Nativity and the Intercession of the Virgin (also restored), stop at the Pokrovskaya bastion and gate, on the riverbank. Here the restoration work of recent years shows how the city walls must have looked centuries ago. (In 1701 Peter the Great ordered the removal of the tower's wooden parts and had the bastion itself stuffed with earth so that it could bear the weight of heavy cannon.)

The bridge at Sovietskaya Square leads into the Zapskovye quarter. The Kozma-and-Demian Church stands close to the bridge. Built in the 15th century, it was badly damaged in 1507 by an explosion of gunpowder stored inside. But its enclosing wall is of rare interest, especially its gate, which resembles a triumphal arch. On Herzen Street is one of the largest churches of 15th-century Pskov, the partly-restored Bogoyavleniye (Apparition of the Lord). On Leon Pozemsky Street, the main thoroughfare of the quarter, the Trubinsky House is one of the masterpieces of lay architecture of the 17th century. The men's and women's apartments had separate dining halls; the former had an adjoining guest room and access to the wine cellar. But the staircase to the garden led from the men's apartments through the women's, so the isolation was not complete.

Opposite the Trubinsky House, the Elijah Church (1677) has an open verandah and a gallery built on high columns. The Postnikov House, on the corner of Leon Pozemsky Street and Moskovskaya, dates from the turn of the 17th and 18th centuries. The Church of the Resurrection also stands on Leon Pozemsky Street (1522). On nearby Varlaamovsky Proyezd lies the Varlaam Church (1495); during the 1615 siege it was transformed into a supporting bastion of the nearby Varlaamovskiye Gates. Finally, visit the Obrazskaya Church (1487), on the Ilyinsky Proyezd.

In the Zavelichye quarter, on the left bank of the Velikaya, the Cathedral of the Savior, within the Mirozhsky Monastery, stands about a mile from the kremlin. The monastery was founded in the 11th century; the cathedral is one of the oldest monuments in Pskov (12th century) and has remained fundamentally unchanged. It is built of limestone and brick; its Byzantine elements are probably due to the taste of Nifont, Archbishop of Novgorod, who initiated the building. Its interesting murals also show a Byzantine influence. The 19th-century restoration did much harm to the murals but more recently some of the original beauty has been regained by skilful work.

The Clement Church, down on the riverbank at the ferry, has more or less preserved its 16th-century form. Close to the bridge is the Church of the Blessed Virgin (1444–1521), and opposite the castle, the Cathedral of St. John the Baptist (or the Cathedral of the Ivanovsky Monastery). The latter, according to tradition, was founded by the wife of Yaroslav, Prince of Pskov. Murdered by her stepson, she was buried in the cathedral.

PRACTICAL INFORMATION FOR

NORTHWESTERN RUSSIA

WHEN TO GO. This district has the same climate as the region northeast of Moscow and therefore the summer is likely to be the best season—especially as there are good facilities for swimming and boating.

GETTING THERE. By train. Trains from Moscow and Leningrad to Novgorod. From Moscow, change at Chudovo. From Novgorod by train to Pskov (240 km., 150 miles).

By boat. To Kalinin by boat on the Volga.

By car and bus. Klin, Kalinin, Vyshny-Volochek, Novgorod are on the Number 1 tourist highway. There is no highway open to tourists from Novgorod to Pskov—but Intourist runs buses on the Novgorod-Riga road.

TOURS. Intourist arranges a nine-hour bus tour to Klin from Moscow. There are two- and three-day tours to Novgorod and its neighborhood and similar tours to Pskov. From Pskov there is a nine-hour tour to Mikhailovskoye, the family estate of the poet Alexander Pushkin.

There are interesting trips out from Murmansk in summer to see the salmon migration, and across the Kola Bay by hydrofoil to view the Arctic coastline.

Hotels and Restaurants

Ivanovo. The only hotels are *Tsentralnaya,* 1/25 Engels Street, 450 rooms, moderate; and *Sovietskaya,* 64 Lenin Prospekt.

Kalinin. *Motel Tver,* 130 Leningrad Highway is best, recent and comfortable; then *Seliger,* 52 Sovietskaya Street; *Volga,* Uritsky Street; *Tsentralnaya,* 33/8 Pravda Street, a modest-sized, five-story hotel.
Restaurants. Aside from hotels you can try *Orel,* Naberezhnaya Stepana Razina, or *Chaika,* opposite the riverboat station.

Murmansk. Two equal-ranking hotels, the *Arktika* at 82 Lenin Prospekt (reported to be quite pleasant, though not luxurious) and the *Severnaya* at 20 Profsoyuzov Street which is reported to be basic, but clean and well heated.
The *International Seamen's Club,* not a hotel, is a social center for visiting sailors *and* tourists. Worth a visit.
Restaurants. We suggest eating at your hotel, but if you're not satisfied, you can always try the *Polyarniye Zori* ("Polar Sunrise") at 17 Knipovich Street, or *Vsetrech* at 28 Aksoldovtsev Street. Both offer special fish dishes.

Novgorod. A choice of four hotels: *Intourist,* 16 Dmitrievskaya Street (tel. 7–5089), 122 rooms. *Sadko,* 16 Yuri Gagarin Street (tel. 9–5170). *Volkhov,* 24 Nekrasov Street (tel. 9–2498). *Ilmen,* Gorky Street.
Camping. *Savino,* Novgorod-6.
Restaurants. In your hotel, or try *Detinets,* set in the medieval kremlin. New but old!

Pskov. *Rizhskaya,* tel. 2–4301/3–3243, first class, 260 rooms. *Oktyabrskaya,* 36 October Prospekt. *Tourist,* on Krasnoarmeiskaya Embankment.
Restaurants. Aside from hotels, try eating at the *Pskov,* 45a Fabritsius Street, or the *Baltika,* at 52 Rizhskoye Chaussée.
At the **Pechora Monastery,** an out-of-town excursion, there are two adequate eating places.

Vyshny Volochek. The *Vyshny Volochek Hotel* on Pervomaiskaya Street, can be used in transit only. Restaurant too.

PLACES OF INTEREST. Kalinin. *Local Museum,* 3 Sovietskaya Street, in the left wing of the Palace. Founded in 1866; closed Tues. *Picture Gallery* in the Church of the Ascension.

Klin. *Tchaikovsky Museum,* 48 Tchaikovsky Street, open 11–5; closed Wed.

Murmansk, *Ethnographical Museum,* 90 Lenin Prospekt: geology, natural history, etc. of the Kola Peninsula. Fascinating. *Museum of Oceanography and Fisheries,* 6 Knipovich Street.

Novgorod. *Historical Museum,* inside the kremlin. *Art Museum,* also in the kremlin (Granovitaya Palata) with a collection of icons and other church treasures gathered from the monasteries and churches. *Openair Museum of Wooden Buildings,* in park near Yuriev Monastery. Churches, houses, peasant huts.

Pskov. *Historical Museum,* in the former Pogankin House.

SHOPPING. Kalinin. *Central Market,* Ploshchad Kommuny; *Department Stores:* 84 Sovietskaya Street and 35 Uritsky Street.

Murmansk. *Khudozhestvenny Salon,* 80 Lenin Prospekt (northern souvenirs, fur, deer-antlers). *Univermag* on Lenin Street is reported to be very well stocked, with quick service.

Pskov. *Souvenirs,* 18 Oktyabrsky Prospekt.

USEFUL ADDRESSES. Pskov. *Tourist Bureau:* 4 Krasnoznamenskaya Street; *Railway and bus station:* Privokzalnaya Square, at the end of October Boulevard.

South of Moscow

Starting from Moscow to the south—either along the Moscow–Yalta highway or from the Kursk railway station in the Soviet capital—the most important stops are Podolsk, Tula, and Kursk. Lesser places deserving exploration include Chekhov, Serpukhov, Yasnaya Polyana, Plavsk, Mtsensk, Verkhnii Lyubazh, Oboyan and Belgorod, south of which the Ukrainian Soviet Republic begins.

Three Writers' Homes

Driving along the Moscow–Yalta highway you will come across the Butovo camping site some 26 km. (16 miles) from Moscow and a little to the right. It is situated on hilly ground among pine trees which keep it pleasantly cool. There is a self-service kitchen, a buffet and shops. The railway station is quite close, making it possible to visit the capital without having to drive there.

Podolsk, less than 40 km. (25 miles) from Moscow, stands on the Pakhra River and has large marble and limestone quarries which have been worked since the 18th century; its coat-of-arms, granted in 1781, carries two crossed pick-axes. It has several gardens and parks and many historical and literary associations. Around the turn of the century, Lenin lived here (on Moskovskaya Street) after returning from his exile. The house where he lived is now a museum. The little estate of Melikhovo, 13 km. (eight miles) from Chekhov (near Podolsk), was the home of Anton Chekhov, the great playwright, who lived here between 1892 and 1898. He was responsible for building the local school and worked as a doctor during a cholera epidemic. The museum contains his personal belongings and manuscripts; there is a monument on the estate.

97 km. (60 miles) from Moscow you reach Serpukhov, with important textile, paint and machine factories. 13 km. (eight miles) to the east, on the banks of the Oka River there is a large Nature Reserve, between the villages of Dubki and Luzhki. It has a special preserve for bison where these rare animals are carefully guarded and registered. Another interesting feature of Serpukhov is the riverside house of the Russian painter Polenov, with a fine collection of paintings by Repin and Levitan. The museum assistants practice flower arrangement and display samples of their art in which they use more than 500 flowers and herbs. The History and Art Museum on Chekhov Street, located in a century-old building, houses a collection of icons and Western European works of art.

Tula lies on either side of the Upa River, a tributary of the Oka. It is one of the oldest industrial settlements of Russia because of the early discovery of its rich iron ore deposits. The arms forged here were famous as early as the 16th century; the first small arms factory was founded by Peter the Great in 1712. By the end of the 19th century, there were 177 workshops and factories in Tula, turning out both weapons and samovars. Among its museums is the Museum of the History of Arms, opposite the kremlin on Lenin Prospekt. Established in 1724, it has a fine collection of Russian arms of all ages as well as many miniatures—well worth a visit.

Less than 16 km. (10 miles) from Tula is Yasnaya Polyana, the home of Leo Tolstoy. Tolstoy's grave, surrounded by oak trees, is in the estate park, on Stary Zakaz Hill. The house contains his portraits by Repin and Kramskoy, a library of 22,000 books in 20 languages, a phonograph presented by Edison, and many other souvenirs. The literary museum is in the building where Tolstoy ran a school for the peasants. Allow plenty of time for this beautiful place—you'll want to linger there and soak up the atmosphere, which really is something special.

As you return from the Tolstoy estate to the highway, you will come to Shchekino, a mining town, next on the road, then Plovsk and—within the Orel region—Mtsensk. Before reaching the town, there is a signpost indicating the road to Spasskoye-Lutovinovo, the Turgenev estate. The turning is marked by a bust of the writer and the estate is 5 km. (3½ miles) from the main road. The estate is now a branch of the Orel Museum with 8 halls of exhibits in the Exile's House (to which Turgenev was exiled in 1852–53 by Czar Nicholas I). The main part of the house was burned down in 1906 but the remaining wings have been restored as they were in 1881 when Turgenev last visited the place. Some of his works were written or completed here, among them *Fathers and Sons.* The park was laid out in 1808; it contains a church and mausoleum.

Mtsensk itself is a swiftly developing industrial city. It is also the scene of Leskov's famous novella, *Lady Macbeth of Mtsensk,* upon which Shostakovich based his opera.

Orel

The next stop is Orel (pronounced "Ahr-yol"), a district capital standing on the upper Orel River. Founded in the reign of Ivan the Terrible, it became an important settlement in the 18th century when the grain destined for Moscow was shipped from here. The first steam engine in Russia was set up in Orel. Today it is an important railway junction and industrial center. During World War II, it was occupied from 1941 to 1943 and liberated after the battle of Kursk.

The Turgenev Museum, of which the estate of Spasskoye-Lutovinovo is a branch, is at 11 Turgenev Street in the Trubitsyn House; it contains not only the great novelist's possessions, but also manuscripts and books left by his friend Belinsky, the critic and reformer. The Granovsky (Local Writers) Museum nearby is also worth a visit. In a hilly part of the town, it is housed in the former home of the historian and writer Timofei Granovsky. It is devoted to the work and life of Turgenev, Leonid Andreyev, the Nobel Prize winner Ivan Bunin and many other outstanding men of letters who were born or lived in the district.

Close to the city park you can visit the Tolstoy House, where the author worked on his novel *Resurrection.*

Orel has one of the Soviet Union's oldest permanent theaters, the Turgenev Drama Theater in Theater Square. It was established in 1815 as a theater of serf-actors by Count Kamensky on his estate a little way outside

Orel; the count, a real tyrant, kept careful records of any mistakes his actors made and punished them severely after each performance. Yet the
company thrived and in a single period of six months produced 18 operas,
15 dramas, 41 comedies, 6 ballets and 2 tragedies; the plays included not
only those of Shakespeare and Schiller and the Russian classics, but also
works by serf-playwrights. The present building dates from 1779 and originally housed the Town Council.

Continuing towards Kursk we first pass Kromy, where the third act
of Mussorgsky's *Boris Godunov* takes place; then come some villages with
unusual names: Kuri (Hens), Butilka (Bottle), Sayka (Breadroll). The district seat Ponyri is famous for its apples, known as *antonovskiye yabloki.*

Kursk and Belgorod

Kursk, one of the junctions of the Moscow–Yalta highway and railway
line, stands in the Dnieper basin, at the confluence of the Tuskor and Seym
rivers. Lying around the city is one of the largest iron ore fields in the
world. It was here that one of the greatest battles of World War II on
Soviet soil took place.

The chronicles mention Kursk as early as the 11th century. But the
Tatar invasion of 1240 destroyed it completely. It was rebuilt in the 16th
century as a frontier fortress against the Crimean Tatars. From the end
of the 18th century it was a district capital but until 1917 it remained mostly a market town. Today it is an industrial center.

The simple easy-to-use gridiron plan of Kursk's streets was preserved
in postwar reconstruction. The center of the city is Krasnaya Ploshchad
(Red Square), with the Lenin Monument and the more important public
buildings. The main streets all converge here, and along them we find the
outstanding sights. Among them, the St. Serge Cathedral in Gorky Street
(which runs parallel with Lenin Street) is the most interesting. It was built
in the years 1752–78 according to a design by Rastrelli. Inside you will
find a fine carved iconostasis, about 55 feet high.

The local picture gallery at 3 Sovietskaya Street (a side street off
Dzerzhinsky Street) is worth visiting; it has several canvases by Repin,
Shishkin, Levitan and Vereshchagin. In the Local Museum (6 Lunacharsky Street running parallel with Dzerzhinsky Street from Red Square),
there are some 50,000 items reaching back to the Stone Age.

The Ufimtsev Museum on Semenovskaya Street is devoted to the inven-
tor and aero-engine constructor who was born in Kursk. He built the
windmill standing beside his house, which is now a club for young engineers.

Traveling from Kursk towards Belgorod, at the 624 km. stone, you can
visit the Park of the Battle of Kursk, where relics of the long and bitter
conflict are preserved. Some deadly souvenirs still lurk underground: in
1957 an immense arsenal was discovered during excavations near the railway station. The shells and bombs have, of course, been rendered harmless.

At the 662 km. stone of the Moscow–Yalta road lies Belgorod, at the
foot of the chalk and limestone hills of the Northern Donets. Its public
buildings and apartment houses are all painted in light colors to suit its
name—"White City." Old Belgorod, which was already known in the 13th
century, was almost completely destroyed in World War II, but has now
been reconstructed and is a district center.

PRACTICAL INFORMATION FOR
SOUTH OF MOSCOW

WHEN TO GO. Late spring and the summer are the best times; the fall is fairly mild and reveals some lovely coloring in the trees.

GETTING THERE. By train: from Moscow (the Kursk Station). From the south via Kharkov.

By car. From Moscow by the Yalta (Number 8) tourist road. Yasnaya Polyana and several other smaller places are off the railroad and only accessible by car or bus.

Hotels and Restaurants

Belgorod. Camping. There is a camping site half a mile to the left of the main road, just south of the town. The site covers 7½ acres and has a buffet, self-service kitchen, hot showers, a laundry, post office, telephone, a sports ground equipped for volleyball and a car-wash and repair shop.

Restaurants. *Urozhai,* Parkovaya Street. *Belgorod Café,* on the main road at the corner of Khmelnitsky and Narodnaya streets.

Chekhov. There is a fairly good restaurant here. Also one at Melikhovo 13 km. (eight miles) away.

Kursk. *Kursk,* 2 Lenin Street (tel. 29–9389) with Intourist bureau and car park; or *Oktyabrskaya,* 72 Lenin Street. *Motel Solovinaya Roshcha* (Intourist), 142a Engels Street.

Camping. At the southern end of the city, 220 yards left from Engels Street, in the Solyanka Park on the River Seym.

Restaurants. *Kursk Café,* in hotel of same name; *Seym,* 6 Solyanka Street.

Mtsensk. *Tourist,* with restaurant and car park, both open all day. Can be visited only in transit on automobile tours.

Orel. *Orel,* 5 Pushkin Street (tel. 5–0589). *Rossiya,* 37 Gorky Street (tel. 7–4550). *Motel Shipka,* 169 Moskovskoye Highway (tel. 3–0704 or 3–0682). Five km. (three miles) out, Intourist facilities.

Camping. 2 miles from the city there is a camping site, off the main Moscow–Simferopol road, 330 yards to the left. Telephone and hot showers, car-wash and repair ramp are available; another 330 yards away on the Tson River there are facilities for fishing and bathing.

Restaurants. *Orlik,* 228 Komsomolskaya Street. *Oka,* 16 Lenin Street. *Tson,* between town and Orel camping site. *Druzhba,* Moskovskaya Street.

Podolsk. A better-than-average restaurant in the center of town.

Serpukhov. *Moskva,* Lenin Square. Can be visited only in transit.

Tula. *Tula,* Lenin Prospekt. *Central,* Sovietskaya Street. Can only be visited in transit.

Restaurant. *Moskva,* in Central hotel.

Voronezh. Try *Rossia* on Teatralnaya Street; then either *Voronezh* or *Don,* both on Plekhanovskaya Street.

Restaurants. Outside hotels, try the *Chaika.*

Yasnaya. The *Polyana* restaurant, just outside the gates of the Tolstoy estate.

PLACES OF INTEREST. Belgorod. *Local Museum,* 42 Frunze Street.

Kursk. *Ufimtsev Museum,* 13 Semenovskaya Street. *Picture Gallery,* 3 Sovietskaya Street. *Local Museum and Planetarium,* 4 Lunacharsky Street.

Melikhovo, 13 km. (eight miles) from Chekhov, is the estate of Anton Chekhov, now a memorial museum.

Orel. *Turgenev Museum,* 11 Turgenevskaya Street. Closed Fri. *Museum of Local Writers,* 7th November Street, No. 24 (in Granovsky's home). Closed Fri. *Local Museum,* 1/3 Moskovskaya Street. *Leskov Museum,* Oktyabrskaya Street (in the writer's house). *Picture Gallery,* 3 Sovietskaya Street.

Podolsk. *Lenin Museum,* Moskovskaya Street. This is a house where Lenin's family lived for some time during the 1890's.

Serpukhov. *History and Art Museum,* 87 Chekhov Street.

Spasskoye-Lutovinovo, the *home of Turgenev,* can be reached by a sideroad which branches off from the main road north of Mtsensk, at the 303 km. stone from Moscow. The turning is marked by a bust of Turgenev and a signpost indicating the way to his former estate.

Tula. *Local Museum,* 68 Sovietskaya Street; *Art Museum,* 44 Lenin Prospekt; *Museum of the History of Arms,* Lenin Prospekt, on the main Moscow-Yalta road, opposite the kremlin. Open 11–3, closed Mon.

Yasnaya Polyana is the *birthplace and home of Leo Tolstoy* lying a mile off the main road, 201 km. (125 miles) south of Moscow. The museum ticket office is at the main gates. Opening hours are 9–5; closed Wed.

THEATERS, CONCERTS, SPORT. Kursk. *Pushkin Drama Theater,* 1 Perekalsky Street; *Summer Theater,* Lenin Street, in the May 1st Garden, opposite the Kursk Hotel; *Puppet Theater,* 99 Lenin Street; *Dynamo Stadium,* 36 Lenin Street; *Trudovye Rezervy Stadium,* 58 Lenin Street, seating 17,000—the Local Agricultural Exhibition is held here between September and November. (Near the Kursk Camping site.)

Orel. *Turgenev Drama Theater,* Teatralnaya Square. *Puppet Theater,* 1/3 Moskovskaya Street in the 18th-century building of the Epiphany Church; *Hippodrome,* near Troitskoye Kladbishche (Cemetery).

Serpukhov. *Drama Theater,* 58/27 Chekhov Street.

Tula. *Gorky Drama Theater,* 51 Lenin Prospekt; *Youth Theater,* 10 Komintern Street; *Puppet Theater,* 78 Sovietskaya Street; *Zenith Stadium,* in the eastern half of the Kremlin area.

SHOPPING. Kursk. *Department Store,* 12 Lenin Street. *Jeweler's,* 2 Lenin Street.

Orel. *Department Store and Souvenirs,* 5 Moskovskaya Street.

USEFUL ADDRESSES. Kursk. *Bus terminal.* Marx Street (north) and 1 Engels Street (south). *Post Office.* Krasnaya Square. *Railroad station.* Privokzalnaya Square.

Orel. *Intourist Office.* 37 Gorky Street.

Byelorussia ("White Russia")

The "White Russian" Byelorussian Soviet Republic is bordered by Poland on the west, Lithuania and Latvia on the north and northwest, with the Russian Federation in the east and the Ukrainian Soviet Republic in the south. Its total area is some 80,154 square miles and it has mild winters and moderately warm summers. Forests cover more than one-third of its total area liberally watered by over 4,000 lakes. The great Dnieper (Dnepr), Niemen (Neman), Pripyat and Berezina rivers flow through it; its wild life includes moose, deer, wild boar, beaver and many species of game birds. It is well-supplied with oil and coal, peat and rock salts.

Byelorussia was once the site of many ancient Russian principalities whose centers were, at various times, Kobrin, Nesvizh, Minsk, Pinsk, Polotsk and Slutsk. It was the Byelorussians who finally defeated the Tatar and Mongol invaders in the battle of Koydanovo (now Dzerzhinsk), barring their way into Western Europe. Napoleon suffered a decisive defeat on the banks of the Berezina. It was the scene of long and bitter fighting during the Second World War and guerrillas were active here throughout the years of German occupation.

The republic has developed considerably both in agriculture and industry. It now has its own engineering, chemical, power and automobile industries. New cities have been built but there are still beautiful old towns, rich in history, to explore. The population (predominantly Slav) has its own distinctive culture, unusual cuisine (rich in mushroom dishes) and its own national drinks.

The major cities are along the Brest–Smolensk highway (which continues to Moscow) and include Brest, Kobrin, Beryoza, Ivatsevichi, Baranovichi, Stolbtsy, Dzerzhinsk, Zhodino, Borisov, Tolochin, Orsha, and Yurtsevo. The capital is Minsk.

Brest

Brest, a mile-and-a-half from the Polish-Soviet border, a busy railway junction and port on the Dnieper-Bug Canal, is also a fairly large center for food production and light industry. The Moscow–Warsaw–Berlin express passes through daily and regular passenger and freight trains leave here for Moscow, Kiev and elsewhere. The Warsaw–Moscow international highway intersects Brest; highways from Lithuania and Transcarpathia, etc., all converge on it.

Although it's quite a sizeable town, its sights can be explored in about two hours. Begin at the railway station, where a memorial tablet marks the defense of the city by a handful of partisans between June 22 and July 2, 1941. They held out for ten long days west of the station, then withdrew into a basement and finally fought their way through the encircling Germans, to reach the forests beyond where they joined the Byelorussian partisans.

From the station, an overpass leads to Lenin Street and a public park. At the main entrance, there is a monument to the war dead above a communal grave. From the park, Lenin Street leads to the Central Square,

where various municipal and regional institutions, a drama theater and the Museum of Local Lore are situated. Moskovskaya Street will take you to the newly-built districts of town.

The Brest Fortress is on the southwestern outskirts. It can be reached from downtown Brest by Lenin Street and the Street of the Brest Fortress Heroes. Here Soviet soldiers held out for almost six weeks in the underground casemates. By then, the German forces had rolled past Brest, advancing as far east as Minsk. The Soviet Army liberated Brest on July 28, 1944 and the fortress was almost reduced to rubble. It has been rebuilt—though it still bears battle scars—and turned into a museum.

An alley leads from the Street of the Brest Fortress Heroes to the northern gate of the Kobrinsky Bridgehead, the largest in the fortress. To the left of the Northern Gate is the Eastern Fort; outside the gate, the alley leads to the bridge spanning the right fork of the Mukhavets. Beyond the bridge is the citadel, erected on a natural island. Left of the alley is the Brest Fortress Defense Museum, opened on November 8, 1956. It has four sections spread over ten halls, illustrating the history of Brest and the Brest Fortress, the Nazi attack, the part played by the defenders of the Fortress in the 1941–45 battles, and, finally, one devoted to war veterans. Portraits, sculptures and photographs complement the historical exhibits and documentary films are shown.

Kobrin and Eastward

Kobrin, an ancient town, stands on either side of the Mukhavets River. It was first mentioned in the Ipatiev Chronicle in 1287 as a fishing settlement. At different times through the years it has belonged to Lithuania and to Poland. Here, on July 15, 1812, the Russians achieved their first victory (albeit temporary) over Napoleon. It is associated with General Alexander Suvorov, whose former estate is now the municipal park: the lime trees date from his time. A monument commemorating the 1812 war stands on the right bank of the river, near the highway.

The Suvorov Military History Museum on Suvorov Street is in the house where the general lived from 1797 to 1800. It contains exhibits associated with his life and activities.

Kobrin has been rebuilt since the last war and is now mainly notable for its food processing industry. The 60-mile-long Dnieper-Bug canal, linking the Mukhavets and Pina rivers, starts in its vicinity. The canal was built between 1775 and 1848 by serf labor; it was reconstructed after 1917 and then again after its partial destruction in World War II.

Beryoza—the name means Birch Tree—is about 97 km. (60 miles) east of Brest. Under Polish rule, the remains of a Catholic monastery here were utilized as a prison; years later, the Nazis established a large concentration camp on the site. Ivatsevichi, 153 km. (90 miles) from Brest, has a large saw mill, but nothing else to recommend it. Kossovo, ten miles further on, is an ancient settlement where the Byelorussian Academy of Sciences operates an experimental station for the study of the conditions and methods of farming on former marsh-land.

Baranovichi 193 km. (120 miles) from Brest, two miles off the main road, was founded in 1870 and is still an important rail junction. Before the Second World War it had a large Jewish population. The two main streets are Sovietskaya and Komsomolskaya. Near the railway station there are extremely dense pine woods and another pine forest has been turned into a park. Near its entrance stands the memorial to Sergei Gritsevets, "twice hero of the Soviet Union", who was killed in the Russo-Japanese War of 1939. Baranovichi (Baranowicze in Polish) has many associations with the Polish poet Mickiewicz.

Stolbtsy, about 225 km. (140 miles) from Brest, is a rapidly growing town, a mile off the main road on the upper reaches of the Niemen River. The countryside is particularly attractive around here: the wide Niemen Valley has meadows and woods stretching to the far horizon. The grave of Avenir Kostenchik, who captained the first heavy military aircraft of the Soviet Union, lies in Stolbtsy. Seven miles away is the village of Nikolaevshchina, birthplace of Yakub Kolas, the Byelorussian folk poet.

Dzerzhinsk (formerly Koydanovo) is a district center for the Minsk Region. Originally it was named after the Tatar leader Koydan who was defeated here in 1241. The first mention of the place is in the 12th century. It was renamed in honor of Felix Dzerzhinsky (1877–1926), born in the nearby village of Petrivolichi. Dzerzhinsky was a close associate of Lenin and a founder of the Cheka, the Soviet Secret Police. His monument stands in the center of town.

The Minsk Sea (a large reservoir) 16 km. (ten miles) before you reach Minsk offers good bathing facilities.

Minsk

Minsk, the capital of Byelorussia, is the republic's biggest industrial, scientific and cultural center. People first settled on the banks of the Svisloch 900 years ago and the city was marked on an old map of the world drawn by the famous Arab traveler Abu Abdallah Muhammed in 1154, when it was already a large and well-known city.

Much of the city was razed to the ground during the war, but the old quarter including the 17th-century cathedral has been under restoration since 1984. Today reconstructed Minsk is a center of heavy and light industry. Yet there remain some old areas of wooden houses, well worth exploring on foot. One lies directly behind the Yubileinaya and Planeta hotels; another is in the Victory Park. A subway opened in 1984. The Byelorussian Academy of Sciences and the Lenin University are the cultural centers; the 12 different faculties have around 35,000 students. The Polytechnical Institute is the second major educational establishment—the Byelorus Film studio is also located in Minsk.

Most foreign tourists usually stay in the Hotel Minsk, where the Intourist offices are housed. The hotel stands on one of the most attractive avenues in the city, the Lenin Prospekt. If you are staying at the Hotel Byelorus, you can easily reach Lenin Prospekt from Kirov Street by taking Krasnoarmeiskaya Street. The first cross-street is Karl Marx Street (running parallel with Kirov Street) and the second is the Lenin Prospekt.

The Lenin Prospekt is the direct continuation of the Brest–Moscow highway and leads from Pobeda ("Victory") Square straight south to the square in front of the railway station.

In the center of Pobeda Square there is a tall gray granite obelisk commemorating the heroes of World War II. It is part of a whole complex of monuments, the work of Zaborsky and Korol, and is a landmark of the city.

Starting along Lenin Prospekt towards the center of Minsk, you can see on the right hand corner of the square, on the river bank, the one-storied house in which the Russian Social Democratic Workers Party held its first congress in 1898. Today it is a memorial museum surrounded by a small park.

The Lenin Prospekt, which is lined with modern apartment houses and public buildings, now crosses the Svisloch River. The next crossing is named after Yanko Kupala, the great Byelorussian poet; a short distance beyond the corner to the right is the literary museum dedicated to his work and life. After passing it, you once again cross the twisting river to reach Kuibyshev Street to the west. After this crossing, you are on the square named after the Paris Commune, dominated by the Opera House. Turning left on Kuibyshev Street, cross still another bridge over the Svisloch, where Kuibyshev Street becomes Herzen Street. At its far end, off Svoboda Square, is the Museum of the Great Patriotic War. On Ratomskaya Street, off Parkovaya Magistral (near the Yubileinaya Hotel), is a monument which commemorates in Russian and Yiddish the Jews of Minsk killed in World War II. According to the Tel Aviv Museum of the Holocaust, this is the only such monument in the Soviet Union.

At the crossing of Lenin Prospekt with Krasnoarmeiskaya Street you will come to the other large square into which Lenin Avenue broadens, called Central Square. It is the heart of the city. If you walk down Engels Road, which crosses Lenin Prospekt on the far (north) side of Central Square, you can reach the Byelorussian Dramatic Theater (named after Yanko Kupala) at the Karl Marx Street crossing.

South of Central Square, the Lenin Prospekt widens out into Lenin Square, dominated by the huge Government Building, the largest and tallest building in Minsk. Lenin's statue (by Manizer) stands in front of it and across the way is the Lenin University complex.

The tourist might like to visit Zhdanovichi, a pleasant recreation area, about 18 km. (11 miles) from the city, with beaches, swimming pools, islands and lakes. Or Lake Komsomol, a dammed-up section of the Svisloch River, right in Minsk, with swimming (changing booths) and boating.

East of Minsk

Minsk is about 225 km. (140 miles) west of the border between Byelorussia and the Russian Republic. As you drive along the Intourist-approved motor route, you cross the Minsk and Vitebsk regions. The important places here are Zhodino, Borisov, Tolochin, Orsha and Orekhovsk.

Zhodino is in the heart of Byelorussia, 48 km. (30 miles) from Minsk, and manufactures heavy vehicles.

Borisov, on the Berezina River, is situated where the Brest-Moscow highway and railway cross the Berezina, the largest tributary of the Dnieper. An important industrial center, it was allegedly founded by Boris, Prince of Polotsk. Between the 14th and 18th centuries it belonged to Lithuania and Poland. North of the town, near the village of Studenka, where remnants of Napoleon's Grande Armée were hastily retreating across the Berezina, the French suffered a serious defeat. The center of the town lies between the river and the railway. Prospekt Revolyutsii, the main thoroughfare, runs through the town from the railway station to the Berezina. There is a fine park and a stadium.

About 560 km. (350 miles) from Brest the road crosses the Kiev-Leningrad Highway. Nearby is Orsha, an ancient Byelorussian town, which was first mentioned in chronicles in 1067 and became part of Russia in the late 18th century. Today it is a large industrial center.

Orekhovsk lies several miles north of the above mentioned highway crossing, in the direction of Leningrad. Once a small town surrounded by swamps, it is now a well-planned town, servicing a peat-burning power station fuelled from the neighboring Osinovsk peat mines.

The last town in Byelorussia on the way to Moscow is Yurtsevo, 116 km. (73 miles) from Smolensk.

PRACTICAL INFORMATION FOR BYELORUSSIA

WHEN TO GO. The best seasons for Byelorussia are spring and fall, though the summer months are pleasant and rarely too hot.

GETTING THERE. By train. The main railroad from Poland runs via Brest, Minsk and Borisov to Smolensk and Moscow.

By car. The main highway crosses the Polish frontier at Brest, then goes to Kobrin, Ivatsevichi, Stolbtsy, Minsk, Borisov, Malyavka and on to the east and Moscow.

By air. Minsk has an airport with direct flights from and to Moscow and Leningrad, plus other major Soviet cities.

TOURS are arranged through Intourist, mostly covering the cities and towns along the Brest-Smolensk highway. It is recommended that those traveling by car or bus should take three or four days for the trip from Brest to Moscow. Individual tours of the area south and west of Minsk can also be arranged. The tours include a visit to the Khatyn Memorial Complex, some 55 km. (34 miles) from Minsk. This marks the site of Khatyn village, where 149 residents were killed by the Nazis, and also commemorates the hundreds of other Byelorussian villages and hamlets burned down during World War II. It was set up in 1969, apparently as a propaganda distraction from Katyn, the site of the massacre of thousands of Polish officers by either the Soviets or the Nazis, according to who tells the story. You might like to make it clear to your Soviet guide that you know Khatyn is not Katyn—but be diplomatic about it. Elem Klimov's recent film *Come and See* is based in every harrowing detail on the fate of the Khatyn villagers.

There are excursions to the Minsk Sea—as the Zaslavskoye Reservoir is known—and to the Minsky camping site on the thickly forested bank of the Ptich River.

Hotels and Restaurants

Beryoza. *Beryoza,* Lenin Street.

Borisov. The *Borisov* restaurant, small but adequate.

Brest. *Intourist,* 17 Moskovskaya Street (tel. 5–1073). *Bug,* 2 Lenin Street. *Belarus,* 150 Shevchenko Boulevard. Only a one-night stay in transit allowed.
Restaurants. *Byelorus,* corner of Pushkin and Sovietskaya streets. Eating house at the Fortress open 10–6.

Kobrin. *Byelorus,* Svoboda Square. Can only be visited in transit.

Minsk. *Yubileinaya,* 19 Parkovaya Magistral (tel. 29–8835 or 29–8024). Modern highrise overlooking attractive square, is best, with 249 rooms. First class. *Planeta* (tel. 23–8416 or 23–8587), adjacent to *Yubileinaya,* 317 rooms. *Minsk,* 11 Leninsky Prospekt, first class with 370 rooms.

Minsky Motel and *Camping Site,* 18 km. (11 miles) outside Minsk on the road to Brest. Set within a forest, this motel has a restaurant and souvenir shop selling local Byelorussian crafts. Nearby is a car service and filling station, post office, open-air cinema and sports ground. (Tel. 99–5140, 22–6380.)

Restaurants. Apart from the hotels, try any of these: *Kamenny Tsvetok,* 12 Tolbukhin Street. *Leto,* 8 Pervomaiskaya Street. *Neman,* 22 Lenin Prospekt, best. *Potsdam,* 2 Lenin Street. *Raduga,* 1–13 Kirov Street. *Teatralnoye,* 34 Gorky Street.

PLACES OF INTEREST. Baranovichi. *A local museum* displays Byelorussian folk art and costumes. (We have elsewhere mentioned the memorial museum at Novogrudok devoted to the life and work of Adam Mickiewicz.)

Brest. The *Regional Museum of Local Lore,* 34 Lenin Street; the *Museum of the Brest Fortress Defense,* Street of the Brest Fortress Heroes (take buses nos. 1, 5 or 12); *the Regional House of Folk Art,* 1 Komsomolskaya Street.

Kobrin. The *Suvorov Military History Museum,* 16 Suvorov Street.

Minsk. *World War Two Museum,* 25a Lenin Prospekt, also known as the Museum of the History of the Great Patriotic War, with 25 halls. *Local History and Folklore Museum,* Karl Marx Street. *Yanko Kupala Memorial Museum,* Yanko Kupala Street. Open 10–5, closed Fri. Housed in the former home of the Byelorussian poet (1882–1942). Ten rooms. *Yakub Kolas Museum,* 66 Lenin Prospekt. Open 9.30–3.30, except Sat. This was the home of another outstanding Byelorussian poet (1882–1956).

Museum of the First Congress of the Russian Social-Democratic Party, 31a Lenin Prospekt. Open 11–6, closed Fri.

State Art Museum, 20 Lenin Street. Open 11–7, closed Thurs.

In nearby **Grushevski,** a small village, important archeological excavations have continued for many years.

THEATERS AND CONCERTS. Brest. The *Drama Theater* is on Lenin Street.

Minsk. The *Trade Unions' Palace of Culture* in Central Square contains a theater. Among several other theaters are the *Bolshoi Theater,* 7 Ploshchad Parizhskoi Kommuny, where opera and ballet are performed and which is the home of the Capella Byelorussian Choir and the Byelorussian Folk Choir; a *puppet theater;* the *Yanko Kupala Byelorussian Theater,* 7 Engels Street; the *Gorky Russian Drama Theater,* 5 Volodarksy Street; a *Youth Theater,* 26 Engels Street; and a *circus* on Lenin Prospekt.

The *Philharmonia Concert Hall* is at 50 Lenin Prospekt.

SHOPPING. The best place for shopping is **Minsk.** The local department store is at 21 Lenin Prospekt. There is a *Children's World Store* at 12 Lenin Prospekt, a gift shop *(Podarki)* at 32 Kolas Street, a sports shop at 16 Lenin Prospekt, a jeweler's at 22 Lenin Prospekt, an antique and art shop at 19 Lenin Prospekt and a florist in the same building.

THE BALTIC REPUBLICS

Estonia, Latvia and Lithuania

The three present-day republics of Estonia, Latvia and Lithuania have a long and checkered history. Lithuania's is perhaps the most distinguished and is characterized by her ancient association with Poland. The other two, Estonia and Latvia, have for centuries been intermittently at the mercy of a variety of powerful neighbors—the Teutonic knights, then the Danes, Poles, Swedes and the Russian Czars and latterly the Soviet Union itself. They enjoyed a brief period of precarious independence between the two World Wars and are now, all three, Soviet republics.

Lying along the Baltic coast in the northwestern corner of the U.S.S.R., in many ways they are different from the rest of this vast empire. They use the latin alphabet (though street signs are also in Russian), their traditions are completely Western, their religion Catholic and Protestant. Of the three, Estonia is the smallest but its capital, Tallinn, offers the most interesting medieval architecture. Latvia, the traditional "work-shop of the Baltic," was an important industrial area in Czarist times, and Riga, too, has some extremely fine architecture. Lithuania, the "land of amber," on the great Amber Road that ran from the Baltic to the Mediterranean, has supplied this mysterious and rare product of the seashore from time immemorial. It has picturesque landscapes, fine monuments in its historic capital, Vilnius, and a magnificent carillon in Kaunas.

Estonia

Estonia lies on the shores of the Baltic and the Gulf of Finland, between the Russian Republic to the east and Latvia to the south. It has an area of 17,413 square miles, including 800 islands and 1,500 small and large lakes. Its population is almost one-and-a-half million of whom 75 percent are Estonians, a people belonging to the Finno-Ugrian group which also includes the Finns and the Hungarians. The 20 percent Russian population lives mostly in the cities and in the oil shale basin. On the western shore of Lake Chud there are some predominantly Russian settlements; these are the descendants of the Orthodox "Old Believers" who fled here in the 17th century. Now, Estonia is the test-bed for many of Mr Gorbachov's economic reforms and social experiments. In 1987 there were over 50 self-financing cooperative enterprises.

Tallinn

Tallinn, the Estonian capital, is the republic's largest industrial and cultural center. It is also an important Baltic harbor. Its climate is tempered by the sea; the coldest month is February, the warmest July. While the days are very short in winter, in summer they stretch well into the nights, especially in the June "White Nights."

In many ways Tallinn is one of the most attractive cities in the Soviet Union. A wonderfully-preserved city of the old Hanseatic League, it has as many atmospheric streets as a really good stage setting. Just across the Gulf of Finland from Helsinki, it is the goal of swarms of Finnish tourists, not always well behaved, and seems to Russian visitors, who also arrive in their thousands, a "little version of the West." Indeed, it may well be the city in which tourists from the West feel most at home. Finnish television even shows B.B.C. programs!

It's hard to lose your way in Tallinn. All you have to do is to use the tallest tower, the steeple of the Oleviste Church, as a landmark. You can start from the Viru Hotel on Viru Square (Viru Väljak). Going down Pärnu Maantee or Estonia Puiestee, past the October 16th Park, the Monument to the Victims of the 1905 Revolution and the Estonian Opera and Ballet Theater, you arrive at Victory Square (Voidu Väljak), which is one of the centers of the New Town. True, the word "new" simply means in this case that these quarters are outside the ancient city walls. They grew up in the mid-19th century. Here you will find the Russian Drama Theater, and the headquarters of the Estonian Association of Fine Arts.

Climbing the promenade up Harju Mägi (hill), you will come to a bastion with a red roof called Kiek-in-de-Kök (Look-Into-The-Kitchen), built in 1470, when it was the tallest edifice in Estonia. From it, watchmen were able to peer into the kitchens of the houses below. It still has some iron cannonballs in the massive walls, souvenirs of the siege of 1577. To the right of the bastion you will see the onion domes of the Alexander Nevsky Cathedral (1894–1900). The nearby tower is the Long Hermann (Pikk Hermann), which now houses government offices.

Before entering the castle area, continue west along Noukogude Street. On the castle side you will see the former Governor's Garden, on the other

FINLAND ·HELSINKI

Gulf of Finland

TALLINN

Kohtla-
Jarve

·Rakvere
Narva

Khiuma

ESTONIAN S.S.R.

Lake
Peipus

·Parnu   Viljanda   ·Tartu

Sarema

Valga·

*Gulf
of
Riga*

Ventspils

Valmiera

Cesis

Pskov

Tukum·   RIGA
Kemeri
Jurmala   LATVIAN S.S.R.

Liepaja·   Jelgava

Rezekne·

Palanga·   Telsiai·

Klaipeda   Siauliai   Daugavpils·

Panevezys·

LITHUANIAN S.S.R.

Ukmerge·

Sovetsk
·Neman   Kaunas

KALININGRAD
Baltiysk   ·Chernyakhovsk   Trakai· VILNIUS

Kapsukas   Minsk

RUSSIAN S.F.S.R.

THE BALTIC
REPUBLICS

—— major roads   – – – republic borders
•—•—• railways   ■ republic capitals

0 miles   50
0 km   50

Druskininkai·   BYELORUSSIA
S.S.R.

Linda Hill. Linda was a legendary lady, the widow of Kalev, hero of an Estonian national epic: an episode of the folk poem supplied the inspiration for Welzenberg's statue on Linda Hill. The semicircular Deer Park (Hirvepark) on one side of the hill is a favorite walk for the people of Tallinn.

From Noukogude Street a stairway leads down on the right to a favorite recreation area, the Toompark, which contains a remnant of the old castle moat, now called Schnelli Tiik. The park stretches as far as the railroad station, where it meets Bastion Square (Tornide Väljak); it has a number of horseshoe-shaped towers in which marksmen used to be stationed. The Patkulli Trepp (stairs) lead up to Castle Hill; their upper end emerges into the courtyard of 3 Ravhakohtu Street, a classical-style building dating from 1792. From here you have a fine view over Bastion Square and of the sea.

Castle Hill

You are now on the Toompea, Castle Hill. In the Middle Ages it was divided into the Great and the Small Castle. The palace, which today houses the Council of Ministers, was the Small Castle, and the rest of the Toompea's area the Great Castle.

"Long Hermann" and the other two surviving bastions of the fortress (Pilstiker and Landskrone), together with the 60-foot-high western, northern and eastern walls, belonged to the Small Castle. This was built in the early 13th century, soon after the Danish conquest, but the system of fortifications you see today dates from the 14th century and was built by the Teutonic Knights to strengthen their hold over the territory they had purchased from the Danes. The Small Castle changed hands several times and underwent several alterations—the most important at the end of the 18th century, during the reign of Catherine the Great, when its eastern wall was demolished to make way for a new Baroque building, and the moat was filled in. Much of the Great Castle was destroyed in the great fire of 1684, and the houses that replaced it were built for the most part in the classical style. The most important surviving monument is the Toomkirk (Cathedral), which was first mentioned in the 13th century. But it, too, has undergone numerous alterations and refurnishings. It has a fine Baroque altar and many interesting tombs.

The most characteristic quarter of Tallinn is the Lower Town. From the courtyard of No. 12 Kohtu Street and the little platform at the end of the same street the whole panorama of the Lower Town unfolds in front of you. Towers and steeples rise above the cluster of red tiled roofs. Below is the bastion of Pikk jalg ("long leg"), opposite the Town Hall: to the left, some distance away, rises the steeple of the Oleviste Church, a familiar landmark. This was the center of ancient Tallinn: the Pikk jalg, whose fortified gate was the only entrance in the Middle Ages to the Toompea; the Town Hall Square, meeting-point of seven streets, and beyond it, the Vanaturg, the Old Market, reached by a short street from the Town Hall Square.

The streets radiating from the Vanaturg all have a history. Vene Street leads to the harbor; Viru Street started where the two gate-bastions now stand; along Harju Street cattle were driven to graze for many centuries. Vene runs left, Viru straight ahead, Harju to the right. Niguliste Street runs from the corner of Harju towards the Pikk jalg and Lühike jalg ("short leg") gates, across Harju Hill.

The steeple of Oleviste Church is flanked by two streets, running parallel, towards Pikk jalg Street. One of them is Lai (Broad) Street, the other Pikk (Long) Street, which once linked the old city center with the harbor.

The Lower Town

You can start an exploration of the Lower Town at the 15th-century Lühike jalg gate, at the junction of Lühike jalg Street and Pikk jalg Street. Next to it you'll notice an iron-studded wooden gate (17th century). Going along Pikk jalg Street you pass the grey limestone of the remains of the former city wall: this was built in 1454 by the municipal council of the Lower Town as a defense against the masters of the castle. The square gate-house of Pikk jalg dates from 1380.

Turning along the flank of Castle Hill towards Bastion Square, follow Nooruse Street, where you can see clear traces of the former fortifications of the city, three-quarters of which are still standing. They were begun in the 13th century, and in their present form date from the 15th–16th centuries. Some of the bastions were named after the town councillors who were the keepers of the keys. But the Saunatorn Tower in Nooruse Street commemorates the baths of the nearby convent. The 13th-century convent's site is now a school, while its medieval cellars are topped by a soft-drinks factory. The convent has in fact housed a school since the 17th century. The assembly-hall of the high school, divided into two Romanesque sections, was once the convent's refectory. The convent church later became an Orthodox cathedral. Its main feature is the Baroque iconostasis, a gift from Peter the Great. Turn left from Nooruse Street into Lai Street. No. 29, a characteristic 15th-century burgher's mansion, is well worth a visit. The entrance to the Museum of Natural History is from its courtyard. The Museum highlights Estonia's fauna, flora and mineral wealth. There is a rich *Herbarium Balticum.*

Passing along Lai Street, turn right into any cross-street and walk down to Pikk Street. Turning left into Pikk Street you'll see "Stout Margaret," a large bastion, built between 1510 and 1529. This was the right-hand defense of the Suur Rannavarar, the Great Sea Gate. "Stout Margaret" and the adjoining building house the Municipal Museum which explores the history of Tallinn since the 17th century. (Earlier history is displayed in the permanent "Old Tallinn" exhibition in the Town Hall.) "Stout Margaret" also houses a large naval museum.

Turning back along Pikk Street, notice to your right the 375-foot-high steeple of the Oleviste Church, named after St. Olaf, King of Norway. Destroyed and rebuilt several times, and restored between 1820 and 1840, it is a fine example of the Gothic style. Continuing along Pikk Street, notice No. 26 (on your left). Now a House of Culture, it used to be the seat of the Society of Blackheads, founded in 1399 by the sons of Tallinn merchants and other bachelors. The members of this society supplied the city's cavalry in times of war. The next house, No. 24 Pikk Street, was once the home of the Olaf Guild, which was founded in the 13th century as a religious body and later became a society of non-German-speaking craftsmen. It survived until 1698.

No. 17, on the other side of the street, was the center of the Great Guild, formed early in the 14th century by the richest merchants; only its members could be elected to the city council. The house was built around 1410 and is a splendid example of Northern Gothic. The white cross against a red background on its facade was the coat-of-arms of both the city of Tallinn and the Great Guild. Inside there are fine vaulted ceilings and rich-ly-decorated columns: the ceremonial hall was the scene of great festivities, including the election of the "Countess of May", a medieval beauty contest. The "Count of May," her consort, had the privilege of freeing one prisoner from the municipal jail. The building was also used for theatrical performances until the beginning of the 20th century. Today it houses the Historical Museum of the Estonian Academy of Sciences. This museum presents the history of the Estonian people from prehistoric times to the present day. It has vast resources of coins, parchments and other docu-ments, archeological finds in abundance, articles of folk art and craft, and over a thousand weapons.

At the next corner you'll see on your left the Church of the Holy Spirit, built at the end of the 14th century, when it was known as the Town Hall Chapel—the oldest Tallinn church that still stands in its original form. It has an old, beautifully-carved clock, installed in 1684, and a magnificent wooden altar, made in 1483 by Bernt Notke, a Lübeck master. Just past the Church of the Holy Spirit, turn left into any of the four streets leading off Pikk Street, and you will find yourself in the Raekoja Plats—Town Hall Square. (Two of these streets are the winding Voorimehe and Saiakäik, so narrow that only pedestrians can use them.) Entering the square by Saiakäik ("White Bread Passage") watch out for a remarkable wrought-iron sign bearing the traditional snake symbol of the apothecary. This is the municipal pharmacist's, in use since 1422.

Town Hall Square was originally called Market Square; excavations have shown that it was a market as long as a thousand years ago. The remains of a 12th century sewage system have also been found, together with pieces of a triumphal arch erected in 1711 for the visit of Peter the Great. The Town Hall, begun in 1317–74 and completed in 1401–4, has been preserved almost intact in its original Gothic form and still serves as the City Hall. Perched on top of its tower you can see a weather vane carved in the shape of a Tallinn municipal guard; this is the Vana (Old) Toomas—or rather, its replica, for the original is kept in the municipal museum inside the Town Hall.

Another fascinating walk starts at the Niguliste (St. Nicholas) Church. This church, built in the 13th century, was dedicated to the patron saint of seamen. In October 1982, only days before restoration had been com-pleted and the church was due to open as a museum a serious fire de-stroyed the steeple and caused internal damage. The steeple has since been rebuilt and the church reopened.

Leaving the church you can walk down Niguliste Street (away from Castle Hill), across Harju Hill as far as Vana Turg and then turn right down Viru Street to Viru Gate. Medieval Tallinn had six gates, all of them bastion-forts with moats and drawbridges. The city walls were protected by an extra moat and other defensive fortifications. In Viru Street you will see two bastions of the 15th-century outer gate.

Continuing your walk, you will soon find yourself back in the New Town, in the Park of October 16, with the Estonian Opera and Ballet The-ater close by. From the parking lot outside the theater a broad promenade leads to Lenini Puiestee (Boulevard) where you can take a No. 1 or No. 3 tram at the stop marked "Forumi" to Kadriorg Park.

Excursion to Kadriorg

Kadriorg (Kateriyna Org, Catherine's Valley) was built in 1718 at the request of Peter the Great in honor of his wife Catherine. It was designed by the Italian architect Niccolo Michetti. One of the original features of the park is the Swan Lake with the statue of F. Kreutzwald, the poet who gave the Estonian national epic, the *Kalevipoeg,* its final form. The Kadriorg Palace was built in 1718–24 in the Baroque style typical of the age. Erected on a hillside, it has two stories in the front and one at the back. The pillared balcony was added later. Today it houses the Estonian State Fine Arts Museum which boasts a fine collection of the Estonian realist school as well as some canvases of Repin and Breughel the Elder. There is also a permanent exhibition of 20th-century Estonian art and sculpture. A few hundred yards away is the House of Peter the Great (open May to October, 11 A.M. to 5 P.M., except Tues). It is a very modest, simply-furnished building with only three light, spacious rooms.

One of the modern buildings in Kadriorg Park, on the Pirita Tee, is an open-air bowl created in 1960 for the Tallinn Song Festival. At 12 and 24 Pirita Tee, beyond the bowl, you will see the pavilions of the National Economic Exhibition. The Pirita Gardening Commune also has a permanent display (closed Sun).

Tallinn's beach and water sports center is at Pirita which you can reach by buses Nos. 1, 8 and 34. There is swimming in fine weather in the sea, but if the waves are too high, you can walk over to the mouth of the Pirita River, where there is a pleasant beach on both banks, with good facilities and cafes. The popular Pirita-Kloostrimetsa motor-racing circuit passes through the pine-woods at the river mouth. Nearby is the huge yachting marina, constructed for the 1980 Olympics, and linked with Tallinn by a new highway. About 15 km. (9 miles) west of Tallinn along the coast is the Estonian Ethnographic Museum. Old peasant farmhouses have been reconstructed in the woods and on Sunday mornings there are folk-dance displays.

Tartu is Estonia's second largest city, and lies on the Emajogi River (which flows into Lake Peipus), some 32 km. (20 miles) from its mouth and about 177 km. (110 miles) from Tallinn. Its German name was Dorpat.

It is Tartu's cultural reputation that is the chief attraction for visitors, tourists and scholars alike. The city is famous for its excellent University which is housed in an early 19th-century classical-style building and has expanded into several specialized institutes. The University has had many outstanding philologists, scientists, physicians and philosophers among its alumni. It has an excellent library, founded in 1802 and housed in the sacristy of the Cathedral of Tartu Castle. The University's Botanical Garden, established in 1803, also attracts many visitors.

Tartu's medieval monuments were destroyed partly by the great fire in 1775 and partly during the Nazi occupation. One of them, destroyed in 1944, was the 14th-century Ivan Church, with three naves.

Parnu and Narva

Pärnu, founded in 1251, is a harbor town and also an important health-resort at the mouth of the River Pärnu on the Bay of Riga. From Tallinn it is 30 minutes by air (summer flights only) and about 2 hours by bus.

Excavations have proved that this site was inhabited in the early Stone Age; many flints, axes and fishing hooks have been found and are on display in the local museum.

Pärnu has a northern climate, with a mild winter and a short and cool summer with a fair amount of rainfall; its two-mile-long sandy beach is nevertheless very popular with Estonians. The town has an important medicinal feature—the mud dredged from the gulf of Riga—and several sanatoria have been built.

Narva lies on the banks of the River Narva, 13 km. (eight miles) from its mouth on the Gulf of Finland. It has been the scene of great battles— the Russian defeat by the Swedes in 1700–1 and the Red Army victory on February 23, 1918. Narva is about 193 km. (120 miles) from Tallinn, 4 hrs. 30 mins. by bus. Its oldest monuments are the castle (14th century) and the Fortress of Ivangorod (built in the 15th century by Czar Ivan III). The City Hall and the former Stock Exchange date from the 17th century, and there are various towers and bastions of the same vintage.

Latvia

The Latvian Republic lies on the Bay of Riga between Estonia and Lithuania. Its inland frontiers also border on Byelorussia and the Russian Republic. It has an area of 24,695 square miles. Of its population of 2.5 million plus, more than 60 percent are Latvians, a quarter Russians, and the rest Byelorussians and Poles. In Czarist times Latvia was one of the most highly industrialized areas of the empire. In 1899 almost half the population of Riga was German.

Riga

The most important Soviet Baltic port after Leningrad, Riga has a long, historic past. The capital of the Latvian Republic, it lies at the mouth of the Daugava River (also known as the Western Dvina). The center of the city is about ten miles from the Bay of Riga. Although Riga is a sizeable city covering almost 90 square miles, its clear layout makes it easy to explore and the TV tower currently under construction on one of islands in the river will be an easy-to-spot landmark. A subway is planned for the future.

A good starting-point for exploration is the River Daugava which is 1,150 feet wide in the city center. Three bridges span the river; most traffic uses the middle one, which is also served by public transport.

The left bank, Pardaugava, has always been the industrial side. On the way from the airport to the city center you will pass the Dzeguzkalna Park; the 60-foot-high hill in the middle is the highest point in the city. The park also has a large open-air theater. The next "green spot" is a cemetery, and behind it the 40-acre University botanical garden. The first river bridge has a landing stage and you will also see several water sports centers here.

Riga's historic sights are on the right bank of the river. If you cross the second bridge you will come to the main seven-mile-long thoroughfare, the Lenin. Lenin Street, called Alexander Street in the last century, divides the right bank into almost-equal areas, cutting across the Vecriga, the Old

City. This district stretches from Komjaunatnes Krastmala, the Daugava Quay, to Padomju Boulevard, which runs parallel with it; the other two edges are marked by Gorky Street (parallel with Lenin) and 13 Janvara Street. Perhaps you will get a clearer idea of the Old City if you remember that it stretches along the canal between the river and the boulevards, in a semicircle that starts and ends at the river Daugava. The short canal was formerly the castle moat. Vecriga is a typical old city; some of its streets are so narrow that you can touch the walls of the houses on both sides.

But beyond Padomju Boulevard, farther away from the river and the Old City, the boulevards and main streets running parallel with the Padomju are wide and shady: the three biggest are Raina, Komunaru and Kirov. Kirov Street crosses Lenin Street at the Latvia Hotel and emerges, beyond Gorky Street, into Kronvalda and Eksporta boulevards, the continuations of Padomju. The other end of Kirov Street runs into Kr. Barona Street (parallel with Lenin Street). Beyond Kr. Barona Street and parallel with it runs Suvorov Street, the continuation of 13 Janvara Street.

If you arrive in Riga by train, you'll find yourself outside the station on the corner of Raina and Suvorov Streets and you will easily find your way. Walking down Suvorov Street toward the river, the first main crossroads you come to is Padomju; turn right and you will find, some way down the street, the Hotel Riga. To reach the Hotel Latvia, simply walk up Kirov Street to Lenin Street, and you will see its huge high-rise block. The somewhat unattractive skyscraper behind the station, incidentally, is the seat of the Latvian Academy of Sciences.

One Castle, Three Museums

Riga offers a wide variety of architectural styles: Romanesque and Gothic, Renaissance and Baroque, Classical and ultramodern. Let's start our walking tour from the old castle:

The castle of Riga (Pils) stands on Pionieru Square, where Gorky Street and Komjaunatnes Krastmala meet. It houses the Riga Pioneer Palace and three museums: the Historical Museum, presenting Latvia's history; the Foreign Art Museum, containing works of Dutch and German masters as well as French graphics and sculpture; and the Rainis Literary Museum. Jan Rainis was Latvia's greatest poet, but the museum is not devoted exclusively to him, other writers are represented and there is a section on the history of Latvian theater.

From Pionieru Square turn into Torna Street. No. 1, on the corner of Arsenal Street, is the Arsenal, a long, low building (erected 1828–32), which includes part of the former city wall and the "Maiden Bastion." Passing it, turn right into Komjaunatnes Iela (not to be confused with Komjaunatnes Krastmala, the riverside walk). On your right is the Church of St. James (or Jacob), originally built outside the city walls in the 13th century. Its parishioners were the Latvian and Livonian inhabitants of the nearby settlements. It has been remodeled several times; but its tall sanctuary and three-naved basilica are still in their original form. The 240-foot-high steeple bears the traces of 16th- and 18th-century restorations. The church opposite is that of Mary Magdalene.

Turning left into Vestures Street at St. James's Church, walk to the corner of Maza Pils Street. Nos. 17, 19 and 21/23 Maza Pils Street, jointly called the "Tris Brali" (Three Brothers), are typical examples of the architecture of medieval Riga. No. 17 is a 15th-century house—the oldest surviving residential building in Latvia. The benches on either side of the gate end in a vertical stone slab bearing the "sign of the house." The ground floor of the house consisted originally of a single room with an open fireplace at its far end. Holes were cut through to the cellar and the upper stories, with a wooden hoist above the openings for the transport of goods into the warehouse. In 1687 a bakery was established here; it has been carefully restored.

Continue back along Maza Pils Street to Komjaunatnes Iela, turn left, then right at the first corner into Smilsu Street, then turn left into Aldaru (Brewer) Street. At the end (No. 11 Torna Street) you come to the Zviedru Varti, Swedish Gate, the only surviving city gate of Riga. It was built in 1698 as an addition to the 13th-century city walls, the adjoining bastion and the neighboring houses. The name "Swedish Gate" refers to this whole complex.

Returning to Smilsu Street, turn left and continue towards the Gunpowder Tower. This was first mentioned by the chroniclers in 1330. Erected on oak foundations, it was rebuilt in 1650, and now houses the Latvian Revolutionary Museum.

Opposite the Gunpowder Tower, turn right into Kaleju Street and walk down towards the river as far as the corner of Zirgu and Meistaru Streets. Turn down Meistaru Street to Amatu Street, pausing en route in front of No. 6, now the home of the Philharmonia; it once housed the Liela Gilde (Great Guild). It has been rebuilt several times though the 14th-century "Munster Chamber," scene of many festivities, has been preserved. In 1521 a smaller chamber was added, the "Bridal Suite". It has many features typical of the late Gothic style.

Continuing down Amatu Street (away from Meistaru), turn right. A few more steps, and you come to 17 Junija Square and the magnificent Lutheran Cathedral (now a museum and possibly still closed for repair). Its building was begun under Bishop Albert in 1211 and 500 years were to pass before it was completed, which accounts for the mixture of architectural styles, including Romanesque and Gothic elements. The Russian Orthodox convent next to the Cathedral is still working. It also houses a Museum of Navigation and History of Riga (entrance from 4 Palastas Street) with good archeological and numismatic collections. The Cathedral itself has a world-renowned organ which still draws large crowds for weekly recitals. It is a marvellous 6,768-pipe structure, built by German craftsmen in 1884 and still one of the largest in the world.

From Palastas walk down Muzeja to Komjaunatnes Krastmala, the river quay. Turning left onto the promenade, look out for a plain residential building just before the corner of Lenin Street. This was once the mansion of Peter the Great, who came to Riga in 1711 and lived here for a while. Originally the Czar had a hanging garden on the roof, where he exercised his "green thumb."

Continue along the quay as far as Marstalu Street (the third turning after Lenin Street); then, turning left into Marstalu Street, notice No. 21, a fine Baroque mansion built in 1696 by Dannenstern, a rich burgher. Further up Marstalu Street, No. 2/4 is the former Reitern mansion (1685), also built by a well-to-do merchant. It still has its original 17th-century facade, with a delicately ornamental portico.

Returning along Marstalu Street past the 18th-century Protestant church, keep turning left, first into Great Kaleju Street then into Sarkanas

Gvardes Street. Notice Nos. 5, 7, 9 and 11, and also No. 10 Vecpilsetas Street. These are 17th-century warehouses. Their frontages are quite narrow but they go a long way back. On the ridge of the double roof you will see the drum of a hoist, and over each main entrance the relief of animals—camels, elephants and other quadrupeds. These served as identifying signs.

From Vecpilsetas Street you can walk down to Audeju Street, turn left, then right at the next corner into Skarnu Street and you will find yourself back in the Middle Ages. The first building on your right (24 Skarnu Street) is the Romanesque-Gothic Church of St. John, first mentioned by the chroniclers in 1297. As it was in a built-up area by the time it was enlarged in 1330 the buttresses had to be placed inside the church. Four alcoves were thus formed and they accommodated the side-altars. At the end of the 15th century the interior was decorated with star-vaults and the church's northern wall was heightened by a 100-foot-high, graduated tympanum. At the end of the 16th century the church was lengthened: to the Gothic nave a new part was added with three naves whose Tuscan pillars display Renaissance features. The Baroque altar dates from the 18th century.

Next door to St. John's church, at 22 Skarnu Street is the Eka Convent, Ek's Home for Widows (Ek was a Mayor of Riga). Built in 1435 as a temporary shelter, it was transformed into a dower house at the end of the 16th century. Its original structure, wooden staircase and former open fireplace have all survived. There is a memorial plaque to the charitable mayor on the facade.

The next building, 10/16 Skarnu Street, was erected in the 13th century. This is St. George's Church, one of the oldest religious edifices in Riga. In the 15th century it became a poorhouse, in the 16th a warehouse. At the end of the 17th century a vaulted passage was added running from the courtyard to the street.

Turning back along Skarnu Street you will see on your right a monumental church. Its main entrance is on Vecrigas Square. This is the 13th-century, late-Gothic Church of St. Peter, patron saint of Riga. Its elegant steeple was the tallest structure in the Old City until Intourist built the 27-story Latvia Hotel overlooking the City and topping the steeple by three feet, to the fury of many of Riga's citizens.

Between the palaces bordering Vecrigas Square there are glimpses of the Daugava embankment. Passing between the palaces, turn right, and the first corner is Lenin Street. Turn up this street and, after passing the Russian Drama Theater and reaching the corner of Padomju Boulevard, you have come to the edge of the Old City.

One final word on the Old City: if you have the chance, stroll through it on a Sunday morning and you will be pleasantly surprised at how many churches are open for worship, and amazed how crowded they are. There are over a dozen Lutheran, Russian Orthodox and Roman Catholic Churches still in use. As well as the Orthodox convent we have mentioned, there is a Catholic seminary with 30 students. A single synagogue, on Peitavas Street, serves all of Riga's 28,000-strong Jewish community, many of whom still speak Yiddish, which has practically died out in other parts of the Soviet Union.

Roaming the Boulevards

Pausing at the corner of Lenina and Padomju, notice at the beginning of Raina (Rainis) Boulevard the Statue of Liberty. Turning left out of Lenin Street, walk into Bastejkalns Park (Bastion Hill) which was built on the site of the former fortifications. It has a fine waterfall, which is illuminated at night. On the far side from Padomju Boulevard, the park is bordered by the municipal canal—a pleasant place to stroll, but beware, sitting on the grassy canal bank can lead to a 5-rouble fine!

Follow the canal north across Gorky Street into Kronvalda Garden, flanked by Kronvalda Boulevard, a continuation of Padomju. The building on the corner of Gorky Street is the Latvian State Drama Theater, where Gorky supervised the production of *The Lower Depths*, in 1904.

On Eksporta, the continuation of Kronvalda Boulevard, notice the Vestura Garden on your right. Peter the Great himself helped to plant it in 1721. In 1873 the first Lativan national song festival was held here. The triumphal arch at the entrance was transferred from Lenin Street in 1935; it commemorates the Russian victory over Napoleon in 1812.

Leaving the Vestura Garden, walk back either along Eksporta or along the parallel Sverdlov Street to Kirov Street; then, turning left, continue south along Kirov which is the outer line of the park and boulevard ring around the Old City. The residential streets beyond it were mostly built in the second half of the 19th century.

No. 10a Gorky Street is the Latvian State Art Museum. Further down Kirov Street you'll pass Komunaru Park on your right. No. 34 Lenin Street the Latvian Supreme Court, is one of the 70 palaces which the Latvian architect Baumanis designed in the 19th century.

Continue along Kirov Street past the Latvia Hotel to the Kirov Park which was laid out in 1816. The park has a rose garden, fountains, an open-air concert-platform, cafes and playgrounds. Turn right out of Kirov Street into Kr. Barona Street. On the corner of Raina Boulevard is the Museum of Natural History. Raina Boulevard and the parallel Komunaru have several important institutions; the Conservatory on the corner of Raina and Kr. Barona, opposite the museum, the University at No. 13 Raina, the Aeroflot office on the corner of Lenin Street (Raina 11) and opposite, on 19 Lenin Street, the Central Post Office. Raina 7 is the Riga City Soviet—the City Hall.

The two important features of Padomju Boulevard are the State Opera and Ballet Theater (No. 3) and, some distance along the other side, at No. 36, the Hotel Metropol.

The Pantheon of Riga

One of the moving, though rather grim, sights of the Latvian capital is the double Pantheon—the Bralu, Cemetery of "Brothers" (or Heroes) and the Rainis Cemetery.

At the bus terminal take No. 4 or 9 to Bralu Kapi, the Bralu Cemetery. The cemetery entrance is by the Berzu Aleja, which branches off on the left. When the road divides into three, continue along the middle one which takes you straight to the entrance of the Bralu Kapi. At its far end is a statue of a female figure symbolizing Latvia; many of the unknown soldiers who fell in battle are buried here.

As you leave the Bralu, you will see on your right the entrance to the Rainis cemetery. Here is the red marble tomb of the great Latvian poet; behind the Rainis monument several outstanding Latvian artists and writers are buried.

Riga's Parks and Resorts

The 500-acre Mezaparks—laid out in 1949—is Riga's main park. It contains a Zoo, an amusement park, the National Economic Exhibition and a Pioneer Railway run by children. There are several open-air theaters and, on Kiso Ezers (Lake), a number of boathouses. The park is accessible from the city by water bus along the Daugava and the Kiso Lake: from the stop outside the two cemeteries by bus No. 30: and from the Old City by tram No. 11, which starts from Gorky Street and runs via Padomju and Kr. Barona.

The "Skansen," the open-air Museum of Peasant Life on the shores of Lake Jugla, occupies almost 200 acres. Lake Jugla is linked by a canal with Lake Kiso; the two lakes are divided by Lenin Street. You can reach Jugla Park by taking buses No. 1, 18 or 19 at the bus terminal, getting off at the Balozi stop and walking down the road that branches off to the right. This brings you to the entrance to Jugla Park.

Riga's seaside beach, Jurmala, is a separate district of the capital, several miles from the city. Over 100 trains daily run there from the main station (Note: permission is sometimes needed to travel there). Jurmala extends for ten miles along the shore of the Gulf of Riga as far as the Lielupe River; it's a two-mile-wide belt of pines and dunes, with sanatoria, hydrotherapy clinics, boarding houses, rest homes, children's camps and small weekend houses. Jurmala is recommended especially for those suffering from high blood pressure; it is also an ideal holiday spot. There is a branch of the Historical Museum here, an open-air theater, and facilities for water sports.

Beyond Jurmala, five km. (three miles) from the Gulf of Riga and about 43 km. (27 miles) from the capital, is the forest resort of Kemeri, which can also be reached by local trains from Riga.

Liepaja is an industrial center and an excellent winter harbor about 225 km. (140 miles) west of Riga. It is an ancient city, mentioned as long ago as 1263 as Portas Liva, because it was surrounded by groves of lime trees.

Kaliningrad

The region of Kaliningrad has, at time of writing, no Intourist facilities and is therefore not visitable as part of the normal tour programs. The area, between Lithuania and Poland, is a mild, lowland countryside, verging on the humid, with fertile soil and extensive forests. Although geographically isolated from the Russian Republic, it forms a part of it.

The city of Kaliningrad, once called Königsberg, was the seat of the dukes of Prussia, who were crowned there. During the 18th century it became the capital of East Prussia and a long-time a bone of contention between Russia and Germany. The city was captured from the Germans, in April 1945, after a two-month-long siege, during which almost all the old town was flattened, including the cathedral with its tomb of Kant. The new city, built in the residential northwestern suburbs, is an important industrial center, as well as being an icefree port, linked with the Baltic by a canal.

Lithuania

Lithuania, known officially as the Lithuanian Soviet Socialist Republic, lies along the Baltic Sea immediately north of Poland, south of Latvia, and across from Sweden. It borders Byelorussia in the east and the Kalingrad Region (former East Prussia) in the west. The land area of 25,173 sq. miles is home to 3.5 million people, 80% of them ethnic Lithuanians and the remainder mainly long-standing Poles and more recent Russian arrivals.

The Lithuanian language belongs to the Baltic group of Indo-European languages (some linguists consider it to be the closest present-day equivalent to the original Indo-European language). The language is different from the surrounding Slavic and Germanic languages, but is very similar to Latvian.

Lithuania's long history reaches back to its establishment as a state in the 14th century. By the 15th century the Grand Duchy had extended southeast as far as the Black Sea. A later union produced the Polish-Lithuanian Commonwealth that lasted for over 200 years until its disintegration in the 18th century. An independent republic formed in 1918 and lasted until 1940. Historically, Lithuanians are closer to Poland and thus to the Latin/Roman Catholic form of Western culture than to the Germanic and Protestant-based culture of the other Baltic countries.

The land consists of flat plains and rolling hills. Most of it is suitable for agriculture, and about half the people live on the land. The urban population is mostly employed in manufacturing: electrical and electronic equipment, food processing, metal work, etc. The climate is moderate with a mean annual temperature of 43°F, with July the warmest month. Summer is never very warm and can be rainy, while a light overcoat is adviseable in spring and fall. Winters can be cold, although the Baltic Sea does tend to moderate the temperature.

Tourists can stay for one night in Klaipeda and Kaunas, and for longer in Vilnius. Intourist also provides one-day trips to Kaunas, Trakai, Druskininkai, and occasionally a few other locations.

Vilnius

The capital covers 100 sq. miles and has a population of about 700,000 inhabitants. Its name first appeared in 1323, although archeological findings indicate inhabitation as far back as 5th century B.C. By the 16th century it was one of the biggest and most important of East European cities. It lost its importance and splendor with the decline of the Grand Duchy of Lithuania, and fell to the plunder of invaders.

The city is on the Neris River and is surrounded on the south and east by wooded hills. The southern, left bank is the ancient and modern center of Vilnius and contains the most interesting sites. The right bank has apartments, the Intourist hotel Lietuva, and a sports arena.

Gedimino Square in the city center is dominated by a neo-Classical building built in 1784. Once the Roman Catholic cathedral, it now houses an art gallery containing mainly 17th- to 19th-century paintings. Its chapels include that of St. Casimir, the only Lithuanian saint; his remains have been removed to Sts. Peter and Paul church. Recent excavations showed that the cathedral is on the site of an ancient pagan temple dedicated to Perkunas, the god of thunder. The remnants of this and early Christian churches are being preserved, and the caskets of royalty, high clergy, and noblemen have been uncovered, some in the excavations of 1931–3 when the cathedral structure was being reinforced (royal insignia disappeared from the cathedral at this time). The lone tower in the square was the cathedral bell tower; it dates from the 13th century. On Sundays the former cathedral is used for organ recitals and concerts.

Castle Hill (Pilies Kalnas) sits at the confluence of the rivers Neris and Vilnele. The bastion on the top is a restored corner tower of the original 14th-century castle. It can be reached from Gedimino Square by a path up the hill. The roof gives a good view, and the tower contains an exhibition of Vilnius' history. At the bottom of the hill (Vrublevskio Street 1) is the Museum of History and Ethnography, the city's main historical museum.

The Old Town

The town's large, interesting old quarter was constructed over five centuries. It stretches south from Gedimino Square, away from the river, with Gorky Street as its main axis. Although the old quarter is being restored, it's still in a state of disrepair. Unlike those of Tallin and Riga, it is not of Germanic origin; the architecture is a synthesis of various West European influences, with Italian dominant.

The old quarter is best explored by foot. In a few hours you should be able to see the most interesting places. From Gedimino Square, take Tallat-Kelpsos Street to Kutuzov Square, where the late-Classical palace was the residence of Vilnius bishops. Later reconstructed in the Russian empire style (1824–32), it became the residence of Russian governors and now houses the Artists' Union. From Kutuzov Square, follow Universiteto Alley to the University area.

The university was founded as a Jesuit College in 1570. In 1579 the university charter was granted by the Polish-Lithuanian king Istvan Bathory and by Pope Gregory XIII: it is the oldest university in the Soviet Union. There are three major inner courtyards: Sarbievijaus, P. Skargos, and M. Pocobuto (this one has a former 17th-century observatory). The arcades give a Renaissance feel to the place. Among the distinguished students here were two famous Poles: the poet Adam Mickiewicz and the recent winner of the Nobel Prize for Literature, Milosz.

Nearby, the recently restored St. John's church now houses the museum of the university's history. From here, turn left on Gorky Street and continue to Pilies Alley. Walk down this quaint street to St. Anna's church, a beautiful example of 16th-century Gothic; it's built with 33 different shapes of brick and still used for Catholic worship. Beside it stands the 16th-century church of St. Bernard. 11 Pilies Street is a memorial museum to Adam Mickiewicz. Most of the architecture here is 17th- and 18th-century.

Return to Gorky Street via Biliuno Street, past the Renaissance church of St. Michael (Svietimo 13), built by 1625, and now housing the Museum of Architecture. Turn left on Gorky Street as far as Antokolskio Street which passes through the old artisan district. Several small souvenir shops (Suvenyrai) and restaurants are along here. "Senas Rusys" is probably the best of these old town restaurants.

The Dailes Muziejus Lithuanian Art Museum is in the former City Hall at 55 Gorky Street; it holds a permanent exhibition of modern Lithuanian art. The hall was rebuilt in 1783 in neo-Classical style, complete with Doric columns. 69 Gorky Street is the massive, stylishly eclectic home of the Philharmonia.

The street ends at the Medininkai Gate—the only one still standing. The gate and wall, once 1 ½ miles long, were built in the early 16th century; the Medininkai is a good example of Gothic and Renaissance architecture. Its traditional name is Ausros Vartai (The Gate of Dawn), and it houses a painting of Our Lady of Vilnius, famous since the 17th century. The shrine is above the street in a small chapel reached through the side door.

Return to Gedimino Square by walking back down Gorky Street to Muziejaus Street. The modern building at no. 2 is Dailes Parodu Rumai (Art Exhibition Hall), a museum of contemporary art with an arts and crafts store. From the Museum of Fine Arts, Muziejau Street leads north toward the river. During World War II this is where the Nazis established the Vilnius Ghetto, between Garelio, Traku, and Muziejaus streets—before the war Vilnius had been an important Jewish cultural and religious center. Turn right on Traku Street, then right on University Alley; reach Gedimino Square via Tallet-Kelpsos Street.

The New Town

If you want to tour the New Town on foot, Gedimino Square is again a good starting point. Walk down Lenin Prospekt, past the Vilnius Hotel. A detour to the right, along Vienuolio Alley, takes you past the popular Dainava restaurant/nightclub to the Opera and Ballet Theater, a good example of modern architecture. Continue to the river and over the bridge to reach the Intourist hotel Lietuva. Returning to Lenin Prospekt you pass a small square containing a statue to the writer Zemaite, and then you come to Lenin Square. This is where the leaders of the 1863 uprising against Russian rule were executed. Across the street from the square are the KGB headquarters, said to have three levels of cellars that extend under the square.

Turn left on Kudirkos Street and climb up Tauras hill for a good view of the city. One of the buildings at the top is the Wedding Palace where marriages are performed. Go left on Kalinausko Street, left on Roziu Street, and descend the stairs to Cvirkos Square. Kapsuko Street leads back to Lenin Prospekt. The tour covers about two miles.

The more interesting places out of the center can be visited by taxi or bus. Taxis are generally inexpensive and are plentiful, especially after working hours when individual drivers can ply for private trade. There are 32 designated taxi ranks; taxis do not cruise looking for passengers.

One of the town's most interesting monuments is the white church of Sts. Peter and Paul. It's reached by walking from Gedimino Square. As you cross the Rover Vilnele, with Olandu Street behind you, you will see the church (it's a 20-minute walk though a less interesting area so you may prefer to take a taxi). The original 14th-century building was renovated in 1668–84 and is still used for worship. It's the most characteristic example of Baroque architecture in Lithuania, with a splendid interior worked on by 200 artists under the direction of the Italian masters Galli and Peretti. It contains more than 2,000 life-size statues and reliefs, as well as the tomb of St. Casimir.

Vilnius is surrounded by several areas of pre-fabricated high-rise apartments. One of these areas, Lazdynai, is considered one of the more successful and its architects were awarded the Lenin Prize. It can be reached by taxi.

Kaunas, Trakai, Klaipeda, Kernave, and Druskininkai

Kaunas is an important industrial center and was the temporary capital between the two wars. Architecturally it is not as interesting as Vilnius. It is a much newer city, with many of its buildings constructed in the 1930s. The old part has ruins of an 11th-century castle at the confluence of the rivers Nemunas (Niemen) and Neris. In City Hall Square the old civic building is now used as a wedding palace. The restored square houses several restaurants, and a souvenir and craft shop.

The basilica nearby has a Gothic chapel that's worth seeing. Further on, the Ciurlionis Museum houses the work of Lithuania's most famous artist, M. K. Ciurlionis, who painted, and composed music, at the turn of the century. Some claim that Kandinsky was influenced by his art. In the nearby Historical Museum there's also a Carillon recital at 11 A.M. on Sundays and holidays.

Laisves Aleja, the main shopping area, is closed to traffic. At the end of the street the Museum of Stained Glass and Sculpture is housed in the former Russian Orthodox Church. Kaunas is a very Lithuanian city and Russian is rarely heard, unlike in Vilnius. The city is also very proud of its Zalgiris basketball team, the winner of the European championship in 1986; it has also been the Soviet Union champion on several occasions.

Trakai, 29 km (18 miles) southwest of Vilnius, has a rebuilt 14th- to 15th-century castle on Lake Galve. Though an important city in the days of the Grand Duchy, it is a small town now. Trakai consists of a cluster of old buildings, including an interesting synagogue, and houses built by Karaites, a tribe of Turkic people who originally served as bodyguards to the Lithuanian dukes. It's a venue for international boating events, and has a training center for local oarsman.

Klaipeda (Memel in German) is an important port on the Baltic. The city has some old buildings of Germanic origin; its newest attraction is a Marine Museum and Aquarium. From Klaipeda a bus excursion to Palanga (29 km or 18 miles to the north) will take you to excellent beaches, crowded in summer with visitors from all over the Soviet Union. Also visit the Museum of Amber in an old mansion surrounded by beautiful parkland. A river resort about 160 km (100 miles) from Vilnius is Druskininkai, a typical Soviet spa with highrise buildings, on the River Nemunan.

At Kernave, about 60 km. (40 miles) north of Vilnius, the ancient capital of Lithuania was unearthed in 1986. It dates from 1279, and will become a museum with cobbled and wood-paved streets, and the remnants of log houses.

PRACTICAL INFORMATION FOR
THE BALTIC REPUBLICS

WHEN TO COME. To **Estonia:** Definitely in the summer, during the "White Nights" in June. Riga (**Latvia**) should be visited early in August for the Festival of Song. The climate is varied but at the end of July and the beginning of August there is little wind and the sea is at its warmest though it never rises above 60°–62°F (17°–18°C). In **Lithuania** July is the warmest month and the only time when you may find it too hot. August is the rainiest.

GETTING THERE. Tallinn. You can reach Tallinn in about 9 hours by train from Leningrad (1 hr. 15 mins. by air) and 19½ hours from Moscow (1 hr. 30 mins. by air). There are connections to all major Soviet cities. Finnish and Soviet steamers sail regularly on the Tallinn-Helsinki Line. You can also travel by car or coach from Leningrad. Tartu is 3–4 hrs. by train from Tallinn, 3 hrs. 15 mins. by bus, 1 hr. by plane (summer only).

Riga is 14 hrs. 45 mins. from Moscow by train (1 hr. 45 mins. by plane), and there are air connections with most other Soviet cities. You can travel from Tallinn by plane, train or Intourist coach.

Vilnius is 1 hr. 30 mins. from Moscow or about 1 hr. from Leningrad by air. Also trains from Moscow (13 hrs.), or from Warsaw.

HOTELS AND RESTAURANTS. A note on regional food: It is generally agreed that the restaurants and the service are better in the Baltic Republics than anywhere else in the U.S.S.R. Each of the three republics has its own specific cuisine; ask the waiter for advice.

Hors d'oeuvres are very good, usually the best part of the meal. Soup and local specialties also will be good, plain meat dishes might be disappointing. Order several different hors d'oeuvres plates to share.

Local specialties in Estonia: *sult* (jellied veal), *taidetud basikarind* (roast stuffed shoulder of veal and *rossolye* (vinaigrette with herring and beets). In Latvia: meat patties, *Alexander Torte* (raspberry-filled pastry strips). In Lithuania *skilandis* (like Canadian bacon) is a local snack meat, in summer cold soup *salti barsciai*. Various potato-based dishes are very popular: *oepelinai* (dumplings), *bulvinai blynai* (potato pancakes), *vedarai* (potato sausage). Also various ravioli-like dishes—*virtinukai*—are popular. *Black Balsam* is a *very* strong local spirit—try it with caution!

Hotel restaurants vary throughout the area, but those in new hotels are generally better than hotels in other parts of the Soviet Union. In Tallinn several U.S./European-style bars (*baar* in Estonian) have opened, serving Western drinks for roubles, but they are pricy. See below.

Riga. *Riga* (Intourist), 22 Padomju. 300 large rooms, centrally located; outer rooms, near main square, get noisy traffic din. Hotel has aged. Food only fair. *Latvia,* (also Intourist establishment), 55 Kirov Street, (tel. 21–1781). 365 rooms, 27-floor skyscraper, 1st class and fairly new; near Old City.

Metropol, 36 Padomju Bulvar (with restaurant); *Daugava*, 38 Kugyu Street.

Restaurants. *Pearl of the Sea (Juras Perle* in Latvian), on the beachfront at Jurmala resort. Beautiful location jutting out over the sand, overlooking Riga Bay. Good food. Western-style floor show and dancing. Be sure to reserve through Intourist in advance. A modest charge is made for reservation. Try seafood fish soups. More expensive than most Soviet restaurants, but not highpriced by world standards.

Blow Wind! (Put, Vejni in Latvian), 18–20 Jauniela Street, around the corner from the Dom Cathedral, off 17th of June Square. One of the best restaurants in the Soviet Union, with excellent cooking, intimate atmosphere, good service. Try *okroshka,* a milk soup with onions, herbs, cucumbers, sour cream; *mestinsh,* a Latvian lemonade-honey drink; and any entrée the waitress recommends. No entry without reservation made through Intourist. Do it when you arrive in Riga. There is a charge for the reservation. Prices are higher-than-average for U.S.S.R. Well worth it. Personally recommended by Editor.

Astoria, 1 ½ blocks from Riga Hotel at top of department store, 16 Audeju Street. Latvian specialties. Good food. Dancing.

Apollo Café, young people's gathering place, with Latvia's best combo.

Staburags, 55 Suvorov Street, is good for fish specialties.

Others: *Kavkaz,* 13 Merkela Street; *Tallinn,* 27 Gorky Street; *Moskva,* 53 Kirov Street; *Daugava,* 7 Stuchkas Street.

Health restaurants: 65 Kirov Street and 9 Suvorov Street.

Cafes. Recommended are *Kafe 12 Stulyev; Petercailis,* 25 Skarnu Iela, open-air in small intimate precinct near cathedral; *Ridzene,* Skarnu Iela.

Tallinn. *Viru,* Viru Square (tel. 65–2070/2081). Scandinavian-style, highrise hotel (22 floors) on edge of old town in downtown Tallinn. Rated deluxe. Finnish-built and furnished. One of the best hotels in the Soviet Union. *Olympia,* 33 Kingissepa Street. 424 rooms on 26 floors. Deluxe rating. *Tallinn,* 27 Gagarin Street (tel. 44–1504). 114 rooms. Rating: first class. Service and food are good. A modern 5-story hotel.

Also: *Palace,* 3 Voidu Väljak; *Europa,* 24 Viru Street.

Restaurants. *Viru Hotel* restaurant, top floor, lovely view, very acceptable food. Bar with selection of western drinks. Often reserved for groups. Reservations essential.

Vanatoomas, at 8 City Hall Square, in the cellar. Very good Estonia food, attractive decor, attentive service. In all, a treat. There are other cellar restaurants near and in the old town; exploring them is recommended.

Others: *Flower Pavilion,* a cafe-restaurant on outskirts, with excellent sandwiches and pastries. *Gloria,* 2 Müürivahe Street. *Kannu Kukk,* 75 E. Vilde Road. *Kevad,* 2 Lomonosov Street. In Pirita, a suburb by the sea, *Pirita,* 1 Merivälja Voidu Väljak.

Cafes. *Moskva,* 10 Voidu Väljak. *Tallinn,* 48 Harju Street, with a garden, on Harju Hill.

Bars. *Mundi* at 3 Mundi Street, cover charge of around 2 roubles include one tiny *Kokteil.* More *Kokteily* cost at least 1 rouble 50 kopeks a shot, and there's a queue to get in. You can buy tickets in advance—before 4 P.M. you stand a chance!

Vilnius. Tourists usually stay in the new *Lietuva,* a good hotel with Intourist services and several restaurants, bars, and a nightclub. Some smaller hotels are also satisfactory: the *Vilnius* (20 Lenin Prospeckt), *Neringa* (23 Lenin Prospekt), and *Draugyste.* The older Intourist *Gintaras* is less desirable.

Restaurants. In the *Lietuva: Seklycia* for ethnic food; *Panorama* bar (22nd floor), restaurant and dancing area. Elsewhere: *Vilnius,* Lenin Pr.; *Draugyste,* M.K.Ciurlionio Street 86; *Gintaras,* Sodu Street 14. For old town atmosphere: *Senas Rusys,* Garelio Street; *Medininkai,* M.Gorky Street 84; *Lokys,* M. Antokolskio 8 (serves moose and boar meat). Otherwise, try the privately run *Stikliai,* near Garelio and Antokolskio streets.

Among the coffee shops, try *Neringa,* Lenin Prospekt 23, as well as some adjacent to restaurants; also *Literatu Svetaine,* Lenin Prospekt 1. Food is also served in nightclubs: in the *Lietuva* hotel; at *Dainava,* Vienuolio 4; and at *Erfurtas* (nightclub is separate from main dining room); and at *Saltinelis,* Zirmunu 106. The nightclub programs are not very interesting.

PLACES OF INTEREST. Kaunas. *M.K. Ciurlionis Gallery; Historical Museum* Donelaitis Street; *Velniu Muziejus* (collection by a private artist of mainly folk art of devil images). Stained glass gallery located in former Russian Orthodox church, (Laisves Blvd.). *Old City Hall* and square. *Catholic basilica.*

Palanga. Amber museum and park.

Riga. *Latvian History Museum, Rainis Literary Museum* and *State Museum of Foreign Art,* in the castle.

Latvian State Art Museum, 10a Gorky Street. Paintings, graphics, sculpture.

Latvian State Natural History Museum, 4 Kr. Barona Street; the oldest in the Baltic area, open 11–5, closed Mon.

Skansen Open-air Museum of 17th–19th century peasant life, beside Lake Jugla. *Museum of Navigation and the History of Riga,* 4 Palastas Street.

Rumsiskes. *Skansen* open-air museum of Lithuanian peasant life. Folk song and theater in summer.

Tallinn. *Gallery of the Estonian Artists' Union,* 6 Voidu Väljak. *State Museum of Natural History,* 29 Lai Street (open 12–7, except Tues.; closed on the last day of every month).

City Museum, 17 Vene Street (open 11–6, except Tues.; Sat. 11–5).

Historical Museum of the Estonian Academy of Sciences, 17 Pikk Street, (open 12–6, except Wed.; Tues. 12–4).

State Fine Arts Museum, Kadriorg Palace, (open 12–7 daily, except Tues.).

Museum of Applied Arts: Pottery and other handicrafts. *Estonian State Maritime Museum,* Pikk Street, in "Stout Margaret" tower. *Estonia Open-air Museum* at Rocca al Mare, 4 km. out of town. Folksong and dances in summer.

Trakai. The *Castle* and *old town.* Boat trip on the lake.

Vilnius. *Museum of History and Ethnography.* Vrublevskio 1, near the Castle. *Art Museum,* 55 Gorky Street.

Art Gallery (Cathedral), Gedimino Square. *Art Exhibition Hall,* Muziejaus 2. *Architectural Museum,* 13 Svietimo Street.

Museum of Lithuanian Folk Art, 2 Rudninku Street. *Adam Mickiewicz Museum,* 11 Pilies Street.

Most Vilnius museums close on Mondays and/or Tuesdays. Check.

THEATERS AND CONCERTS. Riga. *Cathedral* for concerts and organ recitals. *Russian Drama Theater,* 16 Lenin Street. *Latvian Drama Theater,* corner of Kronvalda Boulevard and Gorky Street. *Conservatory,* corner of Raina and Kr. Barona Streets.

State Opera and Ballet Theater, 3 Padomiju Boulevard. *Open-air Theater,* Mezaparks; the scene of the Song Festivals.

Tallinn. *State Drama Theater,* 5 Pärnu Maantee. *Russian Drama Theater,* 5 Voidu Väljak. *State Opera and Ballet Theater,* 4 Estonia Puiestee. *Open-air Musical Theater,* (Lauluväljak), in the Kadriorg Park.

Tartu. *Vanemujne Theater.*

Vilnius. *Opera and Ballet Theater,* average standard. *Philharmonia,* Gorky 69, symphony and chamber music concerts; Sondeckis ensemble and Lietuva quartet are world class. A good city for jazz concerts. Two resident theaters performing in Lithuanian; one in Russian. You can get the dialogue taped in Russian in Lithuanian theaters. *Academic Drama Theater* uses a realistically traditional approach; *Jaunimo Teatras* (Youth Theater) is more experimental and has recently earned some notoriety, especially when directed by Nekrosius. *Art Gallery* (Cathedral) has organ recitals and orchestral concerts on Sundays.

SHOPPING. Amber, linen, and craft and folk art articles are the best buys in the Baltic states. Art objects such as paintings might also be of interest. No export permission is required for items purchased in the dollar shops; however, export permits are required for art objects, amber jewelry, and books purchased in roubles. This can be a problem unless you get local help. Articles exported with such permits also incur export duty of 100% of their value.

Kaunas. *Daile,* in the old Town Hall Square.

Riga. *Souvenirs:* 4 Lenin Street, 9 Teatra Street and Valnu Street (all foreign currency shops). *Souvenirs/jewelry:* 40 Lenin Street. *Arts and crafts:* 52 Lenin Street. *Maksla Art Gallery,* 20 Padomju Boulevard. Most shops close Mon.

Tallinn. The *Central Department Store,* 2 Lomonosov Street (gifts and folk art), *Souvenirs* at Voidu Väljak 8 (open every day), 27 Pikk Street (closed on Sundays), and 6 Viru Street (closed on Sundays). The hard-currency shops in Estonia are called "Turist." There are three in Tallinn: 2 Tekhnika Street, 29 Gagarin Street and 18 Tartu Road (newest and best). *Graphic Design,* a privately run small business, sells the work of good local designers, including stationery items and cards.

Vilnius. *Daile,* 1 Lenin Prospekt, handicrafts. *Souvenirs:* 31 Lenin Prospekt, 6 Antokolskio Street. *Dailes Parodu Rumai,* 2 Gorky Street, art and crafts. *Suvenirai,* 31 Lenin Prospekt and 6 Antokolskio Street.

USEFUL ADDRESSES. Riga. *Intourist:* 22 Padomju Boulevard, in the Riga Hotel. *Railway tickets:* 2 Suvorov Street, 6 Smilsu Street. *Aeroflot City Office:* 11 Raina Boulevard. *Bus terminus:* 13 Janvara Street, near the central station. *Boat landing stage:* Balasta Damvis. *Central Post Office* (long-distance calls): 19–21 Lenin Street. *Telegraph Office:* 33 Lenin Street.

Tallinn. *Intourist:* 27 Gagarin Street, 3 Viodu Väljak. *Rail ticket reservations:* 10 Olevijagi Street. *Air reservations:* 10 Voidu Väljak. (There is a half-hourly Aeroflot bus service from here to the airport.) *Central Post Office:* 20 Suur Karja Street. *Central Telegraph Office:* 9 Vene Street (open 24 hours). Long-distance calls.

Vilnius. *Intourist:* in Hotel Lietuna. *Aeroflot City Office:* 21 Lenin Prospekt. *Railway station:* Gelezinkelio Street (corner of Komjaunimo).

THE UKRAINE AND MOLDAVIA

Breadbasket of the U.S.S.R.

The Ukrainian Soviet Socialist Republic borders on Hungary, Czechoslovakia, Poland, Romania, and the Soviet Republics of Byelorussia, Moldavia and the Russian Federal Republic. The Black Sea forms its southern frontier; the resort area is described in our chapter on the Crimea and Southern Russia.

With an area of 232,046 square miles and a population of more than 50 million in 1983, the Ukraine is the second largest republic in population and the third in size in the U.S.S.R. Forty-six percent of the population is urban; three-quarters are Ukrainian, 21 percent Russians, the remainder Jews, Byelorussians, Moldavians and others. Ethnographically the Ukrainians are Eastern Slavs. They have a strong national consciousness and an independent history. Kiev is the capital.

Ever since the Kievan period of history, the Ukrainian regional dialect has had distinctive features, and Ukrainian is now a separate language—although Russian is also spoken to a greater or lesser extent in all the big cities except Lvov.

It was in Kiev that Christianity first found a foothold in the European part of the present U.S.S.R. (in Armenia and Georgia, Christianity is considerably older), when Prince Vladimir had his people baptized in the river Dnieper in A.D. 988. After the Tatar invasion and the decline of the Kiev Principality (13th and 14th centuries), the Ukraine was held by Poland and Russia, with sovereignty repeatedly changing hands; it was devastated, sometimes completely and sometimes in parts, by the Crimean Tatars. In the mid-17th century the Cossacks, the most militant of the Ukrainian

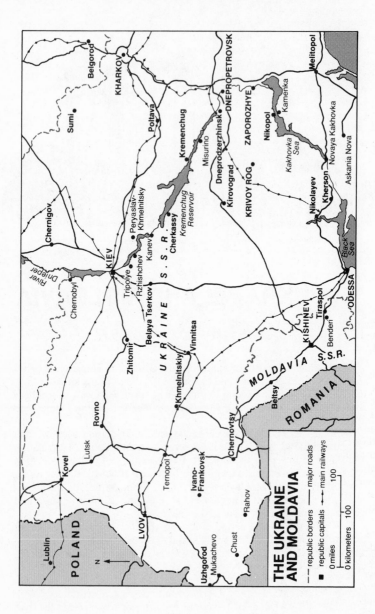

THE UKRAINE
AND MOLDAVIA

----- republic borders ——— major roads
■ republic capitals ←→ main railways

0 miles   100
0 kilometers   100

N ←

population, led by their Hetman, Bogdan Khmelnitsky, won independence from Poland and established their own state, occupying the central part of the modern Ukraine. In 1654 the new state was annexed to Muscovy. Ukrainian nationalism, with its demands for autonomy, had a strong revival early in the 20th century. During the Civil War of 1918–22, Germans, white Russians, Communists and various separatist groups struggled for control of the rich Ukrainian agricultural lands. Proclaimed the Ukrainian Soviet Socialist Republic in December 1917 it was one of the four original republics to form the Soviet Union in 1922. In 1939 the western part of the Ukraine, together with Lvov, until then a part of Poland, was returned to the republic, followed in 1945 by Transcarpathia, which had belonged to Hungary and Czechoslovakia. In 1954 the Crimea was transferred from the Russian Federal Republic and annexed to the Ukraine.

The huge Ukrainian Soviet Republic can be roughly divided into three zones: the forests bordering on Byelorussia in the north; the wooded steppe with oak and beech forests; and the treeless steppe zone with its fertile black soil. The climate is much warmer than that of central Russia. Both industry and agriculture are well-developed; there are also rich deposits of coal, iron ore, natural gas and oil.

The major cities are Kiev, Kharkov, Lvov, Dnepropetrovsk, Lugansk, Uzhgorod, and Mukachevo.

Kiev

Kiev, the capital of the Ukrainian S.S.R., has a population of over two million and is one of the most important industrial and cultural centers in the Soviet Union. It lies on both sides of the Dnieper River; the right bank (western) is hilly, the left an extensive flat plain.

Kiev has developed rapidly in recent decades, absorbing several suburbs, and on the eastern bank of the river a whole new industrial area, the Darnitsa, has sprung up. Machinery plants are the chief industry, with light industries and chemicals coming second in importance. Kiev is also a major road and rail junction, a great river port and a busy airport; and a traditional cultural center with excellent colleges and universities. It is the seat of the Ukrainian Academy of Sciences and numerous research institutes. Its museums are richly endowed, and the city abounds in theaters, opera, ballet and other cultural institutions and entertainments. It is one of the most ancient of "Russian" cities, the original settlement probably dating from the late fifth century, in the chronicles it is described as the "Mother of Russian cities."

Kiev suffered severely during World War II; many irreplaceable architectural and art treasures were destroyed and the city center systematically demolished. Extensive restoration and a 1500th anniversary in 1982 put Kiev firmly back on the map. But the city hit the headlines for all the wrong reasons in April 1986 when the nuclear reactor at nearby Chernobyl exploded. Scientists generally accept that the city is now safe for normal-length tourist visits.

Tours of Kiev—First Tour

Exploring Kiev is best done in four instalments. The starting point of the first tour is the Hotel Dnieper, where many Intourist groups are lodged. It stands at the eastern end of Kreshchatik, Kiev's main boulevard;

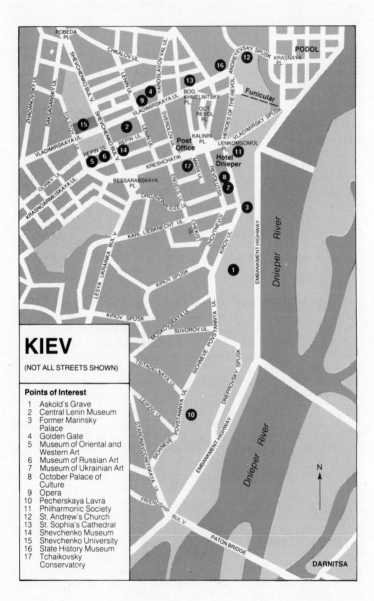

KIEV

(NOT ALL STREETS SHOWN)

Points of Interest

1 Askold's Grave
2 Central Lenin Museum
3 Former Marinsky Palace
4 Golden Gate
5 Museum of Oriental and Western Art
6 Museum of Russian Art
7 Museum of Ukrainian Art
8 October Palace of Culture
9 Opera
10 Pecherskaya Lavra
11 Philharmonic Society
12 St. Andrew's Church
13 St. Sophia's Cathedral
14 Shevchenko Museum
15 Shevchenko University
16 State History Museum
17 Tchaikovsky Conservatory

its entrance is on Lenkomsomol Square, a central location from which the main streets branch off like the points of a star. Opposite is the continuation of the Kreshchatik, the Vladimirsky Spusk, leading down to the river bank; the street to the north, named after the Heroes of the Revolution, leads to the famous St. Andrew's Church, and Kirov Street, leading south, also starts from this square. Lenkomsomol Square is an important traffic center and the terminus of several tram, trolley-bus and bus lines. The Kreshchatik subway station is nearby. An underpass with several branches crosses beneath the square. Opposite the Hotel Dnieper, left of the Vladimirsky Spusk, you can see the building of the Philharmonia (1882).

If you are staying at the Hotel Moskva, you can walk down to the Kreshchatik and turn right, and you will soon reach the Hotel Dnieper. From the old Intourist Hotel on Lenin Street you can get to the Dnieper Hotel via Lenin Street; and from the Hotel Ukraine, via Shevchenko Boulevard, walking downhill and then along the Kreshchatik.

The main street of the Ukrainian capital and its busiest thoroughfare are in a valley (there was once a deep ditch along here) and hills rise steeply on the left-hand side.

Clinging to the hill on this side is the 16-story Hotel Moskva; alongside the hotel October Revolution Street (Zhovtnevoi Revolutsii in Ukrainian) leads up to the top of the hill where the government buildings are situated. At the beginning of October Revolution Street, already a steep slope, you will find the October Palace of Culture. Constructed in 1838–42 as a finishing school for young ladies of the nobility, it was restored and enlarged in 1953–57; its main hall seats over 2,000 and is chiefly used for concerts.

On the other side, the Kreshchatik broadens into Kalinin Square, once the site of the southeastern gate of the city wall, built by Yaroslav the Wise. House No. 2 was once the Noblemen's Diet; today it is a Teachers' Club. The large and elaborate building on the corner of the square and Kreshchatik is the main Post Office.

On the left of the Kreshchatik, Karl Marx Street leads uphill, with the Tchaikovsky Conservatory on the corner. If you turn into Karl Marx Street and follow it up the hill, you come to Ivan Franko Square. Here stands the Ukrainian Drama Theater (built in 1898 and named after the great Ukrainian poet), which has followed the ideas and spirit of the Moscow Arts Theater in its presentation of modern Ukrainian plays.

Back down on the Kreshchatik, you will notice that the odd-numbered side has been made into a sort of parkway with trees, flower beds and benches. The buildings on this side are mostly apartment houses, cinemas, restaurants and hotels—while the other side consists mainly of public buildings and offices. The Kreshchatik underground station (center of the public transport network) is on the odd-numbered side; the largest restaurant in Kiev is in the same building. There is an escalator leading to the booking hall of the Metro (it costs five kopeks to use and this also gives you access to the trains). The escalator on the far side travels a much longer distance and takes you to the hill that rises above the river bank and forms Kiev's administrative district.

Continuing along the Kreshchatik, with its uniformly designed facades, you come to the passage which links the Kreshchatik and Zamkovetskaya Street. The entrance is under an arcade between two wings of a huge building. The building on the far side of the Kreshchatik (with the tall antenna) is the Kiev Radio and Television. On the passage side are Kiev's best shops, among them the Children's Department Store (Nos. 15–17).

Sverdlov Street starts on the opposite side; carrying on farther along the Kreshchatik you come to the Ukrainian Ministry of Culture and then the tall City Council building. A little farther on is the Central Department Store, at the corner of Lenin Street.

Lenin Street climbs the hill rather steeply. Opposite the Central Department Store is the Pervomaiskaya Hotel. At No. 5 Lenin Street is the Russian Drama Theater, which is named after the Ukrainian poetess Lesya Ukrainka. Next comes the Teatralnaya Hotel, and across the street, on the corner of Pushkin Street, the technical bookshop; No. 26 is the Intourist Hotel.

Returning to the Kreshchatik you will see an impressive stairway leading up the hillside to the Druzhba cinema. Then you come to the vast Central Market (Krity Rinok). You are now in Bessarabskaya Square, one of the most important in Kiev. The avenue on the right is the wide Shevchenko Boulevard, with Lenin's statue at the entrance.

The Kreshchatik continues as Chervonoarmiiska (Red Army) Street, another busy main thoroughfare. No. 12 is a permanent exhibition hall for Ukrainian artists. Passing Saksagansky Street you come to the Operetta Theater and then the massive block of the Central Stadium and Sports Palace. It has a covered swimming pool as well as facilities for ice hockey, handball, tennis, football and athletics. The Druzhba Narodov (Friendship of the Peoples) Boulevard, which starts here, leads to the mile-long Paton Bridge. This bridge links the historical quarters of Kiev with the Darnitsa district on the far side.

Second Tour—Monastery of the Caves

Leaving the Hotel Dnieper, turn right into Kirov Street. Next to the hotel is the sociology department of the Ukrainian Academy of Sciences. The building also houses the Institute for the History of Literature and the ground floor is the Academic Bookshop. Still on Kirov Street, climb the slopes of the hill that rises above the Dnieper. The right side of Kirov Street is built-up, while the left is a series of large, well-kept parks. No. 1 Kirov Street, set in one of these parks, is the Republican Library. On the right-hand side, No. 6 Kirov Street, is the Museum of Ukrainian Art. Built in 1898–1900 on the lines of an ancient Greek temple with huge granite steps and a six-columned portico, the museum has a collection of Ukrainian art of the 15th to 19th centuries and of Soviet artists.

Next you pass the headquarters of the Ukrainian Council of Ministers and, a few hundred yards further up, on the left, the Supreme Soviet of the Ukraine with its entrance in the adjoining square. No. 5 across the street is the former Marinsky Palace designed by Rastrelli and built in 1747 as a local residence for the Czar. The upper wooden story, which burned down in 1819, was reconstructed in 1870 and has survived in its 18th-century Baroque form. Outside the palace stands the memorial to the Civil War, with black marble and red granite decorating the mass grave.

On your left, in a park, is the entrance (No. 3 Kirov Street) to the Dynamo Stadium. The other side of the stadium faces on to the Petrovsky Promenade. A bridge divides the former Petrovsky Park into two parks; the northern part is called Pioneer Park and the lower, southern part, Pervomaisky.

In Karl Liebknecht Street (the sidestreet opposite the Supreme Soviet), you will see the headquarters of the Znaniye Educational Society, and in

Rosa Luxemburg Street (Nos. 15–17), the Youth Theater. Chekist Street crosses both these streets further west; here is the Ukrainian Foreign Ministry, and the headquarters of the Composers' Union. The writers, too, have their home nearby at No. 2 Ordzhonikidze Street, which runs parallel with Liebknecht Street towards the Kreshchatik. The editorial offices of several literary reviews are also here. Ordzhonikidze Street passes behind the Ukrainian Drama Theater (the Ivan Franko Theater), and you can see a statue of Ivan Franko himself by Suprun (1956) in the square beyond the theater.

Reaching the end of Kirov Street you come to Moskovskaya Street on your right. This leads eventually into Lesya Ukrainka. On your left, at the corner of Kirov Street and Sichneve Povstannya Street, stands the monument to the Arsenal Workers, commemorating their dead in the Civil War. Sichneve Povstannya Street is named after the January 1917 rising in Kiev. Suvorov Street begins on the right; its left side is a large park in memory of the dead of World War II. A street called Dneprovsky Spusk leads downhill on the left from the park. Here stands the monument to the Unknown Soldier.

On the right of the street named after the January Rising, Citadel Street leads to the Pecherskaya Lavra, the Monastery of the Caves. Nearby is the Museum of the History of the Theater.

The Monastery of the Caves, founded in 1051 by the monks Anthony and Theodosius, comprises a whole series of churches, cathedrals and monuments. Outside the complex of buildings stands the ancient church of the Redeemer of Berestovo, built early in the 12th century by Prince Vladimir Monomakh as a burial place for the princes of Kiev. The founder of Moscow, Yury Dolgoruky, was buried here in 1157. The church is built in characteristic late 11th- and early 12th-century style: a crossdome with six pillars. Its eastern wing, which faces the Dnieper, was added in 1640–44. In 1947 a marble sarcophagus was installed here in memory of Yury Dolgoruky.

The Pecherskaya Lavra is the most important and most famous historical site in Kiev. Most of its buildings have been turned into museums, though some still function as churches. They include the Trinity Church, built over the entrance gate (today 21 Sichneve Povstannya Street), which dates from 1108, and has 18th-century wooden iconostases; the walls of the Upper Monastery, built between 1698 and 1701, stretch from this gateway around the compound. Another gateway is topped by the five-domed All Saints' Church (17th century). The main court of the Upper Monastery centers around the ruins of the Assumption Cathedral, built 1073–89 and destroyed by the Nazis in 1941. The majority of the surrounding houses are 18th century. The bell tower, the highest in the U.S.S.R. (316 ft.), was built in 1731–45; it has been completely restored and the dome regilded. Local legend speaks of the belfry being built by 12 brothers so saintly that heaven aided them—as they worked, the bell tower sunk deeper and deeper into the earth, needing no scaffolding, and when it was finished, it rose again to its full height in a single night!

Of the various museums in the Monastery, the Historical Museum is particularly interesting. Among its exhibits are 17th to 20th-century fabrics, 16th to 19th-century handicrafts, wood carvings, metal work, ceramics—all examples of Ukrainian folk art. Highlights are the delicately painted *krashenki,* Easter eggs.

The St. Anthony Caves contain 73 tombs and three underground churches. In the St. Theodosius Caves there are 47 tombs and another three churches. The two series of caves are quite separate from each other, and are reached by way of a covered gallery. The belfry of the St. Theodosius or Further Caves was built in the 18th century by the architect Stefan Kovnir. The most famous tomb is that of the chronicler Nestor, who died in 1115. Near the refectory walls are the graves of the Cossack leaders Kochubei and Iskra, executed by Ivan Mazepa in 1708.

If you leave the Lavra and walk along Citadel Street you come to Novo-Navodnitskaya Street, which leads to Staro-Navodnitskaya Street and then on to the broad highway of the People's Friendship.

Cross the highway and you will find yourself in the Botanical Garden, which covers some 500 acres and affords beautiful views of the Dnieper and Kiev itself. Here, too, on the bank of the Dnieper, you will see the ruins of the Vydubetsky Monastery. According to archeologists, there was a river ferry here in earliest times. In 1070–77 Vsevolod Yaroslavich, Prince of Kiev, had a monastery built on this spot; only the western side of a part of it, St. Michael's Cathedral (1070–88), has survived, but there are fine murals. In 1701, following a landslide, St. George's Church, a five-domed masterpiece of Ukrainian architecture, was built in its place. The refectory (early 18th century) and the three-storied belfry (1730s–40s) are also interesting. Nearby is the Museum of the Second World War, topped by the gigantic and controversial steel statue of "Mother Russia" which dwarfs the monastery domes on the river bank.

From the Paton Bridge you can return to the hotel by tram or trolley-bus. Or you can walk along the quay until you reach the Dneprovsky Spusk, mentioned earlier. This is one of the sloping roads leading along the riverside parks. Askold's Grave, erected in 1809–10, is a rotunda where, according to legend, a Prince of Kiev was buried in 882. This is perhaps the most picturesque spot in Kiev and a favorite promenade.

One of the park roads leading north will take you to the open-air theater; its sloping amphitheater seats 4,000 people and is used for musical and dance shows and rallies. In the summer there are film shows. Nearby is the Kukushka open-air restaurant.

Descending to the quay again, you can cross by the footbridge (Peshek-hodny Most or Parkovy Most) to the parks on Trukhanov Island and the city's bathing beach. Near the bridge is the monument built by Molensky in 1802–8 to commemorate the charter of the city of Kiev.

You can go back to the Hotel Dnieper by ascending the Vladimirsky Spusk. Nearby, overlooking the river, is the St. Vladimir Monument. Vladimir holds aloft a cross commemorating the conversion of Kievan Russia to Christianity. The monument was erected in 1853.

Third Tour—St. Sophia's Cathedral

To explore the northern and western sections of Kiev, start out along the Street of Revolutionary Heroes walking west. Turn left into Chelyuskintsev Street, and you will find the Planetarium at No. 17 housed in a former Roman Catholic church. This street leads to Kalinin Square. Mikhailovsky and Kalinin Street will take you to Bogdan Khmelnitsky Square, with the statue of the Cossack Hetman who freed the Ukraine from the Poles and later subjugated it to the Russian state. St. Sophia's Cathedral stands behind the statue; like the major part of the Monastery of the Caves, St. Sophia's has also now become a museum.

The cathedral was dedicted in 1037 by Prince Yaroslav the Wise as a mark of gratitude for the battle he won against the Pechenegs, an invading tribe from the east. Here the first Russian library was founded and the earliest chronicles were written. St. Sophia is a stylistic combination of the traditional wooden church and the principles of stone building, with interesting mosaics and frescos in the central part and on the main dome. In the northeast part is the marble tomb where Yaroslav the Wise was buried in 1054. The iconostasis dates from the 18th century.

The bell tower (256 feet) was erected between 1744 and 1852. The Zavorovsky Gate is the main entrance to the Metropolitan's residence and is decorated with elaborate stucco ornamentation. The cathedral's surrounding wall was built in the 1740s. The whole complex is now a museum which also displays architectural models of other ancient Ukrainian and Russian towns, and local archeological discoveries. The entire precincts, as an "ancient monument," are maintained under a preservation order.

Leaving the Sofisky Sobor (cathedral) walk along Streletsky and Polupanov Streets until you reach a small garden containing the Golden Gate, once a part of Kiev's fortifications. The gate consists of two parallel walls built of brick and stone in 1037 by Yaroslav the Wise to guard the main entrance into the city. The arch was topped by the tiny Church of the Annunciation. It was through this gate that Bogdan Khmelnitsky entered Kiev in 1648. The Golden Gate was restored for the city's 1,500th anniversary in 1982.

The far side of the square is the continuation of Vladimirskaya Street. Walking southwest along it you come to the Opera House, then, at No. 57, on your left, to the Kiev branch of the Central Lenin Museum.

At the junction with Shevchenko Boulevard, on your left, is Shevchenko Park, where you can see a statue of the great Ukrainian classical writer erected in 1939 on the 125th anniversary of his birth. The large and impressive building opposite the park, on Vladimirskaya Street, is Kiev University, named after Shevchenko, and founded in 1834. It is flanked by the University Library and the Faculty of Humanities.

The far side of Shevchenko Park borders on Repin Street, which runs parallel with Vladimirskaya. Here there are two museums: No. 9 is the Museum of Russian Art and No. 15 the Museum of Oriental and Western Art. The former covers the 12th to the 17th centuries and includes icons of the Novgorod, Moscow and Stroganov schools; the 18th- and 19th-century rooms also have works by outstanding Russian artists. There is a fine collection of 18th–20th-century china, glass and crystal. The Museum of Oriental and Western Art has a collection that includes works by Bellini, Franz Hals, Rubens and Velasquez.

Passing Repin Street, continue along Shevchenko Boulevard. Between Repin and Pushkin Streets, at No. 12, you will find the Shevchenko Museum, which is devoted to the life and work of the poet. Turn back to cross Vladimirskaya Street again and walk on further northwest and you come to one of the newer but important monuments in Kiev, the Vladimir Cathedral. Built in the 19th century, designed by Beretti and Bernhardt, it has seven gilded domes, three naves and several striking murals.

Further along Shevchenko Boulevard on the left you will see the University Botanical Gardens. Then after a short distance, the boulevard arrives at Pobeda (Victory—Peremogi in Ukrainian) Square. Here you can visit the circus, and shop in the Ukraine State Department Store. Here also is the newest Intourist Hotel (Lybed), one of the country's best.

From here on, the Shevchenko Boulevard continues as the Brest-Litovsk Highway. Along it you will find the Kiev Zoo, which can be reached from Victory Square by trolley-buses No. 5, 6 or 7 and trams No. 2, 9 or 47. Close to it is the Medical Faculty of the University and the Dovzhenko Film Studio.

Fourth Tour

For your final walk, start again from the Hotel Dnieper but follow the Street of the Revolutionary Heroes until you reach Vladimirskaya Street. No. 2 is the Historical Museum. From there turn northeast, down Andreyevsky Spusk. Here is St. Andrew's Church, designed by Rastrelli and built by the Russian architect Michurin between 1744 and 1753, an important example of Russian Baroque architecture. This is the highest point of Old Kiev, overlooking the Podol district, the river and the plain to the east where, tradition says, the Apostle Andrew, who first preached the Gospel in Kievan Russia, erected a cross.

Built at the command of Elizaveta, the pious daughter of Peter the Great, St. Andrew's Church stands on a terrace at the top of a broad flight of steps. Its proportions are perfect. Today the domes are restored in silver-gilt and the walls painted in turquoise and white. The iconostasis was painted by Antropov and local masters. The church has not been used for religious worship since 1961.

Behind the church you can descend the Andreyevsky Spusk into the Lower Town, the Podol. At the foot of the hill turn left into Zelinsky Street and a few steps will take you to Krasnaya (Red) Square. The House of Contracts (Kontraktovy Dom), built here in 1817 expressly as a headquarters for the negotiating and signing of agreements, is an interesting example of the early 19th-century Russian classicist style.

The building on the corner of Red Square and Naberezhno-Nikolskaya Street (designed by Sedel and built in 1735) is a branch of the Academic Library. The courtyard wall has Baroque decorations. The building used to be the home of the Kiev Academy, which was founded in 1701 at the command of Peter the Great, to replace the former Kiev College. It had many distinguished graduates in its time.

Also on Red Square are the ruins of the Bratsky Monastery; the old house in the northwestern corner was Peter the Great's headquarters in 1706 when he prepared the attack on the Swedes, who had advanced to within 25 miles of Kiev.

East of the square, at No. 15 Kreshchatik Quay, which curves in from the river, is the former dormitory of the students of the Kiev Academy, the "Bursa." The ground floor was built in 1778; in 1809–11 two stories were added, with a four-columned gate, and the facade was remodeled in the style of the early 19th-century classicism.

Turning along Kreshchatik Quay towards the harbor, you can see Trukhanov Island on the far side. The island has been developed as an aquatic sports center. A wide promenade lines the riverbank where railway lines and warehouses once stood. Behind the harbor is Pochtovaya Square, a traffic center and terminus for the funicular which links the Lower and Upper Cities. Take the funicular to the Upper City terminal and you are back at the starting point of your tour.

Excursions around Kiev

The permanent Ukrainian Economic Exhibition covers 750 acres on Sorokichya Zhotvnya Prospekt, to the south of the city. It can be reached by No. 11 trolley-bus directly from Lenkomsomol Square.

Pushcha-Voditsa is one of the finest parks in Kiev's green-belt. It extends over 1,875 acres, about 13 miles from the city center. It used to be a hunting preserve and also a refuge from enemies who attacked Kiev. It can be reached by tram No. 25 from the railway station or No. 12 from the Red Square in Podol.

An interesting excursion is to the open-air Folk Architecture Museum on the outskirts of Kiev, near Pirogovka village, which consists of 400 old homes, mills, forges and other structures from all over the Ukraine.

Lvov

Lvov is a regional capital, the traditional economic, transport, cultural and administrative center of the western Ukraine. For six centuries it was the scene of much strife and war between hostile powers, irreconcilable nations and opposing religions. Yet the monuments of the past, their different styles ranging from Ukrainian traditional to Italianate Renaissance, German Baroque and Polish, today form a unique whole. In Ukrainian, the city's name is Lviv.

The statue of the great Polish poet Adam Mickiewicz (by Popiel and Farashcuk, 1905) stands in Mickiewicz Square and has come to be a symbol of Lvov. Also in the square is the Intourist hotel, built in 1901, and close by, the shady promenade of the Shevchenko Prospekt to Rosa Luxemburg Square. The most important monument here is the Roman Catholic Cathedral, dating from 1270–1480, but never completed. It is still used today for services. The old Gothic houses in the square burned down in 1527 but their foundations, ground floors and, here and there, parts of their first floors have survived and been incorporated into more recent dwellings. The cathedral has 18th-century frescos and many decorative carvings and statues dating from the 17th and 18th centuries. The chapels and the 214-feet-high Gothic tower were added between the 16th and 18th centuries. The Boim Chapel, built 1609–17 in Baroque style, belonged to a family of Hungarian origin, whose ancestor was private secretary to King Stephen Batory of Poland and Transylvania.

No. 2 Rosa Luxemburg Square (with its classicist facade) was built in the 18th century. No. 3 dates from 1630.

You entered Rosa Luxemburg Square from the southwest; now you leave it at its northeastern corner, where it is crossed by Russkaya (Russian) Street, the only street where Russian Orthodox believers were allowed to live at the end of the Middle Ages.

No. 2 Russkaya Street dates from the 16th century and has Gothic details. No. 8 is 18th century; notice the four relief carvings symbolizing the occupant's trade. But the most important landmark is the Church of the Assumption, one of the most beautiful in Lvov. After two previous churches had burned down, the present one was built in 1590–1629. In the courtyard there is a bell tower 226 feet high, dated 1572–78, with a bell called Cyril, cast locally in 1783 and weighing almost five tons. The outside walls of the church are decorated with a sculptured frieze depicting Biblical scenes; the interior contains 18th-century sculptures and 17th-

and 18th-century icons. Russian Orthodox services are held here regularly.

Rinok Square

Rinok (Market) Square is like an architectural sampler of the centuries,
so we will describe it in some detail. The old City Hall (now the City Soviet) stands in the center, and almost all the buildings around the edges of
the square are worth close inspection. Of the 44 houses none is less than
200 years old.

No. 2 is a Gothic one-storied house dating from the 16th century, with
a sculpture by Bellon and dolphin-reliefs on its façade. In 1627 this was
the home of the first Lvov post office. No. 4, built in 1577 and known as
the Black House (Chornaya Kamonica), houses a section of the Historical
Museum. (The museum occupies several buildings, including also Nos.
6 and 24 in Market Square.)

No. 6 has also had a varied past. It is called the Korniakt or Sobieski
house; it was built at the end of the 16th century by one of Lvov's richest
burghers, a Greek merchant, who had special permission to erect a broad
facade with six windows instead of the usual narrow frontage. In the 17th
century the Polish King Jan Sobieski bought the house. No. 8 was built
at the end of the 18th century in Classicist style but its front, stylistically
a survival from the 16th century, was later decorated with balconies,
wrought-iron railings and reliefs symbolizing shipping and trade.

No. 12 has also acquired Renaissance features during its long life; the
ornamentation shows the plump-cheeked faces and bold moustaches of
contemporary Polish figures. The portals of No. 14 display a winged lion,
the symbol of Venice, denoting that this was once a diplomatic dwelling;
Antonio di Massari, the Venetian consul, lived here in 1600.

No. 17, built in Louis Quinze style, is noteworthy for its elegance and
air of serene luxury. No. 18 dates from 1523 and was one of the most rich-
ly-decorated mansions of its age. Under the balcony of No. 19 there are
fantastic, half-human, half-animal masks.

No. 23 is massive, almost oppressive in its effect. The details, and decorative elements, the splendid masks, the stylized lions' and angels' heads
belong to the traditions of the Italian Renaissance but their excessive use
and the heaviness of the whole ornamentation betrays German and Flemish influences.

No. 24 is the third section of the Historical Museum; it dates from the
16th century but its front was rebuilt in the 20th. In 1707 Peter the Great
received a deputation of the Stavronigy Brotherhood here and granted
them a charter to sell their books freely in the Ukraine.

No. 28 is a real architectural anthology: its left side still displays the
Gothic arches and flying buttresses of 1510, its Renaissance portico and
window frames are 17th century, while its second story dates from the
Baroque period. Built by an anonymous architect, it has a particular gracefulness and charm.

No. 29, in Classicist style, was built by peasant rebels captured at the
end of the 18th century; as soon as it was finished, they were executed.

Almost the entire northern side of Rinok Square dates from the second
half of the 18th century, but some buildings have earlier elements. The
decorations are especially interesting, ranging from a laurel-wreathed,
bearded head with a lion's body, to the hermit figures supporting the balc-

ony of No. 40, and the grinning stone face with a huge mustache on the façade of No. 41.

Elsewhere in Lvov

Leaving Rinok square at one of the northern corners, you come next to Armyanskaya (Armenian) Street, which is also filled with historical associations. Its most interesting building is the Armenian Cathedral, founded in 1363, with a bell tower dating from 1571. It includes the house where the Armenian Archbishop lived in the 16th century. A 16th-century column topped by a statue of St. Christopher stands in the courtyard. There are many other interesting buildings in the street, especially No. 23, dating from the 18th century, with a Classical façade bearing the signs of the zodiac and the symbols of the four seasons.

From Armyanskaya Street, turn into Krakovskaya, which crosses it behind the Armenian Cathedral. On your right is Daniel Galitsky Street, named after the founder of Kiev. On the square named after the 300th anniversary of the Russian-Ukrainian union stands the Church of the Virgin of the Snows, once the oldest Catholic church in Lvov. It dates from the end of the 13th century.

Reaching Bogdan Khmelnitsky Street, you will notice the Church of St. Nicholas, constructed between the 13th and 18th centuries. Russian Orthodox services are now held here. At No. 63 in the same street, there is another Orthodox church, the Pyatnitskaya, built in 1645, with a very old iconostasis. No. 34 is the St. Onufri Monastery, with a 17th-century church in which Orthodox services are still held; the bell tower and walls are 17th to 19th century. Ivan Fyodorov, the first Russian printer, is buried here. He died in 1583, having produced his first book in 1563 in Moscow, shortly after which he fled from persecution to continue his work in Lithuania and Poland.

This quarter is called Podzamese (Precincts of the Castle); on Bogdan Khmelnitsky Street there is a railway station of the same name. To get to the castle, turn to the right, uphill. There is a No. 12 tram along this route for returning to the October Hotel, if you are staying there.

Zamkovaya Gora (Castle Hill) is the name of the former Prince's Hill where a fortress was built in the second half of the 13th century. Only parts of the southwestern walls remain today. The fortress survived many sieges and occupations; in 1957 Lvov's television mast was erected here in the middle of a park and a playground.

If you have any more time and energy for exploration, you may like to walk down Lenin Prospekt, the most important thoroughfare in Lvov. At No. 15 you can visit the Ethnographical and Handicraft Museum, which has an extremely rich folklore collection. No. 20 the Lenin Museum. At the end of the boulevard, you come to the Lenin statue by Merkurov (1952). Behind it stands the large and impressive Opera House, built between 1897 and 1900.

Another place well worth visiting is the Heroes' Cemetery in Lenin Park (No. 2 tram). Not far from Rinok Square, going eastwards, there is a fine Baroque building, the Church of the Dominican Monastery (1748). Nearby stands the former Royal Arsenal (1630), now used to house the Historical Archives (13 Podvalny Street), and the City Arsenal (5 Podvalny Street) which was built in 1554–56. Another medieval monument is the Gunpowder Tower, opposite the Archives, built in 1554, with walls nine feet thick, now the headquarters of the Architects' Union. All these sights can be reached by trams Nos. 1, 2, 4, 7, 9 or 12.

To the south, on Vechevaya Square, stands the former Benedictine Convent, looking rather like a fortress, and its church, which was built between 1600 and 1630 in Renaissance style by Paolo Romano and Ambrogio. It contains valuable 17th and 18th century artworks.

As well as the Roman Catholic, Armenian and Russian Orthodox churches, the Greek Catholics also had their cathedral in Lvov, sited on a hill in the southwestern part of the city: the St. George Church, built in 1743–60 by Bernardo Meretini; it is a rich storehouse of Ukrainian Baroque, with a splendid equestrian statue of St. George on its roof. Its bell tower contains one of the oldest bells in the Ukraine, cast in 1341.

The Museum of Ukrainian Art, with its fine collection of 14th–18th-century icons, is housed at 42 Dragomanov Street, while the Ivan Franko Museum in Franko Street is in the house where the poet spent the last 14 years of his life.

An interesting open-air Museum of Wooden Architecture has been set up in a park in a Lvov suburb (open 11–7, closed Mondays; ask Intourist for directions).

Kharkov

A regional capital with a population of almost one-and-a-half million, Kharkov is an economic and cultural center accessible by rail, road and air. It is characterized by a preponderance of monumental buildings erected in the last few decades, but it has also several important historical and artistic monuments.

The Lopan River cuts through the city from north to south; near the upper city the little Kharkov River runs into it from the east. The Intourist Hotel is at the beginning of Sverdlov Street. Turning left out of the hotel you soon reach the traffic and architectural heart of the city, the huge Dzerzhinsky Square. Part of it is a regular square, opening on to Sumskaya Street, which leads towards Moscow in a northeasterly direction, while the remainder is a circle from which Lenin Prospekt opens.

Among the huge buildings in the square, the Palace of State Industry catches the eye. Built between 1925 and 1928, it was the first skyscraper in the Soviet Union. The building of the Gorky University, dating from the 30s, was almost totally wrecked during the war but was rebuilt with new ceramic decorations. The Party Headquarters stands at the corner of the square and Sumskaya Street. The seven-storied Hotel Kharkov is on the corner of Dzerzhinsky Square and Trinkler Street.

To the northeast of the main square lies another of Kharkov's main squares, the Tevelev, which was designed in the 1890s by the architect Beketov. The City Hall (now the City Soviet) was erected in 1885 on the corner of what is now Moskovsky Prospekt. Here too is the Tsentralny Restaurant, and several shops.

Kharkov's historical buildings are best approached from Tevelev Square. The fortress that formed the nucleus of the city once stood in the triangle formed by this square, Rosa Luxemburg Square and Proletarian Square. Of its 12 cannon, two can still be seen in the courtyard of the Historical Museum. The Pokrovsky Cathedral on the bank of the Lopan River was built in 1689. The Uspensky Cathedral (1777) on Universitetskaya Gorka has also survived. Situated on top of a hill, it can be seen from every part of the city, by virtue of its prominent bell tower (1841), which commemorates the 1812 victory over Napoleon and has a fine carillon.

Kharkov University was established in the 19th century on the former castle hill. It is now surrounded by a park. The Historical Museum illustrating Kharkov's story is at 10 University Street and is served by trolleybuses Nos. 1, 2 and 4. Kharkov's other great museum is the Fine Arts Museum at 11 Sovnarkomovskaya Street; tram Nos. 5, 7, 10, 11, 20 and A will take you there, as will the trolley-buses 1, 2 and 4. It has 19 halls devoted to Russian and Ukrainian pre-revolutionary art, icons of the Novgorod, Pskov and other schools of the 16th century. There is a good collection of paintings by Repin, who was born at nearby Chuguyev, and Soviet artists are well represented.

Poltava

Lying 129 km. (80 miles) to the southwest of Kharkov, this is the administrative center of the Poltava Region of the Ukraine. The city is of ancient origins; its first mention dates back to the late 12th century.

In 1709 Russian troops, led by Peter I and aided by Ukrainian Cossack detachments, routed the invading army of Charles XII of Sweden near the city. The 17th-century Holy Cross Monastery and the Savior Church still stand, and there are some fine examples of 19th-century public building, notably the administrative offices encircling Round Square.

Poltava has an interesting Museum of Local Lore. The largely rebuilt city has several fine parks, theaters and a philharmonic society.

Vinnitsa

Vinnitsa, 241 km. (150 miles) south of Kiev, is the administrative and cultural center of the region of the same name. It lies in an area famous for folk handicrafts: pottery, embroidery, weaving and carpet-making. Beneath Mayakovsky Street are the ruins of a fortress 600 years old. The origins of Vinnitsa, however, go back much earlier—archeological excavations have proved that Slav tribes inhabited the area in very ancient times. During the war of 1648–54, Cossack troops routed Polish royal forces near Vinnitsa. A commemorative obelisk has been erected on the site of the battle.

Although Vinnitsa, like many cities in the Ukraine, suffered terribly during World War II, some remnants of early 17th-century architecture remain. The city is the birthplace of Ukrainian writer M. Kotsiubinsky, (1864–1913), and the house where he was born and lived is now a museum. Modern Vinnitsa, too, has a Museum of Local Lore, a musical drama theater, a philharmonic society, and is a city of parks.

Down the Dnieper from Kiev to the Black Sea

The great Dnieper River flows through three Soviet republics—the Russian, the Ukrainian and the Byelorussian—and is the third largest river in Europe (after the Volga and the Danube). Rising to the north of Smolensk, in the Valday Hills, it runs past Smolensk, then continues southwest till it reaches White Russia. Here it flows through the town of Mogilyov; its first great tributary is the Berezina. Later it is swollen by the waters of the Sozh and the Pripyat (Pripet), the latter gathering the waters of the huge Pripet marshes. After that for some 885 km. (550 miles), more than half its length, it traverses Ukrainian territory. This is its widest section and it flows through such important cities as Kiev, Dnepropetrovsk and Zaporozhye; its waters are exploited to the full for hydroelectricity with immense dams and power plants.

Many tragic and triumphant episodes in Ukrainian history have been connected with this river; Ukrainian poets, painters and composers have devoted innumerable works to its moods and landscapes; not surprisingly, it has become a national symbol.

There are ample facilities for excursions along the huge river and its tributaries. Cruises from Kiev northwards are unlikely to run for some time in the wake of the 1986 disaster at Chernobyl nuclear power station, about 95 km. (60 miles) north of Kiev. The most popular, most interesting cruise is of 965 km. (600 miles) from the Ukrainian capital to the mouth of the river, to the city of Kherson on the Black Sea. Comfortable fast or slow passenger steamers ply regularly to Kherson; at major points en route there is time for short excursions. Even the express steamers stop for two hours in Dnepropetrovsk and an hour in Zaporozhye, about two-thirds of the way to Kherson.

Leaving Kiev, the boat first starts upstream, then swings south. On the right bank, huge public buildings rise above the parkland, and then you glimpse the domes of the ancient Monastery of the Caves. You pass under the Navodnitsky and Paton bridges—to the left lies the district of Darnitsa—and finally under the railroad bridge, the last landmark of Kiev.

The villages of Osokorki on the left and Korchevatoye on the right are still part of Greater Kiev, but Visenka, on the left, and the vacation settlement of Plyuyi on the right are outside its boundaries. The hills on the right bank begin to rise more steeply. The village of Tripolye takes its name from archeological finds discovered there dating from the Bronze Age to the so-called Tripolye culture of the fourth-to-second millennium B.C.

After Stayki and Kalnoye, you come to the first stop—Rzhishchev. This is the town where in 1654 the envoys of the Czar negotiated the union of Russia and the Ukraine with the Cossack *hetman* (commander), Bogdan Khmelnitsky.

Khodorov, on the right bank, is a small town, founded in 1506; Trakhtimorovo is dominated by the cone-shaped Mount Baturin which rises opposite the harbor of Peryaslav-Khmelnitsky, some eight miles from the river; it was here that on January 8, 1654, the union was voted by a council assembly of Ukrainian nobles.

Grigorovka (another stop) is on the right bank. It was here that, in the autumn of 1943, the Russian troops crossed the Dnieper, in a bitterly contested battle. On the right you will see Kanev, about one mile from the river. This is the home town of the great Ukrainian poet, Taras Shevchenko; he is buried here and there is a large museum devoted to his life and work.

Prohorovka follows on the left bank; a former mansion where both Shevchenko and Gogol were visitors is now the holiday rest home of the Ukrainian Academy of Sciences.

Some 10 km. (six miles) beyond Prohorovka, the river widens into what looks almost like a sea—it is the reservoir of Kremenchug. At the far end is a huge hydroelectric plant. The ship stops on the right, at the mouth of the Olshanka River.

Cherkassy, one of the greenest cities in the Ukraine, is a major administrative and cultural center. Highways and railway lines converge here and there is an airport. The Museum of Local History displays the development of the city since the 16th century, through the Cossack-Tatar wars and later vicissitudes. Since the great reservoir was completed, Cherkassy has become an important river port as well.

Kremenchug is a district capital and a railway junction. Its fortress was built in 1590 against the Tatar marauders and peasant rebels.

The next stop is Misurino, one of the Ukraine's agricultural centers. On the left bank is the port of Perevolochno, where the remnants of the defeated Swedish army tried to cross the Dnieper after the Battle of Poltava (which Peter the Great won). Only King Charles XII and his ally, the Cossack hetman Mazeppa succeeded.

Now the Dnieper reaches the environs of Dneprodzerzhinsk, and traffic on the river becomes much heavier. Dneprodzerzhinsk is a center of the iron and steel industry. It has an interesting Museum of Local History.

Dnepropetrovsk, Zaporozhye and Kherson

Dnepropetrovsk is the next main stop. A regional capital and major railroad junction, it has a large mechanized harbor and an airport. Founded in 1784 by Catherine II and originally called Yekaterinoslav, it has been an industrial town almost since that time.

Its main thoroughfare is the Karl Marx Prospekt, lined with a double row of shady trees. The Shevchenko Park, the favorite recreation area of the city, is on a hill where you can see the poet's statue and the so-called Student Palace, built on the ruins of the former Potemkin Palace (1787–89). The Preobrazhensky Cathedral (1830–35), designed by Zakharov, is also here.

After Dnepropetrovsk, the ship enters Lenin Lake, which covers what used to be dangerous rapids and whirlpools. On the left bank is the Lenin Harbor, close to the great dam of Dneproges, one of the largest hydroelectric installations in the world.

Zaporozhye, a city with a large mechanized port, is the next stop. This, too, is a largely industrial community, built on the site of the former Fort Alexandrovsk. Since 1927 its population has increased tenfold. The Dnieper Power Plant was built next to Khortitsa Island, where the famous Zaporozhskaya Sech, a self-governing Cossack Community, was established in the 16th, 17th and 18th centuries.

In Zaporozhye itself, the main street is the Lenin Prospekt, linking the old and new quarters of the city. There are few historical buildings, but many modern apartment blocks and offices, large parks and gardens.

After Zaporozhye the left bank of the river opens out into a plain crossed by many small streams and dotted with copses and woods. Belenka has a large camping ground for Pioneers (rather like Boy Scouts). After this, the river enters one more huge reservoir, the Kakhovka Sea. The next stop is Kamenka, on the left bank, the center of a large irrigation area. Crossing the reservoir you come to Nikopol on the right bank. Nikopol, a district center, has a Museum of Local History: a settlement on the site was first mentioned in 1530. Between 1638 and 1652 it was the capital of the Zaporozhskaya Sech.

Kherson is your final stop on the Dnieper. Founded as a fortress in 1778, it is both a river and sea port. From here you can visit the new town of Novaya Kakhovka and see the hydraulic power plant, or make an excursion to the steppe preserve at Askania Nova, with its ostriches, bisons, antelopes and wild horses. This is where you leave the Dnieper, but you can take a 300-seat hydrofoil to Odessa, which is only two hours' ride.

Transcarpathia

The Transcarpathian Region (Zakarpatskaya Oblast) is part of the Ukraine and was established on January 22, 1945 as an administrative unit. It extends from the basin of the Tisza River to the ridge of the Carpathians; it is surrounded by Romania, Hungary, Czechoslovakia, Poland and the Lvov and Ivano-Frankovsk regions of the Ukrainian Republic. Until 1914 it was a part of Hungary, between 1918 and 1939 of Czechoslovakia. When Hitler carved up the Czechoslovak state, Transcarpathia passed partly to Ruthenian and partly to Hungarian rule. It was occupied by the Soviet Army in the autumn of 1944. Its population is just over a million, and includes Ukrainians, Russians, Hungarians, Romanians and Slovaks. Its capital is Uzhgorod.

The region can be explored by following the valleys of the various rivers from the Tisza basin to the Watershed Range mountains and springs with their many cataracts and falls. The highest peaks do not rise abruptly but unfold slowly as you gradually climb out of the plain. Your tour will take you through a wonderful region of hills, ravines, steep cliffs, wide valleys, and, in the upper parts, mountain lakes.

After the Caucasus, the Black Sea and the Crimea, Transcarpathia is one of the most popular holiday areas in the Soviet Union. Much of it can be reached by car, but in the mountains the best way is to hike or use whatever local transport is available.

Uzhgorod

Uzhgorod is the largest town in Transcarpathia. It is an important rail and road junction and the best base for exploring the region. Situated on either side of the River Uzh, in the midst of a wine-growing region, Uzhgorod is mentioned in chronicles as early as in the ninth century.

Teatralnaya Square with the Intourist (Verkhovina) Hotel and the opera and drama theater is about halfway between Lenin Square and the castle. Nearby is the Philharmonia Concert Hall, a former synagogue. The square also has an Art Gallery where you can buy souvenirs and gifts made by local artists.

Behind the theater is the river Uzh embankment and a foot-bridge. Turn right here towards Lenin Quay. At the next bridge, turn right into Lenin Square. On either side of the huge City Hall there are other public buildings; on the eastern side the Trade Union house, on the corner of Lenin Quay the medical faculty of the University.

Turning back along Kalinin Street, you pass the Central Post Office overlooking Pochtovaya Square, then reach Koryatovich Square, with its colorful local market. Suvorov Street will take you back to Teatralnaya Square and the Verkhovina Hotel.

You can make another excursion in the opposite direction to climb Castle Hill. The castle dates from the ninth century; Slav Prince Laborets lived here until his murder in 903 by invading Hungarians. In 1312 Uzhgorod was presented by the Hungarian Anjou King Charles Robert to an Italian nobleman, whose family held it until 1692, when it passed to a Hungarian count. After that, it changed hands several times in the course of religious and national wars.

The castle as it stands today has a 16th-century facade; it was reconstructed in 1598 and in 1775 was given to the local bishop, after which it housed a seminary until 1945. A statue of the mythological Hungarian *Turul* bird stands in the garden. The Museum of Local History is at 27 Kremlyovskaya Street, inside the castle.

The slope between the castle and the river is the Gorky Park, with a swimming pool. Turning towards the river bank and walking towards the city center you pass the Botanical Garden and the Pioneer (Children's) Railway, then reach the theater and your hotel.

For your third walk, you might like to climb up the Hill of Glory. Turning into Kladbishchenskaya Street at the corner of Koryatovich Square, near the Hotel Kiev, follow a road that climbs the hill. After passing under a monumental arch, you enter the Cemetery of Heroes, where victims of the last war lie.

There are many long and short excursions and hikes you can take starting from Uzhgorod. The local Intourist office will provide guides, maps and information.

Mukachevo, Chust and Rahov

Mukachevo is a lively town and is another good base for excursions. Standing on the river Latoritsa, it was first mentioned in A.D. 903 when the Hungarians arrived as invaders. After 1919 it became part of Czechoslovakia; it returned to Hungary in 1938, but joined the Soviet Union in 1946.

The most interesting sight is Palanok Castle, on the top of a hill just south of the city. Dating from the 14th and 15th centuries, this 200-foot-high building has served as a prison since 1782. A wooden Russian Orthodox Church stands in Bogomoltsa Street. This was brought from a nearby village in 1927 as an example of early architecture (1777).

Chust (Huszt) is a district center and a busy road junction. The mountain rising above the town is topped by the ruins of a 16th-century castle built to protect the nearby salt mines. The castle was destroyed in 1766 when a bolt of lightning caused gunpowder stored in a tower to explode. The town's Gothic church dates from 1459.

Tyachev is another district center lying on the Tisza River (Theiss) near the frontier with Romania. The road here follows the river through Solotniva, the site of a large salt mine and some interesting caves.

Rahov is at the heart of the Hutsul region. The Hutsuls are a Slav tribe of great antiquity and colorful folk customs. It is an industrial and tourist center. The highway and railway lines lead from here along upper reaches of the Tisza towards its source. On the right is Kvasi, a spa known for its mineral waters. Yasina is 549 meters (1,800 feet) up (in a broad valley) on the bank of the Black Tisza. It has a 200-bed hotel, open in the tourist season, and Hutsul folk art (woodcarvings, embroidery) is on sale here. After this rather large village comes the Yablonitsky Pass (822 meters, 2,700 feet), from where the road continues towards Delatin and Kolomiya.

PRACTICAL INFORMATION FOR THE UKRAINE

WHEN TO GO. As we have indicated, the climate of the Ukraine (except for the mountainous Carpathian region) is much milder than that of Russia. The spring starts earlier and the autumn lasts longer, so April and October are pleasant months for a visit. However, most of the Dnieper river cruises run in the summer months only. There are winter sports facilities in the Carpathians.

GETTING THERE. By train. From the West via Czechoslovakia or Hungary to Uzhgorod and then to Kiev and points east and south. From Moscow and Leningrad to Kiev. From the southwest via Romania. Trains from Eastern Europe to the Ukraine are always full so reservations are advisable, indeed vital if you want sleeping-car accommodation.

By air. Regular connections from Moscow and Leningrad to Kiev.

By car. No. 3 tourist route begins at the Czechoslovak-Soviet frontier and continues via Uzhgorod, Mukachevo to Strij, Rovno, Zhitomir and Kiev. Route No. 7 takes you from Kiev to Kharkov and No. 8 from Moscow directly south to the Black Sea. No. 6 route runs from Kiev to Odessa. (These are the authorized routes for tourists; Intourist will have up-to-date news about changes.)

By boat. Regular sailing to Kiev via Kanev, Cherkassy, Zaporozhye from Kherson and Odessa. Intourist cruises include air travel from London to Kiev and back via Moscow (15 days).

TOURS. Intourist organizes tours to Kiev, Kharkov and Uzhgorod with various stopovers, either as separate excursions or as part of general tours. It also offers a special river cruise down the Dnieper. Up-to-date details are available from Intourist offices.

HOTELS AND RESTAURANTS. A note on Ukrainian food: Ukrainian specialties include soups like *borshch* (beet base) and cutlets of meat fried in egg and breadcrumbs. Chicken Kiev was born here—the white meat of fat hens or capons stuffed with garlic and butter. *Kolbasa*, a long, thick, circular sausage, is always a reliable choice, and ask for *vareniki*, small dumplings filled with sugared sour cream. Ukrainian dishes make lavish but skillful use of garlic, pepper, and vinegar. The wines of Livadia and Massandra are perfectly drinkable, and you may come across a sparkling wine somewhat misleadingly called champagne. Experts also recommend *medivnyk* (spiced honey cake) and *kartoflia solimkoi* (deep-fried matchstick potatoes).

Chernovtsy (formerly Cernauti when part of Romania). *Bukovina,* 141 Lenin Street (tel. 3–8274), five-story, is best, followed by any of following: *Kiev,* 46 Lenin Street; *Radyanska,* 34 Universitetskaya Street; *Dniester,* Kobylianskaya Street; *Verkhovina,* 7 Central Square. *Motel:* two miles east of city.

Campsite at 3 Novoselitskaya Street; 3 small hotels, restaurant, bathing beach.

Restaurants. Aside from hotels, try *Teatralny,* Kotlyarevskaya Street; *Zatyshok,* 6 Zelyonaya Street.

Chop. Try the restaurant of the *Ukraina Hotel,* Privokzalnaya Street.

Donetsk. *Druzhba,* 48 Universitetskaya Street, is best, followed by either the *Ukraina,* 88 Artyoma Street, with 600 rooms, or the *Donbas,* 80 Artyoma Street. *Oktyabr,* 20 Pushkin Prospekt, is not recommended. *Shakhtior,* recent, 15 German Titov Prospekt, 12 floors, 410 rooms, airconditioned.

Restaurants. The following are all average: *Moskva, Troyanda* and *Metallurg,* all on Artyoma Street; then *Sport* on Universitetskaya Street and *Kalmius* on Makeyevskoye Chaussée.

Kharkov. *Intourist,* 21 Prospekt Lenina (tel. 32–0508), moderate. *Mir,* 27a Prospekt Lenina (tel. 30–5543). *Kharkov,* 2 Trinkler Street. *Motel Druzhba,* 185 Gagarin Prospekt (tel. 52–2091).

Campsite. *Lesnaya* at Vysoky Village.

Restaurants. *Tsentralny,* Tevelev Square, and *Teatralnaya* at 2 Sumskaya Street, share top billing. Then either of these: *Lux,* Rosa Luxembourg Street or *Vareniki*

Café, 14 Sumskaya Street, specializing in the Ukrainian national dish, a small dumpling with various fillings.

Kiev. *Rus,* 21 Kuibyshev Street (tel. 20–5091/4255). 22-story, 477 rooms. Fairly recent. *Lybed,* Victory Square (tel. 74–2066/0063). Reported good, with fair service, in 1987. *Intourist,* 26 Lenin Street. Officially classed as deluxe but we call it first-class. Only 43 rooms at last look.

Of equal rank are: *Dniepr,* Lenkomsomol Square (tel. 91–4861/4875). 200 rooms, so-so restaurant, moderate facilities. *Moskva,* 4 October Revolution Street. Skyscraper, 370 rooms; adequate. *Slavutich,* 1 Entuziastov Street. *Ukraine,* 5 Shevchenko Boulevard. 319 rooms, relatively modern; so-so.

Also rans. *Mir,* Goloseyevsky Forest. *Desna,* 46 Milyutinko Street. *Leningradskaya,* 4 Shevchenko Boulevard. *Kiev,* 26/1 Kirov Street. *Pervomaiskaya,* 1/3 Lenin Street. *Teatralnaya,* 17 Lenin Street. *Bratislava* (tel. 57–7233/6866). 365 rooms.

Camping. At Darnitsa on the far bank of the Dnieper. Follow the arrows carefully from the roundabout on the Kharkov road and you will find it on Chernigov Chaussée. The site has a café, a self-service kitchen, showers and laundry facilities.

Restaurants. Quite a good selection in addition to hotels. *Kiev,* 35 St. Vladimir Street; *Abkhaziya,* 42 Kreshchatik; *Metro,* 19 Kreshchatik; *Record,* 5 Suvorovskaya Street; *Dynamo,* 3 Kirov Street (at the Stadium); *Sport,* 22 Chervonoarmiiska Street; and *Stolichny,* 5 Kreshchatik.

Also: *Leipzig,* German specialties (what else?), 30 Volodimirska Street; and *Ostrokvo,* at the Economic Achievements Exhibition.

There are several restaurants which open only in summer and are mostly in the open air: *Poplavok,* Naberezhnoye Chaussée; *Priboy,* on the Rechnoi Vokzal wharf; *Chervoni Mak,* 8 Kreshchatik; *Riviera,* Parkovyi Pereulok; *Automat,* 30 Sverdlov Street; *Kukushka,* near the open air theater; and *Snezhinka,* on Kreshchatik, near Tolstoy Square.

Not far from *Kukushka* is the *Kureni,* where you can get private cabins. Food is excellent, and there's open-air dancing to a good band. There are few tourists; the waiters speak only Russian or Ukrainian. Cover charge 8 roubles includes *zakuski* (starters), and a hot dish, ½ litre of vodka and 200 grams wine. Not bad!

On an island in the river (metro station "Gidropark") is the fairly recent *Mlyn (Watermill) Restaurant.* Turn right out of the station, follow signs for Mlyn about 200 yards through a park. In a converted riverside mill, excellent Ukrainian food. Try *Melnik* Salad first, then *bitki* (meatballs served in a pot). A good local wine is *Perlina Stepu* ("Pearl of the Steppe"). Recommended.

Lvov. *Lvov,* 3 700th-Anniversary-of-Lvov Street (tel. 79–2270). With 226 rooms, it's best of the older hotels and first class (faded). *Intourist,* 1 Mickiewicz Square (tel. 72–6751, 72–5952). Best of newer (relative). First class, moderate, with 98 rooms. Third choice is the *Dnieper,* 45 Pervomaiskaya Square, adequate.

Also-rans. *Ukraina,* 4 Mickiewicz Square. *Narodnaya,* 1 Kosciusko Street. *Kolkhoznaya,* 14 Vossoyedineniye Square.

Restaurants. Best three are—*Moskva,* 7 Mickiewicz Square. *Leto,* 17 Gorky Street. *Pervomaisky,* 17 Lenin Prospekt.

Poltava. Try the *Kiev,* 2 Leningradskaya Street, or the *Poltava,* 19 Oktyabrskaya Street. *Motel Poltava,* 2 Sovnarkomovskaya Street (tel. 3–0024, 3–5747). Intourist.

Restaurants. Either of these two: *Poltava,* 16 Lenin Street or *Vorskla,* on main road out of town towards Kiev.

Uzhgorod. Best is *Kiev,* 1 Koryatovich Street, which boasts an open-air terrace in summer. Then *Verkhovina,* 5 Teatralnaya Square and *Uzhgorod,* 2 Khmelnitsky Square. *Zakarpatye,* (tel. 9–7504/7140). First-class with 309 rooms.

Restaurants. In hotels, or *Konditerskaya Café* on Sholokhov Street is a good bet.

Vinnitsa. *Ukraina,* with an Intourist office, on Lenin Street, is first choice. Second choice, *Vinnitsa,* on same street. *Yuzhniy Bug,* Gagarin Square. *Oktyabrskaya,* Yury Gagarin Square.

Restaurants. In the hotels.

Zaporozhye. Best is *Dnepro,* 202 Lenin Prospekt, with Intourist Office. Then *Teatralnaya,* 23 Chekista Street. *Zaporozhye,* 135 Lenin Prospekt (tel. 33–3184), is also an Intourist establishment.

PLACES OF INTEREST. Kharkov. *Historical Museum,* 10 Universitetskaya Street (with another building). Open 10–6, Closed Tues.
Fine Arts Museum, 11 Sovnarkomvskaya Street. Open 11–7, closed Fri.

Kiev. *Historical Museum in the Monastery of the Caves.* Open 9.30–8, closed Tues. *Ukrainian Theater Museum,* in the Monastery. Open 10.30–5, closed Mon.
Museum of Oriental and Western Art, 15 Repin Street, open 10–5. Closed Fri.
Historical Museum, 2 Volodimirska Street, open 10–6, closed Wed.
Museum of Russian Art, 9 Repin Street. Open 10–6, closed Fri. *Museum of Ukrainian Art,* 6 Kirov Street, open 10–5, closed Fri.
Museum of Historical Jewelry. Archeological treasures.
Shevchenko Museum, 12 Shevchenko Boulevard, open 10–5, closed Tues. Also: *Shevchenko's House,* 8a Shevchenko Pereulok, open 1–5.30, closed Fri. The great Ukrainian poet lived here for some months in 1846.
Lenin Museum, 57 Volodimirska Street. Open 10–7, closed Mon.
Planetarium, 17 Chelyuskintsev Street. *Ukrainian Economic Exhibition,* Sorokichya Zhovtnya Prospekt.
Folk Architecture Museum, near **Pirogovka** village in the suburbs; ask Intourist for details.
Babi Yar (site of massacre of Jews), outside the city. Ask for directions.

Kharkov. *Historical Museum,* 10 Universitetskaya Street (with another nearby building). Open 10–6, closed Tues.
Fine Arts Museum, 11 Sovnarkomovskaya Street. Open 11–7, closed Fri.

Lvov. *Historical Museum,* 4/6 Rynok. Open 11–7, closed Wed. and Sun.
Museum of Ukrainian Art, 42 Dragomanov Street. Open 12–7, closed Mon.
Art Gallery, 3 Stefanik Street. Open 12–7, closed Mon. Large collection includes works by Goya, Rubens, Tintoretto, Titian and many Russian masters.
Lenin Museum, 20 Lenin Prospekt. Open 10–7, closed Mon.
Ethnographical and Handicrafts Museum, 15 Lenin Prospekt. Open 11–6, closed Mon.
Museum of Natural History, 18 Teatralnaya Street. Open 11–5, closed Mon.
Ivan Franko Museum, 152 Franko Street. Open 10–7, closed Tues. Devoted to the life and works of the famous Ukrainian writer.
Yaroslav Galan Museum, 18 Gvardeiskaya Street. Open 12–5, closed Wed, Fri. and Sat. Galan, a publicist and political writer, was murdered in 1949.
Botanical Garden, Shcherbakov Street.
Museum of Wooden Architecture, in a suburb. Ask Intourist for directions.

Mukachevo. *Palanok Castle; Convent; Wooden Orthodox Church,* Bogomoltsa Street.

Uzhgorod. *Local History Museum,* 27 Kremlyovskaya Street, inside the castle. Open 11–7, closed Wed. Sections on natural history and local handicrafts.
There is also an *Art Gallery* inside the castle, open 11–7, closed Mon. Russian and Ukrainian artists.

THEATERS AND CONCERTS. Kharkov. *Lysenko Opera House,* 19 Rymarskaya Street. *Musical Comedy Theater,* 28 Karl Marx Street. *Krupskaya Puppet Theater,* 3 Krasin Street. *Pushkin Russian Drama Theater,* 11 Chernyshevsky Street. *Shevchenko Ukrainian Drama Theater,* 9 Sumskaya Street. *Regional Drama Theater,* 18 Sverdlov Street.

Circus, 17 Krasnogo Militsionera Street.
Philharmonia Concert Hall, 10 Sumskaya Street. *Ukraina Concert Hall,* in the Shevchenko Garden.

Kiev. *Shevchenko Opera and Ballet Theater,* 50 Volodomirska Street. *Ivan Franko Ukrainian Drama Theater,* 2 Franko Square. *Lesya Ukrainka Russian Drama Theater,* 5 Lenin Street. *Musical Comedy Theater,* 51a Chervonoarmiiska Street. *Puppet Theater,* 13 Rustaveli Street.
Philharmonia Concert Hall, 16 Kirov Street (the former Merchants Hall). *Zhovtnevy (October) Palace of Culture.*
Circus, Victory Square. *Cinerama,* 19 Rustaveli Street.

Lvov. *Franko Opera and Ballet Theater,* Torgovaya Square. *Zamkovetskaya Ukrainian Drama Theater,* 1 Ukrainskaya Street. *Russian Drama Theater,* 6 Gorodetskaya Street. *Gorky Youth Theater,* 11 Gorky Street. *Puppet Theater,* Galitsky Street. *Summer Theater,* Khmelnitsky Park, 43 Dzerzhinsky Street.
Concert Hall, 25 Franko Street; the famous Lvov *Trembita* choir performs here.

Mukachevo. *Russian Drama Theater,* Mir Street.

Uzhgorod. *Ukrainian Drama Theater,* Teatralnaya Square. *Philharmonia Concert Hall,* Teatralnaya Square; the home of the Transcarpathian Folk Choir.

SHOPPING. One of the best buys in the Ukraine is the ceramic ware.

Kharkov. *Department Store.* Rosa Luxemburg Street. *Antique and Second-Hand Shops:* 29 Engels Street and 4 Sverdlov Street. *Jewelers:* 16 Trelov Street and 3 Sumskaya Street.

Kiev. *Main Department Store,* 2 Lenin Street, at the corner of Kreshchatik. *Podarki* (Gift Shop), 9 Karl Marx Street and at the corner of Kreshchatik and Shevchenko Boulevard. *Jewelers:* 19 and 53 Kreshchatik. *Porcelain:* 34 Kreshchatik. *Ukrainian Handicrafts:* 23 Chervonoarmiiska Street and 93 Kirov Street. *Dom Knigi* (Bookshop): 30 Kreshchatik. *Bessarabka* (Covered Market), Shevchenko Boulevard.
Kashtan shops are the Ukrainian equivalent of *Beryozkas*—gift shops for tourists. In Kiev they are located at: 27/26 Boulevard Lesya Ukrainka, Monastery of the Caves, Borispol Airport, Prolisok campsite/motel, Hotel Lybed and Hotel Dnieper.

Lvov. *Antique and Second-Hand Shops:* 3 Shevchenko Prospekt (near Intourist Hotel) and 11 Volovaya Street. *Jewelers:* Mickiewicz Square and 29 Lenin Prospekt. *Gift Shop:* 1 Kopernik Street. *Arts and Crafts:* Mickiewicz Square (near Intourist Hotel). *Kashtan Foreign Currency Shop:* 3 Rudenskova Street. *Souvenirs,* Galitskaya Street. *Kolkhoz Market:* 11 Bazaar Street.

Uzhgorod. *Souvenirs, art gallery,* Teatralnaya Square. *Gift Shop,* 10 Suvorov Street. *Jeweler's,* 8 Suvorov Street.

USEFUL ADDRESSES. Kharkov. *Railway Stations:* Yuzhny Vokzal (South), Privokzalnaya Square. (City Ticket office, 7–9 Ufinsky Street.) Trams 1, 9, 11, 14, 17 and 19: trolley-buses 2 and 3. The other two stations are the Vokzal Levada (Sigelnikovsky Street), accessible by trams 13, 14 and 16, and the Vokzal Balashovsky (Pichanovskaya Street) by trams 5, 13, 14, 16. *Bus terminus:* 22 Gagarin Prospekt.
Airport: 13 km. (eight miles) from town. *City terminal:* 2 Rosa Luxemburg Square. Buses start from Kosturensky Street. *Information bureau:* 11 Ufinsky Street. *Central Post Office:* 7 Privokzalnaya Square. Also a recently completed subway system.

Kiev. *Railway Station:* at the end of Komintern Street on Vokzalnaya Square. *City Ticket Office:* Pushkin Street. Trams 2, 6, 7, 10, 13, 25 and 30 serve the station. *Bus Terminus:* Avtovokzalnaya Square, served by trams 9, 10, 24 and trolley-buses 1, 11, 12.

Boat Terminal: Pochtovaya Square, in front of No. 2 Naberezhno-Kreshchatitskaya Street. Local boats serving the environs and excursions boats can be taken from the *Prigorodnaya pristan* landing-stage in front of No. 3 Naberezhnoye Road. Trams: 3, 16, 21, 28, 31 and 32.

Airport: Borispol, 18 miles from the city. City terminal: 6 Karl Marx Street.

Lvov. *Railway Station:* Privokzalnaya Square. (Ticket office: 20 Gorky Street.) Served by trams 1, 6, 9 and No. 1 trolley bus. *Autobus terminus:* 5 Yaroslav Mudry Square.

Airport: about 4 miles from the city. *City terminal:* tickets: 2–5 Pobeda Square. *Information Bureau:* 1 Mir Street. *Main Post Office:* 1 Slovatsky Street.

Spartak Swimming Pool, 49 Instrumentalnaya Street.

Uzhgorod. *Railway Station:* 9 Stantsionnaya Street. *City Ticket Office:* 46 Vossoyedineniye Square. *Bus terminus:* 11 Kirov Street.

Airport: 2 miles from the town, 145 Sovietskaya Street. *City terminal and airport buses:* Koryatovich Square.

MOLDAVIA

The Moldavian Soviet Socialist Republic lies in the southwestern corner of the Soviet Union, between the Prut and the Dniester rivers, on the left bank of the Dniester. The Prut forms the western boundary of Moldavia and Romania while in the north, east and southeast, Moldavia borders on the Ukraine.

Moldavia is a small republic, extending for some 320 km. (200 miles) from north to south and 160 km. (100 miles) from west to east, with a population of just over 4 million.

In pre-Christian times, the rich pastures and wooded slopes of the Carpathian mountains were inhabited by Thracian, and later, by Slav tribes. The Volokh, ancestors of the Moldavians, later left the mountains for the East Carpathian lowlands, where in 1359 they formed an independent principality. For more than 400 years there were waves of foreign invaders. In the 19th century, the territory between the Dniester and the Prut was annexed to Russia; in 1917 Soviet power was established here.

During World War II, Moldavia suffered considerably from the Nazi invasion and occupation. Today it is an industrial and agricultural republic which has undergone considerable development. Moldavian folk art, especially carpets, has become widely known; so has Moldavian music, especially the dances and songs of the Doina Choir, the Zhok Folk Dance Company, and the Fluierash Orchestra of rare folk instruments, which include the *cimpoi* (bagpipe), *fluier, nai* and *tarogato* (ancient clarinet). The orchards, vineyards and wineries produce excellent fruit and wine.

Kishinev

Kishinev, the capital of Moldavia, straddles the River Bik. Its streets and squares are a striking mixture of Western and Eastern elements. Near the banks of the Bik you can still find the Old City, with its picturesque winding alleys and streets. There is much rebuilding going on, though, and gradually the old houses are disappearing. Surrounded by picturesque hillocks planted with flowers, Kishinev's Russian Orthodox Cathedral of the Nativity (opposite the Lenin Monument on Lenin Prospekt) is perhaps the outstanding architectural feature of the Moldavian capital. It was built in 1836; the bell tower dates from 1840. The town's main street is Lenin Prospekt, and the two best hotels are on or close to it. The streets of the new district run parallel with Lenin Prospekt on the Bik River's right bank.

The Fine Arts Museum on Lenin Prospekt has 14 large rooms devoted to Russian, Moldavian and Western European painting, sculpture and applied art. The Pushkin House on Antonovskaya Street, where the poet lived while in exile in Kishinev between 1820 and 1823, is now open as a museum. It was here that Pushkin began working on his long poem *Eugene Onegin.*

Pobeda Square is in the city center. The Mazaraki Church of the Nativity, in the old city, was built in 1852; there is an old synagogue near Armyanskaya Street.

In addition to Kishinev you might like to visit: Tiraspol, one of the centers of Moldavia's canning and wine-making industries. Here on the bank of the Dniester less than 50 miles from Kishinev, you can sample the Moldavian brandies *Yubileiny, Tiraspolsky, Nistru, Doina* and *Solnechy,* and a variety of wines.

Benderi, near Tiraspol, is one of the oldest towns in Moldavia. It has a 17th-century fortress, a fine view of the Dniester, and is famous for its silk mills. Destroyed during the last war, it has been completely rebuilt and now has attractive parks and wide boulevards.

Beltsi, a major industrial center north of Kishinev, produces sugar, vegetables, oil, wines, brandies—and fur coats.

PRACTICAL INFORMATION FOR KISHINEV

WHEN TO GO. Kishinev, standing on the banks of the Bik River, has an average summer temperature of 68–74°F, with a warm autumn and a fairly mild winter.

GETTING THERE. Moldavia can be reached from the Romanian border by rail via Ungheni and by motorway via Leusheni. Kishinev, the capital, is linked by road, rail and air with all the major cities of the Soviet Union.

HOTELS AND RESTAURANTS. *Intourist,* 2 Lenin Prospekt (tel. 52–9083). *Kishinev,* 7 Negruzzi Boulevard. *Moldova Hotel and Restaurant,* 81a Lenin Prospekt.
   Motel Strugurash, 230 Kotovsky Highway (tel. 21–7850, 53–2800); with Intourist facilities, about 6 km. (4 miles) from Center.
   Camping. There is a campsite at Vadu-Lui-Vode, 33 km. (20 miles) out of town.
   Restaurants. Eat in the hotels, or at *Druzhba Café,* 62 Lenin Prospekt. Try *mititeyi,* a Moldavian dish of small sausages containing spice and onions.

PLACES OF INTEREST. *Local Museum,* 82 Pirogov Street, open 12–7, closed Wed. Good collection of carpets and national costumes. *Fine Arts Museum,* 115 Lenin Prospekt. Closed Tues. *Pushkin Museum and Pushkin House,* Antonovskaya Street. Open 11–6, closed Mon. *Russian Orthodox Cathedral,* Lenin Prospekt.

THEATERS AND CONCERTS. *Moldavia Opera and Ballet House,* Lenin Prospekt. *Pushkin Music and Drama Theater,* 79 Lenin Prospekt. All performances in Moldavian. *Chekhov Russian Drama Theater* (formerly a synagogue), 28th June Street.

Philharmonia Concert Hall, at the corner of Komsomolskaya Street. Symphony orchestras, the famous Doina Choir and other national ensembles perform here.

Puppet Theater in the Likurich (Glow-worm) Theater, 121 Kievskaya Street. *Youth Theatre,* 7 Fontanny Lane.

Cinemas—*Patria, Biruinca, Kishinev,* all in city center.

SHOPPING. *Kolhozny Rynok* (market), at the corner of Benderskaya Street and Lenin Prospekt. Sells peasant ware and Moldavian national handicrafts as well as food.

Department Store: 136 Lenin Prospekt. *Podarki (Gift) Shop:* Komsomolskaya Street, at the corner of Lenin Prospekt. *Jeweler's:* 85 Lenin Prospekt. *Secondhand and Antiques:* 36 Pushkin Street.

USEFUL ADDRESSES. *Airport:* 14 km. (nine miles) from the city. *City Terminal:* 132 Lenin Prospekt.

DOWN THE VOLGA

The "Little Mother" from Kazan to Rostov

Matushka—"Dear Little Mother" Volga, as the Russians affectionately call it—is a somewhat contradictory name, for this is the greatest river in Europe, twisting, meandering and flowing from the Valday Hills to the Caspian Sea for almost 2,500 miles, draining an area of a million square miles, and linking five oceans and seas with Moscow through its canals. It is navigable for most of its length until it divides into 80 branches at its vast delta. Yet the Russians call it by a diminutive to express their affection—for, as one of the river captains once put it, "the Volga flows in the heart of every Russian."

To travel its whole length would take a month or more, so Intourist recommends a somewhat shorter cruise, from Kazan along the Middle and Lower Volga and then through the Volga–Don Canal to Rostov-on-Don. From Moscow, a plane will take you to Kazan in a little over an hour. From Rostov, you can return by air to Moscow in less than two hours or you can continue with a visit to the Ukraine or go further south to the Caucasus.

Kazan

Kazan, the capital of the Tatar Autonomous Republic, lies some 1,290 km. (800 miles) east of Moscow. It has a population of around a million. The city is built on the left (eastern) bank of the Volga and is one of the most important industrial and cultural centers in the Soviet Union and a major road and rail junction for traffic from Moscow to the Ural Mountains. Until 1956, when the Kuibyshev Reservoir was built, its harbor was some four miles from the city, but now Kazan is a Volga port in its own right.

Founded in the 14th century, Kazan was once the capital of the Kazan Khanate, annexed to Russia by Ivan IV in the 16th century.

A good place to start your exploration of Kazan is the kremlin (No. 2 trolley-bus to Kuibyshev Square, then No. 1 trolley-bus to the Kremlevskaya stop). Opposite the kremlin entrance is the Tatar State Museum, whose collections present a remarkable survey of the history of the Volga region.

The Spasskaya Bastion, through which you enter the castle, has four levels and with its adjoining walls forms the oldest part of the kremlin (16th century). Originally the fortress only occupied three-quarters of its present area and consisted of the Khan's palace and the mosque (both built of stone) and several other, wooden, buildings. (Kazan also has two 18th-century mosques: the Apanayevskaya and the Mardzhani.) The Church of the Annunciation (1561–62) was designed by the Pskov architect, Postnik Yakovlev. The seven-story Syumbek Tower (17th century) was built by Moscow masters, as was the 19th-century White Palace. Today the White Palace houses the Supreme Soviet and the Council of Ministers of the Tatar Republic.

From the hill next to this palace, or, if you feel like climbing higher, from the Syumbek Tower, there is a fine view of the city. You will see that Kazan lies partly below the level of the Kuibyshev Reservoir and therefore has some 18 miles of protecting dams along its riverfront. In the distance, on a small island, you will see a truncated cone-shaped monument. This is the memorial to the heroic dead of the 1552 siege of Kazan.

Leaving the kremlin by the Spasskaya Bastion, continue along Lenin Street. Here you will find the Kazan Branch of the Soviet Academy of Sciences. In front of the building there is a statue of Lobachevsky, the famous mathematician who studied at the local university and became its rector. Lobachevsky is celebrated in the Soviet Union as the founder of non-Euclidean geometry. Kazan University, by the way, has more than 60 faculties and a library of two million volumes; its former students include Leo Tolstoy—and Lenin.

No. 68 Ulyanov Street is where Lenin lived with his family from October 1888, when he returned from exile. Today the wooden building is the Lenin Memorial Museum, and Lenin's room has been reconstructed with its original furnishings. Maxim Gorky worked in Kazan from 1885 to 1886 as a baker's assistant. The Gorky Museum (10 Gorky Street, take No. 2 trolley-bus to the Dynamo Stadium) has many souvenirs of his stay in Kazan. Nearby, at 13 Gorky Street, is the Kamal Tatar Drama Theater, one of the five theaters in the city (Sharif Kamal was a classic Tatar writer). The Tatar Opera and Ballet Theater stands on Svoboda Square, opposite the Lenin Statue. It is named after Musa Dzhalil, a resistance fighter executed in 1944 by the Nazis in Berlin. He was posthumously awarded a Lenin Prize in 1957 for the poems he wrote while in prison.

Ulyanovsk

Boarding the boat in Kazan, a journey of 11 hours takes you to Ulyanovsk, a regional capital. This is Lenin's birthplace, and here he spent his childhood and youth. As such, it is naturally a Soviet place of pilgrimage.

The squat wooden house on the former Moskovskaya Street (now Lenin Street), now refurbished as the Lenin Memorial Museum, has been visited by several million people.

Previously called Simbirsk, the town adopted the surname of its famous son (Lenin's real name was Vladimir Ulyanov) in May 1924. Simbirsk was founded in 1648 by Czar Alexei Mikhailovich as a frontier fortress; in the 1780s Emelyan Pugachev, the leader of the Pugachev Rebellion, was brought here after his capture and later taken to his execution in Moscow; by then, the city was an important trading centre for the Volga district and in 1796 became an administrative capital. Today it manufactures automobiles, machine tools and electrical equipment.

The best place to start exploring Ulyanovsk is in the center on the right bank. The Lenin Memorial Museum (58 Lenin Street) was the home of the Ulyanov family until 1887, when the founder-to-be of the Soviet Union left to enter the University of Kazan. There are a number of other museums, all devoted to the life and career of Lenin; the central one is at 39 Tolstoy Street. Walking towards the river, you come to the crossroads with Goncharov Street—the main thoroughfare in Ulyanovsk. No. 16 on the left is the birthplace of Goncharov, the author of *Oblomov*.

Crossing into Kommunisticheskaya Street, you reach Lenin Square, which is on the embankment. Before you come to the square you can, if you wish, turn left into Sovietskaya Street, where No. 12 is the former Simbirsk High School, where Lenin studied from 1879 to 1887. A former classroom (next to the assembly hall on the first floor) has been turned into yet another shrine in Lenin's honor.

Opposite the school in the Karamzin Garden you can see the memorial to the first Russian historian, Karamzin, who was born here. Following the park railing along Gimov Street, you come to Ulyanov Street. Lenin's birthplace is No. 12. Today it houses a children's library.

Returning along Ulyanov Street to the corner of Kommunisticheskaya Street, and turning down Kommunisticheskaya Street, you pass the Palace of the Book (a library used by the young Lenin) and then come to Novy Venets (New Wreath) Quay. Nos. 3–4 are known as the Goncharov House, and house the Museum of Fine Arts and Local History. One of the rooms contains souvenirs of the writer's life and work.

Your walk takes you back to Lenin Square, and, at the northern end on the corner of Sovietskaya Street, to the Drama Theater.

The "Sea of Kuibyshev" and Volgograd

From Ulyanovsk you will reach Togliatti in eight hours' sailing. There used to be a small town here called Stavropol, but the building of the huge Kuibyshev Reservoir swallowed it up and its population was transferred to the present-day Togliatti. The city is one of the industrial settlements that have developed around the Kuibyshev Hydroelectric Plant; this is the site of the Italo-Soviet Fiat "VAZ" works, where 70% of Soviet passenger cars are produced, hence the Italian name of the city commemorating the long-time leader of Italy's Communist Party.

Tourists on Volga cruises can take an Intourist excursion to the Lenin Power Works, which were built in 1950–56. The main dam is more than half-a-mile long.

The landscape on either side of this section of the Volga is particularly attractive. On the right the Zhiguli Mountains block the river's course and

it makes a 160-km.-long (100-mile) detour through hills clad with oak and
pine forests. Here it turns east; then, at the Hill of the Royal Grave (Karev
Kurgan) where archeologists have found Scythian burial places, it suddenly curves south. Originally the Karev Kurgan rose well above the river,
but now it barely protrudes out of the Kuibyshev "Sea." On the left you
catch your first sight of the Sokoli Gori (Hawk Mountains) which extend
as far as the city of Kuibyshev. The part you see is called Tip-Tav, and
is even more picturesque than the Zhiguli. Here the Volga narrows at the
Zhiguli Gate, beyond which the holiday suburbs of Kuibyshev begin. Kuibyshev, formerly Samara, is a large industrial city, the wartime capital of
the Soviet Government; but the ship does not stop here. From Togliatti,
there is an unbroken journey of 15 hours to Khvalinsk, which is pleasantly
situated and has an agreeable climate, a sandy beach and other attractions.
From Khvalinsk, you sail straight on to Volgograd, passing Saratov which
is the city of natural gas (a pipeline carries it straight to Moscow). (Here
again there is no stop.) The total journey time to Volgograd is 36 hours.

Volgograd, formerly Stalingrad, was the site of the great, fierce and decisive battle which the Russians consider, with some justification, a turning
point in World War II. The city was totally destroyed in the battle. Today,
Volgograd is a regional capital with a huge power plant and a number
of important industrial plants; the Volga–Don Canal begins close by.
There are direct rail and air connections with Moscow. Spreading for almost 80 km. (50 miles) along the river, the city has vast tracts of industrial
areas. The residential quarters are set apart from these, separated by a
green belt covering well over 20,000 acres.

From Volgograd there are excursions to the Hydroelectric Plant on the
left bank of the river, where a whole town called Volzhsky has been erected. The plant is the largest on the Volga; only those in Siberia can compete
with it in size and output. The reservoir has an area of over 2,000 square
miles.

From the harbor of Volgograd, climb the solemn gray granite steps of
the quay and make your way to the center of the city via Alleya Geroyev
(Heroes' Promenade). The Square of the Fallen Heroes is the center. At
the entrance to the Promenade stands the Fountain of Friendship, while
the road itself is lined with busts of the most famous of the city's defenders.
The Square of the Fallen Heroes has a number of monuments commemorating the dead of the Civil War and World War II. Here too, are several
public buildings: the Intourist Hotel, the House of the Soviets, the Central
Post Office, the Central Department Store and the Gorky Dramatic Theater. It was in the cellar of the department store that Field Marshal Paulus
and his staff surrendered.

The Square of the Fallen Heroes is crossed on the west by Prospekt Mira
(Peace Boulevard). On the corner of Prospekt Mira and Gagarin Street
about three blocks further north is the Planetarium.

By walking along Gogol Street from the Square of Fallen Heroes, you
soon reach the railway station. Close to it (to the south) is Komsomol
Park. Lenin Street leads eastward from the park towards Lenin Prospekt,
the longest thoroughfare in Volgograd. At No. 8 Gogol Street, the corner
of the station square and Gogol Street, a single-story building houses the
Museum of the Defense of the City.

After visiting the museum you might like to inspect the most important
memorial places connected with the Battle of Stalingrad. Walk down the
Promenade of Heroes to the tram station on Lenin Prospekt and take a

tram to Lenin Square. Between the square and the river stands Pavlov House, named after Sergeant Jacob Pavlov, who defended it with a handful of men for 58 days until his group was able to join the Soviet counterattack. Outside the three-storied house is the statue of the Soldier of Volgograd. Beyond Pavlov House toward the river is Flour Mill (Melnitsa) No. 4, which has been left standing in ruins to commemorate the devastation caused by the fighting.

The highest point in Volgograd is the Mamayev-Kurgan, where the front line troops faced each other for five months. You can get to it by taking a bus along Lenin Prospekt. After the battle, 1,200 shell fragments were found for every square yard of this area. At the top of the Mamayev-Kurgan there is a 305-foot-high concrete memorial and a separate colonnaded hall inside which a model panorama of the Battle of Stalingrad has been reconstructed.

Down the Volga–Don Canal

Between Volgograd and the Caspian Sea there is only one important settlement—Astrakhan. This port city is famous for its fish canneries, especially for processing caviar.

The Volga–Don Canal (Lenin Canal) begins some 29 km. (18 miles) south of Volgograd. You'll see a triumphal arch 120 feet high erected to commemorate the mingling of the waters of the two great rivers on the night of May 30, 1952. The first nine locks are still on the Volga: the tenth lowers ships onto the Don. The 13th lock is the entrance to the Tsimlyansk Reservoir which not only feeds the canal and the hydroelectric plant, but also irrigates the Lower Don area, which is often threatened by drought.

On the right as you enter the reservoir (some six miles upstream on the Don—the other way, and not on your cruise) ships sail from the harbor of Kalach for the Cossack village of Veshenskaya, home of Mikhail Sholokhov, the author of the famous "Don" novels. You will turn south down the reservoir and into the bluish-green waters of the Don as you journey towards Rostov, the final stop.

Rostov (officially Rostov-na-Donu) is a regional capital. It lies on the high, right bank of the river, 48 km. (30 miles) from the Sea of Azov. Founded in the 18th century, it is both a river and a sea port and the "Gateway to the Caucasus," the rail and road junction for people traveling from Moscow to the holiday resorts in the Caucasus and on the Black Sea Riviera. By train it is 28½ hours from the Soviet capital, by air 1 hr. 50 mins. The Moscow–Yalta highway branches off at Kharkov towards Rostov; the distance from Kharkov to Rostov is 515 km. (320 miles).

Rostov is a large industrial city, but it has something to offer the tourist, too: the great wheatfields of the surrounding countryside, the fish specialties in its restaurants, and the produce of its champagne factory are all enjoyable. It is well worth visiting the racecourse (at the end of Universitetsky Prospekt), while the traditions of the Cossack past are faithfully preserved in the Museum of Local History (87 Engels Street). Its collection includes the sword of Frederick the Great seized during the Seven Years' War. The Museum of Fine Arts (115 Pushkinskaya) has some splendid canvases by Vereshchagin, Levitan and Repin.

The streets of Rostov are laid out on a rectangular plan around Engels Street. The once busy Pushkin Street has become a pedestrian precinct, with gardens and cafes. The Gorky Theater has an excellent company, while in summer Rostov beach (on the left or south bank) offers good swimming.

PRACTICAL INFORMATION FOR THE VOLGA

WHEN TO GO. Summer, late spring or early autumn are the best seasons. The Intourist cruises are from June to September but regular steamers run year round. The average temperature in summer varies from a maximum of 84°F (29°C) to a minimum of 65°F (18°C). The humidity is low.

HOW TO GET THERE. By air. Regular flights from Leningrad and Moscow to Kazan. The Intourist cruise combines rail and air travel; it takes you by air from London or other Western capitals to Moscow and after two days' sightseeing there, flies you to Kazan. After the river cruise you fly back from Krasnodar to Moscow and then leave the Soviet Union by air after a day's stopover. There are other flights from various points in the Soviet Union to Kazan.

By train. From Moscow to Kazan, then by ship.

By car. From Moscow by Route 8 to Kharkov; from Kharkov by Route 10 to Rostov.

By ship. Extended cruises can be arranged directly from Moscow. The Kazan–Rostov-on-Don cruise takes 11 days. The cruise boat offers various classes of accommodations including all meals and excursions; for current prices check with Intourist. Advance booking is essential.

Salen Lindblad Cruising Inc., 133 East 55th St., New York, N.Y. 10022, have run a 21-day tour of Russia in the past, which includes an 8-day cruise on the Volga, a highlight of which is passing through the 13 giant locks of the Don/Volga Canal. In 1987, costs ran $1,940–$2,540 per person on a share basis (excluding the airfare).

HOTELS AND RESTAURANTS. A note on restaurants. If you travel by boat down the Volga, you will be taking at least your main meals on board. Fish from the Volga is excellent, and the meals are usually ample, though they can be somewhat monotonous. Most of the hotels along the Volga have better than average restaurants.

Kazan. *Kazan,* 9/15 Bauman Street, is the best in town, but by no means outstanding. Centrally located, the restaurant is very popular with locals. Then come either the *Soviet,* 7 Universitetskaya Street or *Tatarstan,* 86 Bauman Street.

Note. At presstime Kazan can only be visited in daytime.

Restaurants. *Parus,* the floating restaurant near the Lenin Bridge. *Vostok,* 13 Kuibyshev Street. *Mayak,* Dekabristov Street. *Tatar Cuisine* (cafe), 31 Bauman Street.

Rostov. Best is *Moskovskaya,* with an Intourist office, at 62 Engels Street. Or *Intourist* at 115 Engels Street (tel. 65–9066/9082/9065); 273 rooms with Intourist services. *Rostov,* 524 rooms, first class, contemporary, but without character. *Don,* 34 Gazetny Pereulok. *Yuzhnaya,* 20 Karl Marx Prospekt.

Camping in Rostov on Novocherkassk Highway, 14.5 km. (9 miles) out.

Restaurants. Eat in hotels or try one of the following: *Druzhba,* 90 Engels Street. *Cosmos,* 128 Engels Street. *Teatralny,* October Revolution Park, fine in summer. *Tsentralny,* 76 Engels Street. *Volgadon,* 31 Beregovaya Street. *Zolotoi Kolos,* 45 Engels Street.

Molodyozhnoye Café, Teatralnaya Square.

Ulyanovsk. Best is *Venets,* 13 Sovietskaya Square (tel. 9–4595), with Intourist office. Then *Volga,* 3 Goncharov Boulevard. *Rossiya,* Marx Street. *Sovietskaya,* 6 Sovietskaya Street.

Restaurants. Eat in hotels.

Volgograd. Equal choice between *Intourist,* 14 Mir Street (tel. 36–4553), and the *Volgograd,* on the Square of the Fallen (Ploshchad Pavshikh Bortsov), (tel. 36–1772).
Restaurants. Try *Leto* in the City Gardens (best in summer), or *Mayak* on the Embankment, and *Molodyozhnoye Café,* 10 Lenin Prospekt.

Novocherkassk. Restaurants. Best is the *Novocherkassk Hotel's* dining room, 90 Podtelkov Street. Then *Yuzhnaya* on Moskovskaya Street, or *Druzhba* on the outskirts of town.

PLACES OF INTEREST. Kazan. *State Museum of Tataria,* 2 Lenin Street. *Gorky Museum,* 10 Gorky Street. *Lenin Museum,* 68 Ulyanov Street.

Rostov. *Local History Museum,* 87 Engels Street. Open 10–6, closed Mon. Interesting stone idols worshipped by nomads in the 11th–12th centuries. The *Planetarium* is in the same building.
Fine Arts Museum, 115 Pushkinskaya Street. Open 10–6, closed Mon. *Museum of the Revolutionary Past and the Glory of Labor,* 2 Guzev Street.

Ulyanovsk. *Lenin Memorial Museum,* 58 Lenin Street. *Lenin's Birthplace,* 12 Ulyanov Street. *Goncharov's Birthplace,* 16 Goncharov Street. *Museum of Fine Arts and Local History,* 3/4 Novy Venets Quay.

Volgograd. *Defense of the City Museum,* 8 Gogol Street. Open daily, except Tues., 11–6. *Battlefield sites,* see this chapter, or ask Intourist for directions.
Local History Museum, 38 Lenin Prospekt, open daily 11–6, except Tues.
Fine Arts Museum, 21 Lenin Prospekt. *Planetarium,* 14 Yury Gagarin Street.

THEATERS, CONCERTS AND CINEMAS. Kazan. *Kamal Tatar Dramatic Theater,* 13 Gorky Street. *Tatar Opera and Ballet Theater,* Svoboda Square.

Rostov. *Gorky Drama Theater,* 1 Teatralnaya Square. *Youth Theater,* 170 Engels Street. *Musical Comedy Theater,* 88 Serafimovich Street. *Open-Air Theater* (Zeleny Teatr), Oktyabrsky Park Revolutsii. *Circus,* 45 Budyonnovsky Prospekt.

Ulyanovsk. *Drama Theater,* corner of Lenin Square and Sovietskaya Street.

Volgograd. *Drama Theater,* The Square of the Fallen. *Theater of Musical Comedy,* 2 Vorovsky Street. *Puppet Theater,* 15 Lenin Prospekt. *Philharmonic,* Embankment. *Circus,* Volodarsky Street.
Cinemas: Pobeda, 1 Kommunisticheskaya Street; *Rodina,* 29 Nevskaya Street; *Novosti Dnya* (newsreels), 4 Heroes' Avenue; *Gvardyeets,* 5 Akademicheskaya Street.

SHOPPING. The large Volga boats all carry souvenir shops; you may be able to pick up items by local craftsmen when you stop en route. There is a large department store on the Square of the Fallen in **Volgograd.**
In **Rostov-on-Don** you will find department stores at 46 and 65 Engels Street; good jewelers at 43 and 58 Engels Street, and a gift shop at 60 Engels Street. The main market is in Oborony Street.

USEFUL ADDRESSES. Kazan. *Intourist Office:* Intourist Hotel (tel. 2–0500). *Aeroflot City Office:* 7 Universitetskaya Street. *Harbor,* at the end of Tatarstan Street (from Kuibyshev Square along Kuibyshev Street).

Rostov. *Intourist,* 62 Engels Street. *Aeroflot,* 68 Engels Street. *Port:* 14 Beregovaya Street. *Railway Station:* Engels Street.

Ulyanovsk. *Intourist:* 13 Goncharov Street. *Aeroflot office:* Sovietskaya Street. *Railway Station:* Privokzalnaya Square.

Volgograd. *Intourist:* 14 Mir (Peace) Boulevard. *Aeroflot Office:* 5 Promenade of Heroes. *Railway station:* Privokzalnaya Square.

THE CRIMEA AND
THE BLACK SEA

From Odessa to Batumi

Tourist brochures often speak of the Soviet Riviera. This is a somewhat misleading description of the northern and northeastern coast of the Black Sea. It is only in the east, at the foot of the Caucasus, that its latitude reaches that of the Mediterranean; and it is only in the Crimea and the coastal areas of the Caucasus that the mountains protect the sea from the cold northern currents. In these regions the vegetation is truly Mediterranean and the attractions are genuine enough—long and seldom-crowded beaches, pleasant if not luxurious hotels, plenty of sunshine, lots to see and do.

Odessa

Odessa, the "Western Gate" of the Soviet Riviera, with its picturesque situation, has been described as the "pearl of the Black Sea." It is connected by regular steamship lines with ports in Romania, Bulgaria, France, Italy, Greece, Turkey, the United Arab Republic and Lebanon. Many foreign tourists prefer to come by rail or air (the 1,530 km. (950 miles) between Moscow and Odessa are covered in 23 hours by express train and 105 minutes by air) and then continue from here by ship on a Black Sea cruise. This takes about 18 hours to Yalta, 45 hours to Sochi and 66 hours to Batumi, the last port on the Soviet coast before the Turkish border.

The best starting-point from which to explore Odessa is the seaside promenade, high above the water. This is the Primorsky Boulevard, with

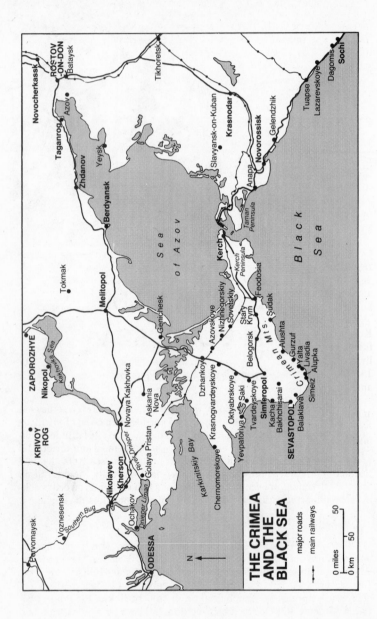

THE CRIMEA
AND THE
BLACK SEA

major roads
main railways

0 miles   50
0 km   50

N

one of the Intourist Hotels, the Odessa, at No. 11 (the other Intourist hotel, the Krasnaya, is at 15 Pushkin Street; these two and the newer Chernoye Morye hotel are recommended for tourists). The walk along Primorsky Boulevard not only reveals the picturesque panorama of Odessa Bay but also introduces you to the city's historical and cultural monuments, many of which you will find on this boulevard and on neighboring streets.

The southern part of Primorsky Boulevard ends at the Pushkin Statue, erected in 1888 by public subscription. The poet spent the years 1823–24 here during his exile, living in a house which is now the headquarters of the Ukrainian Writers' Association.

The palace situated at the far end of the boulevard was once the residence of Count Vorontsov, Pushkin's strict and intolerant boss when the poet was employed as a civil servant. Built in 1826–27 by Boffo, it became the headquarters of the Odessa Soviet after the revolution. Today, restored to its original form, it houses the Odessa Pioneers. Opposite, on the Boulevard, stands a cannon mounted on a wooden carriage which recalls the days of the Crimean War. It was salvaged from the British frigate *Tiger* sunk by shore batteries in 1854.

Close to the boulevard, at 8 Lastochkin Street, stands the fine Odessa Opera House, where Caruso and Chaliapin once sang; its ceiling is decorated with frescos depicting scenes from Shakespeare. Designed in 1884–87 by two Viennese architects (and resembling the Vienna Opera and the Dresden Court Theater), its interior is in Louis XVI style. Tchaikovsky, Rubenstein, Glazunov and Rimsky-Korsakov all conducted here.

Passing the corner of Pushkin Street and Primorsky Boulevard, beyond Kommuna Square, you will see the Archeological Museum with its graceful columns. Dating from 1825, it illustrates the history of the peoples who lived on the northern shore of the Black Sea from ancient times until the 13th century. It also has one of the largest collections of Egyptian relics and exhibits from ancient Greek settlements on the Black Sea.

Farther along stands the impressive, classicist palace of the city Soviet, another Boffo-designed building with some attractive allegorical statuary. No. 9 Primorsky Boulevard used to be the residence of the military commander of the city; today it is the Sailors' Palace. In front of Nos. 7 and 8 the street opens out into the square and two buildings border it in a semicircle. Built in 1827–28 by Melnikov, No. 8 was a private mansion, which in the 1840s became a hotel. No. 7 used to house various offices and, for a while, the municipal library.

The Potemkin Steps

From these buildings a long stone stairway leads down to the harbor. Originally, in 1837–41, Boffo intended this to be the main entrance to the city, with an unusual triumphal arch at the top. These are the famous Potemkin Steps, the scene of the traumatic sequence in Eisenstein's great film in which czarist soldiers massacre the crowd as they descend towards the mutineers from the *Potemkin* anchored in the bay.

From the steps you can see the full panorama of the largest port on the Black Sea. There is another large harbor, built some 24 km. (15 miles) from the city at Sukhoi Liman. This harbor is the base of the Russian whaling fleet, whose headquarters, built in the rather ornate style of the early 1950s, are on the corner of Marx and Deribasovskaya Street. Descending the historic stairway you reach the harbor. At the entrance to the Customs House stands a memorial to one of the Potemkin mutineers.

After visiting the harbor, continue along Primorsky Boulevard (to which you can return by the funicular to the left of the Potemkin steps). Opposite the top of the steps stands a statue of the Duc de Richelieu erected in 1826 in honor of the French aristocrat who was governor of the Novorossisk region from 1803–14. Nearby there is an open-air cafe, where you can take a rest and enjoy the view. Then, between the semicircular houses, you can walk on to the Deribasovskaya, the busiest thoroughfare in Odessa. No. 16 was formerly a college; later Mickiewicz lived here and in 1855–56 the famous scientist Mendeleyev taught at the same institution.

Deribasovskaya Street, with its hotels and shops, leads into the Square of the Soviet Army, in the corner of which stands a bust of Count Vorontsov. Not far from the city center is Shevchenko Park, which can be reached by trolley buses Nos. 2 and 3 and trams Nos. 1, 4, 23, 28. It has many pleasant walks, a stadium, an open-air theater and a beach. On the seashore are some remains of the old Odessa quarantine station. From the park you can walk across the Square of the October Revolution, which used to be the market place.

Your exploration of Odessa would not be complete without a visit to the catacombs which run for several hundred miles under Odessa and its environs. They must be visited with a proper guide as exploring on your own can be highly dangerous. The catacombs have been used as hiding places by revolutionaries and criminals; during World War II they served as a command post for the Resistance and were never occupied by the Germans. A mock-up of the Resistance headquarters can be seen in the Local History Museum (accessible by trolley buses No. 1 and 2 and trams 2, 3, 12 and 23). The Art Museum and the Museum of Western and Oriental Art are also well worth a visit.

Among the numerous scientific institutions in Odessa the distinguished Filatov Clinic of Ophthalmology deserves special mention; also important are the astronomical and geophysical observatory and the laboratory researching increased plant yields. Odessa's university, founded in 1865, is named after Mechnikov, the famous bacteriologist.

Odessa is also a pleasant spa and vacation resort with sandy beaches stretching for some 40 km. (25 miles), a mild climate and plenty of sunshine. The bathing season starts in mid-May and ends around September 25th; September is the sunniest month. As well as the Shevchenko Park Beach there are a number of other spas and beaches. Lermontov is within the city limits, on a high plateau above the seashore. It has a large park, mud baths, hospitals and sanatoria and can be reached by trolley buses 2 and 3 and trams 4 and 28.

Crowding around Odessa are a series of health resorts, some of them dedicated to children. They include Arcadia, Kuyalnitsky, Ukrainsky Artek, Malodolinsky, Chernomorka and October Revolution. A bit farther away (64 km., 40 miles) is Zatoka, a seaside spa with a sandy beach and shallow water. Get there by rail to the town of Bugaz.

The Towns of the "Liman"

Sailing from Odessa towards the Crimea, you see before long the bay formed by the estuaries of the Southern Bug and the Dnieper rivers. In Ukrainian, the bay is called Liman—narrow on the sea side, the peninsula makes a natural barrier some 40 km. (25 miles) long. The three towns Ochakov (at the "gate" formed by the peninsula), Nikolayev (in the mouth of the Southern Bug) and Kherson (on the right bank of the Dnieper) form an almost perfect triangle.

Ochakov is an agricultural and fisheries center. For tourists the nearby excavations some 35 km. (22 miles) from Ochakov are the attraction. The excavations are on the site of the ancient city of Olvia, founded by the Greeks around 2,500 years ago, and now a protected area. A local museum houses archeological finds made over the years.

The second town on the Liman is Nikolayev, an important port and industrial center. Founded in 1788 soon after the Turks were driven out from nearby Ochakov, it was one of the cradles of Russian shipbuilding. The first Russian merchant ship and the first armored cruiser were launched here. Lazarev, the Antarctic explorer, also lived and worked in Nikolayev. The shipyards are still busy. The port is a center of manganese and iron ore export.

The third Liman city is Kherson, lying 24 km. (15 miles) inland from the bay though seagoing ships can enter its river harbor and sail as far upstream as Kiev on the river Dnieper.

Founded in 1778 on the instructions of Catherine the Great, Kherson was intended to be an outpost of the southern steppes and a shipbuilding center. The area was already part of the defense line developed during the 1735–39 Russo-Turkish War. The Alexander Fortification dates from this period and is a characteristic example of 18th-century military architecture. The walls and the main gate are still standing and inside you can visit the former arsenal. Close by is the Basilica of St. Catherine, also 18th century. In 1783 the first ship of the Black Sea Fleet, the *Glorious Catherine,* a 66-gun frigate, was launched here, to be followed by many battleships and merchant vessels. The local history museum has many souvenirs of Field Marshal Suvorov, who supervised the building of the fortifications. An oak tree that he is supposed to have planted to commemorate his victory over the Turks still stands in the center of the city park.

Today Kherson is a major trading port and cultural center.

Near Kherson is a fish reserve in the Dnieper delta and a reservation for steppe animals and waterfowl. Some distance away is the Askania-Nova nature reservation, where large numbers of antelopes, zebras, bisons, llamas, ostriches and other animals roam freely. From Kherson, a short excursion will take you to the mudbaths of Golaya Pristan, 18 km. (11 miles) away, which has a fine park. Or you can make a longer trip to the hydroelectric plant at Kakhovka; here is Novaya Kakhovka, built in the '50s. The Intourist office in Kherson (Intourist Hotel, Svoboda Square) will provide information and make all arrangements for your visit.

The Crimean Coast

Yalta, the best-known Crimean resort, is best approached by sea, skirting the wide arc of the Crimean Peninsula. Coming from Odessa you sail along the western coast, past the softly sloping sandy beach of Yevpatoriya, the majestic rock fortress of Sevastopol, the sheltered bay of Balaklava (where Ulysses once took refuge), and then the long string of picturesque vacation resorts along the southern Crimean shore. Traveling by air or rail you approach the Crimean coast across steppes from the north-east. Simferopol is the end of the railroad and the highway from Moscow. From here, buses and cars will take you along winding roads through the romantic countryside of the Crimea, descending over some 88 km. (55 miles) to the coast. Most of the three million or more tourists who visit the Crimea annually tend to stay in the smaller or larger coastal centers, but there is much to see inland as well.

Simferopol

Simferopol, the regional capital, lies on the banks of the river Salgir, which is rapid and swollen in spring and barely a rivulet in summer. This is the traditional starting or terminal point of Crimean tours. Roads connect the city with the main Crimean resorts. It is 96.5 km. (60 miles) from Yalta, 64 km. (40 miles) from Yevpatoriya, 72 km. (45 miles) from Sevastopol, and 105 km. (65 miles) from Feodosia.

Simferopol has direct rail connections with the mainland, via Dzhankoy in the north and Kerch in the east, and by virtue of its airport and the excellent Crimean road network it is also an important junction for through traffic. From Moscow by rail (express) the journey takes 23 hours, by air less than two hours. From Moscow a 1,500-km. (900-mile) highway leads to the city via Kursk and Kharkov and continues to Yalta.

Simferopol was granted a charter in 1784. Built on the site of a former Tatar settlement, its coat of arms includes a bee hive and bees to symbolize its industriousness. Today the city has a university, numerous research institutes and theaters, and is an important cultural center. The vegetation is tropical and exotic; the terraced city park on the banks of the Salgir is particularly attractive.

A visit to the Local Museum with its specialized Tavrida (Tauria) Library, a collection of some 50,000 books about the Crimea, is very rewarding. The Regional Art Museum, too, is well worth seeing. But the main tourist attraction, in the environs of Simferopol, is Neapolis or Neapol Skifsky, an archeological site in the Valley of Petrovskiy (Peter's Rock), less than a mile from the city, on the Alushta highway. This "Scythian New Town" was the capital of the Scythian state in the 2nd century B.C. It was destroyed by the Huns some 600 years later. Excavations started here in 1827; they revealed many marble and bronze statues, and a large burial ground with stone mausoleums and the graves of 72 Scythian noblemen with gold ornaments and weapons.

The Salgir Reservoir, on the Alushta highway, 3.2 km. (2 miles) from Simferopol, is also a pleasant excursion spot to visit. It has a beach, a boathouse and a lakeside restaurant.

By prior arrangement, you can visit the astrophysical observatory of the Soviet Academy of Sciences. Although 32 km. (20 miles) away it is easily accessible by a regular bus from Simferopol.

From Simferopol to Yalta

Intourist has group excursions from Simferopol along the southern coast of the Crimea and you may find that certain localities can *only* be visited in a group.

You can take a helicopter from Simferopol to Yalta—it seats 10 passengers and the trip takes 20 minutes. There is also a bus and trolley line, or you can drive there yourself. The distance is about 97 km. (60 miles). The winding road first follows the valley of the Salgir River then, passing Lozovoye and Zarechnoye, it climbs a high pass in the Crimean Mountains. This is one of the finest sections of the Simferopol—Yalta road, with the Chatir Dag (Tent Mountain) rising over 1,760 meters (4,500 feet) to your right, and a splendid panorama from the terrace of the Pereval Motel restaurant which you will find on the old highway here.

From here, the road descends quickly to the first large seaside resort, Alushta, almost exactly halfway between Simferopol and Yalta. Less than 16 km. (10 miles) from Alushta stands the Kutuzov Fountain, a monument to the Russian general who lost the sight of one eye in a battle fought nearby in 1774 against the Turks.

Alushta is less sheltered than Yalta because the mountain range is some five miles from the shore; and in the summer the heat is tempered by the mountain breezes. But sunshine hours are very high here and the sea is warmer than at Yalta. The sea bed shelves steeply so swimmers must take great care.

On the hill that forms the city center, the remains of the ancient fortress built by the Byzantine Emperor Justinian some 1,300 years ago are still visible. In the 14th century the Genoese captured the city and turned it into a fortified trading center. The main thoroughfare of the modern resort is Lenin Street, which runs along the shore and is edged with stone balustrades and decorated with flower beds and fountains. The hotels, restaurants, the best shops and the harbor are all on or near this street.

The sanatoria and vacation area is about one mile west of the center. Here, too, there is a camping site with a service station for motorists.

From Alushta you can visit the Chatir Dag. A walk of some two or three hours from the summit will take you to the famous stalactite caves on the northern plateau. The Suuk Koba (Cold Cave) has a cold spring; the Bin-bas Koba (Thousand-Headed Cave) has some splendid rock formations. Another favorite excursion is to Mount Demerdzhi (over 1,219 meters, 4,000 feet), north of Alushta. A longer tour will take you to the Dzhur-Dzhur, 24 km. (15 miles) northeast from Alushta near the village of Generalskoye—this is the finest waterfall in the Crimean, in a picturesque ravine.

Alushta's most interesting sight is the game reservation, officially known as the Crimean State Nature Preserve; its central offices are in the city at 24 Putsatov Street. It can be visited only with an official permit. The reserve covers well over 70,000 acres—it is a huge open-air museum, with ancient trees and a huge variety of native game, Crimean stags, moufflons, gazelles and foxes.

Alushta can be reached from Simferopol and Yalta. There is a water-bus service from Yalta. (Like other spots in the Crimea, it may be barred to individual travellers. Check with Intourist.)

On the way from Alushta to Yalta the road skirts on the left a strangely shaped mountain called Ayu-Dag (Bear Mountain), which looks like a bear bending over the sea. There is a local legend about the mountain: a greedy trio of bruins once tried to drink the Black Sea dry, and a fairy turned the greediest of them to stone. On the summit of Bear Mountain you can still see the ruins of one of the Genoan forts. Adam Mickiewicz, the Polish poet, devoted one of his Crimean sonnets to the Ayu-Dag in 1825.

Here begins Artek, the international children's vacation area, scattered over some five miles. In the summer, Pioneers camp here; while from autumn through spring it is a forest school for children of 10–14 who are tuberculosis-sufferers. Artek consists of several camps, some of them on the seashore (Primorsky). It has various activity centers and its own fleet of small motorboats. A cable-car lift now runs from the sea to the inland camps and pavilions.

Gurzuf is three km. (two miles) from the highway, on a picturesque bay 16 km. (10 miles) from Yalta. It is surrounded on three sides by high mountains, which protect it from cold wind; on the northeast, Bear Mountain, on the north, Babugan-Yayla and Roman-Kos (1,402 meters, 4,600 feet). To the west, Gurzuf is enclosed by the bare cliffs of the Orliny Zalyot ("Where the Eagle Flies"), the nesting place of huge white-headed eagles.

Pushkin spent three happy weeks in Gurzuf in the spring of 1820 and the house of his friend, General Rayevsky, has been restored after being greatly damaged in the last war. A huge cypress stands in the garden. Sitting beneath this Pushkin began his long poem *Prisoner in the Caucasus*. Overlooking the sea at Gurzuf is the Souk-Su Cape with the Chaliapin Cliff, where the great singer liked to perform in the open air, singing to the fishermen.

The former Korovin mansion is now the holiday home of the Soviet Artists' Union. The international youth camp "Sputnik" is also here; the settlement can be approached by bus or waterbus.

Yalta

Yalta, the most popular Crimean resort, lies near the southern tip of the Crimean peninsula, in the valley of the Vodopadnaya and Bystraya rivers, in a horseshoe formed by spurs of the Crimean Mountains. Yalta is a port city and is the administrative center for the 80 sanatoria and health resorts stretching from Alushta in the east to the Baidar Gate in the west. It is linked by regular steamer services with Odessa, Sochi and the more important Black Sea coastal cities. The city is ideally located and has an excellent climate. There are practically no north winds and the average annual temperature is 56°F (13°C). The winters are extremely mild (roses often bloom in the open at Christmas) and the town is rich with acacia, laurel, magnolia, and palm trees, and is surrounded by orchards and vineyards. The mountains are covered with oak and beech forests.

The heat of the summer months is tempered by the sea breezes. The annual sunshine hours equal those of Nice in the south of France. Even in September and October the average temperature is 60°–68°F (15°–20°C.). The bathing season begins in June but the best time is in the early autumn, as the sea water is actually warmer then.

It is, among other things, the most important therapeutic research center on the whole south coast. The Sechenov Climatic and Physiotherapeutic Institute is in Yalta; among many other projects, research is being done here into the therapeutic properties of sun, air and seabathing and of the (undeniably pleasant!) grape-cure. Experiments have proved, according to Soviet sources, that sleeping at night on the seashore is extremely beneficial to TB sufferers. The patients are taken from the sanatoria to the beach at 11 P.M. where they rest under canvas. They are woken at 7 A.M. for gymnastics followed by sunbathing and, in the summer and autumn, seabathing. This climatic therapy has the advantage that the patients can spend an extra eight or nine hours per day in the beneficial sea air.

Another scientific institution in Yalta is the Magarach Central Research Institute of Viticulture and Viniculture, which has worked to improve some 800 varieties of grape and several thousand hybrids from Algerian, French, Italian, Hungarian and Syrian vines. The well-known Vinicultural Combine of Massandra, near Massandra Park, is closely connected with the institute. Its cellars hold some wine bottled in 1775—not for general consumption. You might like to visit the state wine-tasting establishment at 1 Litkens Street to sample Massandra, Livadia and other local wines.

Yalta consists of three more-or-less clearly defined districts: the Old City, whose main thoroughfare is called Roosevelt Avenue; the new city, where the hotels and tourist facilities are, and the former residential district, the Zarechye ("Beyond-the-River"), which is now the sanatoria district.

Yalta's main street is Lenin Street. You reach it by turning left out of Roosevelt Street. It is a seaside promenade and has the most important shops, hotels, restaurants, the post office and a branch of the State Bank. Here, too, is the Polyclinic with its hydrotherapy and balneological departments and 58 other surgeries.

From the promenade, shady walks lead up the mountainside. One of them is Litkens Street (close to the motorboat-harbor) where the Chekhov Theater and Philharmonia Concert Hall stand. Voikov Street also climbs the hillside. Maxim Gorky lived at No. 9 in 1900, while the school on this street used to be supervised personally by Anton Chekhov.

The central section of Lenin Street runs into the city park. A little farther, beyond the bridge over the river Vodopadnaya, it reaches the huge Primorsky Park, renamed Gagarin Park. From the park you can walk down to the city beach and health station.

The Gagarin Park is large and pleasant, with statues of Gorky and Chekhov at the entrance and in its center. On Kirov Street (No. 94) you will find the Chekhov Museum, housed in the villa that the writer himself built in 1898 and where he lived for five years until his final illness. He planted the eucalyptus and Indian lilac trees with his own hands. The museum was privately maintained by Maria Chekhov, Anton's sister, until 1920, when she became its curator, a post she held until she died in 1957. Today it is run by the Moscow Lenin Library, and has recently reopened after extensive renovation and repairs.

Another attraction of Yalta is the Nikitsky Botanical Garden, 6.5 km. (four miles) east of the city, with regular bus and waterbus connections. The garden was founded in 1812 by the Russian natural scientist, H. H. Steven; it rises in terraces from the seashore to the highway and covers some 500 acres. It has been a center for various acclimatization experiments. There are 7,000 trees and plants here, both native to the Crimea and imported from the five continents, and thousands of leaves are preserved in its herbarium. Among its special treasures are a 1,000-year-old pistachio tree, a giant chestnut tree and Baby Ionian willows. Frostresistant oranges and lemons are grown at what is known as the "Citrus Cape." The gardens are open throughout the year.

Another fine excursion can be made to the Uchan-Su waterfall (eight km. (five miles) from Yalta, via Livadia towards the Ay-Petri mountain). There is a regular bus connection for those who don't hike. At the waterfall is a good restaurant with a fine view—the Lesnoi.

Leaving Yalta westwards, at Livadia turn off on to the Bakhchisarai road, which will take you through scented Crimean pine trees to the high plateau. From the bus terminus, a few minutes' walk will take you to the waterfall, which descends into a huge wooded ravine. (*Note:* The waterfall is visible only in the spring and when it is swollen by the autumn rains.)

From the waterfall you can continue along the highway to the Ay-Petri Pass, where there is a fine panorama of the high plateau. A steep path leads from here to the summit. From here you can see the Ayu-Dag, the Bear Mountain of Artek and Gurzuf. The meteorological station of Ay-Petri is three km. (two miles) away.

West of Yalta

Yalta is an excellent center for exploring the other Crimean resorts and cities, as well as the forests and historical monuments of the peninsula. West of Yalta, the spas and holiday resorts along the southern shore of the Crimea follow quickly one after another—Livadia, Oreanda, Mishkor, Alupka, and Simeiz. All are accessible by bus or motor yacht (from Yalta's yacht harbor on Lenin Street, opposite the Polyclinic).

Livadia is only a 45-minute walk from Yalta. It is a picturesque place that was originally an imperial estate, an ideal summer residence near the Meganero springs. There was an early Greek settlement on the site; the artificial "Nymph Mountain" in Livadia Park was shaped in the form of an old sarcophagus. Many courtiers built villas here, but these have now been turned into rest homes and sanatoria and the grounds are a tourist attraction.

The most interesting sight is the Grand or Marble Palace, built by Nicholas II, the last Czar, in Renaissance style in 1911. Here, from February 4 to 11, 1945, Stalin, Roosevelt and Churchill met for the famous Yalta Conference, and here the American delegation stayed. The first floor has been restored as conference rooms, Roosevelt's office, etc., and one of the upper floors houses an exhibition of modern Soviet art.

On the western outskirts of Livadia lies a huge park which is already part of Oreanda, the next resort. Tolstoy spent many hours here beneath the huge and ancient trees. From here you can see the white building of the Nizhnaya Oreanda Sanatorium. After Oreanda, similar buildings follow each other closely. The most attractive spot is the Golden Beach, which is also the terminus of the shorter boat trips starting from Yalta and calling at Livadia. Beyond Golden Beach is one of the most striking sights on the entire Crimean Coast, the Swallow's Nest (Lastochkino Gnezdo). It looks like a medieval castle with bastions and battlements, rising from the sea on the cliffs of Cape Ay-Todor. From Ay-Todor, which also has a lighthouse, the whole Bay of Yalta opens out in front of you. There are the ruins of a 2,000-year-old Roman fortress and a copse of juniper bushes on the northern slope.

Your next stop is Miskhor, which has the mildest climate of all the Crimean Riviera resorts (average July-August temperature 77°F (25°C), in June and September 70°F (21°C), in May and October 61°F (16°C)). Most of its sanatoria are built in Moorish style and favor the same climatic therapy as in other places in the region, with patients spending the night on the seashore, in the open air.

From the park at the Marat sanatorium you can see Gaspra, built on the mountainside opposite, with the gray twin-towered Yasnaya Polyana nursing home where Tolstoy spent several months in 1901–2 and where Gorky visited him several times.

Alupka and Simeiz are twin resorts west of Miskhor, on the steep slopes of the Crimean range. The summit of Ay-Petri (1,128 meters, 3,700 feet) rises over Alupka, the At-Bas ("Horse's Head") over Simeiz (1,097 meters, 3,600 feet). After Yalta these are the most important resorts on the southern shore. Their 22 sanatoria specialize in tubercular patients. One of them is exclusively for children.

Alupka's outstanding feature is the Vorontsov Palace, former home of the Governor General of Novorossisk. It has 150 rooms and took 18 years to build. Its northern elevation is in Tudor style and recalls a medieval castle, while the southern front has distinct Moorish elements. The gates open on to the splendid Lion Terrace, whose six marble lions are the work of Italian sculptors. During the 1945 Yalta Conference, the British delegations stayed here. Today it is a museum, including an art gallery of Russian, Soviet and Western European masters. The 120-acre estate is one of the finest on the southern Crimean coast, with 200 exotic plants and trees. In the Upper Park is the Alupka Chaos, the quarry from which the material for the palace was taken; it is now a picturesque and romantic labyrinth.

The area surrounding Alupka is particularly varied and attractive. The Koshka ("Cat") Mountain to the west of Simeiz is topped by the Simeiz branch of the Crimean Astrophysical Observatory. A little farther to the west is the Krylo ("Swan's Wing") cliff. The nearby Divo ("Miracle") Cliff stretches far out into the sea and provides an excellent vantage point.

Katsiveli lies just west of Simeiz. Rising above the resort of Kastropol, the Devil's Staircase (Chortova Lestnitsa) used to be the only way to reach the pass over the northern ridge of the mountain range, the village of Bayderi and the more distant Bakhchisarai. Pushkin once did the climb—clinging to the tail of his little Tatar horse!

Bakhchisarai

Some 24 km. (15 miles) inland from Yalta, Bakhchisarai can be reached by bus; there are also rail connections from Simferopol or Sevastopol. The former capital of the Girays or Gireys, the old Tatar Khans, Bakhchisarai lies in the valley of the rivers Alma and Kacha. Today it is a district center. Near the railroad station you'll notice a large perfume factory, and some six km. (four miles) from the city, on the road to Sevastopol you can see the tree nursery of the Soviet Agricultural Academy's Botanical Institute. Both can be visited by prior arrangement.

Bakhchisarai, a settlement long before the 13th-century invasion of the Crimean Tatars, has many historical monuments worth visiting. The Historical and Archeological Museum is housed in the former palace of the Khans. It is a setting that inspired both Pushkin and Mickiewicz. The palace was built by Khan Abdul Sahal Girey in 1519; more than two centuries later fire destroyed the original structure but it was rebuilt in 1787 for Catherine the Great when the Crimea was annexed to Russia. The harem is still in its original form, and so is the mosque, which dates from the 1700s; the cemetery of the Gireys has also been preserved—and so has the Fountain of Tears, the famous landmark of Bakhchisarai. There is a richly ornamented Ambassador's Gate, the work of an Italian master imported by Ivan III.

The Russian General Suvorov, who had his headquarters here during the Crimean campaign, is commemorated in a special section of the museum established in 1950, on the 150th anniversary of his death. The Historical and Archeological Museum is also responsible for the 14 cave cities in the neighborhood, or rather, their ruins. Fulla, about three km. (two miles) from the museum, beyond the village of Staroselye is the most interesting. It was inhabited as long ago as the sixth century A.D. The museum will supply you with a guide for group visits. A longer and equally interesting excursion can be made to the medieval fortress of Tepe-Kermen, on a picturesque plateau five miles east of Bakhchisarai. Here there are more than 200 caves, among them a cave church dating from the ninth and tenth centuries.

Sevastopol

Situated just above the southwestern tip of the Crimean peninsula, on the shores of a natural harbor, is Sevastopol, the terminus of the Moscow–Crimea railroad. It is 80 km. (50 miles) from Simferopol by rail or bus, and about 97 km. (60 miles) from Yalta by bus or boat. You may have difficulty getting information from Intourist about visiting Sevastopol—but persevere!

Sevastopol is a treasure-house of historic monuments; some 400 are listed in and around the city, not counting the archeological sites. The more important ones are concentrated in the center.

A good place to start exploring Sevastopol is Istorichesky Boulevard, in the southern part of the city on the site of the former Jason battlements. (All trolley buses will take you to Ushakov Square, while the bus to Kulikovo Pole will put you down at the upper end of Istorichesky Boulevard.) Here, in a tall, round building you will find a circular panorama painted by Roubaud of Munich and depicting the Defense of Sevastopol in the Crimean War (1855). From the tower of the exhibit hall you can enjoy a fine view of the city.

Some 100 yards south of the circular hall you will see a section of Bastion IV as it is called, with seven old cannon; it was here that Tolstoy was promoted lieutenant and began to write the first of his Sevastopol stories in the intervals between the fighting.

About halfway along the boulevard stands the statue of General Totleben who was in charge of the military engineering works during the siege of Sevastopol and commanded the sappers.

From Istorichesky Boulevard you can walk to Ushakov Square which closes the ring formed by Lenin Street, Nakhimov Boulevard and Bolshaya Morskaya—a ring surrounding the hill on which the center of Sevastopol stands.

Turning into Lunacharsky Street you come to Ploshchad Stroitelei (Builders Square). Opposite Gorky's statue is the Cathedral of Peter and Paul (1843), whose classical facade resembles the Theseion of Athens. Today it is a Palace of Culture.

Higher up on the top of the hill stands the former St. Vladimir Cathedral, designed in Byzantine style but badly damaged during World War II. It is no longer used for worship. The highest point of the hill, Nagornaya Square, is dominated by Bondarenko's 65-foot-high statue of Lenin. From here you can walk down to Matrossky (Sailor) Boulevard, where there is a monument to Captain Kazarsky, another naval hero of the Russo-Turkish War of 1829. Here a stairway leads down to Nakhimov Boulevard. No. 9 on the Boulevard is an art gallery, housing a collection that includes works by Repin, Levitan and others; also Western European works of the 14th to 17th centuries, among them a Raphael *Madonna*, canvases by Giordano, Rubens, Sneyders and Ruysdael.

From the adjoining Nakhimov Square, continue along Primorsky Boulevard, the seafront. On the far shore of the bay you will see two stone battery emplacements and various war memorials.

Along Primorsky Boulevard you will find a biological station (founded in 1871) of the Soviet Academy of Sciences, with a museum and an aquarium. Passing the water sports center of the Black Sea Fleet, you come to Nakhimov Square and the striking ceremonial gate of the Grafskaya Pristan (Count's Harbor), which was the private landing stage of Admiral Voinovich, a count and Commander-in-Chief of the Black Sea Fleet. It was here, too, that the Soviet flag was hoisted on May 9, 1944 when Sevastopol was liberated.

Returning to Lenin Street, you can end your first tour by visiting the Museum of the Black Sea Fleet, established in 1869 by public subscription; its present home was opened in 1895. One of the oldest museums in the Soviet Union, it commemorates the long siege of 1854–55 and houses relics of the period. The museum also arranges guided tours, including excursions to Malakhov Hill and Mount Sapun.

Malakhov Hill can be reached by bus or trolley (about four km., two-and-a-half miles) plus a five-minute walk from the terminus. It was the command post of the first defense of Sevastopol. You will see the restored fortifications and the Eternal Flame in honor of Russian and Soviet naval heroes. Memorial tablets mark the spots where Admiral Nakhimov and Admiral Kornilov were mortally wounded. There are a number of other naval and military monuments both here and on Mount Sapun (six km., four miles, south of Sevastopol, on the Yalta road; regular buses from Ushakov Square). Mount Sapun was the scene of the bloody battles of May 1944. A large diorama depicts this struggle and a small local museum of documents and relics can also be visited.

Three km. (two miles) from Sevastopol, the State Historical and Archeological Museum of Khersones (direct bus from Nakhimov Square) houses the heritage of a civilization 2,500 years old. Relics of the ancient Greek city state of Chersonesus are displayed in two sections and several halls.

Balaklava, scene of long and bitter clashes in the 1854–55 Crimean War, is 16 km. (10 miles) south of Sevastopol. Buses start from the city bus terminus, 7 Vosstavshikh Street. Balaklava may not be on Intourist's list of visitable places, but it may be possible to join a group, if there are any.

Halfway to Balaklava, you turn into a sideroad leading to a former monastery and to the rather forbidding seashore cliffs. Here, on the Feolent Cliff, mythology has placed the Temple of Artemis. It was to this spot that the goddess brought Iphigenia to save her from being sacrificed by her loyal father, Agamemnon; this is the setting of Euripides' tragedy, *Iphigenia in Tauris*. The ruins, admired by Pushkin in 1820, have now disappeared.

Returning to the highway, you soon reach the valley of Balaklava and then the city itself. The entrance to the narrow Balaklava bay is protected by red and yellow rocks; the waters are clear and calm even when a storm rages outside the bay.

Balaklava's history can be traced back to the Scythians and one theory ascribes its name to the Scythian King Palak. In the Middle Ages, when it was called Cembalo, the Genoese built a fortress here; its ruins can still be seen on the cliffs. During the Crimean War the British troops had their base here. In World War II there was bitter fighting for the Bezimyannaya

Heights above the city; a monument to the Soviet dead stands at the top of a 600-foot-high stairway.

Western Crimea

Yevpatoriya, an excellent children's resort, lies on the western shore of the Crimean Peninsula near Artek. (Direct rail link with Moscow; with Simferopol by rail and bus; with Sevastopol and Yalta by regular bus connections.) Yevpatoriya can also be reached by boat but, as the port is extremely shallow, landings are made by motorboat. The clear, transparent water warms up very quickly, which makes Yevpatoriya an ideal place for children; the sea bottom shelves gently and gradually, the sand is fine, the beach wide and the sea very clean, so small children can bathe here in complete safety. The season begins in May and lasts through October 1; the annual hours of sunshine are over 2,400. Sunbathing and swimming are both medically supervised.

Yevpatoriya's old city (a few minutes' walk from the harbor) has narrow, twisting alleys, relics of the old, oriental merchants' quarter. Some of the 16th-century battlements have been preserved. The gate through which the marauding Tatars drove their Russian and Ukrainian captives into the fortress still stands. The mosque of the Old City 1552–57) has also survived. To the right of the mosque, on the seafront promenade, stands the cathedral, which was erected in 1898 to commemorate the explusion of the Turks and the liberation of the city. The building is modelled on Hagia Sophia in Istanbul.

Continuing westwards, you come to the late 19th-century New City, once a center for wheat and salt exports. A number of monuments recall the Crimean War and the various struggles during the establishment of the Soviet regime, and during World War II.

At Teatralnaya Square, the New City merges into the health-resort district, which stretches as far as Lake Moynakskoye. The whole area is a single huge park with white sanatoria dotted amid rich foliage. The greenery of Yevpatoriya was planted with considerable effort—there was only a thin layer of sand over the rocky foundation so this had to be replaced by specially imported black soil. The Gorky Promenade on the seafront, and the Frunze Park in the city, are proofs of the success of this painstaking work. The local museum organizes regular tours of the city on foot.

Some eight km. (six miles) from the city is the Mamaiskiye quarry, which has provided much of the limestone used in Yevpatoriya's buildings; the largest quarry in the Crimea, it can be visited in groups by prior arrangement.

Saki is 21 km. (13 miles) east of here, and a little inland. Another well-known spa, it lies on the shore of Lake Saki. Its mud is excellent for arthritic, nervous and vascular complaints—its curative effects were even praised by Pliny. In recent years a medicinal spring has been discovered a few miles from the settlement, and this is used to treat metabolic and digestive complaints. Saki's 80-year-old park has two artificial lakes: the Swan Lake and the Crimea Lake; the former is shaped like the Black Sea, the latter like the Sea of Azov.

East of Yalta

Feodosia, which lies on the hills surrounding its bay, is on the fringe of the Crimean range; beyond it the steppe zone begins. (Feodosia can be reached by rail from Moscow, by bus from Simferopol, 110 km. (68 miles) away, and by ship from the Black Sea Coast, including Yalta. On the way you pass the coast which has already been described between Simferopol and Yalta, the seaside resorts of Gurzuf, Artek and Alushta.) As the mountains are not very high here, Feodosia is exposed to the cold winter and warm spring winds. Its climate is therefore cooler and drier than that of the southern Riviera of the peninsula. Yet it is still an important health resort; its climate is tempered by the sea and there is no frost, even in the coldest months. The summer heat never becomes unbearable. Standing on the top of the Feodosia hills you can see the endless grassy plain to the north, the hills of the Kerch Peninsula to the east and the sea to the south. No wonder Chekhov declared that he could never tire of this panorama—"not in a thousand years!"

The sandy beach is over 16 km. (10 miles) long; the bathing season lasts from June through October. Swimming is particularly pleasant outside the city limits, near the station of Aivazovskaya, where the water is very clear and you can see the bottom at great depths. Close to Feodosia, at the foot of the Lisaya Gora (Bald Mountain), is a medicinal spring. The mud of the nearby Adzhigol Lake (with a strong Epsom salts content) is also used by the local sanatoria.

Feodosia itself is divided into two clearly-marked parts: the old quarter at the foot of Mithridates Hill, and the new city, the coastal health resort. Feodosia was founded by traders from Miletus in the sixth century B.C. Formerly Theodosia, it became Kaffa in the 13th century, when it was a center of the Genoese Black Sea colonies with a famous slave market. These slaves built the harbor and the fortifications, whose ruins—towers, walls, battlements, bridges—have partly survived. The Local Museum, founded in 1811, contains many objects found in the ruins.

Feodosia's name is connected with that of Aivazovsky, a distinguished Armenian painter of seascapes (in the manner of Turner) and battle scenes. His home is now a museum, much enlarged from the original private collection, and there is a statue of the artist in the grounds. The building also houses an art school for children.

From Feodosia you can make an excursion to Sudak, one of the oldest health resorts in the Crimea (48 km., 30 miles, with a regular bus connection).

Halfway between Feodosia and Sudak lies the resort of Planerskoye, picturesquely situated on a spur of the Kara-Dag (Black Mountain) along the shores of the Bay of Koktebel. The Kara-Dag stretches for five miles between the highway and the sea. Many of the coastal cliffs and rocks have fantastic and romantic shapes—and names. Look out for Ivan Razboinik ("Ivan the Bandit"), Chortov Kogot ("Devil's Claw") and Peshchera Piratov ("Pirates' Cave"). Opposite the Kara-Dag, planted way out in the open sea, stands the rock called the Gate of Kara-Dag, whose arch is big enough for a large sailboat to pass under. You can sometimes pick up samples of jasper, agate, cornelian and other semi-precious stones on the shore. The bathing season is from May to October.

Sudak has a bay of its own. A mile south-west of the town you can see a medieval ruined castle perched on a cliff above the sea. The only approach is from the highway to the north. Beside the wall with its 12 bastions stands the citadel of the former "Consul Castle." From here you can have a fine view of the Sudak Valley and the sea. The little town lies in a valley dotted with vineyards, orchards and white houses. The semicircle of the bay is lined by a wide beach. The bathing season lasts from the middle of May through the middle of October. Although July and August are the hottest months, the sea temperature is 68°F (20.2°C) even in September. Sudak is the center of a large agricultural area; the state farm in the Valley of Roses grows many acres of roses and sage.

Kerch

The eastern corner of the Crimean Peninsula is a separate peninsula in itself, about 1,150 square miles in area, protruding far into the sea. This narrow tongue of land, with its eastern neighbors, the Kerch Straits and the Taman Peninsula, separates the Black Sea from the Sea of Azov. The district has important iron ore deposits.

The Kerch Straits linking the Black Sea and the Sea of Azov lie between the Kerch Peninsula and the Taman Peninsula opposite. The straits, which vary greatly in width, are about 40 km. (25 miles) long. Northeast of Kerch is the Crimea–Caucasus rail ferry to the Caucasian side. The straits were originally rather shallow so a canal was dug for ships of greater draught. This made it possible for the Volga–Don canal, built in 1948–52, to link the Black Sea, via the sea of Azov, with the Baltic, Caspian and White Seas.

The city of Kerch sprawls in a horseshoe-shaped bay, and can be reached by rail from Simferopol and Krasnodar, by sea from Odessa, Sochi and Rostov-on-Don, by bus from Feodosia, Simferopol, Sevastopol and Yalta.

Kerch is one of the oldest settlements in the Soviet Union. Founded in the sixth century B.C. by the Greeks, who called it Pantikapaion, it later became the capital of the Bosporan Kingdom. In the fourth and fifth centuries A.D. it came under Byzantine rule; then in 1318 it became a Genoese colony, while from 1475 it was part of the Ottoman Empire until, in 1774, it was annexed by Russia. A visit to the Historical and Archaeological Museum will give you a good idea of the city's history.

Kerch is not only a large port and industrial and cultural center but also one of the main fishing bases in the Crimea. The waters round about are particularly rich in plankton; in winter, when the Sea of Azov cools off, the fish migrate through the straits into the Black Sea and then return again in the spring to the Sea of Azov.

The Caucasus Coast

Crossing the straits to Cape Tuzla, on the Taman Peninsula, you are back in the territory of the Russian Republic. But by the time you have traveled along the several hundred miles of Black Sea coastline from north to south, from Anapa to Batumi, you will also have visited two Autonomous Republics which are in the territory of the Georgian Republic: Abkhazia (capital Sukhumi) and Adzharia (capital Batumi).

As you approach the port of Novorossisk you will see the first foothills of the Caucasus Mountains. These begin south of the large resort of Anapa. These mountains accompany you all the way to Batumi. Novorossisk is a port and an unloading point for goods transported by rail from Rostov and Volgograd, which are transshipped from here along the coast.

At Novorossisk, you join the famous Chernomorskoye Chaussée, the Black Sea coast road built in the 1890's and leading to Sukhumi. One of the road builders was Gorky, who worked here for a while.

The first important resort is Gelendzhik, 40 km. (25 miles) from Novorossisk, with an extremely mild autumn and winter. It has about 30 rest-homes and sanatoria—among them one for members of the Lomonosov University in Moscow. Closeby Dzhanhot (16 km., 10 miles), with its pine-wooded seashore and beach, is equally popular.

At Tuapse (an important oil-port), 193 km. (120 miles) from Novorossisk, the coast road meets the main Armavir–Tuapse–Sochi–Sukhumi railroad. From here the railroad and highway run parallel as far as Sochi, sometimes only a few yards from the blue expanse of the Black Sea, to the right, and the dense Caucasian forests to the left. The various resorts—Gizel-Dere, Dederkoy, Sepsi, Magri, Makopse, Aseba, Lazarevskoye and Dagomis—are all popular favorites with Russian vacationers. To the right of the highway at Lazarevskoye and Dagomis are campsites for motorists. At Dagomis a luxurious complex includes a motel, restaurants, cinema, a medical wing and a sauna. As you approach Sochi the climate becomes more and more subtropical and the oak forests give way to cypresses and yews, palm trees and magnolias. Here the winters are warmer and the summers cooler than in the Crimea. The bathing season lasts from June through the end of October.

Sochi

Sochi is the largest and best known of all the Soviet seaside resorts. It extends for over 32 km. (20 miles) at the foot of the Caucasus Mountains, between the Mamaika and Kudepsta rivers. You can come here from Moscow in two-and-a-half hours by air; the rail journey takes 30 hours. During the high season, trains arrive almost every half-hour from major Soviet cities. By sea the journey from Odessa takes about 45 hours, from Yalta 24 hours. There are bus connections with all the Black Sea resorts.

Sochi owes its popularity to the proximity of the medicinal springs at nearby Matsesta and to its pleasant subtropical climate. The average temperature in January and February is 43°F (6°C), while in summer the heat is tempered by sea breezes. The season begins in mid-June and lasts through mid-October. In the summer and early fall the water becomes very warm (up to 85°F, 29°C). Some of the beaches are pebbly rather than sandy, but they are all well equipped for swimming and sunbathing. Some covered pools have been constructed and are filled with preheated sea-water for winter swimming.

The pleasantest season is the autumn when the humidity falls, there are long hours of sunshine and the mountain winds are warm. Spring comes early to Sochi and the flowers are in full bloom by the end of March.

Founded in 1898, Sochi's real popularity dates from the 1950s. Since then the number of visitors each year has exceeded the total population of the city. Sochi's history can be followed in the Local Museum (29 Ordzhonikidze Street). The sanatoria here are mostly for bronchial, lung and nervous complaints. They are quite palatial, most having their own clinics and beaches, with funiculars linking hillside buildings with the beach. The Avantgard and the somewhat earlier Chaika (Gull) and Lazurny Bereg (Azure Coast) attract the most foreign visitors. Of the older establishments, the Balneological Clinic and the Gorny Vozdukh (Mountain Air) sanatorium are outstanding.

Sochi's harbor building is one of the most attractive in the Soviet Union, with an excellent view from its restaurant. Ships arrive here from other points along the coast and also, via the Volga–Don canal, from Moscow, Leningrad and Murmansk. The Crimea–Caucasus line (Odessa–Batumi) operates throughout the year. There are special cruise lines linking Sochi with the eastern Mediterranean. Short trips can be made in motorboats and hovercraft. The port for these is near the main harbor.

From the harbor you come out into Voikov Street; here you will find the post and telegraph office. The street continues to Kurortny Prospekt, which traverses Sochi from the old Kavkazskaya Riviera Sanatorium in the north to the Sputnik International Youth Holiday Camp in the Matsesta valley to the south, a distance of around 10 km. (six miles). If you stop at the beginning of Kurortny Prospekt and look to the left of the Kavkazskaya Riviera you will see the New City (Noviye Sochi) which grew up in the 1950s between the Mamaika and Sochi Rivers. To the right of the Kavkazskaya Sanatorium, Kurortny Prospekt, with its cypresses, laurel and camphor trees, continues to the city center, lined with hotels and sanatoria.

Between the promenade and the sea front, on Teatralnaya Square, you will find the Sochi State Theater with its 16 columns and allegorical figures of Art, Architecture and Sculpture on its facade. (Sochi also has an open-air theater in the Primorsky Park.) From Teatralnaya Square, steps lead down to the sea. The city beach is near the Primorskaya Hotel. There is a footpath along the sea front from the State Balneological Institute to the Lenin Sanatorium, which takes you through several parks over a distance of some two miles.

On Kurortny Prospekt (take the bus to the Polyclinic stop) lies the Dendrarium (open 10–6). This botanical garden was founded at the end of the last century and extends over 30 acres; more than 1,500 trees and bushes have been planted here from all over the world. There are fountains, basins and statues; the Dendrarium is also an experimental research station, working to improve and increase the flora of the Caucasian Riviera's parks and forests. Another of Sochi's main sights is the Ostrovsky Museum, a memorial museum housed in the writer's home. Some fine excursions can be made in the immediate environs of Sochi and a little farther away.

The Bolshoi Akhun Mountain (579 meters, 1,900 feet) can be reached by car along a winding road. From its high lookout tower you get a panorama of almost the whole Caucasian Riviera, from Tuapse down to Cape Pitsunda. Behind you the snow-covered peaks of the Caucasus seem quite close, though in fact they are some distance away. The Akhun Restaurant, near the lookout, is a very pleasant spot to take a rest.

From Staraya Matsesta (accessible by bus from the center of Sochi), an eight-km. (five-mile) path lined with plantains and lime trees leads to the Orliniye (Eagle) Cliffs and the Agura Waterfalls. The Cliffs and the ravine of the River Agura below them are a most impressive sight. You pass by the three main waterfalls of the Agura, the largest of which drops 90 feet between two immense rocks.

In the valley of the River Hosta, about 24 km. (15 miles) from Sochi (one mile from the resort of Hosta (Khosta), accessible from Sochi by bus and motorboat), there is a forest of yew and box trees, covering some 500 acres on the southeastern slope of the Bolshoi Akhun Mountain. The area is a nature reservation; some trees are 400 years old, and some of the box trees probably date from the birth of Christ.

21 km. (13 miles) from Sochi is the Dagomys Tea Farm, to which a reasonably-priced excursion can be made. Tea is served in delightful sur-

roundings and souvenir packets presented. Also at Dagomys is a pictur-esquely sited tourist complex.

Perhaps the most attractive excursion you can make on the Caucasian Riviera is to Lake Ritsa, high up in the mountains of Abkhazia. The excursion coach from Sochi goes along the shore of the Black Sea, the Cherno-morskoye Chaussée, as far as Gagra, then turns left into the valley of the River Bzipi, following a winding road that runs through forests and ravines. On your left, close to the village of Bzipi, are the ruins of a fortress (10th to 12th centuries) and a Christian church (eighth century). 13 km. (eight miles) from Gagra, just before the Yupsara Gorge, you can stop for a while on the shores of the small Goluboye (Blue) Lake. The lake is a striking deep blue and in places as much as 200 feet deep.

Beyond the lake, at the confluence of the Gega and Yupsara Rivers, the bus enters the Yupsara Gorge. Its high walls soon grow so narrow that only a thin strip of sky remains visible. Caves, pine forests and huge waterfalls follow, then another narrow tunnel-like defile. This brings you out on to a rocky plateau. A few hundred yards farther along, the bus stops outside the boarding house on the lakeshore.

Lake Ritsa lies in a most romantic setting, framed by forest and meadows. Mount Atsetuko rises to 2,290 meters (7,500 feet) and has a snow-capped summit even in July. Another forbidding mountain range to the southeast is the Riukhava, and there are also the twin peaks of Mt. Psegis-va, almost split in two. Lake Ritsa itself is one-and-a-half miles long and about half-a-mile wide. A motorboat will take you on a short cruise, after which you might feel like trying the local specialty—trout.

Matsesta, Hosta and Adler

Sochi's spa, Matsesta (13 km., eight miles from the city center towards Sukhumi), is a recent seaside development. Staraya Matsesta, the old city, lies in the valley of the river Matsesta, but not on the shore—it is situated a little way inland along the river. A good road links the two.

Matsesta's name is of Cherkess origin. It means "Fiery Water," a reference to the hot sulfur springs that have been known here from ancient times. The first baths were built in the early 1900s but there was no real medical supervision until the 1950s when installations were built for treatment of various complaints. The water contains 27 different elements and the wells yield several million gallons a day. The springs spread over 145 km. (90 miles) from Lazarevskoye to Gagra.

Hosta is another pleasant health resort, also with some medicinal sulfur springs, two dozen sanatoria and holiday homes. It boasts a huge plantation of cork trees imported from southern France. The bathing season lasts from July through October.

The airport for Greater Sochi and the last sizeable resort on the coast, still within the territory of the Russian Republic, is Adler, 32 km. (20 miles) from Sochi, at the mouth of the river Mzimta. This is an important agricultural area with numerous tea plantations. One of the collective farms, "Yuzhniye Kulturi," produces flower seeds, trees and ornamental bushes, and supplies large quantities of flowers to other parts of the U.S.S.R. by air. There is a 40-acre arboretum on the alluvial soil of the Mzimta, where more than 500 kinds of trees and bushes are grown.

From Adler you can make a pleasant excursion into the Caucasus, whose snow-covered summits are clearly visible from here, with several around 2,900 meters (9,500 feet). Your destination is Krasnaya Polyana (48 km., 30 miles), at the foot of the Caucasian range, on the river Mzimta, a mountain resort with medicinal springs. The road winds through a wild and picturesque landscape with views as fine as those along the famous Georgian Military Highway. Krasnaya Polyana itself has a lovely park (the former residence of a Grand Duke), with many rare plants. This is the headquarters of the State Nature Reservation of the Caucasus (Southern Section). The reservation covers more than 300,000 acres around Krasnaya Polyana on the northern and southern mountain slopes. The fauna is extremely varied, ranging from the Caucasian heath-cock to the bison, which survives in only two other places in the Soviet Union.

Abkhazia

Abkhazia, a small autonomous republic, begins south of Adler, at the river Psou. Its capital is Sukhumi and more than two-thirds of its territory is mountainous. The highest peak is Domay-Ulgen (3,695 meters, 12,120 feet). This is the area with the largest number of centenarians—some people are reputed to be 140 to 150 years old. A unique local specialty is the Abkhaz song-and-dance ensemble, consisting of these sprightly senior citizens. Their music and dances are very like those of the Basques and other interesting linguistic and folkloric similarities have been noted.

Abkhazia's mountains, with their dense forests, beautiful valleys and wild rivers, begin right on the coast. Paths from the coast lead up through woods of magnolia and cypress, oak and hornbeam to the sanatoria and rest-homes, in which more than 50,000 people stay annually. The climate is subtropical. Gagra, an Abkhazian resort, has the warmest climate in the European part of the Soviet Union. The winters are extremely mild; there is the occasional snowfall, but the snow rarely lies on the ground for more than a day or two.

Apart from tourism, Abkhazia is also noteworthy for its coal deposits, its timber and its subtropical agriculture. Silkworms are cultivated and bees are kept; but the main agricultural areas are along the coastal strip. Tea, tobacco, tropical fruit and grapes are all grown.

Gagra is a health resort lying halfway between Sochi and Sukhumi, reachable by rail, bus and sea. It has an extended seaside park with a great variety of tropical and subtropical trees. The open-air theater and the sports center are also located here. The Gagra mountain range (dominated by the peak of Ah-Had, 2,530 meters, 8,300 feet) surrounds the town like the wall of some ancient amphitheater—the descending terraces contain sanatoria and rest homes concealed in the greenery. The Soviet Government also has several villas and guesthouses here.

Though the atmosphere is humid there is not too much cloud, and there are 200 sunny days per year on average. The bathing season lasts from May through mid-November. There is a long well-equipped beach and, as the sea shelves rapidly, the swimming is excellent.

Gagra was built on the site of the fortress of Tracheia, at the gate of ancient Colchis. Many bastions, ramparts and churches still stand in ruins in and around the city, dating from the sixth, seventh and eighth centuries. Among them are the Marlinsky ruins in the valley of the river Zhoekvara, whose waterfalls are quite spectacular. There are several ravines, caves and underground streams in the limestone of the Gagra mountains. The source of the river Gagripsh is near a stalactite cave with a beautiful spring. It will take you a day to climb from Gagra's subtropical gardens to Mount Mamzdiska (1,830 meters, 6,000 feet), where snow lingers even in summer.

Cape Pitsunda, Gudauta and Akhali Afon

Cape Pitsunda, 24 km. (15 miles) south of Gagra, is one of the newest resorts on the Caucasian Riviera, planned as a second Sochi. Pitsunda's coastal pine woods (300 acres) are a nature reservation. Lake Inkit is a paradise for waterfowl; its shores also boast several mink farms. The fertile soil sustains several plantations of tropical fruit, and fresh figs and passion fruit are on sale in the market. A pleasant sandy beach is another attraction.

The garden city of Gudauta is in a miniature bay on the Black Sea. It can be reached by rail, bus and sea. Surrounded to the north and east by mountains forming a wide semicircle, its climate is similar to that of Sukhumi, though a little less warm, with frost in winter and gentle heat in summer. There is an open-air movie-house here, and a theater. The beach and the fruit market are the largest on the Abkhazian coast.

In the nearby village of Likhny you can see the ruins of an 11th-century Byzantine church and palaces of the old Abkhazian princes.

Akhali Afon, a resort at the foot of the mountains (accessible by rail, bus and ship), was named after a monastery, Novy Afon or New Athos, and was founded by monks from Mount Athos in Greece.

The surrounding mountains protect Akhali Afon from the northern winds, and give it a climate similar to that on the French Riviera, though with rather more sunshine. The little coastal settlement is enclosed by cypresses. Olive groves are scattered on the mountain slopes, and beyond them stands the former monastery, now a sanatorium. From the top of Mount Iverskaya (480 meters, 1,575 feet), which you can climb by a gently rising limestone path you can see as far as the lighthouse of Sukhumi. Two miles from Akhali Afon are the ruins of Prince Hassan Maan's palace. In 1954 the railroad station was moved inland, a little way uphill, and trains also stop at the lake side station of Agaraki.

Sukhumi

Sukhumi is the capital of Abkhazia. It lies on Sukhumi Bay and can be reached from Moscow by rail in 36½ hours and by air in 2 hours 40 minutes; while from Sochi it is 160 km. (100 miles) by rail, bus and ship.

Sukhumi's subtropical climate has been compared with that of southern Spain and Sicily. It is an ideal resort for sufferers from cardiac and lung diseases. Except in December and January the day temperature seldom falls below 54°–61°F (12°–16°C). Spring comes early, in February. The bathing season lasts from April or May through early November. The beach is three-quarters of a mile outside the city, on the Tbilisi road; there are boat and bus connections. The water in Sukhumi Bay is warmer than that of the other Caucasian beaches; there is no tide and there are 2,000 hours of sunshine a year. Early fall is the most pleasant season.

As well as a resort Sukhumi is also an administrative, industrial and cultural center with tobacco and leather factories, shipyards and canneries. It is the site of the Abkhazian Section of the Georgian Academy of Sciences.

The Abkhazian capital has a past going back 2,500 years. Founded by the Greeks in the sixth and fifth centuries B.C. (when it was called Miletos

Dioscurios), it became one of the most important trading ports on the Black Sea. Later a Roman fort was built here. In the city itself you will find interesting historical remains from the 10th, 11th and 12th centuries. The fort in the harbor, dating from the time of Colchis, defended the entrance to Sukhumi from the 10th to the 12th centuries. In the southeastern part of the city, on Chelyuskintsev Street, close to the House of Tourism, stands Bagratid Castle, also dating from the 10th or 11th centuries. This fortress was built by one of the Bagratid rulers of Georgia above the steep banks of the river Besleti, and it offers a fine view of Sukhumi.

On the road to Tbilisi, four km. (two-and-a-half miles) outside Sukhumi, stands the Great Abkhazian Wall, built in the seventh century. It ran as a series of forts for 160 km. (100 miles) between the rivers Kelasura and Mokvi and much of it has been preserved.

A little farther from Sukhumi, in the ravine of the river Besleti, is a multi-arched stone bridge, an interesting 10th–12th century example of Georgian architecture. On the left bank of the river are the ruins of an ancient temple dating from the same period. 18 km. (11 miles) east of Sukhumi, in the village of Dandra, stands another early (restored) church.

The streets of modern Sukhumi are laid out on a regular grid-pattern, the longer streets running parallel with the coast while the smaller side streets climb the mountainside very steeply. Primorsky Boulevard runs along the entire seafront. Where bazaars once stood there are now parks and gardens with palm trees, camphors and cedars, roses and camellias. The promenade is decorated with fountains and obelisks. Reaching Rustaveli Prospekt (a pedestrian precinct) you can follow Sukhumi's main promenade further, to the park with Rustaveli's statue and a large openair movie-house.

Around the middle of Rustaveli Prospekt, steps lead down to the sea; a floating restaurant offers specialties of Abkhazian cuisine. The Prospekt has a whole row of hotels and a Drama Theater, built in Georgian national style.

When you come to the ornamental pillars on Rustaveli Prospekt turn into Lenin Street. At the end of this street you will find the Baratashvili railroad station; the main rail station is outside the city, at the end of Chochua Street, and this is the city halt. At No. 20 Lenin Street you'll find the Abkhazian State Museum, with a varied collection of folklore items including a display illustrating daily life in an Abkhazian village.

The Botanical Gardens of Sukhumi are also on Lenin Street. Founded in 1840, they are a nursery for more than 800 varieties of trees and bushes including a Victoria Regia which flowers for just one day in August.

Trapetsia Mountain is perhaps the most striking peak in the range surrounding Sukhumi. In a park on this mountain there is an Institute of Medical Biology, with a large colony of monkeys and baboons imported from Central Africa, Indonesia and India, who live in the open; by the seventh generation they appeared to be completely acclimatized.

Mount Sukhumi can be reached along Kutaisi Street by climbing some basalt steps or driving up along a highway. The terrace of the restaurant on the summit offers a beautiful panorama. Here, at a Subtropical Plant Research Institute, experiments are conducted into the acclimatization of some 150 varieties of eucalyptus trees.

Some 65 km. (40 miles) from Sukhumi you can see the longest stalactite cave in the Caucasus. (Regular bus service from Ochamchire.) This is the

Avlaskira Cave, the third largest in the Soviet Union. Its "Drapery Chamber" is particularly impressive and it also has an underground stream.

Foreign tourists can arrange visits to the tea and tobacco plantations, orchards and vineyards belonging to nearby collective farms; don't miss the opportunity to taste the "Buket Abkhazii," the famous "Bouquet of Abkhazia" wine.

Batumi

Your final destination on this Black Sea tour is the southern-most city on the Soviet coast, 19 km. (12 miles) from the Turkish frontier—Batumi, capital of the Adzhar Autonomous Republic.

Batumi has the warmest winter, the heaviest rainfall and the most luxuriant vegetation of any place in the entire Soviet Union. From Moscow it is 40 hours 25 minutes by rail, and about three hours by air. It can also be reached by boat from Odessa, Yalta, Sochi and Sukhumi. The humid air and tropical showers have turned Batumi into something like a natural hothouse. The bathing season is from mid-May to mid-November but October is perhaps the pleasantest time for a visit. The winter is also extremely mild; some swimming-pools on the medicinal beaches are filled with preheated seawater.

Exotic trees and bushes growing with amazing speed, dazzling white houses, well-kept gardens and scrupulously clean streets are all typical of Batumi. There is practically no dust.

Of the more modern buildings, the Revolutionary Museum (9 Gorky Street), the pink marble Drama Theater (1 Rustaveli Street) and the Summer Theater (Primorsky Park) are the most important. The Adzhar State Museum (4 Dzhincharadze Street) has many exhibits showing prerevolutionary Batumi, especially the former slum district of Chaoba (Swamp); today this is a modern residential district.

The Primorsky Park is on the seashore and the Pioneer Park (4 Engels Street) provides another pleasant recreation area with a boating lake.

From Batumi you can make a rail or bus excursion to Zelyony Mys (10 km., six miles to the north), the Green Cape health resort. The heavily wooded mountain slopes come down almost to the sea, leaving a narrow strip of excellent beach. This is the site of Batumi's famous Botanical Garden, a large subtropical acclimatization and cross-breeding center.

Also to the north of Batumi are several resorts and sanatoria, many of them open in winter. They include Makhindzhauri, Zelyony Mys and Tsihis-Diri. Kobuleti has a drier climate than Batumi and the bathing season lasts eight or nine months.

North of Kobuleti the railroad and the highway both turn away from the coast but they swing back again at the district center of Ochamchire, continuing through nearby Sukhumi towards Gagra and Sochi.

PRACTICAL INFORMATION FOR THE CRIMEA AND

BLACK SEA RESORTS

WHEN TO GO. The high season in the Crimean and South Russian spas and resorts runs from early May through mid-October and the winter is fairly mild with snow practically unknown and temperatures rarely falling below 32°F. Mid-June through August is worst time to go—over-crowded, too hot and humid, and inadequate airconditioning. So go in the "velvet season", when privileged Russians like to go—September and October. The climate of individual cities is outlined in the text.

GETTING THERE. By train. Most of the places mentioned in this chapter are accessible by rail from Moscow, Leningrad, Kiev, Kishinev, Tbilisi and Yerevan, and are themselves interconnected. It takes 24 hours by train from Moscow to Sevastopol, 32 hours from Leningrad. All trains carry "soft" and "hard" sleeping cars and a restaurant car.

By air. Odessa, Yalta, Simferopol, Sochi, Sukhumi and Batumi all have airports. These are linked to the places mentioned above with rail-connections and also with Baku, Ashkhabad, Dushanbe, Tashkent, Frunze, Alma-Ata, Riga, Vilnius and Minsk.

By car. Odessa can be reached from Central Europe via Chop, Lvov, Zhitomir and Kiev (from Kiev by highway No. 6). Yalta is the terminal of highway No. 8 from Kharkov. Sochi and Sukhumi are on highway No. 10 from Rostov-on-Don via Krasnodar and Novorossisk.

By sea. Cruise routes link Constanza, Varna, Istanbul, Piraeus, Alexandria, Latakia and Famagusta with the Black Sea Coast. Motorships service the routes Marseilles–Odessa–Yalta–Batumi and vice versa; and Vienna–Izmail–Yalta. Odessa can be reached also from ports as varied as Naples, Bari, Dubrovnik, Venice and Genoa.

Hotels and Restaurants

Adler. *Priboi-Gorizont,* 24 Prosveshcheniya Street; 350 rooms, 9 floors. *Adler,* 41 Pervomaiskaya Street. 10 minutes from the sea, shop, café, parking lot, central. *Note.* Adler can only be visited in transit to or from the airport.

Alushta. *Magnolia,* 1 Naberezhnaya. *Tavrida,* 22 Lenin Street. *Note.* Alushta can only be visited in transit.
Restaurants. Either *Poplavok* on Lenin Street, or *Volna* on Naberezhnaya.

Askania-Nova. *Askania,* Krasnoarmeiskaya Street.

Batumi. *Intourist,* 11/1 Ninoshvili Street (tel. 26–61 or 97–331) is best. Set in a garden of palms and flowers, it has 137 rooms on four floors. First class and highly recommended.

Feodosia. Restaurants. For people-watching, *Feodosia,* on the municipal beach; or for just food, *Yuzhny* on Semashko Street.

Gagra. *Gagripsh* is best sited; but if you don't mind being 8 km. (5 miles) outside town, try the *Kholodnaya Rechka Motel* which is near the sea, with cinema, baths and showers, shop, post office, etc. *Note.* Gagra can be visited only in transit.

Gurzuf. Restaurant. The *Gurzuf* on Leningradskaya Street is best.

Kherson. *Intourist,* Svoboda Square, recently opened and best. Then *Pervomaisky,* 26 Lenin Street. *Kiev,* 43 Ushakov Prospekt.
Restaurants. Best is *Kherson* in Pervomaisky Hotel. Then any of *Ogonyok* on Ushakov Prospekt; *Dnieper,* at the harbor; or *Minutka,* on Suvorov Street.

Kobuleti. *Gorizont,* 450 beds.

Novaya Kakhovka. *Druzhba,* 14 Dneprovsky Prospekt (tel. 4–2100).
Restaurant. Try the *Tavriya* on Dneprovsky Prospekt.

Novy-Afon. Restaurant. Try *Psyrtskha,* in the heart of town.

Odessa. *Odessa,* 11 Primorsky Boulevard (Intourist) (tel. 22–5019). One of the nicest hotels in the U.S.S.R., it overlooks the harbor and has a charming courtyard where you can have breakfast under the trees. In the process of refurbishment, due to reopen in 1989. First class, superior.

Next is *Krasnaya,* 15 Pushkin Street, at Kondratenko Street (tel. 22–7220). Also an Intourist hotel. Picturesque red and white exterior, atmospheric. First class, moderate. *Chernoye More,* 59 Lenin Street (tel. 24–2031). Intourist. 195 rooms.

Also-rans. *Arkadya,* 24 Shevchenko Prospekt. 150 rooms, best in this category. *Bolshaya Moskovskaya,* 29 Deribasovskaya Street. *Passage,* 34 Sovietskaya Armiya Street. *Tsentralnaya,* 40 Sovietskaya Armiya Street.

Restaurants. *Ukraina,* 12 Karl Marx Street, is overrated. *Chernomorsky,* 23 Karl Marx Street, reported good. *Yuzhny,* 12 Khalturin Street. *Volna,* in city harbor building.

Pitsunda. There are five Intourist hotels here, each 14-stories high, each open from June through October, the *Apsny, Bzyb, Zolotoye Runo, Mayak* and *Iveria.* Each has dining rooms with European cuisine, bars accepting foreign or Soviet currency, shops, etc. The *Bzyb* has a heated sea-water pool, and guests may rent any kind of sports equipment. Facilities for water-skiing, motor-boating, basketball, tennis, volleyball and—for the indoor types—chess and billiards, concerts and movies (with an open-air cinema as well). This is essentially a health resort.

Pitsunda Motel, 12 km. (7½ miles) out towards the Cape.

Sevastopol. Only possible is *Sevastopol* on Nakhimov Prospekt.

Restaurants. *Volna,* on the sea front, Primorsky Boulevard, is best; followed by *Primorsky* on Lenin Street. In 1982, a three-masted sailing ship, moored in Artillery Bay, was converted into a two-deck floating restaurant.

Simferopol. Best is *Simferopol,* 22 Kirov Street. Then *Airport* which is good for little except transiting. *Ukraina,* 9 Rosa Luxemburg Street. *Moskva,* 2 Kiev Street. *Yuzhnaya,* 7 Karl Marx Street and *Vokzalnaya* at the railway station.

Restaurants. Dining room of the *Simferopol Hotel* is best, followed by *Chaika,* by the reservoir. Also *Dorozhny* at the railway station. *Astoria,* 16 Karl Marx Street. *Otdykh,* in the Kirov Gardens.

Sochi. *Camellia,* 89 Kurortny Prospekt, leads the list. 184 cozy rooms finished in fumed oak. 17 first-class single rooms; 149 first-class double rooms; 18 deluxe two-room suites for two persons. From the Night Stars bar and the Russian Troika tea room on the 11th floor there is a great view. The restaurant serves a wide variety of European, Russian and Caucasian dishes. Dance orchestra and variety; theater booking; large posh and nearby private beach! Next door, at 91 Kurortny Prospekt, is the *Intourist* with 97 rooms.

Magnolia, two buildings, 50 Kurortny Prospekt. A modern 9-story hotel. Rooms have balconies from which there is a good view of the sea. This large hotel is Number Two and almost deluxe.

Zhemchuzhina, 5 Chernomorskaya Street, (tel. 92–2388/4355). Highrise, with 953 rooms, recently opened Intourist hotel, reportedly "adequate" rooms with fine view over beach, good restaurant, two swimming pools, concert hall.

If you get sent to the *Primorskaya,* 1 Sokolov Street, complain. We usually leave out hotels we don't like, but as you are assigned rooms by the bureaucracy, we must report that this one is a dud, 434 rooms and poor service.

Also-rans in Sochi include: *Leningrad,* 2 Morskoi Pereulok; *Yuzhnaya,* Teatralnaya Street; *Kavkaz,* 72 Kurortny Prospekt; and *Kuban,* 5 Gagarin Street.

If you want a good health sanatorium, we can recommend the *Chaika,* at 3 Moskovskaya Street, but Intourist has others on its list as well.

19 km. (12 miles) out of Sochi at **Dagomys** are the 27-story *Dagomys* and the 8-story *Olimpiskaya,* as well as the *Meridian Motel.*

Restaurants. *Cascade Restaurant* in downtown Sochi is best. Good food, colorful atmosphere, dancing. Nice terrace with view of the sea.

Izba Restaurant, outside Sochi on road to Gagra, is second. It is in a re-created Georgian village, in a fascinating setting. Ask your Intourist representative to reserve for you and take you there.

Pazhka Restaurant is beautifully located in a hillside forest about 5 mins. drive from the center of Sochi. Pleasant atmosphere and excellent Armenian dishes.

The following are all about the same in service and atmosphere, so choose according to location: *Gorka,* 22 Voikov Street; *Svetlana,* 10 Pushkinskaya Street; *Goluboye,* 8 Voikov Street; *Dietichesky* (health foods), 10 Voikov Street; *Primorye,* 10 Chernomorskaya Street.

For atmosphere, try *Akhun Restaurant,* on the slopes of Mount Bolshoi Akhun, or *Morskoi* at the passenger wharf.

Sukhumi. Best is the *Sinop Motel,* with Sinop camping site, just outside town on the Tbilisi Highway, among the lush trees and on the beach. Restaurant, shop. The Intourist hotel, called *Abkhazia,* is next, at 2 Frunze Street. Third is the *Tbilisi,* on Dzhguburi Street. Another campsite is at *Gumista,* 5 kilometers out along the Novy-Afon Highway.

Restaurants. Best is *Aragvi* on Mir Prospekt. Next are *Kavkaz,* Frunze Street and *Ritsa,* Lenin Street. The following are about the same and rank next: *Eshera,* corner of Verkhnyaya and Esher streets. *Psou,* Tbilisskoye Chaussée.

For atmosphere, try the *Amra,* Rustaveli Prospekt, on the seafront; *Amza,* on top of Sukhumi Hill; or *Dioskuri,* in the Sukhumi Fortress overlooking the sea.

Yalta. *Oreanda,* 35/2 Lenin Embankment (tel. 32–2034). A first-class Intourist hotel, best in town, coming up for its century; only 30 yards from the sea. In the center of Yalta, with restaurants, cafés, shops, small craft landing stage, wine-tasting center nearby. 3 floors, 94 rooms; restaurant open 11 to 11, café from 8 A.M. Intourist service bureau arranges excursions, reservations, etc. Completely refurbished in 1986 and now runs Intourist holidays in association with Virgin Holidays, a British operator. Clients of Virgin/Intourist get free wine with meals. Resident British representative. Well recommended.

Yalta, 50 Drazhinsky Street (tel. 35–0150/0132). 17 floors, first class, modern, over 1,000 rooms, on hill overlooking the sea. 100 steps down to pebble beach; 10–15 minutes' walk or bus to harbor. Superb view of city, harbor and mountains. Large, excellent dining-room, shops, post office, etc.

Tavrida, 13 Lenin Street, gets a moderate rating for its 113 rooms, and is third best.

Fourth on our list is the *Motel* at 25 Lomonosov Street, overlooking Vodopadnaya River, with restaurant, filling station, etc.

Moderate to inexpensive are: *Ukraina,* 18 Botkin Street, with restaurant open till 11 P.M.; *Yuzhnaya,* 12 Bulvarnaya Street, restaurant also open till 11 P.M.; *Crimea,* 1–6 Moskovskaya Street; and *Gnyozdishko,* Kirov Street (near Chekhov Museum).

Restaurants. The *Oreanda* hotel has a good one. Another nice one is the *Espanola* frigate-bar nearby.

For panoramic views over the city and sea, try one of the following (in order of their proximity to the city): *Gorny Ruchei,* at the cable-car's mountain terminus; *Lesnoi,* on Lake Karagol; *Uchan-Su,* at the Uchan-Su waterfalls up the Ay-Petri mountain; and *Shalash,* at the Baidarsky Gates on the road to Alupka and the west.

Also-rans include: *Aquarium,* Moskovskaya Street, over a small stream; two restaurants in Primorsky Park, both open till 1 A.M., the *Priboi* and *Leto;* and *Otdykh,* a terrace restaurant atop the main port building at the harbor. At all the latter, the atmosphere or view is better than the food, which is at least adequate.

PLACES OF INTEREST. Bakhchisarai. *Historical and Archeological Museum* in the Khan's palace, open 9–5 daily, except Wed.; guides provided. The museum also superintends the 14 cave-dwelling settlements in the neighborhood, including the one at Fulla.

Batumi. *Museum of the Revolution,* 8 Gorky Street. *Local Museum,* 4 Dzhincharadze Street. History of the city and its environs. National costumes.

Feodosia. *Aivazovsky Gallery,* 2 Galereinaya Street, open 12–5, closed Wed. *Local Museum,* contains interesting collection of archeological exhibits from old city.

Kerch. *Historical and Archeological Museum,* 16 Sverdlov Street, open 10–4, closed Wed. Many important local finds; information about excavations now in progress.

Kherson. *Historical Museum,* 16, Prospekt Ushakova, with many exhibits connected with Field Marshal Suvorov.

Odessa. *Archeological Museum,* Kommunarov Square. Open 10–8, closed Wed. *Museums of Art, Local History, Western and Oriental Art. The Catacombs*—ask Intourist for directions; guide compulsory.

Sevastopol. *Black Sea Fleet Museum,* 11 Lenin Street, open 10–5. *Sevastopol Panorama,* Istorichesky Boulevard, open 9–8, closed Mon.
Art Gallery, 9 Nakhimov Prospekt, open 12–6, closed Tues.
Kovalevsky Biological Station of the Academy of Sciences, Primorsky Boulevard. Aquarium and museum open 10–4, closed Mon.
Museum of History and Archaeology of Khersones, 3.2 km. (2 miles) from Sevastopol, open daily 10–5, except Mon. Direct bus from Nakhimov Square, Sevastopol.
Balaklava, scene of Crimean War battle, 16 km. (10 miles) south of Sevastopol. Buses from city terminal, 7 Vosstavshikh Street. Check with Intourist.

Simferopol. *Local Museum,* 18 Pushkinskaya Street, open 10–3, closed Wed. The Neapolis excavations are also part of the museum. These are on the main Alushta Road, not far outside the city; a signpost marked "1 km" points the way.
Art Gallery, 35 Karl Liebknecht Street, open 10–4, closed Tues. *Regional Art Museum.*

Sochi. *Local Museum,* 29 Ordzhonikidze Street, open 10–4, closed Tues. Sections devoted to the natural history of the Caucasus and Black Sea.
Ostrovsky Museum, 4 Ostrovsky Lane, open 10–10, closed Wed. A memorial museum.
Dendrarium, Kurortny Prospekt, open 10–6. Huge botanical garden/experimental research station.
Dagomys Tea Farm, 21 km. (13 miles) from Sochi; excursion through Intourist (10 roubles).

Sukhumi. *Abkhazian State Museum,* 20 Lenin Street, open 9–5. *Monkey Colony,* Baratashvili Street. A large open colony of baboons and macaque monkeys. *Botanical Gardens,* Lenin Street.
The monastery of **Novy Afon,** 18 km. (11 miles) from Sukhumi.

Yalta. *Local Museum,* 21 Pushkin Street, open 10–4, closed Wed. Housed in a former Roman Catholic church.
Chekhov Museum, 112 Kirov Street, open 10–4, closed Tues.
History and Archeology Museum, 3 Zagorodnaya Street, open 10–5, closed Wed.
Literary Museum, 10 Pavlenko Proyezd, open 10–5, Thurs., Sat. and Sun. only.
At **Livadia** 3.2 km. (2 miles) from Yalta; *Grand Palace,* scene of 1945 Yalta Conference.

Yevpatoriya. *Local Museum,* 11 Lenin Street, open 12–7, closed Wed. Interesting natural history section, also an aquarium, with a huge swordfish as its prize exhibit.

THEATERS, CONCERTS AND CINEMAS. Batumi. *Drama Theater* (1 Rusta-veli Street). *Summer Theater* in Primorsky Park.

Kherson. *Musical and Drama Theater,* 7 Gorky Street.

Odessa. In Odessa there is an excellent *Opera and Ballet Theater* at 8 Lastoch-kina Street. The *October Revolution Ukrainian Drama Theater* is at 15 Paster Street, the *Ivanov Drama Theater* at 48 Karl Liebknecht Street.

There is a *musical comedy* theater (50 Karl Liebknecht Street), and the *Ostrovsky Youth Theater,* named after the Russian playwright, is at 12 Tchaikovsky Pereulok. The *Philharmonia Concert Hall,* 15 Rosa Luxemburg Street, dates from 1899. Origi-nally it housed the stock exchange. The *Nezhdanov Conservatoire* is in Ostrovidov Street; the late David Oistrakh and many other leading Soviet musicians have been among its graduates. One of the best Soviet *circuses* is at 25 Podbelsky Street.

Sevastopol. *Lunacharsky Theater,* 6 Nakhimov Prospekt. *Circus,* Korabelnaya Storona, near the Sevastopol wide-screen *cinema.*

Simferopol. *Gorky Drama Theater,* 15 Pushkinskaya Street. *Ukrainian Music and Drama Theater,* 3 Mendeleyev Street. There is also a *puppet* theater.

Sochi. *Theater,* Teatralnaya Square. *Open-air theater,* Primorsky Park, Cherno-morskaya Square. *Circus,* 8 Deputatskaya Street, seats 1180. During the summer season many touring companies and individual performers visit Sochi.

Sukhumi. *Drama Theater,* 1, Pushkin Street. Built in 1952 in Georgian style, it incorporates a waterfall. *Summer Theater,* Kirov Street, in the park.

Yalta. *Chekhov Theater,* 13 Litkens Street. *Philharmonia Concert Hall,* in the same building.

SHOPPING. Local handcrafts, carpets, embroidery, Black Sea Coast and Crime-an silverware can be obtained in the following shops:

Odessa. *Department Store,* 75/73 Pushkin Street. *Podarki (Gift) Shop:* 33 Deri-basovskaya Street. *Beryozka Souvenir Shop:* 19 Deribasovskaya Street. *Book and music shop:* 25 Deribasovskaya Street.

Sochi. *Souvenirs:* 40 Gorky Street. *Art Shop:* Bulevarnaya Street, opposite Mor-skoi Vokzal (Boat Station). *Jewelry:* 26 Kurortny Prospekt. *Market:* 30 Kirpichnaya Street.

Sukhumi. *Department Store:* 52 Mir Prospekt. *Bookshop:* same building. *Jewel-ry:* 1 Lenin Street. *Market:* 7 Tarkhinishvili Street.

USEFUL ADDRESSES. Alupka. *Tourist Office:* 10 Kirov Street. *Paying Guest Service:* 10 Rosa Luxemburg Street. *Railway reservations:* 30 Rosa Luxemburg Street.

Alushta. *Paying Guest Service:* 9 Krasnoflotskaya. *Railroad reservations:* (station in Simferopol) 19 Lenin Street. *Air reservations:* (airport in Simferopol) 13 Lenin Street (telegraph office).

Bakhchisarai. *Railroad station:* some distance from city center, but connection from Sevastopolskoye Road.

Batumi. *Intourist:* 11 Ninoshvili Street. *Harbor:* 2 Primorskaya Street. *Aeroflot:* 42 Marx Street.

Feodosia. *Paying Guest Service:* 23 Kuibyshev Street. *Rail station:* Lenin Boulevard. *Harbor:* Gorky Street. *Rail/air reservations:* 5 Voikov Street.

Gurzuf. *Paying Guest Service:* 26 Leningradskaya. *Rail reservations office:* 19 Leningradskaya.

Kerch. *Rail and air reservations:* 13 Tolstoy Square (nearest airport: Simferopol).

Odessa. *Railroad station:* Privokzalnaya Square (with taxi stand). *Rail tickets:* 21 Marx Street (9–6). *Bus terminus:* 5 Martinovsky Square. *Boat tickets:* 1 Marx Square. *Aeroflot City Office:* 17 Karl Marx Street.

Sevastopol. *Intourist:* 8 Nakhimov Boulevard. *Railroad reservations and sales:* 28 Bolshaya Morskaya. *Boat reservations:* 1 Tamozhennaya. *Air reservations:* (airport in Simferopol) at rail station.

Simeiz. *Railway reservations:* Lenin Boulevard.

Simferopol. *Intourist:* 9 Luxemburg Street. *Railroad station:* at the end of Lenin Boulevard. *Aeroflot Office:* 18 Sevastopolskaya Street.

Sochi. *Intourist:* 91 Kurortny Prospekt. *Railroad station:* Privokzalnaya Square. *Rail reservations:* Gorky Street. *Harbor:* 1 Voikov Street. *Air reservations:* in harbor (nearest airport is Adler).

Sukhumi. *Intourist:* 2 Frunze Street. *Railroad station:* Chochua Street (1½ miles north of city). *Aeroflot Office:* 1 Lenin Street. *Harbor:* 16 Rustaveli Prospekt.

Yalta. *Intourist:* 1–3 Kommunarov Street. *Harbor:* 7 Roosevelt Street. *Railroad reservations office:* 12 Sverdlov Street. *Air reservations:* in the post office in the harbor building.

Yevpatoriya. *Spa administration:* 15 Gorky Quay. *Paying Guest Service:* 44 Revolution Street. *Railroad station:* by tram from Teatralnaya Square (reservations: 15 Revolution Street). *Harbor:* 1 Moryakov Square. *Air reservations:* 14 Gorky Quay (nearest airport: Simferopol).

THE CAUCASUS

Georgia, Armenia and Azerbaijan

The Caucasus, a land of towering mountains and winding valleys, is a varied, colorful part of the Soviet Union—and one that is becoming an increasingly popular tourist destination, thanks to its scenic beauty and the year-round attractions of its invigorating climate. On the narrow strip of land between the Black Sea and the Caspian, snow-covered summits rise above the coast; in a single day one can travel from palm groves to the domain of eternal snow, from fresh, green tea plantations to rocky deserts. The three republics of the Caucasus have much to offer: Armenia has monasteries and chapels dating from the first century, Azerbaijan mosques and minarets almost a thousand years old, Georgia the ruins of 600-year-old castles.

In an area of some 170,000 square miles there is an immense variety of nationalities with different customs, traditions and ways of life—but of these customs, the tradition of hospitality seems to be all-enduring. And the inexorable laws of tribal revenge and masculine domination still linger.

Georgia

To the Russians it is Gruzia; to the Georgians, Sakartvelo—but whatever you call it, it is a country of rare variety and attraction. It is a republic of 26,911 square miles, with more than half of its area lying above 900 meters (3,000 feet), crossed by the towering ranges of the Great and Lesser

Caucasus (highest peak, Mount Elbrus, is 5,642 meters, 18,510 feet). It has some enclosed high valleys like Svanetia, wide basins like Kakhetia; only 13 percent is lowland. A third of its length is bordered by the Black Sea.

Among the more than five million Georgians, 15 major nationalities are registered. The Georgians represent about 70 percent of the population. Within the Republic's territory are two autonomous republics and an autonomous region: the Abkhazian Autonomous Republic (5,375 square miles, capital Sukhumi); the Adzhar Autonomous Republic (1,875 square miles, capital Batumi); and the South Ossetian Autonomous Territory (2,437 square miles). Most of the population live below the 3,000-feet level; the mountain districts are sparsely populated.

This is the area with the greatest concentration of centenarians, whose lives are being studied by a special gerontological institute.

Tbilisi

Tbilisi, the capital of Georgia, stretches along the River Kura for more than 20 km. (13 miles) and has a population of over a million. The city, itself lying high, is surrounded by mountains.

The Suran range, the watershed between the Black Sea and the Caspian, is west of Tbilisi, linking the Kavkasioni range (its highest summit is the 4,938 neter, 15,120-feet-high Kazbek) with the Mesheti Ridge. To the southwest, the spurs of the Trialeti Ridge close the circle; within the city, Mount Mtatsminda rises to 598 meters (1,965 feet). The climate is temperate and continental, with somewhat more precipitation but a less variable temperature than average. Sycamore trees line the streets. July is the warmest and January the coldest month, often with snow, and frost frequently occurs in December, January and February.

Mount Mtatsminda is the highest point of Tbilisi and from the top you get a panoramic view of the surrounding countryside. You can reach it by cable car. The terminal is near the Rustaveli monument, at Elbakidze Street which can be reached by both bus and trolley-bus. There is a stop halfway up where the Mamadaviti (Father David) Chapel stands on a specially-built terrace. Today it is a pantheon honoring the celebrities of Georgian culture. From here you can continue by the funicular or on foot. At the top terminal there are a restaurant, reading and game rooms and children's nurseries. Around the building a large park contains an open-air cinema.

From the summit you can descend on foot, first along the path leading to the Pantheon, then along Besiki Street, emerging on Rustaveli Boulevard, opposite the Hotel Tbilisi. Another, winding, serpentine path passes the resort of Okrokanya; then, along the Kodzhor highway, you reach the Komsomol Promenade, which runs along the Salalaki Ridge. The promenade stretches for almost a mile, lined with cypresses and linden trees. On the town side, a huge aluminum statue, the Deda-Kalaki (Mother of the Town), holds a sword in one hand, a cup in another—the symbolic welcome to foe and friend. On the same side you see the ruins of the former citadel. At the end of the promenade, a one-story brick building houses the Museum of Local History and Ethnography, containing archeological finds, costumes, arms and tools. From Komsomol Promenade, narrow, steep streets lead into the Old Town; but you can also visit on the far side of the mountain the Botanical Gardens, which are a cool, pleasant refuge

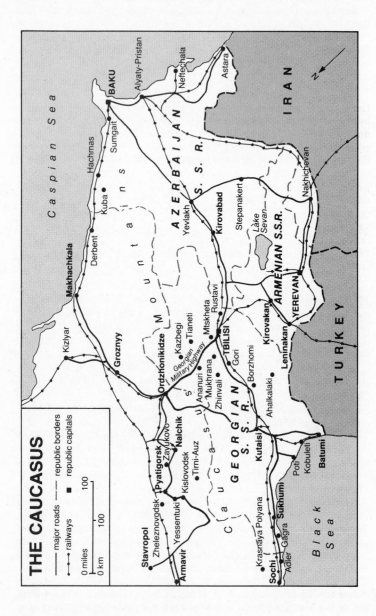

THE CAUCASUS

— major roads — — — republic borders
•—•—• railways   ■ republic capitals

0 miles   100
0 km   100

Caspian Sea

IRAN

BAKU
Alyaty-Pristan
Neftechala
Astara

Sumgait
Hachmas

Kuba

Derbent

Makhachkala

AZERBAIJAN S.S.R.

Yevlakh
Kirovabad
Stepanakert
Lake Sevan
Nakhichevan

ARMENIAN S.S.R.

YEREVAN

Kirovakan
Leninakan

TURKEY

Kizlyar

Groznyy

M o u n t a i n s

Ordzhonikidze
Kazbegi
Tianeti
Mtskheta
Rustavi
TBILISI
Gori
Borzhomi
Ananuri
Mukhrana
Zhinvali
Ahalkalaki

Georgian Military Highway

GEORGIAN S.S.R.

C a u c a s u s

Nalchik
Zavkovo
Tirni-Auz
Kislovodsk

Pyatigorsk
Zheleznovodsk
Yessentuki

Stavropol

Armavir

Kutaisi

Poti
Kobuleti
Batumi

Sukhum

Gagra
Adler

Krasnaya Polyana

Sochi

Black Sea

with a waterfall. Next to the gardens is the former Moslem cemetery, with a number of characteristic funeral monuments.

Descending from Komsomol Promenade you reach the Salalaki District. Its main thoroughfares, Davitashvili Street and Kirov Street, lead to the Inner Town. In Salalaki the most interesting architecture is to be found on Alaverdi Square and on the streets intersecting it.

Tbilisi's Center

The town center is Lenin Square, where, on the north side, stands the Georgian Art Museum. The treasury section (which can only be visited by special request) contains some exquisite gold and silverware. The Museum also has a fine collection of icons, frescos and works by Georgian painters. It was once the Tbilisi Ecclesiastical Seminary; a plaque still records the fact that Stalin studied here from September 1894 to May 1899.

Tbilisi's finest thoroughfare, Rustaveli Boulevard, branches off from Lenin Square. It is a wide, sycamore-lined street with many public, scientific and cultural buildings and hotels; in the evening it is the favorite promenade of the local population. Not far from Lenin Square the boulevard widens. Here is the Pioneers' Palace, formerly the local governor's residence. Opposite stands the Georgian National Museum, opened in 1929. Formerly the Caucasian Museum (founded 1852), it has a particularly rich ethnographical section. Next to the museum are the Shota Rustaveli cinema and the Intourist Hotel, built in the 1870's.

Close by is the Number One High School, with the statues of Ilya Chavchavadze and Akaky Tsereteli in front of it. The school also houses the Museum of Education; the adjoining huge building is the headquarters of the postal administration. (The main post office is on the far bank of the Kura.) Kashvety Cathedral, consecrated in 1910, stands in the center of a large garden on the other side of the boulevard. Behind the cathedral, the Garden of the Communards contains the statues of Gogol, Ketskhoveli and other notables. Before the park, on Rustaveli Boulevard, is the Georgian Art Gallery, which has seasonal exhibitions. It is housed in the former Khram Slavi (Temple of Glory), built in the 1880s to commemorate the conquests of the Russian Army in the Caucasus.

On the corner next to the park is the Hotel Tbilisi, built in 1915. Here the boulevard's straight line deviates at the Rustaveli Drama Theater, which also contains a concert hall. The Rustaveli Drama Company are world famous for their productions of Shakespeare in a bold, original style. They were acclaimed in London and at the Edinburgh Festival in 1979–80.

Nearby is the Paliashvili State Opera, a building in Moorish style, finished in 1896. The Opera House is named after a Georgian composer whose grave is in the garden outside. Their opera and ballet productions are well worth seeing.

On the same side of the boulevard is the Marxism-Leninism Institute and the Lenin Museum. Opposite the institute stand the editorial offices of the *Zarya Vostoka* (Dawn of the East) newspaper. Here the boulevard curves towards the road leading to the top of the Elbakidze Hill. At the end of the boulevard is a rather ornate building housing a cafe and post office. The cable-car station is in its courtyard. Rustaveli Boulevard ends in Rustaveli Square, which has a statue of Georgia's greatest poet, Shota Rustaveli. Just off towards the river is the Iveria Hotel.

Lenin Street is the continuation of Rustaveli Boulevard which divides, not far from the square, into Lenin Street on the right and Melikishvili

Street on the left. In Lenin Street there is, on the right, the open-air cinema, located inside Kirov Park. One entrance to the park is from Lenin Street which stretches to the bank of the Kura. There is another entrance from the river bank side. The Park has a large open-air theater, sports stadia and a Chess Palace. In its southern part, at the end of Niko Nikoladze Street, stands the Lurdzhi (Blue) Monastery which was built in the reign of Queen Tamar, with some of the original 12th-century building surviving. Its once blue roof gave it its name.

Returning to the crossroad, continue along Melikishvili Street. The Hotel Sakartvelo is on the left with a restaurant on the ground floor. The Tbilisi wine cellars are at the bottom of the street, on a little rise to the left. Thousands of bottles of seven hundred different vintages are kept here, including 1806 Tokay and 1714 Kiev vodka. If you can speak Russian the proprietor may show you round this amazing "vinothèque."

The white-domed university building can be seen from the beginning of Melikishvili Street. It stands on Ilya Chavchavadze Boulevard, one of the main arteries of the Vake District. It follows the steep bank of the River Vera, only a block away.

From Chavchavadze Boulevard, a stairway leads into the 300-acre Victory Park, with its fountains, shady walks, open-air cinema and cafes. The Locomotiv Stadium is in the southwestern part of the park. Behind the stadium on the mountain slope is the favorite Tbilisi resort quarter, Tskhneti.

On the other side of the university, the sloping Varazis-Hevi Street leads to the Square of Heroes, an important traffic junction. From here Chelyuskintsev Street leads to the left bank of the Kura and the railway station. Lenin Street crosses the square from north to south, connecting the city center with the Saburtalo district and the Georgian Military Highway. On the north and east side, Heroes' Square is bordered by the slope of the Saburtalo Plateau, on the southwest by a tall mountain. On the southeastern side, the lower stretch of the Vera River and the quay of the Kura can be seen. Turning south, you can see Lenin Street, and, in the distance, the outlines of the Mamadaviti. On the corner of Chelyuskintsev Street and the square a stairway leads to a hill where the municipal circus is located.

On the right of Chelyuskintsev Street are some of the buildings of the Georgian Academy of Science. Cross Chelyuskintsev Bridge to the left bank of the Kura. The street ends at the railway station; from here, another bridge takes us to the Lenin district.

The main street on the left bank is Plekhanov Prospekt. At the corner of Chelyuskintsev Street stands a film studio: The nearby Dynamo Stadium, rebuilt in the 1970s, has a total capacity of 70,000. Ordzhonikidze Park, opposite the stadium, has one of the first Pioneers' Railways, built by schoolchildren and students of the railway engineering college. An open-air theater and cinema, a parachute tower, a library, cafe and planetarium are among the park's other attractions. The Main Post Office is on Plekhanov Prospekt on which also are two typical Tbilisi houses, Nos. 107 and 116. Walking south from Chelyuskintsev Street you will reach the busy Mardzhanishvili Square.

Old Town

The old town is dominated by the castle, built in the fourth century. A few ruins of the citadel or western fort, known as Sahis Tahti (The

Throne of the Shah) have survived on Komsomol Promenade. The castle was a large complex and, beside the courtiers, many artisans and tradesmen lived within its precincts. Southeast of the castle walls a whole town developed. Its former site is most easily reached from Lenin Square by turning into Pushkin Street, then turning right again at the first cross-street. On the main street of the Old Town, in Shavteli Street, we find the Anchiskhati Church, founded in the sixth century and rebuilt several times—most extensively in 1675, when new gateways and a bell tower were added. On the right side of Shavteli Street is the Karis Ecclesia church, built in 1710 on the site of an earlier one. On its western side is a bell tower.

Shavteli Street runs into Irakly Square, center of old Tbilisi. It was the Royal Square where officials listened to complaints, where open-air courts sat, sentences were carried out and royal commands proclaimed. The eastern part is occupied by the police headquarters, formerly the governor's palace. On the north side, at the corner of Shavteli Street, we find the Simon Palace. Most of the old houses have been extensively rebuilt in the 19th century; but part of the palace of King Rustum, next to police headquarters, has survived. This is known as the Mint and has eight vaulted rooms.

Near Irakly Square, on the left side of Sionskaya Street, is one of Tbilisi's oldest and largest churches, the Cathedral of the Assumption. Its 19th-century bell tower with Russian dome is opposite. The original church was built between 575 and 639, but little of that remains. On the left also, just before reaching the Cathedral, there is an early 19th-century caravanserai.

To the south, Sionskaya Street runs into Vakhtang Gorgasali Square, an important traffic junction, linked by a new bridge to the far bank of the river. Vakhtang Gorgasali Street, starting from the square, runs along the river. Behind it is Bannaya (Bath) Street, where there are the remains of a whole row of Turkish-style bath-houses. The newer medicinal baths, which have clinics attached, are back in Vakhtang Gorgasali Street.

On the left bank of the Kura, where the river curves east, there is a steep rocky hill with a small church on top. This is the Metekhi Chapel, the most characteristic sight of Tbilisi. Founded in 1278–83 and reconstructed several times, it was for some time the chapel of the Georgian Catholics. In the 1820's it was turned into a prison; now it is sometimes used as a theater. On the same heights stands the round, bastion-like palace of Daredzha (Darya), the wife of King Erekle (Irakly) II. It is called Sachino (Noble).

Walking along Kura Quay, you can rest in the riverside gardens. At the Verei Bridge is the central bus terminal from which buses leave for every part of Georgia, Armenia and the Northern Caucasus.

The Georgian Military Highway

This road (now to be backed up by a trans-Caucasus rail link) offers the finest tour of the high Caucasus mountains, which have inspired a great many poets. The Military Highway received this name only in the last century, though it is many hundreds of years old. It is the shortest route (210 km., 130 miles), crossing the Caucasus ranges, linking Georgia with the Northern Caucasus and Transcaucasia. Its two terminals are Tbilisi and Ordzhonikidze, capital of the North Ossetian Autonomous Republic. The road from Tbilisi skirts the River Kura, then swings sharply towards Mtskheta. From Mtskheta it runs up to Gudauri and the Cross Pass in the valley of the Aragvi River, then continues in the Terek valley to the plain beyond the Daryal Ravine. This is a spectacular and varied journey, with the landscape and the weather changing almost every mile, through a land of legends and striking beauty.

From Tbilisi you reach the Georgian Military Highway via Lenin Street. The road leads between the fields of the Digom State Farm, passes the Zemo-Avchala Power Plant and makes a sharp turn towards Mtskheta. Not far from the 1927 hydro-electric plant a cliff-top church stands on the horizon—this is Dzhvari.

Mtskheta, some 23 km. (14 miles) from Tbilisi, is one of the most ancient cities in Georgia and was its capital until the 16th century. No more than a village today, once it was a twin city at the confluence of the Aragvi and Kura rivers and excavations have uncovered many valuable and interesting monuments. Here you will find examples of both the styles of ancient church architecture: the basilica and the cruciform domed church. The oldest is the 11th-century Sveti Tskhoveli Cathedral (built around a tiny sixth-century church), dedicated to the Twelve Apostles, with a carved facade and 16th- and 17th-century decorations. There are sixth-century frescoes, 12th-century icons and the church also boasts a "shirt of Christ." It contains the tombs of the last two kings of Georgia and is now the setting for performances of Georgian operas.

About 500 yards northwest from the Sveti Tskhoveli stands the Samtavro Convent, also built in the 11th century. The main church is dedicated to St. Nina, "the Enlightener of Georgia." Not far from the Sveti Tskhoveli, too, are the remains of the so-called Basilica of Antioch, with some parts dating from the fifth and sixth centuries, others much later. Opposite, on the left bank, in the mouth of the Aragvi and Kura, at the summit of the Sagurami ridge's rocky spur, stands the part ruined Dzhvari Church, built in 585–604. Beautifully proportioned, it served as a model for many Georgian churches. Today concerts of Georgian folk music and dancing are given here.

Leaving Mtskheta, you will see on a cliff the ruins of the castle of Bebristsihe (Fort of the Old Man). This was an outpost of Mtskheta built as a defense against attacks from the north.

After Mtskheta the highway runs along the right bank of the Aragvi, descending to the village of Garzis-Hevi, then continues along the undulating Mukhranai Valley. In the next village, Tsitsamuri, a white obelisk marks the spot where Ilya Chavchavadze, the Georgian poet, was murdered on August 21, 1907 by Czarist agents. North of the obelisk, in the village of Saguramo, the poet's former home is a museum.

After Saguramo the highway turns southwest, to Mukhrana. This valley used to be the estate of a great and rich aristocratic family, the Bagrations. Today there are vineyards in this area. In the courtyard of the central administrative building is an 800-year-old oak tree. After crossing the valley, the road reaches the community of Bulachauri. Close to it, on the right bank of the Aragvi, stands the Bodorna Monastery, rebuilt in 1772. There are many caves in the neighborhood which served as temporary refuges for the local people hiding from the hordes of Genghis Khan and Tamerlane. Close to Bodorna, the ruins of a medieval town can still be seen.

Zhinvali lies north of Bodorna, at the meeting of the Psava and White Aragvi rivers. Here, too, there are several ruined castles and watchtowers.

You can now make a detour to Bari-Sabo. A road branching off to the right leads across woods to the village of Bodavi, then over two passes and another couple of villages to Tianeti, in a wide valley. From Zhinvali a side-trip is possible to the town of Duseti and to the scenic Bazaleti Lake, south of it. Duseti became the capital of the Aragvi princes in the 17th century and in the late 18th century was given a municipal charter. The Bazaleti lake, some nine-and-a-half km. (six miles) to the south, has excellent fishing and there is plenty of game in the woods around. In summer, though the water is cold, it offers good swimming (but beware of leeches!). Legend has it that Queen Tamar deposited the cradle of her dead child here and that the lake was created by the tears of the Georgians.

Returning to the Military Highway, eight km. (five miles) from Zhinvali you come to the village of Ananuri with a 16th–18th-century fortress and, inside, the Church of the Assumption, built in 1689. Nearby is the 16th-century Bteba church and at the foot of the hill a domed Armenian church. A little further on is the village of Pasanauri, which has a new Intourist hotel, and an excellent restaurant.

North of Ananuri begins the Mtiuleti region with the highest mountains of the Caucasus. There are forests and Alpine-like meadows; bear, wolf, wildcat and fox roam the woods and the cold streams are well stocked with trout. Mleti is 1,410 meters (4,635 feet) above sea level. Passing across a stone bridge, the road snakes uphill, flanked by a deep ravine. Gudauri, the next village, is on the summit—at 2,158 meters (7,080 feet) the highest habitation along the Military Highway, offering a spectacular view into the valley. To the northeast we see Mount Gud, with the Krestovy Pereval (Cross Pass, 2,389 meters, 7,837 feet) on the right and somewhat farther away the summits of the Red Mountains, with huge rock pillars far behind them. These are Svidi Dzma, Seven Brothers.

After Gudauri the road dips, then, having reached the Devil's Valley, it begins to climb again to the Cross Pass, which is marked by a cross erected in 1824. Beyond the pass is the region of Hevi, the finest section of the road. The narrow valley of the Terek is framed by majestic mountains; the highest is the Kazbek with glaciers covering its flanks. The road now descends to the valley of Baydara, which is usually blocked throughout the winter. Here there are ten important mineral springs.

After passing a few smaller settlements you will arrive in Kazbegi (known in the 19th century as Stepan-Tsminda), center of Mokhavia, a mountain region of Georgia. Excavations have unearthed many bronze and silver vessels, jewels and other objects dating from the sixth century B.C.

The Kazbek, one of Europe's highest mountains, consists of two adjoining peaks, linked by a ridge. Amirani, the Georgian Prometheus, was chained to this soaring summit, according to local legend. The highest geophysical observatory in the Soviet Union stands on the Gergeti Glacier, at the foot of the Kazbek.

West of Kazbek, on a mountain on the left bank of the Terek, is the Trinity (Tsminda Sameba) Church, one of the finest examples of Georgian church architecture. From Kazbegi, a journey of 19 km. (12 miles) will take you to Betlemi which has a large network of caves on several levels. These were lost for a long time and only rediscovered in 1948. Today they are well signposted and lit, and open to tourists.

From Kazbegi the road runs alongside the Terek River, first climbing then descending to the village of Gveleti, near the Gveleti Falls. It descends further to the river, crossing the Devil's Bridge and arriving at the Daryal Gorge, into which the foaming, rushing river is compressed by steep rock walls, stretching for 14 km. (nine miles). Here lie the ruins of the Daryal Fortress, the inspiration of Lermontov's fine poem, *Tamara*.

After the fort, the road on the right leads to the Daryal Sanatorium, that on the left to the village of Chmi. A few miles farther on, Georgia gives way to the North Ossetian Autonomous Republic.

Excursions Around Tbilisi

Turning off from the Georgian Military Highway at the eight-kilometer stone, we reach Digomi, a village that has been inhabited for 2,000 years. Two of its seven original churches have survived; one is St. George's Church, on the outskirts, standing on the right-hand side of the road. It was built in the late 10th or early 11th century. There are some interesting votive tablets and reliefs. The other, the Mother of God Church, is at the northwestern end of Digomi, and is even older.

Kodzhori can be reached on foot from Tbilisi; the footpath is only eight km. (five miles) long, though the distance is more than 16 km. (10 miles) by road. It lies some 1,280 meters (4,200 feet) above sea level. Once it was the favorite summer resort of the Tbilisi nobility. Southwest of it is a ruined castle, dating from the 1600s. A mile to the northeast, on the wooded flank of Mount Udzo, there is a church which was a place of pilgrimage for barren women. The top of the mountain provides an extensive and beautiful view.

Betania is 32 km. (20 miles) west from Tbilisi, with a monastery that is one of the masterpieces of Georgian architecture; its church has ancient portraits of several Georgian kings.

Rustavi, on the banks of the Kura and 26 km. (16 miles) from Tbilisi, is a new industrial center. Its local museum displays interesting finds discovered during its construction.

A good road leads from Tbilisi to Batumi, passing through Gori. This, too, lies on the Kura, and its ancient fortress, the Goris-Tsihe, stands in the center of the town, on a hill rising above the bank of the fast-flowing Liakvi River. It was founded in the first half of the first millennium B.C., but has been rebuilt and altered many times. Gori is Stalin's birthplace and the house where he was born still stands, enclosed within a large, decorative building. On the way to Batumi we also pass Borzhomi, one of the most important health resorts in Georgia, famous for its mineral water. It has a monastery dating from the fifth or sixth century.

On the left bank of the Kura River, 18 km. (11 miles) from the town of Ahalkalaki is Vardzia, the famous cave city. Its caves are on five or six levels and have more than 300 chambers. The church carved directly into the rock dates from the 12th or 13th century and has fine murals.

Kutaisi, Georgia's second largest city, stands on the road linking Tbilisi and Sukhumi. The remains of the Bagrat church and the fortress there date from the 1st century A.D.

The Northern Caucasus

The northern part of the stretch of land between the Black Sea and the Caspian is occupied by autonomous republics which form part of the Russian Federation: Dagestan, Chechen-Ingush, North Ossetia and Kabardin-Balkar. It also includes the Stavropol territory.

The land of mountains, as Dagestan is translated, is a country of narrow valleys and towering cliffs. Most of the villages are in the mountains and are inaccessible for more than half the year. The houses are built very close together, on top of each other, forming strange fortress-like conglomerations. This is the location of Tolstoy's great *Hadji Murat.* Thirty-three nationalities live on the republic's 30,000 square miles; among the most numerous groups are the Lezgins, Avars, Dargins, Kumiks, Tabasaranians and Lakks.

The capital, Makhachkala, is an important port on the Caspian. In 1970 it suffered a devastating earthquake and has been mostly rebuilt. Its hotel is on the shore; it has a theater and a museum with exhibits of the local customs and rich folk art of all the 33 nationalities, especially carpets and jewelry. Kubachi, a mountain village, is famous for its jewelers and metalworkers and there is a good selection of their wares available in Makhachkala—carafes, jars and pots of traditional design.

The other important Dagestan city, Derbent, is also a port—the oldest surviving settlement on the Caspian. It has some fine architectural monuments dating from the 6th to 14th centuries.

The capital of North Ossetia is Ordzhonikidze, also called "The Gateway to the Caucasus", the northern entrance to the Georgian Military Highway. It is a small town which was the scene of bitter fighting during the Civil War. The Revolutionary History Museum is at 50 Kirov Street.

The Kabardin-Balkar Republic boasts within its borders the highest peak in Europe, the 5,642-meter (18,510-foot) Mount Elbrus. Nalchik, the capital, is a health resort and university town, rich in greenery. There is a museum of local history, and close to the city are ancient burial site excavations. Nalchik's main street is Lenin Road, linking Soviet Square and the Square of the 400th Anniversary, commemorating the fourth centenary of Russian rule.

The pride of Nalchik is the city park, which provided the great silver pines decorating Moscow's Red Square. Two peaks rise above the park— the Dih-Tau (Mount Heaven) and the Kostan-Tau (Tent Mountain). The statue of Sora Nogmov, the Kabardin poet who created the Kabardin alphabet and grammar and wrote the *Cherkess Legends,* stands in the center of the park.

Nalchik itself is an important tourist center, from which four main routes branch out. One leads through the Balkar Valley to the Blue Lakes, of which the finest and most mysterious is the Cherek-Koel Tarn. Another route passes through the Bezengi Valley to the Bezengi Ice Wall, which stretches for 14 km. (nine miles) and rises almost vertically. The route through the Chegem Valley winds past huge waterfalls. Finally, the road to Mount Elbrus goes through the Baksani Valley. Much of the latter trip can be taken by bus; from Nalchik the Terskol route passes through Staraya Krepost and Zayukovo (not far from the Baksan Power Plant) to Tirni-Auz, built 1,190 meters (3,900 feet) up, the center of molybdenum and wolfram mining. From here continue through the Baksani Valley. For the walker there are splendid trails in these mountains. One leads to the forest-lined Adir-Su Valley; from here you can proceed to the 3,650-meter (12,000 foot) Adir-Su-Bashi and Cheget-Tau-Chan peaks. The even more picturesque Adil-Su Valley gives access to the Shkhelda Peak (a fantastic ice-palace); thence, through the Dzhan-Tugan Pass, you can reach Svanetia. On the way to Mount Elbrus the first town where the bus stops is

Upper Baksan, with the castle of Prince Ismail Urusiev and his sons. It is a traditional base for Elbrus expeditions.

The next stop is Baksan-Basi-Ullu-Gara, where there is a large mineral spring whose water is bottled and sold all over the Soviet Union. Another 10 km. (six miles) brings you to Terskol, one of the leading winter sport centers in the Soviet Union. A long cable-lift carries you from the Hotel Azau to the summit. There is an intermediate stop at Stary Krugozor.

Mineralniye Vodi

Mineralniye Vodi (Mineral Waters) is the collective name of four well-known Caucasian resorts—Pyatigorsk, Kislovodsk, Yessentuki and Zheleznovodsk—all with a pleasant climate and delightful location, their waters rich in mineral salts, and attracting many vacationers and visitors taking the cure. The resorts are linked by electric trains. In all four resorts there are a number of sanatoria and hotels. The treatments offered include drinking cures and mud baths.

In Pyatigorsk it is worthwhile visiting the Local Museum and the Lermontov Museum (devoted to the poet). There are pleasant walks on the Goryachaya Gora (Hot Mountain), where you can explore the Tsvetnik Park, the Lermontov Gallery or descend on the south side to the caves, among them the Proval, which has a sulfurous lake. You can actually walk underneath the lake bottom. The other interesting features of the town are the Perkal Spring and the tree nursery near Perkal Cliff. From here, less than a mile's walk takes you to the clearing in which Lermontov was killed in a duel on July 27, 1841. The ascent of Mount Masuk is also a traditional Pyatigorsk excursion; the path starts at the museum and it is a comfortable hike of 50 minutes.

Kislovodsk is in a valley, on the banks of the Olkhovka and Beryozovka rivers. There is a beautiful park on the banks of the Olkhovka which has several small waterfalls. From here you can take a trip to the valleys of the Olkhovka or Alikonovka, explore the five huge cataracts of the Honeyed River or Mount Ring (named after its ring-shaped cave), the 1,402-meter (4,600-foot) Great Dzhina Peak and Bermamit. To the north of Kislovodsk, which has no large natural swimming areas, a huge man-made sea is being built, complete with beaches, boathouses, cafes and other tourist amenities.

Apart from its baths, the chief feature of Yessentuki is its spectacular park near the Hotel Mayak. From here you can take an excursion to the Podkumka Gorge and its cave.

Zheleznovodsk lies 576 meters (1,890 feet) above sea level, in the midst of a thick forest. You can climb Iron Mountain (Zheleznaya Gora), which offers a fine view of the district. On Razvalka Mountain the air is always cool, about 10,000 square yards of the mountain having a layer of permafrost, caused by carbon dioxide accumulated in underground caves.

Armenia

The Armenian Soviet Socialist Republic lies on the southern slope of the Armenian Mountains, along the northeastern part of the range, framed by the peaks of the Lesser Caucasus. Its area is 11,502 square miles and its population just over 3 million. It is bordered by Georgia to the north, Azerbaijan to the east, Turkey and Iran to the south.

This is one of the most picturesque and majestic parts of the Caucasus. Its average elevation is 1,370 meters (4,500 feet); even the deepest valleys are 450 meters (1,500 feet) to 730 meters (2,400 feet) above sea level. Spring comes later here; the atmospheric and barometric pressures are different from ordinary.

Yerevan

Yerevan is one of the oldest and most attractive cities in the U.S.S.R. Its situation, its natural features and its colorful buildings all contribute to its beauty. Lying on the Armenian plateau, its elevation is 915 meters (3,000 feet), with a remarkably pure atmosphere. It has hot summer days but cool evenings. In winter it can be very cold and sometimes there is snow, though mild winters are not infrequent. The city is surrounded by mountains; to the south the snow-covered peak of Ararat, on its left the somewhat lower Lesser Ararat (Masis) and to the northwest the four peaks of Mount Aragats. On the north it is bordered by the bleak rocks of the Kanaker Plateau, on the east by the greenery of the villas of the Nork Plateau, on the west by the deep ravine of the Razdan (Zanga) River with its riverside promenades and the vineyards of Mount Dalmin.

Modern Yerevan is a colorful city, its buildings constructed of basalt, marble, onyx and volcanic rock in many styles, yet forming a fairly harmonious whole. Though some of them may look over-decorated, they avoid the monotony of the box-like concrete-and-glass structures of many other cities.

Lenin Square is the center of the city. The dominating building here is the Government Palace, housing the Council of Ministers and the Supreme Soviet of Armenia. Opposite, on the northern side of the square, stand the offices of several ministries. Between the two pink palaces, on the northeastern side of the square, is the House of Armenian Culture, with a huge, arcaded loggia and a large basin with fountains in front of it. This is the home of the Historical Museum and the Armenian National Gallery. The Historical Museum covers the evolution of art on Armenian soil from prehistoric times. On the first floor are works by modern craftsmen and traditional costumes. Also in Lenin Square, on the corner of Amiryan Street, is the Armenian Hotel and the Yerevan branch office of Intourist.

Leaving the Hotel Armenia, turn left along little Amiryan Street and you will reach Lenin Boulevard in a few minutes. Turning left you pass the minaret and mosque built in 1776. This houses the municipal museum illustrating the 2,000-year-long history of the city. Opposite is the Market Hall with its massive wrought-iron railings; it has a striking interior and a very colorful atmosphere. On the other side of the road, before the Market, is the Museum of Modern Art—the only one in the U.S.S.R. Under imaginative and unorthodox direction, its frequently changing exhibits are well worth a visit.

Turning right from Amiryan Street and walking uptown along Lenin Boulevard, you will reach the Armenian Opera House, standing in a park which is a favorite with Armenians. They are often to be seen here engaged in what look like violent arguments but is usually just friendly discussion. The finest street in the city, Barekamutyan, begins at the park. It runs into a broad square, to the left of which Kiev Street starts. This leads to the Great Razdan Bridge, which crosses the river to Ordzhonikidze Boulevard. Turning from the boulevard into the Street of the 26 Commissars, you can reach Shaumyan Square. The Hotel Sevan stands here; the square is linked by a promenade with Lenin Square.

At the north end of Lenin Boulevard a stairway leads to the Matenadaran, the famous Armenian archive—a large collection of manuscripts, complete and fragmentary, in many languages as well as miniatures and some fine rare bindings. Most of the collection originated in the church library of Echmiadzin. A memorial to Mesrop Mashtots, the creator of the Armenian and Georgian alphabets, stands outside.

The Banks of the Razdan

The fast-flowing Razdan (Zanga) River forms a deep ravine near Yerevan. The river's flow has been regulated and pleasant walks have been built along its banks. The shortest way to approach it is through Spandaryan Street to the Bridge of Victory. The other, somewhat more interesting route, is through Kiev Street to the Great Razdan Bridge. After crossing the bridge take a footpath down to the quay. Walking upstream you will reach Abovyan Park, a pleasant recreation area with an open-air theater. The Pioneer's Railway, Ayrenik, will take you to a beach, which has a swimming pool. The river itself has a strong current and the bottom is stony here, so swimming in it is not recommended.

Walking downstream, you will reach the aqueduct. Nearby, on the rocky left bank, there are some remains of a fortress, stormed by Russian troops in October 1827. On the right bank are the Stadium and Shaumyan Park. Near the Aqueduct there is a three-span bridge and on the left bank a large building without doors or windows—the wine cellar of the Ararat Trust. The entrance is round at the back. Opposite, on the far end of the Bridge of Victory, a steep stairway leads to a pink, elaborately decorated building—the brandy stills of Yerevan. Visitors are welcome (by previous arrangement only).

Overlooking the river and Tsitsernakaberd Park in the northwest of the city is the massive monument to the million Armenians slaughtered by the Turks in 1915.

Residential Quarters and Ancient Fortresses

One of the most pleasant recreation areas of the Armenian capital is the Nork Plateau, with its shady trees and villas. You can reach the T.V. tower either by bus or on foot along Abovyan Street and Norki Road. In Abovyan Street, running parallel with Lenin Boulevard, stand the Academy of Sciences and the University. The old observatory is opposite the university in a large park. The new one is not far from Yerevan, at Byurakan, on the side of Mount Aragats.

Abovyan Street, named after a pioneer of modern Armenian literature born nearby, runs into Abovyan Square. Two roads start from here—Kanakeri and Norki. Kanakeri Road leads us to the Kanaker Plateau, from which there is a fine view of the city. (At Kanaker itself, a village now absorbed in Yerevan, is a memorial museum to Abovyan.) Here you can rest in Akhtanak Park and return either by bus or on foot along the Tbilisi highway.

If you set out from Abovyan Square along Norki Road, you will pass a whole row of hospitals and rest homes and come to a residential complex.

Turning right here, you can reach the T.V. tower. From here a forest path leads south to Komsomol Park. South of the park, on the plain, you will see the buildings of Nor-Ares and a bare hill. This is Arin-Berd, the former Urartu fortress, which has been excavated. Stone tablets were found here describing how the son of King Menua built a fortress and founded a city he named Argisti Ervuni. This was the predecessor of present-day Yerevan.

Southwest of Yerevan, on the left bank of the Razdan, is the Karmir-Blur, an Urartu fortress built in the eighth and seventh centuries B.C. Excavations at the foot of the hill, on the southern and western sides, have uncovered the remains of the Urartu city of Teysehaini. This is best visited on Sunday mornings: the bus bound for the race course takes you here from town (get off one stop before the terminal). From here it is only a short walk to the ruins. The hilltop offers a beautiful panorama of Yerevan's buildings and the vineyards and orchards of the Ararat Valley. The Exhibition of Armenian Economy has been laid out near Karmir-Blur; it covers more than 45 acres and has a striking central industrial pavilion.

Armenian Landscapes and Cities

Yerevan is an excellent base for exploring some of Armenia's most typical towns and villages. Nearest and most important is Echmiadzin, some 20 km. (12½ miles) west of Yerevan, which can be reached by car, bus or cycle. The road to Echmiadzin, lined with poplars and peasant flower sellers, begins at the Bridge of Victory and runs on the right bank of the Razdan past vineyards and orchards. There are fine views of Mount Ararat on a clear day. Noah is said to have landed on the peak of Ararat after the Flood and, although the mountain is now in Turkish territory, it remains central to Armenian lore and legend and features in many Armenian paintings.

About 15 km. (9 miles) from Yerevan it is worth stopping to look at the beautiful seventh-century stone church on the right hand side of the road, dedicated to the "virgin martyr" Ripsime, whose remains are thought to be buried in the Sanctuary. The bell tower and surrounding fortifications are a 19th-century addition.

At the 18 km. milestone follow the signpost to the left down a lane leading to the ruined seventh-century Cathedral at Zvartnots. Zvartnots, in its day the largest round church in the world, was sacked by Arab invaders in the 10th century. It is said they wanted no building higher than their own mosque. The ruins contain an unusual sundial and a relief of the architect, Master Ovennes. There is a museum attached.

Echmiadzin, founded as Vargarsapat in A.D. 117 and once the capital of Armenia, is today a busy market town, centre of an agricultural area famous for its fruit, wine and cotton. It is also the religious capital of Armenia, seat of the Catholicos (or Patriarch) and a place of pilgrimage for Christian Armenians from all over the world. When St. Gregory the Illuminator converted King Trdat III to Christianity at the end of the second century, making Armenia the first officially Christian country, he had a vision in which he saw Christ descending from heaven and beating the ground with a golden hammer. On that spot the Cathedral of Echmiadzin (meaning, literally, the "Only-begotten descended") was built in 301. It has been the centre of the independent Armenian church for the last 1700 years.

The present Cathedral was rebuilt in the sixth–seventh centuries and has been added to and embellished ever since. The new marble floor and altar are a recent gift from the Gulbenkian family. Reliquaries (including the lance said to have pierced the side of Christ—one of several in existence) can be seen in the Cathedral Museum. In the courtyard is a fine example of one of the early carved prayer stones to be seen all over Armenia. The nearby Theological Seminary accepts some thirteen young men each year for training to the Priesthood. Worth seeing also is the seventh-century Gayane Convent.

From Echmiadzin, it is worthwhile making a trip to Lake Aygerlich, 16 km. (10 miles) away, accessible by both bus and car. It is a small lake, surrounded by mountains, in a very beautiful setting. There is excellent fishing, and otters are bred in the reeds framing its shores.

To the southeast of Yerevan, some 18 km. (11 miles) distant lie the ruins of Dvin, another former Armenian capital, best reached by car along the Artasat highway.

Garni and Its Environs

Two important Armenian monuments, the Garni temple and the Gegard cave monastery, are only 35 km. (22 miles) from Yerevan by car. The route goes through Avan, Dzhrvezh and Vokhchaberd, twisting through romantic landscapes, along the ridge of the Gegami Range, and descending through a pass into the Garni Valley. In the sheer rock walls of the pass there are caves, today almost inaccessible, though once a regular refuge from invaders.

The Temple of Garni stands on a cliff, near the village, in the steep valley of the Azat River. Its walls are of huge basalt blocks. Once it was the summer palace of King Trdat I, who built it in the first century A.D. Destroyed by an earthquake in 1679, the monument has been excellently restored by Armenian architects in recent years.

The Gegard (Holy Lance) Monastery is only eight km. (five miles) from Garni. After a few loops the road reaches a ravine where the Karmirget River flows far below. A gate-like opening in the rocks is followed by a sudden descent; then the valley narrows and emerges into the Gegard Basin. Its perpendicular walls are honey-combed with caves. The church, built beside the river at the foot of the rock, dates from 1215. It provides access to another building with a roof formed by stalactites. The convent is in a cave adjoining this building; the only way in is through a narrow opening in the roof. It was carved out of the rock by a single craftsman who spent his entire life decorating and enlarging the cave chamber and its smaller alcove, which was used for burials.

Ashtarak, Byurakan and Amberd

Ashtarak is a district center, 19 km. (12 miles) northwest of Yerevan, on the southern slope of Mount Aragats. The whole district has been inhabited from time immemorial and there is hardly a village without some interesting feature. From Semiram (named after the Babylonian Queen) to Kos, the whole area is full of menhirs, cromlechs and dolmens.

Talis is famous for the cuneiform tablets found here. There are ancient burial places and fortifications in Parbi, Orgov, Mungi, Osakan and Egvard. Parbi has one of the oldest Christian basilicas in the world (fourth-century). In the village of Ahtse a fourth-century underground crypt with bas-reliefs has been preserved; it is supposed to be the burial place of the Arshakid rulers. On the road from Yerevan to Ashtarak the Kasan River is spanned by a fifth-century bridge, and on the rock rising above it are the ruins of the fifth-century Tsiranavor Church.

From Ashtarak the highway continues west; after six miles, it begins to twist and turn, leading finally to Byurakan, where there is an important astrophysical observatory. From here you can set out on a pleasant hike. The ascending road reaches the village of Antarur and its fine old oak forest (two miles). The path descending to the west takes you to the valley in which the Arkhansen and Amberd rivers meet. On the heights you can see the restored Amberd Church and Fortress, built in the age of the Bagratid dynasty, with a complex system of underground corridors. On the left bank of the Arkhansen, huge, fish-shaped carved stones, the so-called *visapos,* can be seen. These are several thousand years old, probably relics of a prehistoric water-cult.

Arzni and Environs

Arzni, known for its mineral spring and medicinal baths, lies in the valley of the Razdan River, some 21 km. (13 miles) north of Yerevan, linked by a regular bus service to the capital. Its sanatorium was built in 1925 but its sulfur springs were known long before then. The baths are set in a huge park of pine and chestnut trees. The promenade leads to an impressive waterfall. Towards the north another road takes you to the Egvard highway; a side-road leads to the Arzni reservoir, which is also a boating lake.

Tsakhkadzor is one of the most picturesque valleys in Armenia, some 1,565 meters (5,130 feet) above sea level. From Yerevan you take a train to Razdan and then continue by bus. The Valley of Flowers is the home of several Pioneers' camps, a "city of children." It is possible to put up a tent near the forest springs but the nights are cold and you need blankets or a sleeping bag.

From the valley you can make a half-day excursion to Mount Tegenis, starting from the northwestern edge of the youth camp where the Kecharis, an 11th-century memorial, stands. The path descends to the Tandzhabyur spring, from where a forest trail leads to a valley opening on the left. Here the ascent begins through woods and mountain meadows. From the summit (2,580 meters, 8,463 feet) there is a splendid panorama of much of Armenia. In winter this is a favorite skiing area, with thick, powdery snow, little or no wind and only moderate cold.

Lake Sevan and Leninakan

Some 60 km. (37 miles) from Yerevan, at an elevation of 1,829 meters (6,000 feet), you will find one of the largest mountain lakes in the world—Lake Sevan. Fed by some 30 rivers and streams, it has only one outlet, the Razdan River. The lake has a shoreline of more than 193 km. (120 miles). The Artanas Peninsula narrows the lake at one point to less than eight km. (five miles), dividing it into the Grand and the Little Sevan (the latter is much deeper). It can be reached from Yerevan by train or car. Sevan is a quickly developing town on the western lakeshore.

The Sevan Peninsula is six km. (four miles) from the town; its ninth-century monastery provides some beautiful views. Boating and sailing are best restricted to the morning and late afternoon hours because around noon there is usually a strong wind, often rising to a storm. The water is very cold, so bathing is only for the keen swimmer. In Sevan there is an interesting natural history exhibition in the Institute of Marine Biology.

Not far from Sevan, outside the village of Lohasen, prehistoric cave dwellings have been found and some once-submerged hills have turned out to be Urartu settlements dating from the ninth century. The cuneiform tablets identify King Argisti and the city of Istikuni. The archeologists found an almost complete four-wheeled carriage, bronze vessels, axes, jewels and inlaid daggers, evidence of a highly developed Bronze Age culture.

32 km. (20 miles) from Sevan an ancient cave dwelling at Cape Noratus has been found. Four miles from the cave is the town of Kamo (Nor-Ayazet), founded in the eighth century B.C. and now a center of the fish industry.

Lake Sevan can also be reached from Tbilisi and Baku. On this route, the first Armenian town is Idzhevan, famous for its potters and carpet-makers. From Idzhevan the road leads through the wooded valley of Ak-stafachay to Dilizhan, one of the most pleasant and popular health resorts in the country. It is surrounded by dense pine forests and there are fast mountain streams, waterfalls and bracing air. From here Lake Sevan is only a few kilometers.

Among other Armenian cities we must mention Leninakan, in the northwestern part of the republic, at an elevation of 1,402 meters (4,600 feet). Founded in 1837 by Armenian refugee artisans from Turkey, it has developed into a large city noted for its textile industry and theater life.

Azerbaijan

Azerbaijan occupies the southeastern part of Transcaucasia, on the Caspian Sea. It is bordered by the Russian, Armenian and Georgian republics and by Iran; its northern area lies along the southern slopes of the Caucasus. Near Derbent there is a narrow land bridge, most important in the Middle Ages, for the caravans of Eastern traders passed along this route; the Arabs called it Bab-ul-Abvad (The Gate of the East). Almost half of Azerbaijan's area is a plain. The southwestern part is surrounded by mountains of the Little (Lesser) Caucasus. The flat eastern area is bounded by the Mugan, Mili and Shirvan steppes. The highest peaks are Bazar-Dyuki (4,145 meters, 13,500 feet) and Sag-Dag (3,886 meters, 12,750 feet). At the corner of the Sag-Dag and the Murov-Dag range lies one of the most beautiful features of the country, the Gök-Göl Tarn.

Baku

The Azerbaijan capital is finely situated, built on a hillside around the horseshoe-shaped bay of the Apsheron Peninsula, which stretches out into the Caspian. While its climate is generally mild, it is often plagued by the "Nord of Baku," a wind of devastating strength. Most of the new buildings lie from east to west to lessen their exposure to the wind.

There is little left of old Baku. Its famous oil wells are now on the outskirts and a determined effort has been made to end (or at least limit) pollution. In the 1950s a pleasant promenade was built. It is the busiest spot in the city, with the main thoroughfare, the Boulevard of Oilworkers, running beside it.

The Intourist Hotel stands at one end of the Oilworkers' Boulevard. Next to it is the funicular station. The funicular will take you in a few minutes to the highest point of the city, the Kirov Monument, from where you can see the whole city and its bay.

Baku is a mixture of architectural styles. The rooms of the palace preserve the ancient traditions of Azerbaijani architecture; the flat-roofed ramshackle houses are medieval. Several buildings in the Inner Town date from the turn of the century. One of them is the present-day Marriage Palace, pseudo-French Gothic. It used to be the headquarters of a big industrial concern and later a club for emancipated Turkish ladies. The State Philharmonia (2 Communist Street) was built at the same time in neo-classical style and the Ismailia Palace (10 Communist Street), imitating Venetian Gothic, today houses the Academy of Sciences. The headquarters of the City Council and the Opera (27 Nizami Street) are early 20th-century.

The early constructivist style is represented by the Intourist Hotel on the seashore and the Press Palace on Nizami Square. In contrast, a rather exaggerated, over-decorated oriental style is apparent in the Government Palace on the seashore and the House of Scientists, very close to the Intourist Hotel. Examples of more tasteful, recent architecture, can be seen in the Youth Theater, the observatory and the wide-screen movie theater on Kirov Road.

From the Kirov monument you can descend by an imposing flight of stairs to the shore. The hillside park has an open-air theater, the design of which has cleverly made the most of existing topography.

Starting from the Intourist hotel along the shore, you reach a square with an ornamental fountain and, on the shorter side of the square, the House of Scientists. The Oilworkers' Boulevard begins on the sea side of the square and so does the shore promenade. Here there are an open-air movie theater, several modern restaurants, *chaikhanas* (oriental tea-houses) and facilities for various sports. A miniature Venice has been built here for children, with a maze of boating canals. Visit the big Exhibition Hall and rest a while in the open-air Pearl (Zhemchuzhina) Café, listen to a concert on an open-air stage or watch children's movies (also open-air).

Continuing either by the seashore promenade or by the Oilworkers' Boulevard, you reach Lenin Square.

The Castle

From the Intourist Hotel you can walk in ten to fifteen minutes to the castle district of Baku. It is best to enter by the Shemakha Gate. The streets are so narrow and twisting that in some places you can barely squeeze through between the houses. It is easy to lose your way, but the many slender minarets and the Bastion of the Maiden (Kyz-Kalasy) serve as landmarks.

The Bastion of the Maiden is on the left side of the road leading into the maze from the Shemakha Gate. There are many legends linked with it, most of them centering on unrequited love and a cruel khan, and all of which have a tragic ending. Once it must have stood surrounded by the sea, which has now retreated some 500 yards; it probably dates from the 11th century. The oldest monument in Baku is the minaret of the Mohammed Mosque, the Sinik-Kala, a delicate edifice; its inscription states that it was built in 1093. The Mohammed Mosque itself is much later. The most important part of the castle is the 15th-century Palace of the Shirvan Shahs. It houses the Historical and Architectural Museum of Azerbaijan and consists of several buildings and courtyards. Near the main palace is the Divan Khan, an octagonal, domed hall surrounded by arcades. A huge gate on the southern side is the entrance; the square courtyard is edged by a pillared gallery. There are several other interesting buildings in the castle, including caravanserais, mosques, minarets and baths. Many of the old houses are likely to disappear, but the most important and historical will be restored and preserved.

Nizami Square and Kirov Street

Nizami Square, one of the finest in Baku, is outside the Shemakha Gate, with the statue of Nizami, the outstanding poet of Azerbaijan's Persian literature. Opposite stands the building of the Nizami Literary Museum; its loggia is decorated with the statues of leading Azerbaijan writers. The entrance is from Communist Street. The museum's three halls illustrate the history of Azerbaijan; there are ceramics, miniatures, carpets and paintings dealing with the work of the 12th-century poet.

Behind the Nizami statue is an interesting apartment house called the Monolith. On a smaller square close to the castle wall the statue of Sabir, the great satirist, stands in front of the Academy of Sciences.

On Communist Street, opening from Nizami Square, are the Kirov University of Baku, the local party and government offices and the State Philharmonia.

Kirov Street is one of the main thoroughfares, connecting the hill quarter with the sea. To the left is the Square of the 26 Baku Commissars with a monument and an eternal flame in their memory. Along April 28 Street opening from Kirov Street, or along Lenin Street which crosses it, you reach the railroad station.

Not far from Baku there are the black rocks rising from the Caspian upon which the oil center of Neftaniye Kamni (Oil Rocks) is based. It was in 1949 that the first undersea wells were sunk and since then a whole city has been built upon the iron piles. Neftaniye Kamni can be reached by boat, either directly or from Artyom Island, which is accessible by local train or bus.

Exploring Azerbaijan

Baku is not only the capital, but also the communications center of Azerbaijan. The trains and buses starting from here are an excellent means of visiting the more interesting places in the republic.

You can reach Kirovabad by train and then continue by bus to Gök-Göl, or travel all the way by bus. After leaving the capital, the road passes across the Kobystan Steppe. First journey north, towards Dagestan, along the Hachmas-Derbent highway; from here, the road branches off after Hurdalan westward towards Shemakha-Kirovabad. Soon the first mountains appear. The bus stops first at Maraza with its 15th-century mausoleum (Derk-Baba).

After Maraza the road continues among the spurs of the Greater Caucasus, which, though they do not approach the height of the main peaks, resemble them with their grim cliffs. Shemakha appears in the distance. It was the former capital and one of the oldest settlements of Azerbaijan, the seat of the Shahs of Shirvan, whose court was often visited by the ambassadors of European and Asian powers. The formerly splendid city was several times devastated by earthquakes—by 1902, only 20 buildings survived. The new city was built close to the old one. Outside Shemakha, on the slope of Mount Pirkuli, at a height of 1,380 meters (4,200 feet) one of the largest solar observatories in the Soviet Union is sited.

The road continues toward the Asuini Pass, up through the wine-growing villages of Sagayan and Matrasa. On the right is the rocky ravine of the Harami Ridge with the houses of the town of Ahsu. High up on the mountainside the road passes the mountain village of Baskal, then Mugnali. The pass itself is the finest point of the route.

Descending, the mountains of the Lesser Caucasus on the far side of the Kura Valley can be seen, though they are 160 km. (100 miles) away. West of the pass there is a plain called Kara-Maryam (Black Maria), crisscrossed by mountain streams. On the right side of the highway the Ahsu (White Water) River emerges from a deep valley into the marshland of what was once the Kura's delta. The village of Ahsu is on the riverbank; from here you can get to the district center of Kurdamir, to the village of Kara-Maryam and then to Geokchay and Agdash. These two villages are famous for their huge orchards growing quinces and pomegranates. The grapes of the district are also excellent.

From Geokchay and Agdash continue across the plain and soon cross the Kura, arriving in Yevlah, a developing industrial center with a good restaurant and huge fruit market. After Yevlah the highway and the railroad run parallel for a while. Beyond Kasum-Izmailovo the outlines of the Mingechauri power plant appear. The level of the River Kura is raised by a dam here; beyond it the reservoir stretches for some 65 km. (40 miles).

Villages and railroad stations follow each other, then a monumental tower appears on the right-hand side—the mausoleum of the poet Nizami. From here the road leads along the valley of the Gandzhachay River to the poet's birthplace, the former Gandzha, now called Kirovabad and the second largest city in Azerbaijan. Of its numerous architectural monuments the Dzhuma Mosque is the most interesting, built by the command of Shah Abbas in 1603; you can also see the 13th-century fortress wall, the 17th-century caravanserai and the Dzhavad Khan mosque. Architecturally the Hey-Mam Mosque (built in the 17th, rebuilt in the 19th century) is also significant. The town has a huge park, many gardens and shady squares—and an oil refinery.

After Kirovabad the route continues across the mountains. The mist-wreathed peak of Mount Kyapaz (2,766 meters, 9,090 feet) appears in the distance. The beautiful Gök-Göl Tarn lies amid dense forests at a height of 1,372 meters (4,500 feet), its shores lined with sanatoria and holiday homes.

From Kirovabad continue along the right bank of the Kura, among orchards and vineyards. Samhor is famous for its dry wines. The small town of Tauz stands on the banks of the Tauzchay River. It has a market where good bargains can be found, and a pleasant restaurant. After Tauz you will pass through Akstafa, famous for its wine, then through the ancient village of Kazah. From here the twisting road leads through romantic landscapes and soon reaches the frontier of Azerbaijan and Armenia.

First you will pass the resort of Idzhevan, then in the valley of the Akstafachay, arrive in one of the prettiest resorts in Armenia, Dilizhan, known for its mineral waters and ozone-rich forests. From here it is a short distance to Lake Sevan, from where you can continue to Yerevan.

Nuha, Kah, Ilisu and Belokan-Lagodchi

At Yevlah, the road branches off toward Nuha. Leave Haldan behind you, then cross the bridge of the Aldzhiganchay, with the Mingechauri reservoir on the left of the road. Climbing for some distance, you will reach the saucer-shaped basin of the Adzhinaur lake. A barren plain stretches out to the left of the road; the spurs of the Greater Caucasus rise on the right, among them the Das-Yug. Your road crosses this mountain, then emerges into the valley of the Agrichay River. From here, passing through the fertile Alazan-Agrichay plain, you arrive in Nuha, an important industrial and cultural center which has some interesting monuments, including the castle of the Nuha Khans, dating from the 18th century. Richly decorated both outside and in, it has some remarkable frescos. The caravanserai and the minaret also are well worth visiting.

From Nuha to Kah the road leads among copses and fields. From Kah a wide, steep serpentine road branches off to the resort town of Ilisu, famous for its rich, sparkling mineral springs. There are a castle and mosque built in the 17th century and, Kah's outstanding feature, the Russian fort built in 1856. From here the nature reserve Belokan-Lagodchi is quickly reached, with its wealth of flora and fauna.

Sumgait, Kuba and Hachmas

These locales are best visited by car. From Baku to Sumgait, the distance is 40 km. (25 miles). On the way you will pass the Altava quarry. Sumgait is an industrial center, with modern residential quarters and a fine coastal promenade.

From Sumgait, continue along the Hachmas-Derbent road, crossing the irrigation canal of Samur-Divchini and reaching the dam and the huge Dzherainbatan Reservoir, which is helping to desalinate the soil and turn barren areas into fertile land.

Later along the road there is a large limestone cliff on the left side surrounded by four smaller cliffs. These are called Five Fingers (Bes-Barmak) and are associated with numerous legends; the local folk believe that the spring at their foot produces water only once a week—on Friday, the holy day of Moslems.

The road now turns, then starts to climb. On the right you will see the drilling towers of the Siazan oil field and soon reach the village of Gizib Gurum which is a pleasant halting place. From here you can reach the little town of Divichi in an hour; here the lifeless, dry steppe suddenly ends. A few miles from Divichi the road branches off. On the left, an endless row of poplars leads to Kuba, the town of apple orchards. It is the fifth largest town of Azerbaijan and famous for its carpets. Its buildings are all in oriental style and it has a fine park.

The road that branches off leads towards Hachmas and Derbent. Hachmas is a small place with only one very long street, lined with poplars. Near it the woods begin and north of here you enter Dagestan. If you have the time, you can continue to the 1,500-year-old town of Derbent, to Makhachkala, the Dagestan capital and to Astrakhan, the great port at the mouth of the Volga.

Kizilagachi Reserve and Lenkoran

This excursion is best done by bus, which takes you past several oil fields with a possible stop at the favorite bathing resort for Baku residents, Sihov Beach. The next stop is the town of Primorsk, then Sangalachi, notable for its medieval tower. Next is Salyany, a small town, with several oil wells and a fishery center. From Neftechali, the road leads to the nature reserve of Kizilagachi, rich in flora and fauna. From the village of Massali onward, you are already in a subtropical area, with cypresses, vineyards, lemon and orange groves, rice fields and tea plantations. Its center is the town of Lenkoran, with the experimental subtropical gardens of the Academy of Sciences nearby.

PRACTICAL INFORMATION FOR
THE CAUCASUS REGION

WHEN TO GO. With mountains offering winter sports, lakes and rivers for angling and fishing, medicinal springs and the beaches for swimming, the Caucasus is a year-round tourist attraction. The late spring and early fall are perhaps the most favored seasons.

GETTING THERE. By air. Yerevan is 3 hrs. 35 mins. from Moscow; about 5 hrs. from Leningrad; 4 hrs. from Taskent; 2 hrs. 30 mins. from Odessa; 1 hr. 40 mins. from Sochi; 1 hr. 10 mins. from Tbilisi. Azerbaijan and its capital, Baku, can be reached by plane from Moscow, Kiev, Tashkent and other Soviet cities. The Northern Caucasus is accessible by plane, as is Georgia, whose capital, Tbilisi is linked to the main Soviet centers.

By train. There are rail links into Armenia from the main part of the U.S.S.R., running from Rostov-on-Don via Sochi to Tbilisi and on to Baku. There is also a direct line to Baku via Armavir. From Turkey there is a line from Erzurum via Leninakan. Check before setting out on all these routes, as there are restrictions for tourists.

There are good services to Azerbaijan and its capital Baku from Moscow, Odessa and other main Soviet cities. Tbilisi is, likewise, linked to the rest of the Soviet Union by rail, as is the Northern Caucasus.

By car. There is a road from Tbilisi to Yerevan, while Tbilisi is connected by Intourist routes to many other Soviet centers. From Tbilisi it is possible to make a return trip by Intourist chauffeur-driven car to Yerevan. The journey takes 5–6 hours with stops and costs around 120 roubles.

By boat. The coasts of the Caucasus are served by a network of ferry and other services. However, the disturbances in other neighboring countries (e.g. Iran) make some of the services on the Caspian side difficult to predict. For the adventurous there is—at presstime—a weekly service from Baku to Enzeli on the *Guriev.* Deluxe one-way fare 90 roubles. The *Black Sea Shipping Company* runs ships on a route that covers Odessa–Yevpatoriya–Sevastopol–Yalta–Novorossisk–Tuapse–Sochi –Sukhumi and Batumi. There are about seven journeys weekly from Odessa to Batumi and return, calling at selected Black Sea ports en route. Journey time around $3\frac{1}{2}$ days.

TOURS. Intourist offers several tours of the Caucasus. One takes you to Moscow, Rostov, Kharkov, Pyatigorsk, and Leningrad; departures from Manchester Airport take place early April–late October, and from Gatwick Airport, mid-May through mid-October. Another takes in Tblisi, Baku, and Yerevan as well as Moscow and Leningrad, with similar departure dates.

Winter tours are offered for climbing and skiing in Dombai and Teberda in the Northern Caucasus; in addition there are dozens of local tours which can be arranged either in advance or in the main stopovers of the four tours described above.

TRANSPORTATION. Baku, Tbilisi and Yerevan are the only cities with a subway system. Baku's is said to be earthquake-proof.

HOTELS AND RESTAURANTS. A note on Caucasian food: Georgian cuisine is probably the most subtle and original in the Soviet Union. The standard entrées are usually *shashlik, chicken satsivi, basturma* (a variety of shashlik), *sulguni* (cheese), and *bazha sauce* (of walnuts). *Chicken tabaka* and sausages are the best known specialties. Other delicacies: *khachapuri* (cheese pie), *karabakh loby* (green beans in soured cream and tomato sauce), *tkemali* (sour prune sauce), and *tabaka* (pressed fried chicken). Delicious, fragrant salads—try asking for *tarkhun,* long green leaves with an aroma of aniseed, to accompany kebabs. A tip: if the waiter tells you there is no *"salat"*, ask for *"zyelen"* (greens) and you'll be brought a green salad! There is a difference, at least in Tbilisi's *Iveria Hotel* restaurant. Good Georgian white wine: *Tsinandali;* a good red: *Mukuzani.* Excellent mineral waters (*Borzhomi* the most famous).

In Armenia there are *solyanka* (hot, herbed beef stew), *shashlik,* many kinds of pilaffs and mutton. Excellent wine and heart-warming brandies.

Azerbaijan has at least a dozen kinds of pilaff to offer—the food is always spicy. Try *dovta* (a meat casserole with sour milk), *piti* (soup served in earthenware crockery), *yariakh dalmasy* (meat and rice wrapped in vine leaves, Greek-style); *nur kurma* (roasted meat garnished with pomegranates). Splendid full-bodied red wines, less good white ones.

Baku. *Intourist* is best. First class, comfortable. 63 Prospekt Neftyanikov (tel. 92–1265/1251). 73 rooms, excellent restaurant (by Russian standards); ask waiters for recommendations.

Moskva, 1a 76 Mekhti Gussein Street (tel. 39–2898/3048). 15 floors, 199 rooms. *Azerbaijan,* 1 Lenin Prospekt (tel. 98–9842/9843). 601 rooms. *Yuzhnaya,* 31 Shaumyan Street. Relatively modern. *Baku,* 13 Maligina Street, 744 rooms.

Restaurants. In hotels, or try *Metro,* Gogol Street. *Shirvan,* Kirov Prospekt. *Nargiz,* Karl Marx Gardens.

Gori. *Intourist,* 22 Stalin Prospekt. 54 rooms, swimming pool.

Kazbegi Village. *Kazbegi,* on the Georgian Military Highway near Ordzhonikidze (Intourist). Three floors, 35 rooms.

Kislovodsk. Best is the *Kislovodsk Motel,* outside town by the lake, with filling station, etc. An annexe 3.2 km. (2 miles) further on, named the *Zamok Motel.* Both have restaurants; the Zamok specializes in Caucasian dishes.

Also *Kavkaz,* 24 Dzerzhinsky Prospekt, 246 rooms. *Narzan,* Mir Prospekt.

Restaurants. *Chaika,* 4 Pervomaisky Prospekt, and *Zarya,* Herzen Street, are two favorites. But for scenery or atmosphere try the *Tourist Restaurant* on Lake Kislovodsk (outside town, near the Motel). *Khram Vozdukha* in Nizhni Park. The *Park,* near open-air theater in the Lower Park. *Krasnoye Solnishko,* also in the Lower Park, on Krasnoye Solnishko Hill.

Kutaisi. *Kutaisi,* 5 Rustaveli Prospekt. Four floors, 51 rooms.

Restaurants. Two average places on Rustaveli Street: *Gelati* and *Imeretia.*

Lake Sevan. *Akhtamar,* high on cliff overlooking lake, with three good restaurants. Also *Motel Sevan,* (tel. 42–13). First class, 109 rooms, parking lot for 50 cars. 75 km. (46½ miles) from Yerevan, 100 km. (62 miles) from airport.

Restaurant. If you have a choice at all, try the *Ishkhan* ("King Trout") near the Sevan Monastery.

Mtskheta. *Marani,* one of the new private co-operative restaurants, in a rustic setting with a fragrant open fire. Has its own farm and vineyard. Excellent service.

Nalchik. Either of two equals: *Rossiya,* Lenin Street, or *Nalchik,* Lermontov Street.

Restaurants. These are all in the so-so category: *Kavkaz,* Kabardinskaya Street; *Nalchik,* Respublikanskaya Street and *Dorozhny,* Osetinskaya Street.

Note. Nalchik may not be visited except during the day, as of presstime. Check with Intourist representatives locally.

Ordzhonikidze. The fine new *Vladikavkaz,* 75 Kotsoev Street, near the River Terek and close to the Sunnit Mosque, has 10 floors and 179 rooms. *Motel Daryal,* on the southern outskirts of town in Redant-1 village, is good. A modern, four-story building for 260 guests. Spacious lounges with television on every floor, a bar at ground level. Adjoining restaurant, post office, souvenir shop; set amidst pine grove, with views of the mountains.

Second best in the town itself is *Kavkaz,* 50 Vatutin Street. Third choice is *Intourist,* 19 Mir Prospekt.

Also-rans. *Iriston* and *Terek,* both on Mir Prospekt.

Restaurants. *Otkykh,* Hetagurov Park. *Terek,* Mir Prospekt. *Ogonyok,* Mir Prospekt. For a view and atmosphere, however, try *Gorny Orel,* on top of Mount Lysaya, 11 km. (7 miles) out of town.

Pasanauri. On Georgian Military Highway, 88.5 km. (55 miles) north of Tbilisi, *Intourist,* 60 Lenin Street. New, 32 rooms, excellent restaurant. There is also a restaurant on the main road in from the south.

Pyatigorsk. Best is *Mashuk,* 26 Kirov Prospekt (tel. 53431/52245). With an Intourist office. *Pyatigorsk,* 43 Krainev Street, but only if you are desperate.

Much better are three motels, one on Kalinin Street, another on Lumumba Street (with camping), the newest is *Volna,* 39 Ogorodnaya Street.

Restaurants. *Druzhba* in the Mashuk Hotel is best. Then comes *Kolos,* Shoseinaya Street. *Yug,* Universitetskaya Street, and *Tsentralnaya,* Kirov Street. For atmosphere, try *Lesnaya Polyana,* at the place where Lermontov fought his famous duel.

Stavropol. *Caucasus,* (tel. 32366/39561). First class, six-story, 300 rooms. Otherwise there are two moderate hotels: *Stavropol,* on Karl Marx Prospekt, or *Elbrus,* on Gorky Street.

Restaurants. In hotels, or at two equally modest places: the *Elbrus,* on Marx Street, and the *Gorka,* on Suvurov Street.

Tbilisi. *Iveria,* 5 Inashvili Street (tel. 93–0695/0488) is best, with good food and decent service if you get on the good side of your waiter! A first class, superior hotel, built in 1975. In the center of the Georgian capital, on the bank of the Kura River. 25 deluxe suites, 30 single and 223 double rooms in the first class category. Public rooms air-conditioned. Two restaurants (one on the 16th floor), a cafe, Intourist Service Bureau, and many other facilities. Swimming pool on roof. All rooms have telephones. Complaints about plumbing and heating—or lack of it.

Adjaria, Constitution Square (tel. 36–2716/9822). 22 floors, 300 rooms. Intourist establishment built in the early 1970s. It compares poorly with the Iveria, has a good restaurant but is not well located for tourists.

Tbilisi, 13 Rustaveli Prospekt (tel. 99–7866/7829). 5 floors, 115 rooms, can be rated as moderate, or second class.

Ushba Motel, out of town on the Georgian Military Highway (tel. 51–4922/1681). Better than average.

Restaurants. *Mount Mtatsminda,* dinner for about 10 roubles and a nice view, if you want atmosphere. Best in town itself is probably *Daryal,* 22 Rustaveli Prospekt. The walls are decorated with copies of interesting Georgian "primitive" paintings by Pirosmanishvili. Try their *kuptai* (looks like Georgian bagels), *cheezhi-peezhi* (egg and meat pan omelet).

The other top restaurant is *Aragvi,* Naberezhnaya Street, on the river below the Circus. It is related to the restaurant of the same name in Moscow. Downstairs is recommended.

British students in Tbilisi have recommended the *Khachapuri House,* central but address unknown.

Yerevan. Best is the *Armenia,* 1 Amiryan Street (tel. 52–5393). Has 227 large, but plain rooms. First class, moderate rating. A modern building with restaurant featuring dance bands, cafe, wine cellar and Intourist service bureau.

Next comes the *Dvin,* 40 Paronyan Street, near the river (tel. 52–6348). 15 floors, 297 rooms.

Another Intourist hotel is the *Ani,* 19 Sayat-Nova Prospekt (tel. 52–3961). A high rise building with cafe, bar, cinema and large restaurant. 336 rooms.

Youth Club Hotel (central Yerevan), with sports facilities.

Also-rans: *Sevan,* on Shaumyan Square, and *Erevan,* Abovyan Street.

Restaurants. Outside hotels, four more-or-less equal in standing: *Arabkir,* Komitasa Street; *Aragil,* Victory Park; *Egnik,* Spandarian Square; and *Massis,* Krasnoarmeiskaya Street.

Yessentuki. Not much choice between these three moderate establishments: *Yessentuki,* Karl Marx Street; *Mayak* and *Yalta,* both on Internatsinalnaya Street.

Restaurants. Best place is *Kavkaz,* Internatsinalnaya Street. At a pinch, try the restaurant alongside the railway station.

Zhelenovoksk. Two very modest hotels of equal appeal: *Kavkaz,* Gorky Street, and *Druzhba,* in center of town.

Restaurant. Only place worth mentioning is the *Beshtau,* Tchaikovsky Street.

PLACES OF INTEREST. Baku. *Exhibition Hall,* on the seashore promenade. *Nizami Museum,* Nizami Square, entrance from Community Street.

Historical and Archeological Museum, in the castle. *Mustafayev Museum of Arts,* with works by Azerbaijani, Russian, Soviet and foreign artists of different periods.

Museum of Azerbaijan Carpets and Applied Folk Art. Claimed to be the first museum of this kind, opened in 1972. Carpets and carpet products, embroidery, fine fabrics, ceramics, jewelry, carved wood, stone and bone from ancient times to the present day.

Kislovodsk. *Yaroshenko Museum,* 3 Yaroshenko Street, open 11–6, closed Tues. Devoted to the work of the prominent Russian painter (1846–98).

Sergo Ordzhonikidze Museum, in the Sergo Ordzhonikidze Sanatorium.

Nalchik. *Local Museum,* Lenin Prospekt, open 11–6, closed Sat. *Fine Arts Museum,* 35 Lenin Prospekt, open 11–6, closed Sat.

Ordzhonikidze. *Revolutionary History Museum,* 50 Kirov Street.

Pyatigorsk. *Lermontov Museum,* 9 Buachidze Street, devoted to the life and work of the great Russian poet. *Lermontov's House,* 18 Lermonotovskaya Street. The poet lived here for two months and after he was killed in a duel his body was brought here.

Local Museum, Sacco-and-Vanzetti Street 2, open 10–4.40, closed Tues.

Tbilisi. *Lenin Museum,* 29 Rustaveli Prospekt. *Historical and Ethnographical Museum,* 11 Komosomolskaya Alleya. *Georgian Literary Museum,* 8 Georgiashvili Street.

Tbilisi Art Gallery, 13 Rustaveli Prospekt, open 11–9. *Georgian Art Museum,* 1 Ketskhoveli Street, open 11–9, closed Tues. *Georgian Museum,* 3 Rustaveli Prospekt, open 10–4, closed Mon.

Chavchavadze's House, 22 Ordzhonikidze Street, open 10–6, closed Mon., the home of the outstanding romantic poet of Georgia.

Museum of Children's Toys, 6 Rustaveli Prospekt. *Art Exhibition Hall,* Baratashvili Bridge. *Museum of Georgian Medicine,* 25 Kiacheli Street.

Yerevan. *History Museum,* Lenin Square. *Matenadaran,* Lenin Prospekt.

Museum of Fine Arts, Lenin Square. *Children's Art Center,* Lenin Prospekt. *Museum of Modern Art,* Lenin Prospekt. *Saroyan Museum. House of Folk Art;* exhibits of works by the best folk craftsmen are arranged here.

Erebuni Museum, on the site of the Old City with the remains of the palace of the Urartu King Argishti 1, temples, city walls, water supply system and other structures have survived. There are also displays of bronze and iron tools, weapons, earthenware and jewelry.

The *Armenian People in the Great Patriotic War of 1941–45 Museum. Museum of Martiros Saryan.* Canvases by the famous Armenian artist. *Museum of Ovanes Tumanyan.* Dedicated to the life and work of the Armenian poet.

INTOURIST OUT-OF-TOWN EXCURSIONS. Baku. *Fire Worshippers' Temple Museum.* Dates from the 18th century. 30 km. (20 miles) from Baku. Tour takes 3 hours.

Kobustan Museum-Reserve. Caves lived in by primitive man 10,000 years ago. Unique cave drawings and a museum of excavations. 70 km. (44 miles) from Baku. Tour takes 6 hours.

Zagulba Settlement. Swimming and sunbathing on a beach by the Caspian Sea. 45 km. (28 miles) from Baku. Tour takes 3 hours.

Serebrovsky. One of the major oil fields in Azerbaijan. 35 km. (22 miles) from Baku. Tour takes 3 hours.

City of Shemakha. A tour of the ancient capital of Azerbaijan, and a visit to a state vineyard to include tasting of the famous Shemakha wines. 130 km. (80 miles) from Baku. Tour takes 10 hours.

City of Sumgait. A modern town, founded in 1949. 40 km. (25 miles) from Baku. Tour takes 4 hours.

City of Kuba. Includes a visit to a state fruit and vegetable farm. 200 km. (125 miles) from Baku. Tour takes 16 hours.

Mashtaginsky State Farm of Subtropical Crops. 30 km. (20 miles) from Baku. Tour takes 3 hours.

Pyatigorsk. *Mt. Elbrus Region.* Tourists have an opportunity to reach 3,100 meters by ski-lift to get wonderful panoramic view of Mt Elbrus—the highest summit in Europe. 170 km. (105 miles) from Pyatigorsk. Tour lasts 12 hours.

Dombai Valley. A high-altitude summer and winter resort. 225 km. (140 miles) from Pyatigorsk. Tour takes 12 hours.

Health resort towns on Kislovodsk and Yessentuki. 50 km. (30 miles) from Pyatigorsk. Tour takes 7 hours.

Health resort town of Zheleznovodsk. 25 km. (15 miles) from Pyatigorsk. Tour takes 4 hours.

Tbilisi. *Town of Mtskheta.* A tour of the Dzhvari and Svetitskhoveli Temples (6th century). 70 km. (40 miles) from Tbilisi.

Gori. An old town, the home of Joseph Stalin which is now a museum. The tour includes visits to Mtskheta, the Dzhvari Temple, and the cave town of Uplistsikhe (6th–1st centuries B.C.). 118 km. (74 miles) from Tbilisi.

Village of Pasanauri. Including visits to Mtskheta and the Dzhvari Temple. A tour of 16th–17th century castle. 100 km. (62 miles) from Tbilisi.

Village of Kazbegi and the Krestovy Pass (2,395 meters (7,858 feet) above sea level). The birthplace of the prominent Georgian writer Alexander Kazbegi which is now a museum. The architectural attraction of the village is the Tsminda Sameba (Holy Trinity) Temple dating from the 14th century. 118 km. (74 miles) from Tbilisi.

Yerevan. *Town of Echmiadzin and Zvartnots.* In Echmiadzin visit one of the first Christian churches, as well as the cathedral church, 4th century, with a museum and the Ripsime Temple from the 7th century. Zvartnots has a 7th-century cathedral, 22 km. (14 miles) from Yerevan. Tour takes 3 hours.

Garni-Gegard. Garni has a 1st-century temple, and there is a cave monastery at Gegard. 38 km. (24 miles) from Yerevan. Tour takes 4 hours.

Oshakan. 7th-century church where the creator of the Armenian alphabet, Mesrop Mashtots, was buried. 70 km. (44 miles) from Yerevan. Tour takes 4 hours.

Amberd Fortress and Church. 10th-century palace-fortress, and 13th-century church. 70 km. (44 miles) from Yerevan. Tour takes 8 hours.

Lake Sevan. One of largest mountain lakes in the world; tour also takes in 9th-century churches and the Sevan peninsula. 30 km. (19 miles) from Yerevan. Tour takes 3 hours.

Dilizhan and Agartsin. Dilizhan is a health resort, Agartsin has a 13th-century monastery. 120 km. (75 miles) from Yerevan. Tour takes 8 hours.

Town of Tsakhkadzor (The Valley of Flowers). 12th century Kecharis Monastery, and a big sports camp. 70 km. (44 miles) from Yerevan. Tour takes 6 hours.

Sanain, Akhpat, Odzun. A tour of unique historical monuments dating from the 5th to the 10th centuries. 250 km. (156 miles) from Yerevan. Tour takes 16 hours.

Metsamor. The remains of an ancient observatory dating from the 3rd–1st centuries B.C., and copper smelting furnaces of the same period. 55 km. (34 miles) from Yerevan. Tour takes 5 hours.

THEATERS, CONCERTS AND CINEMAS. Baku. *State Philharmonia,* 2 Communist Street. *Opera House,* 27 Nizami Street. *Children's Theater,* Kirov Avenue. *Open-Air Theater,* on the seaside promenade.

Kislovodsk. *Gorky Theater,* 5 Krasnoarmeiskaya Street. *Concert Hall,* in Verkhny (Upper) Park.

Nalchik. *Drama Theater* in the park.

Ordzhonikidze. *Ossetian Music and Drama Theater,* 18 Naberezhnaya. *Russian Drama Theater,* 1 Lenin Square, founded in 1869. *Puppet Theater,* 3 Lenin Square. *Open-Air Theater,* Kirov Park. *Green Theater* (open-air), Tbiliskoye Chaussée. *Planetarium,* 14 Kirov Street, in an old mosque.

Pyatigorsk. *Musical Comedy Theater,* 17 Kirov Street. *Philharmonia Concert Hall,* in the Lermontov Gallery, Tsvetnik Park. In the Kirov Park, 3 Dunayevsky Street, there is a *planetarium* and an *Open-Air Theater.*

Tbilisi. *Paliashvili Opera House,* 25 Rustaveli Prospekt. *Mardzhanishvili Theater,* 8 Mardzhanishvili Street, named after a well known Georgian theatrical producer. *Rustaveli Theater,* established in 1920, 17 Rustaveli Prospekt. *Griboyedov Russian Drama Theater,* 2/4 Rustaveli. Originally built as a caravanserai, the theater building dates from the 1850's. *Shaumyan Armenian Drama Theater,* 8 Shaumyan Street, opened in 1936. *Russian Youth Theater* in the same building as the Georgian Puppet Theater, 101 Plekhanov Prospekt. *Georgian Youth Theater,* 37 Rustaveli Prospekt.

At 123 Plekhanov is the summer home of the State Symphony Orchestra, the national dance ensemble, etc. Concerts are now mainly given in the new *Philharmonia Concert Hall,* Melikishvili Street. *Vano Saradzhishvili Tbilisi Conservatory,* 8 Griboyedov Street, named after the Georgian singer buried in the Opera House garden. *Concert Hall,* Melikishvili Street.

Abashidze Musical Comedy Theater, 182 Plekhanov Prospekt. *Circus,* Ploshchad Geroyev Sovietskogo Soyuza (Heroes of the Soviet Union Square).

Yerevan. *House of Armenian Culture,* Lenin Square. *Armenian Opera House,* Lenin Boulevard. *Open-Air Theater,* Abovyan Park. *Sports and Concert Hall,* completed in 1984; 9,000 seats in two halls on a hilltop.

Yessentuki. *Theater* in the park.

SHOPPING. The carpets of Armenia and Turkmenia are certainly the best buys in the Caucasus; but wines, brandies, embroideries, miniatures can also be purchased at reasonable prices. The recommended shops are:

Kislovodsk. *Jeweler's,* Karl Mark Prospekt.

Nalchik. *Department Store and Souvenirs,* 15 Kabardinskaya Street; *Jeweler's,* 10 Kabardinskaya Street.

Ordzhonikidze. *Department Store,* 31 Mir Prospekt; *Souvenirs,* 33 Mir Prospekt; *Jeweler's,* 26 Mir Prospekt.

Pyatigorsk. *Department Store,* 1 Oktyabrskaya Street; *Jeweler's,* 42 Dzerzhinsky Street.

Tbilisi. Art Salon, 19 Rustaveli Street, next to the Tbilisi Hotel; *Souvenir Shop,* Lenin Square; *Department Store,* 7 Mardzhanishvili Street. The *Tbilisi Department Store* on Rustaveli at Lenin Square is worth a visit, while the *Souvenir Shop* at 18 Rustaveli is a good one. There is a hard-currency store called *Tsitsinatela,* at 23 Rustaveli, which has some handicrafts from the Caucasus. Wines and liquor are downstairs.

Yessentuki. *Department Store,* 11 Internatsionalnaya Street.

USEFUL ADDRESSES. Kislovodsk. *Baths:* Central, 6 Glavny Prospekt; October Bath, 8 Main Road; mud bath, 5 Krepostnoy Pereulok; *Baths Administration,* 9 Glavny Prospekt. *Tourist office:* 5 Glavny Prospekt.

Pyatigorsk. *Baths:* Lermontov (sulfurous), Tsvetnik Park: Pushkin Bath (upper and lower), Nos. 1 and 2 Kirov Road; radioactive baths, 17 Teplosernaya Street; mud bath, 67 Kirov Street. *Intourist Office,* 26 Kirov Prospekt.

Yessentuki. *Mud bath,* 4 Semashko Street; *Administration,* 15 Andzhiyevsky Street.

Zheleznovodsk. *Baths:* mineral water bath, 6 Gorky Street; Slav baths, Park; mud bath, 2 Pervomaiskaya Street; *Administration,* 4 Gorizontalnaya Street.

THE CENTRAL ASIAN REPUBLICS

Where Tamerlane Held Sway

Central Asia is a plain geographical term which, nonetheless, inspires exotic visions of fearful adventure. Definitely, it has something new to offer the tourist. There are, to be sure, hotels, airports, paved roads, water and electricity, department stores and theaters, yet the climate, the rhythm of life, the dress and the architecture, the traditions and customs are all strikingly unfamiliar to the traveler from the West.

Soviet Central Asia consists of four republics: Turkmenistan, Uzbekistan, Tadzhikistan and Kirghizia. Geographically and ethnographically, moreover, Kazakhstan is also a part, though not officially so. The whole area stretches, north to south, from the Aral-Irtysh watershed to the Soviet-Iranian and Soviet-Afghan borders and, west to east, from the Caspian to the Sino-Soviet frontier.

Four of the five republics are inhabited by people whose languages belong to the Turkish family: the Turkmen, the Uzbeks, the Kazakhs, the Kirghizes and the Kara-Kalpaks. (The last of these form an autonomous republic within the Uzbek Soviet Socialist Republic.) Their languages are so similar that they understand one another and are able to communicate, more or less easily, with the Turks, Azerbaijanis, Tatars and Bashkirs. The language of the Tadzhiks, on the other hand, belongs to the Iranian family, related to Persian. The religion of the Central Asian population is largely Moslem. A good many Russians and Ukrainians also live in the area, especially in Kazakhstan, where, during the 1950s and 1960s, hundreds of thousands of people were sent to open up the so-called "virgin" lands.

Much has been done to develop the culture of the various ethnic communities and the establishment of native arts and literatures as well as to provide modern education, technological know-how and so on. For the visitor, there is a good deal to see—from the immense deserts of Kara-Kum to the cotton-fields of Turkmenistan, the longest irrigation systems in the world, nuclear research centers and hydroelectric plants, local arts and crafts, music and drama.

Turkmenistan

The Turkmenian Republic lies in the southwestern part of Central Asia, bordering on Iran and Afghanistan in the south. It has an area of 188,417 square miles and a population of almost 3 million, of which the majority lives outside the towns. Over 60 percent are Turkmen, the others are mainly Russians, Uzbeks and Kazakhs. More than four-fifths of the republic's area is desert and only a small percentage is irrigated. The Kopet-Dag mountain range stretches along the south and southwest. The principal rivers are the Amu-Darya (the ancient Oxus), the Murgab and the Tedzhen. The mean average temperature in the northern part is −4°C (25°F) in January, 28°C (80°F) in July; in the southern regions, +4°C (39°F), 30°C (86°F) respectively.

Ashkhabad

The capital of the Turkmenian Republic is Ashkhabad. It is the southernmost city of the Soviet Union. Sited in an oasis of the Kara-Kum desert near the Kopet-Dag mountains, it lies only 40 km. (25 miles) from the Iranian border. The winter can be quite cold and the summers extremely hot; the rainy season is in the spring.

The finest view of Ashkhabad can be had from the lower slopes of the Kopet-Dag. It is a long, sprawling city whose houses are almost hidden by trees. Only a few taller buildings emerge from this greenery: the ornamental tower of the textile mill in the northwestern district, the dome of a former mosque, and, in the center, the thin, gilt tower of the Republic's party headquarters.

You can start your exploration on Svoboda Prospekt, the longest and widest thoroughfare, which is around four-and-a-half miles long and lined by acacia, plantain and poplar trees. Small, open irrigation ditches run on both sides—called *aryks,* they are a regular feature of all Central Asian cities.

The eastern section of Svoboda Prospekt leads to a brewery and to metal and glass factories. You pass the Pioneer Palace and the Fine Arts Museum building with its oriental windows and smooth pillars. The Museum contains works by mainly Russian, Italian and French masters, but young Turkmenian painters and sculptors are also represented, and there is a section displaying Turkmenian carpets. The same building houses the Museum of Local History and Ethnography with zoological, botanical and industrial exhibits.

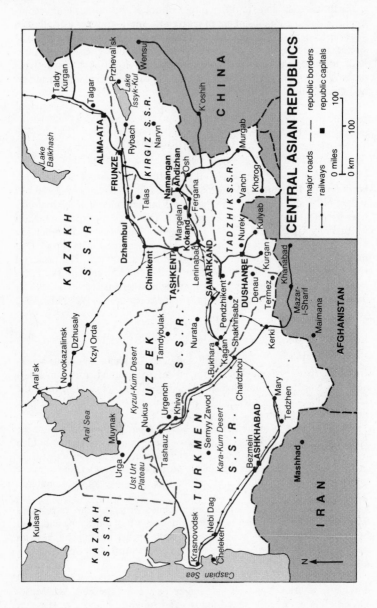

CENTRAL ASIAN REPUBLICS

major roads
railways
republic borders
■ republic capitals

0 miles   100
0 km   100

N

KAZAKH S.S.R.

Lake Balkhash

Taldy Kurgan
Talgar
Przheval'sk
Wensu
Lake Issyk-Kul
ALMA-ATA
FRUNZE
Rybach
K'oshih
CHINA
KIRGIZ S.S.R.
Naryn
Talas
Namangan
Andizhan
Osh
Margelan
Kokand
Fergana
Murgab
Vanch
Khorog
Dzhambul
Chimkent
TASHKENT
Leninabad
SAMARKAND
TADZHIK S.S.R.
Nurek
Kulyab
DUSHANBE
Kurgan
Khanabad
Denau
Termez
Mazar-i-Sharif
Maimana
AFGHANISTAN
Novokazalinsk
Dzhusaly
Kzyl Orda
Tamdybulak
Nurata
Pendzhikent
Shakhrisabz
Kagan
Bukhara
UZBEK S.S.R.
Kyzul-Kum Desert
Kerki
Aral'sk
Aral Sea
Muynak
Nukus
Urgench
Khiva
Serny Zavod
TURKMEN S.S.R.
Kara-Kum Desert
Chardzhou
Mary
Tedzhen
Bezmein
ASHKHABAD
Urga
Ust Urt Plateau
Tashauz
Kulsary
KAZAKH S.S.R.
Krasnovodsk
Nebi Dag
Chelekeñ
Caspian Sea
Mashhad
IRAN

Near the two theaters on the same main street is the Ashkhabad Hotel. Also near here is a huge carpet factory with a small museum displaying samples of its wares.

The race course is on the corner of Svoboda Prospekt and Ostrovsky Street. Races are at least as popular as football matches; the Turkmenians are justly proud of their fast and beautiful Ahaltekin horses, which were praised by Marco Polo. The Agricultural College is at the western end of Svoboda Prospekt, with the Botanical Garden behind it. More than 900 trees and plants are grown here, with many tropical and subtropical varieties. Turn from Svoboda Prospekt into Gogol Street, to reach the government quarter. At 19 Gogol Street is the not very up-to-date Hotel Turk-menistan, with an Intourist office on the ground floor.

The Ashkhabadians are well provided with city parks. The largest are the Komsomol, on the corner of Svoboda Prospekt and October Street, and the Lenin Park, also central.

Firyuza is the favorite resort of the Ashkhabadians. It is some 32 km. (20 miles) from the city, in the Kopet-Dag mountains, 549 meters (1,800 feet) up, reached by bus or car. The road leads across barren fields and sand, then runs along a deep ravine. After the village of Bagir you will reach the Golden Spring, after which the fast-flowing Firyuzinka stream leads you to Firyuza. Its parks and chestnut trees make you forget that you are in the middle of hot, desert-like Turkmenistan.

The Kara-Kum Desert

This is the largest desert in the Soviet Union, with an area of over 218,750 square miles. In recent years it has been transformed considerably by the Kara-Kum Canal, which is still under construction and will link the newly-irrigated lands with the city of Krasnovodsk, some 515 km. (320 miles) northwest of Ashkhabad, on the Caspian.

Krasnovodsk was founded in 1869 as a Russian fortress and port. Built at the foot of the Kuva Dag, laid out like an amphitheater, it later became a traffic junction: the Central Asian railway line leading to Tashkent begins here. More recently it has become the center of one of the largest oil-producing areas in the Soviet Union. Lacking water, its development was restricted until the late 1960s when a huge desalination plant (using atomic energy) was built in the nearby town of Shevchenko, supplying nearby oil towns with electricity and drinking water.

East and north of Ashkhabad, via the oases of Tedzhen and Mary, we reach Chardzhou. This is a river port and textile mill town which stands on the banks of the Amu-Darya, but has little interest for the tourist. Beyond Chardzhou, over the Amu-Darya bridge, Uzbekistan begins.

Uzbekistan

Bukhara and Samarkand are two names that ring in the imagination like those of Istanbul, Isfahan or Shiraz, evoking the poetry of these legendary towns and the glory of Cyrus the Persian, Alexander the Great, the Arabs and the Turks who brought the faith of Islam to this part of the world, the hordes of Genghis Kahn who laid waste to Uzbekistan, and the magnificent reign of Tamerlane (Timur the Lame) who made it the hub of his vast domain. Turkestan—or Central Asia—was conquered by Russia only 100 years ago. Before that, Uzbekistan was divided into three states: the Emirate of Bukhara and the Khanates of Kokand and of Khiva. Feudal in character, these principalities were hotbeds of intrigue and rebellion. Since being taken over by the strong arm of the socialist State, they have undoubtedly gained much in the way of material and social benefits, though some look on the new order with deep misgivings and resent what they see as the cultural straightjacket that has arguably been imposed here as throughout Soviet Central Asia.

Uzbekistan covers a territory of 158,069 square miles, and enjoys a sunny climate with short winters. Its population is made up, besides the Uzbeks proper (60 percent), of Russians, Tatars, Kazakhs and Tadzhiks. The Kara-Kalpaks have an independent republic within Uzbekistan. The countryside is rich in varied and colorful landscapes. To the northwest, the sands of the desert of Kyzyl-Kum are studded with oases, while the south and east is mountain country, with the ranges of Tien-Shan and Pamir-Alay. The north is bounded by the Aral Sea, beyond the famous plain of Ust Urt. Geologists foretell a booming future for this uninhabited plain. Oil, natural gas, coal, rare metals untainted by iron, copper, marble and sulphates are a few of Uzbekistan's natural riches. Industry and agriculture are fast developing; Uzbek wine—once forbidden by the Koran—is even finding its place on the international market. A top-grade cotton grows on the plain, and the republic's emblem today is an open cotton flower. Uzbekistan provides 70 percent of the total cotton output of the U.S.S.R.

Yet the country's artisans still ply the handicrafts passed down from generation to generation: embossed copper, the carpets of Bukhara and of Khiva, the silk tapestry or *suzane,* embroidered headgear. A pity that these artcrafts should be so scarce in the shops. But if you cannot *buy* the folklore, you can enjoy it in the songs and dances of the country. The opera of Tashkent, the Alisher ballet and the Bakhor troupe are worth seeing. There are state schools of music and dance, and 23 theaters. The nation's great men are still honored, among them Alisher Nawai (also Navoi), poet-philosopher of the 15th century, and the leading name of classical Uzbek literature.

The plane lands at Tashkent at the foot of Tien-Shan, the "heavenly mountains." From their snow-topped peaks, melted ice runs down to water the cotton plantations, orchards and vineyards of Uzbekistan.

The country awaits you with a legend, that of Farhad the mason and the princess Shirin. The beautiful princess had vowed to marry whoever brought back growing life to the barren steppe, and food for the hungry. Farhad set to work, hollowing a canal through the rock. But the Persian Shah Khosru, thinking to win the princess by trickery, covered the steppe with carpets of grass that shone green as water in the moonlight; and the Shah said to the princess: "Behold my works." The wind brought Farhad, at work in the mountain, the news of Shirin's betrothal; and sorrow turned him into a rock. When daylight revealed Khosru's treachery, the princess opened her arms to her beloved; but it was too late, and she was changed into a flowing river of tears. A hydraulic dam on the Syr Darya now bears the name of Farhad, and two canals begin at the rock that bears his name.

Tashkent

International tourism is an important economic asset to Tashkent. The city is strategically placed: it was in Tashkent that in January 1966, Ayub Khan, the president of Pakistan, and Mr. Shastri, the Prime Minister of India, met to negotiate a peace treaty. It is a refueling stop for planes en route from Moscow to India, Indonesia, Burma and other countries in Southeast Asia. Although hotel space is still restricted, a number of new large hotels are being built. The airport is modern and well-equipped and has a pleasant-looking transit hotel.

Tashkent is, in fact, a mere stopover while waiting for the flight to Samarkand; but you may as well take a guided tour, and get what entertainment and instruction you may from the guide's earnest salesmanship of the socialist state's achievements. Tashkent is the capital of Uzbekistan, an important economic and cultural center, a town of universities, theaters, museums, parks and palaces (of culture). It is also the biggest communications post of the Soviet Orient, and an important industrial zone. With a population of some 2 million, Tashkent is one of the U.S.S.R.'s largest cities and the only city in Central Asia to boast a subway system, opened in 1977. When completed, its length will total over 30 miles and is claimed to be earthquake-resistant.

On the guided tour, you will be taken to the year-round exhibition of Uzbek achievements in Pobeda Park. On the same outing, you will also pass by the Academy of Science, the State University, and many institutes and research laboratories. Of more interest to the layman is the library of Alisher Navoi, containing over two million volumes, among which are ancient illuminated manuscripts. One interesting visit is to the museum of Uzbek art. It has a few old pieces, but also some recent examples of fine workmanship in good taste. You will be proudly shown one recent acquisition, a truly outstanding sample of embroidery. This ornamental panel, unique of its kind, is the handiwork of 40 embroiderers of Bukhara; the design in gold and silver thread, stitched with amazing lightness and intricacy on a background of blue velvet, calls to mind the craft of the old calligraphers.

And the outing continues, along the wide shaded avenues where the aryks, the oak, mulberry, hazelnut and plane trees freshen the hot summer air. Largest park is the Komsomol, built by the country's youth for the wellbeing and enjoyment of all. If the town seems too new, remember that it was destroyed not long ago by a succession of earthquakes that did not spare the old monuments; few at any rate remain and they are somewhat disappointing. The 1966 quake was particularly severe, with its epicenter right in the city. More than 75,000 families were made homeless. Extensive rebuilding has, however, transformed Tashkent into a Central Asian showcase.

Sightseeing on Your Own

From the airport, a wide highway lined with trees leads into town. The people of Tashkent are particularly proud of their parks and gardens. Most of the inhabitants wear European clothes, except some women, who stick to oriental garb. Men and women alike wear the *tubeteyka,* the small square or round embroidered cap which provides essential protection against the sun.

The center of Tashkent, where you start your exploration, is the Teatralnaya Square; one of its sides is bordered by Lenin Prospekt, the main thoroughfare. Here you will find the Hotel Tashkent, a four-storied, modern building with a roof garden which also houses the Intourist Office. Opposite, occupying almost the whole length of the large square, is the Alisher Navoi Opera and Ballet Theater, named after a distinguished writer, scientist and musician of the 15th century. The theater has a repertoire of classical and native Uzbek operas and ballets. Fountains and colorful flowerbeds surround it. To the left of the Opera House is Pravda Vostoka Street, beginning in the square, and down which you will pass the Shark Hotel and the State Philharmonia Hall. Another park follows, with the city bell tower, then you reach Kuibyshev Street at the beginning of which stands the Uzbek Historical Museum. Continuing along Kuibyshev Street you come to Gogol Street with the Art Museum, whose treasures are described above.

Your second exploratory walk leads from the Hotel Tashkent north along Lenin Street. Cross Karl Marx Street (with the central department store, the Hotel Uzbekistan and the university), then Bratskaya Street and reach one of the finest main streets of Tashkent, Navoi Road, where the Navoi Library is located, leading west. Here the houses are marked by national, local features—especially by large, loggia-like balconies where people sleep outside in the summer heat.

From here, walk along Hamza Street to reach the former Old Town. At Chorsu Square (before Hamza Street) the 16th-century Kukeldash Madrasa rises among the small, flat houses. (A *madrasa* is a Moslem seminary, a school for mullahs.) Not far away to the north is Barak Khan's Madrasa, also 16th-century. It has been described as the "Vatican of Central Asia," since it is the seat of the Mufti, the religious head of the Central Asian and Kazakhstan Moslems. Opposite the madrasa we find a mosque from whose minaret the muezzin calls the faithful to prayer. To visit the mosque is not too difficult for the foreign tourist if he applies to the mullah; but permits are usually restricted to men and you are, of course, expected to remove your shoes before entering. Here also you will see the Gumbazi Barak-Khan, the funeral dome of the Samanids of Tashkent, the ancient local dynasty.

The old town market is also close by; here, in the summer and autumn you can buy melons, grapes and pomegranates—and *samsa,* a pie filled with meat and a considerable seasoning of garlic. The *chaikhana* (tea shop) is also an essential element of all Central Asian markets.

The Hunger Steppe lies southwest from Tashkent. Only 45 or so years ago, nomads roamed here, and there was a little cattle-breeding. Now, a large-scale canal system has turned almost one million acres into fertile agricultural land. You can reach it from Tashkent in about two hours by car, passing through the town of Yangi-Yul. The chief produce is cotton, or, as it is called in Uzbekistan, "white gold," which is exported in large quantities.

Samarkand

"Better one look than a hundred stories." This old oriental proverb seems to fit Samarkand. The modern town at first sight lacks character, but the old center casts a magic spell as you pass through the glazed tile porches of its ancient monuments. Between these legendary walls, time has come to a standstill. The old city seems barely touched by the stark modern surroundings that enclose it.

The oasis of Samarkand lies in the valley of the Zeravshan River. In Uzbek, Zeravshan means "bestower of gold." Taking its source in a great mountain glacier, the river waters all the plain, fully earning its name. According to legend, Samarkand was founded 5,000 or 6,000 years ago by King Aphrasiab. The first written mention of Maracanda—the ancient name of the city—goes back to 329 B.C. In 1971, the town celebrated its 2,300th anniversary.

Passing through on his way to India, Alexander the Great found Samarkand "more beautiful than he had imagined." Tamerlane in the 14th century was the first to make it an imperial capital, and the starting-point of his conquests. He embellished and developed it, and soon it was spoken of by the ancients as "the precious pearl of the world" or "the Eden of the East." It is the monuments of those times that you will visit here.

Under Soviet rule, Samarkand has become an industrial and cultural center, with its university, its chambers of commerce and agriculture, and above all, its karakul breeding research, Uzbekistan being the country of astrakhan. Among its many industries (fertilizers, canning, wines, fruit growing and so on), special mention should be made of its silk, worthy of the name of a once-luxurious city.

The Mausoleums of Shahi Zinda

Placed in the northern suburbs of Samarkand, Shahi Zinda is one of the most remarkable architectural groups of its time. The unequalled craftsmanship of the glazed tiles make of it an outdoor museum of this form of decorative art, peculiar to Islam. The group consists of mosques and tombs built between the 13th and 15th centuries, a cemetery for the great men of the period, mainly army generals and court favorites of Tamerlane. The crippled conqueror, having chosen Samarkand for his capital, wished to make it the most beautiful city in the world. Between them, artists summoned from everywhere built these marvellous monuments which have survived to this day, partly in ruins but priceless still under their gleaming domes.

Leading to the main entrance there is a narrow little street—more like a corridor—flanked by mausoleums built in the 14th and 15th centuries. The first of these is that of Tuglu-Tekin, the daughter of the Emir Hodzham (built 1375–76); the second belongs to Sirin-Bika-Akad, Timur's sister (1385); on the left, the first is the Emir-Zade (1386) and the second the Sadi-Mulk-Alka (1372), the tomb of Timur's niece. The buildings (there are more than a dozen) are decorated with splendid majolica and terracotta tiles.

As they appear today, the tombs of Shahi Zinda barely rise above the earth which once engulfed them. The small rampart behind them clearly shows the depth from which they were dug out. As it is now, the site is a garden walk, bordered by shady arcades and dominated by two turquoise-colored domes, with strips of Koranic writing running along the base. The panels of glazed tiles on the facades, though badly damaged, still evoke past splendor, and the colors on the brick walls shine with undimmed brightness. Suddenly, a small pointed vault frames a little courtyard, almost monastic in its calm. You gaze at a bench, the soft green of a tree, you dream and linger. It is hard to take leave of Shahi Zinda.

Mosque of Bibi Khanym

Another architectural splendor of Samarkand is the Great Mosque, near the center of town, to the east of Registan Square. It was the biggest mosque in Central Asia and one of the most grandiose and beautiful religious monuments of the Moslem world—as much for its size, proportions, and for the harmony and elegance of its design, as for the magnificent quality of the flower patterns on its glazed tiles.

It is called the mosque of Bibi Khanym, whose legend throws a poetic light on the origin of a deeply rooted custom of Islam: the veil worn by Moslem women. Bibi Khanym was a Chinese girl, best beloved of the fierce Tamerlane. In love with her conqueror and ever wishful to please him, she undertook to build a monument of utmost magnificence in his honor while he was away on campaign (1399–1401), and summoned a renowned architect to do her bidding. The master builder fell madly in love with the beautiful Bibi Khanym. The lady turned a deaf ear to his pleadings, but the wily architect threatened to leave his work unfinished unless she granted him a kiss. Faced with this shameless blackmail, Bibi Khanym gave in. But such was the lover's ardor that the guilty kiss left an unmistakable mark, and on his ill-timed return Tamerlane ordered the hapless architect to be put to death. Thereupon, wisely deeming that a woman's beauty was a threat to a man's peace of mind, he ordered all the women in the kingdom to wear veils henceforth.

Of the original minarets, only a few arches remain. The magnificent cupola, though almost in ruins, still shows the gigantic dimensions of the mosque: the entrance to the main room was 140 feet high. In the courtyard there is a huge lectern shaped like an open book, made of marble and richly decorated. Originally it stood inside and the Koran was read from it.

Registan Square and the Gur Emir

Near the mosque of Bibi Khanym, Registan Square marks the center of Samarkand. Framed by the gateways and minarets of three ancient madrasas (15th, 16th and 17th centuries), it is an evocation of oriental poetry in the middle of a modern town. Renewed and restored, these three madrasas are a fascinating example of ancient city planning.

Building of the Registan began early in the 15th century, during the reign of Ulug-Bek. His madrasa was erected between 1417 and 1420. According to tradition, the learned ruler himself taught in this school. Badly damaged in the fratricidal wars of the 18th century, it has now been largely restored.

The Shir-Dor Madrasa was built on the site of the covered bazaar of the hat makers, which was erected at the turn of the 14th and 15th centuries at the express wish of Tuman-Aka, one of the wives of Timur. The madrasa itself was built between 1619 and 1636, and is a copy of the Ulug-Bek Madrasa, though by no means as perfect.

Yalangtus-Bij, the ruler of Samarkand, was also responsible for the third building on the Registan. The foundations of a projected mosque and madrasa were laid in 1646 on the northern side of the square; later it was named Tillya-Kari (Decorated with Gold). It was finished only after the death of Yalangtus. The elaborate murals are particularly fine, though the building was badly damaged in an earthquake early in the 19th century and its famous colored tiles were never replaced.

From the former main square you can set out to visit the Old Town of Samarkand. High mud walls often hide the houses, with only a TV antenna rising above them. The streets are narrow and traffic is rather heavy with cars, donkey carts and cycles all competing. The artisans work in the open or in half-open huts; bread, meat, textiles are sold from stalls and shoemakers, potters, knife grinders and radio mechanics work cheek by jowl. The exotic bazaar is one of the most colorful sights.

You will of course visit the Gur Emir, where lie the Timurid kings: Sultan Mohammed, Ulug-Bek, and the founder of the dynasty, Tamerlane himself, the son of the steppes, whose wish was to be buried in the town which bore witness to his glory. Tamerlane lies under a tombstone of rock jade made to order for him by Ulug-Bek. The Gur Emir is a short walk southeast of the Samarkand Hotel. You can manage on your own by keeping in sight the characteristic fluted dome, outlined from afar against the sky of Samarkand. Over 500 years old, the tomb had suffered rather badly from the ravages of time, but has been carefully restored to its former splendor, perhaps with overmuch zeal. However, the painstaking restoration bears striking witness to the infinite variety of Central Asian decorative art and the imaginative skills of its artists.

If you still have time, go and have a look at the ancient observatory of Ulug-Bek, grandson of Tamerlane. This is now a museum devoted to the work of 15th-century Uzbek astronomers led by Ulug-Bek himself. The Samarkand school of astronomers had immense influence on contemporary Moslem and Arab science. For hundreds of years, eastern and western astronomers made use of the star charts of this scholarly prince. The memory of Ulug-Bek has been perpetuated at the modern observatory not far from Samarkand which also bears his name.

About 48 km. (30 miles) southeast of Samarkand, just across the border in Tadzhikistan, the archeological excavations of the ruins of ancient Pendzhikent are also well worth a visit. A little further out (about 96 km., 60 miles, to the south) is the ancient Uzbek hill town of Shakhrisabz, recently opened to foreign tourists. In the foothills of the Zeravshan Range, at an altitude of about 610 meters (2,000 feet), it contains several fine monuments to the past, among them the remains of the Ak-Sarai Palace (1380–1404), the mausoleum of Jehanghir (14th–15th centuries), the Chor-su covered market (15th century), a town bath (15th century), a mosque, and other ancient monuments. The town is a traditional center of folk-embroidery and pottery.

Bukhara

Of all the ancient places to be visited in Uzbekistan, Bukhara has best retained its exotic charm, with its mud houses and its many religious monuments, madrasas and old mosques. These last, far from having become mere empty shells for sightseeing, have been adapted and are used for a variety of purposes by the locals. The signs of progress are more visible in the television aerials springing from every ancient hovel than in the oil derricks of Bukhara, Khiva, or the drills of Kyzyl-Kum that furnish natural gas to Tashkent, Samarkand and Bukhara. And the spirit of progress is more evident in the free and easy ways of the unveiled women: teachers, doctors, agronomists and so on, than in the few modern buildings. As you may have gathered, the first sight of the romantic Bukhara of your bookish dreams is something of a shock: but do not despair. In spite of these changes, you will be gladdened to see a few old men still wearing the traditional *chupan* of Central Asia. Old Bukhara is not lost.

The town was at the height of its glory in the tenth century, under the Samanids. The capital of the country, it was a center of intellectual ferment renowned throughout the East, the town of Rudaki, the "Adam of poets." It still carries on something of this tradition with its music and drama theater, among the oldest in Uzbekistan. You will come across the old and the new as you stroll at random around Bukhara, and the city will reveal its riches as you explore its corners. You will be surprised at the apparent lack of color compared with, say, Samarkand: most of Bukhara's monuments are made of brick—though patterned with great artistry—and there is little faience.

In recent years much has been done to modernize the city which, until the 1930s, did not have even a proper water supply. The traditional handicrafts—gold embroidery, the curing of hides, etc.—have, however, been encouraged and developed. At the end of the 1950s, one of the greatest fields of natural gas in the world was discovered in Gazli, not far away. The gas is now piped to Tashkent, the Urals and other areas.

Bukhara has an extensive educational system. Traditionally, it was a center of religious learning, with almost 100 madrasas in which 5,000 young men studied for the priesthood; but only two percent of the population was literate. Now there is a teachers' academy, 11 general and several specialized high schools, museums, as well as libraries and theaters. Public buses are crowded, though some locals still prefer the donkey.

Bukhara's area is comparatively small; with the exception of one or two monuments which are on the periphery or outside the city, all its sights can be easily reached on foot. However, to visit even the few most famous ones properly, the tourist needs at least two or three days.

One sight that must be seen is the tomb of Ismail Samani, founder of the Samanid dynasty. This light and graceful building is said to be over a thousand years old.

Turning back towards the center of the city from the mausoleum, you will see on the left a building with four domes. This is the Chashma-Ayub Mazar. (A *mazar* is a place of miracles, usually the tomb of an Islamic saint.) Built in the 12th century, it has four connected chambers, each with a dome. The domes are all of different shapes: one is almost pointed, like a tower.

Not far from this former place of pilgrimage, in the city park, are the regional Theater of Drama and Music and the 18th-century Bolo-Khauz Mosque. The facade of this delicate edifice rests on 20 tall wooden pillars. This was the "court chapel" of the Emirs of Bukhara, which explains the extraordinary splendor of the inner decorations. A miniature minaret and a handsome water basin are part of it. The Bolo-Khauz was built opposite the main entrance of the castle—the Emir's winter residence—and when the ruler went to worship, he walked on thick carpets spread between the two.

On the hill in the middle of town is the Ark or citadel, even older than the Samanid tomb. It has an area of some 8 acres and is a walled fortress. Today the Ark houses a museum which displays Bukhara rugs, gold embroidery, ceramics, embossed copper, and silverwork. Other rooms contain gruesome reminders of the horrors and misery of the Middle Ages.

Crossing the large square, which had a statue of Avicenna (Arab physician and philosopher, A.D. 980–1037) until a recent earthquake, you reach the main part of the Ark. The entrance is flanked by two towers, linked by a corridor with a terrace which was reserved for the court orchestra and the guard. Once upon a time, a hempen whip, symbol of the Emir's power, hung over the entrance. After entering, you will pass through a long, closed corridor; the rooms flanking this dark, sinister passage once served as prison cells and torture chambers. The corridor leads to the Dzhuma Mosque (1819). A short street emerges into the court of the Kush-Begi (Prime Minister) and the Charsu Chapel, and then into the Kurinish-Khana—the "Protocol Courtyard," where the emirs were crowned and where foreign ambassadors were received. One of the buildings contains the Museum of Local History; its second department is in the Zindan, an 18th-century former prison, nearby.

Leaving the Ark, and turning left by the Teachers' College into Communards Street, continue towards the city center, where the majority of the historical monuments are located. On the right of Communards Street stand a huge mosque and a very tall minaret. The first is the Kalyan Mosque (1540–41), one of the most impressive in Central Asia, covering an area of 400 by 250 feet. The large courtyard is surrounded by several rows of galleries. Note especially the portal and the huge dome, decorated in turquoise, rising above the central area.

The Kalyan Minar, built in 1127, was used as a lighthouse for caravans, a watchtower against the enemy, and a minaret for the muezzin's call to prayer. Its superbly decorative cut brick is among the finest you can see.

Close to the Kalyan Mosque and minaret there are the two large domes of a madrasa. (The northern one is completely restored, covered by light blue tiles.) This is the Mir-Arab, built in the first decade of the 16th century, and now a still functioning Moslem seminary. Together with the Kalyan Mosque it forms the Bukhara Forum. It was named after the Yemenite Sheikh Abdullah, who was called Mir-Arab by his people.

Continuing along the Street of the Communards, cross Sovietskaya Street, under a dome called Taki-Zargaron. There were quite a few such domes built in the 16th century over the busiest street crossings for trading purposes. One was where the cap makers sold their wares, others were near the homes of potters and other craftsmen. They provided shade and lessened the congestion of the busy streets. All are different. Under the Taki-Zargaron, jewelers and goldsmiths worked and traded.

Many Madrasas

Close to the Taki-Zargaron stands the early 15th-century madrasa of Ulug-Bek, whose sober lines and harmonious proportions served as model for many other buildings throughout Central Asia. In contrast, all the skills of architects and artisans were put to use to embellish the madrasa of Abdul Aziz Khan opposite; it was built in the middle of the 17th century and decorated with squares of shiny glazed tiles, patterns of cut brick, carved wood and dull glaze earthenware. The reckless artist who decorated a vase with a serpent, in defiance of the Koranic law forbidding images of living beings, paid for the blasphemy with his life.

Leaving this striking building, turn right on Samarkandskaya Street and after a few minutes' walk, on the corner of Pushkin Street, you will come to another madrasa, called Kukeldash. It was built in the reign of Abdullah Khan (1557–98). Its outer walls are distinguished by open balconies or loggias. It used to have 160 cells for the seminary pupils; today it houses the regional archives.

The Kukeldash Madrasa is part of the former merchant center called Liabi-Khauz. Today it is a paved, park-like square with tea-gardens, a favorite place for the Bukharans to sit down and rest. Before walking round the square, continue along Pushkin Street and have a look at the Char-Minar Madrasa, built early in the 19th century. It has a domed, ornamental portal and four tall towers which show the influence of Indian mosque architecture.

The Liabi-Khauz Square was named after the large reservoir in its center, which once provided the Bukharans with water. It was built in 1620. The square is lined with splendid buildings, most of them—except the Kukeldash Madrasa—dating from the 18th century.

On the western side, the square is bordered by the Divan Begi Mosque, on the east by the Divan Begi Madrasa, on the north by the Kukeldash and the Ir-Nazar-Ilchi Madrasas. The last of these was built by a Russian ambassador in Bukhara and largely financed by Catherine the Great. Originally a caravanserai, its facade and first-story arcades are decorated with bird and stag motifs.

Starting from the Liabi-Khauz Square either to the right (towards the Mir-Arab Madrasa) or towards the left, southwards, along Sovietskaya Street, pass again under the domes of the covered bazaars. On the right, the Taki-Tilpak-Furashon arches above the street where headgear and books were once sold; on the left is the Taki-Sarrafon, once the home of money-changers.

From Liabi-Khauz Square you can walk along Lenin and Khmelnitsky Streets to Lenin Square, where the statue of Avicenna now stands (it was moved here after a recent earthquake).

It is well worth exploring the southeastern and eastern parts of Bukhara and the vicinity of the railway station. From the hotel, follow Shevchenko Street as far as the Sayfuddin Bokharzi Mausoleum, built in the 13th century over the grave of a learned sheikh. The first of its two chambers is the *ziarathana* (prayer room), the second the actual crypt *(gur-hana)*.

The nearby Buyan-Kuh Khan Mausoleum is the final resting place of one of the descendants of Genghis Khan, who was killed in 1358 in Samarkand. This, too, has two chambers; the smaller contains his majolica tomb. The four sides of the building have small ornamental pillars and the walls bear rich terra cotta decorations in light and dark blue, violet and white. The modern residential quarter of Bukhara is to the south of the two mausoleums.

Finally, an excursion outside Bukhara to see the summer palace of the last Emir, Said-Alim Khan, is strongly recommended. The Sitore-i-Mahi-Hasa Palace is two-and-a-half miles north, and can be reached by car or bus. Near Said-Alim's summer palace is the palace of his father, Ahid Emir, built in classic Uzbek national style and now used as a hospital.

Khiva

Khiva is in the Kara-Kum Desert, in the oasis of Khorezm, on the left bank of the Amu-Darya River. Excavations show that its history reaches back to the seventh century. This was the capital of the Khivan Khanate from the middle of the 16th century until 1920. Its character has changed little since the Middle Ages, and it has only recently been included in Intourist itineraries. There are no acceptable hotels and services as far as we know. Khiva lies some distance from the Chardzhou-Kungrad railway

line and is best reached by plane from Tashkent via Samarkand to Urgench, the nearest airport. From here, Khiva can be visited only as a one-
day excursion by hired car with guide (cost is 23 roubles at presstime).
This means one or two nights in Urgench, which is 40 km. (25 miles) away.
Alternatively, a day-trip can be made by air from Bukhara, but this is more
difficult to arrange.

An asphalted road runs through the cotton and alfalfa fields, "cuts"
through a thick clay wall—and you come upon the enchanting panorama
of ancient Khiva, its tall minarets glittering in the sun and a multitude
of cupolas topping thousand-year-old mosques and madrasas.

Khiva's streets are a museum of woodcarving (almost every home is
decorated with fancifully carved doors and columns), painting (the Khiva
floral and geometric designs that decorate many minarets and palaces are
world famous), and ceramics (majolica tiles of unsurpassed quality which
have retained all their original vividness of color).

The ancient city of Khiva looks much as it used to in the olden days,
with its narrow streets and roofed bazaars, and is a protected area. There
are more architectural monuments in Khiva than in Samarkand and Bukhara. Many of them have a remarkable history. The old madrasa of Shir-
gazi-khan stands in one of the streets, with the mausoleum of the khan
himself adjoining it. Right opposite the madrasa there is an arch with a
finely-carved wooden gate. In the courtyard you will find another door
inlaid with ivory and behind it, the mausoleum of Pahlavan Mahmud, a
wonderful example of the skill of Khiva architects. The mausoleum, built
of kilned bricks, is adorned with glazed tiles bearing the verses and maxims
by Pahlavan Mahmud, a philosopher, poet and teacher.

The unfinished Kalta-Minar minaret is in the middle of the town. The
Kuk-Minar (Great Minaret) rises 225 feet: a graceful, delicate edifice, it
dates from World War I. The ninth-century Dzhuma Mosque and the
Kutli-Murad-Inak Madrasa have been reconstructed from the original
plans, as they were burned down some 50 years ago. The castle of Kuna-
Ark (12th to 19th centuries), the delicate Tash-Khauli Palace (1830s) and
the Madrasa of Allakuli-Khan (1835) are in many ways superior even to
the Samarkand and Bukhara masterpieces of architecture.

Fergana Basin

This broad, 200-mile-long valley is between the western spurs of the
Tien-Shan mountain. Its territory is divided between the Uzbek, Tadzhik
and Kirghiz Republics and it is easiest to visit from Tashkent, which lies
129 km. (80 miles) to the north. For a longer visit you can now stay at
a hotel in Fergana city.

The Fergana Basin yields about a quarter of the Soviet Union's cotton.
An extensive irrigation system consisting of the Great Fergana Canal, the
Southern and Northern Fergana Canals and several others, provides
water. There is a considerable silkworm breeding industry, lots of fruit
cultivation, and oil, coal and copper ore are also plentiful.

Kokand (some 161 km., 100 miles, from Tashkent) lies along the River
Sokh; in the 18th and 19th centuries it was the capital of the Kokand
Khanate. Two important Uzbek poets, Mukimi (1851–1903) and Hamza
Niazi (1880–1929) were born here. Among its sights the palace of the last
Kokand ruler, Hudoyar Khan, (built in the 1860s) is the most interesting;
it now houses the Local History Museum. The palace has remarkable col-
ored woodcarvings and ceramics.

Fergana (previously called Novy Margelan and Skobelev) is a regional center about 72.5 km. (45 miles) east of Kokand at the foot of the Alay mountains. Founded in 1876, it has an important oil refinery, and factories making fertilizer and artificial silk. Its textile plant was the first in Central Asia. Fergana's park (29 Lenin Street) is also a botanical garden. There are Uzbek and Russian theaters; the Museum of Local History is at 18 Pervovo Maya Street. Intourist offers flights to here from Tashkent.

Margelan is a few miles north of Fergana. An ancient settlement, since the tenth century it has been the center of a flourishing agricultural district. In the 19th century it had several madrasas and about 250 mosques. Today it is the center of the Fergana Basin's silkworm breeding industry. Intourist offer a visit to a silk factory here.

Andizhan is the largest city in the Fergana area. It owes its importance mostly to the fact that this area is one of the most outstanding cotton-growing territories of the Soviet Union. It is an ancient city, mentioned in tenth-century Arab chronicles. It was also a religious center, with innumerable mosques and madrasas. Among the sights, pride of place belongs to the Dzhami Madrasa (276 October Street), with its Romanesque, bricked-up windows and two richly carved towers. The Museum of Local History is at 118 Navoi Prospekt.

Finally, mention should be made of the important, non-Uzbek cities of the Fergana Valley: Leninabad, Tadjikistan's second largest city, lies on the banks of the Sir-Darya, in the southwestern corner of the Fergana basin. For travelers from Tashkent (121 km., 75 miles, to the north) it is the gateway to the whole area. Cotton-growing and silkworm culture have always been the traditional occupations, along with fruit-growing, the mainstay of North Tadjik agriculture.

Tadzhikistan

Tadzhikistan lies in the southeastern part of Central Asia, bordering on Afghanistan and China, separated from Pakistan only by an Afghan corridor of some 20 miles. Its area is 89,438 square miles; the majority of the population are Tadzhiks, with a large number of Uzbeks, Russians, Tatars and Kirghizes. The capital is Dushanbe with a population of over half a million.

Most of Tadzhikistan is occupied by the Pamir Range. Only seven percent of the republic's area is either on a plain or has a lower elevation than 915 meters, 3,000 feet. The valleys in which agriculture is possible lie between the ranges of the Pamir—except in the northern part. In the Eastern Pamir are the highest mountains in the Soviet Union: Communism Peak (6,858 meters, 22,500 feet) and Lenin Peak (6,523 meters, 21,400 feet). The principal rivers of Tadzhikistan are the Syr-Darya, the Amu-Darya, the Vakhsh, the Kafirnigan and the Zeravshan.

Tadzhikistan has seven universities or colleges and it is claimed that illiteracy has been nearly eradicated. The incidence of typhus, malaria and cholera has been drastically reduced. The highest-developed industries are mining (coal, oil, gold, polymetallic ores), machine tools, cotton milling, silk manufacture and food canneries.

The most important agricultural activities are growing cotton, maize and fruit in the valleys, and sheep-breeding by the semi-nomadic peoples in the mountains.

For the time being there is little tourism in Tadzhikistan; yet it is interesting, if you have the chance, to visit this thinly-populated mountain republic, whose hospitable people have a culture that stretches back to the ninth century.

Dushanbe

Dushanbe (earlier called Stalinabad) is the capital of the Tadzhik Republic. It lies on the bank of the Dushanbinka River, in the Hissar Valley, 837 meters (2,475 feet) above sea level. The average temperature in July is 30°C (86°F), in January around freezing point.

It is a completely modern city. Until 1922 it was a village called Dush: the building of the railway in 1929 started its rapid growth. The houses are two- or three-storied: taller buildings are avoided because of the danger of earthquakes, though some which are supposed to be "earthquake-proof" have been erected on Lenin Prospekt.

Most men wear European clothing and so do the women, but some fabrics have oriental patterns and much silk is worn. The Tadzhiks also like the *tubeteyka,* the embroidered skull-cap.

The main thoroughfare is Lenin Prospekt, running for eight km. (five miles) north to south, with most of the important public buildings on or near it. The Prospekt is lined with willows, plane trees, poplars and acacias, with the inevitable aryks, the small irrigation ditches instead of gutters. The other main streets—Ordzhonikidze, Rustaveli and Shevchenko—are also shaded by trees.

Lenin Prospekt begins at the railway station. Opposite is the statue of Kuibyshev, one of the commanders of the Red Army in Central Asia during the Civil War. A few yards away, on the left side, is the Hotel Dushanbe with the Intourist office. Here the Lenin Prospekt forms a square, which contains the Museum of History and Regional Studies with its collection of ancient and modern Tadzhik art. A short walk and a right turn brings you, between Lenin Prospekt and Ayni Street, to the municipal market. From here, a fine panorama of the surrounding high mountains opens to the north, east and south, particularly attractive at dusk. The market (one of two) is delightful—not to be missed.

Continuing along Lenin Prospekt you reach the central Moscow Square, with the Ayni Opera and Ballet Theater and the Hotel Vakhsh.

The next section of the Lenin Prospekt contains the Firdausi Library, with its valuable Eastern manuscripts: next to it are the Philharmonia and concert hall. Almost opposite, the Tadzhik Academy of Sciences is housed in a classical building, while the editorial and printing offices of the Republic's newspapers, and the Central Post Office, are next door.

Here the Lenin Prospekt widens once again into a square. On the left, the tall building of Tadzhik Radio, on the right, one of the largest buildings of Dushanbe, monumental Government House, dominate the square. Nearby is the Hotel Tadzhikistan, down the left side of which (as you face the hotel) runs one of Dushanbe's old streets, leading to the second market. Along the street you'll see traditional flat bread being baked in old ovens, and craftsmen at work.

Farther along Lenin Prospekt you come to Putovsky Street. The central department store is at the crossing and the Russian Drama Theater and the Lakhuti Tadzhik Drama Theater are both close by. If you turn left along Putovsky Street, you soon arrive at the Dushanbinka River, with a bridge leading to the right bank and the newer part of the city.

Returning to Lenin Prospekt, on the left are the Teachers' college and the Avicenna Medical University. Soon you will arrive at a large, well-kept park, also bearing the name of Ayni, the founder of modern Tadzhik literature (1878–1954). There are facilities for swimming and boating.

Excursions from Dushanbe

An excursion along the 97-km. (60-mile) valley of the Vakhsh provides a chance to explore the life and agriculture of a Tadzhik village. (The Hissar Valley does the same.) Surrounded by mountains on three sides, the valley is very sheltered. Cultivated since prehistoric times, it was sparsely settled until the early 1930s, when the Termez-Dushanbe railway line and the Dushanbe-Kurgan-Tube Highway were built. In 1933, the Great Vakhsh Canal was completed and many new kolkhozes and sovkhozes were established in the irrigated areas, while a series of dams was begun on the Vakhsh. From Dushanbe, a good road leads south to the Vakhsh Valley in the direction of the Afghan border, crossing many canals. N.B.: May not be open to foreigners beyond a certain point.

The main produce is cotton, but maize is also grown. This has led to the development of pig-breeding on a large scale even though the Moslem Tadzhiks do not eat pork. Much fruit is also grown here, especially melons and grapes. Lemons are cultivated under glass during the winter (but not in hothouses).

From Dushanbe the best way to see the Vakhsh is by car and Intourist runs a 7-hour excursion. Traveling southwest, you pass across the plain, past well-tilled fields, through the town of Ordzhonikidzeabad and then begin to climb a long and steep road, with 600–900-foot drops on both sides. Nurek, the site of an enormous hydro-electric complex, has no railway; the only access is by road, so it is fairly busy. At Nurek, the Vakhsh is a narrow mountain river, very deep and winding between high mountain ridges. The dam has created a 60-square-mile reservoir, and the hydroelectric plant, when fully operational, will provide an annual output of 10.5 billion kilowatts.

East of Nurek are the heights of the Pamir Mountains—the "Roof of the World." The plateau, glaciers and peaks, all 3,650 to 4,600 meters (12,000 to 15,000 feet) high, are for climbers and alpinists. It is only in the last few years that the final "white spots" have disappeared from the maps and the ultimate secrets of this area have been unlocked. Here the hunt still continues for the yeti, the mysterious and legendary creature that is supposed to represent the missing link between the anthropoid apes and primeval man. The expeditions of the Soviet Academy of Sciences seem to have decided that the yeti does not exist, at least neither in the Tien-Shan nor in the Pamir range. Others, more sanguine, still believe that one day he might be found.

In the hills at Bobo-Tag, 29 km. (18 miles) from Dushanbe, a magnificent 4th–19th-century historical site containing a citadel, two madrasas and a mausoleum as well as other monuments to the area's past, has been restored. Known as the Hissar Fortress, it recently opened to foreign tourists.

At Termez, about 240 km. (150 miles) southwest of Dushanbe, just into Uzbekistan and very close to the border with Afghanistan, a 2,000-year-old Buddhist temple has been discovered and is being excavated. There is a rail link with Dushanbe but Termez is reported not open to foreigners at presstime.

Kirghizstan

Kirghizstan is in the northeastern part of Central Asia and is bordered by China. About 40 percent of its population are Kirghizes and the rest Russians, Uzbeks, Kazakhs and Ukrainians. Most of the inhabitants live in the valleys. The greater part of Kirghiz territory is occupied by the Tien-Shan range. Its highest point is the Victory Peak (Pik Pobedy), 6,803 meters (22,320 feet), but even most of the valleys and plateaus have an elevation of between 1,800 and 2,750 meters (6,000 and 9,000 feet). Only the Chu and Fergana valleys lie lower. The principal river of Kirghizia is the Narin, where a massive new hydroelectric scheme, consisting of five power stations, is nearing completion; its largest reservoir Lake Issyk-Kul. The capital is Frunze.

Large-scale tourism has not yet come to Kirghizia, though it will grow with the development of health resorts around Lake Issyk-Kul.

Within the republic there are regular bus lines (roads are built even to the highest settlements) but many towns can be reached only by air—especially in winter. The sights are of the purely geographical variety—spectacular mountain ranges and valleys.

Frunze

Frunze (until 1926 it was called Pishpek, then renamed after Mikhail Frunze, the Soviet general who was born here) lies in the valley of the Chu River, at the foot of the snow-covered Kirghiz Ala-Tau Ridge, some 7,325 meters (2,400 feet) above sea level. It has severe winters and hot summers, with a mean temperature of 10.2°C (50°F).

Frunze's airport is an extremely busy place. From the airport, Mir Prospekt leads into the center of the city. You pass the University and other institutions. Crossing the small Ala-Archa River and the railway tracks, continue along Belinsky Street, in an industrial area.

Starting from the railway station and the Ala-Too Hotel, Dzerzhinsky Boulevard leads to the center of town. The Boulevard is lined with oak, chestnut, birch and elm trees in thick groves, forming a park-like area. Oak (Dubovy) Park is a continuation of this wide thoroughfare and contains the Krupskaya Russian Theater. From the parks, a tree-lined road leads eastwards to the Kirghiz State Opera and Ballet Theater, which has an excellent dance company. Near the Opera is the Chernyshevsky Public Library, decorated with busts of famous writers.

To the west, Oak Park merges into the Central Municipal Park. At its edge stands Government House, with the domed building of the Kirghiz Academy of Sciences facing it. From Central Park, follow another tree-lined promenade to Panfilov Park. Alongside is the Spartak Stadium.

In the city center, the Fine Arts Museum and the Kirghiz Drama Theater are both on Pervogo Maya Street. On the same street, the birthplace of General Frunze has been turned into a memorial museum. Two modern restaurants are also worth seeing—the Druzhba is on the corner of Ivanitsin and Sopokov streets, a two-storied, all-glass building; the Son-Kul, on the corner of Dzerzhinsky Boulevard and 22nd Party Congress Street, is like an elegant private villa.

About 80.5 km. (50 miles) from Frunze is the 11th-century Burana Tower; Intourist runs a five-hour excursion. Another excursion takes you to the picturesque Ala-Archa Canyon, in the Ala-Too Mountains, 40 km. (25 miles) from Frunze.

Issyk-Kul Lake

"The Kirghiz Sea" (proper name: Issyk-Kul, or "warm lake") can be reached in three or four hours by car or bus. It lies in a basin, 1,583 meters (5,193 feet) above sea level, surrounded by mountains 2,750 meters (9,000 feet) high. Many hot springs rise from great depths in this long, narrow lake which, although it warms up slowly, also retains its pleasant temperature for a long time, reaching 24–26°C (75°–79°F) in the shallow bays.

The Issyk-Kul is said to be the bluest lake in the world. It is very rich in fish, especially carp and perch-pike. Trout weighing over 20 lbs. have also been caught here. Anglers and hunters alike find it a paradise; there are plenty of water fowl, and swans breed freely. Of the 480 km. (300 miles) of coastline, about two thirds are warm, sandy beaches. On the shore and in the nearby mountains many important medicinal springs are being developed; Dzheti-Oguz, Ak-Su Koysara and Cholpon-Ata are already well-established, with some 100,000 visitors every year. Apart from these resorts, there are two towns on the lake: Ribachye is a port; Przhevalsk (previously Karakol) was the first Russian settlement in Kirghizia. You can see a mosque resembling a Chinese pagoda, and a church built by the first Russian settlers. Both of them were constructed of wood without the use of a single nail and are decorated with delicate woodcarvings.

Kazakhstan

Kazakhstan lies in the southwestern corner of Soviet Asia. Its area is 1,064,092 square miles (second largest after the Russian Federal S.R.), its population over 15 million; it could accommodate Germany, France, Spain, Great Britain, Norway and Sweden within its frontiers. More than 40 percent of its population are Russians, about 30 percent Kazakhs and the rest Ukrainians, Tatars, Uzbeks, Uigurs, Koreans, Germans, etc. Many of the non-Kazakh inhabitants moved (or were moved) here in the 1950s to help with the industrialization of the vast territory. The capital is Alma-Ata.

Alma-Ata

Alma-Ata (the Father of Apples) lies in the southeastern corner of the Kazakh Republic, at the foot of the Zailisky Ala-Tau ridge of the Tien-Shan mountain range, on the banks of the Bolshaya and Malaya Alma-Atinka rivers, some 823 meters (2,700 feet) above sea level. Its climate is harsh and cold because of this elevation and the resultant exposure to the cold winds from the north. The average temperature in January is -7°C (19°F) while the summer sees a considerable difference between day and night temperatures—sometimes as much as 20°C (34°F).

The city lies in an attractive and romantic valley and is surrounded on three sides by mountains that rise in terraces. On the lower slopes there are irrigated fields, mostly orchards and vineyards. On the higher slopes, up to 1,646 meters (5,400 feet) wild apricots and other fruit grow. The next zone is the forest, and above 2,560 meters (8,400 feet) there are sub-alpine and alpine meadows. In the more distant areas of the Zailisky Ala-Tau, bears, snow leopards and chamois still roam freely. The tops of the mountains are perpetually covered in snow. Avalanches were quite frequent until in October 1966 a protective ring was created above the city by a huge series of explosions. Earthquakes, however, are still a danger and most of the houses are low-slung (though in recent years earthquake-proof, higher buildings have been erected). Alma-Ata is now a regular feature on Intourist itineraries and the numbers of tourists going there are on the increase.

From the railway station and the airport, both to the north of the city, Red Guardist Road (Krasnogvardeisky Trakt) takes you into the center; it is a twenty-minute journey by car or express bus. Parallel with the road, along many miles, stretches the Baum Park, named after the agronomist who was the first to organize tree-planting in this dusty city.

Traveling along Kommunist Prospekt you reach the center. The road rises, then reaches Lenin Square, with Government House on one side. On Kommunist Prospekt, in a small park, is the Kazakh Drama Theater, an attractive building combining modern architecture with national decorative elements. The Zhetsu Hotel is at No. 55 Kommunist Prospekt; opposite, is the Central Department Store.

From Kommunist Prospekt you can turn into Komsomolskaya Street, which crosses Lenin Square. At the corner of the two streets is the all-glass Children's Department Store. Around the square is the glass pavilion of the souvenir shop, the Central Post Office and the Hotel Alma-Ata. Continuing, turn into Kalinin Street. No. 112 is the Abay Opera and Ballet Theater, which presents traditional Kazakh and classical operas and ballets.

Alma-Ata has several fine, tree-lined boulevards running across the city. Lenin Prospekt has the Pushkin Library; nearby, at 22 Sovietskaya Street, is the Kazakh Art Museum with its collection of modern Kazakh artists and Russian paintings and sculpture. On the corner of Sovietskaya and Shevchenko streets is the Kazakh Academy of Sciences.

Abay Prospekt, which runs east to west, cuts across Lenin Street. This thoroughfare leads to the residential quarters, the western and southwestern districts of Alma-Ata.

The Kazakh capital has a number of great parks. The Gorky Park covers more than 200 acres; it has a boating lake, tennis courts, a Pioneers' railway, a Ferris Wheel and many other attractions. The park named after the 28 Panfilovist Guards contains the tall wooden structure of the former cathedral.

The environs of Alma-Ata have many attractions for the tourist. In the valleys and on the slopes of the Zailisky Ala-Tau, there are chalets for mountaineers. The Medeo winter sports complex, some 20 km. (12 miles) from the city, is also in the mountains; over 100 skating records have been made here, including U.S. Olympic speed skater Eric Heiden's fastest time, apparently helped by the clear mountain air. Intourist runs a three-hour excursion into the mountains around Medeo, including a tour of the sports center.

Other Cities of Kazakhstan

The other Kazakh cities have little significance for the tourist; most of them are quickly-developing industrial and agricultural centers without historical or architectural importance. Most are also best reached by air. A flight from Alma-Ata to *anywhere* will give you an idea of the vastness of this still half-barren land. After you take off, the tall sugar-loaf of the 4,600-meter (15,000-feet) Talgar peak of the Ala-Tau mountains remains within sight for a long time. After some 45 minutes' flight, Lake Balkhash appears—over 650 km. (400 miles) long, and stretching from east to west. Its western part is fresh water while the eastern section is salt. Almost a quarter of all the carp caught in the Soviet Union come from here.

On the northern shore of the lake, the town of Balkhash is a copper-smelting center. Copper ore was found in the mid-1930s near Kounradsky, and the town was built not far from the deposits.

Flying on towards the northwest, you pass over another large city: Karaganda, which is the hub of Central Kazakhstan, a rich coal-mining area. Most of the coal is in the Karaganda Basin. Karaganda also has a number of copper and iron-ore mines (Dzhezkazgan, Atasu, Karsakpay, etc). In the same region there is a small town called Baykonur, which has become famous as the launching point of Soviet cosmonauts.

As you continue northwest from Karaganda, the landscape changes. The gray steppe is replaced by many miles of wheatfields. These are the virgin territories of Kazakhstan. The center is Tselinograd, the former Akmolinsk. Other cities have also been founded: Kustanay and Rudny, where huge iron-ore deposits have been found and the Sokolovo-Sarbay combine has been developed. It is mostly strip-mining, for the ore is not far below the surface.

PRACTICAL INFORMATION FOR CENTRAL ASIA

WHEN TO GO. *Not* in the summer, which can be extremely hot. *Not* in the winter, which is often freezingly cold and without the relief of snow in the lowlands. (The air is very dry, however.) Late spring (April–May) or early autumn (September–October) are the pleasantest seasons, though even then you will encounter extremes in certain spots such as deserts and mountains.

GETTING THERE. This area is best reached by air—trains are not to be recommended for travel in Central Asia. The distances are immense, in summer the heat is hardly bearable and in some districts (for instance Tadzhikistan), the line has to make such detours around the high mountains that 60 miles can easily take half a day. Planes are quicker, more comfortable and not necessarily more expensive.

Alma-Ata can best be reached by plane from Moscow (4¼ hours) or other points, though it does have two rail stations.

Ashkhabad is 3½ hours from Moscow by air. The 13 other Turkmenian cities are also linked by air to the capital, while Ashkhabad has direct connections with all important centers.

Dushanbe is only accessible by air and the flight from Alma Ata or Tashkent is breathtaking, so try to approach this way. You cross soaring peaks (the Tien-Shan foothills) with the high Pamirs visible in the distance most of the way. You drop down into the narrow bowl of Dushanbe in a hair-raising (but perfectly safe) series of circles!

Frunze, the Kirghiz capital, is also hard to reach by train—there is an enormous detour from Tashkent and Alma-Ata. But by plane it is about 50 minutes from Tashkent and 25 minutes from Alma-Ata. The flight from Moscow takes 6½ hours. Within the Kirghiz Republic there is a regular long-distance bus system, but many places, especially in winter, are closed to all but air traffic. The Issyk-Kul lake is 3–4 hours by bus and car from Frunze.

Khiva. The only comfortable way to get to Khiva is by air; it is some distance even from the secondary railroad line from Chardzhou to Kungrad. Planes, trains and buses will also take you from Tashkent to the Fergana Valley. The railroad makes a tremendous detour before it gets to Kokand, the center of the western part of the basin, though from Kokand the other towns can be reached easily and quickly by bus. On the new Tashkent-Kokand highway the bus takes 4–5 hours from the Uzbek capital to Kokand.

Samarkand can be approached from Tashkent, Bukhara and Dushanbe both by train and plane. (Tashkent-Samarkand takes 35–55 minutes by air.) Bukhara has a direct air link with both Tashkent and Samarkand. There is also a train and long-distance bus connection, but it is 290 km. (180 miles) from Samarkand and 644 km. (400 miles) from Tashkent, with the desert lying between these cities. There is also a train connection from Ashkhabad along the Krasnovodsk-Tashkent line.

Tashkent can be reached by train from other Central Asian cities and from Moscow (2½ days) or by plane (Moscow-Tashkent, 4½ hours). (Central Asian time is 3 hours later than Moscow time.) The Hunger Steppe, near Tashkent, can be reached in about 2 hours by car from the Uzbek capital. Traveling by train from Moscow to Tashkent is a most rewarding experience, even if a large part of the route is out of bounds to tourists who cannot break their journey at certain stops. Check with Intourist whether the line is open to foreigners; we have had reports of tourists being refused bookings.

HOTELS AND RESTAURANTS. A note on Central Asian food: Of the five republics in Central Asia, Uzbekistan has the most interesting cuisine. Specialties include skewers of meat grilled over a charcoal fire—*shashliks* (for which either beef or lamb is used, with other ingredients); *tkhumdulma* (a meat croquette encasing a hard-boiled egg); *pakhtakhor* salad (a mixture of chicken, cucumbers, olives, apples, peaches and plums in syrup); soups, such as *lagman* (highly spiced, with meat and noodles), *mstava* (meat soup), *maniar* (another highly spiced clear soup with pieces of meat, egg and noodles). A special kind of bread is called *obi non.* The wines are excellent and the liqueurs fiery (*Aleatiko* is the best known).

Alma-Ata. *Otrar,* 65 Gogol Street (tel. 33–0045). First class, five-story, 190 rooms. Sauna, swimming pool, good restaurant serving Kazakh and European cuisine. Rooms on main street side reported noisy, so try for quieter side. *Zhetsyu,* 55 Kommunistichesky Prospekt (tel. 39–2222/2025). First class, moderate, 5-story, 500 beds, 307 rooms (some with balcony).

Alma-Ata, 119 Panfilov Street. Modern, 8 floors, central. All rooms with balcony. *Ala-Tau,* 142 Kirov Street

Kazakh Aul Summer Tourist Camp, in the Medeo Canyon, about 20 km. (13 miles) out of town in the mountains (tel. 68–8959). 30 beds in 14 yurts—solidly built versions of traditional Kazakh style dwellings with tent-roofs; interiors lavishly decorated with Oriental rugs.

A new 16-floor pyramid-shaped hotel (name unknown) has been built on the shore of Lake Sairan, near Alma-Ata. It includes a cinema, concert hall, swimming pool, sports ground, restaurants and bars. Rooms with views over the Ala-Tau mountains.

Restaurants. *White Swan,* amid the trees by an attractive lake in Gorky Park is best; then *Aral,* also in Gorky Park, or *Issyk,* 133 Panfilov Street.

The *Aul,* at Mount Kok-Tyube, outside the city, offers "a tempting selection of Kazakh cuisine," according to Intourist.

Ashkhabad. Best is *Ashkhabad,* 74 Svobody Prospekt (tel. 57393/90447). *Oktyabrskaya,* in the same street; *Kolkhozchi,* Engelskaya Street; or *Turkmenistan,* 19 Gogol Street. An Intourist hotel with 117 rooms, rated moderate or second class.

Restaurants. In hotels, or try *Gulistan,* Pervomaiskaya Street.

Bukhara. *Amu-Darya,* which it is hoped will be fully operational by 1989, includes 378 rooms, foreign currency bar, tea room, folk-music, barber and beauty parlor. Previous best bet was *Bukhara,* 6 40-Let Oktyabrya Street (tel. 33832/ 31338). 184 rooms. Then *Gulistan* on Lenin Square.

Restaurants. In your hotel, or at the *Bukhara,* 1 Frunze Square.

Dushanbe. *Dushanbe* (Intourist), Ayni Square, is best. 313 rooms, recently opened, rated first-class, adequate. Next is *Tadzhikistan,* 22 Kommunisticheskaya Street (tel. 27–4393). 262 rooms, airconditioned, odd hip-baths! Excellent restaurant serves local dishes. Intourist excursion desk. Also *Vakhsh,* 26 Lenin Prospekt.

Restaurants. In town, the *Pamir,* Kirov Street. For atmosphere and scenery, the *Dushanbe,* at Lake Komsomol; *Leto* (summer only), in the town park; or *Farakhat,* in the park opposite Hotel Tadzhikistan - open-air kebabs, shashliks, etc., serves beer.

An indoor traditional teahouse is the huge *Rokhat* on Lenin Prospekt near the Tadzhik Drama Theater. National dishes; popular with locals. In Putovskaya Street, just across the river, there is a roadside wine bar with attractive trellises. Reported pleasant.

Fergana. *Fergana,* 29 Kommunistov Street. 5 floors, 101 rooms.

Restaurant. *Fergana,* Lenin Street.

Frunze. Best is *Ala-Too,* 1 Dzerzhinsky Prospekt (tel. 22–6041). Comparatively modern, 3 floors, 113 rooms. Opposite the rail station. Second best, Kirghizstan, Panfilov Street.

Restaurants. Try the *Kirghizia,* Kirov Street, *Susamyr,* Kirghizia Street, *Druzhba,* on corner of Ivanitsin and Sopokov Streets, or *Son-Kul,* corner of Dzerzhinsky Boulevard and 22nd Party Congress Street.

Khiva. Restaurants. The only spot to eat here is the restaurant on Gagarin Street. However, in summer another place is open outside the city wall by an artificial lake.

Samarkand. *Samarkand,* 1 Maxim Gorky Street is best. An Intourist operation, it has 10 floors and 184 rooms (many with balconies), and is first-class moderate. Modern in design, it lacks in room service what it has in architecture, and the toilets leave much to be desired. But, still, it is newish and reasonably comfortable. The food is fair. Excellent view from upper floors over the town and the glazed blue domes of the Shahi-Zinda mausoleum and mosque.

Other hotels: *Zeravshan,* 57 Sovietskaya Street. Taxi-rank nearby. *Registan,* 36 Lenin Street.

Restaurants. In your hotel, or try the *Shark,* Kozhevannaya Street.

Shakhrisabz. *Shakhrisabz,* central, tel. 38–61. First class, two floors, 63 rooms. **Restaurant.** In hotel.

Tashkent. Main Intourist hotel is the *Uzbekistan,* 45 Karl Marx Street (tel. 33–3959/7786). First class, 479 rooms, air-conditioned. Finnish decor, restaurant. Intourist bureau, Beryozka shop, post office, bank and swimming pool.

Tashkent, 50 Lenin Street, at Teatralnaya Square. 19 floors, 262 rooms. Quite agreeable and central. *Moskva,* new in 1982. *Shark,* 16 Pravda Vostoka Street. Intourist establishment too, but with less pretension. *Rossia,* Rustaveli Prospekt, is fairly up-to-date.

Also-rans include: *Zeravshan,* 15 Akhunbabaev Street (a bit far away), and *Push-kinskaya,* 18 Pushkin Street.

Restaurants. *Bakhor,* 15 Kuibyshev Street and *Blue Dome Café.*

Urgench. Two modest hotels: *Urgench,* 27 Kommunisticheskaya Street; and *Khorezm,* 2 Al-Biruni Street, 2 floors, 63 rooms.

Restaurant. Only place: *Urgench,* Lenin Street, next to hotel.

TRANSPORTATION. Except in the main cities, taxis are very few and very expensive. The official rate is 20 kopeks a kilometer. As for public transportation, it is practical and very cheap, but is best avoided at the rush hours. Tashkent is the only city in Central Asia to have a subway, reportedly earthquake-proof.

PLACES OF INTEREST. Alma-Ata. *Museum of the Kazah S.S.R.,* in the former cathedral. The history of Kazakhstan from ancient times to the present.

Exhibition of Economic Achievements of the Kazakh S.S.R.

Kazakh Art Museum, 22 Sovietskaya Street. Paintings, sculpture, works of graphic and applied art of Kazakhstan, as well as Russian, Soviet, western European and Oriental art.

Museum of Archaeology. Sections on the Stone, Bronze, Early Iron and Middle Ages.

Kazakh Artists' Union Exhibition Hall. Works by Kazakh and other Soviet artists as well as foreign art.

Museum of Ethnic Musical Instruments.

Ashkhabad. *Museum of History of the Turkmenian S.S.R.* More than 30,000 exhibits relating to the archaeology and ethnography of Turkmenia.

Museum of Fine Arts, 84 Svoboda Prospekt. One of the largest in Central Asia, displaying Russian icons and canvases by Russian, Soviet and foreign artists. Unique carpet collection. At the same address is the *Museum of Regional Studies,* devoted to the history and everyday life of the Turkmenian people.

Exhibition of Economic Achievements of the Turkmenian S.S.R.

Bukhara. *Local History Museum,* within the Ark (castle). Another section of this museum is in the Zindan building nearby. A third section is housed in the Si-tore-i-Mahi-Hasa Palace, 3 km. (2½ miles) from town.

Dushanbe. *Museum of History and Regional Studies,* Lenin Prospekt, near Ayni Square. Local crafts, jewelry, carpets.

Out of town: *Hissar Fortress,* 30 km. (18 miles) away, four-hour excursion.

Fergana. *Museum of Local History,* 18 Pervogo Maya Street.

Frunze. *Fine Arts Museum,* Pervogo Maya Street. *Museum of Applied Art.* Repoussé work, carved wood and *ganch* (a kind of gypsum), marble and carpets.

Zoological Museum. Displays the richly varied fauna of Kirghizia. *Museum of Natural History.* The flora and fauna of the Khorezm region. *Exhibition of Economic Achievements of the Kirghiz S.S.R.*

Frunze House Museum, Pervogo Maya Street. Exhibits devoted to the life of Mikhail Frunze.

Historical Museum. History of the Kirghiz people from the Stone Age to the present day.

Khiva. *Museum of the History of Medicine of Ancient Khorezm.* Among the exhibits are works by the scientists and physicians of ancient Khorezm ibn-Sina and Biruni.

Samarkand. *Museum of History and Museum of Uzbek Art.* Entire old city is a living museum.

Out of town is *Ulug-Bek's Observatory,* with a memorial museum, at the foot of the Chupan-Ata Hill. Intourist will take you there.

At **Pendzhikent,** 48 km. (30 miles) away, visit the Rudaki Museum, rich in archaeological treasures.

Shakhrisabz. *Khujun Handicraft Factory.* Carpets and the traditional headdress of the Uzbek people—*tyubeteikas*—are made here. *Silk Spinning Mill.*

Winery. The most famous local wines are *Shirin* and *Vassarga.*

Out of town: there is an Intourist excursion to a recreation area with tearooms, some 22.5 km. (14 miles) from Shakhrisabz which takes 3½ hours.

Tashkent. *The Exhibition of Economic Achievements of the Uzbek S.S.R.,* Pobeda Park; open 10–6, closed Tues.

Art Gallery (paintings and sculpture), 6 Kuibyshev Street; open 10–6, closed Tues. *Uzbek Art Museum,* Gogol Street. *Alisher Navoi Literary Museum,* 35 Alisher Navoi Street; open 10–5, closed Mon. *Alisher Navoi Library,* 14 Bratskaya Street. *Museum of Decorative Arts,* 15 Shelkovichnaya Street; open 10–5, closed Mon., and Tues. *Textile Factory,* open Mon., Wed., Fri. 10–1; arrange through Intourist.

A *Museum of Carpets* recently opened but no details were available at presstime. The *Botanical Garden* has one of the world's great tulip collections.

TOURS. There are special central Asian tours, arranged by Intourist via Moscow or Leningrad. Tours are organized in Ashkhabad, Alma-Ata, Bukhara, Dushanbe, Samarkand and Tashkent and individual tours can be arranged in the vicinity of these centers. An interesting location is Pendzhikent with its ancient excavations. Can be visited (on day-trip only) from Samarkand. It is now possible to tour Southern Kazakhstan, visiting Djamboul (the ancient city of Taraz), Chimkent with its Museum of Karakul Sheep Breeding, and the mining town of Kentau. Karaganda in central Kazakhstan may also be visited.

THEATERS, CONCERTS, CINEMAS. The opera houses have performances almost every night: recitals, ballet, opera, singing, dancing, and drumming. Seats can almost always be had up to curtain time, from 80 kopeks to 2 roubles. Or Intourist will reserve for you—at 2 roubles only.

Alma Ata. *Kazakh Drama Theater,* Communist Prospekt. *Abay Academic Opera and Ballet Theater,* 112 Kalinin Street. *Film and TV Studio* on Abay Prospekt. *Philharmonic. Circus.*

Ashkhabad. *Turkmenian Theater* and *Russian Drama Theater,* both on Svoboda Prospekt, Botanical Garden (western end of Svoboda Prospekt). *Opera and Ballet Theater. Philharmonic.*

Bukhara. *Musical and Drama Theater,* in the Town Park.

Dushanbe. *Ayni Opera and Ballet Theater,* Moscow Square. *Philharmonia,* Lenin Prospekt (with a concert hall). *Russian Drama Theater,* Lenin Prospekt at Putovsky Street. *Tadzhik Drama Theater,* Lenin Prospekt.

Frunze. *Krupskaya Russian Drama Theater,* Dubovy Park. *Kirghiz State Opera and Ballet,* Dubovy Park. *Kirghiz Drama Theater,* Pervogo Maya Street. *Philharmonic.*

Tashkent. *Alisher Navoi Opera and Ballet Theater,* 31 Pravda Vostoka Street. *Khamza Uzbek Theater,* 2 Uigur Street, presenting Uzbek national plays. *Maxim Gorky Russian Theater,* 28 Karl Marx Street.

Uzbek Philharmonic Orchestra, 10 Pravda Vostoka Street. *Circus,* 46 Lenin Street. *Conservatory,* 31 Pushkinskaya Street.

Rodina Wide-screen cinema, 34 Navoi Street. *Khamza Uzbek Theatre,* 5 Khamza Street. *Mukimi Music and Drama Theater,* 1–87 Almazar Street.

SHOPPING. The souvenir and dollar-currency shops in the tourist hotels offer a choice of several items; prices in the tax-free dollar shops are lower. In Samarkand the bazaar by the *Registan* has souvenir and craft items. The Bukhara market has jewelry, chased copper ornaments, carved wood and alabaster. The most interesting souvenirs in Uzbekistan are the embroidered caps and textiles, often spectacularly colorful and elaborate. Local wines are good too; also enameled silver jewelry. Lacquer ware, carved ivory, ceramics, painted boxes, dolls and pottery are less interesting.

Other best buys in Central Asia are the carpets, but their purchase is a complicated business. We have had reports, furthermore, that some "oriental" carpets on sale in Beriozka shops are made in East Germany. Check the label. Turkmen and Tadzhik skullcaps are also worth purchasing. In Dushanbe, Tadzhik girls do pretty embroidery with gold, silver and silken thread on velvet and other fine cloths. But it's expensive, even in the bazaars.

USEFUL TASHKENT ADDRESSES. *Intourist:* 50 Lenin Street, *Pakhtakor Stadium,* 10 Pakhtakorskaya Street.

SIBERIA

The Wild East

It is only during the last 20 years or so that Siberia has been opened up to the Western traveler—or, at least, a certain part of it has, for there still are vast areas where the foreigner is not welcome. For some years there has been a short-cut route between Tokyo, Moscow and Paris by way of Siberia for a number of airlines, but bookings, at least from Tokyo to Khabarovsk, are reportedly heavy and waiting lists for seats long.

So Eastern and Central Siberia have been put on the tourist map and a whole new world has become moderately accessible to the traveler. Aeroflot advertises Eastern Siberia and has opened up its immense network covering this vast territory. Information about accommodations, travel facilities and so on is becoming routinely more available, and if you are the adventurous type you will enjoy the unusual experience of entering the Soviet Union by its large backyard. After visiting Khabarovsk, Irkutsk and Lake Baikal, you could, if you so wish, proceed via Central Asia to the Black Sea, Moscow and Leningrad.

Siberia's six million square miles offer fantastic variety. Its meridians pass through the icy wastes of the Arctic, through tundra, primeval forest and the endless steppe. Mountains, high plateaux and plains alternate.

Siberia could easily contain the whole of Western Europe. The Trans-Siberian Railway is the longest in the world, while the potential hydroelectric energy of the Siberian rivers is immeasurable—the Angara alone could provide 70 billion kilowatt hours a year. And yet it is only one of the region's rivers which include the Ob, the Irtysh, the Yenisei, the Lena and the Amur. One of the largest hydroelectric plants in the world was constructed at Bratsk on the Angara and some 23 others are being built on the Yenisei.

Siberia's forests are also unimaginably rich. Coal and iron ore deposits are very extensive in some districts of Eastern Siberia and in Western Siberia (Bakchar and Kolpashevo). Siberia contains 90 percent of the U.S.S.R.'s bituminous coal reserves, 75 percent of the iron ore, 80 percent of the timber. Huge oilfields have been discovered near the ancient town of Tyumen, where the Samotlor field is said to be one of the largest in the world and is producing 50 million tons of oil a year; in 1962 rich oil wells were tapped outside the village of Markovo, on the upper course of the Lena, and a whole new town, Neftelensk, has grown up around them. Siberia is also very rich in gold, silver and precious metals, even diamonds. To develop Siberia's vast potential, the Russians are enlisting Western help and contracts are being or have been negotiated with British, U.S., French, German, Japanese and Finnish companies experienced in oil, gas and mineral extraction. The newly opened alternative Trans-Siberian rail link, the B.A.M. (see below) has enabled still more vast areas hitherto inaccessible or at least unexploited to be tapped for their underground riches.

Tourism is, of course, less well developed than elsewhere. Many regions are difficult to reach; others are not yet accessible to the tourist. But you can discover the *taiga,* the primeval forest even on the outskirts of major cities. Some taiga areas still have tigers and bears—though you're unlikely to meet them near the inhabited settlements! The cities have few art treasures and the newer ones are not particularly interesting architecturally, as offices, public buildings and administrative centers have largely been built to the same uniform pattern. Nor was the taste of the rich merchants of pre-revolutionary times very distinguished. In Siberian cities at the turn of the century a good many wooden buildings were to be seen and in the less developed settlements and in the northern districts these are still standing. Most of the cities have one or two theaters, and you'll also find local museums, the occasional art gallery, some fine parks and, almost everywhere, a riverside promenade. Many tourists will feel that a visit to a single Siberian city is sufficient, although both Irkutsk and Novosibirsk are exceptionally interesting in different ways.

Irkutsk

Irkutsk is the capital of Irkutsk Territory which has an area larger than that of France, Holland, Belgium, Austria, Switzerland and Denmark put together. Over 300 years old, it was the final goal of Jules Verne's Michael Strogov—and something of a frontier town. Its University, founded in 1918, was the first institute of higher learning in Eastern Siberia and still has a fine reputation. The city is now firmly on the tourist map. It is an important junction on the Trans-Siberian railway, and planes land and take off regularly. The flight-time from Moscow is seven hours, including a fueling stop at Novosibirsk.

A modern busy city, it has many shady parks; the houses in the center are two-, three- and four-storied, in late 19th-century European neo-Classical style. Many of the old-style wooden houses are being knocked down, but some have been scrupulously preserved. Chocolate-brown in color, with richly-carved, colorfully-painted window-frames, portals and gables, they are the most atmospheric sights of Irkutsk. On summer evenings their inhabitants sit outside on old wooden benches.

Though many of the city's old churches are closed, two remain open as places of worship. The 18th-century Church of the Holy Cross has a fine choir. The Church of the Holy Saviour, on the city's outskirts, has an interesting cemetery containing the grave of Gregory Shelekhov, a roving Siberian merchant who founded Russia's first permanent colony in Alaska in 1784. The graves of some 19th-century exiles and their families are here too, and in the late spring the cemetery is a mass of cherry blossom. Within its walls is the Znamensky Convent, still open, and nearby, the Church of the Apparition of Our Lady. The Local History Museum is a fascinating mix: household utensils, clothing and hunting gear of Eastern Siberia's indigenous people—the Evenks, the Yakuts and the Buryats—together with 19th-century documents of the Decembrist exiles. There is a synagogue at 23 Karl Liebknecht Street, half a block east of Karl Marx Street.

The Siberian oil-refining center, Angarsk, is close to Irkutsk. A long pipeline brings oil from European Russia; but there are also important oilfields around Irkutsk.

Lake Baikal and Area

From the Central Hotel in Irkutsk the landing stage is only five minutes' walk. From here a hydrofoil will take you to Lake Baikal. (You can also go by car as far as Listvyanka, a one-hour drive, passing through some traditional wooden, stockaded villages, on the fringe of the taiga.)

The deep-green woods lining the banks of the Angara open like a gate in front of the boat and the horizon widens to reveal a seemingly endless vista. This is the ancient, sacred sea of the Tunguz tribes, Lake Baikal, shining in dazzling blue. Far away on the horizon, snowy peaks rise mistily. Their lines are delicate, more like a mirage than reality.

A popular Russian song calls it "majestic ocean, holy Baikal." In the language of the Evenki tribe it is also called Lama (Sea) while in the Chinese chronicles it is Pe Hai, Northern Ocean.

Lake Baikal is some 650 km. (400 miles) long and has an area equal to that of Belgium and the Netherlands together. Its width varies between 29 km. and 80 km. (18 and 50 miles). According to the latest measurements, it is more than a mile deep in places. It contains one sixth of all the fresh water in the world, and it is also the world's oldest lake. Soviet scientists claim that the depression was formed in the Tertiary era, 25 million years ago. It lies some 503 meters (1,650 feet) above sea level and the mountains around it tower to 2,750 meters (9,000 feet). Experts are still arguing about its origins and about how seals and sea cows ever came to be in it—not to mention the omul, a white fish of the salmon family which is one of the local culinary specialties. The water is crystal clear; a white sheet thrown into it can be seen clearly at a depth of 90–120 feet. It has hardly any taste, for it contains a negligible proportion of mineral salts. The currents are very slow. It is fed by 336 rivers but has only one outlet, the Angara. The water is cold—even in the hottest summers it never rises above 50–52°F though it rarely freezes before January; then the ice can be 24 or even 36 inches thick. Yet it is a dangerous surface on which to travel for the gases that rise from its depths warm up the water and make the ice unsafe. It is frequently whipped by great storms. The barguzin, the northeast wind, blows along its entire length. The other, even more cruel, wind is the 80 m.p.h. sarma, the northwest wind, which whips the waves up to considerable heights.

At the Limnological Institute at Listvyanka you can hear a lecture on the extraordinary history and ecology of Baikal. The Russians have created a special scientific discipline they call "baikalology." Experts have identified 1200 different creatures which are unique to Lake Baikal, many of them reputed to be survivals which have become extinct elsewhere.

Those who feel inclined to embark on a longer excursion should continue to the station of Bolshiye Koti and explore its neighborhood. It is best to take food and fishing tackle with you. Lake Baikal provides rich and varied sport for the angler. Intourist provides overnight facilities at the Hotel Baikal right on the lakeshore at Listvyanka.

Novosibirsk

Novosibirsk is the largest city in Siberia and the eighth largest in population (third largest in area) in the whole of the Soviet Union. It is the center of the Novosibirsk Territory, an important traffic junction and an industrial center. It is a modern city, laid out on a gridiron plan. The centre of the Inner Town is Red Avenue (Krasny Prospekt), stretching 10 km. (over 6 miles) from the banks of the Ob to the air terminal. Along its less wide section are several parks and well-kept squares. Here, almost every 20th-century architectural style has left its trace. There is a large opera house and a Conservatoire which boasts the only organ in Siberia. A subway opened in 1985.

Novosibirsk has a separate district called Akademgorodok (Science City), 29 km. (18 miles) south, on the Ob River. In 1958 a forest of birches and pines was transformed into a university research center equipped with the finest facilities and staffed by some of the best brains in the country. To attract these people, Akademgorodok is well supplied with consumer goods and its accommodations and cultural facilities are certainly superior to those of most other towns. It has a reputation for comparative liberalism. To balance these attractions, however, the weather is inclement, with summer often oppressive at 90°F while winter can mean 50°F below zero, with four feet of snow. Foreign scientists visit Akademgorodok in considerable numbers, but its inhabitants nevertheless do tend to feel isolated in this Siberian fastness. Your quickest way there is by taxi from Novosibirsk; it is a standard route and cab-drivers enjoy going out there; the fare of 5–6 roubles is a bargain and there are always plenty of taxis back.

Khabarovsk

Khabarovsk is a traffic junction and industrial center, the capital of the Khabarovsk Territory. Flying time from Moscow is 7½ hours.

Built on three hills—called *sopka* locally—each of which is a separate district, Khabarovsk lies on the banks of the Amur where the Ussuri enters the mighty river. The Amur is the second favorite river of the Russians— "Little Father Amur" to "Little Mother Volga." Yet it is a grim river that can smash ships during storms and sweep away villages when it is in flood. The Chinese call it the "Black Dragon." Founded in 1858, the city as it stands today is over a century old and, because of the damage wrought during the Revolution, architecturally it is even younger.

The main thoroughfare is Karl Marx Street, which links Lenin Square with Komsomol Square on the banks of the Amur. There are a few old redbrick houses intermingled with houses and public buildings designed in the Constructivist style of the 1930s. Almost all the important institutions are housed here, as well as the largest hotels.

Komsomol Square, at the far end of Karl Marx Street, has the headquarters of the Amur Steamship Company, a fine building of the *belle époque*. Go on from here to the waterfront and enjoy the view across the river to the treeless steppe, with China in the distance. The river embankment is a favorite walk for the people of Khabarovsk. You may like to know that among Khabarovsk's exports to the world market are Siberian ginseng and Ussuri tigers!

Forty eight km. (30 miles) from Khabarovsk, in Volochayevka, where the Civil War ended, you'll see a large building topped with a huge statue on the summit of the Iyun-Koran mountain. This is the memorial and museum of the Amur partisans.

Bratsk, Barnaul and Yakutsk

The three cities mentioned so far are the most easily accessible to the tourist. The other Siberian cities are presented only briefly here as you are less likely to visit them, although 1–2 night stopovers in Bratsk now feature regularly on Intourist package tours.

The site of Bratsk is over 350 years old and was originally a Cossack fort. There are some interesting cave drawings in the vicinity. The modern city sprang up in the 1960s when one of the largest hydroelectric plants in the world was built here. The Bratsk Sea is a huge (5,000 sq. km.) reservoir; soon after it was completed an aluminum factory and a large timber combine were also erected here. The residential districts are of very recent vintage.

Bratsk is linked to the Trans-Siberian railway by a branch line, which pushes on to Ust Kut and even beyond. There is also a fair road. But the best way of reaching Ust Kut is by plane, from which can be seen the River Angara, which channels the waters of Lake Baikal and the Bratsk Sea into the Yenisei.

Barnaul is the center of the Altaisky Territory. Founded in 1738 when a merchant called Demidov set up a smelting mill on the banks of the Ob River to exploit the silver being mined in the Altai Mountains, it later became an important cultural center. When serfdom was abolished, ending the supply of unpaid labor to the Altai mines, Barnaul began to decline. In more recent years it has begun to flourish again, especially since the opening up of the Virgin Lands. From Barnaul an excursion can be made into the Altai Mountains.

Yakutsk is the capital of the huge Yakutsk Autonomous Republic, an area of over a million square miles. The city was one of the earliest fortresses in Siberia but for a long time only wooden houses were built here. Yakutsk lies in the permafrost zone, where the thermometer can drop to −70°F in January. Large concrete pillars are driven into the soil some 18 feet deep and covered with reinforced concrete in recent construction, enabling quite tall buildings to be erected. The main thoroughfare of Yakutsk, Lenin Street, has many such buildings standing on stilts.

Yakutsk is a major scientific center. Its Frost Research Institute, a branch of the Academy of Sciences, is engaged in essential work for which its location is ideally suited.

Komsomosk, Krasnoyarsk, Abakan and Norilsk

Komsomolsk is on the Amur River, some 322 km. (200 miles) from Khabarovsk. Its building began in 1932, partly using forced labor, in the middle of the taiga, on swampy soil. It is one of the most important industrial centers of the Soviet Far East.

Krasnoyarsk is the center of the Krasnoyarsk Territory. Lying on the banks of the Yenisei River, between the Irkutsk and Novosibirsk regions, it is one of the most important industrial centers in Siberia. The old city is on the left bank, the new town on the right. Founded in 1628, the Cossack fort became a government seat in 1823. Its development was due to the nearby gold mines and to the building of the Trans-Siberian Railway. During Czarist times it was a center for exiles: Lenin spent two months here in 1897.

Six km. (four miles) from Krasnoyarsk are the famous "Pillars," huge (120–270 foot high) columns of rock belonging to outcrops of the Eastern Sayan. They were formed by the combined effect of wind and water. This is a protected area and open to tourists.

About 290 km. (180 miles) south of Krasnoyarsk and two hours' flying time from Novosibirsk, is the modern city of Abakan, recently opened to foreign tourists, where Intourist now provides overnight facilities. Once a scattering of nomad tents in the steppe, it is now a city of wide highways and tall apartment blocks. The Local History Museum contains some forty stone carvings of human and animal figures, which are relics of ancient times. You can't miss them: they are displayed, eerily, on the pavement right outside the museum.

From Abakan, Intourist runs coach trips across the Minusinsk plain, a crossroads on the ancient trade routes from Arabia, Central Asia, China and Tibet, and an area devastated by Genghis Khan's invasion, to Shushenskoye. Here, the original Shushenskoye village (now superseded by a modern settlement) has been reconstructed in every detail to look exactly as it was when Lenin lived there in exile from 1897 to 1900, with his bride Nadezhda Krupskaya.

Another coach trip from Abakan is to the Sayano-Shushenskaya Hydroelectric Station in the Yenisei River valley. The road from the 250-year-old settlement of Maina to the dam site is paved with crushed marble, the only kind of rock to be found in the vicinity. The mountains to your right are also of vari-colored marble, and the River Yenisei itself flows in a marble bed. Weather permitting, the excursion ends with a picnic in the taiga.

Norilsk is one of the major new cities of the Krasnoyarsk Territory in the permafrost region. It has nickel and other metal foundries. Originally a small village, its development gathered pace in the 1950s. Here, too, the buildings are supported on huge pillars driven deep into the ground. Summer brings white nights; in winter, daylight lasts only an hour or two.

Omsk and Tomsk

Omsk, center of Omsk Territory, is situated at the confluence of the Om and Irtysh Rivers. The city—Siberia's second-largest—was founded in 1716 by a military expedition led by Colonel Bukholts. In 1768 a new fort was built on the site of the previous one, then in 1822 it became the seat of the governor of Western Siberia and from 1839 the residence of the Governor General. It was another place of exile—Dostoyevsky did four years' hard labor in its prison. By the early 20th century it had some important industries, mainly textiles and leather; today it is a vast industrial area.

Tomsk, founded in 1604, is one of the oldest cities in Siberia, with a university (established in 1888), a number of colleges and schools and a fine Botanical Garden. Nearby, large-scale excavations have uncovered ancient burial places dating from the Neolithic era, the middle of the first millennium B.C.

Ulan-Ude and Vladivostok

Ulan-Ude is the capital of the Buryat Autonomous Republic, on the banks of the Selenga and Uda Rivers. It was founded in 1666 as the winter quarters of Cossack troops. In 1689 a fortress was built here and in 1775 the city was given its municipal charter as Verkhne-Udinsk; (it was renamed Ulan-Ude in 1934). In March 1920 it became the capital of the Far Eastern Territory. With its mixture of old wooden houses and modern apartment blocks, it still has the atmosphere of a remote, frontier town. The main thoroughfare is Lenin Street, where the shops are.

Vladivostok, founded in 1860 on the shores of the Golden Horn Bay on the Pacific, is the center of the Primorsky (Coastal) Territory. An important strategical base, by 1880 it had become a fair-sized city. Many expeditions started from here and it became particularly important as a naval base during the Russo-Japanese War. Today it is the main base for the Soviet Pacific Fleet. It has a large merchant harbor and is also a center for the whaling and fishing fleets.

The Trans-Siberian Railway

The 9,299 km. (5,778 miles) of railway stretching from the Pacific Coast of Siberia to Moscow is by far the longest continuous track in the world on which through trains are operated. The name "Trans-Siberian Railway" is a purely English invention; to the Russians it is the "Great Siberian." Built between 1880 and 1900 after several decades of debate, it was in its early years a vital and rapid link for Westerners, especially diplomats, who used it to reach the capitals of China and Japan. Today it constitutes the greatest single travel experience a tourist can have, and offers Americans a through route from the Orient to Europe, while Europeans get a fairly cheap and interesting transit to Japan and Hong Kong.

A new "eastern section" of the Trans-Siberian line is now complete running from the town of Taishet to the city of Komsomolsk on the River Amur. The route (some 3,620 km., 2,250 miles) is already in operation. Known as the Baikal-Amur Mainline (the initials B.A.M. are becoming well-known) it is a mammoth engineering undertaking which is opening up vast new areas of Eastern Siberia including the copper deposits in the Udokan area which are said to exceed the combined reserves of the United States, Chile and Zaire. And the new line is some 965 km. (600 miles) from the Chinese border, closer to which the original Trans-Siberian runs for considerable distances. Most important, it provides the final link in a new freight service from Western Europe to Japan, via the Soviet Far Eastern port of Vostochny, relieving pressure on the long-since overloaded Trans-Siberian line.

Tourist trips run on the old, traditional route. For foreigners, the Trans-Siberian doesn't start at Vladivostok, for that is a military port with limited access. The regular ships of the *Soviet Far East Line* come into the port of Nakhodka, about 80 km. (50 miles) to the north, from Hong Kong, Tokyo Bay, and Osaka. A boat train meets the ship (at least twice weekly in summer) and runs for 908 km. (564 miles) to the Soviet Far East city of Khabarovsk. Here passengers must change trains. Eastbound passengers spend a night in Khabarovsk and the next day sightseeing, picking up the boat train in the early evening. Westbound passengers change trains the same day. You can, if you wish, reach Khabarovsk by *Japan Air Lines,* who have weekly flights, but there are reports of long waiting lists on this route.

Day One

That first sight of a Russian train at Nakhodka is an encouraging one, for its green-and-cream cars are airconditioned, offering two-berth sleepers, with a shower between two compartments, an excellent diner, and a powerful electric engine. The train leaves at 7.50 P.M., with dinner served on board. The express arrives at Khabarovsk at 11.35 A.M. the following morning. You change trains here into the *Rossia,* the daily trans-Siberian Express which has come up from Vladivostok and leaves Khabarovsk for its long journey west at 1.10 P.M. on Day Two. There is a dining car all the way. (Confusion is sometimes caused by the fact that Russian timetables use Moscow time, which is seven hours behind local time here. All times given here are local time).

The train itself is less luxurious than the boat express. There are "soft"- and "hard"-class cars, a diner, a baggage car, and three seating coaches for short-haul passengers. "Soft"-class has two or four berths and "hard"-class four. In addition, the "softs" are made up and have full carpeting and sometimes showers between two compartments, while "hard" class passengers must hire their own bedding; there are no showers, only washrooms at both ends of each car. Wide corridors in "soft" are carpeted, with folddown seats, and shaving plugs are placed on the outer walls, so men with electric razors shave in public! Usually one or two of the "S.Z." type two-berth sleepers are attached to this train now, a similar type to those on the boat express. The newest "soft" class sleepers have shower units incorporated in their design with two shower units to each coach. It is planned that the entire *Rossia* trains should have these, but they are being introduced only gradually. You may be lucky. At present, foreigners are accommodated in two-berth first-class and four-berth second-class compartments, according to Intourist. Bed-linen and towels are provided. Meals are provided in the restaurant car for cash payment in roubles only; money *must* be exchanged before starting the journey.

The Trans-Siberian trains, called *Rossia* and numbered One and Two (No. 1 is westbound) run daily from May to September, four times a week in winter. The basic train sets, in red and cream (marked with brass Cyrillic characters on the side denoting "Moscow-Vladivostok"), were built in 1949, and are *not* airconditioned. The train is sealed in winter, with heating by the train attendants stoking stoves; in summer the dry, burning heat of Siberia with plenty of dust about makes travel conditions unpleasant at times. Light indoor clothing is a *must,* but remember also to take along a heavy coat for stops in winter and spring. Normal garb for Russian passengers is very informal: trousers and shirt, often pyjamas. The four-berth compartments are not divided as to sex and it may happen that three men share with a woman, although for tourists boarding with Intourist at Khabarovsk, using airline-type boarding cards, there is an official attempt to avoid this.

Day Two

Day Two sees the Trans-Siberian train rolling across the mighty Amur River and through dry country with the high hills of China never far away. To get the best out of this journey, travelers *must* have a knowledge of the Cyrillic alphabet (it only takes 48 hours to master), for without it they cannot read the timetable displayed in each car and will not know where they are when the train stops. Even more important, they will not know *how long* the stop is going to be. The train adheres very strictly to schedule—it has to, because the Siberian Railway is extremely busy throughout its length. It is double track and boasts C.T.C. (centralized train control) but passes a fast freight every 30 minutes and a number of passenger trains not going the full length of the line. There are 91 stops from Vladivostok to Moscow, 79 of them affecting those passengers who join at Khabarovsk, and the time at stations ranges from one minute to a maximum of 15 (at Sverdlovsk, Novosibirsk and Krasnoyarsk). It is normal to get out and walk up and down the platforms, perhaps to buy things from the station "bazaars" (try ice-cream, chocolate and Russian bread), but only one warning blast is given before the train starts away. The "soft" car attendants try to keep an eye on their passengers to prevent their being left behind. Moscow time is kept throughout the train's run, which can vary up to seven hours from local time. In our description we use local times.

The first stop out of Khabarovsk is at In, a tiny place in the wilds. Ten minutes are allowed. The next stop, at 3.31, is at Birobidzhan, capital of the so-called Autonomous Jewish Region, a bleak and swampy area, but this only lasts two minutes.

As the day wears on the train is rolling smoothly through the dry, hilly country of the Soviet Far East (they do not regard this region as Siberia proper). The dining car is open all day from nine in the morning until ten at night, and its menus are in six languages. Only those items on the huge and optimistic menus which have pencilled prices against them are available. Being a better "shop" than most in the towns and villages through which it passes, the train's diner is often visited by locals who buy soft drinks and ice cream to take away. This can lead to shortages for passengers, and no replacements are made until Irkutsk is reached. Meals are fairly cheap, foreigners paying by means of Intourist coupons purchased in advance (but taking change in roubles and kopeks). The food is fairly good at times, rump steak fried in breadcrumbs apparently being a stable and consistent favorite but recent reports suggest alcoholic drinks are no longer available on the train. Breakfasts are massive affairs, at least for Russians, who seem to visit the diner for four meals a day. Take a chance with the non-tourist menu, it can be good!

Passengers tend to retire early, soon after ten at night, but the car attendants serve tea at that hour. In the "soft" class you can order tea at any time; in the "hard" it is served twice a day. Hot water can also be obtained for your own tea or coffee. The heavy cars, 56 tons on average, rolling on their wide five-foot gauge, ride easily on excellent track (except that after the spring thaw there may be bad stretches) and sleeping is comfortable. A lot depends on your traveling companions!

Days Three and Four

As Day Three brightens and the attendants begin their rounds with the inevitable tea, one has settled into the routine of the Trans-Siberian. It is like traveling in a coastal freighter, with tiny cabins, making a lot of stops in small ports. The wide corridors are the promenade decks and the diner is the saloon. There are parties in the "cabins" and you learn a certain amount of Russian! There are 12-minute stops at Skorodino, 8.09 A.M., and Amazar, 2.04 P.M..

The scenery is mainly upland forests with rivers and lakes often in sight. The ubiquitous silver birch trees are now more in evidence. There is a good exercise stop during the morning when 15 minutes are spent changing engines. The train is now 1,285 km. (800 miles) from Khabarovsk, with 7,173 (4,460) still to do.

For most of the day the train runs along the right bank of the splendid Shilka river. If you are interested in trees and wild life, it is worth sitting on a corridor seat and just watching this little-known part of Siberia unfold. Later, the country becomes very dry again as the train enters the fringe of the Gobi Desert. For most of the evening it runs through arid country with Manchuria and Mongolia well away to the south. Late at night there is a 15-minute stop at the city of Chita, junction for the former Chinese Eastern line to Harbin and Korea.

As Day Four dawns, the train has climbed away from the Gobi region into the Trans-Baikal area, the true Siberia, on one of the last major climbs left in the world. You are crossing the Yablonovy range, little known to Western travelers, where summits reach 2,750 meters (9,000 feet). The train goes through at over 1,220 meters (4,000 feet) and the temperature in winter plummets like a stone—in summer it is noticeably cooler. There is a stop at 6.44 A.M. at Mogzon, then another is made at 10.57A.M. for 12 minutes at Petrovsky Zavod. All around you can see dense forests, the Siberia of fact and fiction. At 1.18 P.M. a stop is made at Ulan Ude, junction for Peking, 12 minutes. Traveling from Moscow, you can book through to Peking on certain days of the week—ask Intourist.

At lunchtime the train nears the fierce Angara River, amid tremendous mountain scenery on the southern side of Lake Baikal. This is the only river to escape from mighty Lake Baikal, into which flow more than 300 rivers.

At 7.55 P.M. there is a 10-minute stop at Irkutsk, where you get a change of linen and towels, and the diner is restocked. Its crew, though, goes right through to Moscow, and so does the electric engine up front. The big city glimpsed from the modern station has been called the "Paris of Siberia"!

Thus ends the more romantic section of the great journey; for the rest, there are some highlights, but mostly a great deal of forest. It is ideal for catching up on sleeping and reading. There are mountains and lakes as Day Four ends on the way from Irkutsk to Zima ("Winter"), with the train still above 900 meters (3,000 feet).

Days Five and Six

Early on Day Five the train stops at Krasnoyarsk, which means both "red" and "beautiful." There are enormous hydro-electric schemes on the river Yenisei hereabouts. All day the Siberian plain unfolds, with its millions of trees, lakes, and streams. Stops are few (only for crew changes) and speed averages 43 m.p.h. At 1.14A.M. you enter highly industrialized Novosibirsk, crossing into the station by the Ob Bridge, longest and most important on the line. Only 32 km. (20 miles) south is Akademgorodok, the Soviet science city.

Going west you see the famous city of Omsk, on the Irtysh River, where the train stops in the early morning of Day Six. This is the junction for the South Siberian Railway. Contrary to popular belief, the Trans-Siberian does not go via Tomsk but misses it by 160 km. (100 miles—you change at Taiga Junction).

There is a run of 12 hours across the plain to Sverdlovsk, an important industrial city in the Urals, where there is a 15-minute stop in mid-afternoon. Soon after leaving it, winding through the comparatively low but rocky Urals, you pass a sign near kilometer post 1,777 (1,100 miles from Moscow), showing Asia to the east and Europe to the West. It is gently downhill through the night, mostly through coniferous forests and wide fields, until the stop at Kirov at 4.51A.M. on Day Seven. This is the last important place till Moscow.

Day Seven

Day Seven goes by, with the train passing through grain fields and forests as it whirls across North Russia, bearing west-south-west towards the capital. This is the day you get your bills for services rendered by the attendants (all those glasses of tea and cups of cocoa). The price is very modest—although they shy at tips, they are happy to accept a present. At 4.40 P.M. (if the train is on time—and it usually is) Moscow's Yaroslavl Station comes in sight and the journey ends amid the bustle of the great Square of the Three Terminals (Komsomol Square).

PRACTICAL INFORMATION FOR SIBERIA

WHEN TO COME. From late spring to early fall, unless you like the cold. It can be pleasantly warm even in October, but be prepared for a cold snap.

GETTING THERE. By air. From Moscow to Novosibirsk; from Novosibirsk to Irkutsk; from Irkutsk to Khabarovsk; from Khabarovsk to Nakhodka by rail. By air from Niigata (Japan) to Khabarovsk. From Ashkhabad to Novosibirsk via Tashkent, also by air.

By train. From Moscow to Nakhodka, stopping in Novosibirsk, Irkutsk or Khabarovsk.

By car. There are no authorized auto routes for foreigners in Siberia.

HOTELS AND RESTAURANTS. Bratsk. Best is first-class *Taiga,* 35 Mir Street (tel. 43–979). With good restaurant and foreign currency bar from 9 P.M. onward. 7 floors, 104 rooms, central. Sumptuous New Year festivities for foreign tourists. *Bratsk,* first class, 9 story, 414 beds, central. Intourist rents a part of this hotel for foreigners.

Restaurants. In hotels.

Irkutsk. Most foreign visitors are accommodated at the *Intourist,* 44 Gagarin Boulevard (tel. 91–353/354/355). Overlooking the Angara River, all rooms with bathroom. Service bureau reported "knowledgeable and helpful" by American and British visitors. Excellent restaurant, see below.

Angara, 7 Sukhe Bator Street. Modern, 7-story, overlooking gardens and a fountain; all rooms with own toilet and shower; good dining room. *Sibir,* 18 Lenin Street. 250 rooms, first-class, moderate.

Restaurants. The *Intourist Hotel* has two large, pleasant restaurants serving the city's best food. Breakfast reported to comprise "marvelous black bread with good, natural butter, spicy sausage and a cheesecake any New York deli could envy." For lunch, which is the main meal of the day, you might get cold or smoked sturgeon from the local rivers, at $2 on the English language menu; $3.40 fried. Caviar, though, is a luxury here as elsewhere in the Soviet Union, at $4.40 a portion of less than an ounce; red salmon caviar is cheaper. Try also Siberian dumplings *(pelmeni)* in soup (under $1) or as a main course ($1.65); stuffed cabbage leaves are good too. The hotel's lounge is the only place we know of in the Soviet Union where visitors have been served whole pots of tea, not a glass or a cup, when they looked thirsty!

The *Angara Hotel's* dining room, where you can eat a meal for about $5 a head, excluding spirits, often serves *omul,* the rare and delicious white fish from Lake Baikal. You may be treated to midnight festivities including champagne, *bliny* (pancakes), dumplings, caviar and smoked salmon, especially at New Year. *The Sibir Hotel* also does a $5 dinner.

Apart from the hotels, the best places to eat are the *Arktika,* and the *Almaz* in Lenin Street. The *Arktika* has standard food but an amusing atmosphere, and is a good place to go dancing. Both of these average $5 a head. There are two ice cream parlors on Karl Marx Street.

Khabarovsk. Two recently built transit hotels are located at the airport. In the city: the new *Intourist,* 2 Amursky Boulevard, near the Lenin Stadium Park (tel. 34–4347, 33–7634). 10 floors, 280 rooms.

Others, comparatively primitive include the *Amur,* 49 Lenin Street (tel. 33–5043), with an Intourist service bureau; the *Tsentralnaya,* 52 Pushkin Street (tel. 33–4759); and last, the *Dalny Vostok,* 18 Karl Marx Street (tel. 33–1434).

Restaurants. Apart from the hotels, the *Ussuri,* 34 Karl Marx Street, shares honors with the airport restaurant.

Listvyanka. *Baikal,* with 112 rooms, many with bath and veranda giving a glorious view over the lake; sauna, ski hire, including skis, poles and boots $2.75 a day, a sled for $1 a day.

Restaurant. The *Baikal Hotel* restaurant is excellent with some unusual local delicacies—lake fish (often perch), salted mushrooms, bilberries and other fruits. The meal can end with a surprise—brown bread and creamy honey is one.

Nakhodka. *Note:* you can only stay in Nakhodka if you are in transit between the U.S.S.R. and Japan or Hong Kong. Only hotel which can be recommended is the *Vostok,* on Tsentralnaya Square.

Restaurant. In hotel, or try your luck.

Novosibirsk. Leader is the *Novosibirsk,* 3 Lenin Street, two blocks from the Opera House (tel. 22–0313). Large and reasonably comfortable; above average food in restaurant; renovated in early 1980s. Next door, *Tsentralnaya* was reported in 1987 to be "a bit antiquated" but to have "spacious, clean rooms and exceedingly good service." Intourist was building a new hotel in the city late in 1987, but we have no completion date at presstime.

Also-ran: *Sibir,* 26 Krasny Prospekt. *Ob,* out-of-town, by river, is newish and looks good.

In the main street of **Akademgorodok,** Ilyich Street, is the *Zolotaya Dolina.* Looks good, river beach not far.

Restaurants. Best outside the hotels is *Snezhinka,* Lenin Street. Or try in "Science City"—you can get into the *Dom Uchenykh* (Scientists' Club) on Morskoi Prospekt where there is a good, subsidized canteen. In the shopping center on Ilyich

Street, also in Akademgorodok, is the circular *Torgovy Tsentr* restaurant which is recommended.

PLACES OF INTEREST. Bratsk. *Local History Museum,* showing the history of the pioneers who developed the Angara basin.

Out-of-town excursions available into the taiga, only 15 km. (9½ miles) from Bratsk city center.

Irkutsk. *Fine Arts Museum,* is the largest in the eastern part of the U.S.S.R., with good representation by Siberian artists.

Local History Museum (two branches, one in a fine church), with colorful artifacts of indigenous Siberian peoples, including some superb richly-carved wooden window-frames that decorated early Siberian dwellings.

Museum of Mineralogy.

Museum of the Decembrists. The exhibits are devoted to the 19th-century noblemen banished to Siberia for having staged an uprising against the Czar in 1825. The homes of two of them—Sergei Trubetskoy and Sergei Volkonsky—still stand.

Khabarovsk. *Museum of Regional Studies,* 21 Shevchenko Street, founded in 1896, exhibits the fauna and flora of the Far East and the taiga. Collections built up by famous explorers.

Far Eastern Art Museum, 45 Frunze Street, displays Russian icons, canvases by Italian, Dutch and Flemish masters—Rembrandt and Rubens among them—and a collection of Chinese and Japanese arts and crafts.

Listvyanka. *The Institute of Limnology* devoted to scientific research into the fauna and flora of Lake Baikal. The four-hour trip by taxi costs about 35 roubles including stops for photographs along the way. Recommended. Cheaper than the Intourist bus on which it is difficult to make unauthorized stops. With a friendly driver you'll be able to drive into villages and talk to passers-by. Take chewing gum, etc.

Novosibirsk. *Art Gallery,* on Sverdlov Square, has a fine collection of Russian art.

Local Lore Museum, nearby, presents a mass of information on Siberia, including plans for the future.

TOURS. Intourist tours are arranged to Novosibirsk, Irkutsk and Bratsk, and you can go to Khabarovosk and finally to Nakhodka, the Soviet port on the Sea of Japan. You can also stay overnight at Abakan.

In Irkutsk you can join special sightseeing tours of the city, a tour of the student quarter and of the Geological Museum of the Polytechnic; also tours to four museums—Natural History, Mineralogy, fine Arts or Nature (each $21); a 3-hour trip to the Irkutsk seed selection station ($27.50); an 8-hour coach trip to Lake Baikal (outward journey only payable in hard currency, returning by hydrofoil, payable in roubles); a trip to the university campus in Bolshiye Koty; and an excursion in the taiga (forests) with picnic ($60). Also, for an extra fee, the Irkutsk Intourist office will organize shooting parties, including bear hunts. An advance payment of $1,100 per person, per day is required, according to reports.

THEATERS, CONCERTS, CINEMAS. Visitors have reported that tours of Siberia don't include enough evening entertainment. It does certainly exist, but you may have to seek it out for yourself.

Bratsk has an *Amateur Art Theater,* and a *Puppet Theater* housed in an exotic wooden building, rather like a fairytale castle.

Irkutsk has *Drama, Musical Comedy* and *Youth* theaters; a *Circus, Cinemas,* a *Philharmonic Orchestra,* Siberia's only *Planetarium* and a fine *Cycling Stadium.*

From 25 Dec. to 5 Jan. Irkutsk celebrates the Russian winter in a festival of sleigh and troika rides, of eating and entertainment. Top-class artists in ballet, opera, concert music and folk dancing perform nightly in the city's theaters.

Khabarovsk has a *Pioneer Theater,* 14 Karl Marx Street; an *Open-air Theater* in the Pioneer Park, 59 Karl Marx Street; a second *Open-air Theater* in the town park. In addition, there is a *Drama Theater,* 92 Dzerzhinsky Street, and a *Musical Comedy Theater,* 21 Shevchenko Street.

Krasnoyarsk has two theaters: The *Pushkin Theater* and a *Puppet Theater.* An *Open-air Theater* performs on an island of the Yenisei.

Novosibirsk has an *Opera House,* a *Musical Comedy Theater,* a *Conservatoire,* the *Red Torch Theater,* the *Village Theater* (with a touring company), a *Children's Theater* and a *Puppet Theater.*
Science City, Akademgorodok, has interesting things going on, if you can find them. Look for posters at the Scientists' Club, which has an *Art Gallery* and *Concert Hall.*

Omsk has a *Drama Theater,* a *Musical Comedy Theater,* a *Pioneer Theater* and a *Puppet* Theater, as well as a university and several colleges. A new *Concert Hall* for organ recitals was opened in the early '80s.

Tomsk has a university (founded in 1888), a *Drama* and a *Puppet Theater.*

Ulan-Ude boasts an *Opera House,* a *Russian Drama Theater* and a *Buryat-Mongol Touring Theater.*

Vladivostok has the *Gorky Theater,* a *Children's Theater, Fleet Theater* and a *Puppet Theater.*

SHOPPING. The best buys in Siberian cities are delicate bonecarvings, jasper and malachite ornaments (if you can find them!) and furs, (sable, marten, kolinsky, ermine, arctic fox, squirrel)—probably no better selection than that available in other Soviet cities, but the salespeople in Siberia may well be more knowledgeable and thus more helpful. Amber is on sale everywhere. **Khabarovsk** has a new shop called *Souvenirs* which sells artefacts by Far Eastern and Far Northern craftsmen.

ENGLISH-RUSSIAN
VOCABULARY

ENGLISH-RUSSIAN VOCABULARY

Although we have tried to be consistent about the spelling of Rusian names in this book, we find the Soviet authorities are not consistent about transliteration of the Cyrillic alphabet into our familiar Latin letters. In Moscow, for example, Intourist spells a street name "Chaikovsky," but in Leningrad it's "Tchaikovsky." We've tried to stick to internationally recognized U.S. and British systems of transliteration, but don't be surprised if you occasionally come across differences like Chekhov and Tchekov, Tolstoy and Tolstoi, Baykal and Baikal, Tartar and Tatar, rouble and ruble—to say nothing of icon and ikon!

We give here some hints on the vital matter of reading Russian signs and on pronunciation, as well as a general English-Russian tourist vocabulary. Reading street names is probably the most important use for even a small knowledge of the Cyrillic alphabet. To help you, a word or two about how they work in Russian. Many Russian streets and squares are named after *people*, but the people's names may appear in different spellings—often they are made into adjectives. Suppose we have a street called Pushkin street, after the poet. The word street, ULITSA in Russian, is feminine (all Russian nouns have a gender; masculine nouns usually ending consonants, feminine in "a" and neuter in "o" or "e"). So you will see the street name as *Pushkinskaya ulitsa,* a feminine form of Pushkin. Pushkin Avenue would be *Pushkinsky Prospekt* in Russian (the word for avenue is masculine). Pushkin Chaussée would be *Pushkinskoye Shosse* (Chaussée is neuter). Don't be worried if you see one of these signs when our guide tells you you are on *Pushkin* street, avenue, etc.—it's the same thing! Almost every Soviet town has its *Leninsky Prospekt*— Lenin Avenue. As a general rule, once you have deciphered the first few letters, you will recognize the name—don't worry about the ending!

Another common way of naming streets is to say, for example, "Street of Pushkin", "Avenue of Lenin" etc.—*Ulitsa Pushkina, Prospekt Lenina* and so on. Here again, the *name* is easy to spot—its ending is not a spelling mistake, just a genitive case form of Pushkin, Lenin, etcetera. If you do get lost, most passers-by will understand if you ask for a street by its English name.

We owe a debt of gratitude to the Government Affairs Institute, Washington, D.C., for their permission to reproduce the Tables of the Russian Alphabet which follow.

THE RUSSIAN ALPHABET

А а	И и	С с	Ъ ъ
Б б	Й й	Т т	Ы ы
В в	К к	У у	Ь ь
Г г	Л л	Ф ф	Э э
Д д	М м	Х х	Ю ю
Е е	Н н	Ц ц	Я я
Ё ё	О о	Ч ч	
Ж ж	П п	Ш ш	
З з	Р р	Щ щ	

The Sound of Russian

Category 1:
Russian Consonants that Look and Sound like English

Russian Letter (Capital)	Russian Letter (Small)	English Letter
Б	б	b
К	к	k
М	м	m
Т	т	t
З	з	z

Category 2:
Russian Consonants that Look Different from Their English Equivalents

Russian Letter (Capital)	Russian Letter (Small)	English Letter
Д	д	d
Ф	ф	f
Г	г	g
Л	л	l
Н	н	n
П	п	p
Р	р	r
С	с	s
В	в	v
Й	й	y

Category 3:
Russian Consonants that Have No English Equivalents

Russian Letter (Capital)	Russian Letter (Small)	Sound
Ч	ч	ch
Х	х	kh
Ш	ш	sh
Щ	щ	shch
Ц	ц	ts
Ж	ж	zh
	ь	soft sign

The Russian Vowels

Russian Letter (Capital)	Russian Letter (Small)	Sound
А	а	ah
Я	я	yah
Э	э	eh
Е	е	yeh
Ы	ы	ih
И	и	i (ee)
О	о	oh
Ё	ё	yo
У	у	u (oo)
Ю	ю	yu

EVERYDAY WORDS AND PHRASES

The most important phrase to know (one that may make it unnecessary to know any others) is: "Do you speak English?" — *Gavaree'te lee vy pa anglee'skee?* If the answer is "Nyet," then you may have recourse to the lists below:

Please	Пожа́луйста	pazhah'lsta
Thank you	Спаси́бо	spasee'ba
Good	Хорошо́	kharasho'
Bad	Пло́хо	plo'kha
I	Я	ya
You	Вы	vy
He	Он	on
She	Она́	anah'
We	Мы	my
They	Они́	anee'
Yes	Да	da
No	Нет	nyet
Perhaps	Мо́жет быть	mo'zhet byt
I do not understand	Я не понима́ю	ya ne paneemah'yoo
Straight	Пря́мо	pryah'ma
Forward	Вперёд	fperyo't
Back	Наза́д	nazah't
To (on) the right	Напра́во	naprah'va
To (on) the left	Нале́во	nale'va
Hullo!	Здра́вствуйте!	zdrah'stvooite!
Good morning!	До́брое у́тро!	do'braye oo'tra!
Good day (evening)!	До́брый день (ве́чер)!	do'bree den (ve'cher)!
Pleased to meet you!	Очень рад с ва́ми познако́миться!	o'chen rat s vah'mee paznako'meetsa!
I am from USA (Britain)	Я прие́хал из США (Англии)	ya preeye'khal eez sshah' (ah'nglee ee)
I speak only English	Я говорю́ то́лько по-англи́йски	ya gavaryoo' to'lka pa anglee'skee
Do you speak English?	Говори́те ли вы по-англи́йски?	gavaree'te lee vy pa anglee'skee?
Be so kind as to show (explain, translate)	Бу́дьте до́бры, пока́жите (объясни́те, переведи́те)	boo'te do'bry, paka-zhee'te (abyasnee'te, perevedee'te)
Excuse my poor pronunciation	Извини́те моё плохо́е произноше́ние	eezveenee'te mayo'pla-kho'ye praeeznashe'nye
I beg your pardon	Прости́те	prastee'te
I want to post a letter	Мне ну́жно отпра́вить письмо́	mne noo'zhna atprah'veet peesmo'
Postcard	Почто́вая ка́рточка	pachto'vaya kah'rtachka

DAYS OF THE WEEK

Monday	Понеде́льник	panede'lneek
Tuesday	Вто́рник	fto'rneek
Wednesday	Среда́	sredah'
Thursday	Четве́рг	chetve'rk

Friday	Пя́тница	pyah'tneetsa
Saturday	Суббо́та	soobo'ta
Sunday	Воскресе́нье	vaskrese'nye
Holiday, feast	Пра́здник	prah'zneek
Today	Сего́дня	sevo'dnya
Tomorrow	За́втра	zah'ftra
Yesterday	Вчера́	vcherah'

NUMBERS

How many?	Ско́лько?	sko'lka?
1	один	adee'n
2	два	dva
3	три	tree
4	четы́ре	chety're
5	пять	pyat
6	шесть	shest
7	семь	sem
8	во́семь	vo'sem
9	де́вять	de'vyat
10	де́сять	de'syat
11	оди́ннадцать	adee'natsat
12	двена́дцать	dvenah'tsat
13	трина́дцать	treenah'tsat
14	четы́рнадцать	chety'rnatsat
15	пятна́дцать	pyatnah'tsat
16	шестна́дцать	shesnah'tsat
17	семна́дцать	semnah'tsat
18	восемна́дцать	vasemnah'tsat
19	девятна́дцать	devyatnah'tsat
20	два́дцать	dvah'tsat
30	три́дцать	tree'tsat
40	со́рок	so'rak
50	пятьдеся́т	pyadesyah't
60	шестьдеся́т	shezdesyah't
70	се́мьдесят	se'mdesyat
80	во́семьдесят	vo'semdesyat
90	девяно́сто	deveno'sta
100	сто	sto
1000	ты́сяча	ty'syacha

INFORMATION SIGNS

Toilet (Gentlemen) (Ladies)	Туале́т (М) (Ж)	tooale't
No smoking!	Не кури́ть!	ne kooree't!
Taxi rank	Стоя́нка такси́	stayah'nka taksee'
Entrance	Вход	fkhot
Exit	Вы́ход	vy'khat
No exit	Вы́хода нет	vy'khada net
Emergency exit	Запасно́й вы́ход	zapasnoi' vy'khat
Stop!	Стоп!	stop!

Pedestrian crossing	Переход	perekho't
Bus stop	Остановка автобуса	astano'fka afto'boosa
tram	троллейбуса	tralei'boosa
trolleybus	трамвая	tramvah'ya
Underground	Метро (М)	metro'
To the Trains	К поездам	k payezdah'm
Way out	Выход в город	vy'khat v go'rat
Ticket Machines	Кассы-автоматы	kah'ssy-aftamah'ty
On, Off	Включён, не включён	fklyoocho'n, ne fklyoocho'n
Telephone	Телефон	telefo'n
Telegraph Office	Телеграф	telegrah'f
Post Office	Почта	po'chta
Chemist's	Аптека	apte'ka
Newspapers, magazines	Газеты, журналы	gaze'ty, zhoornah'ly
Hairdresser's	Парикмахерская	pareekmah'kherskaya
Café	Кафе	kafe'
Restaurant	Ресторан	restarah'n
Dining Room	Столовая	stalo'vaya
Snack Bar	Закусочная	zakoo'sachnaya
Lift	Лифт	leeft
Booking offices	Кассы	kah'ssy
Inquiry office	Справочное бюро	sprah'vachnaye byooró
Waiting room	Зал ожидания	zal azheedah'neeya

AT THE HOTEL

What hotel shall we stay at?	В какой гостинице мы остановимся?	f kakoi' gahstee'neetse my astano'veemsya?
Please get me a taxi	Вызовите мне, пожалуйста, такси	vy'zaveete mne, pazhah'lsta, taksee'
Please have my bill ready	Приготовьте, пожалуйста, счёт	preegato'fte, pazhah'lsta, shshot
First (second, third, fourth...) floor	Первый (второй, третий, четвёртый...) этаж	per'vee (ftaroi', tre'tee, chetvyo'rtee...) etah'sh
What do I do about my luggage?	Как поступить с багажом?	kak pastoopee't z bagazho'm

IN THE RESTAURANT

Give me the menu, please	Дайте, пожалуйста, меню	dai'te, pazhah'lsta, menyoo'
Bring me the bill, please	Дайте, пожалуйста, счёт	dai'te pazhah'lsta, shshot
Please give us a	Дайте, пожалуйста,	dai'te, pazhah'lsta,
knife	нож	nosh
fork	вилку	vee'lkoo
spoon	ложку	lo'shkoo
glass	стакан	stakah'n
plate	мелкую тарелку	me'lkooyoo tare'lkoo

Drinks

cold water	холо́дной воды́	khalo'dnoi vady'
mineral water	минера́льной воды́	meenerah'lnoi vady'
grape, tomato juice	виногра́дного, тома́т-	veenagrah'dnava,
	ного со́ка	tamah'tnava so'ka
whisky, vodka	ви́ски, во́дка	vee'skee, vod'ka
liqueur	ликёр	leekyo'r
lemonade	лимона́д	leemanah't
beer	ли́во	pee'va
tea, coffee, cocoa, milk	чай, ко́фе, кака́о,	chai, ko'fe, kakah'o,
	молоко́	malako'
fruit juice	со́ки	so'kee

Meat

steak	бифште́кс	beefshte'ks
roast beef	ро́стбиф	ro'stbeef
veal chops	отбивну́ю теля́чью	atbeevnoo'yoo telyah'-
	котле́ту	chyoo katle'too
pork chops	свину́ю котле́ту	sveenoo'yoo katle'too
ham	ветчину́	vecheenoo'
sausage	колбасу́	kalbasoo'

Poultry

chicken	цыплёнка	tsyplyo'nka
hazel-grouse	ря́бчика	ryah'pcheeka
partridge	куропа́тку	koorapah'tkoo
duck	у́тку	oo'tkoo

Fish

soft caviar	зерни́стой икры	zernee'stoi eekry'
pressed caviar	па́юсной икры́	pah'yoosnoi eekry'
salmon	лососи́ны	lasasee'ny
cold sturgeon	холо́дной осетри́ны	khalo'dnoi asetree'ny

Vegetables

green peas	зелёный горо́шек	zelyo'nee garo'shek
radishes	реди́ску	redee'skoo
tomatoes	помидо́ры	pameedo'ry
potatoes	картошка	kar'to'shka

Desserts

cake	пиро́жное	peero'zhnaye
fruit	фру́ктов	froo'ktaf
pears	груш	groosh
mandarines	мандари́нов	mandaree'naf
grapes	виногра́ду	veenagrah'doo
bananas	бана́нов	banah'naf

Miscellaneous

white and rye bread	бе́лый и чёрный хлеб	be'lee ee cho'rnee khlep
butter	ма́сло	mah'sla
cheese	сыр	syr
soft-boiled eggs	яйца всмя́тку	yai'tsa fsmyah'tkoo
hard-boiled eggs	яйца вкруту́ю	yai'tsa fkrootoo'voo
an omelette	омле́т	amle't

SHOPPING

Description

good	хоро́ший	kharo'shee
bad	плохо́й	plakhoi'
beautiful	краси́вый	krasee'vee
dear	дорого́й	daragoi'
cheap	дешёвый	desho'vee
old	ста́рый	sta'ree
new	но́вый	no'vee

Colors

white	бе́лый	be'lee
black	чёрный	chyo'rnee
red	кра́сный	krah'snee
pink	ро́зовый	ro'zavee
orange	ора́нжевый	arah'nzhevee
yellow	жёлтый	zho'ltee
brown	кори́чневый	karee'chnevee
green	зелёный	zelyo'nee
light blue	голубо́й	galooboi'
blue	си́ний	see'nee
violet	фиоле́товый	feeale'tavee
grey	се́рый	se'ree
golden	золото́й	zalatoi'
silver	сере́бряный	sere'bryanee

In the shop

Baker's	Бу́лочная	boo'lachnaya
Confectioner's	Кондитерская	kandee'terskaya
Food Store	Гастроно́м	gastrano'm
Grocer's	Бакале́я	bakale'ya
Delivery Counter	Стол зака́зов	stol zakah'zaf
Wine and Spirits	Ви́на—коньяки́	vee'na — kanyakee'
Fruit and Vegetables	Овощи—фру́кты	o'vashshee — froo'kty

Index

Index

The letter H indicates Hotels and other accommodations.
The letter R indicates Restaurants.

General Information

Geographical

MAP

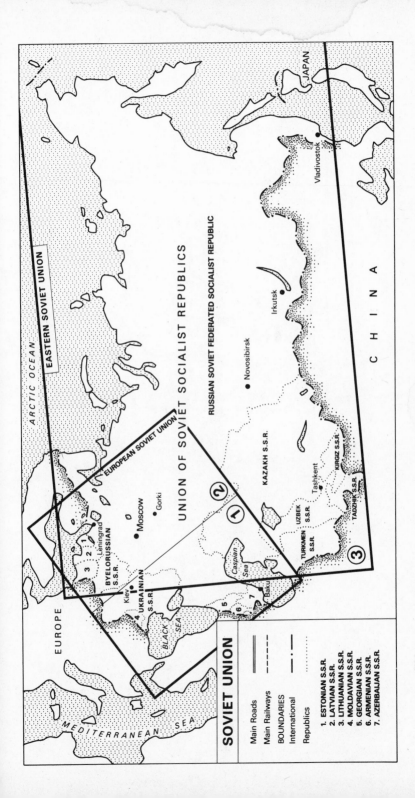

SOVIET UNION

Main Roads	———
Main Railways	- - - - -
BOUNDARIES	
International	— · —
Republics	

1. ESTONIAN S.S.R.
2. LATVIAN S.S.R.
3. LITHUANIAN S.S.R.
4. MOLDAVIAN S.S.R.
5. GEORGIAN S.S.R.
6. ARMENIAN S.S.R.
7. AZERBAIJAN S.S.R.

MEDITERRANEAN SEA

EUROPE

ARCTIC OCEAN

EASTERN SOVIET UNION

EUROPEAN SOVIET UNION

UNION OF SOVIET SOCIALIST REPUBLICS

RUSSIAN SOVIET FEDERATED SOCIALIST REPUBLIC

JAPAN

Vladivostok

Irkutsk

CHINA

Novosibirsk

KAZAKH S.S.R.

KIRGIZ S.S.R.

Tashkent

UZBEK S.S.R.

TADZHIK S.S.R.

TURKMEN S.S.R.

Caspian Sea

Baku

Moscow

Gorki

Leningrad

BYELORUSSIAN S.S.R.

Kiev

UKRAINIAN S.S.R.

BLACK SEA

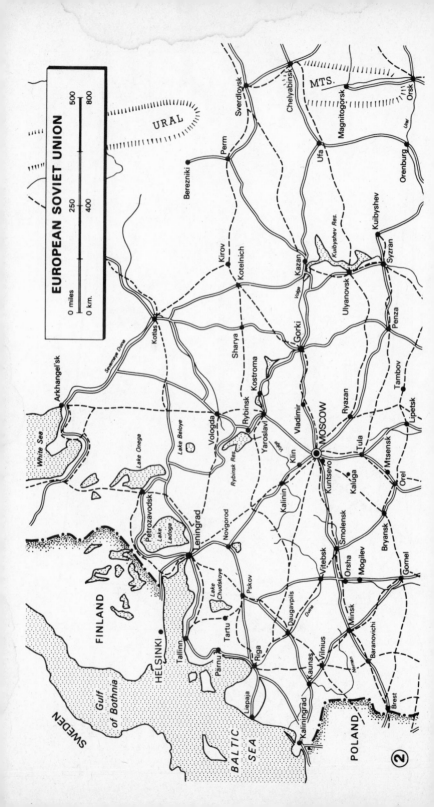

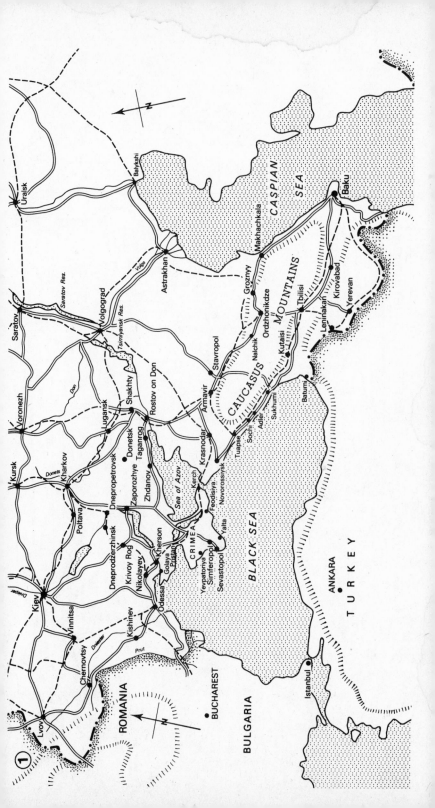

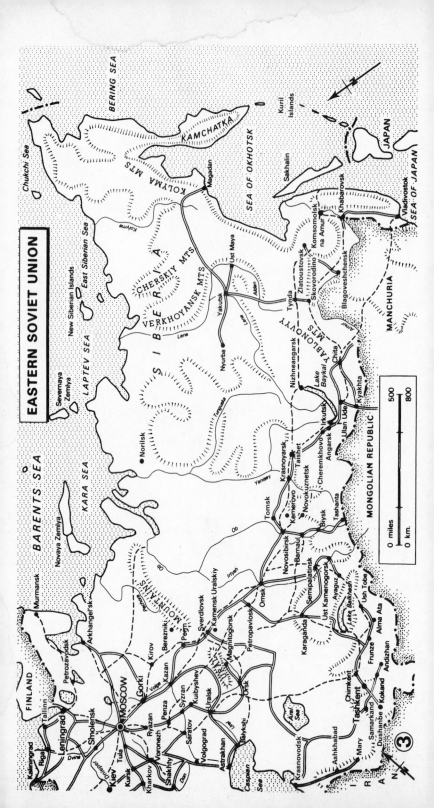

EASTERN SOVIET UNION

Fodor's Travel Guides

U.S. Guides

Alaska
American Cities
The American South
Arizona
Atlantic City & the
  New Jersey Shore
Boston
California
Cape Cod
Carolinas & the
  Georgia Coast
Chesapeake
Chicago
Colorado
Dallas & Fort Worth
Disney World & the
  Orlando Area

The Far West
Florida
Greater Miami,
  Fort Lauderdale,
  Palm Beach
Hawaii
Hawaii (Great Travel
  Values)
Houston & Galveston
I-10: California to
  Florida
I-55: Chicago to New
  Orleans
I-75: Michigan to
  Florida
I-80: San Francisco to
  New York

I-95: Maine to Miami
Las Vegas
Los Angeles, Orange
  County, Palm Springs
Maui
New England
New Mexico
New Orleans
New Orleans (Pocket
  Guide)
New York City
New York City (Pocket
  Guide)
New York State
Pacific North Coast
Philadelphia
Puerto Rico (Fun in)

Rockies
San Diego
San Francisco
San Francisco (Pocket
  Guide)
Texas
United States of
  America
Virgin Islands
  (U.S. & British)
Virginia
Waikiki
Washington, DC
Williamsburg,
  Jamestown &
  Yorktown

Foreign Guides

Acapulco
Amsterdam
Australia, New Zealand
  & the South Pacific
Austria
The Bahamas
The Bahamas (Pocket
  Guide)
Barbados (Fun in)
Beijing, Guangzhou &
  Shanghai
Belgium & Luxembourg
Bermuda
Brazil
Britain (Great Travel
  Values)
Canada
Canada (Great Travel
  Values)
Canada's Maritime
  Provinces
Cancún, Cozumel,
  Mérida, The
  Yucatán
Caribbean
Caribbean (Great
  Travel Values)

Central America
Copenhagen,
  Stockholm, Oslo,
  Helsinki, Reykjavik
Eastern Europe
Egypt
Europe
Europe (Budget)
Florence & Venice
France
France (Great Travel
  Values)
Germany
Germany (Great Travel
  Values)
Great Britain
Greece
Holland
Hong Kong & Macau
Hungary
India
Ireland
Israel
Italy
Italy (Great Travel
  Values)
Jamaica (Fun in)

Japan
Japan (Great Travel
  Values)
Jordan & the Holy Land
Kenya
Korea
Lisbon
Loire Valley
London
London (Pocket Guide)
London (Great Travel
  Values)
Madrid
Mexico
Mexico (Great Travel
  Values)
Mexico City & Acapulco
Mexico's Baja & Puerto
  Vallarta, Mazatlán,
  Manzanillo, Copper
  Canyon
Montreal
Munich
New Zealand
North Africa
Paris
Paris (Pocket Guide)

People's Republic of
  China
Portugal
Province of Quebec
Rio de Janeiro
The Riviera (Fun on)
Rome
St. Martin/St. Maarten
Scandinavia
Scotland
Singapore
South America
South Pacific
Southeast Asia
Soviet Union
Spain
Spain (Great Travel
  Values)
Sweden
Switzerland
Sydney
Tokyo
Toronto
Turkey
Vienna
Yugoslavia

Special-Interest Guides

Bed & Breakfast
  Guide: North America
  1936...On the
  Continent

Royalty Watching
Selected Hotels of
  Europe

Selected Resorts
  and Hotels of the U.S.
Ski Resorts of North
  America

Views to Dine by
  around the World